ANNUAL REVIEW OF IRIS

AUSTRALIA

LBC Information Services
Sydney

CANADA and USA

Carswell

NEW ZEALAND

Brookers
Wellington

SINGAPORE AND MALAYSIA

Thomson Information (S.E. Asia)
Singapore

Annual Review of Irish Law 2000

Raymond Byrne
B.C.L., LL.M., Barrister-at-Law
Lecturer in Law, Dublin City University

William Binchy
B.A., B.C.L., LL.M., F.T.C.D., Barrister-at-Law
Regius Professor of Laws, Trinity College, Dublin

Round Hall Sweet & Maxwell
2001

Published in 2001 by
Round Hall Sweet & Maxwell
43 Fitzwilliam Place,
Dublin 2, Ireland.

Typeset by
Gough Typesetting Services, Dublin.

Printed by
MPG Cornwall.

ISBN 1-85800-262-1

Table of Contents

Preface

In this fourteenth volume in the Annual Review series, our purpose continues to be to provide a review of legal developments, judicial and statutory, that occurred in 2000. In terms of case law, this includes those judgments which were delivered in 2000, regardless of whether they have been (or will be) reported and which were circulated up to the date of the preface. Once again, it is a pleasure to thank those who made the task of completing this volume less onerous.

For this fourteenth voloume of the Annual Review Series the authors are delighted to have had the benefit of specialist contributions on Agriculture and Food Law, Company Law, Contract Law, Defence Forces, Environmental Law, Equity, Evidence, Health Services, Human Rights, Information Law, Labour Law, Land Law, Planning Law, Practice and Procedure, Restitution and Social Welfare included in the volume. The authors continue to take final responsibility for the overall text as in the past, but are especially grateful for the contributions of Raymond O'Rourke in Agriculture and Food Law, David Tomkin and Adam McAuley in Company Law, Eoin O'Dell in Contract Law and Restitution, Declan McGrath in Evidence, Hilary Delany in Equity and Practice and Procedure, Ciaran Craven and Gerard Humphries in Defence Forces, Ubaldus de Vries in Health Services and Employment and Labour Law, Yvonne Scannell in Environmental Law, Garrett Simons in Planning Law, Rosemary Byrne in Human Rights, Estelle Feldman in Information Law and Gerry Whyte in Social Welfare.

Finally, we are very grateful to Round Hall Sweet & Maxwell and Gilbert Gough, whose professionalism ensures the continued production of this series.

Raymond Byrne and William Binchy,
Dublin

November 2001

Table of Cases

Table of Legislation

TABLE OF STATUTORY INSTRUMENTS

Irish Aviation Authority (Noise Certification and Limitation) (Amendment)
  O. 1999 (S.I. No.421 of 1999) 477
Irish Aviation Authority (Terminal Changes) Regulations 1999 477
Irish Aviation Authority (Terminal Charges) Regulations 2000
  (S.I. No.202 of 2000) 477
Irish Aviation Authority (Tethered Balloons, Airships, Free Balloons and
  Kites) O. 1999 (S.I. No.422 of 1999) 477
Irish Water Safety Association (Establishment) Order 1999
  (S.I. No.361 of 1999) 394
Life Assurance (Provision of Information) Regulations 2001
  (S.I. No.15 of 2001) 37
Livestock Marts Regulations 1968 (Amendment) Regulations 2000
  (S.I. No 279 of 2000) 20
Livestock Marts Regulations 1968 (S.I. No. 251 of 1968) 20
Local Government (Planning and Development) Regulations 1994
                Article 17 359
                Article 18 359
Merchant Shipping (Life-Saving Appliances) (Amendment) Rules 1999
  (S.I. No.368 of 1999), ... 478
Money-lenders Act 1900 (Section6(e)) O. 1993 36
National Ambulance Advisory Council (Revocation) Order, 2000
  (S.I. 108/2000) 260
National Ambulance Advisory Council Order, 1998 (S.I. 27/1998) 260
National Beef Assurance Scheme Act 2000 (Census) Regulations 2000
  (S.I. No 415) 19
National Beef Assurance Scheme Act 2000 (Commencement) (No.2)
  O. 2000 (S.I. No.414 of 2000) 392
National Beef Assurance Scheme Act 2000 (Commencement) O. (No. 2)
  2000 (S.I. No. 414 of 2000) 19
National Beef Assurance Scheme Act 2000 (Commencement) O. 2000
  (S.I. No. 130 of 2000) 19, 392
National Minimum Wage Act 2000 (Commencement) O. 2000
  S.I. 96/2000) 291
National Minimum Wage Act 2000 (Prescribed Courses of Study or
  Training) Regulations 2000 (S.I. 99/2000) 293
Netting of Financial Contracts Act 1995 (Designation of Financial Contracts)
  Regulations 2000 (S.I. No.214 of 2000 37
Planning and Development Act 2000 (Commencement) (No. 2) O. 2000
  (S.I. No. 449 of 2000) 332
Planning and Development Act 2000 (Commencement) Order, 2000
  (S.I. 349 of 2000) 331, 332
Plant Breeders' Rights (Form of Certificate) Regulations 1982
  (S.I. No 19 of 1982 18
Plant Varieties (Farm Saved Seed) Regulations 2000 (S.I. No 493 of 2000) 18
Plant Varieties (Proprietary Rights) (Amendment) Regulations 2000
  (S.I. No 490 of 2000) 18
Plant Varieties (Proprietary Rights)(Amendment) Act 1998 (Form of Certificate
  of Plant Breeders' Rights) Regulations 2000 (S.I. No. 492 of 2000) 18

TABLE OF UK LEGISLATION

AUSTRALIA

TABLE OF INTERNATIONAL TREATIES AND CONVENTIONS

Administrative Law

APPROPRIATION

The Appropriation Act 2000 provided as follows. For the year ended December 31, 2000, the amount of supply grants in accordance with the Central Fund (Permanent Provisions) Act 1965 was £16,864,443,000. Under the Public Accounts and Charges Act 1891, the sum for appropriations-in-aid was £1,789,557,000. The 2000 Act also provided that the financial resolutions passed by Dáil Éireann on December 6, 2000 (after the 2000 Budget), which dealt with changes in excise duties on fuels, tobacco and in VAT, would have legal effect provided that, in accordance with section 4 of the Provisional Collection of Taxes Act 1927, legislation was enacted in 2001 (in the Finance Act 2001) to give full effect to the resolutions. The 2000 Act came into effect on its signature by the President on December 15, 2000.

COMMISSION OF INQUIRY

Commission on Child Abuse   The Commission to Inquire into Child Abuse Act 2000 provided for the establishment of the Commission to Inquire into Child Abuse. The Commission, chaired by Laffoy J, was established on May 23, 2000: Commission to Inquire into Child Abuse Act 2000 (Establishment) Order 2000 (S.I. No.149 of 2000). The catalyst for the Commission was a documentary broadcast on RTE in 1998, *States of Fear*, which chronicled abuse in an orphanage in Dublin during the 1950s. The documentary led to enormous discussion in the various media of the extent of abuse in such institutions in the past. The 2000 Act empowers the Commission to investigate child abuse in institutions in the State, including abuse that took place from the 1940s onwards in the State's industrial schools and orphanages. The 2000 Act also enables persons who have suffered such abuse to give evidence to various Committees of the Commission. The 2000 Act provides for the preparation and publication of a report by the Commission containing the results of its investigation and any recommendations it considers appropriate for the prevention of child abuse, the protection of children from it, and the actions to be taken to address any continuing effects of child abuse on those who have suffered it.

One of the key sections of the 2000 Act is section 4, which provides that:

(1) The principal functions of the Commission are, subject to the provisions of this Act—

    (a) to provide, for persons who have suffered abuse in childhood in institutions during the relevant period, an opportunity to recount the abuse, and make submissions, to a Committee,

    (b) through a Committee—

        (i) to inquire into the abuse of children in institutions during the relevant period,

        (ii) where it is satisfied that such abuse has occurred, to determine the causes, nature, circumstances and extent of such abuse, and

        (iii) without prejudice to the generality of any of the foregoing, to determine the extent to which—

            (I) the institutions themselves in which such abuse occurred,

            (II) the systems of management, administration, operation, supervision, inspection and regulation of such institutions, and

            (III) the manner in which those functions were performed by the persons or bodies in whom they were vested, contributed to the occurrence or incidence of such abuse,

    and

    (c) to prepare and publish reports pursuant to section 5.

(2) Subject to the provisions of this Act, the inquiry under subsection (1) shall be conducted in such manner and by such means as the Commission considers appropriate.

(3) The Commission shall have all such powers as are necessary or expedient for the performance of its functions.

(4) (a) The Government may, if they so think fit, after consultation with the Commission, by order confer on the Commission and the Committees such additional functions or powers connected with their functions and powers for the time being as they consider appropriate.

    (b) The Government may, if they so think fit, after consultation with the Commission, amend or revoke an order under this subsection.

    (d) Where an order is proposed to be made under this subsection, a draft of the order shall be laid before each House of the Oireachtas and the order shall not be made unless a resolution approving of the draft has been passed by each such House.

(5) The Commission may invite and receive oral or written submissions.

(6) In performing their functions the Commission and the Committees

> shall bear in mind the need of persons who have suffered abuse in childhood to recount to others such abuse, their difficulties in so doing and the potential beneficial effect on them of so doing and, accordingly, the Commission and the Committees shall endeavour to ensure that meetings of the Committees at which evidence is being given are conducted—
>
> (a) so as to afford to persons who have suffered such abuse in institutions during the relevant period an opportunity to recount in full the abuse suffered by them in an atmosphere that is as sympathetic to, and as understanding of, them as is compatible with the rights of others and the requirements of justice, and
>
> (b) as informally as is possible in the circumstances.'

Section 4 of the 2000 Act clearly indicates a desire to ensure that the traumatic nature of the evidence being recounted by the victims of institutional child abuse be afforded appropriate understanding in recounting their experiences. It is notable that the 2000 Act avoided the use of a tribunal of inquiry as the mechanism for investigating child abuse. This was the subject of some heated debate during the passage of the 2000 Act, reflecting similar concerns outside the Oireachtas that the mechanism of a Commission would not sufficiently publicise the issues being dealt with. The proponents of a Commission argued that a tribunal would not be appropriate as a number of victims might be unwilling to give evidence in a public context and that its was more appropriate to provide the protections ultimately included in the 2000 Act. The 2000 Act provides that Committees of the Commission may take evidence in private from victims of abuse and that the Commission itself may sit in public, including hearing evidence during such sittings. While the Commission was established in May 2000, it was reported that, over a year later, it had been unable to begin its investigative work arising from failure to resolve issues of legal representation: see *The Irish Times*, May 25, 2001.

FREEDOM OF INFORMATION

Bodies subject to 1997 Act The Freedom of Information Act 1997 (Prescribed Bodies) Regulations 2000 (SI No.67 of 2000) prescribed the Courts Service, the Equality Authority and the Ordnance Survey as separate public bodies for the purposes of the 1997 Act (Annual Review 1997, 2-8). They also prescribed the Area Health Boards and the Health Boards Executive established under the Health (Eastern Regional Health Authority) Act 1999 as public bodies under the 1997 Act. The Regulations came into effect on March 9, 2000. The Freedom of Information Act 1997 (Prescribed Bodies) (No.2) Regulations 2000 (S.I. No.115 of 2000) prescribed RTÉ and its subsidiaries as

separate public bodies for the purposes of the Act. They apply the 1997 Act to
non-programme related functions of those bodies only, since programming is
already subject to the Broadcasting Complaints Commission under the
Broadcasting Acts 1961 to 1990. The Regulations came into effect on May 1,
2000.

JUDICIAL REVIEW

Industrial relations enquiry: whether reviewable   In *Ryanair Ltd v. Flynn*
[2001] 1 I.L.R.M. 283 (HC), Kearns J. held that the findings made in an enquiry
under section 38(2) of the Industrial Relations Act 1990 were not amenable to
judicial review. The background was an escalating industrial dispute at Dublin
Airport concerning the pay and conditions of the applicant company's ground
handling agents (GHAs). In a letter to the GHAs trade union, SIPTU, the
company had claimed that its GHAs enjoyed greater pay and conditions than
those in comparable companies at Dublin Airport. SIPTU disputed this claim
and the resulting dispute led to the complete closure of Dublin Airport in
March 1998. The Minister for Enterprise, Trade and Employment then
appointed the respondents to conduct an enquiry into the dispute under section
38(2) of the 1990 Act and furnish a report to the Minister. In response to a
letter from the company, the respondents gave the company an assurance that
any findings of the report would not constitute a form of conciliation or
arbitration.

For the purposes of the enquiry, the Irish Productivity Centre (IPC), a notice
party in the proceedings, were appointed to undertake a study of the pay and
conditions of the company's ground handling employees and of three other
Dublin airport-based companies engaged in broadly comparable duties. The
respondents considered the report from the IPC and concluded in their report
to the Minister that the company's claims that its GHAs enjoyed better pay
and conditions than comparable GHAs was not justified. The company applied
for judicial review seeking, *inter alia*, a declaration that the report prepared by
the respondents was *ultra vires* on the grounds that there were manifest errors
in it, that they had failed to apply rules of natural and constitutional justice in
its preparation and that also sought an order quashing the findings. The two
main issues identified by Kearns J. in his judgment were, first, whether the
contentions and material placed before the Court gave rise to any justiciable
issue and second, in what circumstances should the court intervene by way of
judicial review where 'mistake of fact' was alleged, particularly when those
facts fell within the province of expert bodies.

On the first issue, Kearns J. applied the views of Diplock L.J. (as he then
was) in *R v Criminal Injuries Compensation Board, ex p Lain* [1967] 2 Q.B.
864 that, quite apart from the public law dimension, two other requirements
had to be fulfilled before the Court could intervene by way of judicial review;

namely, there had to have been a decision, act or determination and second, it had to affect some legally enforceable right of the company. In the instant case, Kearns J. held that the matter raised before the court was not justiciable because there was no decision susceptible of being quashed. This was reinforced by the response by the respondents to the company that their enquiry would not constitute any form of medication or arbitration.

On the second issue, Kearns J. held that he should apply the test of reasonableness set out by Henchy J. in *The State (Keegan) v. Stardust Victims Compensation Tribunal* [1986] I.R. 642. He was of the view that the cases where the court could intervene by way of judicial review to correct errors of fact 'must be extremely rare.' He did not accept that the jurisprudence of the courts had developed to the stage where mere factual errors made within jurisdiction could be corrected on judicial review. He was referred to the views expressed in the leading text, Wade and Forsyth, *Administrative Law* (1994 ed.), in which the authors stated that the traditional 'no evidence' rule was being subjected to 'radical development' in some jurisdictions. Kearns J. was referred to the decision of the New Zealand Court of Appeal in *Daganayasi v. Minister of Immigration* [1980] N.Z.L.R. 130, where the Court had quashed an immigration decision by the respondent Minister which had been based on a misleading and inadequate medical report (commissioned by the Minister) concerning the applicant's state of health.

But Kearns J. was not prepared to use this as an analogy for the instant case. He noted that there was a direct conflict of evidence between the parties as to whether the IPC report was factually accurate. He referred to well-established views on the limits to judicial review, such as those of Finlay J. in *O'Keeffe v. An Bord Pleanála* [1993] 1 I.R. 39 (Annual Review 1991, 16-8), and commented that the applicant was asking the Court to be converted into 'a part-time court of industrial relations acting, in effect, as external examiners to experts uniquely qualified to make judgments in complex and delicate matters.' This, he concluded, would be a novel, and inappropriate, extension of the remit of judicial review. Returning to the *Keegan* test of reasonableness, Kearns J. held that, far from being close to being a process that 'flies in the face of fundamental reason and common sense', the procedures followed in the instant case bore the hallmarks of fair play. Thus, there were no grounds on which the court could or should intervene.

TRIBUNAL OF INQUIRY

Refusal to hear evidence in private In *Bailey v. Flood* [2000] I.R. (HC), Morris P. declined to order judicial review of a decision to hear in public certain evidence being tendered before a tribunal of inquiry. The applicants sought judicial review of a decision of the respondent, the sole member of the Tribunal of Inquiry into Certain Planning Matters, which had been invested with the powers of the Tribunal of Inquiries (Evidence) Act 1921. The respondent had refused to make an order pursuant to section 2 of the 1921 Act, to hear the evidence of the applicants' financial affairs otherwise than in public on the grounds, *inter alia*, that the proposed examination was not relevant to the work of the tribunal under its terms of reference.

In refusing the relief sought Morris P. applied the reasonableness test set out by Henchy J. in *The State (Keegan) v. Stardust Victim's Compensation Tribunal* [1986] I.R. 642 and also cited the views in a judicial review challenge to the inquiry chaired by Lord Saville into Bloody Sunday, *R. v. Lord Saville* [1999] 4 All E.R. 860. Thus, he stated:

> The function of the High Court on an application for judicial review is limited to determining whether or not the impugned decision was legal, not whether or not it was correct. The freedom to exercise a discretion necessarily entails the freedom to get it wrong; this does not make the decision unlawful. Consideration of the alternative position can only confirm this view. The effective administration of a tribunal of inquiry would be impossible if it wee compelled at every turn to justify its actions to the High Court.

He noted that the proceedings of a tribunal of inquiry were inquisitorial and in seeking the evidence at issue, the respondent was inquiring into a matter which may have been crucially important, albeit only indirectly, to one of the central disputes before the tribunal. He also commented that it was of fundamental importance that, where possible, the proceedings of a tribunal of inquiry should be conducted in public. On this basis, he declined to grant judicial review.

Similar views had been expressed by the Supreme Court in *Murphy v. Flood (No. 2)*, Supreme Court, January 26, 2000, which concerned a challenge to a ruling in the same tribunal of inquiry. In this case, the respondent had ruled that an affidavit of a deceased party be admitted into evidence before him. The applicant, challenged this ruling and sought a number of reliefs by way of judicial review, including an order that the public be excluded when any witness gave evidence concerning the contents of that document. The High Court and, on appeal, the Supreme Court, refused to grant leave to apply. The Supreme Court held that the rulings were not unreasonable or irrational or flew in the face of fundamental reason and common sense, within the meaning of the *Keegan* test. The Court stated that the admissibility of evidence was purely a matter for the respondent and his decision to admit the evidence could not be said to have been made in breach of the applicant's constitutional rights or to be so unreasonable or irrational as to justify the court in interfering with it.

On the question of a public hearing, the Court noted that section 2(a) of the 1921 Act was couched in the negative, so that a private session of a tribunal of inquiry should be an exception to the general mode of procedure contemplated for hearings before the tribunal. Thus, the tribunal had to be conducted in public unless in its opinion it was in the public interest expedient to hold the hearing in private; this was purely a matter for the tribunal to decide and in the instant case, there was no evidence that the decision not to exclude the public was in any way unreasonable or irrational or in breach of the applicant's constitutional rights.

Agriculture and Food Law

RAYMOND O'ROURKE, Mason Hayes and Curran

ANIMAL WELFARE

Dogs and Cats   The Importation of Dogs and Cats (Amendment) Order 2000 (S.I. No. 56 of 2000) which came into operation on February 29, 2000, allows pet dogs and cats entering the United Kingdom from countries approved under the PETS (Pet Travel Scheme) pilot project, to continue their journey to Ireland, without the necessity of quarantine.

Protection of farming animals   The European Communities (Protection of Animals Kept for Farming Purposes) Regulations 2000 (S.I. No. 127 of 2000) give effect to Council Directive 98/58 concerning the protection of animals for farming purposes. The Regulations require owners and keepers to ensure the proper welfare of their animals. The Regulations do not apply to animals in the wild, intended for use in shows/competitions or laboratory animals used in scientific research.

Hourigan v. Neilan [High Court, Murphy J., November 30, 2000]   The applicant Cornelius Hourigan had been convicted of a number of offences relating to cruelty to animals and the non-burial of carcasses of animals. The offences in relation to cruelty to animals related to the ill-treatment of sheep by not adequately feeding them or shearing them contrary to the Protection of Animals Act 1911, as amended by the Protection of Animals Act 1965. In relation to unburied carcasses the applicant left them in a place to which a dog could gain access contrary to section 24 of the Control of Dogs Act 1986. The applicant was convicted in the District Court and the convictions were confirmed in the Circuit Court. Judicial Review was sought in the High Court on the grounds that the applicant did not get a fair hearing and that the Circuit Court judge did not have the jurisdiction to hear the appeal, as the applicant was not present. The applicant's judicial review was refused as the High Court judged that both the District and Circuit Courts were entitled to have recorded the verdicts in question.

DISEASES OF ANIMALS

Animal nutrition inspections   The European Communities (Animal

Nutrition Inspections) Regulations 2000 (S.I. No. 4 of 2000) give effect to Council Directive 95/53, Commission Directive 98/68 and Council Directive 99/20 which establish conditions and arrangements for official inspections in the field of animal nutrition covering both export and import products. The regulations apply to official animal health inspections but without prejudice to any more specific provisions on inspections in legislation concerning customs, veterinary, animal health and public health inspections.

Brucellosis in cattle   The Brucellosis in Cattle (General Provisions) (Amendment) Order 2000 (S.I. No. 56 of 2000) came into operation on October 29, 2000. The Regulations amend Article 7 of the Brucellosis in Cattle Regulations 1991 (S.I. No. 114 of 1991), in order to permit a veterinary surgeon, without notice being served on the owner, to require an eligible animal or animals to be confined or confiscated to a designated part of the holding for a specified period.

Bovine Tuberculosis   The Bovine Tuberculosis (Attestation of the State and General Provisions) (Amendment) Order 2000 (S.I. No. 161 of 2000), gives effect to Council Directives 97/12, 98/46 and 98/99 regarding health problems affecting intra-community trade in bovine animals and swine so far as they relate to Bovine Tuberculosis. The Order amends the Bovine Tuberculosis (Attestation of the State and General Provisions) Order 1998 (S.I. No. 308 of 1998), by outlining the test to be used to detect Bovine Tuberculosis. The Order also includes procedural changes to veterinary certifications for export where an inconclusive reactor is disclosed at a test and exchanges cattle identity cards of older animals for new bar-coded printed identity cards.

Diseases of Animals Act   The Diseases of Animals Act 1966 (Section 54(2)) (Exemption) Order 2000 (S.I. No. 270 of 2000) add a further exemption to Section 54(2) exemptions in the Diseases of Animals Act 1966 (Appointed Day and Exemptions) Order 1967 (S.I. No. 217 of 1967). Under the 1997 Order it is an offence to sell or export any horned cattle, but this will now be exempted for an animal whose owner has been prosecuted under the Protection of Animals Act 1911 (as amended by the Protection of Animals (Amendment) Act 1965), section 48 of the Control of Dogs Act 1996 or the Protection of Animals Kept for Farming Purposes Regulations 1984 (No. 13 of 1984).

BSE and Specified Risk Materials   The Diseases of Animals (Bovine Spongiform Encephalopathy) (Specified Risk Material) Order 2000 (S.I. No. 331 of 2000) introduces additional controls on specified risk material defined in Article 2 of the Order as the skull, the spleen and any material left attached to the skull or spleen after dissection of the carcase. The European Communities (Specified Risk Materials) Regulations 2000 (S.I. No. 332 of 2000) give effect to Commission Decision 2000/418/EC governing the removal, isolation and disposal of Specified Risk Materials (e.g. skull, spleen, spinal cord) for the purposes of the control of BSE. Specified Risk Material is only permitted to be removed from a carcase at premises licensed under the Abattoirs Act 1998, a slaughterhouse, cutting plant licensed under the European Communities (Fresh Meat) Regulations 1997 (S.I. No. 434 of 1997), a high-risk rendering plant licensed under the European Communities (Disposal, Processing and Placing on the Market of Animal By-Products) Regulations 1994 (S.I. No. 257 of 1994) or a knackery licensed under the European Communities (Knackery) Regulations 1996 (S.I. No. 396 of 1996). The Diseases of Animals (BSE) (Specified Risk Materials) Order 1997 (S.I. No 80 of 1997) and the Diseases of Animals (BSE) (Specified Risk Materials) (Amendment) Order 1998 (S.I. No. 144 of 1998) are revoked. Local authorities will enforce these Regulations within their functional area in accordance with provisions of the Abattoirs Act 1988.

TSE and Animal By-Products   The European Communities (Processed Animal Products) Regulations 2000 (S.I. No. 486 of 2000) give effect to Council Decision 2000/766 concerning protective measures in relation to transmissible spongiform encephalopathies (TSE). Under the Regulations the feeding of animal protein to bovine animals is banned, the import and export of processed animal protein must be done under license and processed animal protein must not be used in the manufacture of animal feedingstuffs.

TSE and Mammalian Animal By-Products   The European Communities (Processing of Mammalian Animal By-Products) Regulations 2000 (S.I. No. 182 of 2000) give effect to Commission Decision 1999/534 concerning the treatment for the processing of animal protein with a view to the inactivation of the Transmissible Spongiform Encephalopathy (TSE) agent. The European Communities (Processing of Mammalian Animal Waste) Regulations 1998 (S.I. No. 62 of 1998) are revoked. Requirements, conditions, processes and validation procedures for plants processing mammalian animal by-products are laid down in Schedules to the Regulations.

Rooney v. Minister of Agriculture [Supreme Court, October 23, 2000 (Appeal Nos. 111/1990 and 224/1991). The plaintiff was a farmer who had initiated proceedings relating to compensation provisions under the Bovine Tuberculosis Eradication Scheme and the Diseases of Animals Act 1966. The proceedings were ultimately dismissed. In this application the plaintiff sought to have the original order set aside as he alleged that one of the judges Mr. Justice Hugh O' Flaherty was biased because he had acted in the past for one of the defendants. The Supreme Court dismissed the action.

FEEDINGSTUFFS

Tolerances of undesirable substances   The European Communities (Feedingstuffs) (Tolerances of Undesirable Substances and Products) (Amendment) Regulations 2000 (S.I. No 36 of 2000) specify that where an undesirable substance exceeds the levels laid down in the European Communities (Feedingstuffs) (Tolerances of Undesirable Substances and Products) Regulations 1998 (S.I. No. 283 of 2000), then the feed material can only be put into circulation if it is intended for use in compound feedingstuffs The product must be accompanied by documents stating that it is to be used in compound feedingstuffs, that it will not be fed unprocessed to livestock and an indication of the amount of the undesirable substance should be specified.

Marketing of compound feedingstuffs   The European Communities (Marketing of Compound Feedingstuffs) (Amendment) Regulations 2000 (S.I. No. 148 of 2000) give effect to Commission Decision 2000/285. This Decision clarifies the situation regarding the prohibition on the use of "sewage" and "sludge" in compound feedingstuffs. Commission Decision 2000/285 states that all wastes obtained from various phases of the urban, domestic and industrial waste water treatment process are not to be used in compound feedingstuffs.

Additives in feedingstuffs   The European Communities (Additives in feedingstuffs) (Amendment) Regulations 2000 (S.I. No 186 of 2000) give effect to Council Directive 96/25 substituting the word "feed materials" for the term "ingredients" in respect of each occurrence in previous Regulations.

Feedingstuffs for particular nutritional uses   The European Communities (Feedingstuffs intended for particular nutritional purposes) (Amendment) Regulations 2000 (S.I. No 187 of 2000) give effect to Council Directive 96/25 substituting the word "feed materials" for the term "ingredients" in respect of each occurrence in previous Regulations.

Protein feedingstuffs   The European Communities (Protein Feedingstuffs) (Amendment) (S.I. No 190 of 2000) give effect to Council Directive 96/25 substituting the word "feed materials" for the term "ingredients" in respect of each occurrence in previous Regulations.

Methods of sampling   The European Communities (Feedingstuffs) (Methods of Sampling and Analysis) (Amendment) Regulations 2000 (S.I. No. 288 of 2000) give effect to Commission Directive 2000/45, which establishes Community methods of analysis for the determination of the presence of Vitamin A, Vitamin E and Tryptophan in feedingstuffs.

FOODSTUFFS

Labelling The European Communities (Labelling, Presentation and Advertising of Foodstuffs) Regulations 2000 (S.I. No. 92 of 2000) revoke and replace the European Communities (Labelling, Presentation and Advertising of Foodstuffs) Regulations 1982 (S.I. No. 205 of 1982) (as amended). They also give effect to EP and Council Directive 97/4 and Commission Directive 1999/10. These Regulations specify the compulsory information that must be contained on a food label – name under which the product is sold; list of ingredients; net quantity in the case of pre-packaged foodstuffs; date of minimum durability; storage conditions; name and address of manufacturer, packager or seller established in the EU; alcoholic strength of beverages containing more than 1.2% by volume of alcohol and quantities and categories of ingredients (QUID) in certain specified circumstances.

Meat products The European Communities (Meat Products and other Products of Animal Origin) (Amendment) Regulations 2000 (S.I. No. 93 of 2000) give effect to Council Directive 97/76 which lays down rules applicable minced meat, meat preparations and certain other products of animal origin. The Regulations impose additional production conditions for stomachs, bladders and intestines; introduce additional labelling requirements and modify the circumstances under which certain derogations from the rules for the processing of meat products can be granted.

Extraction solvents The European Communities (Extraction Solvents in Foodstuffs and Food Ingredients) Regulations 2000 (S.I. No. 141 of 2000) give effect to Council Directive 88/344, as amended by 92/115, 94/52 and 97/60 which lay down specific provisions for extraction solvents used in foodstuffs or food ingredients. Such products may be used in the processing of foodstuffs and may result in the unintentional presence of residues or derivatives in the finished foodstuff or food ingredient. In that case, only authorised extraction solvents in line with these Regulations may be used in such circumstances in order that their use does not endanger human health.

Baby foods The European Commission (Processed Cereal-Based Foods and Baby Foods for Infants and Young Children) Regulations 2000 (S.I. No. 142 of 2000) give effect to Commission Directive 96/5 as amended by Commission Directives 98/36 and 1999/39. The European Communities (Processed Cereal-Based Foods and Baby Foods for Infants and Young Children) Regulations 1998 (S.I. No. 241 of 1998) are therefore revoked. Such foodstuffs must be manufactured from ingredients whose suitability for use by infants and young children has been authorised under these Regulations. The Regulations specify that such products must not contain pesticide residues at a level exceeding

0.01 mg/kg. The Regulations also contain specific labelling requirements for such foodstuffs, in particular with regard to their nutritional composition.

Dioxin contamination   The European Communities (Protective Measures with regard to Contamination by Dioxin in Belgian foodstuffs) (Revocation) Regulations 2000 (S.I. No. 153 of 2000) revoke all the various protective measures taken by the Government with regard to the dioxin contamination of animal feed in Belgium.

Hygiene of foodstuffs   The European Communities (Hygiene of Foodstuffs) Regulations 2000 (S.I. No. 165 of 2000). The Regulations give effect to Council Directive 93/43 and cover all stages of the food chain after primary production and set down obligations on food manufacturers, retailers, hoteliers and restaurant owners to operate their businesses in a hygienic way. The hygiene rules contained in the Regulations cover requirements for premises, rooms where food is prepared, foodstuffs, transportation, equipment, food waste, water supply, personal hygiene and training. Food businesses are obliged to identify any procedure in their activities which is critical to food safety and ensure that adequate safety procedures are identified/reviewed on the basis of the principles developed under the Hazard Analysis and Critical Control Points (HACCP) system. The Regulations also provide for the Food Safety Authority of Ireland to approve Guides to Good Hygiene Practice, which may be used voluntarily by food businesses as a guide to compliance with these Regulations. The Health Board in whose functional area the offence was committed may prosecute an offence under these Regulations. The European Communities (Hygiene of Foodstuffs) Regulations 1998 (S.I. No. 86 of 1998) are revoked.

Food Safety Authority of Ireland's responsibilities   The Food Safety Authority of Ireland Act 1999 (Amendment of First and Second Schedules) (No. 1) Order 2000 (S.I. No. 184 of 2000), lists new food legislation which has been passed and food legislation that has been amended or revoked, which it is the responsibility of the Food Safety Authority of Ireland to ensure is adequately enacted and enforced in Ireland.

Coffee and chicory extracts   The European Communities (Marketing of Coffee Extracts and Chicory Extracts) Regulations 2000 (S.I. No. 281 of 2000) give effect to EP and Council Directive 1999/4, which establishes compositional and labelling standards for coffee and chicory extracts throughout the EU. They came into effect on September 13, 2000 and as of that date, the European Communities (Coffee Extracts and Chicory Extracts) Regulations 1982 (S.I. No 295 of 1982) and European Communities (Coffee Extracts and Chicory Extracts) (Amendment) Regulations 1988 (S.I. No. 102 of 1988) were revoked.

Irradiated foodstuffs   The European Communities (Foodstuffs treated with

Ionising Radiation) Regulations 2000 (S.I. No. 297 of 2000) give effect to EP and Council Directive 1999/2 approximating Member States laws concerning foods and food ingredients treated with ionising radiation and EP and Council Directive 1999/3 which establishes a Community list of foods and food ingredients treated with ionising radiation. The Regulations lay down the general provisions for the treatment of foodstuffs with ionising radiation including labelling rules, as well as the conditions for the approval and control of irradiation facilities.

Product liability extension to agricultural products   The European Communities (Liability for Defective Products) Regulations 2000 (S.I. No. 401 of 2000) give effect to Council Directive 1999/34 which extends the Product Liability Directive 85/374 to cover primary agricultural products (such as meat, cereals, fruit and vegetables) and game. The Regulations came into operation on 4th December 2000. The food producer or importer is required to pay compensation if the injured party can prove a casual link between the damage sustained and the defect, without the injured party having to prove negligence on the part of the food producer or importer. The injured party has 3 years within which to seek compensation and the producer's liability expires at the end of 10 years from the date at which the producer put the product into circulation. This extension puts an end to the difficulties, which often arose determining the dividing line between primary agricultural products and processed food products.

Beef labelling   The European Communities (Labelling of Beef and Beef Products) Regulations 2000 (S.I. No. 435 of 2000) give effect to the beef labelling system established by EP and Council (EC) Regulations 1760/2000 and 1825/2000 which specify that operators must maintain adequate up-to-date plans so as to ensure that the compulsory traceability statements indicated on their labels (factory approval number and traceability code) are accurate. The Regulations provide for approval of additional voluntary labelling claims. The European Communities (Labelling of Beef and Beef Products) Regulations 1998 (S.I. No. 31 of 1998) and the European Communities (Labelling of Beef and Beef Products) (Amendment) Regulations 1998 (S.I. No. 230 of 1998) are revoked.

Additives, colours and sweeteners   The European Communities (Additives, Colours and Sweeteners in Foodstuffs) Regulations 2000 (S.I. No. 437 of 2000) give effect to EU directives on food additives in general and those covering colours and sweeteners in particular. Only food additives, colours and sweeteners, which are authorised in line with the various provisions of these Regulations, are permitted to be used in foodstuffs. The Regulations revoke the European Communities (General Provisions on the Control of Additives and in particular Colours and Sweeteners for use in Foodstuffs) Regulations 1995 (S.I. No. 344 of 1995)

Purity criteria for additives   The European Communities (Purity Criteria on Food Additives other than Colours and Sweeteners) (Amendment) Regulations 2000 (S.I. No 434 of 2000) amend the European Communities (Purity Criteria on Food Additives other than Colours and Sweeteners) Regulations 1998 (S.I. No. 541 of 1998). These Regulations implement Commission Directive 98/86, which amends Commission Directive 96/77, which lays down specific purity criteria for food additives other than colours and sweeteners as set out in Council Directive 95/2. The Regulations establish new purity criteria for some categories of additives listed in Council Directive 95/2 (mainly emulsifiers and stabilisers).

Drinking water   The European Communities (Drinking Water) Regulations 2000 give effect to Council Directive 98/83 on the quality of drinking water intended for human consumption. The Regulations prescribe quality standards, sampling frequency, methods of analysis, and the provision of information to consumers, which will apply in relation to certain supplies of drinking water. The Regulations come into effect on January 1, 2004. The European Communities (Drinking Water) Regulations 1988 (S.I. No. 81 of 1988) are revoked.

Infant formulae   The European Communities (Infant Formulae and Follow-on Formulae) (Amendment) Regulations 2000 (S.I. No. 446 of 2000) give effect to Commission Directive 1999/50 on infant formulae and follow-on formulae. They amend European Communities (Infant Formulae and Follow-on Formulae) Regulations 1998 (S.I. No 243 of 1998) by establishing a maximum residue level of 0.01 mg/kg for these products.

Materials in contact with food   The European Communities (Materials and Articles intended to come into Contact with Foodstuffs) (Amendment) Regulations 2000 (S.I. No. 475 of 2000) give effect to Commission Directive 1999/91 amending for the fifth time Commission Directive 90/128 relating to plastic materials and articles intended to come into contact with foodstuffs. The Regulations amend the list of plastic materials permitted to be used in packaging that comes into contact with foodstuffs.

MILK QUOTA

The European Communities (Milk Quota) Regulations 2000 (S.I. No. 94 of 2000) replace the European Communities (Milk Quota) Regulations 1995 (S.I. No. 266 of 1995), as amended. The Regulations put in place from April 1, 2000 arrangements for the operation of the milk quota and super levy regime in Ireland up until 31 March 2008. The Regulations are introduced in accordance with the provisions of Council Regulation (EEC) No. 3950/92 as amended particularly by Regulation (EEC) No. 1256/99 and Commission Regulation (EEC) No. 536/93. The Regulations introduce substantially new arrangements for the transfer of milk quotas and continue with some modifications of the 1995 Regulations in relation to the registration of milk purchasers and the establishment, collection and payment of the super levy.

Maher v. Minister of Agriculture [High Court, Carroll J, December 15, 2000]   The European Communities (Milk Quota) Regulations 2000 (S.I. No. 94 of 2000) were challenged with regard to their validity. In particular the applicants challenged Regulation 5 (restrictions on the transfer of milk quota), Regulation 6 (exemption for certain family transactions), Regulation 7 (exemption for certain transactions where the Minister grants a certificate to transfer quota), Regulation 26 (restructuring of milk quota) and Regulation 27 (temporary transfer of milk quota limited to one year only, two in exceptional circumstances). The three applicants for a number of years had each leased their land and milk quota to third parties. They therefore challenged provisions in the European Communities (Milk Quota) Regulations 2000, which would necessitate them obtaining special permission from the Minister of Agriculture to continue to lease their land and milk quota in this fashion. They argued that these changes to the milk quota and super levy regime in Ireland were not in line with the EU legislation covering milk quotas and therefore the Minister of Agriculture was acting contrary to their proprietary rights under the Constitution. The High Court ruled that the European Communities (Milk Quota) Regulations 2000 do not go beyond what is required under EU law. The Minister of Agriculture was therefore fully entitled to make the decision that milk quotas should be transferred when possible, to active milk producers, this policy being in accordance with the stated policy under the EU Milk Quota Regulations. The applicants case therefore failed.

NATIONAL STUD

National Stud (Amendment) Act 2000   This provides the National Stud with company powers to sell or lease any part of the facilities in Co. Kildare but they must seek the prior consent of the Minister of Agriculture. The share capital of the National Stud has been established at £30 million. The National Stud is also given the powers to borrow an amount not exceeding £30 million once they obtain the approval of the Minister of Agriculture and the consent of the Minster of Finance. Finally, the National Stud is given powers to acquire shares and to enter into join ventures subject to any condition that may be imposed by the Minister of Agriculture or the Minister of Finance.

PLANT HEALTH

Organisms harmful to health   The European Communities (Introduction of

Organisms Harmful to Plants or Plant Products) (Prohibition) Regulations 2000 (S.I. No. 59 of 2000) introduce the provisions of Commission Decision 1998/842 strengthening existing prohibitions on the import of various potato varieties from Egypt. The European Communities (Introduction of Organisms Harmful to Plants or Plant Products) (Prohibition) (Amendment) (No. 2) Regulations 2000 (S.I. No 135 of 2000) implement the provisions of Commission Decisions 1999/355 and 1999/516. The Regulations ban the importation of *"Anoplophora glabrip ennis"* (Motschulsky) from China (excluding Hong Kong). The Regulations also implement provisions of Commission Decision 2000/23, which extends the expiry date for protected zone status in a number of Member States in respect of the harmful organism *"Erwinia amylovora"*. The European Communities (Introduction of Organisms Harmful to Plants or Plant Products) (Prohibition) (Temporary Provisions) Regulations 2000 (S.I. No. 189 of 2000) prohibit without approval of the Department of Agriculture the import into Ireland of tomato plants *"Lycopersicion lycopersicum"*, other than seeds so that they meet the requirements of Commission Decision 2000/35 in relation to the Pepino mosaic virus. The European Communities (Introduction of Organisms Harmful to Plants or Plant Products) (Prohibition) (Amendment) (No. 3) Regulations 2000 (S.I. No 434 of 2000) implement provisions of Commission Decision 2000/568, which strengthen existing controls relating to the import of certain potato varieties from Egypt.

Plant protection products The European Communities (Authorisation, Placing on the Market, Use and Control of Plant Protection Products) (Amendment) Regulations 2000 (S.I. No. 366 of 2000) give effect to Commission Decisions 2000/10, 2000/49, and 2000/50 which provide for the inclusion of the active substances – *fluroxypyr, metsulfuron-methyl, prohexadione-calcium* – respectively in Annex 1 of Council Directive 91/414 as implemented into Irish law by the European Communities (Authorisation, Placing on the Market, Use and Control of Plant Protection Products) Regulations 1994 (S.I. No. 139 of 1994).

Pesticide residues The European Communities (Pesticide Residues) (Cereals) (Amendment) Regulations 2000 (S.I. No. 459 of 2000) amend existing Regulations by the fixing of new maximum levels of pesticide residues in and on cereals though amendments to Annex II of the European Communities (Pesticide Residues) (Cereals) Regulations 1999 (S.I. 181 of 1999). The European Communities (Pesticide Residues) (Foodstuffs of Animal Origin) (Amendment) Regulations 2000 (S.I. No. 460 of 2000) amend existing Regulations by the fixing of new maximum levels for pesticide residues in and on foodstuffs of animal origin through amendments to PART A and PART B Annex II and further amendments to Annex I and Annex II of the European Communities (Pesticide Residues) (Foodstuffs of Animal Origin) Regulations 1999 (S.I. No. 180 of 1999). The European Communities (Pesticide Residues)

(Fruit and Vegetables) (Amendment) Regulations 2000 amend the European Communities (Pesticide Residues) (Fruit and Vegetables) Regulations 1989 (S.I. No. 105 of 1989) by the fixing of new maximum pesticide residues levels in and on fruit and vegetables contained in Annex II of the 1989 Regulations. The European Communities (Pesticide Residues) (Products of Plant Origin including fruit and vegetables) (Amendment) Regulations 2000 (S.I. No. 462 of 2000) amend existing regulations by the fixing of new maximum pesticide residue levels in products of plant origin including fruit and vegetables contained in Annex II of the European Communities (Pesticide Residues) (Products of Plant Origin including fruit and vegetables) Regulations 1999 (S.I. No. 179 of 1999)

Plant varieties (proprietary rights)   The Plant Varieties (Proprietary Rights) (Amendment) Act, 1998 (Commencement) Order 2000 (S.I. No 489 of 2000) stipulates that the 1998 Act will come into force on December 14, 2000. The Plant Varieties (Proprietary Rights) (Amendment) Regulations 2000 (S.I. No 490 of 2000) implements certain amendments and extensions to the Plant Varieties (Proprietary Rights) Act 1980 such as the crop species to which the grant of rights applies, the duration of rights, fees to be charged and the repeal on a number of previous regulations regarding Plant Varieties (Proprietary Rights). The Plant Varieties (Proprietary Rights) (Amendment) Act 1998 (Section 19(2)) Order 2000 (S.I. No. 491 of 2000) designates the varieties of any plant genus or species to which the farm saved seed exemption in Section 19(2) of the Plant Varieties (Proprietary Rights) (Amendment) Act 1998 applies. The Plant Varieties (Proprietary Rights) (Amendment) Act 1998 (Form of Certificate of Plant Breeders' Rights) Regulations 2000 (S.I. No. 492 of 2000) prescribes the form of certificate for the granting of Plant Breeders Rights as specified in section 15(2) (a) of the Plant Varieties (Proprietary Rights) (Amendment) Act 1998. The Plant Breeders' Rights (Form of Certificate) Regulations 1982 (S.I. No 19 of 1982) are therefore revoked. The Plant Varieties (Farm Saved Seed) Regulations 2000 (S.I. No 493 of 2000) will enable breeders of plant varieties to collect royalties on the plant varieties they have bred and developed and which are used for farm saved seed. Under this Regulation, farmers retaining a portion of their harvest for re-sowing may be required to pay the holder of a Plant Breeders' Right a royalty fee. Small farmers as specified in Council Regulation 2100/94 concerning Community Plant Variety Rights are exempt from the payment of royalties. The plant species covered by these Regulations are Cereals, Fodder plants, Oil and Fibre plants (excluding flax) and Potatoes.

RETIREMENT OF FARMERS

The European Communities (Retirement of Farmers) (Amendment) Regulations 2000 (S.I. No. 330 of 2000) amend Article 13 of the Farmers Retirement Scheme

(S.I. No 116 of 1974) which provides for increases in the annuity payable under the scheme. These Regulations increase the amount of annuity to £3,960 (married rate) and to £2,641 (single rate) for the 12 months commencing May 1, 2000.

TRADE IN ANIMALS

Bovine animals and swine (trade)   The European Communities (Trade in Bovine Animals and Swine) (Amendment) Regulations (S.I. No. 5 of 2000) amend Regulation 4 of the European Communities (Bovine Animals and Swine) Regulations 1997 (S.I. No. 270 of 1997) by specifying that in the case of a bovine animal intended for export in future it will be necessary that the animal's current status, identification and origin is confirmed by the Department of Agriculture.

Bovine animals (identification)   The European Communities (Identification and Registration of Bovine Animals) (Amendment) Regulations 2000 (S.I. No. 46 of 2000) provide for amendments to the design of animal passports in respect of bovine animals registered from January 1, 2000 and also to extend the list of breed codes to be registered in the national animal registration database.

National Beef Assurance Scheme Act 2000   This Act establishes the National Beef Assurance Scheme, the purpose of which is to provide additional guarantees about the safety of Irish cattle and beef following the BSE crisis. The Scheme applies to all persons engaged in the primary production and processing of cattle and beef (farmers, marts or assembly centres, dealers, live exporters, slaughterhouses, meat processors and bovine animal feed manufacturers or traders). Under the Act, only persons meeting the prescribed standards will be approved to participate in the cattle, beef and feedingstuffs industry. These standards are set out in the Second Schedule of the Act. The Act provides for the mandatory inspection, approval and registration of all participants. Under the National Beef Assurance Scheme, the existing animal identification and tracing database is to be enhanced by the recording of data on all cattle movements by means of a new initiative known as the Cattle Movement Monitoring System (CMMS). The National Beef Assurance Scheme Act 2000 (Commencement) Order 2000 (S.I. No. 130 of 2000) designated May 29, 2000 as the date when Part V (increase in penalties under Diseases of Animals Act 1966, the Livestock Marts Act 1967 and the Slaughter of Animals Act 1935) of the Act would come into operation. The National Beef Assurance Scheme Act 2000 (Commencement) Order (No. 2) 2000 (S.I. No. 414 of 2000) designated December 22, 2000 as the date when sections 20-22 (cattle census) of Part II of the Act came into operation. The National Beef Assurance Scheme Act 2000 (Census) Regulations 2000 (S.I. No 415) enabled a census to be taken of all bovine animals on December 31, 2000. The Regulations defined the scope of the census, the persons required to complete Herd Reconciliation forms for the purpose of the census and how the information would be provided to the computerised Cattle Movement Monitoring System (CMMS).

Assembly centres The European Communities (Assembly Centres) Regulations 2000 (S.I. No. 257 of 2000) give effect to those sections of Council Directive 97/12 relating to assembly centres. Assembly centres cater for animals being exported to other EU Member States. The Minister of Agriculture may either refuse to grant an approval or revoke an approval for an assembly centre if he or she is satisfied that the provisions of these Regulations or the Council Directive have not been complied with. The Regulations detail the facilities which must be available at such centres and specify that only bovine animals that have been tagged, have a passport and health documents, are free of tuberculosis, brucellosis and leucosis or swine that are properly identified may be admitted to these assembly centres. Owners of such centres must keep records on all animals utilising the facilities. Regulation 12 of the European Communities (Trade in Bovine Animals and Swine) Regulations 1997 (S.I. No. 270 of 1997) is thereby revoked.

Livestock marts The Livestock Marts Regulations 1968 (Amendment) Regulations 2000 (S.I. No 279 of 2000) revoke regulation 19 of the Livestock Marts Regulations 1968 (S.I. No. 251 of 1968) requiring livestock marts to have their conditions of sale approved by the Minister of Agriculture.

Bulls: breeding permits The Control of Bulls for Breeding (Permits) (Amendment) Regulations 2000 (S.I. No. 284 of 2000) which are made under the Control of Bulls for Breeding Act 1985, provide for the continuation of the granting of permits to persons to keep unregistered bulls for breeding purposes and to extend permits already issued under the previous Control of Bulls for Breeding (Permits) (Amendment) Regulations 1998 (S.I. No. 425 of 1998) until October 31, 2002.

Veterinary checks The European Communities (Veterinary Checks on Products Imported from 3rd Countries) Regulations 2000 (S.I. No. 292 of 2000) give effect to Council Directive 97/78 which lay down the principles governing the organisation of veterinary checks on products entering the EU from third countries. The Regulations require that such products must be presented at an approved border inspection post having given 24 hours written notice beforehand. The Regulations also provide for the appointment of authorised officers to carry out the inspections and for the prosecution of offences. After an inspection a veterinary surgeon will certify the results and a declaration will be provided stating that the products comply with the Regulations. The Regulations came into operation on September 25, 2000. The European Communities (Fees on imports of products of animal origin from third countries) Regulations 2000

(S.I. No. 301 of 2000) extend and consolidate the list of products of animal origin from third countries for which fees are levied in respect of veterinary checks at border inspection posts. The Regulations revoke the European Communities (Fees on imports of products of animal origin from third countries) Regulations 1995 (S.I No. 231 of 1995) and came into operation on October 9, 2000.

WILDLIFE

Wild birds The Wildlife (Wild Birds) (Open Seasons) (Amendment) Order 2000 (S.I. No. 280 of 2000) amends the Open Seasons list of huntable species of wild birds by extending the hunting season for the *Greylag Goose* and *Canada Goose* from September 30, 2000 to October 15, 2000 on a countrywide basis.

Wildlife (Amendment) Act 2000 [No. 38 of 2000] The Act makes a large number of amendments to the principal Act – the Wildlife Act 1976. The amendments cover the functions of the Minister for the Arts, Heritage, Gaeltacht and the Islands in relation to wildlife, powers in relation to the acquisition of land and rights agreements, extinguishment of easements, the designation by the Minister for the Arts, Heritage, Gaeltacht and the Islands of "Natural Heritage Areas", the protection of flora, wild birds and wild animals, restrictions that may be placed upon activities like shooting, hunting etc so as to protect wildlife and the regulation and control of wildlife dealing.

Commercial Law

BANKRUPTCY

Advertisement   In *Bank of Ireland v. D.H.* [2000] 2 I.L.R.M. 408 (HC), Laffoy J. granted the petitioner in a bankruptcy petition an order for the substitution for service of notice of the petition by public advertisement. She held that where the act of bankruptcy relied on is failure to comply with a bankruptcy summons issued by the court, the court has jurisdiction under Order 76 rule 25 of the Rules of the Superior Courts 1986 to order that notice of the petition be given by public advertisement. She added that this mode of service should only be resorted to if other modes have not proved feasible.

Proposal to creditors: whether reasonable   In *In re N.C., an Arranging Debtor*, High Court, November 26, 1999, Laffoy J. approved the proposal put forward by the petitioner to his creditors, which had been unanimously accepted by the creditors at a private sitting. She emphasised that, in determining whether to approve such a proposal, the Court has to have regard to the protection of the public and of the commercial community.

She applied the principles in *In re C., an arranging debtor* [1926] I.R. 14 and *In re J.H., an arranging debtor* [1962] I.R. 232, to the effect that if the requisite majority of creditors accepted the proposal made by an arranging creditor, their judgement ought normally to be accepted, provided that the debtor's conduct had been unimpeachable. In the instant case,) evidence had come before the Court by way of affidavit from one of the creditors that the debt which it claimed had arisen due to fraudulent conduct on the part of N.C., was not in fact the case.

Laffoy J. also dealt with a connected matter, namely that the indebtedness of N.C. was inextricably linked to the management and business of a company, of which N.C. was a director, and which was now in receivership. She held that the protection of the public and of the commercial community, which had to be a factor which the Court should have regard to when determining whether to approve a proposal under section 92 of the Bankruptcy Act 1988, would be adequately met by the making of a disqualification order under section 160 of the Companies Act 1990. She considered that this would be more appropriate than a restriction order under section 150 of the 1990 Act because if N.C. was adjudicated bankrupt he would be debarred from being an officer of a company while an undischarged bankrupt. She pointed out that the Court could make a disqualification order against any person for such period as it thought fit. Finally,

Laffoy J. commented that, by submitting to an order under section 160 of the 1990 Act, N.C., although not admitting to any specific form of misconduct, was implicitly admitting to past conduct which made him unfit to be concerned in the management of a company.

Application to annul: delay in applying   In *O'Maoileoin v. Official Assignee*, High Court, December 21, 1999 Laffoy J. declined to grant an application for an annulment brought by the applicant, who had been adjudged a bankrupt in 1987. The applicant grounded the application on the basis that the verifying affidavit of the petitioning creditor had not been signed or sworn by him in the presence of a Commissioner for Oaths. The evidence indicated that the applicant had become aware of the defect in the petitioning creditor's affidavit as early as March 1995, but had not sought to apply for an annulment until the end of 1999. In dismissing the application, Laffoy J. held that she should apply the same principles as in determining whether a claim in civil proceedings should be dismissed for want of prosecution, as exemplified in *Primor plc v. Stokes Kennedy Crowley* [1996] 2 I.R. 459 (Annual Review 1995, 401). In the instant case, she held that since the knowledge which formed the basis of this application had been known to the applicant for 4½ years, the delay in initiating the application was inordinate and inexcusable. And since it was the applicant's conduct which hindered the application, the balance of justice was in favour of not allowing the bankrupt to prosecute the application.

Time limit: proof of debts   In *In Re Kelly (Matthew), a bankrupt*, High Court, December 20, 1999, Laffoy J. considered to what extent extensions may be granted to the time limits in the Bankruptcy Act 1988 for proving a debt in a bankruptcy. The background was as follows. In 1981, the High Court had made an order declaring Mr Kelly personally liable for all the debts of a company. In 1984, the Revenue Commissioners petitioned to have Mr Kelly adjudged a bankrupt, claiming that some £2 million was due in respect of unpaid taxes from him. The Official Assignee fixed July 1997 as the last day on which creditors proofs of debt were to be received by him. The Revenue Commissioners applied to have a proof of debt admitted after the deadline of July 1997. A member of the Criminal Assets Bureau swore the affidavit grounding the application. Mr Kelly argued, *inter alia*, that there had been excessive delay in bringing the application and that the Revenue Commissioners were statute barred from collecting a debt which the High Court had adjudicated upon. Mr Kelly also argued that the 1981 High Court order had created a debt in favour of a company, and not the Revenue Commissioners, and as such, they could not collect it. Laffoy J. largely accepted these arguments.

She held that a provable debt against which time is running but which has not been statute barred at the date of adjudication remained provable in the bankruptcy even after the ordinary limitation period had elapsed. Such was a necessary corollary, she held, to section 136 of the 1988 Act, which provides that the effect of adjudication on the creditors' remedies is to limit their remedies to their rights under the 1988 Act itself. Applying this principle, she held that in respect of one of the debts, the Revenue Commissioners had only missed the Official Assignee's original deadline by one day, and that an extension of time was allowable in respect of that debt. However, she considered that a delay of 2½ years in bring the application to extend time in respect of two of the other debts was inordinate and inexcusable and the Court would not exercise its discretion to extend time in respect of those debts. She added that since the Revenue Commissioners had not been a party to the order in 1981 for Mr Kelly to pay monies to the official liquidator of the company, they had no entitlement to enforce any of the declarations made in the order of 1981 in its favour.

CONSUMER PROTECTION

Consumer Information: airfares   The Consumer Information (Advertisements for Airfares) Order 2000 (S.I. No.468 of 2000), made under the Consumer Information Act 1978, provides that advertisements for airfares must give the total price payable by the purchaser for the airfare, and the availability of the airfare advertised. The Order came into effect on

Prices: alcoholic drinks   The Prices Stabilisation Order 2000 (S.I. No.209 of 2000), made under section 22A of the Prices Act 1958, as inserted by the Prices (Amendment) Act 1965, authorised the making of Orders to impose controls on the price of drink. The Retail Prices (Beverages in Licensed Premises) Order 2000 (S.I. No. 210 of 2000), made pursuant to the Stabilisation Order 2000, provided that the prices charged for certain listed alcoholic drinks in any particular part of a licensed premises shall be those obtaining and displayed on May 15, 2000. This 'drinks price freeze' was made as part of the government's attempts during 2000 to combat inflation. The Order had effect for six months, from July 6, 2000 and was not renewed in January 2001 when it lapsed. Although there had been suggestions from the drinks industry that the Order might be challenged for being potentially discriminatory in application, no legal challenge to the Order emerged in the six months during which it operated.

Time sharing contracts   The European Communities (Contracts for Time Sharing of Immovable Property – Protection of Purchasers) (Amendment) Regulations 2000 (S.I. No.144 of 2000) amended the European Communities (Contracts for Time Sharing of Immovable Property – Protection of Purchasers) Regulations 1997 (Annual Review 1997, 59) and further implemented Directive 94/47/EC. It ensures that the purchaser's option to obtain a timeshare contract in his or her language is provided for; that contracts are drawn up in the language

where the timeshare property is situated; introduce penalties for non-compliance
with the provisions of the 1997 Regulations; and ensure that the purchaser is
not deprived of the protection afforded by the 1994 Directive if the property
concerned is situated within the territory of a Member State. The 2000
Regulations came into force on May 25, 2000.

Unfair terms in consumer contracts The European Communities (Unfair
Terms in Consumer Contracts) (Amendment) Regulations 2000 (S.I. No.307
of 2000) amended the European Communities (Unfair Terms in Consumer
Contracts) Regulation 1995, which had implemented Directive 93/13/EEC.
The 2000 Regulations provide that consumer organisations set up for the
purpose of protecting consumer rights, such as the Consumer Association of
Ireland, may seek an order in the High Court to prevent breaches of the
Regulations. The 2000 Regulations came into effect on October 2, 2000. The
1995 Regulations, as amended by the 2000 Regulations, are discussed
separately below, 40.

COPYRIGHT AND RELATED RIGHTS

The Copyright and Related Rights Act 2000 put in place a modern regime of
statutory protection for copyright and related rights. The 2000 Act replaced
(largely with effect from January 1, 2001: see below) the Copyright Act 1963
and a number of Ministerial Regulations made under the European
Communities Act 1972 which had implemented some, but not all, of the State's
obligations as an EU Member State. But the 376 sections of the 2000 Act is
much more than a consolidation of the previous legislative provisions in this
area. It also introduces entirely new concepts in Irish law, including moral
rights as well as other provisions which attempt to deal with the copyright
issues connected with new forms of technology and communication. In this
respect, the 2000 Act provides for a more effective regime of civil remedies
and criminal penalties than was the case under previous legislation. By including
this new regime, the drafters intended to ensure that they were fully sufficient
to deter copyright theft, bearing in mind the economic and cultural
consequences of such theft for the 'information society.' Other innovations in
the 2000 Act include civil protection for performers' rights and for rights in
performances and non-original databases in line with the best EU and
international standards. Indeed, the international dimension is writ large in the
2000 Act.

EU and international dimension The 2000 Act seeks to implement all
relevant EU directives in the field of copyright and related rights, including
those already implemented by previous Regulations but extending to other
Directives not already implemented. The 2000 Act gives effect to: Directive

91/250/EEC on the legal protection of computer programs; Directive 92/100/ EEC on rental right and lending right; Directive 93/83/EEC on copyright of satellite broadcasting and cable retransmission; Directive 93/98/EEC on the term of copyright; and to Directive 96/9/EC on the legal protection of databases. At a wider international level, the 2000 Act brought Irish law into conformity with all obligations incurred under, for example, the WTO Agreement on Trade Related Intellectual Property Rights (the TRIPS Agreement), the Berne Convention, the Rome Convention, the World Intellectual Property Organisation (WIPO) Copyright Treaty, and the Performances and Phonograms Treaty. This extensive list of international agreements is testimony to the global trade-related context within which copyright and related rights now exist. Indeed, it was accepted during the passage of the 2000 Act in the Oireachtas that the absence of such a modern legislative framework had led to some criticism of the State by leading international trading partners; some commentators had suggested that if the lacuna had persisted it might have affected the ability of the State's industrial development bodies to attract continued foreign investment from MNCs in the IT sector. Be that as it may, the 2000 Act cannot be seen entirely as a reaction to such perceived criticism, since it is part of the gradual updating of the legislation on intellectual property rights, which have included the Patents Act 1992 (Annual Review 1992, 41- 6) and the Trade Marks Act 1996 (Annual Review 1996, 68-76). The process will be completed when the Industrial Designs Bill 2000 is enacted.

Copyright in general   Part II of the Copyright and Related Rights Act 2000 deals with the traditional rights of copyright. Section 17 of the 2000 Act provides:

(1) Copyright is a property right whereby, subject to this Act, the owner of the copyright in any work may undertake or authorise other persons in relation to that work to undertake certain acts in the State, being acts which are designated by this Act as acts restricted by copyright in a work of that description.

(2) Copyright subsists, in accordance with this Act, in- (a) original literary, dramatic, musical or artistic works, (b) sound recordings, films, broadcasts or cable programmes, (c) the typographical arrangement of published editions, and (d) original databases.

(3) Copyright protection shall not extend to the ideas and principles which underlie any element of a work, procedures, methods of operation or mathematical concepts and, in respect of original databases, shall not extend to their contents and is without prejudice to any rights subsisting in those contents.

This is largely in line with the Copyright Act 1963, with the exception of the extension to non-original typographical arrangements (listings) and original databases.

Section 23 of the 2000 Act deals with ownership of copyright. It provides that, in general, the author of a work shall be the first owner of the copyright. To this general principle, there are a number of important exceptions:

(a) Where the work is made by an employee in the course of employment, in which case the employer is the first owner of any copyright in the work, subject to any agreement to the contrary,

(b) Where the work is the subject of Government or Oireachtas copyright,

(c) Where the work is the subject of the copyright of a prescribed international organisation, or

(d) the copyright in the work is conferred on some other person by an enactment.

The exception concerning employees is, in turn, subject to a further important exception. Section 23(2) provides:

> Where a work, other than a computer program, is made by an author in the course of employment by the proprietor of a newspaper or periodical, the author may use the work for any purpose, other than for the purposes of making available that work to newspapers or periodicals, without infringing the copyright in the work.

This provides some additional copyright protection to journalists, at least insofar as their work might be used as the basis for a book, for example.

Section 24 of the 2000 Act provides for a general 70 years duration for copyright protection in the various classes of copyright work, first introduced in the European Communities (Term of Protection of Copyright) Regulations 1995, which implemented Directive 93/98/EEC (Annual Review 1995, 48-9), discussed in *Sweeney v. National University of Ireland Cork t/a Cork University Press* [2001] 1 I.L.R.M. 310, below. Sections 25 to 32 of the 2000 Act provide for other durations in respect of specific matters, and a 50 year rule applies, for example, to broadcasts.

Section 37 of the 2000 Act outlines the rights of a copyright owner in relation to a work, including the exclusive right to authorise the copying or reproduction and making available to the public or adaptation of the work subject to the provisions of the Act itself. Section 40 of the 2000 Act states that 'making available to the public of a work' comprises any of the following:

(a) making available to the public of copies of the work, by wire or wireless means, in such a way that members of the public may access the work from a place and at a time chosen by them (including the making available of copies of works through the Internet);

(b) performing, showing or playing a copy of the work in public;

(c) broadcasting a copy of the work;

(d) including a copy of the work in a cable programme service;

(e) issuing copies of the work to the public;

(f) renting copies of the work;

(g) lending copies of the work without the payment of remuneration to the owner of the copyright in the work,

Section 40 states that such acts are lawful only where any relevant royalty has been paid to or permission obtained from the copyright holder. In effect, where such has not been obtained, section 40 contains a list of potential copyright infringements. By including reference to the Internet, the 2000 Act makes clear that the kind of copying facility available on sites such as Napster (prior to its being injuncted in the United States) would clearly be in breach of the 2000 Act. For a critical view of this aspect of the 2000 Act, see Denis Kelleher, Gazette, Law Society of Ireland, April 2001.

Of course, as with the 1963 Act, the 2000 Act does provide for a limited number of exceptions or derogations from what would otherwise be the absolute rights of the copyright owner. These are, principally, the 'fair dealing' exceptions in favour of research and private study (section 50), criticism and review of works (section 51) and incidental inclusion of copyright material in another work (section 52). There are also limited exceptions in favour of educational and library and archival use (sections 53 to 71) as well as certain uses in public administration, such as parliamentary and judicial proceedings, statutory tribunals or government activities (sections 72 to 76).

Moral rights   Part 3 of the 2000 Act also introduces for the first time in Irish law provision for moral rights. Section 107 provides that the author of a work has the right to be identified as the author and that right shall also apply in relation to an adaptation of the work. This is referred to as the 'paternity right.' It is notable that this phrase was not gender proofed to provide that it could be referred to as the 'maternity right.' This right is subject to a number of exceptions in section 108 (principally any act that is authorised by other provisions of the 2000 Act itself). Subject to this, section 109 provides that the author of a work has the right to object to any distortion, mutilation or other modification of, or other derogatory action in relation to, the work which would prejudice his or her reputation and that right shall also apply in relation to an adaptation of the work. This is referred to as the 'integrity right' (which is also subject to some exceptions in sections110 and 111).

Dealing, assignment and licensing The 2000 Act contains important provisions governing dealings in copyright interests, including assignment and licensing. Thus, section 120 provides that the copyright in a work is transmissible by assignment, by testamentary disposition or by operation of law, as personal or moveable property.

Remedies and enforcement The 2000 Act provides for extensive remedies for infringement of copyright interests. On the civil side, the Act contains 'notify and take down' provisions. These provide that if copyright infringing material is being carried on a service, such as an Internet service, and the rights owners inform the service providers that infringing material is being carried on that service, the service providers will be obliged to remove that material as soon as is practicable. The 2000 Act also introduces more effective criminal sanctions than the Copyright Act 1963, which, as indicated was one of the principal weaknesses in the statutory regime prior to the 2000 Act.

Performance rights Part III of the 2000 Act introduced for the first time in Irish law a regime of rights, exceptions and sanctions in respect of performers' rights and rights in performances. This is broadly parallel to those provided for in relation to copyright by Part II. The rights protected under this Part may broadly be described as the exclusive right of a performer to authorise the copying or making available to the public of his or her performance and recording rights. Recording rights involve the rights of persons who have exclusive recording contracts with performers, such as record producers, to protection from illicit recording. Part III represents the introduction into Irish law for the first time of a comprehensive regime of protection for this type of right. This includes direct legal protection for performers and producers against illicit direct recording of live performances, that is, what is often described as bootlegging. Part IV of the 2000 Act, on performers' moral rights, provides for a regime of moral rights protection for performers in relation to their performances which is parallel to that provided for authors of copyright works under Part II.

Databases Part V of the 2000 Act provides for a new regime of protection for non-original databases as required by the EU Database Directive, 96/9/EC. Non-original databases are databases the creation of which does not involve significant intellectually creative input. Examples are simple alphabetical lists, such as telephone directories. These would have been protected up to now under Irish law by copyright as literary works. However, the database directive requires that a higher standard of originality be applied to databases if they are to qualify for full copyright protection. Thus, Part V provides a more limited form of protection for databases no longer meeting the copyright originality standard in line with the rules set out in the Database Directive.

Jurisdiction of Controller Part VI of the 2000 Act, on the jurisdiction of Controller of Patents, Designs and Trade Marks, makes provision for and expands the role of the Controller as a tribunal for the resolution of certain disputes regarding copyright licensing schemes.

Technological protection measures Part VII of the 2000 Act, on technological protection measures, provides copyright rightsholders with rights and remedies against persons who unlawfully circumvent technological measures designed to protect certain copyright materials. An example of this would be producing counterfeit smart cards for tapping into encrypted satellite broadcasts and cable programmes. Another example is the removal of identifying rights management features, such as digital fingerprints and other electronic markers, from copyright materials.

Commencement and detailed Orders and Regulations The Copyright and Related Rights Act 2000 (Commencement) Order 2000 (S.I. No.404 of 2000) brought the following provisions of the 2000 Act into force on January 1, 2001: Part 1 (except section 10(2) in so far as it applies to section 56 of the Copyright Act 1963); Part II (except sections 98, 198 and 199;) Part III (except section 247); Part IV; Part V; Part VI; and Part VII. As can be seen, this represents the overwhelming majority of the 2000 Act. The following Orders and Regulations under the 2000 Act have also been made: the Copyright and Related Rights (Recording of Broadcasts and Cable Programmes for Archival Purposes) (Designated Bodies and Classes) Order 2000 (S.I. No.405 of 2000); the Copyright and Related Rights (Provision of Modified Works) (Designated Bodies) Order 2000 (S.I. No.406 of 2000); the Copyright and Related Rights (Recording for Purposes of Time-shifting) Order 2000 (S.I. No.407 of 2000); the Copyright and Related Rights (Works of Folklore) (Designated Bodies) Order 2000 (S.I. No.408 of 2000); the Copyright and Related Rights (Educational Establishments and Establishments to which Members of the Public have Access) Order 2000 (S.I. No.409 of 2000); the Copyright and Related Rights (Educational Establishments) Order 2000 (S.I. No.410 of 2000); the Copyright and Related Rights (Material open to Public Inspection) (International Organisations) Order 2000 (S.I. No.411 of 2000); and the Copyright and Related Rights (Librarians and Archivists) (Copying of Protected Material) Regulations 2000 (S.I. No.427 of 2000).

ELECTRONIC COMMERCE

The Electronic Commerce Act 2000 was enacted to remove in a relatively simple manner any existing legal impediments and uncertainties that have arisen as a result of the onset and continuing growth of e-commerce (or e-business or any number of similar titles, such as 'etailing', as opposed to retailing, or B2B to describe transactions between businesses and B2C to describe consumer transactions). As was stated when the 2000 Act was being progressed through the Oireachtas, the 2000 Act was not intended to introduce a new legal framework for e-commerce, it is an enabling Act. Some of the provisions of the 2000 Act were based on the Electronic Signatures Directive, 1999/93/EC, and it also attempted to take account of directives that were still in draft form at the time of its legislative passage. The Act was passed into law on its manual signature by the President, though an electronic signature ceremony (which had no legal status) was also given much publicity at the time. The Electronic Commerce Act 2000 (Commencement) Order 2000 (S.I. No. 293 of 2000) brought the Act into effect on September 20, 2000.

Equivalence between electronic and paper world   Part 2 of the 2000 Act (sections 9 to 28) provides, in effect, for equivalence between the electronic and paper world. Section 9 lays down the fundamental principle on which the Act is founded, namely:

> Information … shall not be denied legal effect, validity or enforceability, solely on the grounds that it is wholly or partly in electronic form, whether as an electronic communication or otherwise.

Consumer and defamation laws   By way of clarifying the scope of section 9, section 15 of the 2000 Act provides that all electronic contracts are subject to all existing consumer law and that the role of the Director of Consumer Affairs in such legislation is to apply equally to consumer transactions within the State, whether conducted electronically or non-electronically. Similarly, section 23 provides that all provisions of existing defamation law shall apply to all electronic communications within the State, including the retention of information electronically. The question might arise whether the reference to existing law in section 23, which clearly covers the statutory rules in the Defamation Act 1961, is sufficiently wide to capture relevant common law rules as well.

Exclusions   Section 10 provides that the following are, at least initially, excluded from the scope of the 2000 Act:

- the law regarding the creation, execution, amendment, variation or revocation of a will codicil or any other testamentary instrument to which the Succession Act 1965 applies
- a trust; or an enduring power of attorney
- the law governing the manner in which an interest in real property (including a lease) may be created, acquired, disposed of, or registered, other than contracts for the creation, acquisition or disposal of such interests;
- the law governing the making of an affidavit or a statutory or sworn

declaration, or requiring or permitting the use of one for any purpose, or

• the rules, practices or procedures of a court or tribunal.

The reasoning behind section 10 was that it was felt that the technology and systems were not yet at a stage where they could cope with the execution of such transactions electronically. Nonetheless, the Minister for Public Enterprise is empowered by the Act to make Regulations to extend the application of the legislation to these excluded categories, subject to the consent of the relevant Minister; in the case of providing for on-line access to courts, this would be the Minister for Justice. Where this occurs, section 22 of the 2000 Act provides for the admissibility of electronic information as evidence in legal proceedings. In the meantime, the Courts Service, for example, is engaged in a significant 'E-programme' aimed at introducing more widespread use of IT in the court system (including a pilot study for on-line use of the small claims procedure in the District Court). No doubt, developments in the United Kingdom implementing the next phase of the post-Woolf reforms will be influential in the future of this programme and the ultimate extension of the 2000 Act to court proceedings and the implementation of section 22 of the 2000 Act.

Similarly, section 11 provides that nothing in the Act shall prejudice the operation of:

(a) any law relating to the imposition, collection or recovery of taxation or other Government imposts, including fees, fines and penalties,

(b) the Companies Act 1990 (Uncertificated Securities) Regulations 1996(S.I. No.68 of 1996) or any Regulations made in substitution for those Regulations,

(c) the Criminal Evidence Act 1992, or

(d) the Consumer Credit Act 1995, or any Regulations made thereunder, and the European Communities (Unfair Terms in Consumer Contracts) Regulations 1995 (S.I. No.27 of 1995).

This in no way hinders for example, the Revenue Commissioners from dealing electronically with their customers: it is designed solely to ensure that the substantive aspects of the laws referred to are not captured by the 2000 Act.

Validity of electronic contracts In keeping with section 9, section 19(1) of the 2000 Act provides:

> An electronic contract shall not be denied legal effect, validity or enforceability solely on the grounds that it is wholly or partly in electronic form, or has been concluded wholly or partly by way of electronic communication.

Similarly section 22 provides that electronic contracts, writing or signatures cannot be denied admissibility as evidence on the sole ground that it is electronic evidence, provided that it is the best evidence which can be reasonably obtained.

Formation of contracts by electronic means Section 19(2) of the Act provides that:

> The formation of a contract, an offer, acceptance of an offer or any related communication . . . may unless otherwise agreed by the parties, be communicated by means of an electronic communication.

This general principle is followed up by a number of specific rules. Thus, section 20 provides that where an electronic communication is sent which requires an acknowledgement, until the acknowledgement is received the communication will be treated as if it had never been sent (this clearly indicates that the 'postal rule' will not apply). Section 21 details the conditions of dispatch and receipt of electronic communications. Essentially, it provides that a communication is sent once it enters the first information system outside the control of the originator (such as the Internet) and is received once it enters the recipient's system.

Electronic writing and records Section 12(1) of the 2000 Act states:

> If by law or otherwise a person or public body is required ... or permitted to give information in writing ... the person or public body may give the information in electronic form, whether as an electronic communication or otherwise.

This can extend to giving information such as making an application, a claim, a request, an unsworn declaration, lodging an objection or recording or disseminating a court order. Section 12 also sets out basic requirements that writing in electronic form must meet. At the time the writing was given, the author must reasonably expect that the writing be accessible for subsequent reference. A distinction is made between the requirements of public and private bodies. In essence, this allows public bodies to lay down their requirements before being obliged to receive writing electronically. Private bodies require the consent of the recipient to use electronic writing.

It should be noted that section 24 provides that nothing in the 2000 Act shall be construed as *requiring* any person or public body to use electronic communications. Indeed, sections 10 and 11 exclude from the 2000 Act various activities, such as the registration of titles and court procedure as outlined in rules of court.

Section 17 of the 2000 Act relates to the generation of original documents electronically, while section 18 provides for the electronic retention and production of records electronically. Where they are so generated or retained, the Act requires that a number of conditions must be complied with, including that there must be 'a reliable assurance as to the integrity of the information.' The exceptions in sections 10 and 11 of the 2000 Act should also be noted in this context.

Electronic signatures and encryption Section 13(1) of the 2000 Act provides that electronic signatures may be used wherever a signature is required by law or otherwise. Section 13(2) provides that an electronic signature can only be used where the person or public body to whom the signature is given consents to its use. Similarly, section 14 allows for signatures to be witnessed electronically. In this case 'advanced electronic signatures' must be used because they offer a higher level of authenticity, which is considered appropriate for documents that need to be witnessed. An advanced electronic signature is defined as an electronic signature uniquely linked to the signatory, capable of identifying the signatory, created using means that are capable of being maintained by the signatory under his, her or its sole control, and linked to the data to which it relates in such a way that any subsequent change of the data is detectable. Section 16 provides for an electronic method of meeting the requirement for a seal using electronic signatures. Again, in both sections 14 and 16, these electronic methods can only be used with the consent of the public body or person who requires the signature to be witnessed or the document to be sealed.

Section 27 of the 2000 Act deals with the confidentiality of deciphering data and provides that:

> Nothing in this Act shall be construed as requiring the disclosure of unique data, such as codes, passwords, algorithms, private cryptographic keys or other data, that may be necessary to render information or an electronic communication intelligible.

This focuses on the security and integrity of the encryption systems needed to implement provisions such as sections 13, 14 and 16.

Offences for fraudulent use of electronic signatures and signature creation devices Section 25 of the 2000 Act provides for a number of offences for the fraudulent use of electronic signatures, signature creation devices and electronic certificates. Section 26, which was added to the legislation during its passage through the Oireachtas, provides for activities partly outside the State, in effect, for the extra-territorial application of the Act. Given the nature of the Internet, in particular, it was accepted that the systems used to commit offences may well be located outside the State. Section 27 lays down the investigative procedures for the offences created in the previous sections.

Certification services Part 3 of the Act (sections 29 and 30) provides for matters relating to the service providers who issue electronic signature certificates or provide other services related to electronic signatures, and is based on the 1999 Electronic Signature Directive, 1999/93/EC. These service providers are known in the Act as certification service providers. To meet the needs of the IT sector and the specific requirements on reliability and confidentiality in the 2000 Act, the emergence of electronic signature certification services has already begun. Section 29 empowers the Minister for Public Enterprise to prescribe accreditation and supervision schemes for certification service providers. The 2000 Act does not require prior authorisation before such a business begins, but provides that the government may put in place a scheme for the accreditation and supervision of certification service providers. It was felt that the potential for liability of certification service providers, which is dealt with in section 29, for failure to ensure appropriate verification of such signatures would be sufficient to result in the voluntary arrangements becoming, *de facto*, mandatory. The final shape of the direct supervision scheme has yet to be determined, but these supervision service providers will be accredited by the National Accreditation Board (NAB), the State's accreditation body which is a division of Forfas. Indeed, the accreditation scheme developed by NAB for the 2000 Act has become a model for similar schemes in other European states.

Domain name registration Part 4 of the 2000 Act (section 31) empowers the Minister for Public Enterprise to place the registration of Irish Internet domain names on a statutory basis 'for the purpose of easy comprehension, fairness, transparency, avoidance of deception, promotion of fair competition and public confidence.' Currently, this is organised on a non-statutory basis by the Internet Corporation for Assigned Names and Numbers, in conjunction with regional entities. The two-letter code assigned to Ireland for domain names is 'ie.' This is based in ISO 3166-1 (Codes for Representation of Names of Countries and their Subdivision) of the International Organisation for Standardisation. As was stated during the Oireachtas debate on the 2000 Act, the Irish domain name is a national resource which should be managed in the public interest as in the interests of the Internet community.

FINANCIAL SERVICES

Consumer credit: list of credit institutions The Consumer Credit Act 1995 (Section 2) Regulations 1999, the Consumer Credit Act 1995 (Section 2) (No.2) Regulations 1999 (S.I. No.392 of 1999) and the Consumer Credit Act 1995 (Section 2) Regulations 2000 (S.I. No.113 of 2000) further supplemented the list of credit institutions to which the Consumer Credit Act 1995 apply.

ICC Bank The main purpose of the ICC Bank Act 2000 was to provide for the disposal by the Minister for Finance of his shares in the Bank; in effect to provide for its privatisation. It also increased the authorised share capital of ICC Bank plc and made provision in relation to certain guarantees of the borrowing of ICC Bank. The 2000 Act also provided for the repeal of the ICC Bank Acts 1933 to 1997. With the exception of sections 3, 5 and 7, the 2000 Act came into effect on 7 December 2000: ICC Bank Act 2000 (Commencement) Order 2000 (S.I. No.396 of 2000). The sale of the ICC Bank to Bank of Scotland was completed in early 2001.

Moneylender: exemption for loan on property In *Wise Finance Company Ltd v. Hughes*, Supreme Court, November 12, 1999, the plaintiff company had advanced £25,000 to the defendant, which had been secured by a charge on property in Co. Longford. The loan was not repaid and the plaintiff sought an order for possession in the High Court. The defendant claimed, *inter alia*, that the loan was invalid as the plaintiff had no licence to carry on the business of money lending under the Money-lenders Acts 1900 and 1933. This ground was accepted by Laffoy J. in the High Court and, as a result, the plaintiff's claim was dismissed (Annual Review 1998, 27). However, in a later case, Laffoy J. accepted that she may have been *per in curiam* in her judgment (Annual Review 1998, 28). This was confirmed when the plaintiff appealed on the grounds that its business came within the provisions of Art.2(1)(a)(iii) of the Money-lenders Act 1900 (Section 6(e)) Order 1993 (Annual Review, 1993, 48). This exempts from the licensing requirements of the 1900 and 1933 Acts any business involved in lending money for use for the purposes of purchasing, developing or otherwise dealing with land whether or not the loan is secured on land or for some other purpose where the loan is secured on land whether with or without other security. It was accepted that the 1993 Order had not been raised or relied on in the High Court by the plaintiff.

The Supreme Court considered that the commitment letter and printed standard form which the plaintiff had supplied to the defendant fell well short of what was required by the terms of the relevant Article in the 1993 Order. This was because it went no further than demonstrating that in the case of some transactions the loan was so secured, but there remained no evidence as to the extent to which the business of the plaintiff consisted wholly or mainly of such transactions. Nonetheless, the Supreme Court allowed the appeal and remitted the matter to the High Court on the undertaking of the plaintiff that it would confine its claim for interest from the date of the Order appealed from to the date of the determination of the matter at the rate of interest allowed by the court. The Court held that it was for the High Court to determine in the light of whatever evidence was furnished whether the plaintiff in fact came within the provisions of Article 2(1)(a)(iii) of the 1993 Order and it would also be open to the defendant to rely on the other grounds raised by him in the High Court. It also ordered the plaintiff to pay all the defendant's costs to date.

Netting of contracts   The Netting of Financial Contracts Act 1995 (Designation of Financial Contracts) Regulations 2000 (S.I. No.214 of 2000), made under the Netting of Financial Contracts Act 1995 (Annual Review 1995, 40) designated certain types of contracts as financial contracts for the purposes of netting. They came into effect on June 30, 2000.

INSURANCE

Disclosure of information and supervision of insurance intermediaries   The Insurance Act 2000 had two main objects. First, it made provision for the disclosure to potentially insured persons of information by insurers and insurance intermediaries in relation to life assurance and non-life insurance products. It thus made substantial amendments to the Insurance Act 1989 (Annual Review 1989, 44-7) in order to implement Directive 92/96/ EEC. The long-awaited detailed Regulations on disclosure, especially in connection with life insurance policies, first envisaged in the 1989 Act, ultimately emerged in 2001: Life Assurance (Provision of Information) Regulations 2001 (S.I. No.15 of 2001). The second object of the 2000 Act was to provide for the authorisation and supervision of insurance intermediaries by the Central Bank of Ireland. To this end, it amended the Investment Intermediaries Act 1995, to provide for the application of the 1995 Act to insurance intermediaries. The change in regulatory control followed collapses of insurance intermediaries and it was concluded that the arrangements under the 1995 Act were not sufficiently strong to ensure consumer confidence. The Insurance Act 2000 (Commencement) Order 2000 (S.I. No.472 of 2000) brought the Act into effect on 1 January 2001.

Insurance undertakings in group The European Communities (Supplementary Supervision of Insurance Undertakings in an Insurance Group) Regulations 1999 (S.I. No.399 of 1999) introduced additional requirements to be met by insurance undertakings within the European Economic Area by obliging such undertakings to provide information to the supervisory authorities on intra-group transactions. They came into effect on January 1, 2001.

Reinsurance business The Insurance Act 1989 (Reinsurance) (Form of Notification) Regulations 1999 (S.I. No.437 of 1999), made under the Insurance Act 1989 (Annual Review 1989, 44-7) prescribe the form of notification to be made to the Minister for Enterprise, Trade and Employment by companies wishing to carry on the business of reinsurance within the State. They came into effect on December 30 1999.

INTELLECTUAL PROPERTY

Copyright and Related Rights Act 2000 The Copyright and Related Rights
Act 2000, which replaced the Copyright Act 1963, is discussed separately, **25**,
above.

Copyright: injunction In *Sweeney v. National University of Ireland Cork t/a
Cork University Press* [2001] 1 I.L.R.M. 310, the plaintiff was granted an
interlocutory injunction preventing the defendant from publishing extracts from
the works of James Joyce in an anthology of Irish literature which the defendant
proposed to publish. The case involved the consequences of the revival of
copyright in Joyce's works, as a result of the European Communities (Term of
Protection of Copyright) Regulations 1995, which implemented Directive 93/
98/EEC (Annual Review 1995, 48-9) (see now section 24 of the Copyright
and Related Rights Act 2000, above). Copyright in Joyce's works had lapsed
in 1992 under the 50 year rule in the Copyright Act 1963, but had been revived
in 1995 under the 70 year rule introduced by the 1995 Regulations. The
defendant had initially sought the permission of Joyce's estate to publish the
extracts, but when a dispute arose over the fee requested, the defendant sought
to include extracts from an anthology of Joyce's works which had been
published in 1997. The author of the 1997 anthology claimed that it was exempt
from the revival of copyright under the 1995 Regulations on the grounds that
substantial preparations had been made on the anthology prior to the 1995
Regulations came into effect. Thomas Smyth J. accepted that the substantive
case might disclose that the defendant was entitled to publish the extracts
from the 1997 anthology, but in the interlocutory application he concluded
that the balance of convenience favoured granting an injunction to the plaintiff.
Perhaps not surprisingly in view of the subject matter of the case, the decision
attracted considerable publicity. Ultimately, the defendant decided to publish
its anthology, Pierce, *Irish Writing in the 20th Century: A Reader* (Cork
University Press, 2001) without any extracts from Joyce.

Electronic Commerce Act 2000 The Electronic Commerce Act 2000 is
discussed separately, 30, above.

Trademark registration: confusion In *Montex Holdings Ltd v. Controller of
Patents, Designs and Trademarks* [2000] 1 I.L.R.M. 481, O'Sullivan J. refused
the plaintiff's application for registration of the word 'Diesel' as a trademark
for use in connection with clothing. The plaintiff had applied to the Controller
to register the word on the ground that ownership of the mark and goodwill
vested in the plaintiff. The second defendant had filed a notice of opposition,
claiming that it had the ownership of the mark and goodwill attached to it.
Registration of the mark was refused by the Controller and the plaintiff appealed
by way of special summons. The plaintiff submitted that the wrong test had

been applied by the Controller in interpreting section 19 of the Trade Marks Act 1963, which prohibited, *inter alia*, any registration which would, by reason of its being likely to deceive or cause confusion or otherwise, be disentitled to protection in a court of law (see now section 8 of the Trade Marks Act 1996: Annual Review 1996, 68-9).

Referring to *Albassam Trademark* [1995] RPC 511, O'Sullivan J. applied the test that ownership of a trade mark vested in the party first using it in this jurisdiction. In the instant case, the plaintiff had established a sufficient user prior to the date of application to entitle it, *prima facie*, to be registered as owner, but the second defendant had also established a sufficient user prior to that date to entitle it to *locus standi*. On the competing interests of the two parties, therefore, he was not satisfied on the evidence before it that the plaintiff's proposed user of the mark was bona fide. He noted that the clear and unambiguous meaning of the words of section 19 of the 1963 Act (and section 8 of the 1996 Act) excluded registration where it was established that use of the mark would have involved confusion, deception or otherwise, thereby disentitling such use to protection in a court of law. In that respect, the use of the same word on the same type of garments for distribution into the same market had to raise the likelihood that a substantial number of persons would be confused, at least in the sense that they would be left in doubt as to whether these were the goods of the plaintiff or the second defendant. The decision is under appeal to the Supreme Court.

INTERNATIONAL TRADE

Export of dual-use (civil and military use) goods The European Communities (Control of Exports of Dual-Use Goods) (Amendment) Regulations 2000 (S.I. No.98 of 2000) amended the 1999 Regulations to enable the Minister for Enterprise, Trade and Employment to grant a general authorisation in respect of a type or category of dual-use goods which is listed in Annex I, but which is not contained in Annex IV, of Council Decision 94/942/CFSP as last amended. The 2000 Regulations came into effect on March 24, 2000.

International Development Association The International Development Association (Amendment) Act 2000 enables the Government to make a total payment of IR£20 million to the Twelfth Replenishment of the International Development Association.

Multilateral Investment Guarantee Agency The Multilateral Investment Guarantee Agency (Amendment) Act 2000 amended the Multilateral Investment Guarantee Agency Act 1988 (Annual Review 1988, 3-4) to enable the Government to subscribe 281 shares in the 1998 Capital Increase of the

Multilateral Investment Guarantee Agency (MIGA). The MIGA was established in 1988 as a member of the World Bank Group. Its main object is to provide insurance cover or direct foreign investment in developing countries.

Trade sanctions: Indonesia   The European Communities (Ban on the Supply to Indonesia of Equipment Which Might be used for Internal Repression or Terrorism) Regulations 1999 (S.I. No.357 of 2000) provide for penalties for infringements of Council Regulation (EC) No.2158/1999 which introduced a ban on the supply to Indonesia of equipment which might be used for internal repression or terrorism.

Trade sanctions: former Yugoslavia   The European Communities (Revocation of Trade Sanctions Concerning the Federal Republic of Yugoslavia (Serbia And Montenegro) and Certain Areas of the Republics of Croatia and Bosnia-Herzogovina) Regulations 2000 (S.I. No.60 of 2000) revoked the 1993 and 1995 Regulations (Annual Review 1993, 63 and Annual Review 1995, 49) which had provided for trade embargoes against Serbia, Montenegro, Croatia and Boznia-Herzogovina. The 2000 Regulations, which were made after the ending of the Kosovo conflict but before the full rapprochement with Serbia in 2001, came into effect on March 2, 2000.

MEASUREMENTS AND METROLOGY

Units of measurement   The European Communities (Units of Measurement) (Amendment) Regulations 2000 (S.I. No.143 of 2000) amended the 1992 Regulations (Annual Review 1992, 46), as last amended in 1998 (Annual Review 1998, 36), to give effect to Directive 99/103/EC for a period of ten years. They updated the definitions of some units of measurement in line with the decisions of the *Conférence Génerale des Poids et Mesures,* the International Organisation for Standardisation and the International Council of Scientific Unions. The 2000 Regulations were deemed to come into effect on January 1, 2000.

UNFAIR TERMS IN CONSUMER CONTRACTS

The European Communities (Unfair Terms in Consumer Contracts) (Amendment) Regulations 2000 (S.I. No.307 of 2000) amended the European Communities (Unfair Terms in Consumer Contracts) Regulations 1995, which had implemented Directive 93/13/EEC. The 2000 Regulations provide that consumer organisations set up for the purpose of protecting consumer rights, such as the Consumer Association of Ireland, may seek an order from the High Court to prevent breaches of the Regulations. The 2000 Regulations came into effect on October 2, 2000. In light of the amendment of the 1995 Regulations, it is appropriate to outline their provisions here.

The 1995 Regulations apply to consumer sale of goods and supply of services contracts only. They have a civil and criminal element; the civil element stating that contracts in breach of its terms are not enforceable while the criminal law element empowers the Director of Consumer Affairs to initiate criminal prosecutions where there is non-compliance with its terms. Because the 1995 Regulations apply to sale of goods and supply of services contracts, there is some overlap with the Sale of Goods and Supply of Services Act 1980. For criticism of the method of implementing the 1993 Directive, see Murphy, "The Unfair Contract Terms Regulations: a Red Card for the State" (1995) 13 ILT 156.

Sale of goods and supply of services   In general, Regulation 3 of the 1995 Regulations provides that they apply to any term in a contract concluded between a seller of goods or supplier of services and a consumer. However, Schedule 1 to the Regulations specifies that they do *not* apply to:

    (a) any contracts of employment;
    (b) any contract relating to succession rights;
    (c) any contract relating to rights under family law;
    (d) any contract relating to the incorporation and organisation of companies or partnerships;
    (e) any terms which reflect—
        (i)   mandatory statutory or regulatory provisions of Ireland, or
        (ii) the provisions or principles of international conventions to which the Member States or the Community are party.

These exclusions are roughly in line with the exclusions from the definition of contracts for the supply of services in the Sale of Goods and Supply of Services Act 1980. Thus, the 1995 Regulations apply mainly to sale of goods and supply of services contracts.

Consumer contracts   By contrast with the 1980 Act, the 1995 Regulations apply to consumer contracts only. Regulation 2 of the 1995 Regulations defines a 'consumer' as a natural person (that is, an individual) who is acting for purposes which are outside his/her/its business sections. 'Seller' and 'supplier' are defined as a person who is acting for purposes related to his/her/its business sections The word 'business' is defined as including a trade or profession and the activities of any government department or local or public authority. These definitions are, again, broadly in line with those in the 1980 Act. However, the fact that 'consumer' is defined in the 1995 Regulations as a 'natural person' clearly excludes companies from ever being considered as a consumer, whereas it is possible that a company may be 'dealing as consumer' under the 1980

Act: see *R & B Customs Brokers Co Ltd v. UDT Ltd and Saunders Abbott Ltd* [1988] 1 All E.R. 847.

Pre-formulated standard form contracts   Regulation 3 provides that the 1995 Regulations applies to contracts that have not been individually negotiated. Regulation 3(4) states that this refers to contracts which have been drafted in advance and the consumer has therefore not been able to influence its substance, in particular 'a pre-formulated standard contract.' Regulation 3(5) states that the fact that a specific term or any aspect of a term has been individually negotiated shall not exclude necessarily exclude the application of the Regulations to the rest of the contract if an overall assessment of the contract indicates that it has not been individually negotiated. Regulation 3(6) states that the onus is on any seller or supplier who claims that a term was individually negotiated to show that it was.

Unfair terms not legally binding on consumer   Regulation 6(1) of the 1995 Regulations is critical since it provides that 'an unfair term in a contract concluded with a consumer by a seller or supplier shall not be binding on the consumer.' Regulation 6(2) provides that the contract shall continue to bind the parties, if it is capable of continuing in existence without the unfair term. This approach seems to be close to stating that unfair contract terms are void, to use the language of the 1980 Act, but the 1995 Regulations are, in fact closer to applying a 'fair and reasonable' test when they are examined in more detail.

Definition of unfair term: significant imbalance between parties   Regulation 3(2) provides that, for the purpose of the 1995 Regulations, a contractual term is unfair if:

> contrary to the requirement of good faith, it causes a significant imbalance in the parties' rights and obligations under the contract to the detriment of the consumer, taking into account the nature of the goods or services for which the contract was concluded and all circumstances attending the conclusion of the contract and all other terms of the contract or of another contract on which it is dependent.'

Unfair terms – good faith   Regulation 3(3) states that, in determining whether a term satisfies the requirement of good faith, regard must be had to the matters listed in Schedule 2 to the 1995 Regulations, which specifies:

> In making an assessment of good faith, particular regard shall be had to
>
> — the strength of the bargaining positions of the parties,
> — whether the consumer had an inducement to agree to the term,

— whether the goods or services were sold or supplied to the special order of the consumer, and
— the extent to which the seller or supplier has dealt fairly and equitably with the consumer whose legitimate interests he has to take into account.

This list of factors is remarkably similar to those in the Schedule to the 1980 Act, used in determining whether an exclusion clause is 'fair and reasonable'. Presumably, a similar weighing of these factors would be appropriate to the 1995 Regulations.

Plain language/contra proferentem Regulation 5(1) of the 1995 Regulations provides that in the case of contracts where all or certain terms offered to the consumer are in writing, the seller or supplier must ensure that terms are drafted in plain, intelligible language. Regulation 5(2) provides that, where there is a doubt about the meaning of a term, the interpretation most favourable to the consumer shall prevail. This is very like the common law principle of *contra proferentem*.

Price v. service – insurance contracts Another provision of the 1995 Regulations, Regulation 4, also discussed the requirement for plain language, though it is hardly written in very clear terms. Regulation 4 states:

A term shall not of itself be considered to be unfair by relation to the definition of the main subject matter of the contract or to the adequacy of the price and remuneration, as against the goods and services supplied, in so far as these terms are in plain, intelligible language.

This provision is intended to apply, for example, to insurance contracts. A feature of many insurance company's policies is that they limit or restrict liability, that is, the payment to be made under a policy is subject to a ceiling. This is directly related to the risk covered (the subject matter of the contract) and this in turn would have been a major factor in deciding the premium charged by the insurance company. Regulation 4 of the 1995 Regulations indicates that the balance made by the insurance company between the restriction on liability, the risk and the premium is not of itself to be regarded as unfair under the 1995 Regulations, provided the insurance contract is written in plain language. An example of this provision being applied can be fund in Marrinan Quinn (ed.), *Insurance Ombudsman of Ireland: Digest of Cases 1992-1998* (Insurance Ombudsman of Ireland, 1998). This Digest of Cases of the first Insurance Ombudsman of Ireland contains an adjudication by her (Case 95) in which she applied the general 'good faith' test in the 1995 Regulations and also the exclusion for insurance policies in Regulation 4. This was in the context of an exclusion in a travel policy for medical expenses incurred in the State: it was held that the exclusion in this case did not fall foul of the 1995 Regulations. Nonetheless, reflecting the special nature of the Ombudsman's role, she recommended an *ex gratia* payment of £200 to the insured.

Unfair terms – approach to be taken by courts   While Regulation 6(1) provides that 'unfair terms' shall not be binding on a consumer, a court must go through a number of steps in order to declare that the 'unfair term' in not applicable. These steps are:

• is the contract one to which the 1995 Regulations apply, or are the exceptions in Schedule 1 relevant?
• is the contract a consumer contract?
• was the contract term not one individually negotiated?
• does the term create a significant imbalance between the parties?
• was the term negotiated contrary to the requirement of good faith, taking account of the factors in Schedule 2?
• was plain, intelligible language used?
• are the specific examples in Schedule 3 and the exceptions mentioned there relevant?

Overlap between 1995 Regulations and 1980 Act   It is worth noting that there are some unfortunate overlaps between the Sale of Goods and Supply of Services Act 1980 and the 1995 Regulations which have not been dealt with when the 1995 Regulations were made. For example, the 1995 Regulations apply to consumer sale of goods contracts (the 1980 Act applies to consumer and non-consumer contracts), but the 'good faith' test seems less strong than that in the 1980 Act, since the 1995 Regulations leave open the possibility that such an exclusion would pass the 'good faith' test whereas the 1980 Act simply bans certain exclusion clauses outright. Presumably, where the 1980 Act applies, it takes priority over the 1995 Regulations, applying the *generalia specialibus non derogant* principle of statutory interpretation. Of course the definition of 'unfair terms' is more wide-ranging than the exclusion clauses to which the 1980 Act applies, and in those cases the 1995 Regulations would take priority. As to contracts for the supply of services, the 1980 Act applies a 'fair and reasonable' test in consumer supply of services contracts; in that respect, the 1995 Regulations are broadly similar.

Unfair terms – Schedule 3 list The general tests of 'good faith' and 'significant imbalance . . . to the detriment of the consumer' is the controlling test under the 1995 Regulations, subject to the particular example relevant to insurance contracts referred to in Reg.4, discussed above. The 'significant imbalance' test is very general, but the Regulations provide some specific examples which give a clearer picture of their scope. Schedule 3 to the 1995 Regulations sets out '[a]n indicative and non-exhaustive list of the terms which may be regarded as unfair' under the Regulations. Although Schedule 3 is not, therefore, a complete list of 'unfair terms' it probably comes quite close. The English Office of Fair Trading (OFT) has indicated that the following are the most common types of unfair terms:

- entire agreement clauses: these exclude from a contract anything said by a salesperson or agent of a company
- hidden clauses: terms and conditions not brought to the consumer's attention before making a contract
- penalty clauses: for example where the company can retain a deposit in the event of the consumer being in default but where no equivalent penalty applies to the company
- exclusion clauses, many of which still try to exclude liability for a wide range of defaults by the seller/supplier
- variation clauses: giving the seller/supplier the right to increase the price without any realistic right to the consumer to withdraw from the contract.

Schedule 3 to the 1995 Regulations deals with all of these common unfair contact terms among the following 17 types of terms.

(1) Excluding or limiting liability for death or personal injury

(2) Excluding liability consumer's rights, including set-off, where there is total or partial non-performance

(3) Agreement binding on consumer but compliance by seller/supplier matter for will of seller/supplier

(4) Seller/supplier retaining deposit, but no equivalent for consumer

(5) Disproportionate penalties

(6) Seller/supplier may dissolve contract and/or retain deposit but no equivalent for consumer

(7) Termination of indefinite contract without reasonable notice (unless serious grounds)

(8) Automatic extension of fixed duration contract

(9) Irrevocably binding consumer without reasonable opportunity to become aware of terms

(10) Seller/supplier unilaterally altering terms without valid reason

(11) Seller/supplier unilaterally altering characteristics of product/service without valid reason

(12) Price variation/increase solely determined by seller/supplier

(13) Allowing seller/supplier interpret contract terms

(14) Seller/supplier limiting responsibility for actions of agents

(15) Consumer required to fulfil all his/her obligations, but seller/supplier not

(16) Seller/supplier allowed transfer responsibilities and reduce guarantees to consumer

(17) Limiting consumer's procedural legal rights

Choice of law: exclusion of Regulations　Regulation 7 of the 1995 Regulations provide that they apply notwithstanding any contract term which attempts to apply the law of a non-EC Member State in order to deprive a consumer of protection under the 1993 Directive, as implemented in the 1995 Regulations.

Enforcement: Director of Consumer Affairs and consumer associations Regulation 8 of the 1995 Regulations empowers the Director of Consumer Affairs to apply to the High Court for an order prohibiting the use of any term in contracts concluded by sellers or suppliers adjudged by the Court to be an unfair term. As amended by the European Communities (Unfair Terms in Consumer Contracts) (Amendment) Regulations 2000 (S.I. No.307 of 2000), Regulation 8 also provides that consumer organisations set up for the purpose of protecting consumer rights, such as the Consumer Association of Ireland, may seek such an order also. Regulation 10(5) provides that, in the exercise of its jurisdiction under Regulation 10, the High Court 'shall take account of all the interests involved and in particular the public interest.' This is similar to the powers conferred on the Director and the High Court by the Consumer Information Act 1978 and the European Communities (Misleading Advertisements) Regulations 1988, discussed in *J.O'Connor (Nenagh) Ltd v. Powers Supermarkets Ltd (t/a Quinnsworth Ltd)*, High Court, March 15, 1993 (Annual Review 1993, 64-6). Finally, Regulation 11(5) provides that a person who obstructs or impedes an authorised officer of the Director or the Minister for Enterprise, Trade and Employment in the enforcement of the Regulations shall be guilty of an offence and is liable on summary conviction to a fine not exceeding £1,500.

Company Law

ADAM MCAULEY and DAVID TOMKIN
Dublin City University Business School

THE RULE IN *SALOMAN v. SALOMAN*

Shinkwin v. Quin-Con Ltd and Quinlan [2001] 2 I.L.R.M. 154. Quinlan ran and controlled a company. Quinlan was the company's sole shareholder. The company employed the plaintiff. The plaintiff was seriously injured at work and took an action against both the company and Quinlan. The High Court held that the company and Quinlan were negligent. The High Court awarded the plaintiff £304,000. The company was uninsured and had no assets. Therefore, Quinlan was liable for the entire £304,000. Quinlan appealed to the Supreme Court.

In the Supreme Court, Fennelly J. held that a person may be the sole effective and controlling shareholder in a company and yet have no involvement or control over the day-to-day operations of the business of this company. Such a shareholder will not be held liable for the negligent acts of the company which injure a company employee. To hold otherwise would disregard the separate legal character of the company, the principle of limited liability and the rule in *Saloman v. Saloman* [1897] A.C. 22.

Fennelly J. held that although Quinlan could not be held liable for the plaintiff's injuries in his capacity as sole shareholder and controller, Quinlan could be held personally liable where the plaintiff proved that Quinlan managed the factory, and in particular, supervised the plaintiff. The evidence was that Quinlan managed the factory and supervised the plaintiff, a point which Quinlan conceded in cross-examination.

Fennelly J. found that Quinlan had placed himself in a relationship of proximity to the plaintiff. Quinlan had personally taken on a young and untrained person to work in a factory managed by him. Quinlan had put the plaintiff to work upon a potentially dangerous machine over which Quinlan exercised control to the extent of giving some albeit completely inadequate instructions. Fennelly J. held that Quinlan owed a duty of care to warn the plaintiff of these obvious dangers. Fennelly J. held that Quinlan was negligent because he had failed to warn of these obvious dangers.

Fennelly J. distinguished this case from *Sweeney v. Duggan* [1997] 2 I.R. 531, see Annual Review 1997, 110-111. In *Sweeney*, an employee was injured when working in a quarry. The employee successfully sued his employer, a company. However, the company was uninsured and had no assets. The employee sued the company and its sole shareholder and quarry manager,

Duggan. The employee claimed that the company and Duggan were legally obliged to obtain employer's insurance. The Supreme Court held that the company had no implied contractual or tortious duty to insure its employees. The Supreme Court held that as the company had no such liability, neither could its principal director/shareholder. Fennelly J. noted that the plaintiff here had claimed directly against Quinlan personally. Quinlan's actions had brought about a personal relationship of proximity and thus a duty of care, subsequently breached. Fennelly J. dismissed the appeal.

A company may only act through human beings authorised to do so, such as a director or employee. People who involve themselves in company business should ensure that the company is liable for what they do on behalf of the company. The *Saloman* decision does not preclude an individual who is a shareholder from owing a personal duty of care to others, including a company employee.

DIRECTORS

Fiduciary duties of company directors   *Anois Couriers Ltd v. Philip Hannigan*, High Court, July 28, 2000. A director has a fiduciary relationship with the company and owes fiduciary duties to it. A director should not place himself or herself in a position in which there is a conflict between his or her fiduciary duties to the company and his or her personal interests. Such a conflict arises where a company director diverts a business opportunity away from the company to himself or herself or to another company with which he or she is associated.

In this case, the plaintiff was a company engaged in the courier business. The defendant was a director of the plaintiff company. Two investors acquired the plaintiff company. The defendant remained on as director and in effect the general manager of the plaintiff company. The plaintiff company learnt that the defendant had become involved in another courier business. The plaintiff company claimed that the defendant had recruited two of its employees and was trying to divert customers from the plaintiff to the other courier business. The plaintiff company wrote a letter to the defendant expressing its concerns. The defendant resigned as director of the plaintiff company.

The plaintiff company sought to restrain the defendant from soliciting business from the plaintiff's customers, from soliciting employees of the plaintiff, from diverting to the other courier business any business advantage belonging to the plaintiff and from using any confidential information.

In the High Court, Morris P. held that a director should not place himself or herself in a position in which there is a conflict between his or her fiduciary duties to the company and his or her personal interests. A director cannot exploit the company's assets, opportunities or information for personal gain, without the informed consent of the company. Morris P., relying on *Canadian*

Aero Services Ltd v. O'Malley [1967] 2 A.C. 46, held that a conflict arises where a company director diverts a business opportunity away from the company to himself or herself or to another company with which he or she is associated. Morris P. held that the director's duty may not be terminated by his or her resignation. The duty will be breached where the former director takes a business opportunity derived from his or her position as director of the company. The duty is not breached if the former director can show that the business opportunity came to him personally and was unrelated to his former connection with the company. Morris P. held that if a director resigns, he must notify the company of his resignation.

Morris P. then turned to consider the criteria which should be applied to the granting of an interlocutory injunction. Morris P. held that there was a fair issue to be tried, were the plaintiff company's allegations made out. Morris P. decided that damages would not sufficiently compensate the plaintiff company.

Morris P. considered where the balance of convenience lay. Morris P. held that a director's fiduciary duty is not absolute. Otherwise it would be an unlawful restraint of trade. Morris P. held that here, the defendant's duty of confidentiality would have expired three months after the date of his resignation. Morris P. held that the plaintiff company would be irreparably harmed if the plaintiff could prove the course of action which the defendant was pursuing. Morris P. held that if an interlocutory injunction were granted, this would prevent the defendant soliciting customers. However, Morris P. held that the defendant's potential loss was overcome by the plaintiff company's undertaking as to damages for the period of the interlocutory injunction.

Morris P. concluded that the balance rested in favour of granting the interlocutory injunction for three months by which date the defendant's duty not to compete with the company would have expired.

This case highlights the necessity to state expressly in every director's contract the precise nature of the director's obligation not to compete with the company, including the extent of the director's duty following resignation, retirement or removal. In so drafting such clause, care must be taken to safeguard the company's business on the one hand and balance this consideration against the former director's entitlement to carry on the same or similar business. To settle such a contractual term by way of injunction and possible later plenary action is expensive and with some forethought, unnecessary.

Spring Grove Services (Ireland) Limited v. Denis O'Callaghan, Seamus Desmond and National Linen Limited, High Court, July 31, 2000. In the High Court, Herbert J. stated that a director owes fiduciary duties of good faith, fair dealing and honesty to the company of which he or she is a director. These duties encompass a duty not to compete with the company, a duty to act in the best interests of the company and a prohibition on using confidential information otherwise than for the benefit of the company.

Commencement of restriction period   *Duignan v. Carway and Others*, High
Court, July 27, 2000. Proceedings for restriction orders against former directors
of a company were initiated in 1994. This application was issued in 1994. The
former directors sought dismissal of these proceedings on two grounds. First,
the five-year restriction period commenced on the date the application was
issued, and this period had now expired. Second, there had been inordinate
and inexcusable delay in proceeding with the application.

In the High Court, O'Donovan J. rejected both grounds. First, O'Donovan
J. held that section 150 of the Companies Act 1990 is clear and unambiguous:
the five-year restriction period commences from the date of the making of the
High Court order.

Second, O'Donovan J. held that where there had been an inordinate and
inexcusable delay, the court has a discretion to allow the proceedings to continue
if the balance of justice favours this: *Primor plc v. Stokes Kennedy Crowley*
[1996] 2 I.R. 459. O'Donovan found that there was inordinate and inexcusable
delay in prosecuting these proceedings. O'Donovan J. held that even where
there has been such delay, the court can allow these proceedings to continue,
if the balance of justice favours this the court can allow the proceedings to
continue where the balance of justice favours this.

O'Donovan J. held that the court has no discretion to allow proceedings to
continued in two circumstances. First, the delay has given rise to a substantial
risk of the former directors receiving an unfair trial. Second, the delay is likely
to cause or has caused serious prejudice to the former directors. O'Donovan J.
held that the delay in prosecuting these proceedings had caused general, but
not specific prejudice to the directors. O'Donovan J. was of the opinion that
the directors could deal with the allegations at the full hearing. In reaching his
conclusion as to where the balance of justice lay, O'Donovan J. considered
where the balance of justice lay, and held that this public interest overrode any
general prejudice which the directors might suffer on account of the delay and
that the public interest requires that unsuitable persons should not hold
directorships. O'Donovan J. dismissed the respondents' motion.

Duties of directors, restriction order and shadow director   *In Re Vehicle
Imports Ltd*, High Court, December 6, 2000. This involved an application for
restriction orders against three individuals. The first two were husband and
wife, both directors of the company. The third individual, D, it was claimed
was a shadow director of the company.

The husband had been a director of two other companies. However, the
husband was not involved in keeping those companies' books of accounts nor
overseeing any of their other company law obligations.

In 1996, the husband met D, a certified accountant. D offered to act as the
company's accountant if the husband took a lease in the premises in which D
practised. The husband and D agreed that D would take charge of the company's
financial and accounting affairs.

D opened a bank account for the company. The husband provided a personal guarantee. The husband was the only signatory of company cheques. The husband signed blank cheques that were later filled in by D. D was responsible for the company's lodgments. D opened a second company bank account secured by another personal guarantee given by the husband. The overdraft for this second account reached £150,000 in less than five months. D advised the husband to re-mortgage his family home in order to raise further finance for the company.

D received £105,000 from the company in a fourteen-month period. The husband was unable to explain why D had received such a sum. D never informed the husband that the company was insolvent. The husband was unaware of the extent of the company's indebtedness to the Revenue Commissioners. The High Court addressed two issues. First, was D a shadow director? Second, whether the court should impose a restriction order on both husband and wife.

In the High Court, Murphy J. explained that the Companies Act 1990 defines a shadow director as a person in accordance with whose directions or instructions the directors of a company are accustomed to act. However, the 1990 Act provides that a person who gives advice to the directors in his or her professional capacity on that ground alone cannot be a shadow director.

Murphy J. identified two aspects of the husband's uncontroverted evidence that tended to prove that D was a shadow director. First, D filled in blank cheques signed by the husband. Second, D arranged the opening of two bank accounts in the company's name and recommended to the husband that he should guarantee the borrowings on these two accounts. Murphy J. admitted that D could refute this evidence by showing that that he was in fact the company's landlord and accountant and was merely providing professional services to a company in difficulty. Murphy J. noted that D's affidavit explained that he had initially acted as the company's landlord and later as the company's accountant. However, Murphy J. found that D's failure to deny that he was a shadow director in his affidavit as ominous. It will be remembered that D was a certified accountant. Murphy J. stated that the maxim ignorance of the law is no defence could not apply to a person recognised by the Companies Acts as qualified to audit books of account. Murphy J. preferred the husband's evidence as to the role played by D to that of D himself. Murphy J. held that this was *prima facie* evidence that D was a shadow director. Such evidence had not been rebutted. Murphy J. was of the opinion that it was appropriate in the circumstances to make a restriction order against D, the shadow director. However, Murphy J. decided to grant a stay of 21 days so that D could apply to court for relief under section 152.

Murphy J. considered whether restriction orders should be made against the husband and wife. Murphy J. adopted the six headings for director's duties contained in *Barings Plc. & Others Secretary of State for Trade and Industry v. Baker & Others* [1999] 1 B.C.L.C. 433 at 435-436 and more extensively detailed at 486-489.

First, each individual director owes a duty to the company to inform himself or herself about the company's affairs and to join with his co-directors in supervising and controlling them.

Second, the Board of Directors might delegate specific tasks and functions, subject to the provision of the company's articles of association. Some degree of delegation was almost always essential if the company's business was to be carried out efficiently. There was a clear public interest in delegation by those charged with the responsible for managing the company.

Third, the duty of an individual director does not preclude the director delegating functions or tasks. However, the delegation of a certain function does not mean that the director was no longer under any duty in relation to the discharge of that function, even though the person to whom the function had been delegated appeared both trustworthy and capable of discharging that function.

Fourth, the Board and individual directors remain responsible for delegated function and retain a duty of supervision and control. The extent of that duty depends on the facts of each particular case, as will the question of whether this duty has been breached.

Fifth, a person who accepted the office of director of a particular company undertook the responsibility of ensuring that he understood the nature of the duty a director was called upon to perform. That duty would vary according to the size and business of that particular company and the experience or skills which the director held himself or herself out to have in support of appointment to the office of director. The duty included that of acting collectively with other to manage the company.

Sixth, where there was an issue as to the extent of a director's duties in any particular case, the reward which he or she was entitled to receive or might reasonably have expected to receive from the company might be a relevant factor in resolving that issue. The higher the level of reward, the greater the commensurate responsibilites might *prima facie* reasonably be expected.

Murphy J. considered the absence of books and records or the inadequacy of any proper books and records during the company's existence. Murphy J. divided this period into two. First, the period when D was responsible for keeping the company's books and records. Second, the period when the husband lost contact with D and the husband took charge of the company's books and records. The husband was at all times the only signatory of company cheques. Murphy J. rejected as incredible the husband's claim that he had not seen bank statements during this second period. Murphy J. refused to accept the husband's crude attempt to exonerate himself by blaming D because D had no contact with the company during this period and thus was not responsible for keeping the books and records. Even if the husband could show that D as a shadow director was responsible for keeping its books and records, Murphy J. held that the responsibility to keep a company's books and records falls upon every director. Each director is jointly and severally liable for breaches of this duty. Murphy J. decided to impose a restriction order against the husband.

Murphy J. considered whether to impose a restriction order against the wife. Murphy J. held that the wife was a director of the company and must fulfil her duties as such, despite her lack of involvement in the company. Murphy J. held that one of the duties of a director was to take reasonable steps to be and remain informed of the company's affairs. Murphy J. held that this duty applied to non-executive directors: *In Re Hunting Lodges Limited* [1985] I.L.R.M. 75. Murphy J. distinguished between the way in which the husband and wife had discharged their dutiess as directors. The wife had opposed further increasing the company's borrowings. Murphy J. was of the opinion that this was a responsible position for the wife to take in the circumstances of the case. Accordingly, Murphy J., considering the duties of directors to the company and its creditors, decided with some hesitation not to impose a restriction order on the wife.

This is the first recorded Irish judgement explaining the circumstances in which a person may be held liable as a shadow director. When it is alleged that a professional person has participated in company management so as to constitute himself or herself a shadow director, the burden of proof shifts to that professional person to prove to the court that his or her involvement was restricted to giving professional advice. This case reiterates the principle that the burden of proof lies on the director to establish one of the statutory defences to the making of a restriction order. It will be well-nigh impossible for such a director to successfully invoke any of these defences where the company's books and records have not been properly kept. On restriction orders, see Annual Review 1995, 79-85, Annual Review 1996, 120-123, Annual Review 1997, 119-120, Annual Review 1998, 53-54 and Annual Review 1999, 25-26.

Directors' failure to keep proper books of account   *In Re Ashclad Ltd*, High Court, April 5, 2000. The liquidator of a company found substantial errors and omissions in the company's books. Two directors had managed the company. The relevant omissions included large cheques made payable to cash for which the company received no recorded benefit. The liquidator, in a vain attempt to have his queries answered, brought the director before the Master of the High Court for examination.

The liquidator claimed that the deficiencies in the company's books created substantial uncertainty as to the company's assets and liabilities of the company and impeded the orderly winding up of the company. The liquidator estimated that 80% of his time and that of his staff was spent trying to remedy these deficiencies.

In the High Court, Geoghegan J. adopted Shanley J.'s approach to liability for failure to keep proper books of account articulated in *Mehigan v. Duignan* [1997] 1 I.R. 341, see Annual Review 1996, 115-120. Geoghegan J. held that the liquidator had discharged the necessary proofs for an order declaring the directors personally liable for some or all of the company's debts under section 204 of the Companies Act 1990. Geoghegan J. held that as a matter of probability that sums amounting to at least £100,000 were wrongly withdrawn from the company and appropriated for other purposes. Geoghegan J. costed the time spent by the liquidator in trying to ascertain the company's assets and liabilities as a consequence of the directors' failure to keep proper books of account. Geoghegan J. held the directors liable for this cost: £12,000.

Geoghegan J. declared that the directors were personally liable for a total of £112,000 of the company's debts. This failure resulted in substantial uncertainty as to the company's assets and liabilities, and/or impeded the orderly winding up of the company and/or contributed to the company's inability to pay all of its debts. In addition, Geoghegan J. imposed restriction orders on the two directors.

This case distinguishes between two aspects of a director's personal liability for failure to ensure that proper books of account were maintained. First, such a director will be liable for the accountancy costs incurred by the liquidator in making good deficiencies in the company's books of accounts. Second, there is the more complex question of liability for transactions for which the company appears to have received no benefit. A director will be liable for such debts unless the director can demonstrate that the company did indeed receive some benefit.

Service of summons on managing director *O'Shea v. Director of Public Prosecutions*, High Court, November 30, 2000. A summons against a company director is not served by leaving it with a company employee, even if served at the company's place of business

The managing director of a company was charged with driving a car in excess of the speed limit. He gave his private address and the address of the company's business address to the Garda member who stopped him. The gardaí attempted to serve the managing director at the company's business address. Each time they did so, the managing director was away. Ultimately, the gardaí served the summons on another person in the company's employ. The case proceeded and the managing director was convicted.

The managing director brought a challenge to his conviction, on the grounds that the service of the summons on the company employee could not be deemed proper service on the driver.

Murphy J. held that although service of a summons on a company could be effected by serving the company secretary, a director of a company could not be said to have been served with a summons, where it was left with another company employee. Hence the managing director's challenge was upheld and his conviction quashed.

Interrogatories and directors *Money Markets International Stock Brokers Ltd (in liquidation) v. Fanning and Others*, [2000] 3 I.R. 215, [2001] 1 I.L.R.M.

1. An officer of a company may be required to answer an interrogatory not only on the company's behalf, but also concerning his or her conduct as a company officer. Directors, present or former, cannot escape answering interrogatories on the grounds that the information sought is not withing their personal knowledge. They must also answer interrogatories concerning all company matters for which they are legally responsible as company directors.

The plaintiff was a stockbroking company. The defendants were former directors of the company. The company was placed in liquidation. The liquidator claimed that these defendants had defrauded the company. The liquidator delivered a number of interrogatories seeking to establish how the fraud was perpetrated. Two of the defendants refused to answer these interrogatories claiming that they had no personal knowledge of the information. It should be noted that the defendants were not being asked to answer these interrogatories on behalf of the company. The interrogatories were addressed to each of them in their personal capacities

In the High Court, O'Sullivan J. held that a person must answer interrogatories in the following two circumstances. First, the information is within his or her personal knowledge. Second, the person has or had legal responsibility over subordinates with personal knowledge. O'Sullivan J. held that the defendants fell within this second circumstance. They had delegated to others tasks for which they were legally responsible as directors. Therefore, the directors were obliged to answer the interrogatories even though it was those delegated with the tasks who had personal knowledge.

INSPECTIONS AND INVESTIGATIONS

Appointment of authorised officer   *Dunnes Stores Ireland Ltd, Dunnes Stores (Ilac Centre) Ltd and Margaret Heffernan v. Gerard Ryan, The Minister for Enterprise, Trade and Employment, Attorney General and Ireland*, High Court, July 6, 1999. In the High Court, Kinlen J. held that the Minister for Enterprise, Trade and Employment had validly appointed an authorised officer to two companies in the Dunnes Stores group. However, Kinlen J. held that authorised officer had exercised his function *ultra vires* when he sought the production of company records and documentation, see Annual Review 1999, 36. The plaintiffs and defendants appealed against this decision.

Dunnes Stores Ireland Ltd, Dunnes Stores (Ilac Centre) Ltd and Margaret Heffernan v. Gerard Ryan, The Minister for Enterprise, Trade and Employment, Attorney General and Ireland, Supreme Court, 8 February, 2000 In the Supreme Court, Keane C.J. found that Kinlen J. had failed to consider the claim that the Minister's power to appoint an authorised officer was unconstitutional. The Supreme Court allowed the appeal, setting aside the High Court order. The Supreme Court remitted the proceedings to the High Court for a determination on all the issues raised.

Dunnes Stores Ireland Ltd, Dunnes Stores (Ilac Centre) Ltd and Margaret Heffernan v. Gerard Ryan, The Minister for Enterprise, Trade and Employment, Attorney General and Ireland, High Court, July 29, 2000. These proceedings focussed on one issue: whether the Minister's reasons for appointing an authorised officer were sufficient. The Minister claimed that it was necessary to appoint an authorised officer to examine the companies' books and records in order to determine whether an inspector should be appointed, whether there had been tax evasion, intentions to defraud creditors or members and conduct unfairly prejudicial to members, and past illegalities.

In the High Court, Butler J. held that the Minister's reasons were insufficient. First, there was insufficient evidence warranting the appointment of an authorised officer to examine the books and documents in order to determine whether an inspector should be appointed. Second, the Companies Act 1990 allows the Minister to pass evidence obtained by an authorised officer to certain specified competent authorities. However, the Revenue Commissioners were not then listed as competent authorities. Butler J. drew support for this proposition from the fact that it had later been necessary to amend Companies Act 1990 to add the Revenue Commissioners to the list of competent authorities. Third, no shareholder in the Dunnes Stores companies had claimed oppression or an intention to defraud him or her. Butler J. held that the Minister could not appoint an authorised officer on this ground in the absence of such a complaint. Shareholders in the Dunnes Stores companies had reconciled their differences and gone their separate ways prior to the appointment of the authorised officer. Fourth, the Companies Act 1990 allows the Minister to appoint an authorised officer if there are circumstances suggesting the company is breaking or will break the law. Butler J. explained that the 1990 Act does not permit the appointment of an authorised officer where the illegality is past.

Butler J. held that before the High Court could overturn a public authority or official's decision, the impugned decision must be fundamentally unreasonable and contrary to common sense and thus *ultra vires*: *The State (Keegan) v. Stardust Victims Compensation Tribunal* [1986] I.R. 642 at 658 *per* Henchy J.. Butler J. held that the Minister's decision to appoint an authorised officer was fundamentally unreasonable and contrary to common sense and thus *ultra vires*.

Despite this finding that authorised officer was thus invalidly appointed, Butler J. went on to consider whether the authorised officer had acted reasonably in seeking a meeting with the officers of the Dunnes Stores companies to discuss his request for books and documents. Butler J. held that the request for the meeting was a reasonable one. Was the request for documents reasonable? Butler J. held that it was not. The authorised officer sought production within four days of an "enormous" volume of documents, including copies of all audited accounts of Dunnes Stores company since incorporation. Butler J. held that four days was unreasonably short considering the volume of documents sought.

Since the request for the production of company books and records may be a prelude to seeking the appointment of an inspector, the 1990 Act requires that the Minister must be of the opinion that one of the specified grounds exists before he or she can exercise this executive power. The determination as to whether such executive powers have been exercised validly is a function of the judiciary.

Butler J. holds that the Minister's power can not be exercised in a vacuum. The Minister must point to circumstances substantiating his or her opinion as to the necessity for the appointment of an authorised officer within one or more of these specified grounds. However, Butler J.'s approach seems to misinterpret or rewrite two of the four grounds put forward by the Minister. The first is that the company's affairs are being conducted with an intent to defraud the creditors or any other person, in this case the Revenue Commissioners. Butler J. rejects this ground because the Minister could not pass any information relating to tax evasion to the Revenue Commissioners. However, with respect, this consideration appears irrelevant. The Minister's ability to pass information to a specified competent authority is not a statutory prerequisite to the appointment of an authorised officer on this particular ground. The second was that the company's affairs were conducted with intent either to defraud its members or treat some of them in an unfairly prejudicial manner. Butler J. assumes that the Minister cannot intervene on this basis in the absence of a complaint by as member. There is no reference in the statutory provision to the necessity of a complaint from a member, before the Minister can appoint an authorised officer.

This case raises the question as to the nature of the evidence required before the Minister can appoint an authorised officer. It is clear that the Minister cannot act on the basis of a hunch or rumour. The Minister must have *prima facie* evidence that one or more of the eight grounds specified in section 19(2) of the Companies Act 1990 exist.

MEETINGS

Notices of directors' meeting and shareholders' meeting   *Colthurst and Tenpis Ltd v. La Touche Colthurst and Colthurst*, High Court, February 9, 2000. Proper notice for both directors' and shareholders' meetings is essential. It is irrelevant that any vote at such meetings is a conclusion. Where there had been a deliberate failure to give notice of a meeting of either directors or shareholders, any resolutions passed at these meeting are invalid.

The second plaintiff was a private company. The first plaintiff held 49% of the shares in this company, his wife held 1% of the shares and the second defendant held the remaining shares. The first plaintiff, his wife and second defendants were directors of the company. There were various legal disputes between the parties. The first plaintiff and defendants entered into a settlement resolving these disputes. The settlement was contained in a court order. The first plaintiff decided to challenge this settlement and join the company as a co-plaintiff. The first plaintiff and his wife wrote a letter as directors and shareholders of the company authorising a firm of solicitors to institute these proceedings in the company's name and represented that both directors' and shareholders' meetings had been properly convened and held and the necessary resolution passed.

In the High Court, McCracken J. held that the second defendant had not received notice of these board meetings and general meetings.

The first plaintiff claimed that the second defendant was not prejudiced by this failure. The first plaintiff and his wife at all times have outvoted the second defendant. McCracken J. dismissed the first plaintiff's explanation. McCracken J. was satisfied that this failure to give notice was a deliberate step taken to conceal the plaintiff's intention to issue proceedings against the defendants.

McCracken J. held every shareholder of a company and its auditor is entitled to notice of every general meeting. In view of this, the purported resolution was invalid, thus the company had been improperly joined as a co-plaintiff.

Though the decision may be seen as a triumph of empty procedure, it is a useful reminder that if people choose to conduct their business through the vehicle of a company, they must abide by the concomitant obligations imposed by company law and the provisions of the Memorandum and Articles of Association, see Annual Review 1999, 27-29.

LIQUIDATION

Winding up petition *In Re Millhouse Taverns*, High Court, 3 March, 2000. Where a creditor knows that the company has a substantial and reasonable defence to the creditor's claim, the courts do not permit the winding up jurisdiction to become a forum for resolving disputed debts: see *Truck and Machinery Sales Ltd v. Marubeni Komatsu Ltd* [1996] 1 I.R. 12 and Annual Review 1996, 107-113. The sum claimed must be certain and incapable of dispute. A winding up petition is not a legitimate means of seeking to enforce payment of a debt that is *bona fide* disputed.

In the High Court, Finnegan J. held that the company had failed to establish that it had a substantial and reasonable defence to the petitioner's claim that would enable it to defeat the entire of the claim brought against it. Finnegan J. was satisfied that the company was unable to pay its debts and accordingly made an order winding up the company.

The Investor Compensation Act 1998 and administrator/liquidator *In Re Money Markets International Stockbrokers*, High Court, May 12, 2000. The Investor Compensation Act 1998 establishes an investor compensation scheme.

The Act 1998 incorporates a company (I.C.C.L.) whose function is to process expeditiously compensation claims by clients of investment firms.

I.C.C.L. is obliged to pay each eligible investor a sum equal to his or her compensable loss. This duty arises where a court has ruled or decided that the investment firm's financial circumstances precluded an investor from suing the investment firm for return of money and investment instruments. The responsibility for identifying eligible investors in such an investment firm and for computing the compensation due to each eligible investor falls on the investment firm's "administrator". A liquidator appointed to an investment firm by the court automatically becomes its administrator.

An administrator is obliged to deliver to I.C.C.L., as soon as practicable, the names of eligible investors, a statement of the net loss of each such investor and a statement of the compensable loss of each such investor.

An administrator may apply to court to determine any question in relation to his or her functions under the 1998 Act. In this case, the administrator was unable to furnish a definitive statement of the names of eligible investors, a statement of the net loss of each such investor and a statement of the compensable loss of each such investor. The administrator had prepared a draft interim statement identifying 89 eligible investors with the computation of their respective exact net losses and compensable losses. However, the administrator was unable to compute the net losses for the purposes of the 1998 Act, because of the possible implications of the issues which had to be determined by the court in winding up. Therefore, the administrator calculated approximate net losses. These represented the lowest possible amount which each eligible investor could claim to be his or her net loss in the event that the various issues before the court were decided against the investors.

In the High Court, Laffoy J. held that the statutory definition of a court ruling covers the court order for the winding up of an investment firm. Laffoy J. noted that the 1998 Act makes no provision for the administrator to make an interim statement. However, the E.C. Directive to which the 1988 Act owes its origins and the 1998 Act itself stresses the need to have the expeditious settlement of claims of eligible investors. Laffoy J. held that the 1998 Act must be interpreted in light of this imperative. Laffoy J. held that the administrator has the power to deliver an interim statement. Laffoy J. made an order deeming that the administrator's interim statement constituted a statement for the purposes of the 1998 Act.

The administrator's statement is prepared on the basis of the company's books and records maintained by the directors. Consequently, the administrator is not responsible for the accuracy of these company's records. Laffoy J. held that the administrator's statement must accordingly contain an appropriate disclaimer.

Stockbroking companies and the protection of clients' funds *In Re Money Markets International Stockbrokers*, High Court, May 23, 2000. Section 52 of the Stock Exchange Act 1995 gives effect to the State's obligations under Article 10 of Council Directive 93/22 EEC of May 10, 1993. This Directive seeks to protect the money and investment instruments of clients of stockbroking firms entrusted to or held by such firms. Section 52(5)(a) of the 1995 Act provides that no liquidator, receiver, administrator, examiner or creditor can have recourse or right against a client's money or investment instrument until all claims of the client against his or her money or investment instrument have been satisfied in full.

In the High Court, Laffoy J. held that the effect of section 52(5)(a) is to ring-fence the funds in the client account and preserve them for the client creditors who provided them. In this case, there was a sum of £1.2 million in the client account. This sum comprised lodgements of significant sums of money over the years by the stockbroking firm. Laffoy J. held that the £1.2 million was "client's money" within the meaning of section 52(5)(a). Laffoy J. held that the clear and unambiguous meaning of section 52(5)(a) is that the beneficial claims of client creditors have to be satisfied in full before anyone else has a call on funds.

APPLICATION FOR SECURITY FOR COSTS

When may a defendant seek security for costs from a company plaintiff?

Section 390 of the Companies Act, 1963 provides that if a limited company is plaintiff in any action or other legal proceedings, any judge having jurisdiction in any matter, may, if it appears by credible testimony that there is reason to believe that the company will be unable to pay the costs of the defendant if successful in his defence, require the plaintiff company to provide sufficient security to cover these costs and may stay all proceedings until the security is given, see Annual Review 1998, 62-64.

Wexford Rope & Twine Co. Ltd v. Gaynor and Modler, High Court, March 6, 2000. In the High Court, Barr J. explained that a court will be inclined to make an order for security for costs against a plaintiff company where it is admitted or proved that the plaintiff company will be unable to discharge the costs if the action is unsuccessful and the defendant has a *prima facie* defence to the plaintiff's claim. The court will not make an order for security for costs against the plaintiff company where the plaintiff company can prove the existence of "special circumstances".

In this application, the plaintiff company sought to rely on two special circumstances. First, the plaintiff company's inability to pay the defendant's costs arose from the alleged wrongdoing of the defendant complained of in the plaintiff company's action. Second, the defendant has delayed in seeking security for costs. Barr J. held that the plaintiff company had failed to establish either of these special circumstances and made an order against the plaintiff company requiring it to provide security for costs

Ochre Ridge Ltd v. Cork Bonded Warehouses Limited and Port of Cork Company Limited, High Court, December 20, 2000. The plaintiff company agreed to purchase a leasehold interest in a warehouse from the first defendant. A dispute arose between the plaintiff and the first defendant. The plaintiff company sued the first defendant seeking an order of specific performance. The first defendant sought an order for security for costs against the plaintiff company under section 390 of the Companies Act 1963. It claimed that the plaintiff company was a shelf company and had no assets.

In the High Court, O'Neill J. held that that the issue was whether the plaintiff company would be solvent on the day that its claim proved unsuccessful. The issue was not whether the plaintiff company was solvent on the date of application for security for costs. O'Neill J. held that the plaintiff company would be unable to pay the defendant's costs were the plaintiff company's claim to be unsuccessful.

O'Neill J. held that the burden of proof now shifted to the plaintiff company to establish special circumstances that would move the court to refuse to order the plaintiff company to provide security. The plaintiff company sought to rely on one such special circumstance. The plaintiff company argued that it would be unable to pay the defendant's costs only because of the alleged wrongdoing of the defendant complained of in the plaintiff company's action.

O'Neill J. identified two elements to this special circumstance. First, did the plaintiff have an arguable cases that its inability to pay the defendant's costs arose from the defendant's alleged wrongdoing complained of in the plaintiff's action? The first defendant admitted that the first plaintiff company had made an arguable case. Second, is there a *prima facie* case of a causal connection between the defendant's alleged wrongdoing and the plaintiff company's inability to provide security? O'Neill J. concluded that the plaintiff company's financial status was inextricably linked to the merits of the claims made by it. It was immaterial that the plaintiff company's impecuniosity would arise in the future at the time when the first defendant obtained judgement in its favour. O'Neill J. was satisfied that the plaintiff company had demonstrated special circumstances and refused to order the plaintiff company to provide security for costs.

Locus standi of a company and security for costs *Village Residents Association Ltd v. An Bord Pleanála, McDonald's Restaurants of Ireland Ltd and Kilkenny Corporation* [2001] 2 I.L.R.M. 22. In 1999, the High Court ([2000] 2 I.L.R.M. 59) granted leave to Village Residents Association Ltd (Village Ltd) to challenge by way of judicial review An Bord Pleanála's decision to grant planning permission to McDonald's Restaurant (McDonald's). The High Court rejected a challenge by McDonald's to Village Ltd's *locus standi*.

McDonald's issued a motion seeking security for costs against Village Ltd pursuant to section 390 of the Companies Act 1963. Village Ltd admitted that if it lost the proceedings, it would have insufficient funds to discharge an order for costs made against it at the conclusion of the proceedings. McDonald's argued that the *locus standi* of a private company formed solely to conduct litigation was dependent on the provision of security for costs.

In the High Court, Laffoy J. considered Keane J.'s judgement in *Lancefort Ltd v. An Bord Pleanála* [1998] 2 I.L.R.M. 401 at 442. Laffoy J. held that a mechanism for obtaining security for costs is to be taken into account when the *locus standi* of a company is challenged because the principle of limited liability immunises the members of the company from an order for costs. Laffoy J. held that the *bona fides* of such a company's members requires cautious consideration where they resist an application for security for costs against the plaintiff company. Laffoy J. agreed with Morris J. in *Lancefort Ltd v. An Bord Pleanála* [1998] 2 I.R. 511 at 517 that an application for security presents an opportunity for the company's members to demonstrate their commitment to the company's challenge by providing the necessary funds.

Laffoy J. held that a court will be inclined to make an order for security for costs against a plaintiff company, where the plaintiff company admits that it would not be able to pay costs made against it at the conclusion of the proceedings. However, the court may refuse to order security for costs if the plaintiff company can prove special circumstances make this inappropriate.

Laffoy J. found that the plaintiff company had failed to prove the existence of any special circumstances and made an order requiring security for costs. Laffoy J. stayed all further proceedings until this security was given.

Conflicts of Law

JURISDICTION

Tort and Contract In *Rye Valley Foods Ltd v. Fisher Frozen Foods Ltd*, High Court, May 10, 2000, O'Sullivan J. applied the principle, set out by the Court of Justice in *Kalfelis v. Bankhaus Schröder* [1988] E.C.R. 5565, that the concept of 'matters relating to tort, delict or quasi-delict' in Article 5:

> must be regarded as an autonomous concept which is to be interpreted, for the application of the Convention, principally by reference to the scheme and objectives of the Convention in order to ensure that the latter is given full effect.
>
> In order to ensure uniformity in all the Member States, it must be recognised that the concept of 'matters relating to tort, delict and quasi-delict' covers all actions which seek to establish the liability of a defendant and which are not related to a 'contract' within the meaning of Article 5(1).

In the instant case, the Irish plaintiff company, which, in the context of a well-established commercial relationship, had been supplied in England with bean sprouts by the defendant company for use in its food processing business in County Monaghan, sought to sue the defendant in Ireland for breach of contract and for negligence in tort. O'Sullivan J. held that the Irish courts did not have jurisdiction to hear the claim in contract. The obligation forming the basis of the proceedings had been to deliver bean sprouts in accordance with the contract. Delivery had occurred in England. The wider ongoing commercial relationship between the parties did not alter this fact.

As to the claim sounding in tort, counsel for the plaintiff submitted that the breach of the alleged duty of care was a separate and independent cause of action and was not related to the contract and in particular was not related to the overall contractual relationship which was, in truth, the expression of the full commercial reality of the transactions between the parties. The defendant's duty of care, he argued, arose from its knowledge of the plaintiff's requirements over the years which was independent of its knowledge of those requirements arising out of the instant transaction or under the related contractual obligations.

O'Sullivan J. did not agree. He stated:

With regard to plaintiff's claim sounding in tort, in my opinion it is clearly related to the contract. One of the purposes of the Convention was to avoid or reduce situations where legal proceedings arising out of the same transaction might be instituted in different Member States. That is why, in my view, the Court of Justice in *Kalfelis* decided not only that the concept of 'tort, delict or quasi-delict' was to be independent of similar concepts in individual Member States, but also that it covered all actions seeking to establish liability of a defendant which are not related to a 'contract' within the meaning of Article 5(1).

In this context, O'Sullivan J. referred to the following paragraph from the opinion of the Advocate General in *Kalfelis*, acknowledging that it did not, in terms, form part of the judgment of the Court:

> In other words, it is thus appropriate to conclude that where there are overlapping grounds ... only Article 5(1) will determine the jurisdiction of the Court, since the matters relating to contract will 'channel' all the aspects of the dispute.

Prorogation of jurisdiction   In *Bio-Medical Research Ltd t/a Slendertone v. Delatex S.A.* [2000] 4 I.R. 307, an attempt by the plaintiff company to characterise the terms of its contract with the defendant company as involving a selection of Irish jurisdiction under Article 17 of the Brussels Convention was unsuccessful in the High Court and on appeal to the Supreme Court. The defendant company was French; it sold the products of the plaintiff company, which was Irish, throughout France. The crucial issue in dispute between the parties was whether an exclusive distribution agreement was in place.

In Case 24/76 *Estasis Salotti di Colzani Aimo and another v. RUWA Polstereimaschinen GmbH* [1976] E.C.R. 1831 the Court of Justice had counselled caution in this context:

> The way in which that provision is to be applied must be interpreted in the light of the effect of the conferment of jurisdiction by consent, which is to exclude both the jurisdiction determined by the general principle laid down in Article 2 and the special jurisdictions provided for in Article 5 and 6 of the Convention.

> In view of the consequences that such an option may have on the position of the parties to the action, the requirements set out in Article 17 governing the validity of clauses conferring jurisdiction must be strictly construed.

> By making such validity subject to the existence of an 'agreement' between the parties, Article 17 imposes on the court before which the

matter is brought the duty of examining, first, whether the clause conferring jurisdiction upon it was in fact the subject of a consensus between the parties, which must be clearly and precisely demonstrated.

The purpose of the formal requirement imposed by Article 17 is to ensure that the consensus between the parties is in fact established.

Applying these principles to the facts of the instant case, Fennelly J. (Keane C.J. and Murray J. concurring) could not identify a choice of jurisdiction sufficient to warrant the application of Article 17:

None of [the terms of the printed conditions] m contains any reference to distribution, exclusive or otherwise, or even to the fact that the goods are being sold for resale in France. They have all the appearance of standard conditions regarding the sale of goods and nothing more. It would require a very strained interpretation to apply them to the question of the exclusivity of an agreement for distribution of goods sold in another Member State of the European Community. This is, as agreed, a matter of Irish law.

Forum non conveniens In *D.C. v. W.O.C.*, High Court, July 5, 2000, the plaintiff claimed that the defendant, a fellow employee, had raped her and subjected her to sexual assault when they travelled to Stockholm in the course of their employment. She sought damages in tort. Both parties were Irish domicilaries. The defendant entered an appearance under protest for the purposes of contesting jurisdiction. He argued that, on the grounds of *forum non conveniens*, the proceedings should be litigated in Sweden.

Finnegan J. was satisfied that the affidavits filed on behalf of the defendant disclosed circumstances which would justify granting the relief sought if the common law ground of *forum non conveniens* survived the incorporation into Irish law of the Brussels Convention of 1968 by the Jurisdiction of Courts and Enforcement of Judgments (European Communities) Act 1998 where both parties were domiciled in a contracting state.

Since, however, both parties were domiciled in a contracting state, there was no jurisdiction to stay the proceedings on the ground that it would be more convenient and less expensive to have the issues litigated in Sweden. The position was that the courts in Sweden would be obliged to decline jurisdiction under Article 21.

Finnegan J. quoted from paragraph 78 of the Schlosser Report on the Convention (of which Irish courts had judicial notice by virtue of section 4(2)(b) of the 1988 Act), which puts matters beyond dispute:

Article 21 expressly prohibits a Court from disregarding the fact that proceedings are already pending abroad. For the rest the view is expressed that under the 1968 Convention the contracting states are not only entitled to exercise jurisdiction in accordance with the provisions laid down in Title Two, they are also obliged to do so. . . Where the courts of several states have jurisdiction the plaintiff has deliberately been given a right of choice, which should not be weakened by application of the doctrine of *forum conveniens*.

Further support for this view could be found in *Boss Group Limited v. Boss France S.A.*, [1996] 4 All E.R. 970.

Finnegan J. distinguished the English Court of Appeal decision in *Re Harrods (Buenos Aires) Ltd* [1992] Ch. 72 and the Irish Supreme Court decision in *Intermetal Group Ltd v. Worslade Trading Ltd* [1998] 2 I.R. 1. The former case was concerned with the entitlement of a person being sued to have proceedings stayed on the basis of *forum conveniens* where the plaintiff was not domiciled in a contracting state. It was there held that the common law jurisdiction to stay survived in such circumstances. The decision was of no assistance to the plaintiff since each of the parties in the instant action was domiciled in a contracting state. Likewise in the latter case the first named plaintiff was domiciled in a non-contracting state and in these circumstances it was held that the convention had no application. The decisions were in accord with Article 4 of the Brussels Convention of 1968, which provides as follows:

> If the defendant is not domiciled in a contracting state the jurisdiction of the Courts in each contracting state shall, subject to the provisions of Article 16, be determined by the law of that state.

SOVEREIGN IMMUNITY

In the Practice and Procedure Chapter, below 378, Hilary Delany and Raymond Byrne analyse *Adams v. Director of Public Prosecutions*, High Court, April 12, 2000, affirmed by Supreme Court, March 6, 2001. The issue of sovereign immunity did not fall for consideration on appeal.

ADMIRALTY

Under the International Convention Relating to the Arrest of Seagoing Ships, signed in Brussels on 10 May 1952 and incorporated into Irish law by the Jurisdiction of Courts (Maritime Conventions) Act 1989 (Annual Review 1989, 69 et seq.), a 'sister ship' arrest may be ordered by the court where it is established that the plaintiff has a 'maritime claim' and that the claim arose in respect of another ship which is owned by the person who was, at the time when the maritime claim arose, the owner of the ship.

In *M.V. Tirgu Frumos: Gourdo-Michalis Maritime S.A. v. The Owners and All Persons Claiming an Interest in the M.V. Tirgu Frumos*, High Court, May 12, 2000, two issues arose as to whether the grounds for a 'sister ship' arrest had been established. The first concerned the nature of a 'maritime claim'. Article 1 of the Convention defines it as a claim arising out of, *inter alia*, an 'agreement relating to the use or hire of any ship whether by charter party or otherwise.'

In the instant case, a joint venture agreement between the parties provided that the vessels referred to in Annex 1 of the agreement, 'will be entered into bare boat charter between Petromin and/or their nominees and the subsidiary company'. One of the vessels named in the Annex was a bulk carrier being built in a shipyard in Romania which was due for delivery to Petromin within a year.

The second issue was more substantial. The defendants denied that they were the owners of the vessel in the circumstances described in Article 3 of the Convention. Article 3 provides as follows:

> (1) subject to the provisions of paragraph 4 of this Article and of Article 10 a claimant may arrest the particular ship in respect of which the maritime claim arose or any other ship which is owned by the person who was at the time when the maritime claim arose the owner of the particular ship even though the ship arrested be ready to sail ...

In the instant case, the claim arose when there was a failure on the part of the defendants to deliver the vessel in accordance with the agreement.

The onus lay on the plaintiff to establish to the satisfaction of the court on the balance of probabilities that the two vessels were in fact in the ownership of the same company at the relevant time.

On the evidence, the plaintiff failed to discharge that burden. Morris P. rejected the plaintiff's submission that the ownership in the vessel whilst under construction 'passed piecemeal to the building owner'. Morris P. was satisfied that:

> Logically whilst staged payments were required during the construction of the vessel which would give the building owner rights in the vessel, the ownership of the finished product would pass only on the completion of the contract and the payment of the final instalment.

> If therefore the breach of the agreement and the maritime claim arose on the failure of Petromin to deliver the vessel as required under the joint venture and if by then the contract for the construction of the vessel had already been rescinded, I am satisfied that the vessel was not in the ownership of Petromin and accordingly there is no entitlement in the plaintiff to [an] order [for 'sister ship' arrest].

JUDICIAL REVIEW

In *Adams v. Director of Public Prosecutions*, High Court, April 12, 2000, Kelly J. rejected the contention that the High Court had an inherent jurisdiction to order the service of judicial review proceedings out of the jurisdiction. Counsel for the plaintiff conceded that no such jurisdiction arose under Orders 11 or 11a of the Rules of the Supreme Court in *Brennan v. Lockyer* [1932] I.R. 100. So far as the possibility of an inherent jurisdiction was concerned, Kelly J. considered that Egan J.'s judgment in the Supreme Court decision of *Fusco v. O'Dea* [1994] 2 I.R. 93 gave a negative answer. Counsel argued that there was an emerging phenomenon in many countries of transnational public law. Kelly J. considered that such authority as existed on this issue suggested the contrary. In Kelly J.'s view, judicial review in Ireland stopped short at its territorial boundaries.

The Supreme Court affirmed on March 6, 2001. We shall examine McGuinness J.'s judgment in detail in the 2001 Review. We need merely note here that the manner in which she addressed this issue was somewhat more qualified than that of Kelly J.

DIVORCE

The whole basis of the law relating to jurisdiction and the recognition and enforcement of decrees relating to matrimonial matters in Europe has been transformed by Council Regulation (EC) No. 1347/2000 of May 29, 2000, which came into force on March 1, 2001. In essence it introduces a test based on one year's habitual residence. This radical measure, which has caused considerable controversy, will be examined in detail in the 2001 Review.

In *PK (otherwise C) v. TK*, High Court, April 14, 2000, Murphy J. held that a divorce obtained in New York in 1980 should be recognised under Irish private international law rules as the wife, an American citizen, was domiciled there at the time. He did not resolve the question whether the wife had 'reverted to her domicile origin or chose New York as a domicile of choice ....' The wife had come to Ireland to study in 1959, having been reared in New York. (The judgment is silent on her exact age or on the domicile or domiciles of her parents. It notes that they had lived in New York for at least ten years prior to her birth. The ascription in the judgment of a New York domicile of origin must have been based on the view that the state of domicile of her father, or possibly of both her parents, was New York.) The parties had married in New York in 1963, where they stayed for a few months before returning to Ireland. The husband was Irish; nothing in the judgment suggests that his domicile at all relevant times was Irish. From 1963 until 1972 the parties lived together in Ireland, the wife looking after their three children (born in 1964, 1965 and 1969). The family went to Maine in 1972, where the wife took up a full-time academic appointment. They returned to Ireland in 1974. The marriage was then going through a difficult period. By 1977, the marriage had broken down. The wife went to New York in that year. The parties entered into a separation agreement in November 1977, under which the husband had custody of the three children until September 1978, after which time the wife was entitled to have custody of one child (to be named by mutual agreement). The agreement did not provide for maintenance for the wife.

The 1980 divorce decree, obtained by the husband, incorporated the 1977 separation agreement in the judgment. The wife was living in New York at the time of the divorce. She still maintained rent controlled accommodation there at the time of the Irish proceedings in 2000, wherein the wife sought a divorce under the 1996 Act, arguing that the New York divorce should not be recognised as she had been domiciled in Ireland at that time.

The wife's central argument was that she had been driven by financial and social pressures to go to New York as she had little or no employment prospects in Ireland in 1977 and her husband's behaviour towards her 'made it difficult socially as well as financially to remain in Ireland'. She explained her participation in the 1980 divorce on the basis that she was looking for financial support through it (in respect, apparently, of the child who was living with her, under the terms of the agreement) on account of the 'lack of legal structures in Ireland.' She attributed her retention of her New York apartment, while she worked in the United States for some periods, to the fact that she had no security and would otherwise risk homelessness.

Murphy J. rejected the wife's claim that she was domiciled in New York at the time of the divorce. His analysis is worth recording:

> In the present case there are no written statements, nor indeed any independent evidence of the [wife]'s statement of domicile. Neither is it claimed that she had a domicile of dependency once she married the [husband].

> There is no doubt that she was resident in Ireland from the time she commenced her studies in 1959 to her separation and return to New York in 1977, other than the period of two years in …. Maine. However, being here as a student, and acquiring a passport, does not of itself prove domicile.

> However, though not all of her children were born in this jurisdiction, maintaining a family home from 1963 to 1977 does provide evidence of *animus manendi*. One assumes that this may have been the basis for a domicile of dependency in the past.

> However, that is no longer the position since *C.M. v. T.M (No. 2)* [1990] 2 I.R. 52. A wife needs to prove that she has abandoned her domicile of

origin to a domicile of choice. It may very well be that this proof is satisfied so long as a wife remains married and resides primarily in the domicile of her choice.

In the present case the overwhelming evidence is that, after the separation agreement of 1977 .... the [wife] either reverted to her domicile of origin or chose New York as a domicile of choice by maintaining her residence there for the past twenty-two years. While it is clear that the issue of domicile is of January 1980 when the divorce decree was obtained, it is significant that the [wife], in going back to New York in 1977 to seek employment and agreeing to the terms of the separation agreement whereby custody would be given substantially to her husband, was reverting to the security of her domicile of origin.

It seems from this passage that Murphy J. was of the view that the wife's domicile was that of New York, either because, being her domicile of origin, it had never been replaced by an Irish domicile of choice, or, if it had, because the wife had again acquired a New York domicile this time, by choice. Murphy J.'s two references to her reverting to her domicile of origin might possibly suggest a view on his part that the wife had abandoned an Irish domicile of choice and not acquired any other domicile of choice, even in New York, in which case her New York domicile of origin would revive to fill the vacuum: see Binchy, *Irish Conflicts of Law* (1988), pp. 74-7. Two factors support this interpretation. First, Murphy J.'s express reference to New York as her domicile of origin, rather than as a domicile of choice, indicates that its character as her domicile of origin was considered to be relevant. It is true that Murphy J. spoke of the wife's reverting to that domicile rather than of its revival. As a matter of historical narrative, if she was acquiring it as a domicile of choice she was indeed reverting to *the state of* her domicile of origin. To speak of her reverting *to her domicile of origin* might be considered to connote a juridical rather than factual transition. As against this, Murphy J.'s statement that the wife, in returning to New York, 'was reverting to *the security of* her domicile of origin' (emphasis added) would suggest that what he had in mind was in the factual domain. A second factor supporting the interpretation of Murphy J's observations as indicating a holding of a revival of the wife's domicile of origin is that the wife had averred that, after her return to New York in 1977, she had lived in various parts of the United States, in which she had never obtained permanent pensionable employment. This suggests a lack of clear intention on her part to live indefinitely or permanently in New York, thus weakening the notion that she had acquired a domicile of choice there.

Since Murphy J. held that the New York divorce should be recognised, he did not have to address the question whether the residence-based approach favoured by McGuinness J. in *G McG v. DW* [2000] 1 I.L.R.M. 107 should be endorsed.

Murphy J. went on to reject the wife's argument that she had been acting under duress in not opposing the divorce. Duress is a ground for non-recognition of a foreign decree: *Gaffney v. Gaffney* [1975] I.R. 133; Binchy, *op cit.*, pp. 286-7. In 1978 the wife had sent her husband a moving letter (quoted in the judgment), indicating a hope that her husband would initiate divorce proceedings as quickly as possible. Moreover, her lawyer had invoked the decree in 1987 when seeking to enforce its provisions as to maintenance for her youngest child. (This would seem more a matter supporting an estoppel argument rather than one of duress seven years previously.)

GUARDIANSHIP OF CHILDREN

The Protection of Children (Hague Convention) Act 2000 gives force in the State to the 1996 Hague Convention on Jurisdiction, Applicable Law, Recognition, Enforcement and Co-operation in Respect of Parental Responsibility and Measures for the Protection of Children. The Act applies to children under the age of eighteen; it is concerned with 'measures directed to the protection of the person or property of the child' – in essence what is embraced by the concept of guardianship in Irish law. It is not concerned with such matters as adoption, maintenance or succession.

Habitual residence is the basic rule for jurisdiction. This is so even where a child has been abducted: in such circumstances the courts of the habitual residence before the abduction retain jurisdiction. The *lex fori* is the basic choice of law rule. A broad requirement of recognition and enforceability in other contracting states is prescribed, with a machinery of designated central authorities which has a precedent in earlier conventions on maintenance and child abduction. S. 12 of the Act makes it clear that nothing in the legislation affects the application in the State of the Child Abduction and Enforcement of Custody Orders Act 1991.

We shall give an extensive analysis of the legislation in the 2001 Review. It should be noted that its effect is partially eclipsed by Council Regulation (EC) No. 1347/2000 on jurisdiction and enforcement of judgments in matrimonial matters and in matters of parental responsibility for children of both spouses, which we shall also examine in the 2001 Review.

INTERNATIONAL CHILD ABDUCTION

Rights of custody   In *M.S.H. v. L.H.* [2000] 3 I.R. 390 the question arose as to the application of the provisions of the Hague Convention to parents in custody. Could it be argued that such a parent, by virtue of his or her lack of day-to-day contact with her or her children, lost his or her right to custody where, so far as the domestic law of the state of habitual residence was concerned, the parent retained a legal right to custody?

The Supreme Court, affirming Herbert J., thought not. The case concerned an application by an English father, in prison in England since 1997, having been convicted of an offence involving drug dealing, for the return of his two children from Ireland, where they had been taken by their English mother, to whom he was married.

McGuinness J. (Hardiman and Geoghegan JJ. concurring) did:

> not accept that the clear position of the father in English law can be negatived or nullified by the fact that, due to his imprisonment, he is not at present playing a large part in the physical day to day care of the children. There are many circumstances in which one parent may have a low level of input into the day to day physical care of a child. It could not be that that fact alone would deprive that parent of a legally established right of custody. Still less could it be right for this Court to hold because a parent is serving a term of imprisonment he or she is divested of a legally established right of custody of his or her children.

> The situation in *In re P. and W.: W.P.P. v. S.R.W.* [2000] 4 I.R. 401 is not comparable, since in that case the parties were divorced and Court orders governed the custody and access arrangements. In that case it was clear that the father had right of access only.

Accepting, therefore, that the father had the legal right to custody, was he 'actually exercising the custody rights' at the time of the removal as Article 13 (a) required? Again McGuinness J. agreed with Herbert J.'s conclusion. Herbert J. had quoted from paragraph 72 of the Report of Madame Perez-Vera, where she explained that the burden of proving that the requesting parent was not exercising rights of access fell on the abducting parent. Herbert J. did:

> not understand Professor Perez-Vera in these paragraphs or in any part of her report to be advancing the proposition that it is not sufficient for persons seeking relief under Article 12 of the Hague Convention to establish that the particular custody right upon which reliance is placed and which is alleged to have been breached by the other party was exercised by them but that such persons must in addition in every case establish that they were to some extent taking immediate care of the person of the child at the date of the alleged wrongful removal.

> Should this be the case, then persons under a disability, for example, a person serving a term of imprisonment, persons incapacitated by sickness or accident and persons whose occupation necessitates long absences from home such as mariners would all be deprived of the benefits of the Hague Convention in the case of an unauthorised removal

of their children. In my judgment this could hardly have been the intention of the Contracting States in entering into this agreement on the civil aspects of international child abduction.

McGuinness J. observed:

> Whether or not [the father] was seeing his children at the highest frequency permitted by the prison authorities (a matter on which this Court has no evidence either way), it is clear that he was exercising his right to see them and to maintain his relationship with them. In addition his application to the Oldham County Court to obtain a Prohibited Steps Order was a clear exercise of his right of custody. Failure to exercise rights of custody must be clearly and unequivocally established. In my view, the [mother] has not discharged the burden of proof required and I consider that Article 13(a) does not apply in this case.

It would seem from this analysis that a parent who is in prison and who did not avail himself or herself, to some degree at least, of the opportunity to take an active role in his or her children's lives could find Article 13(a) raised successfully as a bar to the return of the children. Whether that active role would have to involve actual visits to the prison is not clear from the judgment. Presumably other lines of communication and involvement, such as letters, the sending of books or participation in the children's education or even recreational interests might suffice.

Where does this leave a parent who suffers from a disability that renders it impossible for him or her to exercise any rights of custody? On one view, it could be argued that a parent can be met with the Article 13 bar only where, having an opportunity to exercise these rights, he or she neglects to do so. On the other hand, Article 13(a) does not speak in terms of normative judgment: it provides that the authorities are not bound to order the return of a child if the person having the care of the person of the child '*was not actually* exercising the custody rights' at the relevant time (emphasis added). A disabled parent who *could* not exercise these rights surely cannot deny that he or she *was* not actually doing so.

The tenor of the analysis of both Herbert J. in the High Court and McGuinness J. in the Supreme Court suggests that there would be a futility in seeking to ensure that the rights of the imprisoned, the disabled and the otherwise compulsorily absent parent should be preserved under Article 3 as rights of custody only to be lost under Article 13(a) where the same compulsion led to their non-exercise. Perhaps the court could fall back on the fact that Article 13 removes an obligation to return which would otherwise arise and hold that a court, even though not under that obligation, should exercise its discretion to order a return where the only reason for the non-exercise of the applicant parent's right to custody was that the parent lacked the capacity (through external or internal circumstances) to do so. As against this, it may be argued that Article 13(a) treats the non-exercise of such rights as the basis for the establishment of a bar to the obligation to order a return and it does not require the court to interest itself in the reason for that non-exercise. There could well be excellent reasons for the non-exercise, apart altogether from circumstances of incapacity, which involve no criticism of the applicant parent.

Grave risk of harm Article 13 of the Hague Convention relieves the court of the obligation to order the return of a child who has been wrongfully removed or retained where the party opposing the return establishes that:

> There is a grave risk that his or her return would expose the child to physical or psychological harm or otherwise place the child in an intolerable situation.

In *M.S.H. v. L.H.* [2000] 3 I.R. 390, the mother of two children whom she had taken to Ireland from England in breach of a court order argued that their return there would place them in an intolerable situation. She claimed that their father, who was in prison, had taken one of the children as cover when he was dealing heroin and had been violent to her.

McGuinness J. (Hardiman and Geoghegan JJ. concurring) did not accept the mother's argument. She stated:

> The difficulty with the [mother's] evidence of risk, in my view, is that it is indeed very general and lacking in detail; indeed it highlights the paucity of factual evidence on either side as to the circumstances of the children either before they left England, during their residence in Galway, or prospectively if they return to England. This situation serves to illustrate the wisdom not only of the policy of the Hague Convention but also of the former rule that the question of the welfare of children is best decided by the Courts of the jurisdiction with whom they have the closest real connection, in general the Courts of their habitual residence. All the evidence which is so lacking in this Court and in the Court below will be readily obtainable in the English Court which already has seisin of the matter.

McGuinness J. did not accept the submission of counsel for the mother that the phrase 'grave risk' could be disjoined or separated from the latter part of the sentence in Article 13(b):

> It seems to me that the meaning of subparagraph (b) must be that either there is a grave risk that his or her return would expose the child to physical or psychological harm or there is a grave risk that his or her return would otherwise place the child in an intolerable situation. The

requirement that there should be a grave risk applies to both situations.

Access rights In *In re P. and W.; W.P.P. v. S.R.W.* [2000] 4 I.R. 401, the Supreme Court held that Article 21 of the Hague Convention was the appropriate vehicle for protecting rights of access and that the main machinery of the Convention was concerned with the enforcement of custody rights. Accordingly a wrongful removal of a child in breach of access rights would not be a wrongful removal or retention for the purposes of Article 3. In contrast, Article 21 is a mere pale imitation, lacking the sanctions that apply to interference with custody rights.

In the instant case the father of children who had been taken from California by their mother, their full legal custodian, to Ireland sought to invoke Article 5. Under the law of California, following a court order, he had right of access. He contended that this right, by implication, prohibited their removal without his prior consent or an order of the court. The Supreme Court considered it 'at least doubtful' that such removal would be unlawful under Californian law.

Article 5 provides in part that:

> [r]ights of custody shall include rights relating to the care of the person of the child and, in particular, the right to determine the child's place of residence …

Counsel for the father argued that the father's right to be notified of the mother's decision to alter their children's place of residence was itself a 'right of custody' within the meaning of the Convention.

Keane J. (McGuinness and Hardiman JJ. concurring) was unable to accept that proposition:

> No doubt a parent who has the right to determine the child's place of residence but who may not have the right to the physical custody of the child is regarded, by virtue of that article, as having a 'right of custody' which is protected by the Convention. The affidavits as to Californian law do not suggest that the plaintiff enjoyed any such right: on the contrary, they proceed on the basis that the defendant, as the parent having custody, was entitled to determine the minors' place of residence
> ….
>
> The exercise of the right to determine a child's place of residence may, of course, be restricted by the order of the court awarding custody to one parent by prohibiting the removal of the child from the jurisdiction of the court without the further leave of the court or the consent of the other parent. In such a case … the removal of the child, without such leave and without the consent of the other parent may constitute a breach of a right of custody vested in the court. In this case, however, we are

concerned with an order which gave the plaintiff rights of access only. It is clear, in my view, that the appropriate machinery for enforcing such rights is Article 21 of the Convention. To order the return of children and their custodial parent to the jurisdiction in which they were formerly habitually resident merely so as to entitle the non-custodial parent to exercise his rights of access is not warranted by the terms of the Convention.

Constitutional Law

COMMUTATION POWER

Article 13.6 of the Constitution provides that:

> [t]he right of pardon and the power to commute or remit punishment imposed by any court exercising criminal jurisdiction are hereby vested in the President, but such power of commutation or remission may also be conferred by law on other authorities.

Section 23 of the Criminal Justice Act 1951 gives this power to the government, which in turn may delegate it to the Minister for Justice.

In *The People (DPP) v. Finn*, Supreme Court November 24, 2000, the long-standing practice of the judges in the Central Criminal Court and the Circuit Court of including in custodial sentences a provision for review after a certain time was held to violate Article 13.5.

Keane C.J. (Murphy, McGuinness, Hardiman and Fennelly JJ. concurring) stated:

> [T]he essential legal frailty of the review procedure is not that it deprives the Executive of its statutory power to commute or remit the sentence during that period. It is that, when the review date arrives, the Central Criminal Court or the Circuit Court, on being satisfied that the relevant conditions have been met, suspends the balance of the sentence and orders the release of the convicted person, it is in substance exercising the power of commutation or remission which the Oireachtas has entrusted exclusively to the government or the Minister for Justice to whom the power may be delegated. The Minister cannot, of course, in exercising that power do what the court purports to do at the review stage, i.e. impose a suspended sentence which would normally involve the convicted person being returned to prison on foot of the order of a court in the event of his being convicted of further offences or breaking other conditions attached to the sentence. But if one looks to the substance of the order made by the court at the review date it is clearly an order which releases the convicted person before the completion of the sentence which the judicial arm of government considered appropriate at the sentencing stage and must, accordingly, be regarded as, in all but name, the exercise by the court of the power of commutation

or remission which, during the currency of the sentence imposed by the court, is vested exclusively in the Executive.

The making of such orders is not merely inconsistent with the provisions of s. 23 of the 1951 Act: it offends the separation of powers in this area mandated by Article 13.6 of the Constitution. That provision expressly vests the power of commutation or remission in the President but provides that the power may also be conferred by law on other authorities. Since under Article 15.2.10° of the Constitution the sole and exclusive power of making laws for the State is vested in the Oireachtas, it was for the legislative arm alone to determine which authorities other than the President should exercise that power. In enacting s. 23 of the Criminal Justice Act 1951, the Oireachtas conferred the power of commutation or remission on the government or, where it delegated its power, the Minister ...

It would seem to follow that the remission power, despite its essentially judicial character, once vested under the Constitution in an executive organ, cannot, without further legislative intervention, be exercised by the courts.

DEFAMATION

In the Torts Chapter below, 456, we examine *O'Brien v. Mirror Group Newspapers Ltd*, Supreme Court, October 25, 2000, in which the relationship between the constitutional protection of free speech and the European Convention's equivalent guarantee was addressed.

DELAY IN CRIMINAL PROSECUTION

In the Criminal Law Chapter, below, 77 *et seq.*, we examine the developing jurisprudence on delay in criminal proceedings, expanding on the implicit constitutional right to reasonable expedition, under Article 38.1

EDUCATION

In *Sinnott v. Minister for Education*, High Court, October 4, 2000, Barr J. held that the State had failed in its constitutional obligation to provide a twenty-three-year old adult with severe autism and mental and physical dysfunction with education and training appropriate to his particular situation. He made wide-ranging orders as to his future care. He also awarded his mother damages in respect of the unconstitutional failure by the State. The Supreme Court reversed Barr J. on July 2001. It held that the State's obligation did not extend into adulthood. It also favoured a more restrained relationship between the organs of State so far as the scope of judicial orders was concerned. This highly controversial decision will be analysed in detail in the 2001 Review.

EQUALITY

In *Riordan v. An Taoiseach* [2000] 4 I.R. 537, the Supreme Court gave short shrift to the applicant's claim that Article 40.1 required the Executive to inform the public of all public service posts before deciding how they should be filled. The post in questionof that of vice-president of the European Investment Bank, for which the former Mr Justice O'Flaherty was nominated but ultimately withdrew. Keane C.J. (Murphy, McGuinness, Geoghegan and McCracken JJ concurring) considered it:

> sufficient to say that even the most expansive construction of Article 40.1 could not support the proposition that the guarantee of equality required the imposition of such constraints on the executive in making recommendations of this nature.

FAMILY

The decision of McCracken J. in *North Western Health Board v. H.W. and C.W.*, High Court, October 27, 2000 contains an important analysis of the limit of parental autonomy in decision-making as to the welfare of children. The issue was a straightforward one. The plaintiff Health Board, in conjunction with other health boards and the Department of Health, provided a screening service for parents of new-born infants to test for the presence of fair metabolic conditions and one endocrine condition in the children. These conditions could cause severe mental handicap, intercranial bleeding and eye damage. The risk of their occurring was one in several thousand. The process, commonly known as the PKU test, involved the extraction of drops of blood from the infant's heel, having punctured the skin with a lancet. If one of these conditions was discovered, it would be treatable by diet control or medication but, if not, once the damage had been caused by the condition, it was usually irreversible. It was thus 'immediately considered of great importance to have the condition diagnosed at as early a stage as possible'.

It was not mandatory for parents to provide their consent for the test though only about six cases a year occurred where parents refused to have the test carried out. In the instant case the defendants refused to permit the test to be effected by invasive measures on the basis of what they described as their 'strong religious belief that nobody is allowed to injure anybody else'. They had no objection to the test being carried out by non-invasive means on hair and urine samples.

The plaintiff took legal proceedings, seeking declarations that it was in the best interest of the infant that the test be carried out on him and that the defendants' refusal to provide their consent was a failure on their part to vindicate the personal rights of their son. It also sought an injunction restraining the defendants from impeding the execution of the test and a mandatory injunction requiring them to furnish their consent.

The constitutional and statutory framework was easy to identify. Articles 41 and 42 of the Constitution defined the State's relationship with the family and specifically, in the case of Article 42, with the parents. Section 3 of the Child Care Act 1991 prescribed the function of health boards to provide the welfare of children in their areas who were not receiving adequate care and protection. The plaintiff argued that the benefits of the screening process clearly outweighed the drawbacks: all that was involved was a pinprick carrying absolutely minimal risk of harm to the infant in contrast to the possible seriousness of any of the condition which would otherwise go unmonitored.

The defendants replied that the legislature in Ireland and the legislatures of every other country had not chosen to make this screening process compulsory. They contended that 'the rights of the family, and therefore in the case of a young infant, the parents, must take precedence under the Constitution over the rights of the child unless there is an exceptional case where the parents, for physical or moral reasons, have failed in their duty towards the chil[d]'. Their counsel pointed to the fact that parents made decisions for their children all that time and had 'a right to be wrong'; they certainly were not bound to act in accordance with generally accepted principles or generally accepted medical opinion.

McCracken J. refused the relief sought by the plaintiff. He agreed with the defendants' submission on the general criterion for State intervention into the area of parental decision-making:

> Article 42.5 is quite clear that such jurisdiction must only exist in exceptional cases 'where the parents for physical or moral reasons fail in their duty towards their children'. This provision clearly justifies State intervention in certain cases, but only in exceptional cases and only where there has been a failure by the parents in their duty for physical or moral reasons.

McCracken J. observed that:

> Article 41.1 places the family in a very special position as being the natural primary and fundamental unit group of society. It also provides that the family possess rights which are antecedent and superior to all positive law. It is indeed probably the provision in the Constitution which comes nearest to accepting that there is a natural law in the theological sense. There have been a number of cases which have spoken

of a hierarchy of rights under the Constitution, but the wording of Article 41.1 certainly would appear to place the rights of the family and therefore presumably the rights of the parents in relation to their children, very high up in this hierarchy.

There was no doubt that medical opinion would emphatically state that it was in the infant's best interest to have the PKU test done. The question which McCracken J. had to answer was whether this objective benefit to the infant overrode the rights of his parents, in effect, to decide that they did not want him to have the discomfort of a pinprick in his heel, they being prepared to take the risk that he did not suffer from any of the relevant conditions.
    McCracken J. observed:

> Parents constantly make decisions of this nature, and subject their children to risks which objectively may not be justified, and which may have disastrous results. Examples outside the medical field may be decisions to allow a child to cycle to school on a busy road, or decisions to allow a teenager to find his or her own way home from a disco. Of course, in extreme cases the putting of children into a situation of risk may justify State intervention, but such cases would be extreme, and therefore exceptional cases. In the medical field, the State provides many facilities for the protection of children, such as inoculations and vaccinations, but it does not compel the parents to have their children inoculated or vaccinated. There is in fact a far stronger case to be made that some vaccinations should be compulsory in the common good where the vaccination is against an infectious disease such as diphtheria or meningitis, but the State have chosen to leave it to the decision of the parents to have these vaccinations.

McCracken J. distinguished the Supreme Court decision of *Ryan v. Attorney General* [1965] I.R. 294. There, the State had sought to impose a treatment of water for the common good, and one individual had attempted to prevent the entire nation from having the benefit of fluoridation.
    The initial case is quite the opposite:

> Here the State is providing a service to the public in general, which will not be affected by the outcome of these proceedings. In the *Ryan* case, one suspects the result would have been very different if Mrs Ryan had simply sought a declaration that she and her family were not bound to drink from the common water supply, and that in effect is the argument being made by the defendant[s] in the present case.

In a crucial passage, McCracken J. disposed of the central issue:

The framers of the Constitution used the word 'exceptional' in Article 42.5, and one must assume that they did so after very careful consideration. Indeed, the use of that word is totally consistent with the provisions of article 41.1. There are of course cases in which the State may interfere with parental rights, and many of these are detailed in the Child Care Act, 1991. They are exceptional cases. In my view, the decision in the present case by the defendants, who are acknowledged to be caring and conscientious parents, could not be said to constitute an exceptional case, even though the general medical opinion would be quite clear that such decision was wrong. If the State were entitled to intervene in every case where professional opinion differed from that of the parents, or where the State considered the parents were wrong in a decision, we would be rapidly stepping towards the Brave New World in which the State always knows best. In my view, that situation would be totally at variance with both the spirit and the word of the Constitution.

McCracken J. concluded his analysis by reflecting on the respective functions of the organs of the State. The State had not chosen to use its laws to protect the infant in the manner envisaged by Article 40.3.2° (assuming, contrary to his holding, that the parents' refusal to consent to the test constituted an injustice to their son):

> The State, through the plaintiff as an organ or body set up by the State, appears to be asking the Court to undertake the obligation imposed by the Article. If the State believes that it has an obligation to make it unlawful for parents to refuse to allow their children to undergo tests such as this, the State, through the Oireachtas, could so provide in legislation. That legislation could then be tested in the Courts for its constitutionality.

This decision is clearly of very considerable importance. It reasserts a broad remit of parental decision-making at a time when cultural trends might be regarded as moving in the opposite direction so far as health policy is concerned. It is not easy to speak with confidence about these trends but some interesting dissonances to be noted. On questions of what might be called conventional health issues, such as obesity, alcohol, smoking and dental health, there seems to be a broad social acceptance of the propriety of the role of the State, even where this interferes with particular parental philosophies. On larger issues of life and death, such as euthanasia and abortion, or issues relating to religious values, there is a discernible reluctance to acknowledge with equal enthusiasm the role of the State in the context of parental decision-making. In the instant case, the parents invoked a religious basis for their objection. McCracken J. noted it but did not enlarge upon this element.

A question arises as to the relationship between public and private law in this context. It may be argued that the parents were guilty of negligence towards their son in refusing to permit the test. If he developed one of the conditions, he could well succeed in an action for negligence against them. *In Hanrahan v. Merck Sharp & Dohme (Ireland Ltd* [1988] I.L.R.M. 629, the Supreme Court acknowledged that the corpus of tort law served the function of protecting constitutional rights. Only if a particular tort was 'basically ineffective' in affording that protection, should the court resort to an ancillary remedy for infringement of constitutional rights. Is an infant who is the victim of negligence which may result in injury to him bereft of a remedy until the injury actually occurs or should the court be pro-active in protecting him by means of a mandatory injunction which will remove the risk of injury? McCracken J. was reluctant to surrender parental decision-making to the agencies of the State but where the decision in question is (let us assume) one that violates the parents' duty of care towards their child, is the court to stand idly by? Would the position be any different if some third party – a grandparent, for example – sought to protect the infant's interests by resort to the courts?

Within the confines of constitutional law, it could be argued that the issue in the instant case was not confined to a dispute between parents and an agency of the State. The infant child had constitutionally protected rights – to health and bodily integrity – which required recognition and vindication.

IMMIGRATION

In *Article 26 Reference Re Illegal Immigrants (Trafficking) Bill 1999*, Supreme Court, August 28, 2000, the constitutional validity of sections 5 and 10 of the Bill was upheld. Section 5 precludes any person from questioning the validity of certain decisions made under the immigration code save by way of application for judicial review within fourteen days of his or her being notified of the decision, unless the High Court considers that there is 'good and sufficient' reason for extending the period. Section 10 amends the Immigration Act 1999 by giving the Minister for Justice power to require people subject to deportation orders to present themselves to a member of the Garda Síochána, produce travel documents required for deportation and reside at a particular district or place pending deportation. It also widens the power of arrest without warrant where a member of the Garda Síochána with reasonable cause suspects that persons subject to a deportation order have destroyed their identity documents, intend to leave the State and enter another state without lawful authority or intend to avoid removal from the State.

Counsel assigned to attack the validity of these provisions argued that section 5 infringed the constitutional right of all persons of access to the courts on the basis that the time for taking judicial review proceedings was too short, in view especially of the State's dispersal policy and the lack of access to legal advice.

The Court did not agree. Keane C.J., for the Court, stated:

> There is a well established public policy objective that administrative decisions, particular those taken pursuant to detailed procedures laid down by law, should be capable of being applied or implemented with certainty at as early a date as possible and that any issue as to their validity should accordingly be determined as soon as possible ... Furthermore, it may be inferred from the Bill and surrounding circumstances that the early establishment of the certainty of the decisions in question is necessary in the interests of the proper management and treatment of persons seeking asylum or refugee status in this country. The early implementation of decisions duly and properly taken would facilitate the better and proper administration of the system governing seekers of asylum for both those who are ultimately successful and ultimately unsuccessful.
>
> For these reasons, the Court is of the view that the State has a legitimate interest in prescribing procedural rules calculated to ensure or promote an early completion of judicial review proceedings of the administrative decisions concerned. However, in doing so, the State must respect constitutional rights and in particular that of access to the courts.
>
> Accordingly, the court is of the view that there are objective reasons concerning the public interest in the certainty of the validity of the administrative decisions concerned on one hand the proper and effective management of applications for asylum or refugee status on the other. Such objective reasons may justify a stringent limitation of the period within which judicial review of such decisions may be sought, provided constitutional rights are respected.
>
> The test is not whether a more extended period of time within which to seek leave to apply for judicial review (whether slightly longer or very much longer) would permit the same policy objectives to be attained
> ....
>
> [P]rocedures of the courts may be regulated by law. It is a matter of policy and discretion for the legislature to choose the appropriate limitation period. The legislature is not obliged to choose the longest possible period that might be thought consistent with the policy objective concerned. However, in exercising that discretion the legislator must not undermine or compromise a substantive right guaranteed by the Constitution such as the right of access to the courts. Where a limitation period is so restrictive as to render access to the courts impossible or excessively difficult it may be considered unreasonable ... . therefore unconstitutional.
>
> In applying that test in this case, the court acknowledges that there are likely to be cases, perhaps even a very large number of cases, in

which for a range of reasons or a combination of reasons, persons, through no fault of their own, ... are unable to apply for leave to seek judicial review within the appeal limitation period, namely fourteen days. This is a situation with which the courts deal on a routine basis for other limitation periods. The fourteen days time limit envisaged by the Bill is not the shortest with which the courts have had to deal.

Moreover, the discretion of the court to extend the time to apply for leave where the applicant shows 'good and sufficient reason' for so doing is wide and ample enough to avoid injustice where an applicant has been unable through no fault of his or hers, or for other good and sufficient reason, to bring the application within the fourteen day period. For example counsel assigned to the court have argued that the complexity of the issues, or the deficiencies and inefficiencies in the legal aid service, may prevent the applicant from being in a position to proceed with his application for leave within the period of fourteen days.

However, where this has occurred through no fault of the applicant, it may be advanced as a ground for extending the time for applying for leave for judicial review ....

The court is satisfied that the discretion of the High Court to extend the fourteen day period is sufficiently wide to enable persons who, having regard to all the circumstances of the case including language difficulties, communication difficulties, difficulties with regard to legal advice or otherwise, have shown reasonable diligence, to have sufficient access to the courts for the purpose of seeking judicial review in accordance with their constitutional rights.

The court does not therefore consider the limitation period to be unreasonable as such and its repugnancy to the Constitution has not been established.

Whilst no one could cavil at the formal logic of this analysis, it may seem somewhat removed from the flesh-and-blood human situation in which asylum seekers find themselves. Their problems are of a systemic nature which do not easily translate into the perception, on which section 5 is based, that they may occur exceptionally to individual asylum seekers. Again the court adopted a formally correct position in holding that, merely because it was possible or likely that the judiciary would be called on to exercise this 'exceptional' jurisdiction frequently, this meant that the provision was necessarily unconstitutional. As a matter of human experience, however, litigants who genuinely are the victims of systemic failure will find it hard to convince courts to exercise a purportedly exceptional jurisdiction in a way that in practice contradicts the legislative perception that the jurisdiction should be exercised rarely.

So far as section 10 of the Bill was concerned, the court rejected the argument that it created a species of unconstitutional preventive detention. Keane C.J. stated:

> Common sense suggests that there will always be cases where an immigrant who has gone through, or had an opportunity to go through, all the application and appeal procedures for asylum or for leave to remain in the country on humanitarian grounds will still attempt to evade the execution of a deportation order.
>
> Depending on the country of origin, travel arrangements may be extremely difficult to put in place and powers of detention between the making of the deportation order and in advance of the deportation itself may well be necessary in some instances.

Keane C.J. went on to refer to several considerations which mitigated the potential for abuse of this detention power.

One may wonder whether an apprehension that a person may 'attempt to evade the execution of a deportation order' can be sufficient reason to deny that person of his or her liberty. Formally, the intervention is not punishment for a crime not committed but surely that is what it is in substance? Liberty should not be sacrificed to administrative concerns, however reasonable these concerns may be.

PROCEDURE

In the Practice and Procedure Chapter, below, 378, Hilary Delany and Raymond Byrne analyse two recent decisions of the Supreme Court, *Blehein v. Murphy* [2000] 1 ILRM 481 and *Dunnes Stores (Ireland) Co v. Ryan*, Supreme Court, February 8, 2000, on the circumstances in which that Court will consider constitutional issues which had not been argued in the High Court.

PROPERTY

Garrett Simons, in the Planning Law Chapter, below, analyses the Supreme Court decision in *In re Article 26 of the Constitution and Part V of the Planning and Development Bill 1999* [2000] 2 I.R. 321.

RIGHT TO VOTE

In *Breathnach v. Ireland* [2000] 3 I.R. 467, Quirke J. held that denying prisoners the right to vote violated their right to equal treatment under Article 40.1. Quirke J. reasoned as follows:

Whilst the applicant's right to vote in national and other elections is a limited and qualified right ... it is nonetheless a constitutionally protected right. The State has, by its laws, vindicated the same limited but constitutionally protected rights of other categories of its citizens who for one reason or another are unable to attend at polling stations in order to vote in national and other elections. That vindication has been achieved by the enactment of laws providing postal voting facilities for such citizens.

It has been acknowledged by the State that the extension of a system for postal voting to citizens (such as the applicant) who are lawfully detained within the prison population would not impose undue administrative demands upon the State but nonetheless no such legislative provisions have been enacted by or on behalf of the State.

The sanctions imposed upon the applicant by the Special Criminal Court in respect of the offences with which he has been lawfully convicted comprised sentences of various terms of imprisonment. The loss of the applicant's right to vote in national and other elections was not, at the time of his conviction, a sanction which was prescribed or permitted by law in respect of the offences of which the applicant was convicted. Accordingly, the applicant retains his constitutionally protected right to vote at '... an election for members of Dáil Éireann' and his legally protected right to vote in Presidential, European and Local Government elections. Furthermore he is entitled to exercise that right provided that his exercise does not impose unreasonable demands upon the authorities who are lawfully detaining him. It has been acknowledged that the authority that is lawfully detaining the applicant is the State.

Quirke J. concluded that the failure on the part of the State to provide for the applicant, 'as a citizen of the State amongst the prison population', the necessary machinery to enable him to vote violated Article 40.1.

The Supreme Court reversed on appeal on July 11, 2001, invoking the more indulgent approach evident in *Draper v. Attorney General* [1984] I.R. 277. We shall discuss the Supreme Court decision in the Annual Review 2001.

Contract Law

EOIN O'DELL, Trinity College, Dublin.

BREACH

The best way to win a case is to win on the facts. In a breach of contract action, the best way for a defendant to win is to show that he did not in fact breach his contract. That is precisely what the defendant succeeded in doing in *Allianz France Iardt v. Minister for Agriculture,* Supreme Court, May 17, 2000. Two brokers had assisted the Minister's advisor in the placing of insurance, which the Minister eventually placed with the plaintiff. However, when the Minister made a claim, the plaintiff sought to repudiate the policy and the Minister therefore commenced proceedings against its advisor who in turn commenced proceedings against the brokers. In the High Court, Morris P. held that each of the brokers had responsibility for placing the Minister's insurance, but, on appeal, the Supreme Court, (Keane C.J., Barron and Hardiman JJ.) held that the agreement between the Minister's advisor and the brokers was that one would secure underwriters in the English market and the other in the French, and that as the insurance had been placed with a French company, the broker who was solely and exclusively responsible for placing the risk on the English market did not act as placing brokers in respect of the placing, handling, management or renewal of the Minister's insurance policy with the plaintiff. Although the Minister might be able successfully to allege that the broker who placed the risk with the French company was in breach of contract and thus responsible for the Minister's loss, the defendant was not.

On the other hand, a party who can't easily win on the facts might try to win on the law, as by arguing that the contract did not in fact impose the obligation which the other party is seeking to argue was breached. In *Scanlon v. Ormonde Brick,* High Court, July 21, 2000, Barr J., the defendant seemed to adopt such a strategy, though unsuccessfully. The plaintiff sold property to the defendant, and reserved "out of the said lands any coal deposits, pillars or otherwise exposed in the course of the Purchaser's works and shall have the right to mine and remove any such deposits". Barr J. held that "expose" here means "made available for removal", as it was when the defendant, having removed shale or fireclay from the land, left the remaining coal pillars covered by a thin layer of shale, even though the coal was not then literally exposed. The plaintiff had mined some coal, but then a dispute arose between the parties, and the defendant prevented the plaintiff from continuing to do so. Thereafter, the coal on the defendant's land was subject to large scale commercial pilfering. Barr J. held that the defendant was bailee for the plaintiff's coal, and owed the plaintiff a duty to take reasonable steps to prevent loss to the plaintiff (by analogy with *Sheehy v. Faughnan* [1991] I.L.R.M. 719 (HC; Barron J.)) which it had failed to do, and was thus liable in damages.

Breach of conditions and conditions precedent   Breach of contract will not of itself terminate a contract; rather, it gives rise, in favour of the party not in breach, first to a right to damages and/or specific performance, and second, if the breach is sufficiently serious (as of a breach of a condition) to a right to bring the contract to an end; unless and until that latter right is exercised, each party's contractual rights and obligations continue to subsist (see the Annual Review 1995, 201; Annual Review 1998, 138-150). However, the parties might make the contract subject to a condition precedent, by which the contract would not be binding unless an agreed specified event occurs. If one party has the obligation to bring that event about, and fails to do so, then the main contractual obligations simply do not arise (see, *e.g.*, *Macklin & McDonald v. Graecen & Co* [1983] I.R. 61 (SC)).

Hence, there is an important practical difference between a breach of condition and a breach of a condition precedent; in the former case, contractual obligations subsist and continue until discharged; in the latter, they simply never arise. It has been something of an open question, of great practical importance, as to whether the obligation on the purchaser of real property to pay a deposit is merely a condition of the contract of purchase or a condition precedent to such a contract. If the former, then non-payment of the deposit will not of itself discharge the contract, and, unless discharged, the vendor can have specific performance against the purchaser; whereas, if the latter, then non-payment will prevent the contract from coming into existence in the first place, and there is nothing of which the vendor can have specific performance. The better view is that the obligation to pay the deposit is a condition of the contract rather than a condition precedent to it. There were *dicta* to this effect in *Millichamp v. Jones* [1982] 1 W.L.R. 1422 (Warner J.); the question had been left open in *Kramer v. Arnold* [1997] 3 I.R. 43 (SC) 60 (*per* Keane J.) and in *Damon v. Hapag-Lloyd* [1985] 1 W.L.R. 435; whilst in *Mytong v. Schwab-Morris* [1974] 1 W.L.R. 331 Goulding J. held that a condition as to payment of a deposit did in fact constitute a condition precedent. Professor Clark has commented that the *result* was fair as "the defendant purchaser had registered a caution against the vendor's property and this result meant that the caution could be removed" but Clark went on to argue that the *reasoning* of Goulding J. is open to question: "the purchasers duty to pay a deposit is part of he purchaser's contractual obligations, rather than an external condition upon which the contract's very existence will turn" (201). There is much force in this criticism, so the fact that the matter has been put beyond doubt in this jurisdiction by Finnegan J. in *Blackall v. Blackall* [2000] 3 I.R. 456 (HC), and put beyond doubt in a manner entirely consistent with principle, is warmly to be welcomed. In that case, Finnegan J. preferred *Millichamp* and held that the clause requiring the payment of the deposit in the instant case was merely

> a term of the contract non-performance of which would entitle the
> vendors to rescind immediately but so long as they refrain from so
> doing the contractual obligations of both vendor and purchase remain.
> ([2000] 3 I.R. 456, 463)

On the facts the notice to terminate by two of three co-owner-vendors was
insufficient as all three had to agree for it to be valid, and specific performance
was ordered.

ESTOPPEL

In *Aer Rianta v. Ryanair,* High Court, December 5, 2000, Kelly J., the plaintiff
sought summary judgment against the defendant for airport landing charges
(which are – pursuant to section 39 of the Air Navigation and Transport
(Amendment) Act 1998 – recoverable as a simple contract debt). The defendant
sought to resist on the grounds that negotiations between the parties had resulted
in either a variation of the landing charges scheme in the defendant's favour,
or a collateral contract to that effect; but Kelly J. held that the documents
exhibited by the defendant did not substantiate either contention. The defendant
also claimed that representations by the plaintiff during the course of the
negotiations estopped the plaintiff from pursing the action. As the routes to
which the charges related commenced on February 7, 1997, Kelly J. held that
correspondence subsequent to that date could not be relied upon to found the
promissory estoppel claim, presumably because if the relevant actions predated
the representations, the actions could not be said to have happened in reliance
upon the representations. Hence, Kelly J. awarded summary judgment to the
plaintiffs.

FRUSTRATION

Frustration occurs "whenever the law recognises that without default of either
party a contractual obligation has become incapable of being performed … or
because the circumstances in which performance is called for rendered it
something radically different from that which was undertaken by the contract"
(*Davis v. Fareham* UDC [1956] A.C. 696 (HL) 729 *per* Lord Radcliffe; *Codelfa
Construction v. State Rail Authority of NSW* (182) 149 C.L.R. 337 (HCA);
Bates v. Model Bakery [1993] 1 I.R. 359; [1993] I.L.R.M. 22 (SC); *Neville v.
Guardian Builders* [1995] 1 I.L.R.M. 1 (SC) (see the Annual Review 1994,
134-140)). The consequence is that the contract is automatically discharged
by the frustrating event (see *Hirji Mulji v. Cheong Yue SS* [1926] A.C. 497

(HL)) and the parties are released from their obligations in the future; accrued rights and liabilities remain, unless the frustration works a total failure of consideration, in which case the parties can have restitution of the benefits already transferred under the now discharged contract (see *Fibrosa v. Fairbairn* [1943] A.C. 32 (HL)).

"Much discussion is to be found in the cases as to the so-called theoretical or juristic basis of the doctrine of frustration" (Treitel *Frustration and Force Majeure* (Sweet & Maxwell, London, 1994) 578). For example, according to Lord Loreborn in *Tamplin v. Anglo-American Petroleum* if the parties "must have made their bargain on the footing that a particular thing or state of things would continue to exist ... a term to that effect will be implied" ([1916] 2 A.C. 397 (HL) 404; see also *Constantine v. Imperial Smelting Corp* [1942] A.C. 154 (HL) 163 *per* Viscount Simon). This was the basis of the doctrine stated by Blackburn J. in *Taylor v. Caldwell* (1863) 3 B.&S. 826, 836; 122 E.R. 309, 313, the case which established that frustration could relieve parties from their contractual obligations, and which was followed on this point in *Gamble v. Accident Assurance Company* (1871) I.R. 4 C.L. 204, 216 *per* Pigot C.B.; *cp. Cummings v. Stewart (No 2)* [1913] 1 I.R. 95, 116-118 *per* O'Connor M.R. In other words, frustration discharges the contract because a term is implied into the contract that it will have this effect. It is a theory which has its adherents, especially among those who take a similar view of the operation of mistake (see especially Smith "Contracts - Mistake, Frustration and Implied Terms" (1994) 110 L.Q.R. 400, discussed in the 1999 Review, 87-100) but the speech of Lord Loreborn has been the subject of much criticism (see, *e.g., Denny, Mott & Dickson v. Fraser* [1944] A.C. 265 (HL) 274-275 *per* Lord Wright; *Davis v. Fareham* [1956] A.C. 696 (HL) 728 *per* Lord Radcliffe) and it is now rejected (*Atisa v. Aztec AG* [1983] 2 Lloyd's Rep. 579, 586): if the term is implied even where the parties did not and would not have addressed their minds to the prospect of a frustrating event, then the court is no longer attempting to give effect to the parties' intentions, and is instead itself simply imposing the solution on the parties. A famous example demonstrates the absurdity of the implied term theory:

> A tiger has escaped from a travelling menagerie. The milkgirl fails to deliver the milk. Possibly the milkman may be exonerated from any breach of contract; but even so, it would seem hardly reasonable to base that exoneration on the ground that 'tiger days excepted' must be held as if written into the milk contract. (*Scott v. Del Sel* 1922 SC 592, 597 *per* Lord Sands; *Davis v. Fareham* [1956] A.C. 696 (HL) 720 *per* Lord Reid).

As a consequence, some judges have argued that when an unforeseen event occurs, the court should simply impose a just solution upon the parties (see, *e.g., Hirji Mulji v. Cheong Yue SS* [1926] A.C. 497 (HL) 510 *per* Lord Sumner;

Denny, Mott & Dickson v. Fraser [1944] A.C. 265 (HL) 274-275 *per* Lord Wright; *Constantine v. Imperial Smelting Corp* [1942] A.C. 154 (HL) 186 *per* Lord Wright). Unsurprisingly, such a technique attracted itself to Lord Denning. In *British Movietonenews v. London and District Cinemas* he said that in "frustration cases ... the court really exercises a qualifying power – a power to qualify the absolute, literal or wide terms of the contract – in order to do what is just and reasonable in the new situation" ([1951] 1 K.B. 190 (CA) 200), although, on appeal in that case, the House of Lords rapped him on the knuckles for these views ([1952] A.C. 166 (HL) 183 *per* Viscount Simon). As Treitel has pointed out, the theory "does not purport to explain why the courts sometimes abandon the doctrine of absolute contracts: it simply asserts that they do so" (Treitel, 581).

More simply, Lord Haldane (dissenting) in *Tamplin v. Anglo-American Petroleum* was of the view that when a frustrating event has occurred "the foundation of what the parties are deemed to have had in contemplation has disappeared and the contract itself has vanished with that foundation" ([1916] 2 A.C. 397, 406), but as Treitel points out, the metaphor of foundation is many cases unhelpful; for example, how "can one tell whether passage through the Suez Canal is the 'foundation' of a charterparty?" (Treitel, 582, plainly contemplating cases like *Tsakiroglou v. Noblee Thorl GmbH* [1962] A.C. 93 (HL)). As a consequence, Treitel argues that the real basis of the courts' power to discharge a contract for frustration lies simply in the fact that the contract on its proper construction does not cover the relationship between the parties on the facts as they have become (Treitel, 582; see *Davis v. Fareham* [1956] A.C. 696 (HL) 720-721 *per* Lord Reid; 726-729 *per* Lord Radcliffe; *National Carriers v. Panalpina* [1981] A.C. 675 (HL)). There is much to be said for this view, as it simply states that the contract is discharged by operation of law when the frustrating event occurs, without recourse to fictional implication of terms, unprincipled analysis of just results or fruitless searches for the foundations of the contract.

Irish cases have tracked this development without committing to any alternative to the implied term theory. The doctrine was referred to in *Byrne v. Limerick SS Co* [1946] I.R. 138 (HC) in which Overend J. held that the plaintiff's contract of employment with the defendant was not frustrated by the defendant's failure to obtain approval for the plaintiff to work on the defendant's ship in an English port. In *Mulligan v. Browne,* High Court, July 9, 1976, Gannon J.; Supreme Court, November 23, 1977, Kenny J. in the Supreme Court set out the competing views without choosing between them because the event which was sought to be relied upon as working the frustration had been provided for by the parties; and as it was foreseen, it did not amount to a frustration at all. In the High Court in *Neville v. Guardian Builders*, many of the English cases above were cited to Murphy J. to demonstrate "how far the courts ... ha[ve] moved from the implied term as the basis for the doctrine of frustration to an objective test based on the construction of the contract"

([1990] I.L.R.M. 601 (HC) 614) but Murphy J. made no comment on the issue. Furthermore, Blayney J. in the Supreme Court in the same case, following the lead of Lord Wilberforce in *Panalpina* ([1981] A.C. 675, 693-694) rather than attempt to choose between various theories which shaded into one another, chose instead to focus on whether circumstances had radically changed the nature of the parties' contractual obligations ([1995] 1 I.L.R.M. 1 (SC) 7-8).

This lack promised to be filled, according to Clark and Clarke *Contract Cases and Materials* (2nd ed., Gill & Macmillan, Dublin, 2000) xii, by "the fascinating analysis of the judicial basis of frustration in ... Murphy J's judgment" in *Zuphen v. Kelly Technical Services (Ireland) Ltd* [2000] E.L.R. 277 (HC). The defendants carried out network maintenance and development for Eircom, and hired the plaintiffs on one year contracts as extra staff for projected work from Eircom which failed to materialise. The defendants claimed that this frustrated their contracts with the plaintiffs. It is clear that if the plaintiffs themselves had become unable to work, this could have frustrated their contracts of employment (see, *e.g.*, *Flynn v. Great Northern Rly Co (Ireland) Ltd* (1953) 89 I.L.T.R. 46 (HC; Budd J.)), and although not every difficulty in the employer's way in employing the employee will amount to a frustration (see, *e.g.*, *Byrne v. Limerick SS Co* [1946] I.R. 138 (HC; Overend J.)) the sinking of the ship upon which the employee is serve will do so (*Kearney v. Saorstát and Continental Shipping* (1943) I.R. Jur. Rep. 8 (Davitt J.)). In *Zuphen*, Murphy J. considered it "inappropriate ... to apply a strict contract law approach to employment disputes. Attempts to so apply tend to obscure the social implications of certain kinds of conduct or events by reducing them to legalistic principles" ([2000] E.L.R. 277, 291). It is unclear what he meant by a "strict contract law approach" in this context, although it seems that it was the doctrine of frustration which Murphy J. regarded as embodying the strict approach on the facts of *Zuphen*. However, in the history of the evolution of the doctrine of frustration, the strict approach of the absolute nature of contractual obligations (see *Pardine v. Jane* (1647) Aleyn 26; 82 ER 897) was ameliorated by the development of the doctrine of frustration exemplified in *Taylor v. Caldwell* and, in Ireland, in *In re Carew* (1851) 3 I.R. Jur. 323. It seems therefore that, far from being a comment on the doctrine of frustration, Murphy J.'s *dictum* amounts simply to the proposition that the law ought to be sensitive to the position of employees. In any event, relying on the *Neville* statement of the *Davis v. Fareham* definition of the doctrine of frustration set out at the start of this section, he held that the plaintiffs' contracts with the defendants had not been frustrated by the defendants' failure to obtain the projected work from Eircom. "The basis of the doctrine of frustration ... is that there is a supervening event which must be so unexpected and beyond the contemplation of the parties, even as a possibility, that neither party can be said to have accepted the risk of the even taking place when contracting" ([2000] ELR 277, 290; *cp. Byrne* (above)), and the contract between the parties had not become entirely incapable of performance. However, although he identified "contradictory Irish authorities providing alternative explanations as between the implied contract theory and/or true construction theory" of frustration, he did not provide any resolution of this "uncertainty as to its theoretical basis" ([2000] E.L.R. 277, 284-285). As yet, there is therefore no unequivocal Irish authority accepting that the basis of the courts' power to discharge a contract for frustration lies simply in the fact that the contract on its proper construction does not cover the relationship between the parties on the facts as they have become. It is an entirely rational basis which ought to be adopted at the first possible opportunity. It is only to be regretted that the opportunity in *Zuphen* was not taken.

INCORPORATION

Where parties enter into a short term contract, and after the time specified in the contract has passed, continue with their contractual relationship, then the terms of the written contract will often continue to apply, subject to any necessary modifications and to actually agreed oral terms. In *Dower v. Radio Ireland* [2000] E.L.R. 1 (HC: Carroll J.) the defendant engaged the plaintiff on a three month contract for services which contained an arbitration clause. The plaintiff continued to work for the defendant for a further three years. For Carroll J. there was no valid reason why the parties did not continue to be bound by the same terms as set out in the original written contract, it being reasonable that the parties would consider their relationship to continue on the same basis as before subject only to the changed working schedules and remuneration. The written terms were thus incorporated into the parties' oral contract, and the arbitration clause was enforced.

In *Bio-Medical Research t/a Slendertone v. Delatex,* Supreme Court, December 21, 2000, Fennelly J. (Keane C.J. and Murray J. concurring) held that printed terms included with invoices may – depending on the proof of a practice to that effect – become binding (referring to Case C-106/95 *MSG v. Les Gravières Rhénanes SARL* [1997] E.C.R. I-911). This is because the terms of the invoices are incorporated in their contract by the parties' course of dealing *inter se*. If the contract has been agreed between the parties, and the invoice comes later with the delivery of the goods, terms stated on the invoice will not alter the terms of the contract (*cp., e.g., Olley v. Marlborough Court* [1949] 1 K.B. 342), though a long and continuous course of dealing in which an invoice is always shipped and accepted may incorporate the terms of the invoice into the contract (*Kendall v. Lillico* [1969] 2 A.C. 31 (HL); Swanton "Incorporation of Contractual Terms by a Course of Dealing" (1988) 1 *J.C.L.* 223).

MISREPRESENTATION

In any claim for misrepresentation, the plaintiffs must demonstrate "that there was a representation of fact, that that representation was untrue and that the plaintiffs were induced to enter into the settlement by reason of the representation" (*Colthurst v. Colthurst,* High Court, February 9, 2000, McCracken J., at p 3). The plaintiff sought to have set aside, on the grounds of misrepresentation, an agreement which had purported to settle five sets of proceedings between the parties. It was not alleged that the misrepresentation was made fraudulently or negligently, so the plaintiff accepted that the only available remedy was rescission (see, *e.g., Redgrave v. Hurd* (1881) 20 Ch. D. 1 (CA)). Applying his admirably concise definition of an actionable misrepresentation to the facts, McCracken J. held that although there had clearly been a representation, it was neither untrue nor had the plaintiff (who believed it to be untrue) relied upon it. In fact, McCracken J. found that the plaintiff had made a conscious decision to trade off this issue for the other benefits he would gain from the settlement (p 6).

Whilst a misrepresentation will of itself be sufficient to set a contract aside, if it is either fraudulent or negligent it will also sound in damages for the torts respectively of deceit or negligent misrepresentation. A plaintiff who seeks damages for such a negligent misrepresentation must, according to McGuinness J. in *Wildgust v. Bank of Ireland and Norwich Union Life Assurance Society,* Supreme Court, April 13, 2000 (also discussed in the Practice and Procedure chapter, 000-000) plead that the defendant owed the plaintiff a duty of care, that the defendant represented a fact or facts to the plaintiffs, that the representation was untrue, and that the plaintiffs relied upon the misrepresentation to their detriment. The second, third and fourth elements here correspond with McCracken J.'s definition in *Colthurst*; the addition of the first element here – the duty of care, which is breached by the misrepresentation – is the additional factor which justifies the claim for damages in tort (on misrepresentation generally, see Carey (2001) 8 *C.L.P.* 131). In *Wildgust*, the plaintiff and his wife had a life assurance policy with the Norwich Union, the premia for which were paid monthly by direct debit. However, due to a breakdown in the direct debit system, one debit was unpaid and the policy lapsed, and the Norwich Union refused to pay out on the death of the plaintiff's wife. The policy was a security for a loan made by Hill Samuel Merchant Bankers, and the plaintiff claimed that the defendant had negligently misrepresented to Hill Samuel that the policy had been reinstated. In the High Court, Morris P. declined to non-suit the plaintiff on this claim but ordered the plaintiff to amend its pleadings to clarify its negligent misrepresentation claim and to bear the costs of the proceedings to date (see the Annual Review 1999, 157, 168-174). On appeal, McGuinness J. (Denham and Murphy JJ. concurring) held that the plaintiff's statement of claim failed to set out a claim of negligent misrepresentation under the principles in *Hedley Byrne v. Heller* [1964] A.C. 465 (HL):

It does not state the duty of care owed by the ... [Norwich Union] to the Plaintiffs. It does not state that the communication in question was made to the Plaintiffs, or at least to agents of the Plaintiffs. It does not state that the Plaintiffs, or indeed Hill Samuel Bank Limited, relied on the communication or that Norwich Union knew that they would rely on it; nor does it clearly set out that the Plaintiffs acted to their detriment in reliance on the communication. It does not even set out that the communication was untrue. All of these things would be normal elements in the pleading of a claim negligent misstatement and are material facts rather than matters of law.

Nevertheless, she held that during the course of the proceedings in the High Court, the Norwich Union was made aware in general terms of the nature of the plaintiff's claim, and any consequent prejudice would not have survived a short adjournment to allow for the amendment of the pleadings. In the circumstances, the case should have continued before the Morris P. and should return to him, where the costs of the trial to date should be treated as part of the costs of the proceedings as a whole, to be dealt with by the judge at the conclusion of the trial.

PRACTICE AND PROCEDURE

Improperly commencing a private law claim at public law   A recent theme of this section of the Review (see Annual Review 1998, 178-182; Annual Review 1999, 116-120) has been to decry the increasing ventilation in the judicial review procedure of contractual issues which are exclusively matters of private law and ought therefore to be taken by means of plenary summons. There are many possible reasons for this development.

First, the judicial review procedure has many advantages over the plenary summons procedure, and parties may seek to gain such advantages. By itself, this is an illegitimate reason for a private law claim to proceed at public law, and it ought to be resisted by the judiciary.

Second, on some sets of facts, there may be uncertainty as to whether judicial review or plenary summons is the appropriate procedure in the circumstances; this reflects the fact that the scope of the judicial review is in many respects unclear despite attempts at clarity provided by *Murphy v. Turf Club* [1989] I.R. 172 (HC: Murphy J.; applying *R v. Panel on Takeovers and Mergers; Ex Parte Datafin Plc* [1987] Q.B. 815 (CA); on which see Clarke "Accommodating the Special Needs of the Financial Markets. *R v. Panel on Takeovers and Mergers; Ex Parte Datafin Plc* (1987)" in O'Dell (ed.) *Leading Cases of the Twentieth Century* (Round Hall Sweet & Maxwell, Dublin, 2000) 366, 368-379). There are of course difficult borderline cases, but some will be clear. If the issue is purely a matter of contract, then the private law plenary summons procedure is the appropriate one, even if the defendant is in some sense a public body. For example, it is clear that the rules of a club or a sporting organisation constitute a contract binding the members of the club or organisation, and that breach of such rules is remedied in private law action for breach of contract (see, *e.g.*, *Bolger v. Osborne* [2000] 1 I.L.R.M. 250 (HC: Macken J.) discussed in Annual Review 1999, 117-118). Hence, in *Moloney v. Bolger,* High Court, December 6, 2000, Herbert J.) the plaintiffs' claim against the Leinster Branch of the IRFU was taken as a breach of contract action, though on the facts, their claim for interlocutory relief failed (see also *Dundalk AFC v. FAI National League,* High Court, May 2, 2000). If, on the other hand, the issue relates to the exercise of a public law power, then the public law judicial review procedure is the appropriate one, even if the exercise of the public law power has an impact upon a contract between the parties: the real grievance is in respect of the exercise of the public law power, and the remedy sought should be directed accordingly. For example, section 13 of the Civil Service Regulation Act 1956 provides for the power to suspend a civil servant, and it is appropriate to seek judicial review of the exercise of that power, as the unsuccessful applicants did in *Gavin v. Minister for Finance,* Supreme Court, April 12, 2000; Keane C.J., (Murray and Geoghegan JJ. concurring)). Thus, for example, in *Carr v. Minister for Education* [2000] E.L.R. 78 (HC; Morris P.) (discussed in Annual Review 1999, 119-120) the real question was whether section 7 of the Vocational Education (Amendment) Act 1944 provided the Minister with the power he purported to exercise. Morris P. in the High Court held that it did not, and, on appeal, the Supreme Court affirmed ([2001] 2 I.L.R.M. 272 (SC)). Hence, the real issue was the exercise of public law powers, and it was successfully challenged by way of judicial review. However, the private law contractual employment relationship between the applicant and her employer was raised by the employer, who was a second respondent to the application, and the Supreme Court accepted that it could have regard to the applicant's alleged breaches of this contract in determining whether discretionary public law remedies ought to be withheld. In the event, Geoghegan J. (Keane C.J., McGuinness, Hardiman and Fennelly JJ. concurring) held that they should not, but pointed out that this would not preclude the employer from seeking a remedy at private law for the applicant's alleged breaches of her contract.

Claims against schools often seem to fall along the disputed borderline. In the case of purely private primary and secondary schools, the matter is plainly one of contract between the pupils' parents and the schools. Most primary schools and many secondary schools are state-funded but often privately owned (see Glendenning, *Education and the Law* (Butterworths, Dublin, 1999) 30-30); the relationship between such schools and their pupils and pupils' parents in principle is exactly the same as in the case of private schools, and therefore redress ought to be sought in the private law procedure of the plenary summons rather than by means of judicial review. Neither the fact that the pupils or parents by and large do not in such schools pay may make a contract difficult to spell out, nor the fact that state aid is provided to such schools, ought to alter the conclusion that a private law action is appropriate. Indeed, the essentials of the relationship should not alter if the school is state owned rather than privately owned, as for example in the case of the "small number" (Glendenning, 30) of State and special schools in the primary sector, or the much larger number of vocational schools in the secondary sector. In this latter instance, the involvement of a Vocational Education Committee might in some cases render a public law action against, for example, an *ultra vires* decision of the VEC appropriate, but the private law essentials of the relationship between school, pupils and parents remain the same, and in matters reflecting that relationship, private law actions are the appropriate route for redress. Furthermore, in the case of comprehensive or community schools established under a deed of trust, Murphy J. in *O'hUallachain v. Burke* [1988] I.L.R.M. 693 (HC) held that the "relationship of course between the Board of Management and the principal and the other staff of the college or indeed between the students and the Board of Management are matters of comment and matters to be determined in accordance with private law" ([1988] I.L.R.M. 693, 702). Hence, students challenging suspensions from schools ought to pursue the matter by plenary summons (consider *Wright v. Board of Management of Gorey Community School,* High Court, March 28, 2000 where O'Sullivan J. refused an injunction to reinstate two suspended students pending full trial of the action). Nevertheless, it seems to have been accepted that some issues of school discipline are amenable to judicial review (*Murtagh v. Board of Governors of St Emer's School* [1991] 1 I.R. 482 (HC: Barron J.; and SC); *Student A and Student B v. Dublin Secondary School,* High Court, November 25, 1999, Kearns J.).

On the other hand, there ought to be less difficulty in spelling out a contract of employment between a teacher and a school (see Glendenning, chapter 11) and thus in characterising a dispute between a teacher and a school as a private law matter. Nevertheless, in *Tobin v. Cashell,* High Court, March 21, 2000 Kearns J. quashed the decision of the respondent Community School purporting to dismiss the applicant teacher. The matter was pursued by way of judicial review, notwithstanding that the passage from the decision of Murphy J. in *O'hUallachain v. Burke* set out above was quoted by Kearns J. (though as part of a longer extract directed to another purpose).

Third, many of the cases involve allegations on the part of the applicants that the respondents have failed to follow fair procedures, an allegation with undoubted public law overtones (and occasionally is properly constituted as a public law action against an administrative decision: see, *e.g., Carr* (above); see also, in this context, *Sheriff v. Corrigan* [2000] E.L.R. 233 (SC)). However, it is clear that a term that an employer must follow fair procedures in suspending or dismissing an employee, if not expressed in contracts of employment, is implied into them (see *Glover v. BLN* [1973] I.R. 388 (SC); *Tierney v. An Post*

[2000] 2 I.L.R.M. 214 (SC)). An action against an employer to restrain a suspension or for wrongful dismissal is an action for breach of that (express, or more often, implied) term; it is a breach of contract action, and as such attracts not judicial review but private law procedures. Hence, in *McGrath v. Minister for Justice* [2000] E.L.R. 15 (HC; Morris P.) the plaintiff's successful claim arising out of his suspension from his employment as a Garda was properly taken by way of plenary summons. In *Charlton v. HH The Aga Khan's Studs Société Civile,* High Court, February 22, 2000, Budd J. the plaintiff alleged unfairness in the defendant's disciplinary procedures for breach of contract (plainly a *Glover* implied term) in a breach of contract action. Again, in *Howard v. UCC* [2000] E.L.R. 8 (HC: O'Donovan J.) the plaintiff was in dispute with the defendant university, and in this application, she obtained interlocutory injunctions precluding the university from removing her from the position of Head of the Department of German and from appointing anyone else to the post. Although alleging breach of fair procedures by a body established by statute, the issue was nevertheless properly pleaded as one of breach of her contract of employment, and it proceeded at private law by way of a plenary summons. Similarly, in *Moloney v. Bolger* (above) one of the plaintiffs' claims was that the respondents had failed to follow fair procedures in their relegation of a the plaintiffs' club, a claim quite properly made in plenary and not judicial review proceedings.

Failing to adopt the proper procedures can have significant procedural consequences, as is illustrated by *O'Leary v. Minister for Transport, Energy and Communications* [2001] 1 I.L.R.M. 132 (SC). The plaintiff commenced what in substance was a wrongful dismissal action against the defendant by means of judicial review. However, the High Court had ordered on consent that the action be adjourned to be heard as plenary proceedings and that a statement of claim and defence be served. The plaintiff then sought to amend his pleadings. There is a less stringent test to amend in plenary proceedings pursuant to Order 28 Rules of the Superior Courts (RSC) than in judicial review proceedings pursuant to Order 84 of the Rules of the Superior Courts (ironically, this is one of the few occasions upon which plenary proceedings are more advantageous than judicial review proceedings; it might even be said that being in essence confined to the grounds upon which leave for judicial review was obtained is the price to be paid for the advantages of the procedure). However, Kelly J. in the High Court ([2000] 1 I.L.R.M. 389) refused the plaintiff leave to amend, but on appeal, the Supreme Court reversed. McGuinness J. (Denham and Barron JJ. concurring) commented

> It is in some ways difficult to understand why he took this course [that is, why the applicant had commenced his proceedings by way of judicial review]. On general principles there is no reason why he should not have sought relevant and effective reliefs in connection with his alleged dismissal by way of plenary proceedings for wrongful dismissal rather

than by seeking an order of *certiorari*. I have no doubt that this aspect of the matter was present in the mind of the learned Smyth J. when he made the consent order of 14 July 1997 directing that the action be adjourned to be heard as plenary proceedings and that a statement of claim and defence be served. In my view from that point onwards the action should in effect be regarded as plenary proceedings. The learned High Court judge was, therefore, correct in his approach ... where he held that he would treat the application as to it fell to be dealt with solely under O 28 r 1 and without reference to the fact that these were judicial review proceedings. ... [As to the actual amendment sought to be made, it should have been allowed] ... the learned High Court judge's view of the application continued to be influenced by the origin of the proceedings in judicial review and by the standards which the court should, and does, apply in regard to judicial review proceedings. ([2001] 1 I.L.R.M. 132, 141-142).

In principle, private law proceedings which are in substance breach of contract actions ought not to be maintainable by way of judicial review, notwithstanding that the alleged contract-breaker is a creature of public law. Had *O'Leary* been commenced by means of plenary summons – as it ought to have – then this problem would simply never have arisen. In *Tierney v. An Post* [2000] 2 I.L.R.M. 214, 217, Keane C.J. chose to reserve for another day the issue as to whether such breach of contract actions are maintainable by way of judicial review. Echoing last year's sentiments, this other day cannot come soon enough to sort out the procedural muddle in which many of the cases are currently mired.

Release   Section 17(1) of the Civil Liability Act 1961 provides that the release of, or accord with, one concurrent wrongdoer shall discharge the others if such release or accord indicates an intention that the others are to be discharged. For the purposes of the Act, a wrong includes a breach of contract (section 2), so that a wrongdoer includes a party in breach of contract. In *ACC Bank v. Malocco* [2000] 3 I.R. 191, Laffoy J. explained the effect of section 17 in the context of a breach of contract as follows:

> ... if the settlement agreement indicates an intention that the other is to be discharged, the settlement agreement effectuates his discharge, but, if it does not, he gets the benefit of the settlement agreement and his liability is reduced accordingly. ... As to whether an accord or settlement agreement 'indicates', within the meaning of that word in s17, that a co-debtor is to be discharged, it seems to me that it does so indicate if such an outcome is agreed expressly or by necessary implication ... [and] the onus is on the defendant [asserting the discharge] to establish such intention. ([2000] 3 I.R. 191, 201).

The common law on the point had none of the clarity of section 17: a release of one of several joint-tortfeasors automatically released the others (*Duck v. Mayeu* [1892] 2 Q.B. 511), because the cause of action was wholly destroyed; whereas a mere covenant not to sue one of several joint-tortfeasors did not preclude the plaintiff from proceeding against the others (*Cutler v. McPhail* [1962] 2 Q.B. 292).

The defendant and his wife had breached a contract of loan with the plaintiff. Proceedings by the plaintiff against the defendant's wife had been settled. The plaintiff commenced these summary proceedings against the defendant. Laffoy J. held that section 17 raised a fair and reasonable probability of a real or *bona fide* defence (applying *First National Bank v. Anglin* [1996] 1 I.R. 75 (SC)) and sent the matter for a full plenary hearing.

Delay When parties agree a price for certain work, and then it is discovered that extra work needs to be done, interesting questions arise, as to whether there was a misrepresentation as to the nature of the work to be done, whether there was a mechanism in the contract by which a claim for extra work could be make, whether there was consideration for any variation (*e.g., Williams v. Roffey* [1991] 1 Q.B. 1 (CA)), or whether, if there is no contractual claim, there could nevertheless be a claim in restitution (upon a *quantum meruit*). Such issues arose in *Cotter v. Minister for Agriculture,* High Court, November 15, 1992; Supreme Court, April 1, 1993, but their resolution in that case is not without difficulty (see O'Dell (1998) 20 *D.U.L.J.* (*n.s.*) 264, 274-276; to the discussion of *Miles v. Wakefield* [1987] A.C. 539 (HL) there, see now also *Carr v. Minister for Education* [2001] 2 I.L.R.M. 272, 288-291 *per* Geoghegan J.). Such issues arose again in *Hughes v. Moy Contractors,* High Court, January 25, 2000, Morris P., but as the claim was dismissed for delay the legal issues remain unresolved; (on the other hand, in *Silverdale & Hewitt's Travel Agencies Ltd v. Italiatour Ltd,* High Court, November 7, 2000, Finnegan J. declined to strike out for delay the plaintiff's breach of contract action relating to the sale in Ireland of travel packages to the 1994 world cup).

PRINCIPLES OF INTERPRETATION

As Keane J. pointed out in *Kramer v. Arnold* [1997] 3 I.R. 43 (SC) 55 (see the Annual Review 1997, 221-229) "... in any case where the parties are in disagreement as to what a particular provision of the contract means, the task of the court is to decide what the intention of the parties was, having regard to the language used in the contract and the surrounding circumstances". This was the principle which underpinned an important statement of the principles of interpretation to be applied where the relevant contractual documentation is voluminous rather than contained in a single discrete document provided by Laffoy J. in *UPM Kymmene Corporation v. BWG Ltd,* High Court, June 11,

1999 (see Annual Review 1999, 108-110). In such circumstances, the "general rule of construction is that all the statements must be considered in their entirety, and in their bearing on one another, the primary object being to ascertain whether the conjoint effect of the whole complex representation is true or false on the facts". The plaintiff had purchased shares, "on the basis of the [defendant's] balance sheet … but subject to the disclosures listed in the Disclosure Letter …", an appendix to which contained three letters from the defendants' pensions advisor, stating the basis on which pension benefits were being funded. Reading all of these documents together, Laffoy J. in the High Court had held that the defendant had unambiguously represented the true state of under-funding of the pension fund and was not therefore in breach of any warranty in the contract. In the Supreme Court, April 4, 2000) Murphy J. (Murray, McGuinness, Hardiman and Geoghegan JJ. concurring) dismissed the appeal, leaving undisturbed her important statement of principle.

Contra proferentem In *Blackall v. Blackall* [2000] 3 I.R. 456 (HC) (see also the Breach section, above, 87-89) Finnegan J. reiterated that in "the event of an inconsistency a clause in the contract must be construed *contra proferentem*" ([2000] 3 I.R. 456, 463). An obligation to pay a deposit was expressed to apply "on or before the date of the sale" of property; the contract defined "date of sale" but not "date of the sale". However, having regard to what Keane J. had held in *Kramer v. Arnold* set out above, Finnegan J. concluded that "… the word 'the' in [the deposit clause was] … included in error and in construing the contract I am entitled to reject the same and should do so".

***Contra proferentem* and time of the essence** Although the *contra proferentem* rule ultimately ceded the field in *Blackall*, it had a greater impact in another judgment of Finnegan J. in *Sunreed Investment Ltd v. Gill,* High Court, June 3, 2000. The parties had entered into a contract for the sale of land in which the plaintiff purchasers "expressly agree[d] that any date specified for completion … shall be absolute and unchangeable", thereby making time of the essence of the contract. On 11 March 2000, the defendant vendor served notice requiring completion of the purchase "not later than 12.00 on March 31, 2000" provided that the plaintiff accepted this notice "in writing by noon on Monday 13, March 2000". On March 31, by 12.00 noon, the plaintiffs had not taken any steps to complete; at 12.11 the defendants' solicitors faxed the plaintiffs that the agreement for sale was at an end. At 12.25 a representative of the plaintiffs attended at the defendants' solicitors office with view to completing, but the defendants declined to complete. The plaintiffs sought specific performance.

If the reference in the notice making time of the essence referred to 12.00 noon, then the defendant would have been entitled to take this position (*Union Eagle v. Golden Achievement* [1997] A.C. 514 (PC); see also *United Yeast v. Cameo Investments* (1977) 111 I.L.T.R. 13). As a consequence, the defendants sought to have the plaintiffs' claim struck out.

However, the plaintiff, in seeking specific performance contrasted the reference to "12.00 on 31st of March" with the reference later in the notice to "noon on Monday 13th March", raising the prospect that the former referred to 12.00 midnight and not 12.00 noon. Given that the notice ought to be construed *contra proferentem* Finnegan J. was not satisfied that the plaintiff would necessarily fail on this point, and declined to strike the matter out.

Ejustem generis In *Moran v. Orchanda,* High Court, May 25, 2000, McCracken J., the plaintiff sought specific performance of a contract for the sale of a licensed premises subject to an abatement of purchase price to take account of an error made by the defendants' accountants in stating turnover. The abatement would have been justified under Condition 33 of the General Conditions of Sale, but they are subject to the Special Conditions, one of which provided that, in "the event of the vendor not being able to satisfy the purchaser with regard to any matter relating to planning permission, licensing, or title (or any other matter), then in such event the vendor shall be entitled to rescind this contract" (Clause 8), and in reliance upon this condition, the defendant sought to rescind the contract. *In re Jackson and Haden's Contract* [1906] 1 Ch. 412 (CA) provides in effect that the vendor's power to rescind in such situations must be exercised reasonably and in good faith, and that such a condition "must be read (as against the person who are taken to have introduced it and introduced it for their benefit) as not applying to ... something arising wholly and solely out of their own recklessness in the manner in which they have formulated the contract" ([1906] 1 Ch. 412, 421 *per* Collins M.R.). McCracken J. held that the defendants' accountants acted reckless in giving a certificate of turnover in circumstances where the defendants had not kept any records and there was nothing which would have enabled the accountants to verify the estimates of turnover which they purported to certify. On this basis, McCracken J. held that the defendants could not rely on clause 8. But he continued that he had "serious doubts as to applicability of clause 8 to a representation of this nature, and ... [that] there is a good deal of merit in the plaintiffs' contention that the clause should be construed *ejustem generis*, and its application ... restricted to matters similar to planning permission, licensing or title" though he did not have to reach a conclusion on the issue. In the event, he ordered specific performance with an abatement of purchase price.

The *ejustem generis* principle is more usually deployed in the interpretation of statutes, but the application of the *contra proferentem* rule would achieve the same effect. If Clause 8 of the special conditions, which is inserted for the benefit of the vendor, is interpreted strictly against the vendor then the right of the vendor to rescind in "the event of the vendor not being able to satisfy the purchaser with regard to ... (or any other matter)" would be confined to other matters of the same nature as matters "relating to planning permission, licensing, or title". One obfuscating Latin maxim is enough; it is not necessary to introduce another to achieve this just result.

SPECIFIC PERFORMANCE

In *Honiball v. McGrath,* High Court, March 23, 2000, Kearns J., the defendants' predecessors in title established a retirement village in the grounds of a large Georgian house. Their brochure promised a wide range of activities, facilities and services at the development, especially in the house. "In short, the brochure promised a version of heaven on earth to purchasers who became lessees of bungalows in the village" (p.4). For about five years, a later operator used the upstairs floor of the house as a nursing home. On foot of the brochure, in 1990, the plaintiff leased a bungalow from this operator. In parallel with the lease, the parties also entered into a care contract under which the plaintiff was to pay an annual charge for care services. However, the retirement village was not a success, and the defendants purchased it from a receiver, intending to reside with their young family in the large house, and to run and develop the retirement village. As a consequence, the defendants sought to put a new care service in place which would replace the original care contracts

The plaintiffs sought specific performance of the original lease and care agreements and an injunction restraining the defendants from residing in the large house. Kearns J. dismissed their applications. He held that, although nursing home facilities were maintained in the house by one operator of the village, there was nothing in the brochure or the original care agreement to impose upon any operator such as the defendant an obligation to continue to provide such facilities. As to the variation of the original care contract, he held that the contract was "a most unfortunate piece of legal drafting" (p.28) but concluded that it did contain a mechanism allowing variation which had been properly followed by the defendants. The plaintiffs argued that they access rights to the house with which the defendants residence would interfere, but Kearns J. held that no such rights arose from the brochure or bungalow lease and that any such rights which might have arisen under the original care contract persisted after its variation. He also held that there was nothing in the planning permissions for the village to preclude the defendants from residing in a portion of the house and that, even if there were, it would not confer any right of access upon the plaintiffs.

SUBJECT TO CONTRACT

The phrase "subject to contract" – that "fatal rubric", as Keane J. described it in *Jodifern v. Fitzgerald* [2000] 3 I.R. 321 (SC) 327 – had long been the cause of much confusion, not to say distress, before the decision of the Supreme Court in *Boyle v. Lee* [1992] 1 I.R. 555; [1992] I.L.R.M. 65 (SC) which in effect decided that for so long as negotiations are continuing, and the phrase is used, it precludes both a final formal agreement and reliance upon any document bearing the words as a note or memorandum in writing for the purposes of section 2 of the Statute of Frauds (Irl) 1695. As Barron J. put it in *Jodifern v. Fitzgerald*, if a party "wishes to negotiate in correspondence, but does not at the same wish to enter into an enforceable contract, this can be avoided by heading the letter or, if appropriate, any other form writing" with the words "subject to contract" ([2000] 3 I.R. 321, 331). Indeed, he emphasised that it would be better to use this phrase, simpliciter, rather than the composite "Subject to Contract/Contract Denied" which was at issue in the case itself and is common conveyancing usage in this jurisdiction (*ibid.*).

If, however, the phrase is not introduced until after an agreement has been reached, then it can have no effect. This, it seems, is what the plaintiffs sought to argue had occurred in *Jodifern v. Fitzgerald* [2000] 3 I.R. 321 (SC). The case exemplifies a clear pattern reflected in many cases this year: plaintiffs seek specific performance of a contract for the sale of land; defendants seek to have the claims struck out on the basis that the negotiations were "subject to contract"; but the courts decline to strike out on the basis that the arguments against the effect of subject to contract on the facts are not doomed to failure. However, even though the arguments are not doomed to failure, their chances of success at trial cannot be high.

In *Jodifern v. Fitzgerald*, the parties had signed draft agreements for the sale of land for £2m, to come into effect at a later date to be agreed. The plaintiffs subsequently paid a deposit of £150,000; but the solicitors for the defendant vendors headed all of their subsequent correspondence "Subject to Contract/Contract Denied", and then sought to withdraw from the sale, but the plaintiffs then sought specific performance. McCracken J. in the High Court, July 28, 1999 (see Annual Review 1999, 107) struck the claim out on the grounds, first, that no completed agreement had been reached as the draft agreements had never come into effect, and second, that, even if they had, the defendant's solicitors' use of the words "Subject to Contract/Contract Denied" precluded any writing from constituting a sufficient note or memorandum for the purposes of the Statute of Frauds, applying *Boyle v. Lee* [1992] 1 I.R. 555; [1992] I.L.R.M. 65 (SC). On appeal, the Supreme Court (Hamilton C.J., Keane, Murphy, Barron and Murray JJ.) reversed. Keane J. focussed simply on the signed draft agreement, and pointed out ([2000] 3 I.R. 321, 327-328) that, in the words of Lord Blackburn in *Rossiter v. Miller* (1877-1878) 3 App. Cas. 1124, 1151 (in a passage cited with approval by Kenny J. and the Supreme Court in *Law v. Roberts* [1964] I.R. 292)

> the mere fact that the parties have expressly stipulated that there shall afterwards be a formal agreement prepared, embodying the terms, which shall be signed by the parties does not, by itself, show that that they

continue merely in negotiation. It is a matter to be taken into account in construing the evidence and determining whether the parties have really come to a final agreement or not. But as soon as the fact is established of the final mutual assent of the parties so that those who drawn up the formal agreement have not the power to vary the terms already settled, I think the contract is completed.

If there were, in the present case, such an agreement, and it or a note thereof did not contain the phrase subject to contract so that the terms of the Statute of Frauds would be satisfied, then, for Keane J, the present case would be outside *Boyle v. Lee.* As this claim was not doomed to failure, it was allowed to proceed.

Barron J. similarly regarded the signed draft agreement as raising sufficient issues to justify a trail of the action. However, in the course of his judgment, he commented, *obiter*, that the phrase "subject to contract" has its negativing effect only when placed at the head of the letter and continued that if it is contained instead in the body of the document "it is a matter of construction of the writing as a whole whether it is intended to deny the existence of a concluded agreement" ([2000] 3 I.R. 321, 331). This is a thoroughly regrettable *dictum* which ought to be repudiated by the Supreme Court at the first opportunity. Having in *Boyle v. Lee* forcibly rejected those cases which had sought to make the effectiveness of the phrase "subject to contract" a matter of construction (in particular *Tiverton v. Wearwell* [1975] Ch. 146 (CA): *Kelly v. Park Hall School* [1979] I.R. 340 (SC); *Casey v. Irish Intercontinental Bank* [1979] I.R. 364 (SC)) in favour instead of a clear policy that the phrase necessarily denies the existence of a contract (see *Mulhall v. Haren* [1981] I.R. 364 (HC; Keane J.), this attempt by Barron J. to carve out another exception in favour of construction threatens to undo all the good work of the judgments in *Boyle v. Lee*. Indeed, inconsistently, immediately after stating his unfortunate *dictum*, Barron J. articulates that very policy, in language strong enough to call his prior sentence into question: "there cannot be a valid note or memorandum in writing of an agreement when at the same time such note or memorandum denies that any such agreement exists" (*ibid.*). Quite so. As a consequence, the phrase "subject to contract" should have its negativing effect where-ever and when-ever it is used in documents in the course of negotiations.

The emerging pattern was repeated in *Supermac's v. Katesan (Naas) Ltd* [2001] 1 I.L.R.M. 410 (SC) (noted Whelan (2001) 8 *C.L.P.* 103; see also *Silverstone Designs v. Ryan,* High Court, January 17, 2000, Smyth J.; referred to in High Court, February 28, 2000, Smyth J.). Two documents recorded a purported agreement to sell six premises and associated business assets. The background correspondence between the parties' solicitors was all marked "subject to contract"; the two documents were drafted by a mediator between the parties and not signed by them; and they did not specify the amount of a deposit or a completion date. Nevertheless, the sale of five of the properties was completed; but when a dispute arose in relation to the sixth, the plaintiffs sought an order of specific performance. Macken J. in the High Court, March 15, 1999, had dismissed the defendants' application to strike out the plaintiffs' claim; on appeal, the Supreme Court affirmed: Hardiman J. was not confident that the plaintiffs' claims would of necessity fail and allowed the matter to proceed to trial, Geoghegan J. delivered a judgment to similar effect, Denham J. concurred, and the appeal was dismissed.

The defendants asserted that the use of the phrase "subject to contract" by the parties' solicitors precluded the existence of a contract, but Hardiman J. demurred:

> ... it is plainly arguable that the use of this rubric by the solicitors does not preclude the existence of a 'done deal' between the parties themselves, which the plaintiffs contend for. In so far as it is contended that the plaintiffs are estopped by the use of the rubric from asserting a completed and enforceable agreement, this seems to me to be plainly a matter for evidence at the trial. ([2001] 1 I.L.R.M. 410, 408).

Geoghegan J. concurred that it could not possibly be said at the preliminary stage that the documents in question were definitely not intended to constitute a concluded contract ([2001] 1 I.L.R.M. 410, 423). Reference was made by Geoghegan J. to *Jodifern v. Fitzgerald* but only for what was said by Barron J. about striking out, not for this issue. As with Barron J.'s attempt in that case to carve out an exception to what was said in *Boyle v. Lee*, the judgments of Hardiman and Geoghegan JJ. here have the potential to undercut a rule which has a clear policy base, where indeed those policy reasons strongly pull against exceptions. It may be that the issue is properly one for evidence at trial, but at trial it should take strong evidence, such as a subsequent completed contract, to displace the effect of the use of the phrase "subject to contract"; anything short of this means that the parties were still negotiating and no contract finally eventuated.

The standard pattern was repeated in *Moran v. Oakley Park Developments,* High Court, March 31, 2000, O'Donovan J. The defendants had orally agreed to build and sell a house for £101,000 and the plaintiffs paid a booking deposit of £2,500. The plaintiffs argued that this agreement had been reduced to writing, but subsequent correspondence seemed to make the agreement "subject to contract". The defendant built the house according to the plaintiff's specifications, but then declined to sell it to them, and the plaintiffs sought specific performance. The defendants, relying *inter alia* on *Mulhall v. Haren* and *Boyle v. Lee*, argued that the use of the phrase "subject to contract" prevented an enforceable contract from having come into existence, and sought to have the claim dismissed, either pursuant to Order 19, rule 28 (RCS) or pursuant to the inherent jurisdiction of the court, on the grounds that the claim did not disclose a reasonable cause of action or that the claim was frivolous or vexatious. The plaintiffs submitted that it was open to the court to conclude that the parties had entered into an oral contract which was backed by acts of part performance, in particular the construction of the house according to the plaintiffs' requirements. O'Donovan J., admitting to some reservations, declined to strike out the claim and sent the case for plenary hearing. With respect, the only matter pleaded which would have justified this finding is the subsequent reduction of the oral agreement to writing.

In the end, the moral of *Jodifern*, *Supermac's* and *Moran* seems to be that relying on "subject to contract" to have a specific performance claim struck out is unlikely to succeed, though in accepting that some decidedly spurious arguments were not doomed to failure, the courts may have been too lenient: certainly, it has the effect of unnecessarily undercutting *Boyle v. Lee*.

Deposit Another aspect of *Boyle v. Lee* was also at issue in *Supermac's v. Katesan*. The defendants asserted that the lack of agreement on a deposit was fatal to the plaintiffs' assertion of a concluded oral agreement, but Hardiman J. demurred. In *Boyle v. Lee* Finlay C.J. had said that the "amount of a deposit to be made … is too important a part of a contract for the sale of land in the large sum of £90,000 to be omitted from a concluded and complete oral agreement" ([1992] 1 I.R. 555, 571; [1992] 1 I.L.R.M. 55, 65). Here, Hardiman J. commented that there "is no doubt that an agreement in relation to a deposit is usual in concluded contracts for the sale of land. But the cases prior to *Boyle v. Lee* demonstrate that it is not invariable" ([2001] 1 I.L.R.M. 410, 406; referring to *Barrett v. Costelloe,* High Court, July 13, 1973, Kenny J.; noted (1973) 107 *I.L.T.S.J.* 239) and *Black v. Kavanagh* (1973) 108 I.L.T.R. 91, and he considered it at least arguable that Finlay C.J. did not speak for a majority on this point in *Boyle v. Lee* ([2001] 1 I.L.R.M. 401, 407). Geoghegan J. went further in his analysis of this aspect of *Boyle v. Lee*. He pointed out that while McCarthy and Egan JJ. did not consider a deposit essential, this was in effect a minority view with which Finlay C.J. (Hederman J. concurring) and O'Flaherty J. did not concur, and subjected the judgments of Finlay C.J. and O'Flaherty J. to a detailed examination which led him to the conclusion that, on the evidence in that case,

> the question of a deposit was still to be negotiated and that it was intended to be a term of the agreement. In my view Finlay C.J.'s reference to the importance of a deposit in such a transaction was simply a comment on credibility. He was taking the view that once the deposit was still to be negotiated that meant there was an actual term of the contract still to be negotiated and therefore there was no concluded contract. The views of O'Flaherty J, although expressed differently, are not dissimilar. ([2001] 1 I.L.R.M. 401, 414).

Because there were many permutations of the importance of a deposit – Geoghegan J. identified five that the parties may have agreed – the absence of a deposit did not mean that the plaintiffs' claim was bound to fail, and Geoghegan J. allowed it to proceed to trial.

TERMS

Not only are terms added by the law (terms implied in fact, terms implied by law, terms imposed by statute) but terms are often removed from a contract by the common law (see, e.g., *Interfoto v. Stiletto* [1988] 1 All E.R. 348 (CA), or the 'fundamental breach' exclusion clause cases, see, *e.g.*, the Annual Review 1995, 199-201) by statutory instrument (see, *e.g.*, the European Communities (Unfair Terms in Consumer Contracts) Regulations 1995 (S.I. No. 27 of 1995)) or by statute (see, *e.g.*, the Sale of Goods and Supply of Services Act 1980). *APH Manufacturing v. DHL* [2001] 1 I.L.R.M. 224 (HC: Finnegan J.) is a good example of this last category. Property of the plaintiffs was damaged whilst being transported by air by the defendants. The contract between the parties was partly oral and partly in writing, incorporating various documents, including the defendants' standard terms and conditions, an airwaybill relating to the specific carriage and incorporating a hold harmless agreement which purported to exclude the defendants' liability, and faxes between the parties. The carriage was subject to the terms of the Warsaw Convention (implemented into Irish law by the Air Navigation and Transport Act 1936, as amended). Article 23 of the Convention rendered null and void any term which purported to relieve a carrier of liability or to fix a limit on liability lower than that provided by the convention. As this was the purport of the airwaybill and hold harmless agreement, Finnegan J. applied Article 23 and held them ineffective.

UNDUE INFLUENCE

The decision of the Supreme Court last year in *Carroll v. Carroll* [1999] 4 I.R. 241; [2000] 1 I.L.R.M. 210 (SC) (discussed in Annual Review 1998, 186-189 and Annual Review 1999, 121-125; noted Hourican "The Presumption of Undue Influence and the Relevant Duties of Solicitors" (2000) 6 (1) *C.P.L.J.* 18) is important for many reasons, in particular for emphasising the policy basis upon which equity raises the presumption of undue influence and for clarifying the position of solicitors who advise both parties in impugned transactions. On the other hand, however, though actual and presumed undue influence are distinguished, the circumstances in which the presumption will arise are not further divided into those relationships which will automatically give rise to the presumption, and those in which, though they will not automatically give rise to it, nonetheless it arises because of the individual facts of the individual relationship. This can be remedied if *Carroll*, far from being treated as the leading and exclusive modern statement of the applicable principles, is instead seen simply as the most recent case in a long line of applicable authority not only in Ireland (*Kirwan v. Cullen* (1854) 2 I.R. Ch. Rep. 322 (Lord St Leonards LC); *Provincial Bank of Ireland v. McKeever* [1941] I.R. 471; *McMakin v. Hibernian Bank* [1905] 1 I.R. 306; *Grealish v. Murphy* [1946] I.R. 35 (HC, Gavan Duffy J.); *Gregg v. Kidd* [1956] I.R. 183 (HC, Budd J.); *Harris v. Swordy,* High Court, December 27, 1967, Henchy J.); *McCormack v. Bennett* (1973) I.L.T. 127 (HC, July 2, 1973, Finlay J.); *O'Flanagan v. Ray Ger* (1963-1993) Ir. Co. Law Rep. 289 (April 28, 1983, HC, Costello J.); *Leonard v. Leonard* [1988] I.L.R.M. 245 (HC, McKenzie J); *RF v. MF* [1995] 2 I.L.R.M. 572 (SC, October 24, 1985, Henchy J.); *Bank of Ireland v. Smyth* [1995] 2 I.R. 459; [1996] 1 I.L.R.M. 241 (SC); *Bank of Nova Scotia v. Hogan* [1996] 3 I.R. 239; [1997] 2 I.L.R.M. 407 (SC)) but also elsewhere in the common law world (*e.g. Johnson v. Buttress* (1936) 56 C.L.R. 113 (HCA); *R (Protcor) v. Hutton* [1978] N.I. 139 (NI CA); *National Westminster Bank v. Morgan* [1985] A.C. 686 (HL); *Geffen v. Goodman Estate* [1991] 2 S.C.R. 353 (SCC)), to say nothing of the veritable torrent of cases which apply these general principles in a three party context (see Annual Review 1993, 194-209, Annual Review 1995, 235-239 and Annual Review 1996, 219-227). The recent decision of Smyth J. in the High Court in *Moyles v. Mahon,* October 6 2000 (noted Wall (2001) 6 (2) *C.P.L.J.* 47) reflects many of the strengths and weaknesses of *Carroll*.

Moyles v. Mahon concerned the classic fact structure of an elderly disponer seeking to rescind gifts made to a younger family member, *viz.* two gifts of property made by a father to the daughter who supported him and gave him somewhere to stay during unhappy difficulties with his wife. The first deed was drawn up in 1991, and transferred some land. The plaintiff's own solicitor both fully advised him about the effects of the deed and also referred him to another solicitor who likewise fully advised him. The second deed was drawn up in 1994, and concerned that portion of the family home which the plaintiff had obtained in matrimonial proceedings. Again, he was fully legally advised, this time by the solicitor he had instructed in the matrimonial proceedings. After a meticulous examination of the evidence, Smyth J. found no infirmity in the legal advice, drawing a stark contrast with *Carroll*; in particular, all three solicitors were concerned that he had not sought to protect his position by taking rights of revocation, of maintenance and support, and/or of residence. Furthermore, Smyth J. found that the plaintiff knew his own mind, and intended to follow it, whatever advice was given. In this respect, he found it very similar to *McCormack v. Bennett*; in particular, in respect of the 1994 deed, although the plaintiff had left the property to the defendant in his will, Smyth J. found that the plaintiff wanted and was determined to have finality by transferring it to her outright by deed. As a consequence, he found that the plaintiff had in fact fully consented to the execution of both deeds, and therefore rejected the plea of undue influence. All this must be unexceptionably right. However, as in *Carroll*, the various strands of equitable doctrine are not fully disentangled.

Some of his analysis is consistent with rejecting a plea of actual undue influence, some with the presumption of undue influence, and within the passages on this latter topic, there is great ambiguity as to whether he considered himself to be dealing with a case where the presumption arose automatically, or by virtue of the circumstances of the individual relationship.

Finally, both transfers were improvident, in that the plaintiff received nothing in return. Smyth J. found that whilst he may have expected that his daughter would continue to look after him, he never expressed this wish to the solicitors, and there was no agreement between the plaintiff and defendant to this effect. It is clear that the fact that a transaction is improvident in this sense is insufficient to justify setting it aside for undue influence. However, there is – as recognised by Denham J. in *Carroll* – in Irish law a doctrine of improvidence, independent of undue influence. It is a doctrine of some antiquity (*Butler v. Miller* (1867) I.R. 1 Eq. 195; *Slator v. Nolan* (1876) I.R. 11 Eq. 367; *O'Rorke v. Bolingbroke* (1877) 2 App. Cas. 814 (HL); *Rae v. Joyce* (1892) 29 L.R. (Ir.) 500; *Kelly v. Morrisroe* (1919) 53 I.L.T.R. 145 (Pim J.)) indisputably established as an element of the modern law by the judgment of Gavan Duffy J. in *Grealish v. Murphy* [1946] I.R. 35 (HC; discussed in Clark "An Everyday Tale of Country Folk (Not!). *Grealish v. Murphy* (1946)" in E O'Dell (ed.) *Leading Cases of the Twentieth Century* (Round Hall Sweet & Maxwell, Dublin, 2000) 149), a hugely influential decision which has been cited and applied many times since (*Lydon v. Coyne* (1946) 12 I.R. Jur Rep 63 (O'Byrne J.); *Gregg v. Kidd* [1956] I.R. 183 (HC, Budd J.); *Nyland v. Brennan,* High Court, December 19, 1970, Pringle J.; *Haverty v. Brooks* [1970] I.R. 214 (HC, McLoughlin J.); *Smyth v. Smyth,* High Court, November 27, 1978, Costello J.; *JH v. WJH,* High Court, December 20, 1979, Keane J.; *O'Flanagan v. Ray Ger* (1963-1993) Ir. Co. Law Rep. 289 (April 28, 1983, HC, Costello J.); *Noonan v. O'Connell,* High Court, April 10, 1987, Lynch J.; *McGonigle v. Black,* High Court, November 14, 1988, Barr J.; *McQuirk v. Branigan,* High Court, November 9, 1992, Morris J.; *Tobin v. Cassidy,* High Court, November 3, 1988, Keane J.; *Carroll v. Carroll* [1999] 4 I.R. 241; [2000] 1 I.L.R.M. 210).

For present purposes, *Grealish v. Murphy* is important for the fact that although the plea of undue influence failed, as it did in *Moyles v. Mahon*, that of improvidence succeeded. In *Grealish v. Murphy*, the plea of undue influence failed because of the absence of victimisation; as Professor Clark puts it, all there is on the facts "is a foolish, imprudent and short-sighted old man entering into a foolish, imprudent and short-sighted agreement, the very circumstances that Lindley LJ [in *Allcard v. Skinner* (1887) 36 Ch. D. 145 (CA) 161] referred to as being *invalid* factors in triggering relief *via* undue influence" (*Leading Cases,* 156, emphasis in original). On the other hand, Gavan Duffy J. held that equity "comes to the rescue whenever the parties to a contract have not met on equal terms" (*Grealish v. Murphy* [1946] I.R. 35, 49), and that, as a consequence, "the court must inquire whether a grantor, shown to be unequal to protecting himself, has had the protection which was his due by reason of his infirmity, and the infirmity may take various forms" (*ibid.*). Although the doctrine of improvidence has subsequently been applied to protect elderly plaintiffs (*e.g. Grealish v. Murphy* itself, *Gregg v. Kidd, Carroll v. Carroll*), it is usually their age in combination with other factors such as bereavement, loneliness and ill-health (*Gregg v. Kidd, McGonigle v. Black, Carroll*) mental infirmity or incapacity (*Noonan v. O'Connell, Tobin v. Cassidy*) which calls equity to the rescue. There is less reason for such a rescue mission where there is substantial consideration for the transaction (*Nyland v. Brennan, Haverty v. Brooks*) or where there is comprehensive legal advice (*Nyland, Smyth v. Smyth*). On this basis, whilst an improvidence argument might get to the starting blocks on the basis of the plaintiff's age, there are strong headwinds against it from the substantial amount of independent legal advice which he received and the fact that he was a strongwilled old man determined to have his way, and there is no other factor such as ill-health or mental infirmity to bring it down the track to the finishing tape. In the circumstances, though such a plea had been successful in *Grealish v. Murphy*, an improvidence plea would almost certainly not have been a runner in *Moyles*.

Coroners

Farrell, *Coroners: Practice and Procedure* (Round Hall Ltd, 2000) provides the first comprehensive overview of the coroners system in Ireland and is a welcome publication. It is also timely, coming in a year when significant proposals for reform of the Coroners Act 1962 have been made in the *Report of the Review of the Coroner Service* (December 2000), the full text of which is available on the Department of Justice's website, www.justice.ie (which also contains a comparative research paper on coronial law and the function of inquests). The Review came about arising from widespread dissatisfaction with the 1962 Act, including the well-publicised difficulties with using the inquest procedure as a means to establish the true extent of suicide in Ireland. In other important aspects of the procedure, some of the case law discussed below (and in previous Annual Reviews) underlines the need for substantial reform. For some insightful criticism of the limitations contained in the 1962 Act, see Cusack, 'The Coroner's Court' 1 *Medico-Legal Journal of Ireland* 82 (editorial).

Application by Attorney General for injunctive relief In *Attorney General v. Lee* [2001] 1 I.L.R.M. 553, the Supreme Court affirmed the general or residual jurisdiction of the High Court (and, on appeal, the Supreme Court) to enforce the law by way of injunction or other suitable remedy, on the Attorney General's application as guardian of the public interest. But the Court also pointed out that the jurisdiction should be exercised only in 'exceptional circumstances, as had been stated by Costello J. in *Attorney General v. Paperlink Ltd* [1984] I.L.R.M. 373. In the *Paperlink* case, an injunction had been granted in circumstances where the defendant was carrying on a postal business in breach of the Post Office Act 1908 but where the penalties for breaching the 1908 Act were completely inadequate. In the *Lee* case, the defendant, the widow of the deceased person, had refused to attend a coroner's inquest into his death. Section 38 of the Coroners Act 1962 provides that in such circumstances, the coroner could certify to the High Court that the person was in contempt and a summary trial would then be instituted in the high Court. This form of 'summary' contempt provision had been held in breach of Article 38.5 in *In re Haughey* [1971] I.R. 217, and was thus not activated by the coroner in the instant case. The coroner had written to the Chief State Solicitor indicating that the defendant was 'an essential witness' and that the deceased's family were 'adamant' that the defendant attend. The Attorney General subsequently applied to the High Court for a mandatory injunction to require the defendant's attendance. The High Court granted an interlocutory injunction in the form requested, but the Supreme Court reversed. While accepting that the jurisdiction to grant such relief existed, the Court considered that this was not a suitable case in which to invoke it. Although the coroner had stated that the defendant was an essential witness, it did not consider that there was sufficient evidence on which this assertion was based; and it also noted that, while the deceased's family's wishes should be taken into account, the question of whether a witness should be called was a matter solely for the coroner's judgement, and it concluded that the family's views may have weighed too heavily with the coroner in the instant case.

Anonymity of witnesses In *Morris v Dublin City Coroner*, High Court, October 8, 1999, Kinlen J. held that a coroner had no power under the Coroners Act 1962 to allow for the anonymity of witnesses in an inquest. The applicants had applied for judicial review of the respondent's decision to allow members of the Gardaí give evidence at the inquest of the deceased. The Gardaí were to be allowed give evidence anonymously and would be identified only by a code letter. The applicants also challenged a decision to admit certain ballistic reports with similar anonymity. The respondent contended that section 29(1) of the 1962 Act made a clear distinction between every deposition or note of the names and addresses of witnesses taken at an inquest and that a deposition did not have to be signed or the person who made it be identified. The applicants objected to these procedures, contending that an inquest was a public hearing and that the Gardaí concerned ought to give evidence in person. In granting the reliefs sought, Kinlen J. stated that, while it was desirable that a request for anonymity should be investigated by the respondent, it was not for the Gardaí to personally claim it. He noted that there was no precedent in this jurisdiction to allow for anonymity in an inquest, though such had been allowed under the legislation applicable in Northern Ireland. He acknowledged that such a power could be necessary for national or personal security reasons, but that it was for the legislature and not the courts to remedy the lacuna.

Link between vaccination and death: whether within coroner's remit In *Eastern Health Board v Dublin City Coroner*, High Court, December 14, 1999, Geoghegan J. held that it was not within the remit of a coroner under the Coroners Act 1962 to investigate any suspected connection between a vaccination and subsequent death. The applicant health board sought judicial review concerning an inquest being held by the respondent coroner into the death of a man who suffered from mild mental retardation. The deceased's family claimed that the death was caused by a reaction to a vaccination when he was a child. The health board were not notified of an intention at the inquest to investigate a connection between the vaccination and the death and the board claimed that it was not part of the respondent's remit to pursue such an investigation under the 1962 Act. Geoghegan J. agreed. He stated that the issues were so important that, even though the health board was out of time in seeking judicial review, the court's discretion should be exercised in favour of allowing the application to be made and determined on its merits. Turning to the substantive point raised, Geoghegan J. re-iterated the views of the Supreme Court in *Green v McLoughlin*, Supreme Court, January 26, 1995 (Annual Review 1995, 240) that the coroner was solely concerned with the proximate cause of death; as indeed is the case under British legislation, although differing in other respects (see *Reg. v. Coroner for North Humberside and Scunthorpe* [1995] 1 Q.B. 1, to which he referred). In the instant case, the death had been caused by pneumonia. Thus, any conceivable link with the vaccination was too nebulous and indirect to make it appropriate for an investigation by the coroner.

Criminal Law

McAuley and McCutcheon, *Criminal Liability* (Round Hall Ltd, 2000) is a welcome addition to the burgeoning Irish criminal law library, providing a comprehensive overview and critique of the 'general law' of criminal liability. As will become evident in this chapter, the text began immediately to be judicially cited with approval and to form the basis for judicial reappraisal of elements of the general law: see, for example, the discussion of provocation in *The People v. Davis* [2001] 2 I.L.R.M. 65, 121-123, below.

ARREST

Arrest without warrant   In *Director of Public Prosecutions v. Bradley*, High Court, December 9, 1999, the defendant had been charged in the District Court with assault on a Garda, contrary to section 2(1)(b) of the Non-Fatal Offences Against the Person Act 1997. The defence submitted that there was no power of arrest for such an offence and that the arrest was unlawful. The prosecution accepted that the Criminal Law Act 1997, which granted a general power of arrest, did not apply, as the offence in this case was not punishable by a term of imprisonment of 5 years or more. The prosecution submitted that the question whether there was a lawful arrest was immaterial to the matters before the District Court. The case came before the High Court by way of consultative case stated, on the question whether the District Court was entitled to dismiss, where the accused alleged his constitutional right to liberty had been violated, where proof of valid arrest was not an essential ingredient in proving the offence. It was accepted that proof of a valid arrest was not an essential proof under the relevant provision of the 1997 Act.

McGuinness J. held that whether an arrest is illegal can only be of relevance where proof of a valid arrest is an essential ingredient to ground a charge. As a general rule, the District Court's jurisdiction to embark on any criminal proceeding was not affected by the fact that the accused had been brought before the court by an illegal process. One exception, not the case here, was where the circumstances were such that there had been a deliberate and conscious violation of constitutional rights. She considered that it seemed unlikely that the unlawful arrest here would require the court to refuse to embark on the hearing. If a person alleged that his constitutional rights were infringed in procedures adopted in bringing him before the court, the District Court had jurisdiction to hear the submission and take such steps as it considered proper. She accepted that the judge here clearly acted correctly in hearing evidence and submissions and in stating a case for the High Court. It remained for him to decide whether or not to dismiss the case. McGuinness J. added that he should only decline to embark on the hearing if he considered there had been a deliberate and conscious violation of the defendant's rights as outlined by the Supreme Court in *Director of Public Prosecutions v. Murphy* [1999] 1 I.L.R.M. 46.

BAIL

Commencement of 1997 Act   The Bail Act 1997 (Commencement) Order 2000 (SI No.118 of 2000) brought all remaining provisions of the Bail Act 1997 (Annual Review 1997, 277-83) into effect from May 15, 2000.

Pending appeal   In *The People v. Corbally* [2001] 2 I.L.R.M. 102, the Supreme Court gave guidance on the factors to be taken into account in deciding whether to grant bail pending an appeal against conviction, as aspect of bail law not affected by the Bail Act 1997, above. In *Corbally*, the Court held that bail can only be granted pending an appeal against conviction where there is some 'definite or discrete ground of appeal' which is of such a nature that there is a 'strong chance of success' in the appeal itself. In an appeal against sentence, bail might be granted where the sentence imposed at trial is about to expire or where there is some other special circumstance, but in such cases the jurisdiction to grant bail should be exercised sparingly. In all such applications, the onus is on the applicant to establish the basis for granting bail. In the instant case, the applicant had been convicted of a number of offences in the Circuit Criminal Court, including possession of firearms and ammunition with intent to endanger life. The Court noted that the applicant's appeal against conviction did not involve a specific point, but was likely to range over a number of different facets of the trial, the availability of witnesses and inconsistencies in evidence tendered at trial. On this basis, the applicant had not made out a case for being granted bail.

CONTEMPT OF COURT

Attorney General's letter to President of Court not contempt   *Attorney General v. McDonnell*, High Court, March 29, 2000 concerned a rather unusual case of alleged contempt. The respondent judge of the District Court had initiated contempt of court proceedings against the Attorney General, arising from certain difficulties which had arisen during the course of extradition proceedings. In the course of the hearing, the respondent had indicated that the Attorney General's Scheme of legal aid did not apply to extradition cases in the District Court. This was despite assurances from counsel on behalf of the Attorney to the contrary. The extradition proceedings were then adjourned and, before the adjourned date, a letter was sent to the President of the District Court by the Attorney General's office stating that the Attorney General's Scheme was applicable. On hearing of this letter, the respondent judge considered that this amounted to an interference with his judicial functions and constituted contempt of court; and he purported to attach the Attorney for contempt under section 9 of the Petty Sessions (Ireland) Act 1851. The Attorney then applied to the High Court for judicial review the contempt motion. Kearns J. granted an order of *certiorari* quashing the respondent's order.

Applying the approach taken by Kelly J. in *Application of Byrne*, High Court, December 21, 1998 (which was a *habeas corpus* application arising from the same extradition case), Kearns J. held that, in light of the Attorney's position as a constitutional officer, it was the general and correct approach of the courts to adopt assurances given to them by the Attorney without question and it was no part of the function of a District Court judge to probe into the *vires* of the Attorney. In this respect, the respondent should have accepted the Attorney's assurances that legal representation would be provided under the Scheme. To refuse thereafter to make a recommendation under the Scheme was erroneous and unjustifiable. Kearns J. considered that it was even less appropriate to direct that the contempt hearing would take place on the same day that the motion was initiated. In so directing and in purporting to rely on section 9 of the Petty Sessions (Ireland) Act 1851, the respondent had also been in error, since section 9 of the 1851 Act was clearly confined to contempt *in facie curiae*. The letter sent by the Attorney could not, in any circumstances, be regarded as a contempt as it was quite normal for the Attorney to communicate with the President of a particular division of the courts in relation to matters within that jurisdiction. Indeed, Kearns J. thought that it was impossible to think of a more appropriate person to whom such a letter could have been written. The letter did nothing more than clarify the application of the Scheme to extradition matters in the District Court and could by no stretch of the imagination be construed as a comment on the respondent's conduct of an extradition matter or an attempt to exercise pressure on the judge in the proceedings. Thus, no question of contempt arose, let alone contempt in the face of the court.

Interlocutory orders In *Charlton v. H.H. The Aga Khan's Studs Societe Civile*, High Court, February 22, 2000, the contempt arose against the following background. The plaintiff had been employed as a secretary with the defendant for 27 years. In 1998 she was informed that an inquiry was being held into alleged improper use of the defendant's property. The plaintiff then sought interlocutory relief on the grounds that she was not being afforded basic fair procedures and that the person conducting the inquiry, the defendants' personnel manager, would infringe the principle against bias, *nemo judex in causa sua*. An interim injunction was granted to the plaintiff preventing the holding of an inquiry and the defendant was ordered to pay her salary and pension pending the trial of the action. The plaintiff then brought a motion for attachment and/or committal of the defendant and the person holding the inquiry, alleging contravention of the High Court order. Budd J. declined to order attachment, but he was prepared to award the costs of the motions to the plaintiff.

He accepted that there had been an attempt to proceed with an inquiry into the alleged deletion of computer files on the part of the defendants, and that this could only have proceeded by ignoring the meaning of the words in the judgment and orders made or by arrogant obduracy or reckless insouciance. He concluded that the defendants were in clear contempt of both the court orders. Budd J. ascribed this to misguided zealousness on the part of the defendants' personnel manager and misconceived notions of the interests of his employer. He felt it would certainly be open to the Court to make orders to attach and commit and to order sequestration of the defendant's assets and to strike out the defendant's defence. However, he accepted that the courts were always reluctant to impose a prison sentence, feeling that the rebuke implicit in this judgment would suffice in the circumstances, Budd J. ended by emphasising that it must be understood that he could not countenance disregard or defiance of court orders. On this occasion, the Court's concern at the defiance of its orders would be reflected in the orders in respect of costs.

Prejudicial photographs of and comment on accused   The issue of media comment on the demeanour of a defendant and the publication of photographs of a defendant in handcuffs in high-profile criminal trials arose in two cases in 2000. In *The People v. Davis* [2001] 2 I.L.R.M. 65, the Court of Criminal strongly disapproved of the publication in various media of photographs of the defendant in handcuffs as he was being brought to and from the Central Criminal Court on a charge of murder, on which he was convicted. The Court considered that such publications were in contempt of court as being likely to prejudice the trial of the accused. In the instant case, the Court held that the evidence against the defendant was so overwhelming that the prejudicial coverage did not make his trial unsatisfactory: see 121, below. Nonetheless, the Court emphasised that the contempt jurisdiction should be invoked in such cases. Delivering the Court's judgment, Hardiman J. noted that reg.17 of the Rules for the Government of Prison 1947 provides that a prisoner being brought to court from prison should be exposed to public view 'as little as possible' and that this provision mirrored international model rules for prisons of more recent origin. The Court abhorred the growing tendency for the media to publish such photographs, and while it noted that the Irish media did not yet participate in the media-friendly staged-managed 'perp walks' familiar in the United States (whether involving John deLorean or Mike Tyson), it clearly wished to nip this possible development in the bud. It noted the views of Brennan J. in *Estelle v. Williams* 425 US 501 (1975) that to identify the accused in this manner is likely to deprive him or her of the dignity associated with the presumption of innocence. The Court noted that, in the instant case, the trial judge had made a number of requests in this regard, but they had been ignored; clearly a more strict approach in the future may emerge as a result of the comments of the court.

A similar issue arose in another highly-publicised murder trial in the Central Criminal Court in April 2000, *The People (DPP) v. Nevin*. In this case, the trial judge, Carroll J., imposed reporting restrictions on the print media, prohibiting them from publishing 'colour pieces' which referred to the defendant's demeanour, dress, reading material or other similar matter. Carroll J. strongly criticised some of the media coverage of the defendant's appearance in court, which extended to her choice of nail varnish and reading material, though she concluded that the coverage was not prejudicial to a fair trial and was more in the nature of comment that failed to respect the defendant's dignity. It is notable that the restrictions did not apply to radio or television, though it might be said that the coverage in those media had been less sensational. In his article discussing the restrictions, Simon McAleese, 'Reporting Restrictions' *Gazette*, Law Society of Ireland, May 2000, describes in detail the judgment of Carroll J. in the case. He suggests that the restrictions imposed may be in conflict with the right to freedom of expression in Article 10 of the European Convention on Human Rights as interpreted by the European Court of Human Rights in *News Verlags GmbH v. Austria* (European Court of Human Rights, February, 2000). In the Austrian case, a blanket ban on the publication of a photograph which, it was accepted, had no prejudicial element, was found by the Court to be in breach of Article 10 of the Convention because the restriction on freedom of expression it imposed was not necessary in the interests of the administration of justice. It is at least clear from this decision that blanket restrictions on publication would not be acceptable; but more limited restrictions, as envisaged in the *Davis* case and, possibly, in the *Nevin* case, may be justifiable. It could be argued that the comments of Carroll J. that the media coverage in *Nevin* was not prejudicial would be difficult to justify in light of the *News Verlags* case, but that the restrictions actually imposed were justified in the highly charged atmosphere that surrounded the trial.

Sub judice: publication between conviction and sentence In *Kelly v. O'Neill*, Supreme Court, December 2, 1999, the Supreme Court held that the *sub judice* rule continues to apply in the period between conviction and sentencing in a criminal trial. In this case, the applicant had been convicted by a jury in May 1993 on drugs offences and the trial judge had postponed sentencing for some days. Before the sentencing hearing, an article appeared in The Irish Times, written by the first respondent, whose contents, the applicant claimed, were malicious lies which destroyed the possibility of a dispassionate assessment of his case. The trial judge fined the respondents for contempt of court and this was appealed to the High Court. On a case stated, the Supreme Court was asked whether it could be a contempt of court to publish an article in the terms of that complained of after the case had passed from the jury's seisin, and whether, given the right to freedom of expression of the press, the publication of the article in question could ever constitute a contempt of court when published after conviction and before sentencing. The Supreme Court answered the questions posed in the affirmative.

The Court accepted that the contempt jurisdiction should not be lightly invoked by the courts and that freedom of expression, guaranteed protection by the Constitution, should not be curtailed save to the extent necessitated to protect the administration of justice. The Court noted that contempt of court was committed when a person publishes material which is calculated to interfere with the course of justice; thus, it was not a necessary ingredient of the offence that it actually results in such an interference. The Court also pointed out that, under the Constitution, freedom of expression was not an absolute right. In addition, the applicant, though found guilty, was still entitled to the constitutional guarantee in Article 38.1 of a trial in due course of law. In that respect, a temporary restraint on a publication of this nature was not disproportionate, when weighed in the balance against the damage which could be done to the administration of justice if the media were to have unrestricted licence, subject only to the law of defamation, to comment freely and publish material, however untrue and damaging, concerning a trial at a stage when it was still in progress. On that basis, the Supreme Court confirmed the contempt conviction, thus restricting the burgeoning development of 'background' stories until sentencing has been completed. Of course, where the sentence to be imposed is mandatory, as in murder cases, the restrictions imposed in this case will be minimal.

DEFENCES

Provocation: subjective test   The completely subjective nature of the provocation test in Irish law has been addressed again by the Court of Criminal Appeal in a number of cases. In *The People v. Kelly* [2000] 2 I.L.R.M. 426, the defendant had been convicted of murder on a majority of 10 to 2. He had pleaded provocation in his defence. On appeal against conviction, he argued that the quotations from the case law on provocation used by the trial judge in his charge to the jury appeared to contradict the subjective test to be applied. It was pointed out that the jury foreman had asked the judge twice to redirect on the issue of provocation. The Court of Criminal Appeal, in quashing the conviction and ordering a new trial, gave some guidance on the test and on the need to avoid direct quotations from some of the case law.

The Court accepted that the trial judge had charged the jury on the lines laid down in the relevant case law, beginning with *The People v. MacEoin* [1978] I.R. 27, and had stressed that the test as to whether the defendant had been provoked was a subjective one and not an objective one. Indeed, as the Court pointed out, Ireland differed from all other common law countries in that it had adopted a purely subjective test in relation to the issue of provocation in a murder trial. The problem with the relevant cases, the Court noted, was that certain passages from them appeared to apply a subjective test to the question whether the accused was so provoked that he lost control, and then to apply an objective test to the defendant's reaction to being so provoked. These sentences had to be placed in context and it would make no sense to suggest that a man who had been so provoked that he lost self-control should measure his reaction and use no more than reasonable force in response. Thus, the Court held that a trial judge dealing with a plea of provocation in a murder trial should follow the case law but might not find it necessary or helpful to the jury to quote from it.

The Court also drew an important contrast between the defences of provocation and self-defence. The latter presupposed the existence in the accused of a calculating mind, even if it was a mind operating under stress. The former presupposed the existence of a mind subject to a sudden and temporary loss of self-control, rendering the accused so subject to passion as to make him for the moment not master of his mind. Thus, in a provocation plea, it was not sufficient for the defence merely to show that the accused lost his temper or that he was easily provoked or drunk, though all these could be factors in the situation. The loss of control had to be total and the reaction must come suddenly and before there was time for passion to cool. The reaction could not be tinged by calculation and had to be genuine. To justify the plea of provocation there must be a sudden unforeseen onset of passion, which totally deprives the accused of his self-control for the moment.

Applying this principle, the Court concluded that if a jury found that an accused was so provoked, their duty was to bring in a verdict of manslaughter rather than murder. If they found that the prosecution had convinced them beyond reasonable doubt that the provocation alleged could not or did not provoke the accused to the extent that he totally lost self-control, then their duty was to bring in a murder verdict. However, if they still entertained a reasonable doubt that the accused may have been sufficiently provoked by the matters alleged as totally to lose self-control, then their duty was to come to a verdict of manslaughter. In the instant case there was a serious danger, the Court held, that the jury may have received inconsistent messages from the judge's charge and there was a risk that the conviction was unsafe. The verdict was quashed and a re-trial ordered. A similar approach was taken by the Court in *The People v. Heaney*, Court of Criminal Appeal, January 17, 2000.

In *The People v. Davis* [2001] 2 I.L.R.M. 65, the Court returned to the issue again, applying the approach taken in *The People v. Kelly* [2000] 2 I.L.R.M. 426. On this occasion, the Court also suggested that some aspects of the subjective nature of the test might be in need of clarification, or at least in need of restating in light of modern conditions. The Court acknowledged that some of its comments were *obiter*, because in the particular circumstances, it was satisfied that the defendant in *Davis* was completely unable to raise any question of provocation. In *Davis* the defendant had admitted repeatedly and savagely kicking and beating the deceased, with whom he was living, but that he had been 'vexed' and 'in a rage' because she had been out of the house drinking during the day when he considered she should have been at home minding her children. The Court pointed out that being in a rage fell far short of provocation and that, even with the low threshold of proof inherent in the subjective test, the defendant had failed to meet the burden on him of raising the defence. Indeed, the Court felt that the evidence against the defendant was so overwhelming that a conviction was justified even in the face of some prejudicial media coverage of the trial (discussed separately, 118, above).

The Court also commented that some of the published comment on the subjective test probably over-estimated the difficulty for the prosecution since the *MacEoin* case of dealing with the defence where it was raised. As the Court noted, both in the *Kelly* and *Davis* cases, the requirements for establishing the defence were re-stated by emphasising the burden on the defendant, and that not every assertion of the existence of provocation would be sufficient to have it considered by a court.

In addition to acknowledging this refinement, the Court also strongly suggested the need to fully restate the law on provocation in the light of modern conditions. In view of the overwhelming evidence in the instant case, it acknowledged that its comments on provocation would be *obiter*, but it nonetheless proceeded to make important comments on the matter. The Court cited with approval the discussion of the defence in McAuley and McCutcheon, *Criminal Liability*, Round Hall Ltd, 2000, 851. The authors had noted that, historically, the defence had arisen as an exception to the principle that one is bound by one's actions and that some concession to human nature must be made where events rob a person of their normal self-control. In *Davis*, the Court thought that the element of the defence as a concession should be acknowledged. Second, the Court felt that its basis in policy considerations should be acknowledged, in particular that the policy considerations may change from time to time. It referred approvingly to the view expressed in McAuley and McCutcheon, above, that the subjective test could not have been intended to be used by persons who espoused morally repugnant views. Thus, a white supremacist should not be allowed to justify attacking a non-Aryan merely because the non-Aryan spoke to the supremacist before being spoken to. Similarly, the Court commented that the development of 'road rage' as a phenomenon should not be permitted to allow the perpetrators of such violent behaviour to depart from the minimum degree of self-control which citizens are entitled to expect from each other. One wonders whether the court was fully aware that such suggestions appear to re-introduce, albeit using different language, an element of objectivity which the Court in *Kelly*, above, had been at pains to avoid. It is also unclear to what extent the Court in *Davis* intended that changes in society should be taken into account in each case in which provocation is pleaded. As a converse to the limits on the defence inherent in the Court's suggestions, perhaps evidence might be introduced on the provocative effects, especially on women, of long-term abusive behaviour. If it could be established that such long-term abuse had the same effect as a 'short' provocative episode, would the defence not arise? And, if it could be shown that such long-term abuse created a reasonable apprehension of imminent risk to one's own life, might the distinction sought to be drawn between provocation and self-defence in the *Kelly* case collapse? As the Court in *Davis* acknowledged, perhaps these issues require ventilation in another court that might rule authoritatively on the matter. Indeed, it is worth noting that the Law Reform Commission proposes to examine the whole area of defences in criminal law as part of its *Second Programme* of law reform, which it agreed in December 2000.

DELAY

Assault   In *Director of Public Prosecutions v. Arthurs* [2000] 2 I.L.R.M 363, Kearns J. granted an order of prohibition where he concluded that the delay in question arose from the failure of the State to provide sufficient resources to the court system to ensure a speedy summary disposition. The defendant had been charged with an assault offence allegedly committed in October 1995. He was arrested and detained on that day, and then arrested and charged with the offence in August 1996 on foot of a warrant issued in June 1996. In October 1996 he elected for summary trial and the judge of the District Court consented to summary disposal in December 1996. The case was listed for hearing in April 1997. Due to the length of the court lists the case was adjourned a number of times until January 1998. The defendant objected to the case being heard on the grounds of excessive delay and applied for a dismissal, but was refused. On consultative case stated, the central question was whether the judge was correct in finding that the State's explanation that the failure to get a hearing date in over two years was because of the difficulties with court lists amounted to an explanation to the judge's satisfaction for any delay and did not prejudice the defendant. In answering this issue, Kearns J. held that the trial judge had erred in not dismissing the case.

Kearns J. noted that the defendant must satisfy the court that his case passed one of two tests. The first is to show he has suffered or is likely to suffer an actual specified prejudice, or that the length of the delay is so inordinate or excessive that the necessary inference is that there is a real risk of an unfair trial. The second test focussed on the causes for the delay rather than the specific or inferred effect which the delay might have on the defence, and envisaged circumstances relating to the state's conduct of the proceedings, ranging from extreme *mala fides* to overcrowded courts. In themselves these factors could constitute breaches of the constitutional right to a speedy trial, he held.

He went on that there was an obligation on the State to make adequate provision to ensure that an accused can have an expeditious trial. The selection of certain offences as suitable for summary trial carried an implication that the time scale for the completion of such trials should generally be shorter than for trials on indictment. In the instant case, he accepted that, while the delay of two years and three months was excessive in summary proceedings, it was not such that it gave rise to a necessary inference that the trial would be unfair through frailty of recollection of witnesses and he could not infer that the defendant would be prejudiced in the conduct of his defence by the delay.

As to the second test, however, where there were repeated delays in getting the case on, there was an inescapable inference that these delays were the result of a failure by the State to have provided adequate resources so that the District Court could deal with the cases before it. The State's failure to have made provision for the expeditious conduct of District Court cases, which constituted nine months of the total delay, was an unwarranted invasion of the defendant's constitutional right to an expeditious trial. Notwithstanding the absence of evidence of actual or presumptive prejudice, he held that the District Court was obliged to prevent such an invasion of that right and should have acceded to the request not to allow the trial to proceed. The judge was not correct in law in finding that the application for a dismissal on the grounds of delay should be refused. It is notable that the judge took the view that delays in obtaining a court hearing was due to lack of resourcing by the State. It might be argued that, at least in some instances, delays may be due to poor administration rather than necessarily lack of resources by the State, though in the absence of any such explanation by the prosecution in this case it must be taken that the conclusion reached by Kearns J. is the correct explanation (It is notable that, in a lecture on the future of the courts in the 21st Century, published in the April 2001 *Bar Review*, the Chief Justice suggested that poor administration could be the explanation for some delays in the court system).

In *Mulready v. Director of Public Prosecutions* [2001] 1 I.L.R.M. 382, McGuinness J. appeared to take a less stringent view of the effects of delay in a summary case. In that instance, she declined to prohibit summary charges (not specified in her judgment) alleged to have been committed in April 1997 and in respect of which a summons had been issued in October 1997, but in connection with which a court hearing was not scheduled until January 1999. While she accepted that there had been unacceptable delays, she considered that the balance between the applicant's right to a fair trial and the community's interest in having the case proceed favoured proceeding with the trial. She followed the summary of the relevant principles set out in Kelly J's judgment in *McKenna v. Presiding Judge of the Dublin Circuit Criminal Court*, High Court, January 14, 2000, below.

In *Director of Public Prosecutions v. Ferguson*, High Court, December 21, 2000, Ó Caoimh J. held that a delay of less than one year between applying for a first summons alleging assault contrary to section 2 of Non Fatal Offences Against the Persons Act 1997 and its actual return date (three summonses on the same count had been applied for) did not justify dismissal of the charge. He was of the view that, while some of the delays had not been fully explained, they were not inordinate and did not justify an inference of prejudicial delay.

Fraud   In *McKenna v. Presiding Judge of the Dublin Circuit Criminal Court*, High Court, January 14, 2000, Kelly J. declined to prohibit a trial on grounds of delay against the following background. The applicant had been returned for trial for fraud offences, alleged to have been committed between mid-1991 and 1992. A complaint had been made to the Gardaí about the applicant's alleged activities at the end of 1992. He was arrested in February 1994 and the file was submitted to the Director of Public Prosecutions for his directions in November 1994. The applicant was again arrested and brought before the District Court in June 1998. His claim for prohibition related to the delay between the complaint to the Gardaí and his first arrest, and the delay between that arrest and his second arrest in June 1998.

On the first period of delay, Kelly J. held that, since the charges in this case were not straightforward, and there had been work done on the matter in the 14 months between the complaint and first arrest, no legitimate criticism could be made of that delay. He accepted that the period of four years and four months between the applicant's first and second arrests was the most significant period of delay. The delay up to submission of the papers to the Director of Public Prosecutions could not in all the circumstances be regarded as inordinate, he held. But queries raised by the Director's office with the Gardaí were not dealt with in a timely fashion and there had been delays involving counsel which were inordinate and only partly explained. An unexplained delay was an inexcusable delay, and in all the circumstances the cumulative delay was inordinate and inexcusable. No blame could be attributed to the applicant for the delays and he did not obstruct the investigation. But while there had been inordinate and inexcusable delay in the prosecution of the charges, the applicant had not shown that such delay gave rise to a real risk of an unfair trial. No actual prejudice had been shown, and the circumstances were not such as to give rise to an inference that the risk of an unfair trial had been established as a reality. Kelly J. took into account that the applicant had been on bail and so no question of oppressive pre-trial incarceration arose. Nor were there were circumstances which placed the case into a special category, such as might arise in sexual abuse cases, of which Kelly J. noted *B v. Director of Public Prosecutions* [1997] 3 I.R. 140 (Annual Review 1997, 289) or *O'R v. Director of Public Prosecutions* [1997] 2 I.R. 273 (Annual Review 1997, 290).

Sexual offences   In *S v. Director of Public Prosecutions*, Supreme Court, December 19, 2000, the Supreme Court reviewed again the case law. In this case, the applicant, a consultant surgeon had been charged by summons in December 1996 alleging offences of indecent assault relating to eleven male youths who had been his patients. The majority of the charges related to offences alleged to have occurred between 1971 and 1979, with one charge relating to 1962 or 1963 and the final offence alleged to have taken place in 1982. The majority of the youths concerned were in their later teenage years at the time of the alleged offences; the youngest was between 9 and 11 years of age at the time of the alleged offence. The applicant at all times and in particular during interviews with members of the Garda Síochána denied all the allegations made against him and he pleaded not guilty to the offences in the District Court. The judge of the District Court held that the allegations were fit to be tried summarily and accepted jurisdiction in the matter. This decision was never subsequently challenged. The applicant later applied for an order of prohibition on the ground of unconscionable delay and prejudice. The principal ground on which he sought prohibition was the lengthy delay between the alleged commission of the offences and any possible trial of the appellant. This was rejected in the High Court (Geoghegan J.) and, on appeal, by the Supreme Court.

The first point considered by the Court was whether the case was to be treated differently from previous similar cases because the applicant is to be tried summarily in the District Court. In other words, did the time limit of six months prescribed under s.10 of the Petty Sessions (Ireland) Act 1851 apply here? The Court held it did not, by virtue of section 7 of the Criminal Justice Act 1951, which excluded the six month time limit for scheduled offences (of which the indecent assault was one). The Court applied the dicta of Blayney J. in *Director of Public Prosecutions v. Logan* [1994] 3 I.R. 254 (Annual Review 1994, 231-3)on the correct interpretation of section 7 of the 1951 Act.

On the general delay issue, the Court stated that the approach should be same where the trial is to take place in the District Court rather than before a jury, because the context is the same - a sexual offence or offences against a child or a young person, a long delay in making any complaint to the proper authorities, an explanation of the reasons for that delay, the obvious difficulty for the accused person in preparing and presenting his or her defence. In this context, the Court cited with approval the comments of Denham J. in *P.C. v. Director of Public Prosecutions* [1999] 2 I.R. 25 (Annual Review 1999, 127, 128, 130).

Fundamental principles at the heart of a constitutional society are at the kernel of this case. These principles and constitutional rights have to be weighed and balanced by the court. They include the community's right to legal issues being determined in the courts; to have criminal charges processed through the courts; the right and duty of the prosecutor to bring to the courts for adjudication allegations of serious child sexual abuse alleged to have taken place; the community's right to have its society protected, especially its most vulnerable - children. Also at the core of this case is the rule of law; the right of the applicant to a fair trial; the right of the community to the rule of law for all, including the applicant.

The Court accepted that it must balance the rights of the alleged victim or victims, and the right of the community to prosecute offences, against the right of the accused to a fair trial, bearing in mind that this includes the right to a trial with reasonable expedition. In doing this, it must have regard to the question whether the delay of the complainant in making the complaint was in reality attributable to the alleged perpetrator. That delay may have arisen from the authority, undue influence, or what was described by Denham J. as 'dominion' exercised by the accused person over the complainant or complainants. The Court also quoted *in extenso* the views of Keane J. (as he then was) in the *P.C.* case. Keane J. stated:

> The delays may also be more readily explicable in cases where, not merely is the person concerned significantly older than the complainant at the time of the alleged offences, but occupies a particular role in relation to him or her e.g. as parent, step-parent, teacher or religious. In such cases, dominion by the alleged perpetrator over the child and a degree of trust on the part of the child may be more readily inferred.

This is not to say that the court in dealing with applications of this nature must disregard the presumption of innocence to which the accused person is entitled But the issue is not whether the court is satisfied to any degree of proof that the accused person committed the crimes with which he is charged. The issue in every such case is whether the court is satisfied as a matter of probability that the circumstances were such as to render explicable the inaction of the alleged victim from the time of the offence until the initiation of the prosecution. It is necessary to stress again that it is not simply the nature of the offence which discharges that onus. All the circumstances of the particular case must be considered before that issue can be resolved.

Manifestly, in cases where the court is asked to prohibit the continuance of a prosecution on the ground of unreasonable delay, the paramount concern of the court will be whether it has been established that there is a real and serious risk of an unfair trial; that, after all, is what is meant by the guarantee of a trial 'in due course of law'. The delay may be such that, depending on the nature of the charges, a trial should not be allowed to proceed, even though it has not been demonstrated that the capacity of the accused to defend himself or herself will be impaired. In other cases the first enquiry must be as to what are the reasons for the delay and, in a case such as the present where no blame can be attached to the prosecuting authorities, whether the court is satisfied as a matter of probability that, assuming the complaint to be truthful, the delay in making it was referable to the accused's own actions.

If that stage has been reached, the final issue to be determined will be whether the degree to which the accused's ability to defend himself has been impaired is such that the trial should not be allowed to proceed. That is a necessary enquiry, in my view, in every such case, because, given the finding that the delay is explicable by reference to the conduct of the accused is necessarily grounded on an assumption as to the truth of the complaint, it follows that, in the light of the presumption of innocence to which he is entitled, the court asked to halt the trial must still consider whether the degree of prejudice is such as to give rise to a real and serious risk of an unfair trial.

Applying these principles, the Court accepted that the applicant did not occupy a position of dominance in the complainant's personal lives comparable to that of a father or a person with continuing contact. However, in view of the large disparity in age between the appellant and the complainants, who were still relatively young and immature and his position as a consultant surgeon the delay in reporting was justified. The Court acknowledged that criticisms have been made in general of diagnosis and psychological assessment of sexual abuse which is alleged to have occurred many years ago and noted that Hardiman J. had surveyed a number of these criticisms in his judgment in *J.L v. Director of Public Prosecutions*, Supreme Court, July 6, 2000, the main criticisms being directed against the psychological phenomena of repression of memory and recovered memory. However, in the instant case, the expert witness had not been cross-examined or challenged on his evidence. As to whether the applicant had established that there was a real danger of an unfair trial, the Court did not consider that his difficulties in defending the case after the undoubtedly long lapse of time established that a trial in these circumstances would not possess the character of a fair trial as required by the Constitution. On these grounds the Court dismissed the application for prohibition.

DETENTION IN GARDA CUSTODY

Custody Regulations In *The People v. Smith*, Court of Criminal Appeal, November 22, 1999, the defendant had been found guilty of rape and sexual assault and sentenced to 12 years and four years, respectively. At the time of his arrest, the defendant had been very drunk. He made an incriminating statement to Gardaí the following day. He alleged that he had been assaulted by the Gardaí, that he was not in a fit state to be interviewed, that he was questioned by more than two Gardaí and that there had thus been a breach of regulation 12(3) of the Criminal Justice Act 1984 (Treatment of Persons in Custody in Garda Síochána Stations) Regulations 1987. The Court of Criminal Appeal refused leave to appeal against conviction but granted leave to appeal against the sentence and suspended the last six years of the term.

The Court considered that there was adequate evidence to support the findings that the defendant had been in a fit state to be questioned, that the statement had not been induced by fatigue and that it had not been brought on by the stress of the interview. Thus, the statement was voluntary. On the 1987 Regulations, the Court held that regulation 12(3) should be construed as providing that during the course of an interview, while those present remain the same, only two members of the Gardaí may actually question the suspect. In this respect, it accepted that a breach of regulation 12(3) had occurred during the question and answer session. Of course, the Court noted that a breach of the 1987 Regulations is not of itself sufficient to exclude what the defendant had said in his statement and the Court was not prepared to interfere with the decision to admit it.

On the sentencing element, the Court held that the trial judge had failed to give adequate consideration to the mental disorder of the applicant induced by alcohol abuse and so varied the sentence as indicated.

EXTRADITION

Corresponding offence: conspiracy and conspiracy to defraud In two recent extradition cases, the question of corresponding offences in connection with charges of conspiracy to defraud arose. In *Myles v. Sreenan* [1999] 4 I.R. 294, Geoghegan J. ordered extradition to England in a case involving conspiracy to defraud. Geoghegan J. held that the ingredients of the offence of conspiracy to defraud and the meaning of 'defraud' had been so clearly established over centuries (as in *Scott v. Metropolitan Police Commissioner* [1975] A.C. 819) that the question of uncertainty did not arise. He thus saw no reason why the common law of offence of conspiracy to defraud would not have been carried over under the Constitution of 1937. Geoghegan J. added, *obiter*, that certain types of vague conspiracies which might have been regarded as an offence at common law might now be regarded as too uncertain to render them triable under the Constitution; but this did not arise in the instant case.

The question was considered again by the High Court and, on appeal, the Supreme Court in *Attorney General v. Oldridge* [2000] 2 I.L.R.M. 233 (HC); [2001] 2 I.L.R.M. 125 (SC). The respondent had been brought before the District Court in an extradition application alleging that he had aided and abetted others to carry out schemes to defraud certain banks and companies in the United States. Counsel for the Attorney General confirmed that the only corresponding offence in Irish law would be conspiracy to defraud, contrary to common law. In the High Court, Kearns J. held that the extradition should not proceed, for two reasons. First, the relevant facts and events in the context of any supposed conspiracy took place prior to the involvement of the respondent and for that reason he held that the facts did not disclose the offence of conspiracy to defraud as had been the case in *Myles v. Sreenan* [1999] 4 I.R. 294, above. Second, Kearns J. held that since there was no prescribed minimum or other penalty for the offence of conspiracy to defraud contrary to common law, the offence failed to meet the minimum penalty threshold requirement in the Extradition Treaty between the State and the United States, the Washington Treaty. On both points, the Supreme Court reversed and ordered the respondent's extradition.

Delivering the leading judgment in the Supreme Court, Keane C.J. referred to the two slightly different threshold requirements under the 1965 Act and the Washington Treaty. Section 10(1) of the Extradition Act 1965 provides that, in general, 'extradition shall be granted only in respect of an offence which is punishable under the laws of the requesting country and of the State by imprisonment for a maximum period of *at least one year* or by a more severe penalty.' This is subject to any contrary provision in an extradition treaty. The Extradition Act 1965 (Part 2) (No.22) Order 1987 gave effect to the 'Washington

Treaty', the extradition treaty between Ireland and the United States. Article II of the Treaty provides that an offence is only extraditable between the two states 'if it is punishable under the law of both contracting parties by imprisonment for a period of *more than one year*, or by a more severe penalty.' Thus, as Keane C.J. pointed out, the punishment threshold provided for in the 1965 Act is lower than that provided for in Article 2 of the Washington Treaty. Where section 10 of the 1965 Act is the only applicable provision, a person can be extradited if the relevant offence is punishable by imprisonment for at least one year. Under Article 2 of the Treaty, he or she can be extradited only where the relevant offence is punishable by a period of more than one year. While the latter was the relevant provision in the present case, it was clear to the Court that, whichever was applied, the threshold requirement was met. The offences with which the respondent was charged in the United States each carry a maximum penalty of five years imprisonment. The corresponding offence in Ireland, that is, conspiracy to defraud, was a common law misdemeanour punishable by imprisonment for life or any lesser term.

On the question of correspondence, the Court also differed from Kearns J. Keane C.J. quoted with approval the view of Henchy J. for the Supreme Court in *Hanlon v. Fleming* [1981] I.R. 489 that the court must look at the factual components of the offence specified in the warrant, regardless of the name given to it, and see if those factual components, in their entirety or in their near entirety, would constitute an offence which, if committed in this State, could be said to be a corresponding offence of the required gravity. The Supreme Court held that it was clear that the acts charged against the respondent would correspond in Irish law to the offence of conspiracy to defraud which, the Attorney General argued was an offence under Irish law. The Court quoted with approval the view expressed in McAuley and McCutcheon, *Criminal Liability* (Round Hall, 2000) that, while the definition of conspiracy to defraud is 'undoubtedly hydra-headed… its incriminating features have been clearly and consistently delineated by the courts for at least two centuries.' Keane C.J. also agreed with the view of Geoghegan J. in *Myles v. Sreenan* [1999] 4 I.R. 294, above, that the offence had been carried over on the enactment of the 1937 Constitution. On this basis there was a corresponding offence and extradition should proceed.

Corresponding offence: section 4 rape   In *Stanton v. O'Toole*, High Court, December 7, 1999 O'Donovan J. ordered the extradition of the applicant to Scotland. He had been charged with committing acts of buggery and other sexual assaults on a woman, and these were described in the Scottish indictment as constituting 'rape contrary to common law.' In the District Court, the order granting his extradition stated that the offences charged corresponded to rape under section 2 of the Criminal Law (Rape) Act 1981, that is the historical common law definition. O'Donovan J. considered that this was not the case, but was nonetheless satisfied that the offences charged corresponded with rape contrary to section 4 of the Criminal Law (Rape) (Amendment) Act 1990, which had introduced the wider rape offence (see Annual Review 1990, 258-62). He pointed out that it was open to the High Court on review of an order made by a District Court judge to confirm that order even though the High Court was satisfied that the offence specified in the order was not a corresponding offence. As in the *Oldridge* case, above, O'Donovan J. quoted with approval the view of Henchy J. for the Supreme Court in *Hanlon v. Fleming* [1981] I.R. 489 on the approach to be taken in determining correspondence.

Political offence: escape from custody   In *Quinlivan v. Conroy* [2000] 2 I.L.R.M. 515, Kelly J. ordered the applicant's extradition to England, notwithstanding that the applicant was probably entitled to avail of the early release regime under the Criminal Justice (Release of Prisoners) Act 1998, enacted after the Good Friday Agreement (Annual Review 1998, 118-27). The applicant had escaped from prison custody in England in 1991 while on remand and the United Kingdom authorities sought his extradition in respect of that escape. The applicant contended that he had been arrested in respect of political offences, and thus ought not to be amenable to extradition. He also submitted that an agent of the United Kingdom government authorities had facilitated his escape from custody. He contended that an Irish court would not convict someone whose escape from custody was facilitated by an agent provocateur and thus there was no correspondence of offences. He also further argued that he was entitled to avail of the early release of prisoners provisions contained in the Good Friday Agreement; and that it would therefore be a fruitless exercise to extradite him, as he would be entitled to release by July 2000, less than three months after the High Court hearing. Nonetheless, Kelly J. refused to order his release from custody.

In view of the arsenal of weaponry available to and the potential methods to be employed by the applicant, there was a potential loss of civilian lives which denied him the right to avail himself of the political exemption under section 50 of the 1965 Act. Applying the test in *McGlinchy v. Wren* [1982] I.R. 154, he held that the applicant's activities did not fall within a category which could, on any reasonable view, be regarded as political, either in itself or its connections. Neither did he consider the applicant's escape from custody to be a political offence because of the vicious means used in its commission; it was thus an offence which was captured by section 4 of the Extradition (European Convention for the Suppression of Terrorism) Act 1987. In addition, the applicant had failed to discharge the onus of proof on him that there was no correspondence. Finally, Kelly J. noted that the applicant had to be a convicted prisoner in order to benefit from any early release scheme. The scheme did not interfere with the notion that persons who were accused of offences had first to be tried for them, and on that basis the 1998 Act was not to be extended to persons awaiting trial, or awaiting extradition.

FIREARMS AND OFFENSIVE WEAPONS

Decommissioning of arms and explosives: Northern Ireland   The Decommissioning Act 1997 (Decommissioning) (Amendment) Regulations 2000 (S.I. No. 134 of 2000) amended the 1998 Regulations (Annual Review 1998, 202), which made detailed provision for the decommissioning of arms in accordance with the 1997 Act (Annual Review 1997, 301-2) and for the functions of the Independent International Decommissioning Commission. They came into effect on May 18, 2000.

Firearms certificates for non-residents   The Firearms (Firearm Certificates for Non-Residents) Act 2000 makes permanent provision for the granting of firearms certificates for non-residents, primarily for those engaged in hunting. The 2000 Act replaced the Firearms (Temporary Provisions) Act 1998, which was enacted to deal with the decision in *National Association of Regional Games Council v. Minister for Justice and Minister for Agriculture*, High Court, June 12, 1998 (Annual Review 1998, 4). In that case, Quirke J. had held that the respondent Ministers had acted *ultra vires* the Firearms Act 1925 and the Wildlife Act 1976, respectively, in the procedures adopted for granting firearms certificates and hunting licences to persons not ordinarily resident within the State. The 1998 Act remedied this on a temporary basis and the 2000 Act provides for a permanent arrangement.

The 2000 Act amended section 3 of the Firearms Act 1925, governing the granting of firearm certificates to persons ordinarily resident outside the State, whether for hunting or sporting purposes or for shooting species where such shooting is not prohibited by law, for example, vermin, or for other purposes. It also amended the Wildlife Act 1976, primarily in regard to the granting of hunting licences for persons ordinarily resident outside the State. After a two year transitional period (during which the Minister for Justice retains the jurisdiction to grant such licences), such licences will in the future be granted on application to the local superintendent of the Garda Síochána. The 2000 Act introduced for the first time a combined firearm certificate/hunting licence which will be available to non-residents for the purpose of hunting hares or protected wild birds. A separate hunting licence from the Minister for Arts, Heritage, Gaeltacht and the Islands (who has responsibility under the Wildlife Act 1976) will still be required for non-residents who wish to hunt deer as is the case for residents of the State at present.

NON FATAL OFFENCES

Assault: effect of abolition of common law offences   In *Grealis v. Director of Public Prosecutions* [2000] 1 ILRM 358 (HC); Supreme Court, May 31, 2001, the High Court and, on appeal, the Supreme Court dealt with an aspect of the abolition of the common law offences of assault by the Non-Fatal Offences Against the Person Act 1997 (Annual Review 1997, 304-13). It also dealt with the connected provisions of the Interpretation (Amendment) Act 1997 (Annual Review 1997, 283-5).

The Non-Fatal Offences Against the Person Act 1997 came into effect in August 1997, and summonses had been issued against the applicant in September 1997 alleging common assault and assault occasioning actual bodily harm committed in May 1997. As mentioned, the 1997 Act had abolished the common law offence of assault but contained no transitory arrangements permitting the prosecution of persons alleged to have committed abolished offences prior to its coming into force. On this basis, in the High Court McGuinness J. held that since there was no common law offence of assault when the summonses were issued, the prosecutions could not be lawfully taken. This view of the Non-Fatal Act 1997 was upheld by the Supreme Court in 2001, to which we shall return in the 2001 Review. McGuinness J. had also held that the offence of assault occasioning actual bodily harm was a statutory offence and that the summons on this charge could proceed. On appeal, the Supreme Court held that assault occasioning actual bodily harm was a common law offence, and that since it too had been abolished by the 1997 Act, the applicant could not be prosecuted on that charge either. We will also return to this aspect of the Supreme Court decision in the 2001 Review, but we note briefly here that the decision had the effect of prohibiting a number of other assault summonses issued in late 1997.

The other aspect of the case dealt with the connection with the Interpretation (Amendment) Act 1997. This Act had been passed to provide some element of transitional arrangements for charges made in respect of common law offences abolished by the Non-Fatal Act 1997 where such prosecutions were brought after the Interpretation (Amendment) Act 1997 was enacted, in December 1997. It was clear that the Interpretation Act was intended to apply prospectively only. Nonetheless, in *Grealis* the High Court found it unconstitutional. On appeal, the Supreme Court reversed and found the Interpretation (Amendment) Act 1997 to be valid. We will also deal with this aspect of the Supreme Court judgment in the 2001 Review, but the effect is that summonses issued after December 1997 for common law assaults alleged to have been committed before August 1997 (when the Non-Fatal Act 1997 came into effect) would appear to be valid.

Sexual assault: whether different offence from assault   In *O'C v. Governor Of Curragh Prison* [2000] 2 I.L.R.M. 76 (HC) the applicant attempted to raise the same issues as had been dealt with in *Grealis*, above, in this instance in connection with the offence of indecent assault. But Geoghegan J. held that this offence was not affected by the abolition of the common law offence of assault in the Non-Fatal Offences Against the Person Act 1997. The applicant had pleaded guilty to a count of indecent assault 'contrary to the common law as provided for in section 10 of the Criminal Law (Rape) Act 1981.' Geoghegan J. held that indecent assault remained a separate common law offence from common assault and was thus not affected by the abolition in the 1997 Act of common law assault. As permitted by the Supreme Court in *The People v. McDonagh* [1996] 1 I.R. 565 (Annual Review 1996, 274-8), he took account of the 'pre-parliamentary material' which preceded the 1997 Act, especially the Law Reform Commission's proposals in this area. From this, it was clear that the 1997 Act did not abolish indecent assault, which remained a common law offence. On the relevant authorities, Geoghegan J. also held that section 10 of the Criminal Law (Rape) Act 1981 was essentially a sentencing provision. Thus, the applicant's claim to be released from custody was dismissed.

PROCEDURE

Attendance of prosecution witness   In *Geaney v. Director of Public Prosecutions,* High Court, December 8, 1999, O'Sullivan J. applied the Supreme Court decision in *O'Regan v. Director of Public Prosecutions* [2000] 2 I.L.R.M. 68 (Annual Review 1999, 239-241) that the prosecution was not bound to call as a witness or to procure the attendance in court of persons who made witness statements to the Gardaí. The prosecution's duty was discharged once it had made available all relevant information in their possession in relation to a certain witness and once a reasonable opportunity had been afforded to the defendant to arrange for the attendance of that witness.

Consolidation or joinder of counts: effect   In *Conlon v. Kelly*, High Court, December 14, 1999, the applicant had been tried in the Circuit Criminal Court on fraudulent conversion charges, and a new trial was directed after the jury failed to agree a verdict. Prior to the trial the applicant had been charged with further similar but distinct counts and been sent forward for trial, but these had not been dealt with in the trial. Leave was granted by the respondent judge of the Circuit Court to 'consolidate' in one indictment the charges on which the applicant had already been tried and the additional charges on which he had been sent forward for trial. The applicant sought judicial review of this order and argued that if there was to be a retrial before a jury he should be tried on the same indictment and no additional counts could be added, and that the effect of uniting both sets of counts was prejudicial and would be in breach of his constitutional rights. The Director of Public Prosecutions argued that rather than a consolidation of the bills there had in fact been a joinder of charges which was reasonable in the circumstances. McGuinness J. agreed with this analysis. She held that although the term 'consolidation' had been used in both the orders made by the respondent Circuit Court judge, in fact the purpose and effect of the orders was the joinder of a number of additional counts in the bill of indictment. In the instant case the applicant had neither been acquitted or convicted on the original counts and made no objection to a new trial on these counts. This was not a case such as the well-known *Connelly v. Director of*

Public Prosecutions [1964] A.C. 1254, where additional counts were based on the same offences or similar offences arising out of the same facts. Here, they were different offences alleged to have been perpetrated on different victims and with different evidence, so that the applicant could in any event apply for a separate trial on the different counts.

Copy documents: admissibility   In *Carey v. Hussey* [2000] 2 I.L.R.M. 401 (HC) Kearns J. dealt with the admissibility in evidence of copy documents in the following context. At a hearing before the respondent judge of the District Court, it was alleged that the applicant had breached a safety order. A photocopy of the original order was produced; the applicant objected to its reception into evidence and the respondent adjourned the case to produce the original order. The applicant then sought an order of prohibition. In dismissing the application, Kearns J. noted that the Criminal Evidence Act 1992 confers on a judge a wide discretion to accept copies, photocopies or facsimile copies as admissible evidence in criminal proceedings and that section 30 of the 1992 Act confers jurisdiction on a District Court judge to determine the manner in which he or she shall deem a copy document to be duly authenticated. He also held that it was well within the discretion of the respondent judge to decide to adjourn a case at hearing, albeit subject to the rules of fair procedures, which had not been breached in the instant case.

Dismissal order in summary trial: effect   In *Director of Public Prosecutions v. Martin*, High Court, May 19, 2000, the respondent judge of the District Court had dealt with a drink-driving prosecution under section 49 of the Road Traffic Act 1961. The solicitor for the defendant submitted on a number of ground that the charge should be dismissed, including that the summons before the Court had not been signed by the appropriate District Court Clerk or by any District Court Clerk. The respondent replied: 'Mr. O'Sullivan, that was your trump card.' The respondent then proceeded to dismiss the charge, though she commented to the prosecuting Garda in court: 'There he is gone running, I hope he knows you can come again.' The order of the court recited the charges and concluded as follows: 'Was adjudged as follows: Dismissed.' Despite this order, the prosecution brought a fresh prosecution as the case was still within the six months time limit under the Petty Sessions (Ireland) Act 1851 (as the comment of the respondent in court had anticipated). The defendant in the case sought an order of prohibition, while the Director of Public Prosecutions sought an order of *mandamus* directing the prosecution to proceed. Kinlen J. granted the order of prohibition and refused the *mandamus*. He pointed out that, because the District Court had been a court of record since the passing of section 13 of the Courts Act 1971, the formal order drawn up in the case represented the outcome of the case, rather than the verbal comment of the respondent which appeared to envisage that a fresh prosecution was possible. Kinlen J. emphasised the need to ensure the accuracy of the court order in view of the court's status as a court of record. On this basis, he concluded that there had been a full hearing of the case and that it had been dismissed, rather than 'struck out without prejudice', which would have been the appropriate form if the court had intended a fresh prosecution to be possible. In the circumstances, the defendant in the case was entitled to plead *autrefois acquit* and to obtain an order of prohibition.

District Court area amalgamation: whether retrospective In *O'Brien v. O'Halloran*, High Court, November 16, 1999, Kearns J. held that a District Court Variation Order could not operate retrospectively to validate proceedings which were bad for want of jurisdiction. The applicant had been charged with a drink-driving offence under the Road Traffic Acts 1961 to 1995. The summons had been issued for the Listowel area, but it purported to return him for trial to Abbeyfeale District Court. At the hearing of the case in September 1998, he contended that since Abbeyfeale was in a different District Court area from the Listowel District Court area and was not within one mile of it, the court lacked jurisdiction to try him. The respondent judge adjourned the matter to November 24, 1998. On October 7, 1998, the Minister for Justice signed the District Court Districts and Areas (Amendments) and Variation of Days (Number 5) Order 1998 (SI No.376 of 1998), which amalgamated the Listowel and Abbeyfeale District Court areas. The 1998 Order purported to validate retrospectively any proceedings initiated though not completed prior to its commencement. On the return trial date in November 1998, the applicant was convicted and disqualified from driving for two years. Kearns J. quashed the conviction on judicial review.

He held that before a District judge can deal with a matter in any way, he had to be satisfied that he had jurisdiction, and that requirement existed even for the purpose of adjourning matters. IN the instant case, the respondent had no jurisdiction to do anything other than strike out the summons when objection was taken to jurisdiction in September 1998. Nor could the adjournment power in the District Court Rules 1997 be invoked in aid of a situation where there was a complete lack of jurisdiction. He also held that the provisions of the 1998 Order could only relate to business which was properly initiated and outstanding prior to the commencement of the order and could not be interpreted as making good a want of jurisdiction. He noted in this context the well-established presumption of the courts against retrospective legislation, particularly in criminal matters. On this basis, the conviction was quashed.

Fair procedures: no remittal In *Nevin v. Crowley*, Supreme Court, February 17, 2000 the Court quashed a conviction in circumstances where fair procedures had not been applied in the trial court, in particular in relation to the cross-examination of prosecution witnesses. In this instance, the Court took the view that the prosecution could not be acquitted of all the blame for some, at least, of what went wrong at the trial. On this basis, where the applicant had already endured enough, the proper exercise of the court's discretion required that the case should not be remitted to the District Court, applying the principles in *Sweeney v. Brophy* [1993] 2 I.R. 202 (Annual Review 1992, 268-70).

Jury trial: vetting by questionnaire   In *Director of Public Prosecutions v. Haugh*, High Court, May 12, 2000 the Director successfully challenged an order made by the first respondent, a judge of the Circuit Court, concerning a questionnaire which had been prepared for distribution to potential jurors in the pending trial of the second respondent. The second respondent was a former Taoiseach, Charles Haughey, who had been charged with obstructing the activities of a tribunal of inquiry, the McCracken tribunal, which had investigated him. The tribunal of inquiry had attracted enormous publicity and it was argued that the second respondent could not obtain a fair trial arising from the adverse comment on his activities in the various media. His defence lawyers argued that, to overcome the potential prejudice, a questionnaire should be distributed to potential juries which would include questions concerning their general knowledge of the second respondent and of the tribunal of inquiry in question. The respondent trial judge agreed to have such a questionnaire distributed, but a Divisional High Court (Carney, Laffoy and O'Donovan JJ.) held that this would constitute an unacceptable interference with the normal rules concerning jury selection under the Constitution and the Juries Act 1976. The High Court concluded that any alleged prejudice from the adverse media publicity concerning the second respondent could be dealt with at the trial in the more conventional form of appropriate directions from the judge to the actual jury selected that they must base their decision on the evidence presented in court. The Court may have been influenced in this approach by the potential for the lengthy pre-trial jury selection processess to be found in the United States. For the time being, at least, such processes remain unlikely to be adopted in Ireland. It may be noted that the issue or prejudicial publicity arose in the case later in 2000: see *Director of Public Prosecutions v. Haugh (No.2)*, High Court, November 3, 2000, below 138.

Majority jury verdict : statement by jury foreman   In *The People v. Higginbotham*, Court of Criminal Appeal, November 17, 2000, the defendant had been convicted of dangerous driving causing death by majority verdict of a jury. Section 25(2) of the Criminal Justice Act 1984, which introduced majority verdicts, requires that the jury foreman state in open court whether the verdict is unanimous or by majority, and the relevant number if the latter is the case. In this case the jury foreman had not done so. The Court of Criminal Appeal re-iterated the view in *The People v. Ryan*, Court of Criminal Appeal, 12 July 1999 that section 25(2) of the 1984 Act was mandatory and that failure to comply vitiated a majority verdict. As to whether a re-trial should be ordered, the Court held that, on the evidence, a properly instructed jury could not have been entitled to return a verdict of guilty, unanimously or by majority, so that if the correct procedures had been followed a conviction should not have been properly recorded. Thus, a retrial was not appropriate in the instant case.

Separate trials: similar fact evidence   The issue of separate trials arose directly in *The People v. Kelly*, Court of Criminal Appeal, December 13, 1999. The defendant had been tried on four counts involving three different individuals of indecent assault and attempted buggery. He was convicted on the two counts of attempted buggery and sentenced to seven years on each count. He sought leave to appeal against conviction and sentence and the grounds that the counts in relation to different boys should have been tried separately. The Court of Criminal Appeal allowed the appeal and quashed the convictions. In essence the case turned on whether similar fact evidence was admissible across the range of offences being tried. Referring, *inter alia*, to the House of Lords decision in *R. v. Boardman* [1975] A.C. 421, the Court held that such evidence may be admitted in two main types of cases: (a) to establish that the same person committed each offence because of the particular feature common to each; or (b) where the charges are against one person only, to establish that offences were committed. The Court also stated that the admissibility of such evidence must be against the background of the general principles that the rules of evidence should not be allowed to offend common sense and that only where the probative value of the evidence outweighs its prejudicial effect may it be admitted. Applying these principles, the Court held that the joinder of the various counts was incorrect, since the evidence did not establish that there was the necessary nexus to justify them being heard at the same time.

Stay on trial: prejudicial publicity   In *Director of Public Prosecutions v. Haugh (No.2)*, High Court, November 3, 2000, Carroll J. declined to quash a decision of the respondent judge of the Circuit Court to stay a criminal case, *The People v. Haughey*. This was a prosecution of a former Taoiseach for allegedly obstructing the McCracken Tribunal of Inquiry. One count alleged that he did so by asserting in a letter to the Tribunal of March 1997 that he had not received any payment in cash or in kind of the nature referred to in the terms of reference of the Tribunal, which assertion he knew to be false. Arising from the substantial publicity attaching to the prosecution, counsel for the former Taoiseach applied to strike out the indictment or for a permanent stay or to postpone the trial until such time, if any, as the unfairness created by adverse pre trial publicity abated. In June 2000, the respondent refused a permanent stay, but granted a stay without leave of the Court. In coming to this conclusion, the respondent stated:

> I believe that by virtue of the sustained prolonged and repetitive nature
> of the attacks made against the character and reputation of the accused
> in relation to matters which I believe might well influence a jury in its
> deliberations, should these charges be permitted to proceed to trial in

> this climate of opinion... there is a real and substantial risk that he
> would not receive a fair trial. I believe the degree of vilification is such
> and the depth of feeling against the accused is such that I would not be
> at all confident that it could be obviated or cured by instructions, direc-
> tions or warnings by a trial judge no matter how strong they might be.

On judicial review, Carroll J. did not consider that the respondent had fallen
into such an error as to amount to unreasonableness under the *Wednesbury*
principle in *Associated Provincial Picture Houses Limited v. Wednesbury
Corporation* [1948] 1 K.B. 223, as approved of by the Supreme Court in *The
State (Keegan) v. Stardust Victims Compensation Tribunal* [1986] I.R. 642
and *O'Keeffee v. An Bord Pleanála* [1993] 1 I.R. 39. Accordingly, she declined
to interfere with the order made, pointing out that the 'fade factor' had already
begun to set in and that a further application to lift the stay might be made to the
trial judge.

Time limit: summons In *Murray v. McArdle*, High Court, November 5, 1999,
Kelly J. applied the case law concerning the overlap between the complaint
procedure under s.10 of the Petty Sessions (Ireland) Act 1851 and the
administrative procedure set out in section 1 of the Courts (No.3) Act 1986.
The applicant had been convicted of a number of offences under the Road Traffic
Acts 1961 to 1995. The offences were alleged to have occurred on May 10,
1997 and a summons was issued on October 24, 1997 pursuant to the Courts
(No.3) Act 1986. The applicant sought to quash the convictions on the ground
that the respondent judge of the District Court had acted without jurisdiction in
that no lawful complaint had been made in respect of the complaints within six
months of the alleged offences as required by the Petty Sessions (Ireland) Act
1851. Kelly J. dismissed the application.

Applying the principles set out by the Supreme Court in *Director of Public
Prosecutions v. Nolan* [1990] 2 I.R. 526 and by McGuinness J. in *National
Authority for Occupational Safety and Health v. Gabriel O'Brien Hire Ltd*
[1997] 1 I.R. 543, he held that there are two ways in which a defendant may be
summoned before the District Court: the procedure under the 1851 Act and the
procedure involving a request for the issue of a summons under the 1986 Act. In
the latter case, a complaint is not made at the time the summons is sought, the
complaint being made to the District Court when the summons is listed for
hearing. He went on to state, applying the *Nolan* case, that where proceedings
are instituted using the procedure in the 1986 Act, the application for the summons
must be made within six months of the date of the alleged offence and there is
no bar to the prosecution if the date upon which the summons is returned before
a District Court and the case first brought before him is more than six months
from the date of the alleged offence. This may also explain why the 1986 court
procedure is the overwhelmingly favoured method of instituting criminal
proceedings in the District Court.

ROAD TRAFFIC

Dangerous driving causing death: circumstantial evidence In *Director of Public Prosecutions v. Lafferty*, Court of Criminal Appeal, February 22, 2000, the Court upheld a conviction for dangerous driving causing death, contrary to section 53 of the Road Traffic Act 1961, where evidence as to the manner in which a car was being driven at a relatively short time before the accident was admitted. The defendants had been found guilty of dangerous driving causing death and been sentenced to three years each. In refusing their applications for leave to appeal, the Court held that evidence as to the manner in which a car was being driven at a relatively short time before the accident was admissible as circumstantial evidence in a prosecution for dangerous driving causing death. The Court applied the Australian decision in *R. v. Horvath* [1972] V.R. 533 in this respect. The Court also held that it was sufficient that the dangerous driving was one of the causes of death

Random road checks In *Director of Public Prosecutions v. O'Connor*, Supreme Court, November 17, 1999 the defendant, who was driving a vehicle registered in a foreign State, had been stopped in a random road check and had failed to produce a certificate of insurance. He was charged with failure to produce a certificate, contrary to section 69A of the Road Traffic Act 1961, as inserted by the European Communities (Road Traffic) (Compulsory Insurance) Regulations 1975, which implemented Directive 72/166/EEC, the first Directive on Motor Insurance. Section 69A of the 1961 Act provides that a Garda may demand of a person having charge of a vehicle such as in this case to produce evidence that the vehicle is covered by insurance. On a case stated to the High Court, it was held that the Gardaí were entitled to make a demand of proof of insurance providing that the District Court judge was satisfied that it was a random check. On appeal, the Supreme Court affirmed. The Court held that the 1975 Regulations were aimed primarily at removing border controls but it was also clear that all blanket or systematic checks on foreign registered cars are to be avoided, random checks may be permitted but if checks are to be random they should not be aimed against foreign registered cars only. While the purpose of the 1972 Directive and 1975 Regulations was to place foreign registered cars and their drivers, so far as practicable, in the same position as domestically registered cars and their drivers it was not the intention to confer upon foreign registered and their drivers any form of privileged position. Thus, random checks of such vehicles were permitted, just as was the case with domestically registered vehicles.

SEARCH AND SEIZURE

Warrant bad on its face In *Simple Imports Ltd v. Revenue Commissioners*,

Supreme Court, January 19, 2000, the Supreme Court held invalid the seizure of items on foot of a search warrant which on its face indicated that it had been issued on a basis not authorised by statute. In this case, the warrants had been purportedly issued under the Customs Consolidation Act 1876 and the Customs and Excise (Miscellaneous Provisions) Act 1988. The search had been for indecent, obscene or pornographic material. The application for a declaration that the warrants were unlawful was dismissed in the High Court, but on appeal the Supreme Court reversed. The Court considered the case law on this area, including *Byrne v. Grey* [1988] I.R. 31, *Reg. v. Inland Revenue Commissioners, ex p Rossminister* [1980] A.C. 952 and *Attorney General of Jamaica v. Williams* [1998] A.C. 351. The Court considered that, on the evidence before the judge of the District Court who issued the warrant, he could not have been satisfied on the basis of the information provided by the customs officer that, viewed objectively, the cause or ground relied upon by the officer for his suspicion was reasonable. Given the necessarily draconian nature of the powers conferred by the customs legislation, a warrant issued in such circumstances could not be regarded as valid. On this basis, the warrant was quashed.

SENTENCING

Leniency: appropriate sentence at time of appeal   In *The People v. Egan*, Court of Criminal Appeal, December 18, 2000, the Court emphasised that, in exercising its jurisdiction under the Criminal Justice Act 1993 to review the leniency of sentences, it applies two essential principles. First, the trial court must have fallen into an error of principle before it will intervene to substitute a different sentence. Second, if the trial court fell into error, the Court will substitute a sentence which is appropriate at the time of the appeal, not at the time when the original sentence was imposed. Thus, on this second point, the passage of time from the original sentencing date to the appeal date may justify not interfering with the actual sentence imposed. This was the situation in the instant case. In February 2000, the defendant had been sentenced to 12 months imprisonment, having pleaded guilty to gross indecency, buggery and harassment; all but 3 months of the sentence was suspended. The Court accepted that the trial judge had erred in principle, but that the circumstances of the defendant had changed since then and the Court concluded that this justified leaving the sentence to stand.

By contrast, in *The People v. Melia*, Court of Criminal Appeal, November 29, 1999, the Court held that a nine year sentence, with the final year suspended, imposed on the defendant, who had pleaded guilty to a number of offences, including aggravated sexual assault, false imprisonment and robbery, met the test of being unduly lenient within the meaning of section 2 of the Criminal Justice Act 1993. At the time of sentencing, the defendant was 32 years old and had a number of previous convictions, including a six-year sentence for rape in 1991. The Director submitted that, apart from the plea of guilty, there were no mitigating factors in the circumstances of the case. The Court of Criminal Appeal agreed and substituted a sentence of 12 years. The Court considered that each of the offences of aggravated sexual assault in this case was extremely serious, and if the defendant was being sentenced for only one of these offences he would inevitably have received a reasonably significant custodial sentence. A sentence of 9 years, even with the final year suspended, was undoubtedly such a sentence, but it did not reflect the gravity of the entirely separate offences to which the defendant had pleaded guilty. Further, in light of the defendant's previous conviction for rape and a six-year sentence and the probation officer's ominous assessment of the defendant, the Court concluded that it was clear that the sentence here was unduly lenient. The Director had thus discharged the onus of showing a substantial departure from the norm and a sentence of twelve years was appropriate.

Incest   In *The People v. D.H.*, Court of Criminal Appeal, February 1, 2000, the Court reduced a sentence of 12 years to one of eight years where the defendant had pleaded guilty to three counts of incest. One sentence of 12 years and two sentences of four years had been imposed on the three counts. The Court accepted that it had to take cognisance of the increased maximum sentence introduced by the Criminal Law (Incest Proceedings) Act 1995. But in the instant case, mitigating factors of importance included a plea of guilty, the fact that there was one victim only, that the defendant had been held not to be a danger to others, that he was not a paedophile, that he had attended a Granada course and obtained some insight into his behaviour and now felt remorse, that there was no physical violence and that he had had an inadequate family background. In all the circumstances of the case, therefore, the Court was of the view that the sentence of 12 years imprisonment was an error in principle and reduced it as indicated.

Suspension on condition to keep the peace   In *Dignam v. Groarke*, High Court, November 17, 2000, McCracken J. quashed the respondent's decision to re-impose a sentence of detention on the applicant for failure to keep the peace and be of good behaviour. The applicant, a young offender, had originally been sentenced to four years detention. On a review of the sentence, he was released into the custody of the Probation and Welfare Service, subject to keeping the peace and being of good behaviour. The matter was later re-entered on the basis that the applicant had breached the probation conditions, and the respondent re-imposed the four year detention sentence. On judicial review, McCracken J. quashed the order. He accepted that the respondent was not required to enter into a criminal trial on the re-entering of the case. Nonetheless, he considered that the respondent was required to deal with the mater by applying the principles of fair procedures, as the Supreme Court had held in the context of revocation of temporary release in *The State (Murphy) v. Kielt* [1984] I.R. 458. In the absence of such procedures, McCracken J. quashed the respondent's decision.

Tax returns: fine imposed   In *The People v. Redmond*, Court of Criminal Appeal, December 21, 2000, the Court declined to interfere with a sentence under the Criminal Justice Act 1993 on grounds of leniency. The defendant had pleaded guilty to failure to make returns of income tax over a ten year period. For the first five years, he was fined £500 for each year and £1,000 per year in respect of the second five years. The trial judge took into account that the defendant had already paid civil penalties under the tax code in respect of the income tax assessments which had been raised on his income (after they had been revealed in a highly publicised tribunal of inquiry). The Court of Criminal Appeal considered that the trial judge had not fallen into error, and indeed it noted that the prosecution had conceded that the trial judge was entitled to take into account the civil penalties paid by the defendant. The Court added that it would, for example, be unreal and unjust to exclude from the sentencing process in a larceny case that restitution had been made or damages paid.

Updated reports on applicant   In *The People v. M.S.*, Court of Criminal Appeal, February 1, 2000, the Court of Criminal Appeal held that its jurisdiction under the Courts of Justice Act 1924 included the power to consider up-to-date reports and to vary the sentence by suspending, if considered just, the latter part of a sentence on conditions determined by the Court. The defendant had pleaded guilty to rape and was sentenced to six years imprisonment. The complainant had refused to give evidence and if the defendant had not pleaded guilty the prosecution would have collapsed. The defendant had no previous convictions and his actions were out of character. On his application for leave to appeal, the Court of Criminal Appeal sought up to date reports on him. The Director of Public Prosecutions argued that the Court of Criminal Appeal may only consider such reports if it found that the trial judge had erred in principle in the sentence imposed. The Court disagreed and allowed the application for leave to appeal and adjourned the appeal itself until it received up-to-date reports. The Court took the view that the fundamental principle underlying the Courts of Justice Act 1924 was that it conferred on the Court the power and jurisdiction to do justice in the case before it. The court was satisfied that a just sentence may have elements of rehabilitation included in it. In the instant case, the applicant had successfully completed a treatment programme, which illustrated this element most appropriately. Further, a sentence may incorporate an element of protection of society; protection of society may sometimes be best achieved by a supervised release after treatment rather than a later release with no treatment or supervision.

Defence Forces

CIARAN CRAVEN and GERARD HUMPHREYS

OVERSEAS MISSIONS

The dispatch of further armed contingents of the Permanent Defence Force to serve with United Nations missions overseas was approved by the Dáil in respect of INTERFET (International Force East Timor) and KFOR (Kosovo Force) (See, Annual Review, 1999 169-170).

INTERNATIONAL HUMANITARIAN LAW

Following on the incorporation of the Geneva Conventions by the Geneva Conventions Act 1962, the Genocide Convention by the Genocide Act 1973 (see, Humphreys and Craven, International Humanitarian Law in *Military Law in Ireland*, Round Hall, 1997, 262-281) and the protocols to the 1949 Geneva Conventions by the Geneva Conventions (Amendment) Act 1998, Annual Review, 1998, 234-236), both the 1984 Convention against Torture and Other Cruel, Inhuman or Degrading Treatment or Punishment and the 1994 Convention on the Safety of United Nations and Associated Personnel were incorporated into domestic law in 2000. Penal sanction and questions of jurisdiction are addressed in both Acts.

United Nations Convention against Torture   The Convention against Torture and Other Cruel, Inhuman or Degrading Treatment or Punishment, adopted by the General Assembly of the United Nations on December 10, 1984 resolution 39/46) was incorporated into domestic law by the Criminal Justice (United Nations Convention against Torture) Act 2000. Article 2 of the Convention requires each signatory state to take effective measures, whether legislative, administrative, judicial or otherwise, to prevent acts of torture in any territory under its jurisdiction. It further provides that no exceptional circumstances whatsoever, whether a state of war or a threat of war, internal political instability or any other public emergency may be invoked as a justification of torture. And, it also provides that the defence of superior orders – whether from a superior officer or a public authority – may not be invoked to justify any torture. In compliance with the provisions of article 4 of the Convention, the Act of 2000 provides that all acts of torture, any attempt to commit torture and acts which constitute complicity or participation in torture are criminal offences, punishable by such penalties that take into account their grave nature.

Thus, section 2 of the Act provides that it is an offence, punishable on conviction on indictment, by life imprisonment, for a public official, irrespective of nationality, to carry out an act of torture on a person, whether within or outside the State. Any person, other than a public official, who carries out at act of torture on another person, at the instigation of, or with the consent or acquiescence of, a public official is similarly guilty of the offence of torture. Again, there is no jurisdictional limitation arising from the nationality of the person accused or the place where the torture was carried out. For example, a foreign national in Ireland may be tried for the offence of torture committed in his own country of origin or any other place.

For the purposes of this offence, a public official includes a person acting in an official capacity. The definition clearly extends to military officers, whether exercising command or staff functions. The statutory definition of torture mirrors almost exactly the definition contained in article 1 of the Convention. The Act defines torture as an act or omission by which severe pain or suffering, whether physical or mental, is intentionally inflicted on a person for such purposes as (a) obtaining information or a confession from the person tortured or another person, (b) punishment for an act which the person tortured or another person has committed or is suspected of having committed, or (c) intimidation or coercion of the person tortured or another. This obviously extends to extracting confessions and other information, reprisal punishments and acts generally aimed at subjugating communities and suppressing dissent. However, the list is not framed in exhaustive terms and the offence is capable of being committed in analogous situations. The offence is also committed if the acts are carried out for any reason based on any form of discrimination – extending to so-called 'ethnic cleansing' or any discrimination-based collective punishment.

Although superficially unremarkable, the statutory limits of what constitutes torture – whether in the Convention or the Act – are not totally devoid of definitional problems. Thus, for example what is meant by 'severe' pain or suffering is not further specified. Whereas an objective approach to the issue might usefully be considered appropriate to a determination as to whether the 'test' is met, given the range of individual vulnerabilities to suffering – whether physical or mental – such a 'test' hardly seems capable of addressing the mischief at which the Convention and the Act are directed. But, the requisite *mens rea* is expressed in terms of intention. Accordingly, if the intention of the accused was only to inflict 'minor' pain or suffering, e.g. to induce mild distress, but, because of the particular vulnerability of the individual, severe suffering was caused, it may not be possible to assert that he was guilty of the offence of torture. In addition, the Act (but not the Convention) provides that omissions intentionally inflicting such pain or suffering are caught within the terms of the offence. Many acts are capable of being characterised as either positive acts or omissions, e.g. withholding food or failing to feed a person. Pure omissions, however, could also arise from an institutional or collective governmental failure to evacuate a particular area that was, for example, contaminated, with the result that those who were left suffered 'severe' pain and suffering. If the failure to evacuate were to arise from an ethnic or other bias, the offence of torture would seem to be committed, on a plain reading of the statutory definition, were it not also for the requirement for an intention to inflict suffering. Arguably, an intention to inflict 'severe' suffering cannot arise by mere passive public or governmental omission. If this is correct, it would appear to be in conformity with the objectives of the Convention.

The intentional infliction of severe pain or suffering, whether mental or physical, arising solely from, inherent in or incidental to, lawful sanctions does not fall within the ambit of the definition of torture in both the Convention and the Act of 2000. Although, perhaps, relevant in determining whether or not certain penal sanctions of a foreign state fall within the definition of torture, it is difficult to envisage that the intentional infliction of severe suffering as part of our regime of lawful punishment would pass constitutional muster. Whereas this caveat arises directly from the wording of the final sentence of article 1 of the Convention, it should be noted that the Convention refers to 'pain or suffering' – not 'severe pain or suffering' and is silent as to whether or not it was intentionally inflicted. Indeed, on one reading, the conceptual thrust of the actual wording of the provisions of article 1 seems to point to the exclusion from the definition of torture such pain and suffering that is not intentionally caused. This, however, cannot be correct given that in some jurisdictions corporal punishment is an accepted part of the 'normal' penal regime. What is prohibited is the intentional infliction of pain and suffering outside of the range of 'normal' penal sanctions, provided that any pain or suffering so permitted does not fall within the prohibited range of conduct otherwise outlawed by the Convention. On a strict construction, the Convention prohibits *any* infliction of *severe* pain or suffering. But, unlike the Convention, the Act of 2000 excludes all intentional acts inflicting *severe* pain or suffering arising solely out of the imposition of penal sanctions. This seems to create a lower threshold for the exclusion of certain acts from the definition of torture and, in the context of the title to the Convention (which refers to cruel, inhuman or degrading treatment or punishment), could be regarded as defeating part of the objective of the Convention, the obligations imposed on the State by article 16 notwithstanding. That article requires the State to undertake to prevent, in the jurisdiction, other acts of cruel, inhuman or degrading treatment or punishment which do not amount to torture as defined when such acts are committed by, or at the instigation or with the consent or acquiescence of, a public official. Furthermore, it seems anomalous to have incorporated any such exclusion, without qualification in terms of jurisdictional application, having regard to our constitutional norms.

Section 3 of the Act provides that it is an offence to attempt or to conspire to commit the offence of torture or to do any act with the intent to obstruct or impede the arrest or prosecution of another person, including a public official, in relation to the offence of torture. Neither territorial nor nationality limitations apply and, like an offence under section 2, offences under section 3 are punishable on conviction on indictment by imprisonment for life.

Proceedings for an offence under the Act of 2000 may be taken in any place in the State and the offence, for all incidental purposes is treated as having been committed in that place. Offences are triable only in the Central Criminal Court and, once a person is charged under the Act, no further proceedings may be taken save by, or with the consent of, the Director of Public Prosecutions. However, no proceedings may be taken pursuant to the provisions of section 38 of the Extradition Act 1965 (in respect of the trial, in this jurisdiction, of an Irish citizen for an offence committed abroad) where an act constitutes an offence under that section and the Act of 2000 (section 5). (An identical provision is found in section 5 of the Criminal Justice (Safety of United Nations Workers) Act 2000.

Insofar as military law is concerned, a limited court-martial has no jurisdiction to try a person subject to military law for an offence under the Act of 2000 (section 6(b) amending the Defence Act 1954, section 192(3)(c) as amended by the Genocide Act, 1973 section 5). However, a general court-martial does have such jurisdiction, but only where the offence was committed on active service (section 6(b) amending the Defence Act 1954 section 192(3) as amended by the Genocide Act 1973, section 5). Any such person is liable, on conviction by court-martial, to imprisonment for life (section 6(a) amending the Defence Act 1954, section 169 as amended by the Criminal Justice Act 1990, section 7). The exercise of the court-martial's jurisdiction is contingent on the consent of the civil authority where the offence relates to a person not subject to military law, irrespective, is seems, of whether or not the offence was committed on active service. In the case of other so-called 'civil offences' ordinarily, the consent of the Superintendent of the Garda Síochána within whose district the offence is committed is required (Defence (Civil Authority with respect to Courts-martial) Regulations, 1954), (see, generally Humphreys and Craven, *Military Law in Ireland*, 134). Having regard to the provisions of section 5 of the Act of 2000, however, it seems that the consent of the Director of Public Prosecutions would be required where the offence alleged is under that Act.

The Act of 2000 (sections 7 and 9) also amends the Extradition Acts 1965 to 1994, to comply with the requirements of articles 3 and 8 of the Convention:

(i) prohibiting extradition where there are substantial grounds for believing that if the person is extradited he may be subjected to torture (section 11 of the Act of 1965),

(ii) prohibiting surrender of a person under order of the Minister (for Justice) if he is of the opinion that the extradition of the person whose surrender is requested would involve transit through any territory where there is reason to believe that he may be subjected to torture (section 33(3) of the Act of 1965),

(iii) prohibiting endorsement for execution of an extradition warrant by the Minister or the High Court where there are substantial grounds for believing that the person may be subjected to torture (section 44(2) of the Act of 1965 as amended by the Extradition (European Convention on the Suppression of Terrorism) Act 1987 section 8),

(iv) directing the release of a person where the High Court is of the opinion that there are substantial grounds for believing that the person, if removed from the State, may be subjected to torture (section 50(2) of the Act of 1965 as amended by the Extradition (European Convention on the Suppression of Terrorism) Act 1987 section 9), and

(v) scheduling offences under the Act of 2000 as offences that are not to be regarded as political offences (First Schedule to the Extradition (Amendment) Act 1994.

In addition, section 4 of the Act (and article 3 of the Convention) prohibits the expulsion or return of a person to another state where the Minister is of the opinion that there are substantial grounds for believing that the person would be in danger of being subjected to torture. For this purpose, the Minister must take into account all relevant considerations including, where relevant, the existence in the other state of a consistent pattern of gross, flagrant or mass violations of human rights. Issues of interpretation, on which no guidance is given either in the Convention or the Act are legion. The interpretative issues arising from an approach dependent on so many qualifying adjectives are legion.

The Act of 2000 effects minor amendments (section 8) to the Criminal Procedure Act 1967 and (section 10) includes offences under the Act of 2000 in the list of offences for which bail may be refused.

Overall, the Act of 2000 is primarily concerned with the prosecution of offences in relation to torture. However, the Convention also imposes obligations on the State in relation to the provision of mutual assistance by parties to the Convention in criminal matters arising thereunder (article 9). Disputes between state parties as to the interpretation or application of the Convention are required to be resolved by negotiation and, if necessary, arbitration, subject to any reservation made at the time of accession (article 30). There is further an obligation on the State to keep under systematic review interrogation rules, instructions, methods and practices as well as arrangements for the custody and treatment of persons subjected to any form of arrest, detention or imprisonment within the jurisdiction, with a view to preventing torture or other forms of cruel, inhuman or degrading treatment or punishment (articles 11 and 16). A prompt and impartial investigation is required to be proceeded with by the State authorities, wherever there is reasonable ground to believe that an act of torture or other form of cruel, inhuman or degrading treatment or punishment has been committed in the jurisdiction (articles 12 and 16). The State is similarly required to ensure that a person who alleges that he has been subjected to torture or other forms of cruel, inhuman or degrading treatment or punishment in the jurisdiction has the right to complain to, and to have the case promptly and impartially examined by, the authorities. A further obligation is imposed on the State to ensure that the complainant and witnesses are protected against all ill-treatment or intimidation as a result of the complaint or any evidence given (articles 13 and 16). In addition, the Convention requires the State to ensure in its legal system that the victim of an act of torture obtains redress and has an enforceable right to fair and adequate compensation, including the means for as full rehabilitation as possible. Where torture has resulted in death, the Convention further provides that an entitlement to compensation is to arise on the part of the victim's dependants, although these provisions do not affect any rights existing under national law (article 14). No such requirements arise in respect of other forms of cruel, inhuman or degrading treatment or punishment. In this jurisdiction, the common law rules on intentional and negligent infliction of suffering and the prevailing constitutional norms should generally be sufficient to give effect to these requirements of the Convention. If disability cannot be established, and the limitation period has expired, however, they may be inadequate having regard to obligations imposed by article 14 of the Convention. The exclusionary rule of evidence set out in article 15 of the Convention (in relation to the admissibility of statements made as a result of torture) is already well established as part of our system of criminal procedure. Such statements are to be deemed admissible, however, against a person accused of torture as evidence that the statement was made. A statement obtained as a result of other forms of cruel, inhuman or degrading treatment or punishment might well also be excluded in this jurisdiction, although the Convention does not make any such stipulation, providing that its provisions are without prejudice to any national law prohibiting such treatment or punishment (article 16).

Of relevance to the Defence Forces, the Convention further requires that education and information regarding the prohibition against torture are fully included in the training of civilian and military police, medical personnel, public officials and others who may be involved in the custody, interrogation or treatment of any person arrested, detained or imprisoned and that the State includes this prohibition in the rules or instructions issued to them (article 10).

Section 11 of the Act provides that the members of the Committee against Torture established under article 17 of the Convention and a conciliation commission set up under article 21 are to be accorded such privileges and immunities as are necessary for the independent exercise of their functions in the same manner and to the same extent as are experts performing missions for the United Nations as provided for in the Diplomatic Relations and Immunities Act 1967. The Committee consists of 'ten experts of high moral standing and recognised competence in the field of human rights', to be elected by the state parties. Article 19 of the Convention requires the state parties to submit to the Committee, through the Secretary-General, reports on the measures taken to give effect to their undertakings under the Convention, one year after the entry into force of the Convention with supplementary reports every four years. Each report, which is transmitted to all the state parties, is considered by the Committee which may make such general comments thereon as it considers appropriate. These are then forwarded to the state concerned which may respond with any observations, if it chooses. Articles 20 to 22, in turn, provide for the investigation of 'well-founded' indications of torture being systematically practised in the territory of a party to the Convention and allegations by one state against another, or by an individual against a state, that it is not fulfilling its obligations under the Convention.

Convention on the Safety of United Nations Personnel   The United Nations Convention on the Safety of United Nations and Associated Personnel of December 9, 1994 was incorporated into domestic law by the Criminal Justice (Safety of United Nations Workers) Act 2000. Article 7 of the Convention provides that United Nations and associated personnel, their equipment and premises are not to be made the object of attack or of any action that prevents them from discharging their mandate. It further requires all state parties to the Convention to take all appropriate measures to ensure the safety and security of all United Nations and associated personnel and, in particular, to take all appropriate steps to protect such personnel deployed in their territory from specified crimes. The state parties to the Convention are required to co-operate with each other and the United Nations in the implementation of the Convention, particularly in circumstances where a host state is unable to take the required measures. In compliance with the provisions of article 14 of the Convention, the Act of 2000 provides for the prosecution of offences against United Nations workers, their premises and vehicles. And, in compliance with the provisions of article 9, the Act schedules the relevant offences and provides for their punishment by such penalties that take into account their grave nature.

Thus, section 2 of the Act provides that it is an offence for a person, outside the State, to do an act to, or in relation to, a United Nations worker that, if done in this jurisdiction, would constitute any of the following:

(i)   the common law offences of murder, manslaughter or rape;

(ii) offences under the provisions of the Non-Fatal Offences against the Person Act 1997, i.e. assault, assault causing harm, assault causing serious harm, threats to kill or cause serious harm, poisoning, endangerment and false imprisonment;

(iii) sexual offences under the provisions of the Criminal Law (Rape) (Amendment) Act 1990, i.e. sexual assault, aggravated sexual assault and rape under section 4 of the Act, or

(iv) any offence under section 2 (causing explosion likely to endanger life or damage property) of the Explosive Substances Act 1883.

Section 3 provides that it is an offence for a person, outside the State, to do an act in connection with an attack on a United Nations premises or vehicle that if done in this jurisdiction, would constitute any of the following:

(i) any offence under section 2 (causing explosion likely to endanger life or damage property) of the Explosive Substances Act 1883, or

(ii) offences under the provisions of the Criminal Damage Act 1991, i.e. damaging property, threats to damage property, possessing any thing with intend to damage property.

What constitutes an 'attack' for the purposes of section 3, however, is unclear. Article 9 of the Convention requires that 'a violent attack' on a premises or vehicle likely to endanger the person or liberty of a United Nations worker should be a criminal offence under national law. It is difficult to contemplate when an attack might not be characterised as violent. In any event, attacks on empty United Nations premises or the destruction of empty United Nations vehicles where there is no risk to the life, limb or liberty of United Nations workers are not caught by the Convention. Nor, it seems, are such attacks where the risk is to civilians who are not capable of being classified as United Nations workers. Nevertheless, offences against property, even if empty, if committed as part of an attack, are included in our incorporation of the terms of the Convention. But, mere criminal damage to United Nations property, not part of an attack (involving, it is presumed, some element of orchestration, however primitive), e.g. the breaking of a window by a drunk, could hardly be considered to fall within the scope of a section 3 offence. It should be noted that a premises, in this context, includes both the official premises and private accommodation of a United Nations worker and a vehicle means any means of transportation of such a worker, extending, obviously to include everything from bicycles to helicopters and jet aircraft.

On conviction, under section 2 or 3, a person is liable to that penalty to which he would have been liable if the act had been carried out in the State. However, it is an offence under section 4 of the Act of 2000, punishable on conviction by imprisonment for up to ten years, for a person to make a threat to commit an act that is an offence either under section 2 or 3 and to intend that the person threatened fears that it will be carried out, if done in order to compel a person to do or to refrain from doing any act. Unlike section 2 or 3 offences, a section 4 offence may be committed by a person either in or outside the State. Although the Convention (article 9) also requires the criminalisation of an act that constitutes participation as an accomplice in attacks on UN personnel and property, or in an attempt to commit such attacks or in the organising or ordering of others to commit such attacks, this is not expressly set out in the Act of 2000.

For the purposes of these offences, the definition of a United Nations worker (in accordance with the provisions of article 1 of the Convention) is not confined to those engaged on UN operations as generally contemplated but extends to include any person who, at the time of the alleged offence, was:

(a) engaged or deployed by the Secretary-General as a member of the military, police or civilian component of a United Nations operation,

(b) present in an area where a United Nations operation was being conducted as an official or expert on mission of the United Nations, one of its specialised agencies or the International Atomic Energy Agency (IAEA) or

(c) assigned, with requisite UN agreement, by a government or inter-governmental organisation or engaged by the Secretary-General, a specialised agency of the UN or the IAEA or deployed by a humanitarian non-governmental organisation or agency, under agreement with the Secretary-General, a specialised agency or the IAEA to carry out activities in support of the fulfilling of a mandate of a UN operation.

The specialised agencies referred to are those established by intergovernmental agreement and having wide international responsibilities in economic, social, cultural, educational, health, and related fields and brought into relationship with the United Nations pursuant to the provisions of article 63 of the UN Charter, e.g. ILO, UNICEF.

Insofar as the definition of a United Nations operation is concerned, it extends to an operation established by a competent organ of the United Nations in accordance with the UN Charter and conducted under UN authority and control where:

(i)   the operation is for the purpose of maintaining or restoring international peace and security (i.e. Chapter VI and peace-keeping operations), or

(ii) the Security Council or the General Assembly has declared, for the purposes of the Convention, that there exists an exceptional risk to the safety of the personnel participating in the operation (e.g. weapons inspectorates operating in hostile environments).

Specifically, Chapter VII (peace enforcement) operations in which any of the UN personnel are engaged as combatants against organised armed forces are excluded from the scope of the Convention (Article 2) and the Act of 2000. The exclusion, however, is expressed to be limited to those operations to which the laws of war apply. Given the nature of the United Nations Organisation, one would have considered that even if the peace enforcement operation were to be against organised, but irregular, forces the laws of war would still, of necessity, apply. Furthermore, the Convention (and Act) applies only to operations conducted under UN authority *and* control. Operations by regional organisations (e.g. NATO) carried out with UN approval but not under UN control, accordingly, are excluded.

For the purpose of the exercise of jurisdiction in relation to an offence under the Act of 2000, section 5 provides that the offence is deemed to have been committed within the area of the Dublin Metropolitan District. (An identical provision is found in section 38 of the Extradition Act 1965, in relation to offences committed abroad by Irish citizens). Offences are triable in any court of competent jurisdiction and, once a person is charged under the Act, no further proceedings may be taken save by, or with the consent of, the Director of Public Prosecutions. However, no proceedings may be taken pursuant to the provisions of section 38 of the Extradition Act 1965 (in respect of the trial, in this jurisdiction, of an Irish citizen for an offence committed abroad) where an act constitutes an offence under that section and the Act of 2000 (section 5). (An identical provision is found in section 5 of the Criminal Justice (United Nations Convention against Torture) Act 2000). Where, in any proceedings under the Act, a question arises as to whether a person was a UN worker or an operation was a UN operation, a certificate signed by, or with the authority of, the Minister for Foreign Affairs and stating any fact relating to the question is deemed to be evidence of that fact. Article 17 of the Convention imposes a guarantee of a fair procedures and further provides that any alleged offender is entitled to communicate, without delay, with the nearest appropriate representative of the state of which he is a national or which is otherwise entitled to protect the person's rights. Where an accused is stateless, he is entitled to communicate with the representative of that state which, at his request, is willing to protect his rights. An accused is also entitled to be visited by the appropriate state representative. The final outcome of any prosecution is required to be notified to the Secretary-General, who then transmits the information to the other state parties to the Convention (article 18).

Insofar as military law is concerned, a limited court-martial has no jurisdiction to try a person subject to military law for an offence under the Act of 2000 (section 6(b) amending the Defence Act 1954, section 192(3)(c) as amended by the Genocide Act 1973, section 5 and as amended by the Criminal Justice (United Nations Convention against Torture) Act 2000 section 6(b)). However, a general court-martial does have such jurisdiction, but only where the offence was committed on active service (section 6(b) amending the Defence Act 1954 section 192(3) as amended by the Genocide Act 1973, section 5 and as amended by the Criminal Justice (United Nations Convention against Torture) Act 2000 section 6(b)). Any such person is liable, on conviction by court-martial, to any punishment assigned for the offence or any less punishment awardable by a court-martial (section 6(a) amending the Defence Act 1954, section 169 as amended by the Criminal Justice Act 1990, section 7 and as amended by the Criminal Justice (United Nations Convention against Torture) Act 2000 section 6(a)). As noted in the discussion above in relation to the Convention against torture, the exercise of the court-martial's jurisdiction is contingent on the consent of the civil authority where the offence relates to a person not subject to military law, irrespective, is seems, of whether or not the offence was committed on active service. Again, however, having regard to the provisions of section 5 of the Criminal Justice (Safety of United Nations Workers) Act 2000, it seems that the consent of the Director of Public Prosecutions would be required where the offence alleged is under that Act.

The Act (section 8) also amends the First Schedule to the Extradition (Amendment) Act 1994 by providing that any offences under the Act of 2000 are not to be regarded as political offences. It also effects minor amendments (section 7) to the Criminal Procedure Act 1967 in respect of murder, attempted murder and conspiracy to commit murder and (section 9) includes any offence under the Act of 2000 in the list of offences for which bail may be refused. Section 10 provides for the defence of double jeopardy, where a person has otherwise been convicted or acquitted outside the State of an offence in respect of an act that also constitutes an offence under the Act of 2000.

The Act of 2000 is primarily concerned with the prosecution of offences committed against UN workers. However, the Convention also requires the taking of all practicable measures to prevent preparations, within the jurisdiction, for the commission of crimes against UN workers (whether inside or outside the State) (article 11), in relation to the communication of information regarding alleged offenders and victims (article 12) and the provision of mutual assistance by parties to the Convention in criminal matters arising thereunder (article 16). Disputes between state parties as to the interpretation or application of the Convention are required to be resolved by negotiation and, if necessary, arbitration, subject to any reservation made at the time of accession (article 22). The Convention also provides for the identification of UN personnel and vehicles (article 3) and imposes a duty to ensure their safety from any attack or action that prevents the discharge of the mandate (article 7) and to release or return UN workers who are captured or detained (unless otherwise provided in an applicable status of forces agreement) (article 8). Of relevance to the Defence Forces, the Convention further requires the dissemination of the Convention as widely as possible and, in particular, the inclusion of its study (as well as relevant provisions of international humanitarian law) in programmes of military instruction (article 19).

Of further relevance to military law is that nothing in the Convention affects the applicability of international humanitarian law and universally recognised standards of human rights in relation to the protection of UN operations and workers or the responsibility of those workers to respect those laws and standards. Furthermore, the Convention does not affect (i) the rights and obligations of states (consistent with the UN Charter) in relation to consent to entry of persons into their territories, (ii) the obligation of UN workers to act in accordance with the terms of the mandate of a UN operation, (iii) the right of a state to withdraw its personnel from a UN operation to which it had voluntarily contributed, (iv) the entitlement by such personnel to compensation for death or injury attributable to peace-keeping service or (v) the right to act in self-defence. The Convention requires that the state within whose territory the UN operation is conducted (the host state) and the UN are to conclude, as soon as possible, an agreement on the status of the operation and all personnel so engaged including *inter alia* provisions on privileges and immunities for military and police components (a status of forces agreement) (article 4) and that any state in whose territory UN workers and their equipment are in transit or temporarily present in connection with a UN operation is to facilitate their unimpeded transit to and from the host state (article 5). Without prejudice to such privileges and immunities as they may enjoy or to the requirements of their duties, UN workers are required to respect the laws and regulations of both the host and transit states and to refrain from any activity incompatible with the impartial and international nature of their duties (article 6).

Education

Fair procedures   In *Student A and Student B v. Dublin Secondary School*, High Court, November 25, 1999, Kearns J. evinced a reluctance to interfere with the decision of a school to expel two students where he was satisfied that the school had in general terms been fair in their treatment. The plaintiffs, who were both final year students at the defendant secondary school, sought an interlocutory injunction to restrain it from expelling them because they had been discovered using cannabis while at a party off school property. They claimed that it was difficult to make alternative arrangements for schooling and that their constitutional right to education had been interfered with, while fair procedures had not been observed. Kearns J. made an order adjourning the action, to enable further submissions to be made on the plaintiffs' behalf.

Kearns J. reviewed a school's traditional authority to exercise discipline over pupils, as described in *Fitzgerald v. Northcote* (1865) 4 F & F 656, which derives from the *in loco parentis* doctrine through parental delegation. In the present context, he noted that there was no general discretionary power of expulsion but only one for reasonable cause.

He was of the view that the courts will only interfere in the administration of discipline in schools where the school authorities or teachers exceed their powers or when decisions made by the Secretary General under section 29 of the Education Act 1998 were appealed to the courts by way of judicial review or if the sanction administered failed to pass the test of reasonableness. Kearns J. noted that provisions of the Education Act 1998, which provided for an appeal procedure, did not apply to the defendant school which had applied for but had not obtained recognition as a secondary school from the Department of Education because there were already a large number of schools in the area. He commented that where, as here, Department of Education Guidelines or the provisions of the Education Act 1998 did not apply to a particular school, it was important for such schools to have clear rules of conduct and to ensure that parents and pupils were made fully aware of such rules and disciplinary policy. It would be prudent for schools to adopt a practice of requiring parents to read and sign such rules, particularly where it related to behaviour of students off the school premises.

Moving to the penalty imposed in the instant case, Kearns J. cited with approval the decision of Finlay P. (as he then was) in *State (Smullen) v. Duffy and Ors* [1980] I.L.R.M. 47. He stated that, when determining whether a particular sanction was appropriate, the gravity of the offence involved and its implication for the safety and welfare of the other pupils were all matters which had to be taken into account. An immediate suspension might be necessary to maintain discipline within a school, particularly if the pupils are placed in physical danger. In that respect, he held that 'there could be no doubt' but that the school was entitled to take an extremely severe line in relation to drug use, even of 'soft' drugs, because any slippage of discipline in that regard could have the most deleterious implications for the student user, other students and the school generally. A 'zero tolerance' line of approach was not unreasonable in such circumstances.

Kearns J. accepted that expulsion was the most draconian punishment a school could impose and such were the implications of expulsion, particularly for a final year student, that such decisions could be properly regarded as quasi judicial in nature. But the kind of offence in the instant case had to be regarded as falling into the category where both pupils and parents alike had to reasonably expect a school authority to take serious action in the event of transgression. He held that, once a court decided that a school had in general terms been fair, it should not lightly interfere with the autonomy of the school or do anything which would have the affect of damaging its capacity to discipline its students, given that the school, with its vast experience, usually knew best. Accordingly, it would not be appropriate for a Court to state whether the punishment should be suspension or expulsion in an individual case unless there appeared to be a want of any reasonable basis for the decision of the school authority. He accepted that there could be no doubt in the instant case that the adverse consequences of the penalty imposed were very considerable.

Kearns J. concluded that the defendant school had fallen into error in one respect. The evidence indicated that a view had been formed by the headmaster that he had no option but to expel the plaintiffs. This, in Kearns J's view was an erroneous belief, because any form of automatic expulsion was in breach of an essential requirement of natural justice that a person be allowed address the question of penalty before same was imposed, as set out in cases such as *Flanagan v. University College Dublin* [1989] I.L.RM. 469 (Annual Review 1988, 14-15) and *McAuley v. Garda Commissioner* [1996] 1 I.R. 208 (Annual Review 1996, 403-4). Accordingly, Kearns J. adjourned the matter to enable the plaintiffs and their parents the opportunity of addressing the school's Board of Governors prior to the possibility of any more lengthy suspension or expulsion.

In *Wright v. Board of Management of Gorey Community School*, High Court, March 28, 2000, O'Sullivan J. declined to interfere by interlocutory relief where two students had been suspended on suspicion of drug use. It is also notable that he expressly declined to have the matter dealt with on an *in camera* basis. The plaintiffs were brothers who had been suspended by the defendant from their school on suspicion of being engaged in drug abuse. They applied for an interlocutory injunction seeking their reinstatement in the school until the trial of their action in which they claimed, *inter alia*, that unfair procedures had been adopted against them by the Board which involved a breach of their constitutional rights. They also sought to limit the reporting of their names and their school.

Before dealing with the substantive application, O'Sullivan J. held that, in the absence of clear jurisdiction, he felt bound to obey the spirit and letter of Article 34.1 of the Constitution to the effect that justice "shall be administered in public" save in special and limited cases as may be prescribed by law. This approach is in line with the decision of Laffoy J. in *Roe v. Blood Transfusion Service Board* [1996] 1 I.L.R.M. 555, which we criticised as being somewhat inflexible: Annual Review 1996, 139-42. Given the sensitivity of the issues, and the youth of the students, the approach taken by Kearns J. in the *Student A and Student B* case would seem preferable.

Turning to the substantive issues in the *Wright* case, O'Sullivan J. held that, in the case of a school, the requirement of maintaining discipline and authority meant that the obligation of fair procedures did not demand something approaching the formality of a courtroom situation even where expulsion, which was the ultimate sanction with very serious consequences for the person expelled, was open for consideration. He accepted that the plaintiffs had established a fair question to be dealt with at the trial and that damages would not be an appropriate remedy to either party in this case, but he concluded that the balance of convenience favoured the refusal of the plaintiffs' reinstatement. He was of the view that if the plaintiffs were reinstated and they lost their action, enormous damage would have been done to the authority and policy of the school, faced with the grave responsibility of dealing with any threat from drug abuse. On the other hand if the injunction was refused and the plaintiffs eventually won their case, they would in all probability in the meantime have had access to appropriate schooling.

EDUCATION AND TRAINING QUALIFICATIONS (OTHER THAN DEGREES)

The Qualifications (Education and Training) Act 1999 established the National Qualifications Authority of Ireland and the Further Education and Training Awards Council and also defines their functions. The Act dissolved the National Council for Education Awards (NCEA) and amended both the Labour Services Act 1987 and the Regional Technical Colleges Act 1992. The 1999 Act came into effect on February 26, 2001: Qualifications (Education and Training) Act 1999 (Commencement) Order 2001 (S.I. No.57 of 2001). One of the main purposes of the 1999 Act is to provide for a more systematic recognition and validation regime for academic and vocational qualifications, other than primary degrees, such as National Certificates and National Diplomas formerly accredited by the NCEA, now replaced by the National Qualifications Authority of Ireland (NQAI). In addition the 1999 Act provides for recognition of national vocational qualifications, which will replace the formalised apprenticeship arrangements formerly administered by FAS.

INSTITUTES OF TECHNOLOGY (REGIONAL TECHNICAL COLLEGES)

Institute of Technology, Blanchardstown The Regional Technical Colleges (Amendment) Act 1999 provided for the dissolution of Institute of Technology, Blanchardstown Limited and the formation of The Institute of Technology, Blanchardstown and amended the Vocational Education Act 1930 in relation to the composition of Vocational Education Committees; to be commenced by Ministerial Order.

PRIMARY AND SECONDARY LEVEL: EDUCATION ACT 1998

Introduction and commencement of 1998 Act The Education Act 1998 is an enormously significant landmark in the regulatory framework for educational services at first and second level in the State. The 1998 Act is the first comprehensive legislative regulation of this area and may be seen against the background of comparable legislation for the third level sector, the Universities Act 1997 (Annual Review 1997, 354-64). The Education Act 1998 (Commencement) Order 1999 (S.I. No. 29 of 1999) brought sections 2 to 6, 13, 25, 26, 36, 37 and Parts VIII and IX of the 1998 Act into effect from February 5, 1999. The Education Act 1998 (Commencement) (No.2) Order 1999 (S.I. No.470 of 1999) brought sections 7, 9, 14-17, 19-24, 27, 28, 30, 31, 33-35, and Part VII of the 1998 Act into effect from December 23, 1999. The Education Act 1998 (Commencement) (No.3) Order 2000 (SI No.495 of 2000) brought the remaining sections of the Act, sections 1, 8, 10-12, 18, 29 and 32, into force on December 22, 2000. This latter Commencement Order might be described as somewhat extravagant, since section 1 of the 1998 Act had provided that, in the absence of a Commencement Order, any provisions of the Act not already in force would come into effect at the latest two years after the passing of the 1998 Act, that is, on December 23, 2000. The (No.3) Commencement Order thus had the effect of bringing the sections in question into force one day early (at a time when all first and second level schools were, no doubt, shut).

General objects Section 6 of the 1998 Act sets out the general objects of the Act. It requires every person concerned in its implementation to have regard to 'the following objects in pursuance of which the Oireachtas has enacted this Act':

(a) to give practical effect to the constitutional rights of children,
including children who have a disability or who have other special
educational needs, as they relate to education;

(b) to provide that, as far as is practicable and having regard to the
resources available, there is made available to people resident in
the State a level and quality of education appropriate to meeting
the needs and abilities of those people;

(c) to promote equality of access to and participation in education
and to promote the means whereby students may benefit from
education;

(d) to promote opportunities for adults, in particular adults who as
children did not avail of or benefit from education in schools, to
avail of educational opportunities through adult and continuing
education;

(e) to promote the right of parents to send their children to a school
of the parents' choice having regard to the rights of patrons and
the effective and efficient use of resources;

(f) to promote best practice in teaching methods with regard to the
diverse needs of students and the development of the skills and
competencies of teachers;

(g) to promote effective liaison and consultation between schools and
centres for education, patrons, teachers, parents, the communities
served by schools, local authorities, health boards, persons or
groups of persons who have a special interest in, or experience
of, the education of students with special educational needs and
the Minister;

(h) to contribute to the realisation of national educational policies
and objectives;

(i) to contribute to the realisation of national policy and objectives
in relation to the extension of bi-lingualism in Irish society and in
particular the achievement of a greater use of the Irish language
at school and in the community;

(j) to contribute to the maintenance of Irish as the primary community
language in Gaeltacht areas;

(k) to promote the language and cultural needs of students having
regard to the choices of their parents;

(l) to enhance the accountability of the education system, and

(m) to enhance transparency in the making of decisions in the
education system both locally and nationally.

Functions of Minister   Section 7 of the 1998 Act deals with the functions of
the Minister for Education. These are:

(a) to ensure that there is made available to each person resident in the State, including a person with a disability or who has other special educational needs, support services and a level and quality of education appropriate to meeting the needs and abilities of that person,

(b) to determine national education policy, and

(c) to plan and co-ordinate—
    (i) the provision of education in recognised schools and centres for education, and
    (ii) support services.

It also requires the Minister:

(a) to provide funding to each recognised school and centre for education and to provide support services to recognised schools, centres for education, students, including students who have a disability or who have other special educational needs, and their parents, as the Minister considers appropriate;

(b) to monitor and assess the quality, economy, efficiency and effectiveness of the education system provided in the State by recognised schools and centres for education, having regard to the objects provided for in section 6 and to publish, in such manner as the Minister considers appropriate, information relating to such monitoring and assessment;

(c) to lease land or buildings to any person or body of persons for the purpose of establishing a school without prejudice to the establishment by patrons of schools which are situated on land or in buildings which are not leased to them by the Minister, the extension and further development of such schools when established and the recognition of such schools in accordance with section 10 of the 1998 Act; and

(d) to provide support services through Irish to recognised schools which provide teaching through Irish and to any other recognised school which requests such provision.

Patron of school Section 8 of the 1998 Act provides that (a) the person who, at the commencement of the section, is recognised by the Minister as the patron of a primary school; and (b) the persons who, at the commencement of this section, stand appointed as trustees or as the board of governors of a post-primary school and, where there are no such trustees or such board, the owner of that school, shall be deemed to be the patron for the purposes of the Act. It also provides that the patron of a school shall carry out the functions and exercise the powers conferred on the patron by the Act, deed, charter, articles of management or other such instrument relating to the establishment or operation of the school. The most significant functions in this respect are the appointment of the board of management of the school under section 14 of the 1998 Act: see below.

Functions of a recognised school   Section 9 of the 1998 Act provides that a recognised school shall provide education to students which is appropriate to their abilities and needs. It also requires that it shall use its available resources to:

> (a) ensure that the educational needs of all students, including those with a disability or other special educational needs, are identified and provided for,
>
> (b) ensure that the education provided by it meets the requirements of education policy as determined from time to time by the Minister including requirements as to the provision of a curriculum as prescribed by the Minister in accordance with section 30,
>
> (c) ensure that students have access to appropriate guidance to assist them in their educational and career choices,
>
> (d) promote the moral, spiritual, social and personal development of students and provide health education for them, in consultation with their parents, having regard to the characteristic spirit of the school,
>
> (e) promote equality of opportunity for both male and female students and staff of the school,
>
> (f) promote the development of the Irish language and traditions, Irish literature, the arts and other cultural matters,
>
> (g) ensure that parents of a student, or in the case of a student who has reached the age of 18 years, the student, have access in the prescribed manner to records kept by that school relating to the progress of that student in his or her education,
>
> (h) in the case of schools located in a Gaeltacht area, contribute to the maintenance of Irish as the primary community language,
>
> (i) conduct its activities in compliance with any regulations made from time to time by the Minister under section 33,
>
> (j) ensure that the needs of personnel involved in management functions and staff development needs generally in the school are identified and provided for,
>
> (k) establish and maintain systems whereby the efficiency and effectiveness of its operations can be assessed, including the quality and effectiveness of teaching in the school and the attainment levels and academic standards of students,
>
> (l) establish or maintain contacts with other schools and at other appropriate levels throughout the community served by the school, and
>
> (m) establish and maintain an admissions policy which provides for maximum accessibility to the school.

Recognition of schools Section 10 of the 1998 Act deals with the criteria on which a school is recognised. Section 10 provides that a school that, on the commencement of section 10 (December 22, 2000), was in receipt of funds provided by the Oireachtas in respect of:

    (a) the education activities for students of that school, or
    (b) the remuneration of teachers in that school,

is deemed to be a school recognised in accordance with the Act.

    Otherwise, section 10(1) of the 1998 Act provides that, on a request being made for that purpose, the Minister may from time to time designate a school or a proposed school to be a school recognised for the purposes of this Act. Section 10(2) provides that the Minister may designate a school or a proposed school to be a school recognised for the purposes of the Act where the Minister, on a request being made for that purpose by the patron of a school or a proposed school, is satisfied that:

    (a) the number of students who are attending or are likely to attend the school is such or is likely to be such as to make the school viable,

    (b) in the case of a proposed school, and having regard to the desirability of diversity in the classes of school operating in the area likely to be served by the school, the needs of students attending or likely to attend the school cannot reasonably be met by existing schools,

    (c) the patron undertakes that the school shall provide the curriculum as determined in accordance with section 30,

    (d) the patron agrees to permit and co-operate with regular inspection and evaluation by the Inspectorate,

    (e) the school complies, or in the case of a proposed school shall comply, with health, safety and building standards as are determined by law and any further such standards as are determined from time to time by the Minister, and

    (f) the patron agrees that the school shall operate in accordance with such regulations as may be made by the Minister from time to time under section 33 and... with any other terms and conditions as may reasonably be attached to recognition by the Minister.

Withdrawal of recognition While existing schools are deemed to be recognised schools under section 10 of the 1998 Act, section 11 of the 1998 Act specifies that recognition can be withdrawn where the requirements of section 10 of the Act are not being complied with by any school. In such event, the Minister must arrange to make alternative and appropriate education facilities available for those students who were enrolled in the school.

Annual funding of schools   Section 12 of the 1998 Act provides that the Minister, with the concurrence of the Minister for Finance, shall determine and publish in each school year criteria by which any class or classes of recognised schools or centres for education are to be funded in the following school year from monies provided by the Oireachtas. It also provides that such criteria shall allow for the payment of additional monies to recognised schools having regard to the level of educational disadvantage of students in the schools. A grant or grants shall not be made unless the school is a recognised school at the date that such grant or grants are to be made. It also provides that where, on the commencement of section 12, arrangements are in place whereby grants are provided by the Minister to a body of persons which disburses such grants to two or more recognised schools, nothing in the 1998 Act is to operate to alter such arrangements except with the agreement of that body or its successor.

Schools Inspectorate   Section 13 of the 1998 Act provides that the Minister shall appoint a Chief Inspector and others Inspectors. One of the general functions of the Inspectors are to support and advise recognised schools, centres for education and teachers on matters relating to the provision of education. In specific terms, they:

    (i) shall visit recognised schools and centres for education on the initiative of the Inspectorate, and, following consultation with the board, patron, parents of students and teachers, as appropriate, do any or all of the following:

   (ii) may conduct assessments of the educational needs of students in recognised schools and advise those students, their parents and the schools as appropriate in relation to the educational development of those students,

  (iii) shall advise teachers and boards in respect of the performance of their duties, and, in particular, assist teachers in employing improved methods of teaching and conducting classes, and

  (iv) shall advise parents and parents' associations.

In addition, they must

(a) evaluate the quality and effectiveness of the provision of education in the State, including comparison with relevant international practice and standards, and to report thereon to the Minister;

(b) conduct research into education and to provide support in the formulation of policy by the Minister;

(c) promote excellence in the management of, teaching in and the use of support services by schools and in the procedures for consultation and co-operation within and between schools and centres for education;

(d) evaluate the effectiveness of the teaching, development, promotion and use of Irish in schools and centres for education and to report to the Minister on those matters;

(e) advise the Minister on any matter relating to education policy and provision, including the curriculum taught in recognised schools, assessment and teaching methods.

These functions must be seen in conjunction with the role of the welfare (school attendance) officers appointed under the Education (Welfare) Act 2000: see below.

Boards of management of schools Section 14 of the 1998 Act provides that it shall be the duty of a patron, for the purposes of ensuring that a recognised school is managed in a spirit of partnership, to appoint where practicable a board of management the composition of which is agreed between patrons of schools, national associations of parents, recognised school management organisations, recognised trade unions and staff associations representing teachers and the Minister. Section 14 also specifies that the board of management appointed by the school patron will be a corporate body, capable of suing and being sued in its own name.

Section 15 specifies that the board of management 'shall... manage the school on behalf of the patron.' It also provides that, in carrying out its functions the board shall:

(a) do so in accordance with the policies determined by the Minister from time to time,

(b) uphold, and be accountable to the patron for so upholding, the characteristic spirit of the school as determined by the cultural, educational, moral, religious, social, linguistic and spiritual values and traditions which inform and are characteristic of the objectives and conduct of the school, and at all times act in accordance with any Act of the Oireachtas or instrument made thereunder, deed, charter, articles of management or other such instrument relating to the establishment or operation of the school,

(c) consult with and keep the patron informed of decisions and proposals of the board,

(d) publish, in such manner as the board with the agreement of the patron considers appropriate, the policy of the school concerning admission to and participation in the school, including the policy of the school relating to the expulsion and suspension of students and admission to and participation by students with disabilities or who have other special educational needs, and ensure that as regards that policy principles of equality and the right of parents to send their children to a school of the parents' choice are respected and such directions as may be made from time to time by the Minister, having regard to the characteristic spirit of the school and the constitutional rights of all persons concerned, are complied with,

(e) have regard to the principles and requirements of a democratic society and have respect and promote respect for the diversity of values, beliefs, traditions, languages and ways of life in society,

(f) have regard to the efficient use of resources (and, in particular, the efficient use of grants provided under section 12 [of the 1998 Act]), the public interest in the affairs of the school and accountability to students, their parents, the patron, staff and the community served by the school, and

(g) use the resources provided to the school from monies provided by the Oireachtas to make reasonable provision and accommodation for students with a disability or other special educational needs, including, where necessary, alteration of buildings and provision of appropriate equipment.

Section 16 of the 1998 Act provides that the patron may, subject to the consent of the Minister, dissolve a board of management 'for good and valid reasons.' Section 17 of the 1998 Act provides that the patron shall, at the request of the Minister, dissolve a board of management where the Minister is satisfied that the functions of a board are not being effectively discharged or for other reasons stated in the section.

Section 18 if the 1998 Act requires the board of management to keep all proper and usual accounts and records of all monies received by it or expenditure of such monies incurred by it and shall ensure that in each year all such accounts are properly audited or certified in accordance with best accounting practice. This does not apply to a school established or maintained by a vocational education committee.

Section 19 provides that where the Minister or the patron is of the opinion that the functions of a board are not being effectively discharged, the Minister or the patron, as the case may be, shall inform the board of that opinion and the reasons therefor. Having considered any representations by the board, the Minister or the patron, as the case may be, may authorise any person or persons as the Minister or the patron may deem appropriate to report to the Minister or the patron or both the Minister and the patron on any matter arising from or relating to the operation of that board.

Section 20 requires a board of management to establish procedures for informing the parents of students in the school of matters relating to the operation and performance of the school.

Section 21 of the 1998 Act requires the board of management to prepare a school plan, which must identify how the school will manage and maintain the education needs of its students, thus indicating its compliance with, for example, section 10 of the 1998 Act.

Functions of Principal and teachers Section 22 of the 1998 Act provides that the Principal of a recognised school and the teachers in a recognised school, under the direction of the Principal, shall have responsibility, in accordance with the Act, for the instruction provided to students in the school and shall contribute, generally, to the education and personal development of students in that school. In particular, they must:

(a) encourage and foster learning in students,
(b) regularly evaluate students and periodically report the results of the evaluation to the students and their parents,
(c) collectively promote co-operation between the school and the community which it serves, and
(d) subject to the terms of any applicable collective agreement and their contract of employment, carry out those duties that—
    (i) in the case of teachers, are assigned to them by or at the direction of the Principal, and
    (ii) in the case of the Principal, are assigned to him or her by the board.

Sections 23 and 24 provide that the board of management will appoint a principal and teachers to the school.

In addition to the functions of a Principal in section 22, section 23 of the 1998 Act provides that the Principal shall:

(a) be responsible for the day-to-day management of the school, including guidance and direction of the teachers and other staff of the school, and be accountable to the board for that management,
(b) provide leadership to the teachers and other staff and the students of the school,
(c) be responsible for the creation, together with the board, parents of students and the teachers, of a school environment which is supportive of learning among the students and which promotes the professional development of the teachers,
(d) under the direction of the board and, in consultation with the teachers, the parents and, to the extent appropriate to their age and experience, the students, set objectives for the school and monitor the achievement of those objectives, and
(e) encourage the involvement of parents of students in the school in the education of those students and in the achievement of the objectives of the school.

School terms Section 25 provides that the Minister may, from time to time, following consultation with patrons, national associations of parents, recognised school management organisations and recognised trade unions and staff associations representing teachers, prescribe (a) the minimum number of days in a school year during which a school shall be open to receive students and provide them with instruction, (b) the minimum number of hours of instruction in a school day or in a school week, and (c) any matters related to the length of the school year, the school week or the school day and the organisation and structure of such year, week or day.

Parents' association Section 26 provides that the parents of students of a recognised school may establish, and maintain from among their number, a parents' association for that school. It provides that a parents' association shall promote the interests of the students in a school in co-operation with the board, the Principal and teachers.

Information to students and student council Section 27 provides that a board of management shall establish and maintain procedures for the purposes of informing students in a school of the activities of the school. It also provides that students of a post-primary school may establish a student council to promote the interests of the school and the involvement of students in the affairs of the school, in co-operation with the board, parents and teachers.

Grievance and other procedures Section 28 provides that, following consultation with patrons of recognised schools, national associations of parents, recognised school management organisations and recognised trade unions and staff associations representing teachers, the Minister may prescribe procedures in accordance with which—

> (a) the parent of a student or, in the case of a student who has reached the age of 18 years, the student, may appeal to the board against a decision of a teacher or other member of staff of a school,
> (b) grievances of students, or their parents, relating to the students' school (other than those which may be dealt with under paragraph (a) or section 29), shall be heard, and
> (c) appropriate remedial action shall, where necessary, be taken as a consequence of an appeal or in response to a grievance.

It also provides that, in prescribing procedures for these purposes, the Minister must have regard to the desirability of determining appeals and resolving grievances in the school concerned.

Appeals from grievance procedure Section 29 of the 1998 Act provides for an appeals procedure where a board or a person acting on behalf of the board—

> (a) permanently excludes a student from a school, or

(b) suspends a student from attendance at a school for a period to be prescribed for the purpose of this paragraph, or

(c) refuses to enrol a student in a school, or

(d) makes a decision of a class which the Minister, following consultation with patrons, national associations of parents, recognised school management organisations, recognised trade unions and staff associations representing teachers, may from time to time determine may be appealed in accordance with the section.

In such cases, the parent of the student, or in the case of a student who has reached the age of 18 years, the student, may, within a reasonable time from the date that the parent or student was informed of the decision and following the conclusion of any appeal procedures provided by the school or the patron, in accordance with section 28, appeal that decision to the Secretary General of the Department of Education and Science. The appeal will be heard by an appeals committee appointed under the section, comprising an Inspector and such other persons as the Minister considers appropriate.

The appeals committee's procedures must ensure, *inter alia*, that:

(a) the parties to the appeal are assisted to reach agreement on the matters the subject of the appeal where the appeals committee is of the opinion that reaching such agreement is practicable in the circumstances,

(b) hearings are conducted with the minimum of formality consistent with giving all parties a fair hearing, and

(c) appeals are, in general, dealt with within 30 days from the date of the receipt of the appeal by the Secretary General.

Curriculum Section 30 of the 1998 Act provides that the Minister may, from time to time, following such consultation with patrons of schools, national associations of parents, recognised school management organisations and recognised trade unions and staff associations representing teachers, as the Minister considers appropriate, prescribe the curriculum for recognised schools, namely:

(a) the subjects to be offered in recognised schools,

(b) the syllabus of each subject,

(c) the amount of instruction time to be allotted to each subject, and

(d) the guidance and counselling provision to be offered in schools.

Teaching through Irish Section 31 of the 1998 Act provides that the Minister shall establish a body of persons to plan and co-ordinate the provision of textbooks and aids to learning and teaching through the Irish language.

Educational disadvantage Section 32 provides that the Minister shall by order, following consultation with patrons, national associations of parents, recognised school management organisations, recognised trade unions and staff associations representing teachers and such other persons as the Minister considers appropriate, establish an educational disadvantage committee, to advise him or her on policies and strategies to be adopted to identify and correct educational disadvantage.

Regulations   Section 33 of the 1998 Act empowers the Minister, following consultation with patrons, national associations of parents, recognised school management organisations and recognised trade unions and staff associations representing teachers, to make Regulations for the purpose of giving effect to the Act. These may deal with:

(a) the recognition of schools and the withdrawal of recognition from schools;

(b) the making of grants by the Minister to schools and centres for education;

(c) the appointment and qualifications of persons who are to be employed as teachers in schools or centres for education;

(d) the inspection of schools;

(e) the building, maintenance and equipment of schools;

(f) the length of the school year, school week and school day;

(g) admission of students to schools;

(h) access to schools by school attendance officers and other persons;

(i) access to schools and centres for education by students with disabilities or who have other special educational needs, including matters relating to reasonable accommodation and technical aid and equipment for such students;

(j) procedures for the promotion of effective liaison and co-operation by schools and centres for education with—

(i) other schools and centres for education,

(ii) local authorities (within the meaning of the Local Government Act 1941),

(iii) health boards (within the meaning of the Health Act 1970), and

(iv) voluntary and other bodies which have a special interest in education, in particular, education of students with special educational needs;

(k) appeals, and

(l) the curriculum of schools.

Education support centres Section 37 provides that the Minister may recognise a place as an education support centre. Such centres shall provide services for schools, teachers, parents, boards and other relevant persons which support them in carrying out their functions in respect of the provision of education.

National Council for Curriculum and Assessment Section 39 provides for the establishment by the Minister of the National Council for Curriculum and Assessment. The object of the Council, as set out in section 41, will be to advise the Minister on matters relating to the curriculum for early childhood education, primary and post-primary schools, and the assessment procedures employed in schools and examinations on subjects which are part of the curriculum. Sections 42 to 48 of the 1998 Act contain detailed provisions on the staffing and operation of the Council.

EXAMINATIONS AND REGULATIONS

Part VIII of the 1998 Act (sections 49 to 53) deals with examinations and the regulations attaching to them. The relevant examinations are those listed in the Second Schedule to the 1998 Act and any other specified by order of the Minister. The examinations listed in the Second Schedule are:

> Leaving Certificate Examination
> Junior Certificate Examination
> Technological Certificate Examination
> Trade Certificate Examination
> Certificate in Commerce Examination
> Ceardteastas Gaeilge Examination
> Teastas i dTeagasc na Gaeilge Examination
> Typewriting Teachers Certificate Examination
> Commercial Instructors Certificate Examination.

Section 51 of the 1998 Act provides that the Minister may make regulations as he or she from time to time considers appropriate for the effective conduct of examinations. These may include:

(a) the preparation of an examination paper and other examination materials,

(b) procedures at places where examinations are conducted, including the supervision of examinations,

(c) the marking of work presented for examination,

(d) the issuing of results of examinations,

(e) the charging and collection of fees for examinations,

(f) the terms under which candidates may appeal against the results of an examination and the procedure for such appeals,

(g) the penalties to be imposed on a person who acts in breach of regulations made by the Minister or who otherwise misconducts himself or herself in respect of an examination, and

(h) the designation of places where examinations may be held.

Section 52 contains a list of offences connected with the conduct of examinations together with penalties which may be imposed on conviction. On summary conviction, a fine not exceeding £1,500 and/or six months imprisonment may be imposed. On conviction on indictment, a fine not exceeding £5,000 and/or two years imprisonment may be imposed. The offences created are where a person:

(a) knowingly and without lawful authority publishes an examination paper or part of such paper to any other person prior to the holding of the examination concerned,

(b) has in his or her possession without lawful authority an examination paper or part of such paper prior to the holding of the examination concerned,

(c) carries out any duties relating to the preparation of examination papers and knowingly and without lawful authority provides a candidate for an examination or any other person with information concerning the material prepared by him or her in the course of those duties with the intention of conferring an advantage upon a candidate over other candidates,

(d) knowingly and wilfully credits a candidate with higher marks than the marks to which that candidate was entitled with the intention of conferring an advantage on that candidate over other candidates,

(e) knowingly and maliciously credits a candidate with lower marks than the marks to which that candidate was entitled,

(f) personates a candidate at an examination or knowingly allows or assists a person to personate a candidate at an examination,

(g) knowingly and maliciously destroys or damages any material relating to an examination,

(h) knowingly and maliciously obstructs any candidate or a person engaged in the conduct of an examination or otherwise interferes with the general conduct of an examination,

(i) knowingly and without lawful authority alters any certificate or any other record, including a record in machine-readable form, containing the results of an examination, or

(j) knowingly issues or makes use of any certificate or other document which purports to be a document issued by the person or body under whose authority the examination was conducted and to contain the results of an examination knowing that those results are false.

Refusal of access to certain information   Section 53 of the 1998 Act provides that notwithstanding any other enactment the Minister may refuse access to any information which would enable the compilation of information (that is not otherwise available to the general public) in relation to the comparative performance of schools in respect of the academic achievement of students enrolled therein. This includes:

(i)   the overall results in any year of students in a particular school in an examination, or

(ii) the comparative overall results in any year of students in different schools in an examination.

This would appear to prevent the compilation of so-called 'league tables' of schools performances in the State, though this is, at the time of writing, subject to a judicial review hearing in the High Court where the question arises whether such information should be made available under the Freedom of Information Act 1997 (Annual Review, 1997, 2-8).

Section 53 also empowers the Minister to refuse access to information relating to the identity of examiners.

Establishment of bodies to provide services related to education   Part IX of the 1998 Act (sections 54 to 59) provides for the establishment by the Minister, with the concurrence of the Government, of bodies to perform functions in or in relation to the provision of support services in the education sector.

PRIMARY LEVEL

Non-recognition of Steiner school   In *O'Shiel v. Minister for Education*, High Court, April 16, 1999, the plaintiffs claimed that the Minister was obliged to provide funding for a Steiner primary school. While ultimately unsuccessful in this claim, Laffoy J. made some favourable comments in their favour.

The plaintiffs were a family, parents and children, who were attending a school in County Clare which operated under the ideology of Rudolph Steiner. The parents of the children had raised the money required to run the school. They then applied to the Minister for Education for funding for running the school. The Minister refused to recognise the school for funding purposes. The Minister stated that recognition was refused on the grounds that only one of the school's teachers was a qualified teacher under the rules as they then applied, prior to the Education Act 1998 (see above), and also because of problems with the teaching of the Irish language.

The plaintiffs claimed that the Minister had infringed the right to free primary education under Article 42 of the Constitution in that they failed to recognise and thereby fund the school. They contended that they were entitled under Article 42 of the Constitution to choose to have their children educated using the Steiner method of education, and that the State was obliged to respect that choice. In reply, the Minister stated that he had not interfered with the plaintiffs' choice in regard to their preference of the Steiner method and that there was no obligation on the Minister to fund education in accordance with the parents' choice. The Minister did in fact fund 15 schools within a 12-mile radius of the plaintiffs' school and thus had discharged his obligation to provide free primary education in that particular part of County Clare. It was also argued that the State was entitled to take into consideration the lack of recognised qualifications amongst the teaching staff at the school, and the absence of a credible programme of instruction in Irish.

As indicated, Laffoy J. refused the reliefs sought. Nonetheless, she did express some views that were favourable to the plaintiffs. She noted that if the school did not exist, there would be no diversity of choice of primary education in County Clare and it would pervert the clear intent of the Constitution to interpret the obligation on the State in Article 42 as merely obliging them to fund a single system of primary education which was on offer to parents on a 'take it or leave it' basis. Such an interpretation would render meaningless the guarantee of parental freedom of choice. Laffoy J. was of the opinion that in order to fulfil its constitutional obligation to provide for free primary education, the State had to have regard to and had to accommodate the expression of parental conscientious choice and lawful preference. Thus, it was incumbent on the State to incorporate in any scheme of primary education measures to ensure that need and viability were properly assessed and that there was accountability. She opined that the correct interpretation of Article 42 was somewhere between the two polarised positions adopted by the parties. She was of the view that, where the pre-1998 Act non-statutory Rules with regard to recognition diminished the plaintiffs' constitutional rights, those Rules were invalid to that extent.

She accepted that it was undoubtedly proper for the Minister to prescribe standards in relation to academic competence, nature and duration of training, when deeming a person to be eligible to be a teacher in a primary school in the State, and there was no conflict between the imposition of those standards and the provisions of the Constitution. Nonetheless, the requirement that teachers at the school conform to prescribed standards of qualification would negative the plaintiffs' lawful preference.

Laffoy J. held that if there was a reasonable solution available to sort out the dispute between the plaintiffs and the State, the failure of the Minister to adopt it would constitute a breach of the plaintiffs' constitutional rights. She went on to say that there should have been a more searching and pro-active response from the Minister to the school's application for recognition.

She concluded that, in their application of the Rules with regard to recognition, the defendants had not infringed the plaintiffs' constitutional rights under Article 42.4. An obligation to provide a minimum primary education to children had to include the teaching of the Irish language to a minimum standard and the requirement in the Rules that teachers teaching in recognised primary schools should have a proficiency in Irish was a valid provision under the Constitution. Since there was no provision in the school to provide adequate instruction in Irish, either to the basic national level or even to the 'Steiner' requirement, the Minister was thus entitled to withhold recognition from the school as the teaching of the Irish language was wholly inadequate. The recognition issue must now also be considered in the light of the Education Act 1998: see above.

SECONDARY LEVEL

Appointment of teachers to denominational secondary schools   In *Greally v. Minister for Education*, High Court, January 29, 1999, the plaintiff unsuccessfully challenged the constitutionality of a scheme which provided for the selection of teachers for second level Roman Catholic denominational schools. The plaintiff, a practising Catholic and teacher, alleged that the scheme infringed Article 44.2.2° of the Constitution and meant he was unable to pursue a career as a teacher in the Catholic school system, despite the fact that he had relevant qualifications.

Under the terms of the non-statutory scheme in question, every secondary teacher in Ireland was equally eligible for membership of the selection panel under which a person was appointed a teacher in a Catholic school, provided he or she fulfilled certain conditions. To be appointed to the panel, a teacher, who did not have to be a Roman Catholic, had to be able to persuade a Catholic school to employ him for the requisite period. The plaintiff had not been appointed to the necessary temporary posts which would qualify him and therefore was not placed on the panel.

Geoghegan J. stated that qualifying for membership of the panel did not involve an enquiry into a person's religious beliefs or as to whether they practised their religion. The sole requirement was proof of satisfactory service for specified periods in Roman Catholic schools. This was prima facie a much fairer system than one which enquired into religious beliefs and practices and the arrangements under this scheme were no different from any other part of the State's education and funding policy. In addition, the plaintiff's inability to obtain the relevant posts was not grounded in any discriminatory or unconstitutional practice

He was of the opinion that the plaintiff's right to earn a livelihood had not been infringed. Because a person had a right to a particular livelihood, it did not mean that he had a right to receive employment from any particular employer. The first named defendant, the Minister for Education, had no interest in preventing Catholic employers from employing anybody they wished. The conditions in the scheme were conditions laid down by those employers in consideration of their agreement to honour the system and in assertion of the right to maintain denominational schools. The Minister had not prevented the plaintiff from achieving panel rights. Rather, the plaintiff had failed to achieve a position on the panels because of his inability to get employment on a temporary basis in Catholic schools. Therefore the panel system was not haphazard, arbitrary or unfair, nor did the scheme require implementation on a statutory basis.

Geoghegan J. concluded that the State was not required to adopt a funding scheme for secondary teachers which had the effect of destroying the denominational nature of schools requiring funding. Finally, Geoghegan J. noted that, since proceedings had been issued, the plaintiff had procured an excellent teaching post in a community school and the evidence did not establish that his long-term career prospects had been adversely affected by the matters of which he complained. Nor had his pension entitlements been adversely affected.

SCHOOL ATTENDANCE

Compulsory school attendance   In *Director of Public Prosecutions v. Best* [2000] 2 I.L.R.M. 1 (SC), the defendant had been prosecuted in the District Court under the School Attendance Act 1926 for failure to send her children to a primary school. She argued that the children were receiving suitable elementary education in a manner other than attending school, which is a defence to such a prosecution. She also relied on the relevant provisions of Article 42.1 of the Constitution concerning the role of parents in providing education to their children. The schools District Inspector found as a matter of fact that the children were not in receipt of suitable elementary education of general application *viz. á viz.* the primary school curriculum, in particular as regards instruction in the Irish language. On a consultative case stated, the question posed was whether the District Court judge was prevented in law from pronouncing a formal order of conviction in view of the fact that the Oireachtas had not to date defined what constitutes a suitable elementary education under section 4(2)(b) of the School Attendance Act 1926. The Supreme Court held that the judge was not so prevented.

The Court was of the view that, since the Irish language was designated by the Constitution as the first official language and the fact that a knowledge of it is a precondition to at least some forms of employment, it could not be said that its absence from a curriculum cannot be taken into account in determining whether the education of the child reaches the constitutional standard. When giving her decision the District Court judge would be doing so in the light of the evidence tendered. The Court considered that the fact that the Oireachtas had not embodied the minimum constitutional standard in legislation would not in any way prevent her from arriving at a fair and objective decision in the case.

The Court further held that the right of the child to be educated would be seriously violated if the State, although satisfied that teaching methods were patently inadequate, could not intervene simply because the curriculum purported to be taught approximated, for example, to the primary school curriculum. In this respect, the Court declined to follow dicta to the contrary in *In re the School Attendance Bill 1942* [1943] I.R. 334. On the cautious approach of the Court to overruling its previous decisions, see *Attorney General v. Ryan's Car Hire Ltd* [1965] I.R. 642, *Mogul of Ireland Ltd v. Tipperary (NR) County Council* [1976] I.R. 260 and *State (Lynch) v. Cooney* [1982] I.R. 337.

The Court was of the opinion that the absence of a definition of suitable or minimum education could not affect the decision of the court. In each case it is a question of mixed law and fact to be decided on the basis of the criteria indicated and the evidence adduced before it whether the education being provided is the minimum required for that child. In that respect, the Court crucially held that the onus of proof lies on the defendant to make out the statutory defence under the 1926 Act by adducing appropriate evidence as to the education of which the children are in receipt and the evidential burden in making the defence was the balance of probabilities test.

The Court reiterated the long-established view that the Constitution is a living instrument and it must be construed as of its time. Thus the standard of a 'certain minimum education' may vary according to the time in issue, and the standard must be the relevant one for its time. The common good places a priority on the children's right to receive a certain minimum education, intellectual and social. The Court stated that the standard is a question of fact which must be decided in view of factors including actual conditions in the community and having regard to, *inter alia*, the physical and intellectual capacity of the children. The minimum education must be conducive to the child achieving intellectual and social development and not such as to place the child in a discriminatory position.

The Court concluded that the District Court judge should, whilst recognising the parental and family rights, at the same time acknowledge the child's constitutional rights and the duty of the state as guardian of the common good. An education which creates a discriminatory situation for a child may establish circumstances where the rights of the child and the interest of the common good outweigh considerations of the family and parental rights. The decision must now be considered in the light of the updated provisions in the Education (Welfare) Act 2000: see below.

STUDENT WELFARE AND SCHOOL ATTENDANCE

The Education (Welfare) Act 2000 has a number of objectives. It provides for the first time a national system of school attendance and minimum education. It provided for the establishment of the National Educational Welfare Board which has overall responsibility, subject to Ministerial policy, for the implementation and operation of the 2000 Act. The 2000 Act also provided for the repeal of the School Attendance Acts 1926 to 1967. While section 1(2) of the 2000 Act provides that it will, in general, require Commencement Orders to come into effect, section 1(3) of the Act also provides that a default date of two years after its passing (that is, July 5, 2002) applies for any sections of the Act not in operation by that date. This is line with the default provisions of the Education Act 1998: see above. The National Educational Welfare Board was established on an interim basis in May 2001, but at the time of writing (July 2001) no Commencement Order for any provisions of the Act have been made.

It is important to note that the 2000 Act goes beyond being a mere replacement for the School Attendance Acts. The National Educational Welfare Board is empowered to develop, co-ordinate and implement school attendance policy so as to ensure that every child in the State attends a recognised school or otherwise receives an appropriate education. The Board will appoint education welfare officers to work in close co-operation with schools, teachers, parents and community/voluntary bodies with a view to encouraging regular school attendance and developing strategies to reduce absenteeism and early school leaving. The educational welfare officers will focus in particular on children at risk and those who are experiencing difficulties in school in order to resolve any impediments to their regular attendance at school. Alternative schooling will be sought for students who have been expelled, suspended or refused admittance to a school.

The Board will maintain a register of children receiving education outside the recognised school structure and will assess the adequacy of such education on an ongoing basis. School registers, attendance records, codes of behaviour and attendance strategies will be used by school authorities to promote regular attendance and foster an appreciation of learning among the student population. Thus, schools will be required to prepare and implement a code of behaviour, setting standards of behaviour and disciplinary procedures for the school.

Parents are required to ensure that their children attend a recognised school or otherwise receive an appropriate minimum education. Thus, the 2000 Act provides that parents must send their children to a recognised school on each school day or otherwise ensure that they are receiving an appropriate minimum education. Where a child is absent from school on a school day, the parents are required to notify the principal of the school of the reasons for such absence. Where parents decide to educate their child in a place other than a recognised school, the parents shall apply to have their child registered with the National

Educational Welfare Board and shall comply with such conditions as may be stipulated by the Board. The 2000 Act provides that parents may appeal a decision of the Board regarding the registration of their child.

As an indication of other connected changes in policy, the 2000 Act provides for raising the minimum school leaving age from 15 to 16, or the completion of three years of post-primary education, whichever is the later. Provision is also made for the continuing education and training of young persons of 16 and 17 years of age who leave school early to take up employment. It provides for the registration of early school leavers with the National Educational Welfare Board and for the Board to assist them in availing of appropriate educational and training opportunities. It also prohibits employers from employing early school leavers who are not registered with the Board for this purpose, and requires employers to notify the Board when they employ an early school leaver. This involves amendments to the Protection of Young Persons (Employment) Act 1996 (Annual Review 1996, 543-5).

UNIVERSITIES

Trinity College Dublin   The Trinity College Dublin (Charters and Letters Patent Amendment) Act 2000 was a Private Act which amended the Charters and Letters Patent establishing Trinity College Dublin, the sole constituent college of the University of Dublin. The 2000 Act should be seen against the background of the Universities Act 1997 (Annual Review 1997, 354-64), which had, as a Bill, sought to provide that the Trinity College Dublin charters would, in effect, be subject to the general provisions of its terms; this provision was abandoned in the final text of the 1997 Act (Annual Review 1997, 361). The 2000 Act, which departs in some respects from the general model in the 1997 Act, may thus be seen as a legislative compromise made in order to complete a reform of the regulatory arrangements between the universities and the State, particularly where State funding is concerned. The debates during the passage of the 2000 Act provided an opportunity for discussion on the role of the university in the 21st Century; and these debates were particularly intense in the Seanad where Trinity College Dublin is represented by three members.

Environmental Law

YVONNE SCANNELL, Law School, Trinity College, Dublin

INTRODUCTION

There were relatively few developments in Environmental Law in 2000 if one excludes Planning law. Legislative developments described in previous issues of the *Annual Review* described the legislature's accomplishments in establishing a framework for controlling pollution of the various environmental media and the management of chemicals, fleshing out the details of framework legislation and implementing EC Directives. The debate has now moved on to more intractable problems and political issues such as sustainable development and the integration of environmental policies into others policy objectives such as agriculture, transport and energy are now emerging as the dominating themes in environmental law. Judicial cases addressing these are more usually resolved in the context of land-use controls, usually in the planning system, because lawyers and the public are more familiar with the potential uses of the planning legislation for achieving their objectives. The potential of other areas of environmental law to ensure the sustainability of development and the practical implementation of EC environmental law has yet to be explored.

A major development in 2000 was the publication of the OECD *Environmental Performance Review of Ireland* (www.oecd.org/env). This concluded that despite progress in some areas, notably in reducing industrial pollution, pollution intensities in Ireland are high compared to those in other European Countries. Major challenges concern environmental pressures from energy production and agriculture (particularly intensive livestock rearing), public infrastructure such as waste water treatment, waste, transport and urban sprawl. Ireland is advised to implement environmental policies in a more cost effective way and to increase efforts to build a more modern environmental infrastucture. The OECD reviewers recommended that the User- Pays and the Polluter- Pays principles should be applied to water use. (At present householders are not universally required to pay water charges) The Report concluded that Ireland had a modern and coherent body of environmental law and that it was transposing nearly all EC Directives into national law very thoroughly.

AIR

The EPA published a review of *Emissions of Atmospheric Pollutants in Ireland*

1990 to 1998 in August. This reported that Ireland produces the highest levels of ammonia, methane and nitrous oxides per head of population in the EU. Agriculture is the major source of these emissions. The State is not on target to meet commitments under the Kyoto Protocol and carbon dioxide emissions have increased by 30% from 1990-98, mainly due to the rapid growth in the industrial sector and transport emissions. The rapid growth of emissions of atmospheric pollutants means that Ireland has to ensure that there is no further growth in some of the greenhouse gasses until 2010.

The National Climate Change Strategy (www.environ.ie) was published in November 2000. It sets out a methodology for extricating economic growth from growth in greenhouse gases. The Strategy proposes, measures *inter alia*,

– to introduce greenhouse gas taxation prioritizing CO2 emissions on a phased, incremental basis. The details of this are to be examined by a Tax Strategy Group.

– to engage in international emissions trading as a supplement to, and not as a substitute for domestic action. It is arguable that this proposal will not encourage the maximum reduction of domestic emissions at the most economical cost or indeed, will not facilitate the maximum reduction of global, as distinct from national, emissions of greenhouse gases. It is, however, more consistent with general EC policies on greenhouse gas reductions. Some policy makers fear that possibilities for reducing greenhouse gases by international trading of emissions might encourage the richer nations to take advantage of emission credits in poorer countries and to avoid ethical obligations to undertake more costly projects to reduce emissions at home. A separate report by the Emissions Trading Group was published in November 2000. The main strategies proposed are:

– to prohibit the use of coal to generate electricity at Moneypoint in County Clare. Money point is the largest single emitter of industrial greenhouse gas emissions.

– reducing methane emissions from agriculture by reducing livestock numbers by 10% by 2010.

– reducing emissions from transport by a balanced range of measures dealing with fuel efficiency, demand management and modal shift.

– more stringent requirements for house insulation where fiscal incentives are given for new houses.

– improved spacial and energy use planning and better insulated and more energy efficient building through review of the Building Regulations.

A Cross-Departmental Climate Change Team has been established to implement the *National Climate Change Strategy*, to engage in consultative arrangement with Social Partners and to promote an Awareness Campaign on climate change
    The Air Pollution Act, 1987 (Environmental Specifications for Petrol and

Diesel Fuels) Regulations 2000 (S.I. No. 72 of 2000) were enacted to give effect to part of the EC *Auto Oil Programme* in implementing Directive 98/70/EC on the quality of petrol and diesel fuels. New standards apply limits of 1% for benzene and 42% for aromatics.

The Air Pollution Act 1987 (Marketing, Sale and Distribution of Fours) (Amendment) Regulations 2000 (S.I. No. 278 of 2000) ban the sale of bituminous coal in six additional restricted areas and amend the Air Pollution Act, 1987 (Marketing, Sale and Distribution of Fuels) Regulations 1998. The European Communities (Agricultural or Forestry Type Approval) Regulations 2000 (S.I. No. 188 of 2000) implement the provisions of a number of EC Directives relating to the type approval of forestry tractors and components.

DANGEROUS SUBSTANCES

The European Communities (Introduction of Organisms Harmful to Plants or Plant Products) (Amendment) (No.2) Regulations 2000 (S.I. No.135 of 2000) implement the provisions of Commission Decisions 99/353/EC and 99/315/EC and Commission Directive 2000/23/ EC on emergency measures against the dissemination of *anoplophora glabripennis (notschulsky)* as regards China, excluding Hong Kong,

HORIZONTAL INSTRUMENTS

Freedom of Information The Freedom of Information Act 1997 (Prescribed Bodies) Regulations 2000 (S.I. No. 355 of 2000) prescribe a number of bodies, including the Local Government Computer Services Board and the Irish Water Safety Association, as separate public bodies for the purposes of the Act.

Environmental Impact Assessment The European Communities (Environmental Impact Assessment)(Amendment) Regulations 2000 (S.I. No. 450 of 2000) were enacted in order to transfer the functions of certifying EIA of local authority developments from the Minister for the Environment and Local Government to An Bord Pleanala. Subjecting local authority development for which EIA is required to the same procedures as the private sector for EIA should enhance the transparency of the development consent procedures and increase public confidence in the planning system.

Cases have arisen in Scotland and in England about decisions made by Ministers on development consent matters in which they have an interest. This usually consists of implementing a particular policy or securing a particular type of development or some other public benefit. The House of Lords in *R (Alconbury Developments Ltd) v. Secretary of State for the Environment* [2001] 2 All E.R. 929 held that it was not a violation of Article 6(1) of the European

Convention on Human Rights ("in the determination of his civil rights and obligations ...everyone is entitled to a affair and public hearing...by an independent and impartial tribunal established by law) when a Minister decided an appeal against a decision on a planning application basically because, although the Minister was not an independent and impartial tribunal, he was democratically accountable and his decisions were subject to judicial review . This decision has been widely criticized (frequently by arguing that the English judicial review process does not ensure *adequate* judicial control of administrative decisions) in the academic literature. (It should be noted that in *Alconbury* Lord Slynn merged the test of reasonableness in *Wednesbury* [1947] 2 All E.R. 680 with the test of proportionality and in *R v. Secretary for State for the Home Department, ex parte Daly* [2001] 3 All E.R. 433 he proposed an approach in judicial review which allows for a much closer examination of the merits of executive decisions than has hitherto been the case in England). It looks as if the *Wednesbury* test is being revised in England. Given the even more limited scope for judicial review of the merits of decisions in Ireland after *O'Keeffe v. An Bord Pleanala* [1993] I.R. 39, and the higher thresholds set for testing unreasonableness, *Alconbury* should not be followed here in cases where public authorities take decisions affecting citizens civil rights where they have an interest or, if followed, the scope of judicial review of administrative decisions should be enlarged.

INTERNATIONAL

The Sea Pollution (Hazardous and Noxious Substances) (Civil Liability and Compensation) Act 2000 gives effect to the International Convention on Liability and Compensation for Damage in connection with the Carriage of Hazardous and Noxious Substances by Sea 1996 (HNC) and the 1996 Protocol to the International Convention on the Limitation of Liability for Maritime Claims 1976. The Convention provides for compensation for loss of life or personal injury, loss or damage to property, environmental damage and for the costs of preventative measures arising from incidents involving a range of substances classified in various international codes as hazardous or noxious. These include materials, which are explosive in nature such as liquefied gases, corrosive acids, volatile chemicals, aromatic liquids, and certain solid materials, which generate dangerous gases when carried in bulk.

The HNC convention complements legal provisions on civil liability and compensation for oil pollution contained in the Oil Pollution of the Sea (Civil Liability and Compensation) Acts 1988 to 1998. Oil pollution damage is still covered by the 1969 Convention as amended. Payments of compensation under HNC are administered under the same regime applicable to compensation for oil pollution damage, i.e. the Shipowners' Liability and Compensation Fund.

WASTE

The EPA published the second report on the *National Waste Database* for 1998 in March 2000. It provides statistical information on the generation and management of solid waste and an inventory of waste disposal and recovery facilities throughout the State.

The Waste Management (Licensing) Regulations 2000 which consolidate earliest regulations made in 1997 and 1998 under the Waste Management Act 1996 came into effect on 26 June 2000. The new Regulations substantially reproduce the earlier regulations but they improve the administration of waste management law by providing that a single waste licence may be obtained for the operation of mobile waste treatment plants at a number of specified locations which may be reviewed to authorize operations at unspecified location or reflect the completion of operations at a specific location. Standards for mobile and fixed facilities are the same. The Regulations deal with the application procedures for waste licences, reviews of licences and appeals against decisions on licences and fees for making them.

The Hazardous Waste (Amendment) Regulations 2000 (S.I. No.73 of 2000) amend the Hazardous Waste Regulations 1998 (S.I.No.165 of 1998) to give effect to Council Directive 98/10/EC adapting to technical progress Council Directive 91/157/EEC on batteries and accumulators containing certain dangerous substances. Commission Directive 98/101/EC prohibits the marketing of all batteries and accumulators containing more than 0.0005% of mercury by weight, including those cases where batteries and accumulators are incorporated into appliances. Button cells and batteries composed of button cells with mercury content of more than 2% by weight are exempted from this prohibition.

The European Communities (Protection of Workers) ((Exposure to Asbestos) (Amendment) Regulations 2000 (S.I. No. 74 of 2000) give further effect to Council Directive 87/217/EEC relating to the prevention and reduction of environmental pollution by asbestos. The amendments alter the plan which must be prepared before demolition involving asbestos is undertaken, and lengthen the time for which medial records and the occupational health register must be maintained.

The Diseases of Animals (Bovine *Sprongiform Encephalopathy*)(Specified Risk Materials) Order 2000 (S.I. No. 331 of 2000) introduces further controls on specified risk material. This order is complemented by the European Communities (Specified Risk Material) Regulations 2000 (S.I. No. 332 of 2000) which deal with the removal, isolation and disposal of specified risk material for the purposes of Bovine *Sprongiform Encephalopathy* (BSE). These materials must be disposed of in licenced facilities by a special process. The European Communities (Processing of Mammalian Animal By-Products) Regulations 2000 (S.I. No. 182 of 2000) implement Council Decision 99/534/EC concerning the heat treatment for the processing of animal protein with a view to the inactivation of transmissible *sprongiform encephalopathy*

WATER

Directive 91/676/EEC on nitrates from agricultural sources. requires, *inter alia*, that measures be taken to identify Nitrate Vulnerable Zones and to implement programmes for improving water quality in those zones. Vulnerable groundwaters were identified in five counties as being polluted or susceptible to pollution by nitrates from agricultural sources and county councils in these areas have been asked to prepare information so that the Minister may designate vulnerable areas as NVZ's.

The European Communities (Quality of Water Intended for Human Consumption) (Amendment) Regulations, 2000 (S.I.No.177 of 2000) amend the European Communities (Quality of Water Intended for Human Consumption) (Amendment) Regulations, 1988 and apply the standards set in Directive 80/778/EEC to waters supplied in private group water schemes. It had previously been assumed that the Directive only applied to waters supplied by public sector undertakings because the European Court of Justice had held in *European Commission v. Belgium* (Case C- 42/89 [1992] 1 C.M.L.R. 22) that Directive 80/778/EEC did not apply to water from private sources. This decision was widely criticized and it appears that the Directive is now to be interpreted as applying to public and private water supplies. The 1988 Regulations were also amended to require action programmes for improving the quality of water supplied for human consumption where it does not meet EC standards. Private water schemes must secure full compliance with quality standards related to public health by December 31, 2003 and with all quality standards by December 31, 2006.

The European Communities (Drinking Water) Regulations, 2000 (S.I.No.439 of 2000) will come into operation on January 1, 2004 and will replace the abovementioned Regulations on that date. These regulations transpose Council Directive 98/83/EC on the quality of water for human consumption. The Regulations:

– set standards in relation to water quality for drinking, cooking, food preparation, other domestic purposes and food production (other than natural mineral waters, bottled water, certain medicinal products and exempted supplies which are mostly regulated under other legislation.) Limits are set for 48 parametric values grouped into three categories viz. microbiological, chemical and indicator parameters. Much more stringent parameters are set for lead which must be reduced from 50ug/l to 10 ug/l by December 2013 while an interim value of 25ug/l will apply from January 1, 2004. Provision is made for temporary derogations from standards where there is no risk to human health and these must be permitted by the Environmental Protection Agency. Ireland has set more stringent standards than those in the Directive

for ammonium and fluoride. Time limits are set for compliance with standards
by sanitary authorities and private water suppliers,

– prescribe penalties where a private water supplier does not comply with a
notice served by a sanitary authority,

– simplify and rationalize the monitoring regime into check monitoring and
audit monitoring.

The EPA's annual *Report on Drinking Water* 1999 made under section 58(2)
of the Environmental Protection Agency Act 1992, published in 2000 indicated
that Irelands drinking water had compliance levels of about 99% for key
parameters of heavy metals, ammonium, nitrates and nitrites. Compliance with
coliform parameters was achieved by 96% of samples from public supplies
which were free of faecal coliforms and 92% of these were free of all coliforms.
Group water supplies continue to experience problems in complying with
coliform standards and only 62% complied although this was 4% better than
the level of compliance in the previous report. The Rural Water Programme
which will invest £55 million in upgrading them in 2001 is addressing problems
with group water schemes.

WILDLIFE (AMENDMENT) ACT 2000

This Act was passed to amend and extend the Wildlife Act, 1976 and to provide
for connected matters. The main objectives are to provide statutory protection
for Natural Heritage Areas (NHAs); to enable the NHA mechanisms to provide
statutory protection for important geological and geomorphological sites,
including fossil sites, to enhance the conservation of wildlife species and their
habitats; to enhance controls in respect of hunting and introduce new powers
to regulate commercial shoot operators; to ensure or strengthen compliance
with international agreements and, in particular, enable ratification of the
Convention on International Trade in Endangered Species (CITES) and the
Agreement on the Conservation of African-Eurasian Migratory Waterbirds
Agreement (AEWA);to introduce substantial fines for contravention of the
Wildlife Acts 1976-2000 and introduce prison sentences in addition to those
fines; to enable the Minister to act independently of forestry legislation in
some matters such as the acquisition of land by agreement; to strengthen the
protective regime for Special Areas of Conservation (SACS) by ensuring that
protection will in all cases apply from the time of notification of proposed
sites and to give specific recognition of the Minister's responsibilities in regard
to promoting the conservation of biological diversity, in the context of Ireland's
commitment to the UN Convention on Biological Diversity.

If the Oireachtas was serious about ensuring protection for wildlife (and
the efficient delivery of legal services) it should have consolidated all wildlife
legislation. Instead it has enacted yet another statute which can only be

understood by referring to earlier legislation. No less than 47 of the 75 sections in the Wildlife (Amendment) Act 2000 are amending sections. This will confuse and frustrate people dealing with wildlife legislation and increase the transaction costs of implementing it.

JUDICIAL CASES

Waste Management   The decision on *Wheelbin Services Limited v. Kildare County Council*, High Court, December 21,1999 raised an interesting question relevant to waste management law. Section 33 o f the Waste Management Act 1996 obliges each local authority to collect, or arrange for the collection of, household waste within its functional area unless certain conditions specified in section 33 (2) and 33(6) apply. Section 33 (4) empowered, but did not oblige, local authorities to collect or arrange for the collection of waste other than household waste. The Act therefore gave local authorities discretion to place the burden of commercial and industrial waste collection and disposal wholly or partly with the private sector. Several local authorities have exercised this discretion with unseemly alacrity, notwithstanding the severe shortage of waste disposal and recovery facilities in the country and the practical difficulties in getting environmental authoritisation for them. The problem in this case arose because Kildare County Council, like many others, was running out of landfill capacity for waste. In order to conserve existing capacity at its only landfill, which was almost full, it decided to reduce the amount of commercial waste that it would accept there. Wheelbin, a commercial waste collector which used the Council's landfill, had its allocation reduced by 15%. This could be viewed as either an attempt by the Council to conserve landfill capacity and/or as an incentive to the commercial sector to devise better waste management practices than disposal to landfill which is the least preferred option for waste management in EC and Irish law. However the latter motivation could hardly have been uppermost in the Council's mind because no such reduction had apparently been imposed on the Council's own subcontractors who collected commercial waste.   Wheelbin sought an interlocutory injunction to prevent the Council from abusing its dominant position in the refuse business in Kildare contrary to section 5 of the Competition Act 1991. It argued that the Council, as the owner of the only landfill in Kildare, did not charge a landfill charge to its own customers and that it had therefore a competitive advantage over others in the waste business. The Council argued that they had a statutory obligation under section 33 of the Waste Management Act 1996 to collect most of the household waste in Kildare, that they were running out of landfill capacity and that they had arranged for the diversion of some of the plaintiff's waste from North Kildare to specialized waste disposal facilities in Dublin. Wheelbin however could not dispose of sewage sludges in Dublin because they had to be mixed with household waste in order to minimize environmental nuisances.

Although the Court (O'Caoimh J.) held that there was a fair issue to be tried, he refused the interlocutory injunction on the balance of convenience having regard to the fact that the Council had made some alternative arrangements for the Wheelbin.and that damages would adequately compensate it if it could be demonstrated at a full hearing that the refusal of access to the Kildare landfill was in breach of the Competition Act 1991. The learned judge also considered that to grant the plaintiff's claim would itself distort competition in North Kildare because the Council would be open to similar claims from other contactors competing with Wheelbin. If that happened, the Council would be unable to fulfill its obligations under the Waste Management Act 1996. This was a very pragmatic decision but it failed to address why the Council should be permitted to discriminate against private commercial waste collectors and it is surely not sufficient to say that several wrongs can make a right.

Habitats   *Murphy v Wicklow County Council .v Minister for Arts, Heritage, Gaeltacht and the Islands and the Minister for the Environment.* The decision in *Murphy v Wicklow County Council and the Minster for Arts, Culture, the Gaeltacht and the Islands*, Supreme Court December 13,1999 (only available in 2000) concerned an appeal against a High Court decision to refuse an interlocutory injunction preventing the construction of a motorway through the Glen of the Downs. Murphy alleged that Wicklow County Council (WCC) had not complied with Directive 92/43/EEC on the protection of natural habitats and of wild flora and fauna and the European Communities (Habitats) Regulations 1998 (S.I. No 23 of 1998) which purport to implement it.

The Glen of the Downs was a nature reserve that had been put on the Candidate List for designation as a Site of Community Importance and ultimately as a Special Area of Conservation (SAC) under the Habitats Regulations and Directive. . Murphy alleged that article 6 (3) of the Directive required that the proposals for road widening, being "a plan or project" should be subjected to an "appropriate assessment" of the implications for the site in view of the site's conservation objectives and that the EIS prepared *before* the site was selected as a Candidate SAC was not such an assessment.

An "appropriate assessment" was required for "operations and activities" in Candidate List sites under Regulation 14 of the Habitats Regulations 1997 but the definition of "operations and activities" in Regulation 2 excluded local authority developments. Murphy claimed that this exclusion of local authority development from Regulation 14was, *inter alia,* a failure to implement the Directive properly and that WCC was accordingly bound by article 6.3 of the Directive. WCC argued that the objectives of the requirement for an "appropriate assessment" were in substance achieved by the EIS lodged with the its application under Part 1X of the Local Government (Planning and Development) Regulations 1994 to the Minister for the Environment for permission to carry out the works. They relied on the decision in *Mc Bride v. Galway County Corporation* [1998] 1 I.R. 485. But Murphy considered that this EIS did not address the *European* importance of the site because it was submitted before the site was put on the Candidate List. While O'Sullivan J. in the High Court (December 13,1999) conceded that habitats legislation might be stricter than wildlife legislation as to what might constitute "an appropriate assessment", he refused leave to apply for judicial review because Murphy's application had not been made promptly. The effective date from which time began to run was the date of designation of the site as a proposed Special Area of Conservation. In a further (supplementary?) judgment on December 15, 1999, O'Sullivan J. refused to refer the case to the European Court of Justice under article 234 of the European Treaty because he had already determined the matter two days earlier and because he did not consider that a decision by the ECJ was necessary to enable him to make a judgment, a precondition for a reference to the ECJ under Article 234.

O'Sullivan J.'s decisions were appealed to the Supreme Court. Murray J. (Hamilton C.J., Keane, Murphy and Denham JJ. concurring) delivered judgment. The court held that the Glen of the Downs, not having been placed on the list at Community level, was not subject to article 6(3) of the Habitats Directive because article 4(5) of the Directive expressly provided that that a site should be subject to Article 6(3) "as soon as" it is placed on a list of sites of Community importance. (The European Commission designates sites of Community importance -usually from Candidate list sites- and it had not, or had not yet, selected the Glen o f the Downs as one). Consequently the Court held that under *European law*, the obligations in article 6(3) did not apply to the road-widening project. Neither did they apply under national law because of the exclusion of local authority development from the definition of "operations and activities". This was the only conclusion the Court could have arrived at because of the clear words of the Directive.

Article 6 obligations had been applied to many "operations and activities" as defined in Regulation 2 of the Habitats Regulations and excluding local authority developments) in Candidate list sites under Regulation 14 of those Regulations but this was because the Minister in purporting to implement the Directive had given sites governed by Regulation 14 a higher level of protection than the Directive required. The court held that she was entitled to do this as a matter of national policy. One must question this conclusion on the Minister's entitlement. The Habitats Regulations acquired their immunity from constitutional scrutiny in so far as they affect the constitutional rights of citizens because they were "necessitated" by the obligation to give effect to European law. The restrictions of property rights consequent on designation as a *Candidate list site, as distinct from a site of Community importance,* are clearly not necessitated by the obligations to give effect to European law (except perhaps where the site hosts a priority habitat or species- see below) and must therefore be constitutionally suspect. But this is by the way.

Murphy also argued that since the State was in breach of its obligation under the Directive to transmit the list of Candidate sites to the Commission by May 1995, it should not be allowed to profit from its own wrong and that the site in question should be treated as being subject to the obligations in the Habitats Directive. Similar arguments had succeeded before the European Court of Justice in *EC Commission v. Germany* (the *Leybucht* Case) [1991] 1 E.C.R. 883 and in *EC Commission v. Spain* [1993] E.C.R. 1-4221. After analysing the requirements for designation as a site of Community importance, Murray J. dismissed this argument concluding that there was no factual or material basis on which it could be determined at the date of judgment that the site in question would have been, or will be in the future be, adopted as a site of Community importance and become a designated site. This was the correct conclusion on the facts of the case because in *Leybucht*, Germany had conceded that the habitat concerned should have been designated as a Special Protected Area (SPA) under Council Directive 75/449/EEC on the conservation of wild birds and in *EC Commission v. Spain,* the Marismas de Santona were factually worthy of designation as a SPA and there was much independent and scientific evidence to this effect. This was not the case for the Glen Of the Downs.

The court also held that there was no need to refer the case to the European Court of Justice because the issues raised did not raise a question of interpretation of European law.

This was the second (*Dubski v. Drogheda Port Company*, Annual Review 1999, 208 was the first) of what may be predicted to be many cases on the Habitats Directive to reach the Supreme Court. The Habitats Regulations are seriously defective in the manner in which they implement the Directive, and despite being alerted to the many deficiencies in them, the Minister for Arts, Culture, the Gaeltach and the Islands has not yet reformed them except as indicated in the next paragraph.

Section 75 of the Wildlife (Amendment) Act 2000 now defines a Candidate list site notified to relevant parties under Regulation 4 of the Habitats Regulations, or a Candidate list site as amended under Regulation 5, as a European site thereby extending the protective regime for European sites in the Habitats Regulations to mere Candidate list sites. This means that a local authority carrying out development on a Candidate list site is now obliged under Regulation 29 of the Habitats Regulations to ensure that an appropriate assessment of the implications for the site in view of the site's conservation objectives is undertaken where it proposes to carry out development to which Part 1X of the Local Government (Planning and Development) Regulations 1994 applies. This amendment was probably motivated by a recognition that Candidate list sites *hosting priority habitats and species* ought to be subject to the obligations in Article 6(3) of the Directive. (See this argument in Scannell, Cannon, Clarke and Doyle, The *Habitats Directive in Ireland* (Centre for Environmental Law and Policy, 1999) at 91-3, 128) but it goes further than required by European law in protecting *all* Candidate list sites.

Equity

HILARY DELANY, Law School, Trinity College, Dublin

TRUSTS

Quistclose / Constructive Trusts   An issue in relation to whether a trust arose was considered by Carroll J. in a judgment dealing with the third of five issues ordered to be tried arising out of the liquidation of Money Markets International Stockbrokers Ltd in *In the Matter of Money Markets International Stockbrokers Ltd* delivered on October 20, 2000. The court was required to consider whether K. and H. Options Ltd should be entitled to claim a sum against client funds of MMI for option premia in respect of settled stock exchange transactions. Having made debit entries in the individual client's accounts, the money due to K. and H. Ltd was not always withdrawn from the general client account and in the period preceding the liquidation of MMI, money unpaid to K and H, which should have been withdrawn from the general client account, amounted to approximately £321, 620. MMI had a statutory obligation under the Stock Exchange Act 1995 to hold client's money in a section 52 account in an institution specified by the Central Bank. In her judgment on the first issue arising in the case, Laffoy J. had held that the meaning of section 52(7)(a) was that the beneficial claims of client creditors had to be satisfied before anyone else, even a contributor to the ultimate balance, had a call on the funds.

Counsel for K. and H. claimed that a trust had been created in its favour in the client account in respect of money for premia for completed stock exchange transactions and that it had a proprietary claim against these monies. He claimed that once allocated, the money belonged in equity to K. and H., although he conceded that in a mixed fund the company could not claim to be paid 100%. In support of this proposition he cited *Barclay's Bank Ltd v. Quistclose Investments Ltd* [1970] A.C. 507 and also referred to the decisions in *Carreras Rothman Ltd v. Freeman Matheus Treasure Ltd* [1985] Ch. 207 and *General Communications Ltd v. Development Finance Corporation of New Zealand Ltd* [1999] 3 N.Z.L.R. 406. Based on the principles set out in these cases, counsel on behalf of K. and H. claimed that the entry in the individual clients account by MMI crystallised K. and H.'s interest in the money. Alternatively, it was claimed that a constructive trust in favour of K. and H. arose on the basis that it would be inequitable to deny it as the clients were in debt to K. and H. and would be unjustly enriched if the company were put to the expense of suing individual clients. Counsel on behalf of the investors argued that K. and H. could not have a proprietary right in a fund where there were client investors who owed no money to K. and H. and that the company could not acquire such an interest in the fund as there was no specific fund identified and no properly constituted trust.

Referring to the earlier judgment of Laffoy J. in the case, Carroll J. stated that she did not think that the judgment went so far as to say that no person whatever could make a claim against the section 52 account until the client creditors were paid. However, if there were no trust in relation to the section 52 account monies, there was no basis for the claim made by K. and H. Carroll J. said that in her opinion the debit entry in an individual client account cannot be construed as a declaration of trust. None of the clients created any trust in favour of K. and H. and there was no separate fund designated for the payment of share premia, unlike in the cases referred to by counsel for K. and H. The money coming from the client account had to be paid to K. and H. or it remained client money; as Carroll J. stated 'no halfway house arrangement was possible'.

Carroll J. further held that it was not possible to impose a constructive trust on the grounds of unjust enrichment or any other equitable ground. The client creditors of MMI had the share premium payments deducted from their account before their net credit balance was calculated and they had already suffered a loss in respect of this as their contractual liability to pay K. and H. remained. Carroll J. concluded by saying that she was not suggesting that there are circumstances in which a person not named specifically in section 52 of the Act of 1995 can make a claim against an individual client account in a section 52 account and that she proposed to leave that question for a case where there was a basis for making a claim against the beneficial interest of a client creditor.

The relationship between trustees and beneficiaries   An interesting issue relevant to the relationship between trustees and beneficiaries in relation to management of trust property arose in *Bank of Ireland v. Gleeson*, Supreme Court, April 6, 2000 although in the circumstances the court had to decline to answer the issues raised in a special summons which had sought directions from the High Court as to whether the applicant bank ought to have proceeded to complete a contract entered into by it as trustee against the will of the beneficiaries, represented by the respondent. The respondent had objected to the completion of the sale on the basis that the ground rents legislation did not apply to the property in question and contended that accordingly the bank was not obliged to sell it to the Commissioners of Public Works at a price calculated in accordance with that legislation. Murphy J. observed that the view put forward by the respondent had the support of certain observations made by O'Flaherty J. in *Metropolitan Properties Ltd v. O'Brien* [1995] 2 I.L.R.M. 383 and said that the respondent claimed that the sale of the property by the bank would involve it in a breach of trust. Having regard to the objections raised by the respondent beneficiary, the bank instituted proceedings by way of special summons seeking the directions of the High Court. Murphy J. stated that the answer to the question posed in the special summons depended essentially on the question of whether the contract for sale was enforceable by the Commissioners against the bank. If the bank was bound by the contract and neglected to perform it, liability and costs would be incurred which would obviously be detrimental to the interests of the beneficiaries. However, as Murphy J. pointed out, the question of whether the bank as trustee was bound by an obligation apparently imposed upon it by the contract for sale was a matter which could only be resolved in proceedings between the bank and the Commissioners. As those parties were not before the court, the issue could not be determined and until it was, it was impossible for the Supreme Court to express any opinion about the obligations of the trustee to the beneficiaries under the settlement in relation to the sale of the premises. In these circumstances Murphy J. stated that Morris P. had been entirely correct in declining to answer the question posed in the special summons.

EQUITABLE REMEDIES

Interlocutory injunctions   There have been a number of decisions delivered over the past year dealing with applications for interlocutory injunctions and in general the courts have tended to apply established principles. Two of these cases related to disputes which arose in an employment context and in the first, *Philpott v. O'Gilvy and Mather Ltd*, High Court, Murphy J., March 21, 2000 the plaintiff sought an injunction restraining the defendant from giving effect to his purported dismissal from his post as creative director of the defendant advertising agency. Counsel for the defendant relied on the decision of the Supreme Court in *Parson v. Iarnrod Éireann* [1997] E.L.R. 203 as a ground for dismissing the application in which it had been held that employees must choose between suing at common law and claiming relief under the Unfair Dismissals Act. In addition, the Supreme Court had held that the traditional relief at common law in such cases was a claim for damages and that any declarations sought would be in aid of the common law remedy and had no independent existence apart from such a claim. While in the case before the court the plaintiff had not sought to pursue a remedy under the Unfair Dismissals Act, Roderick Murphy J. expressed the view that the *Parson* decision was relevant in so far as the pleadings were concerned. He stated that if the traditional relief at common law for unfair dismissal was a claim for damages then the plaintiff might also have been entitled to declarations and injunctions in aid of his common law remedy but if such equitable relief had no independent existence apart from the claim for damages for wrongful dismissal then it seemed that there was no other free standing relief which could be claimed at law or in equity. In these circumstances, Murphy J. concluded that the plaintiff was not entitled to the relief claimed.

In *Howard v. University College Cork*, High Court, O'Donovan J., July 25, 2000 the High Court considered an application made by the plaintiff for interlocutory injunctions restraining the defendant from taking any steps to remove her from her post as head of the Department of German at University College Cork or from appointing a person other than the plaintiff to the post. O'Donovan J. referred to the decision of the Supreme Court in *Campus Oil Ltd v. Minister for Industry and Energy* [1983] I.R. 88 and said that all he was required to consider was whether there was a fair question to be tried, not whether there was a probability that the plaintiff would succeed on any particular issue. He concluded that there were fair questions to the tried, first as to whether the defendant was obliged to observe fair procedures when considering the determination of the plaintiff's role as head of department, and secondly, whether the plaintiff had legitimate complaints in relation to the defendant's investigation of allegations of impropriety which had been made against her. In relation to the adequacy of damages, O'Donovan J. made reference to the fact that if the relief were granted at the interlocutory stage and it was subsequently determined that the decision was unlawful, it would be extremely difficult if not impossible for a trial judge to assess a sum for damages which would adequately compensate the plaintiff for the injury to her reputation. In assessing where the balance of convenience lay, O'Donovan J. acknowledged that there was considerable unrest within the department, but expressed the view that appointing a new head at this stage in the proceedings was likely to create greater difficulties and could place an 'intolerable burden' on the trial judge. In these circumstances, O'Donovan J. concluded that the balance of convenience demanded that the status quo be maintained and he rejected the submission made by the defendant that granting the interlocutory relief would cause the college irreparable harm.

Similar principles were applied the High Court, albeit with a different result, in *Wright v. Board of Management of Gorey Community School*, High Court, O'Sullivan J., March 28, 2000 in which the plaintiff schoolboys, who had been suspended on the grounds of allegations relating to the use of drugs, sought reinstatement in their school until the trial of the action in proceedings in which they claimed that unfair procedures had been adopted against them which involved a breach of their constitutional right to education. Having regard to the fact that there was room for argument that the charges and details of the evidence on which they were based only became known to the boys and their parents in the course of proceedings before the school board, O'Sullivan J. stated that he was prepared to accept that a fair question arose to be dealt with at the trial. He then moved to consider where the balance of convenience lay, noting that this was clearly a case where damages would not be an adequate remedy on either side. The plaintiffs submitted that unless they could return to school, they might be left without education as there was no guarantee that another school would take them in and the defendant contended that it was essential, given the importance of maintaining discipline, that the plaintiffs should not be permitted to return to school pending determination of the issues. O'Sullivan J concluded that the balance of convenience clearly favoured the refusal of the plaintiffs' reinstatement and made reference to the enormous damage which would be done to the authority and policy of the school if he were to allow the suspension to be lifted and the plaintiffs subsequently lost their action. On the other hand if he refused the interlocutory relief sought by the plaintiffs, they would in all probability have access to appropriate alternative schooling pending the trial. In these circumstances, O'Sullivan J. decided to refuse the interlocutory injunction sought.

Established principles relating to interlocutory injunctions were also applied by the High Court in *Eircell Ltd v. Bernstoff,* High Court, Barr J., February 18, 2000 which concerned a dispute between the plaintiff and a group of local people in relation to the erection of a mobile phone mast. The defendants sought relief restraining the plaintiff from continuing with the erection of the mast and the plaintiff sought an interlocutory injunction restraining the defendants from interfering with the plaintiff's use and enjoyment of the site of the mast. In relation to the first issue, Barr J. held that the defendants were not entitled to the relief claimed pursuant to section 27 of the Local Government (Planning and Development) Act 1963. As regards the plaintiff's claim, Barr J. was satisfied that there was sufficient evidence before the court in relation to the controversy about a right of way to establish that there was a fair issue to be tried. In assessing where the balance of convenience lay, Barr J. had regard to a number of factors, including the adequacy of damages and the conduct of the parties. Barr J. suggested that damages would not constitute an adequate remedy from the plaintiff's point of view if it suffered an on-going loss of business and on the other hand he was of the view that no significant relevant loss would be suffered by the defendants pending the trial. In addition, in his opinion it was proper for him to take into account the 'reprehensible' conduct of the defendants in seeking to intimidate other persons and conversely, the 'fair and reasonable behaviour' of the plaintiff and its agents. In these circumstances, Barr J. was satisfied that the balance of convenience favoured the granting of the relief sought by the plaintiff and that it should be permitted to activate the mast as part of it mobile phone network.

Another example of the application of the *Campus Oil* principles is the decision of the High Court in *Local Ireland Ltd v. Local Ireland-Online Ltd.,* High Court, Herbert J., October 2, 2000 which concerned a claim in relation to alleged passing off. Herbert J. made reference to the fact that despite the suggestion by counsel for both sides that the outcome of the application for interlocutory relief was likely to determine the dispute there was no agreement to treat the hearing of the motion as the trial of the action and in these circumstances, having regard to the *Campus Oil* principles, he was not entitled to inquire into the merits of the case or to consider the probabilities of success of any party at the trial of the action. Provided the plaintiffs had shown to the satisfaction of the court that there was a fair *bona fide* question to be tried between the parties and that the continuance of the defendants' activities until the trial of the action was likely to cause substantial injury for which a subsequent award of damages would not be adequate compensation, Herbert J. stated that he was obliged to determine the application solely on the balance of convenience.

Having considered the evidence, Herbert J. stated that the plaintiffs had made out a *bona fide* case to be tried in a number of respects and he was further satisfied that damages would not be an adequate remedy for either party. He therefore had to consider whether on the facts of the particular case, the damage suffered by the plaintiffs should the court decline to make the order sought would on the balance of probability be greater than the damages suffered by the defendants should the court grant the interlocutory relief. In this regard he noted the fact that the defendants would not be excluded from the market in the relevant services should the court grant such relief and that they would be at liberty to continue to offer these services under a new business and domain name. Herbert J. also made reference to the fact that there was no doubt about the value of any undertaking in damages which the plaintiffs might make whereas there was no evidence which would enable to the court to conclude that the defendants had a similar ability to meet a future award of damages against them. In the circumstances, Herbert J. concluded that the balance of convenience clearly lay in granting rather than refusing the injunctive relief sought by the plaintiffs.

A case in which a mandatory interlocutory injunction was sought is *Downey v. Minister for Education and Science*, High Court, Smyth J., October 26, 2000 in which the plaintiff minor, who had been diagnosed as autistic, sought finance to enable his next friend and father provide for primary education suitable to his needs. It was submitted on behalf of the plaintiff that the decisions in *O'Donoghue v. Minister for Health* [1996] 2 I.R. 20 and *Sinnott v. Minister for Education*, October 4, 2000 had established a constitutional obligation on the part of the State to provide for free basic elementary education for all children as would enable them to make the best possible use of their inherent and potential capabilities and that the State therefore had an obligation towards the plaintiff in this respect. It was contended on behalf of the defendant that '*prima facie* you do not obtain injunctions to restrain actionable wrongs for which damages are a proper remedy' (*per* Lindley L.J. in *London and Blackwell Railway Co. v. Cross* (1886) 31 Ch. D. 354, 369) and that this was a case in which an injunction was not a suitable remedy. Counsel for the plaintiff argued in reply that the court can and does in appropriate cases oblige a defendant to make payments to a plaintiff pending resolution of a case and referred to *Courtney v. Radio 2000 Ltd* [1997] E.L.R. 198. Smyth J. commented that the *O'Donoghue* and *Sinnott* cases were clearly distinguishable on the facts and did not necessarily conclude the issue of liability in the case before him. He also stated that the *Courtney* case was one in which a contractual right stated to have been infringed left the complainant without a means of livelihood and that it could also clearly be distinguished from the case before him. Smyth J. concluded that he had considered the balance of convenience and that in his view damages and not an injunction were 'at the fulcrum of the motion' and he refused the relief sought.

A final case in which the principles relating to the grant of mandatory interlocutory injunctions were considered is *de Burca v. Wicklow County Council*, High Court, Ó Caoimh J., May 24, 2000. The background to the application before the court was that the applicant had been granted leave to apply for judicial review to seek various relief relating to obligations on the part of the local authority in respect of the collection and management of domestic waste. The applicant sought relief in the form of a mandatory interlocutory injunction to oblige the respondent to continue to collect domestic waste pending the resolution of the action. It was argued on behalf of the respondent that the applicant had failed to establish that there was a fair issue to be tried or that the balance of convenience favoured the granting of an injunction. Counsel on behalf of the respondent submitted that in so far as the relief sought was a mandatory order it must be possible to specify with a sufficient degree of particularly precisely what action was required to comply with its terms. In addition, counsel referred to a number of authorities which suggested that where an interlocutory injunction of a mandatory nature is sought the case has to be unusually strong and clear. Ó Caoimh J. stated that he would apply the appropriate test set out by the Supreme Court in *Campus Oil* and expressed the opinion that the applicant had raised a fair question to be tried. However, he added that he was inclined to accept the view expressed by Murphy J. in *Bula Ltd v. Tara Mines Ltd* to the effect that he would be reluctant to hold that the granting or withholding of a mandatory injunction at the interlocutory stage should be related to the strength of the applicant's case as it was difficult to make any real assessment of the strength of a case at this stage in the proceedings. Ó Caoimh J. made reference to the fact that the applicant had failed to demonstrate that at a personal level she had been deprived of a waste collection service and that no alternative was available to her. He therefore concluded that the balance of convenience favoured the respondent and that interlocutory relief should be refused.

Mareva injunctions   A 'Mareva' injunction may be granted to prevent a defendant from removing assets from the jurisdiction or from disposing of them within the jurisdiction in a manner likely to frustrate the plaintiff's proceedings. However, where such an injunction has been granted, an application may be brought on a defendant's behalf to have the order varied to allow certain payments to be made, as happened in *Criminal Assets Bureau v. S.H.*, High Court, O'Sullivan J., March 15, 2000. The defendants sought an order varying the terms of the Mareva injunction to allow for payment out of monies required for a business run by the second named defendant, for accountants' fees to challenge the plaintiff's tax assessment, for legal costs involved in the proceedings before the court and to pay for goods purchased by the first named defendant after the Mareva injunction had been made. In relation to the first item, O'Sullivan J. stated that he was prepared to accede to the defendants' request to vary the injunction subject to a stipulation that the defendants should present an invoice for the amount required to the plaintiff's solicitors or its agent and that payment be made with the approval and under the supervision of its agent. In addition, O'Sullivan J. was prepared to vary the injunction made to allow payment of legal expenses taxed on a solicitor and client basis. However, he expressed the view that the part of the application dealing with accountants' fees was 'quite unsatisfactory' and he refused the application to vary the terms of the order to meet that claim and the amount sought in relation to goods purchased by the first named defendant.

Anton Piller orders   'Anton Piller' orders were developed as a means of dealing with cases where there is a serious risk that a defendant may destroy or otherwise dispose of material in his possession which may be of vital importance to the plaintiff if he is to establish his claim at a trial. An Anton Piller order requires the defendant to consent to a plaintiff, attended by his solicitor, entering his premises to inspect and if necessary take away any documents or articles specified in the order. Such an order is obtained on an *ex parte* basis and applications are often heard *in camera* as secrecy will be of the essence if the order is to have the required effect and if the defendant is forewarned he will in all likelihood take steps to frustrate the plaintiff's intentions. A number of aspects relating to such orders have recently been considered by the High Court in *Microsoft Corporation v. Brightpoint Ireland Ltd* [2001] 1 I.L.R.M. 481.

The plaintiff companies which carried on the business of software development and production claimed that they were the creators of specific computer software programmes which were entitled to the protection of the Copyright Act 1963 as amended and the Intellectual Property (Miscellaneous Provisions) Act 1998. The plaintiffs brought the action not only on their own behalf but also on behalf of the Business Software Alliance. The plaintiffs contended that the defendant company, which distributed and secured telephones, had infringed its legal rights and specifically alleged that the company had engaged in the unlawful copying, use, distribution, possession and networking of its software programmes. On June 2, 2000, Quirke J. granted the plaintiffs interim injunctive relief and made an Anton Piller order in their favour requiring the defendants to deliver up all infringing copies of computer programmes and other items and to allow the plaintiffs' representatives to enter their premises for the purpose of inspecting and preserving software and documents. The order was executed at the defendants' premises that evening and the defendant subsequently brought a motion seeking wide ranging reliefs while the plaintiff sought interlocutory relief following upon the interim relief already granted. Smyth J. commented that the essence of an Anton Piller order is surprise and that the publication of the existence of such an order in advance of its execution could weaken or deprive it of its element of surprise. The case law and in particular the decision in *Columbia Picture Industries Inc. v. Robinson* [1986] 3 All E.R. 338 supported the view that an affidavit in support of the application for the order ought to err on the side of excessive disclosure because in the case of material which falls into the area of possible relevance, the judge and not the plaintiff should decide what is relevant. However, on the facts Smyth J. was satisfied that there had been full and proper disclosure as to the circumstances of the case and that there was strong *prima facie* evidence of dishonest conduct by the defendants which indicated a strong probability that they would be likely to destroy records.

In relation to the defendant's argument that the Anton Piller order was oppressively and excessively executed, Smyth J. stated that the conflict of evidence as to what had happened in the course of its execution could only be resolved by an oral hearing and that he was not disposed to setting the order aside given this conflict. The defendant also contended that the plaintiffs through their agents had failed to advise the defendant as to its right against self-incrimination, but given the assertion made on the defendant's behalf that the company was complying with the law, the issue of self-incrimination could not arise and Smyth J. found that this was not a basis for setting aside the Anton Piller order. A further point was raised in relation to whether the plaintiff should be required to provide a list of the items and documents seized. Smyth J. commented that while it might have been a sensible thing at the time of the inspection for an agreed list or inventory of the items taken to have been made and signed, there was no obligation on the plaintiffs to provide a list as requested by the defendant. However, he said that as there was an obligation to preserve all copies taken under the Anton Piller order, the furnishing of a list was a courtesy which should have been accorded. In this regard Smyth J. stated that the law on this issue was properly put by Scott J. in *Columbia Picture Industries Inc. v. Robinson* where the latter had stated that it is essential that a detailed record of the material taken should be made by a solicitor executing an Anton Piller order before the material is removed from the premises. Smyth J. concluded on the basis of the documentary evidence before him that the making of the Anton Piller order was justified and that the subsequent conduct in the case was not such as could be regarded as contemptuous or as to warrant the relief sought by the defendant. He therefore dismissed the defendant's motion and granted the relief sought by the plaintiff, also directing that until the final determination of the action neither party should make any communication in the media of the matters at issue.

Undue influence   Gifts or agreements concluded on a voluntary basis or on the basis of wholly inadequate consideration are liable to be set aside in equity where they have been given or made as a result of the exercise of undue influence over the donor or party of whom advantage has been taken. In addition, a gift or transfer may be deemed to be improvident because of the circumstances in which it was made and may be liable to be set aside on that basis. These issues were considered by the High Court in *Moyles v. Mahon*, High Court, Smyth J., October 6, 2000 in which an elderly plaintiff sought to have a voluntary transfer of 11 acres of land to his daughter, the defendant, set aside on the grounds of undue influence and on the basis of claims that the transaction was an improvident one. The evidence was that the plaintiff and the defendant, with whom he was living at the time, had visited the former's solicitor who gave advice to the plaintiff in relation to the proposed transaction, which the court was satisfied was of an independent character. The solicitor suggested to the plaintiff that as the transaction was a voluntary conveyance, he should obtain further legal advice and another solicitor spoke to the plaintiff alone and satisfied himself that the plaintiff was aware of what he was doing. Another solicitor who also acted for the plaintiff gave evidence that she was satisfied that the plaintiff understood the nature of the transaction and wanted to proceed with it and Smyth J. stated that he found as a fact that the decision to proceed was 'a free act of the plaintiff'. It was submitted on behalf of the plaintiff that there was a presumption of undue influence and that the nature and quality of the legal advice had been deficient. However, it was contended on the defendant's behalf that the principles set out by the court in *McCormack v. Bennett* (1973) ILT 127 applied and that the legal advice given had been quite adequate and sufficient. Having considered the evidence, Smyth J. concluded that the deeds in question had not been executed as a result of undue influence and that the plaintiff had not been suffering from any mental or physical infirmity at the time, which prevented him from understanding the nature and consequences of the deed. In addition, he was satisfied that the plaintiff had had the benefit of independent legal advice. While Smyth J. expressed the view that the deeds were on their face improvident because the plaintiff had disposed of his interest in the property without valuable consideration, he was also satisfied that the plaintiff had exercised a spontaneous act of free will. He was satisfied that the plaintiff had not been susceptible to influence and that while at the time of the execution of the deeds he might have been in a vulnerable position, he had shown himself to be determined and resilient. In these circumstances, Smyth J. was satisfied that the plaintiff's claim had not been established.

Evidence

DECLAN McGRATH, Trinity College Dublin

BURDEN OF PROOF

Discharging the Burden of Proof Whether the prosecution has discharged the legal burden upon it to prove the guilt of the accused beyond a reasonable doubt is decided by the tribunal of fact at the end of the case after both parties have adduced evidence. It necessarily follows that this decision will be based upon all the evidence adduced in the case, including that adduced by the defendant and this was confirmed in *People (DPP) v. Byrne*, Court of Criminal Appeal, June 7, 2000.

One of the grounds of appeal of the applicant against his conviction for handling stolen goods was that the trial judge should have told the jury that the evidence adduced on behalf of the defence should only be considered if, having first considered the evidence on behalf of the prosecution, they were satisfied that it pointed to the guilt of the applicant beyond a reasonable doubt. The Court of Criminal Appeal was, however, satisfied that there was no substance to this ground of appeal. It said that the jury were entitled to, and indeed bound to, consider all the evidence in the case and not merely the evidence adduced on behalf of the prosecution for the purpose of determining whether it had discharged the burden upon it of establishing the guilt of the accused beyond a reasonable doubt.

Identification of the accused A straightforward application of the principle that the prosecution bears the burden of proving every fact essential to its case (*see AG (McLoughlin) v. Rhatigan* (1966) 100 I.L.T.R. 37 and *Woolmington v. DPP* [1935] A.C. 462, [1935] All E.R. 1) can be seen in *DPP v. Crimmins*, High Court, Ó Caoimh J., June 8, 2000.

The accused, who had been charged in the District Court with a charge of assault contrary to section 2 of the Non-Fatal Offences Against the Person Act 1997 failed to turn up at the hearing and a case was stated by the District Judge as to whether she could convict an accused of a criminal offence if the accused was not physically present or formally identified in court as being the offender. Ó Caoimh J. emphasised that it was only if the District Judge was satisfied that all essential elements of the offence charged had been proved beyond a reasonable doubt that she could proceed to convict the accused. Thus, if the District Court heard evidence satisfying it beyond all reasonable doubt that the injured party was assaulted in accordance with the charge against the accused and that the assault was perpetrated by the accused, it could proceed to convict the accused. The learned judge went on to clarify that if a trial in the District Court proceeded in the absence of an accused, the same essential proofs needed to be satisfied by the prosecution as where the accused was present. Hence, if the accused was not identified physically, the Court would have to be otherwise satisfied that the evidence related to the accused and that the evidence was such as to prove his guilt beyond all reasonable doubt. Turning to the facts of the instant case, he held that if the District Judge was satisfied that the accused was known to the injured party (or any other witness) at the time of the alleged offence, and evidence was given by the injured party or some other witness showing that the accused had committed the assault alleged, then the Court could proceed to convict the accused notwithstanding the fact that there had not been any physical identification of the accused in court.

Section 4(2) of the Criminal Justice Act 1964 Section 4 of the Criminal Justice Act 1964 deals with the intention required for murder and subsection (2) contains a presumption to the effect that: "the accused person shall be presumed to have intended the natural and probable consequences of his conduct; but this presumption may be rebutted". Although it has been suggested that this subsection could be construed as placing a legal burden on the accused to rebut this presumption on a balance of probabilities (see O'Higgins & O'Braonáin (1991) 1 ICLJ 113 and (1992) 2 ICLJ 179), it was held in *People (AG) v. Dwyer* [1972] I.R. 416 and *People (DPP) v. Murray* [1977] I.R. 360 that it merely places an evidential burden on the accused and that the onus of proving, beyond a reasonable doubt, that the presumption had not been rebutted is on the prosecution.

In *People (DPP) v. Cotter*, Court of Criminal Appeal, June 28, 1999, one of the grounds on which the applicant sought leave to appeal against her conviction for murder was that the trial judge had suggested in his charge that an onus lay on the applicant to rebut the presumption in section 4(2) on a balance of probabilities. The Court was satisfied that the trial judge had erred in this regard even though he had recharged the jury in response to a requisition, making it clear to them that the prosecution bore the burden of proving the guilt of the accused beyond a reasonable doubt and that no onus rested on the applicant. The Court pointed out that this redirection was divorced from the recitation of the facts of the case whereas the erroneous directions had been given in the context of the facts and it was, therefore, of the view that these were likely to have weighed more heavily in the jury's minds than the redirection. Accordingly, the Court concluded that the conviction was unsafe and proceeded to quash it.

The Court took the opportunity to express its appreciation of the difficulties in properly charging a jury as to the application and effect of the presumption contained section 4(2). It acknowledged that, no matter what form of direction is adopted, it more often than not gives rise to an awkwardness of expression which the trial judge must be careful to ensure does not lead to confusion.

Nevertheless, while accepting that it was not possible to lay down any hard and fast formula, it proceeded to suggest the following model direction:

> If you are satisfied beyond a reasonable doubt that the presumption of intending the natural and probable consequences of conduct has not been rebutted then that presumption applies and you may convict of murder. If, however, you are not so satisfied, then you must have a reasonable doubt as to whether or not the presumption applies and you should acquit of murder. There is no onus on the accused to establish anything. You must consider all the evidence including that of the accused and you ask yourselves has the prosecution satisfied you beyond a reasonable doubt that the presumption has not been rebutted and therefore applies and depending on your answer you proceed accordingly to convict or acquit of murder.

Whether this direction will actually elucidate the presumption for the average juror must be a matter of some doubt.

Summing up The decision in *People (DPP) v. Cremin*, Court of Criminal Appeal, ex tempore, May 10, 1999, illustrates once again the ease with which a trial judge may fall into err if he or she attempts to elucidate the concept of a reasonable doubt when summing up to the jury. The trial judge had directed the jury that the onus was on the prosecution to prove the guilt of the accused and that the onus never shifted onto the accused. However, he then went on to say that this did not mean that doubt on any one matter entitled the accused to be acquitted. The Court of Criminal Appeal thought it probable that what the trial judge meant to convey was that doubt on a peripheral matter, a matter which is not in any sense an essential ingredient in the charge, would not prevent the jury from arriving at a verdict of guilty. However, this was not what he had said and his charge in this regard was capable of leaving the jury under the mistaken impression that a doubt, even in respect of an essential aspect of the case, would not entitle the accused to an acquittal. This of course was clearly erroneous and departed from the model charge laid down in *People (AG) v. Byrne* [1974] I.R. 1 where it was stressed that the jury should be told that "the accused is entitled to the benefit of the doubt and that when two views on any part of the case are possible on the evidence, they should adopt that which is favourable to the accused unless the State has established the other beyond a reasonable doubt".

This misdirection was of some significance in the instant case given that the facts were not simple or straightforward and the jury had been presented with totally conflicting versions of what had happened. It was also compounded by the failure of the trial judge in dealing with the issue of self-defence to make it clear that the burden of proof remained at all times on the prosecution to satisfy the jury beyond a reasonable doubt that the accused was not entitled to be acquitted on the grounds of self-defence (see *People (AG) v. Quinn* [1965] I.R. 366). In the circumstances, the Court quashed the conviction and ordered a retrial.

Duress   It is well established that an accused bears an evidential burden to raise the defence of self-defence but, once this burden is discharged, the legal burden of proving beyond a reasonable doubt that the accused did not act in self-defence devolves upon the prosecution (see *People (AG) v. Quinn* [1965] I.R. 366 and *People (AG) v. Byrne* [1974] I.R. 1). The decision of the Court of Criminal Appeal in *People (DPP) v. Kavanagh*, Court of Criminal Appeal, May 18, 1999 confirms that the same principles apply to the affirmative defence of duress.

In *Kavanagh*, the central ground of appeal advanced by the appellant against his conviction by the Special Criminal Court for various offences arising out of the false imprisonment of the former Chief Executive of National Irish Bank, Mr James Lacey, was that the Court had misapplied the law in relation to his defence of duress. He contended, firstly, that the Court had erred in failing to accede to the application made to it for a direction at the end of the prosecution case. However, the Court was satisfied that the Special Criminal Court had correctly applied the principles laid down by the English Court of Appeal in *R v. Galbraith* [1981] 2 All E.R. 1060, [1981] 1 W.L.R. 1039 in relation to applications for directions. It, therefore, proceeded to consider the alternative submission that the Special Criminal Court had mis-directed itself at the conclusion of the case as to the incidence of the burden of proof in relation to the defence of duress.

In dealing with this contention, the Court began by endorsing the following passage from Archbold, *Pleading, Evidence and Practice in Civil Cases* (36th Edition), p.21, as a correct statement of the law:

> Where a defence of duress is relied on, the defendant, either by cross-examination of the witnesses for the prosecution or the evidence called on his behalf or by a combination of the two, must place before the Court such material as makes the issue fit and proper to be left to the jury. The evidential burden is therefore on the defendant. Once, however, he has succeeded in doing this the ultimate or persuasive burden is on the Crown to destroy the defence in such a manner as to leave in the minds of the jury no reasonable doubt on the question whether the defendant can be absolved on the grounds of the alleged compulsion.

The appellant sought to rely on a number of passages in the judgment of the Special Criminal Court which, it was contended, suggested that there was a burden on the accused to substantiate his defence of duress. However, the Court said that it was clear from the judgment of the Special Criminal Court that, having examined all the evidence and correctly applied the law, it had been satisfied that the appellant had not been acting under duress and that the facts which he asserted as constituting duress were simply untrue.

Provocation   In *People (DPP) v. Davis*, Court of Criminal Appeal, 23 October 2000, the law in relation to provocation was re-stated by the Court. It emphasised that an accused bears an evidential burden to raise the defence and that the issue of provocation will not, automatically, be left to the jury simply because it is asserted:

> We entirely accept that the burden on the defendant is not a heavy one but it necessarily involves being able to point to evidence of some sort suggesting the presence of all the elements of provocation…the burden which rests with the accused is to produce or indicate evidence suggesting the presence of the various elements of the defence. This can be produced either through direct evidence or by inference on the evidence as a whole, but before leaving the issue to a jury the judge must satisfy himself that an issue of substance, as distinct from a contrived issue, or a vague possibility, has been raised.

The Court went on to state that the determination of this preliminary issue as to whether there is sufficient evidence of the defence such that the issue can be left to the jury is one to be determined by the trial judge on the basis of an assessment of the evidence. In making this determination, the trial judge has to bear in mind that questions as to the credibility of evidence, as opposed to its existence, are for the jury and not for him. He or she also has to bear in mind that, before provocation becomes an issue in the case fit to be left to the jury's determination, there must be evidence (direct or inferential) suggesting the presence of all the elements required for the defence. In this regard, it was suggested that a useful approach might be for the judge to consider whether or not a jury would be perverse in finding, on the evidence available, that there had been provocation available. In the instant case, the Court was of the view that the evidence fell far short of meeting the requirements for permitting the issue of provocation to go to the jury.

The placing of an evidential burden on an accused to raise any affirmative defence which goes beyond a mere denial of the prosecution case (see *DPP v. Collins* [1981] I.L.R.M. 447) is designed to act as a filter to prevent unmeritorious defences being raised and put to the jury leading to unjustified acquittals. Traditionally, the courts have taken quite a generous approach towards determining whether an accused has satisfied this evidential burden and it has not proved to be a difficult threshold to meet. For example, in *People (DPP) v. Clarke* [1995] 1 I.L.R.M. 355 (Annual Review 1994, 169), O'Hanlon J. left the issue of self-defence to the jury even though he was of the view that it was only theoretically open to the jury to acquit the accused on this ground. The decision in *Davis* may, therefore, be of some significance insofar as it seems to indicate that a trial judge should engage in a more stringent appraisal than may have been previously the case of whether an accused has actually adduced evidence which satisfies the elements of the affirmative defence and raises it in a substantive way.

Standard of proof In *People (DPP) v. Cotter*, Court of Criminal Appeal, June 28, 1999, issue was also taken on appeal with regard to a passage in the trial judge's charge wherein he disagreed with the proposition, stated in the closing address of counsel for the defence, that the standard of proof which had to be met by the prosecution in the case was one of moral certitude. The trial judge corrected what he considered to be mis-statement of the law and, in his summing up, instructed the jury that what was required was something short of a mathematical or moral certainty and that the appropriate standard of proof to which they had to be satisfied was proof beyond a reasonable doubt.

The Court of Criminal Appeal was satisfied that the trial judge had been quite entitled to reject the concept of moral certitude as the appropriate standard of proof and to insist instead on the well-established standard of beyond a reasonable doubt. In doing so, the Court once again confirmed its strong preference for instructing the jury in terms of what Kenny J. in *People (AG) v. Byrne* [1974] I.R. 1 described as the "time-honoured formula" of telling the jury that the prosecution has to prove the guilt of an accused beyond a reasonable doubt.

EXAMINATION OF WITNESSES

Complaints in sexual cases The definitive statement in relation to the admission and use of complaints in sexual cases is to be found in *People (DPP) v. Brophy* [1992] I.L.R.M. 709 (Annual Review 1992, 252) where the Court of Criminal Appeal distilled the following propositions from the authorities:

(a) Complaints may only be proved in criminal prosecutions for a sexual offence.

(b) The complaint must have been made as speedily as could reasonably be expected and in a voluntary fashion, not as a result of any inducements or exhortations. Once evidence of the making of a complaint is admissible then particulars of the complaint may also be proved.

(c) It should always be made clear to the jury that such evidence is not evidence of the facts on which the complaint is based but to show that the victim's conduct in so complaining was consistent with her testimony.

(d) While there is mention in one of the older cases, *R v. Osborne* [1905] 1 K.B. 551, of a complaint being 'corroborative of the complainant's credibility' this does not mean that such a complaint amounts to corroboration of her testimony in the legal sense of that term but as pointing to the consistency of her testimony. Corroboration in the strict sense involves independent evidence that is evidence other than the complainant's evidence.

The application of these principles was considered by the Court of Criminal Appeal in a number of decisions in 2000.

In *People (DPP) v. Gavin*, Court of Criminal Appeal, July 27, 2000, the appellant had been convicted of sexual assault and one of his grounds of appeal related to the admission of a complaint made to a garda who had arrived shortly after the alleged assault. The garda gave evidence that the complainant had told him that he had awoken to find the appellant in his bed with his hand on the complainant's groin. However, at no point in his testimony had the complainant made any reference to an assault of this nature.

McGuinness J, delivering the judgment of the Court, stated that it was clear from the exposition of the law in *Brophy* that the purpose of admitting evidence of a complaint is to demonstrate consistency on the part of the complainant, i.e. that he or she gave the same account in the immediate aftermath of the incident complained of as was given in evidence at the trial. In the instant case, she was of the view the complaint which had been admitted did not meet this primary criterion because there were crucial differences between the terms of the complaint and the testimony of the complainant at the trial. She rejected, in that regard, the contention made by the prosecution that there was sufficient consistency in that both descriptions were of sexual assaults.

Furthermore, it was held that the trial judge had erred in directing the jury as to the use which could be made of the complaint. He drew their attention to the inconsistency between the complaint and the testimony of the complainant and stated that this was a conflict of fact which the jury had to reconcile. However, it was clear from the decision in *Brophy* that the complaint itself was not evidence of the truth of its contents and that this should have been made clear to the jury. Furthermore, the trial judge had failed to make it clear to the jury that the complaint did not amount to corroboration. The Court, therefore, allowed the appeal and quashed the conviction of the appellant.

An issue as to the consistency of a complaint with the testimony of the complainant was also raised in *People (DPP) v. Jethi*, Court of Criminal Appeal, *ex tempore*, February 7, 2000 but a different conclusion was reached on the facts. The applicants had been convicted of assault and sexual assault and one of the points raised on appeal was that the complaint made to a friend of the complainant the day after the alleged assault was not in identical terms with the evidence which she gave at the trial. The precise nature of the inconsistencies is not apparent from the judgment but they were characterised by the Court as minor in nature and explicable upon the basis of faulty recollection. Barrington J. stated that the primary significance of a complaint is that it indicates that the rape or sexual assault complained of was something to which the complainant did not consent. In the instant case, the principal issue before the jury was that of consent and, although the complainant may have been hazy in her recollection about peripheral matters, on the central fact that she had been assaulted against her will, she was perfectly clear. The trial judge had drawn to the attention of the jury in sufficient detail the inconsistencies complained of and, in the circumstances, the Court dismissed this ground of appeal.

Finally, reference should be made to the decision of the Court in *People (DPP) v. Moloney*, Court of Criminal Appeal, *ex-tempore*, November 8, 1999. At the trial, the applicant had objected to the admission of a complaint on the basis that it had not been made at the first reasonable opportunity and that it was not voluntary. However, the trial judge, having considered all the circumstances, ruled that it was admissible and the Court, on appeal, refused to interfere with this decision which it said was open on the facts. Lynch J. stressed that each case must, to some extent, depend upon its own facts and that the trial judge was in the best position to decide the facts.

The admission of complaints in sexual cases has been criticised by some commentators as anomalous but is explicable by reference to the historical development of the offence of rape. Cross (*Cross on Evidence* (7th ed.), p.282) has explained that:

> In the Middle Ages is was essential that the victim should have raised the hue and cry if an appeal of rape were to succeed. By the beginning of the eighteenth century, when the modern law of evidence was beginning to take shape, the absence of complaint was no longer an absolute bar to success, but Hawkins still referred to the strong presumption against a prosecutrix in a case of rape if she made no complaint within a reasonable time of the alleged offence. If the absence of such complaint could tell against a prosecutrix it seemed to follow that the fact of having made a complaint ought to tell in her favour, and if failure to complain could be proved by the defence then the fact of making a complaint should be capable of proof by the prosecution.

It follows that the central purpose for the admission of complaints in sexual cases is to show consistency and to negative any inference of consent. Because of this, it has been held that if the complainant does not give evidence, then the complaint is not admissible, there being no testimony with which the complaint can be consistent (*Sparks v. R* [1964] A.C. 964, [1964] 1 All E.R. 727; *Ugle v. R* (1989) 167 C.L.R. 647). It further follows, as held in *Gavin* and the English decision of *R v. Wright* (1987) 90 Cr. App. R. 91 that if the terms of the complaint are actually inconsistent with the testimony of the complainant, then there is no basis for its admission.

Cross-examination on sexual history   Section 3(1) of the Criminal Law (Rape) Act 1981 (as amended by section 13 of the Criminal Law (Rape) (Amendment) Act 1990) contains an important restriction on the admissibility of evidence of the previous sexual history of a complaint in sexual cases. It provides that no evidence can be adduced or question asked in cross-examination by or on behalf of an accused person about any sexual experience (other than that to which the charge relates) of a complainant with any person (including the accused) except with the leave of the judge. Leave can only be granted by the trial judge where he or she is satisfied that it would be unfair to the accused person to refuse to allow the evidence to be adduced or the question to be asked, i.e. if he or she is satisfied that the evidence might give rise to a reasonable doubt on the part of the jury as to whether the accused is guilty (section 3(2)). Given the increasing number of prosecutions for sexual offences in recent years, there is a notable and surprising paucity of authority as to the application of this section. It is, therefore, disappointing that the Court in *People (DPP) v. Moloney*, Court of Criminal Appeal, ex-tempore, November 1999, did not avail of the opportunity presented to it to give guidelines as to its application.

One of the grounds of appeal advanced by the applicant in that case was that the trial judge had erred in not permitting cross-examination of the complainant on her previous sexual history. However, this submission was dismissed by the Court in a cursory fashion on the basis that cross-examination as to previous sexual history is primarily related to the question of consent which did not arise in the instant case where the complainant was 14 years of age. Further, the view was taken that the issue of consent could only arise where it is accepted that some form of sexual activity had taken place and here the accused denied that anything had ever happened. It might be noted that, while the Court is correct in asserting that, in the great majority of cases, previous sexual history will be relevant, if at all, to the issue of consent, such evidence can be admitted if sufficiently relevant to any issue in the case (see *R v. Viola* [1982] 3 All E.R. 73, [1982] 1 W.L.R. 1138).

Rebuttal evidence   The general rule in criminal proceedings is that both the prosecution and the defence must adduce all the evidence on which they wish to rely before the close of their respective cases (*R v. Rice* (1963) 47 Cr. App R 79). However, a trial judge has a discretion to allow a party to adduce evidence after its case has closed where it is in the interests of justice to do so. In *People (AG) v. O'Brien* [1963] I.R. 65, Davitt P., delivering the judgment of the Supreme Court, held that, while neither party in a case is entitled to adduce further evidence after its case has closed, circumstances could occur which would justify the recalling of a witness by a trial judge after the side calling him has closed their case. He enjoyed a discretion in that regard, the exercise of which depended on "the course of the trial, the facts of the case, and other matters which can be fully and properly appreciated only by the trial judge himself".

A good example of circumstances justifying the exercise of this discretion can be seen in *People (DPP) v. Leahy*, Court of Criminal Appeal, *ex tempore*, February 14, 2000. The applicant had been charged with a number of counts of fraud involving the uttering of forged documents and the obtaining of money by false pretences at various financial institutions. In the course of the prosecution case, it was alleged that the fingerprint of the applicant had been found on one of the bank drafts at issue in the case. However, the applicant while giving evidence sought to explain the presence of his fingerprint on the bank draft on the basis that a garda officer, when questioning him about another matter, had produced a number of bank drafts to him, and it was in this way that his fingerprint had come to be upon the bank draft. The trial judge then permitted the prosecution to recall the relevant garda witness to give evidence that the bank drafts which he had produced to the applicant on the previous occasion did not contain the draft on which the fingerprint had been found and, thus, the fingerprint could not be explained away in that fashion.

While the Court accepted that a trial judge generally has to be vigilant before allowing the prosecution to adduce evidence after it has closed its case, it was of the opinion that this was an appropriate case for the judge to have exercised his discretion to allow the evidence in. This was because the prosecution could hardly have anticipated the evidence and, even if it had, it was not evidence which a trial judge would normally have permitted the prosecution to use as part of their case because it would have disclosed to the jury that the applicant had been investigated in relation to another matter by the gardaí. In the circumstances, the Court was satisfied that the trial judge had been perfectly entitled, in the interests of justice, to admit the rebuttal evidence.

Fair procedures　In a number of cases, most notably in *State (Healy) v. Donoghue* [1976] I.R. 325, the courts have emphasised the importance of affording accused persons fair procedures in the trial of offences against them. A trial must be conducted in accordance with the requirements of natural and constitutional justice including the principle of *audi alterem partem*. Thus, an accused must be given an adequate opportunity to challenge the evidence against him or her and a conviction will be quashed if this is not afforded (see, for example, *Gill v. Connellan* [1987] I.R. 541).

In *O'Donnell v. O'Connell*, High Court, Morris P., November 29, 2000, the applicant sought various reliefs by way of judicial review arising out of the trial of a number of licensing offences. It was alleged that the respondent District Judge had relied on matters which were not in evidence before the court or, at least, had given the impression of have been influenced by such matters in dealing with the charges before him. Morris P. succinctly stated the relevant principles as follows:

> I am satisfied that at the hearing of a prosecution there is a clear obligation upon the trial judge to not only confine his considerations to the matters actually before the court but to ensure that no reason is given to promote

a belief that matters extraneous to the actual prosecution are being taken into account in reaching his decision.

Therefore, to allow an accused person to believe that extraneous matters were being taken into account in the determination of the issues before the court was a breach of fair procedures.

HEARSAY

Documentary hearsay In *People (DPP) v. Byrne*, Court of Criminal Appeal, 7 June 2000, the applicant, a motor dealer, had been convicted of handling a motor car knowing or believing it to be stolen arising out of the sale by him of a car which it was alleged comprised of the chassis of a crashed car and the body shell of a vehicle which had been stolen from another motor dealership.

At the trial, evidence was given by a number of witnesses relating to the importation of the stolen vehicle, its delivery to and subsequent theft from the relevant motor dealership as follows: (i) by an employee of National Vehicle Deliveries Ltd who produced a form with his signature relating to an examination of the car at Rosslare wherein he recorded its chassis and engine number; (ii) by a lorry driver based on a signed daily transport sheet of delivery by him of that car to the relevant motor dealership; (iii) by an employee of the motor dealership who inspected the vehicle and signed a form acknowledging receipt of the vehicle and containing its chassis number; (iv) by an officer of the Revenue Commissioners as to the results of his examination of the reconstructed vehicle and the mis-match between the various vehicle identification numbers; and (v) by an authorised officer attached to the Motor Taxation Office who produced the original records relating to the reconstructed vehicle. The main ground of appeal was that the trial judge had erred in admitting this evidence which the applicant contended was inadmissible hearsay. In reliance on the decision of the House of Lords in *Myers v. DPP* [1964] 2 All E.R. 881, it was submitted that evidence should have been given by the persons who actually complied the documents concerned and, since the prosecution had failed to produce a certificate pursuant to section 6 of the Criminal Evidence Act 1992, this evidence was inadmissible.

The Court, in a judgment delivered by the Chief Justice, held that the trial judge had been correct in ruling that the prosecution were not obliged, in the circumstances of the case, to produce a certificate pursuant to section 6 of the 1992 in order to render the evidence of these persons admissible. Each witness identified a document which he had personally filled in or signed. Further, the documents produced by the authorised officer of the motor taxation office and the officer of the Revenue Commissioners were properly admitted in evidence, although not compiled by the officers concerned, as documents properly in the custody of public officers. Accordingly, the principles laid down in *Myers* were of no application and it was not necessary for the prosecution to pray in aid the Criminal Evidence Act, 1992.

Given the fact that the case raised issues similar to those in the landmark English decision of *Myers* and the paucity of modern Irish authority, the extreme brevity with which the hearsay issue is dealt with is disappointing. Indeed, the issue is disposed of in such a summary manner that it is difficult to determine the precise basis for the Court's decision and to follow its reasoning.

While the ultimate decision would seem to be correct, the reasoning in *Byrne* is terse and requires some expansion. The facts in *Byrne* are not dissimilar to those in *Myers*. In that case, the accused had been charged with fraud involving the passing off of stolen cars as models re-built from wrecks. This was done by substituting the identifying numbers of the stolen cars for those of the wrecked cars. It was not, however, possible to change the vehicle identification number cast in the engine block and the prosecution case rested on the discrepancy between the numbers which could be changed and the number of the engine block. In order to establish the relevant combination of numbers, the prosecution called as a witness the custodian of the manufacturer's records which had been complied by unidentified workmen working on the assembly line. Notwithstanding, that the records were undoubtedly reliable and that no oral testimony would have been credible, the House of Lords held that the records were inadmissible hearsay and should have been excluded. The decision in *Myers* was reversed in England by the Criminal Evidence Act 1965 which provided for the admissibility of certain hearsay statements contained in business records. Similar provisions were introduced in this jurisdiction in Part II of the Criminal Evidence Act 1992.

The crucial difference between *Myers* and *Byrne* and the reason why the Court was satisfied that it was not necessary to rely on the provisions in Part II relating to business records was that, in the case of each witness, he gave evidence in relation to a document containing information which he personally had compiled and which, in some cases, he had signed. The records themselves were and remained hearsay being out of court documents adduced to prove the truth of their contents but the testimony of the witnesses in court, based on those records was not hearsay. The evidence of the various witnesses did not, therefore, fall foul of the hearsay rule but, rather, provides a good example of witnesses being allowed to refresh their testimony from a document which was made or verified by the witness contemporaneously with the transaction to which it refers. (see *Northern Banking Co v. Carpenter* [1931] I.R. 268 and *Lord Talbot de Malahide v. Cusack* (1864) 17 I.C.L.R. 213).

It is not apparent from the judgment of the Court of Criminal Appeal but it seems unlikely that the witness had any independent memory of the events to which the various records related or that the records actually jogged their memory. Thus, the records would have been used as an encapsulation of past recollection recorded to refresh testimony on the basis, *per* Kennedy C.J. in *Northern Banking Co* that, "[i]f the witness can say that, from seeing his own writing, he is sure of the fact stated therein, such statement by him is admissible in evidence of the fact". It must be acknowledged, though, that this category of 'past recollection recorded' constitutes an exception to the hearsay rule in all but name. The witness by swearing to the accuracy of the written document which he or she uses to refresh his or her memory invests the out of court statement with sufficient reliability to justify its reception in evidence. The fact that it is the oral testimony of the witness rather than the written document which constitutes evidence in the case is a matter of form only.

Proceeds of crime   In *Criminal Assets Bureau v. Craft*, High Court, O'Sullivan J., July 12, 2000, objection was taken to the admission of hearsay evidence pursuant to section 8 of the Proceeds of Crime Act, 1996 (see Annual Review 1996, 321) on the basis that it deprived the defendant of the opportunity to cross-examine the garda as to his sources. In accordance with the rule that the court should reach constitutional issues last, O'Sullivan J declined to deal with this submission insofar as the constitutionality of section 8 was impugned. However, he did go on to observe that the evidence at issue was peripheral in nature and was not central to the allegations made.

PRIVILEGE

Banker/Customer relationship   In *Cooper Flynn v. RTE* [2001] 1 ILRM 208, Kelly J. made it clear that although a duty and right of confidentiality exists between a banker and his customer this was not to be equated with an entitlement to any form of privilege.

Without prejudice privilege   In order for a claim of without prejudice privilege to succeed, it must be shown that a communication was made: (i) in a *bona fide* attempt to settle a dispute between the parties; and (ii) with the intention that, if negotiations failed, it could not be disclosed without the consent of the parties. In order to demonstrate that these conditions have been met and, thereby, bring a communication within the scope of the privilege, parties will almost invariably label it as 'without prejudice'. However, these words "possess no magic properties" (*O'Flanagan v. Ray-Ger Ltd*, High Court, Costello J., April 28, 1983, p.13) and where a claim of privilege is disputed, the court will examine the document and the circumstances surrounding its genesis in order to ascertain whether the claim for privilege is properly made (see *South Shropshire District Council v. Amos* [1987] 1 All E.R. 340, 344).

The foregoing principles were applied in *Ryan v. Connolly*, High Court, Kelly J., February 29, 2000. The case involved the trial of a preliminary issue as to whether the defendants were estopped from raising the Statute of Limitations as a defence to the plaintiff's claim. In order to ascertain whether the claim of estoppel had been made out, Kelly J. examined correspondence between the plaintiff's solicitors and the insurance company representing the defendant, notwithstanding that it was headed "without prejudice". He said that it was clear from the authorities that the mere attaching of this label to correspondence did not make such letters privileged and that the Court had to examine the letters to see whether they fell within the rubric of privileged correspondence. Having examined the letters, he was satisfied that they were not privileged, notwithstanding the fact that most of them were headed "without prejudice".

Taking evidence for use outside the State   Section 51 of the Criminal Justice Act 1994 makes provision for the Minister for Justice to nominate a judge of the District Court to take evidence from a person on foot of a request for assistance from a court or tribunal exercising criminal jurisdiction outside the State in connection with criminal proceedings that have been instituted or a criminal investigation that has been carried on in that country. The procedures to be applied in the taking of such evidence are set out in the Second Schedule to the 1994 Act. It provides that the judge shall have the like powers for securing the attendance of a witness for the purpose of the proceedings as the District Court has for the purpose of any other proceedings before that court and that the judge may take evidence on oath. It is further provided in rule 3 that a person cannot be compelled to give in the proceedings any evidence which he could not have been compelled to give, *inter alia*, in criminal proceedings in the State.

The proceedings in *de Gortari v. Smithwick* [2001] 1 I.L.R.M. 354 arose out of the decision of the Minister to nominate the President of the District Court to take evidence from the applicant, a former President of the Republic of Mexico, on foot of a request for assistance from an investigating magistrate in France. When the matter came on before the respondent, the applicant answered most of the questions put to him but refused to answer certain questions on the basis of his desire to maintain his privacy and confidentiality in relation to his personal financial affairs. The respondent ruled that the applicant was obliged to answer the questions and the applicant sought judicial review of that decision.

Counsel for the applicant submitted that the investigation being carried out by the investigating magistrate was at a comparatively early stage in that no charges had yet been brought. It was, therefore, comparable to the stage in this jurisdiction where the police were interviewing possible witnesses, or indeed suspects, during the course of a preliminary investigation and prior to charging any person with an offence. Given that the applicant was not an accused person but simply a potential witness in the proposed French criminal proceedings, it was submitted that the applicant should have the same general right to silence as would a person being interviewed by the police in an interview governed by the Judges' Rules in this jurisdiction.

McGuinness J. stated that the procedure established by section 51 of the 1994 Act was *sui generis* and rejected the analogy sought to be drawn by counsel for the applicant with a trial or with investigations conducted by the gardaí. She accepted the submission made by counsel for the Minister for Justice that the

Judges' Rules were designed to control investigations carried out by the police and could not be imported by implication into a statutory procedure laid down by the Oireachtas where a witness was being examined under oath by a judge of the District Court. Having regard to the fact that the applicant was obliged to attend to give evidence, the learned judge was satisfied that his position was not comparable to that of an accused who could not be compelled to give evidence. He was, rather, in the same position as a witness and witnesses at common law did not enjoy a general right to silence but were obliged to answer any question put unless he or she could rely on the privilege against self-incrimination.

The conclusion that the entitlement of a witness under the section 51 procedure to refuse to answer a question was confined to the exercise of his privilege against self-incrimination was reinforced by a consideration of rule 3 which made explicit provision for the privilege of witnesses. She had no doubt that the Oireachtas intended that a witness under the section 51 procedure was to be compellable both in the sense of attending the proceedings and in the sense of answering the questions put and that the 1994 Act should be interpreted insofar as is possible to fulfil that purpose. It might be pointed out, however, that this conclusion was undermined to some degree by her holding that there was no provision in the 1994 Act or otherwise for any penalty to be imposed in the event of a witness refusing to answer questions.

Turning to the question of whether the privilege against self-incrimination was available to the applicant, she took the view that rule 3 in the Second Schedule clearly covered the situation where the applicant's answer to a particular question would tend to incriminate him in the State. However, she went on to state that it is necessary that a foundation for the privilege be laid and she endorsed in this regard a passage from the judgment of Lord Denning MR in *In re Westinghouse Electric Corporation (No. 2)* [1977] 3 All E.R. 717, 721:

> If a witness claims the protection of the Court, on the grounds that the answer would tend to incriminate himself and there appears reasonable ground to believe that it would be so, he is not compellable to answer. ... Note that a witness is only given this protection if he can satisfy the Court that there is reasonable ground for it....It is for the judge to say whether there is reasonable ground or not. Reasonable ground may appear from the circumstances from the case or from matters put forward by the witness himself. He should not be compelled to go into detail because that may involve his disclosing the very matter to which he takes objection. But if it appears to the judge that, by being compelled to answer, a witness may be furnishing evidence against himself, which could be used against him in criminal proceedings, or in proceedings for a penalty, then his objection should be upheld.

It was clear from this passage that if the applicant in the instant case was able to establish some realistic prospect or possibility of his being proceeded against in this jurisdiction as a consequence of answers he might give to the questions posed by the respondent, he would be entitled to claim a right not to answer the questions as a consequence of the existence of the common law privilege against self incrimination. However, in order to invoke this protection he would, as a witness under oath, have to satisfy the respondent that there were reasonable ground for the belief that his answer could be used against him in criminal proceedings. To date, the applicant had failed to do this and had not put forward any evidence either in the District Court or in the instant proceedings to ground the claim that his potential answers would tend to incriminate him either in this State or in France. He was not, therefore, entitled to any relief on that ground.

Anton Piller Order   In *Microsoft Corporation v. Bright Point Ireland Limited* [2001] 1 I.L.R.M. 540, the defendant, relying on *Access Floors Inc v. Boswell* [1991] Ch. 512, sought to set aside an Anton Piller order obtained by the plaintiffs on the ground, inter alia, that the plaintiffs, in executing the order, had failed to advise the defendant as to its right against self-incrimination. However, Smyth J. pointed out that, in the instant case, the defendants insisted that it was fully compliant with the law. If this was indeed the case, then the question of self-incrimination simply could not arise and, accordingly, this was not a basis for setting aside the Anton Piller Order.

CORROBORATION

Corroboration warning in sexual cases   Section 7 of the Criminal Law (Rape) (Amendment) Act 1990 abolished the mandatory corroboration warning in respect of sexual complaints making it a matter instead for the discretion of the trial judge to decide, having regard to all the evidence, whether the jury should be given the warning. The enactment of this section was, at least to some extent, attributable to the criticisms of many commentators, especially feminists, that the traditional corroboration warning which was grounded on assumptions about the mendacity of female complainants, was misogynistic in conception and demeaning to women (see, for example, Temkin, "Towards a modern Law of Rape" (1982) 45 M.L.R. 399, 418). However, given that the requirement to give a warning had been a judicially created rule reflecting the views and prejudices of judges, it was feared by some commentators such as Caroline Fennell ([1990] ICLSA 32-16) that:

> The chosen route to reform may have just the appearance or form of change, while the requirement reasserts itself in substance in practice as the same factors considered to justify the original rule, might also be deemed to justify a continual exercise of their discretion by the judiciary.

Those fears seemed to have been realised with the decision in *People (DPP) v. Molloy*, Court of Criminal Appeal, July 28, 1995, where, in a judgment delivered by Flood J., the Court criticised the trial judge for initially deciding not to give a corroboration warning:

> The Court is deeply concerned with the undoubted inconsistency in the attitude and approach of the jury. It is all the more concerned by the fact that the trial Judge in his charge to the jury makes no reference whatsoever to corroboration and the need for corroboration in sexual offences and of the danger to act [*sic*] without corroboration. The Court is fully aware and alive to the fact that there is no statutory obligation on the trial Judge to warn the jury of the dangers of acting on the Complainant's evidence alone in the absence of corroboration.

> Nonetheless, this Court is of the view that where the charge is essentially supported by the evidence of the Complainant alone without collateral forensic evidence or any other form of corroboration, it is a prudent practice for the trial Judge to warn the jury that unless they are very very satisfied with the testimony of the Complainant that they should be careful not to convict in the absence of corroborative evidence.

Although these comments were, strictly speaking, *obiter*, because the trial judge did subsequently issue a warning following a requisition, they seemed to indicate a very firm view on the part of the Court as to the continued desirability of giving a corroboration warning, at least where there is no corroboration. As such, the decision seemed to significantly undermine the reform effected by section 7 and constituted something of a 'shot across the bows' of trial judges who might be inclined to exercise their discretion not to give a warning.

The approach taken in *Molloy* stood in stark contrast to that taken in Australia and in England in respect of similar reforms enacted in those jurisdictions. In *Longman v. R* (1989) 168 C.L.R. 79, the High Court of Australia considered the proper construction of section 36BE of the Evidence Act 1906 (WA) which had been amended to abrogate the warning. It took the view that the purpose of the section was to remove sexual complainants from the categories of suspect witness and that by doing so, it overrode the reasons underpinning the warning. Thus, sexual complainants were no longer to be viewed as a suspect class and it was inappropriate for judges to continue to give juries a general warning grounded in curial experience that allegations of sexual offences are easy to make or more likely to be fabricated than other classes to allegations.

Closer to home, the decision of the English Court of Appeal in *R. v. Makanjuola* [1995] 3 All E.R. 730 contains an even more trenchant rejection of the contention that the reasoning underpinning the warning has any continued validity. At issue in that case was the interpretation and effect of section 32(1) of the Criminal Justice and Public Order Act 1994 which abrogated the mandatory corroboration warnings with respect to both accomplices and sexual complainants. Lord Taylor C.J. emphasised that:

> The circumstances and evidence in criminal cases are infinitely variable and it is impossible to categorise how a judge should deal with them. But it is clear that to carry on giving "discretionary" warnings generally and in the same terms as were previously obligatory would be contrary to the policy and purpose of the 1994 Act. Whether, as a matter of discretion, a judge should give any warning and if so its strength and terms must depend upon the contents and manner of the witnesses evidence, the circumstances of the case and the issues raised. The judge will often consider that no special warning is required at all. Where, however, the witness has been shown to be unreliable, he or she may consider it necessary to urge caution. In a more extreme case, if the witness is shown to have lied, to have made previous false complaints, or to bear the defendant some grudge, a stronger warning may be thought appropriate and the judge may suggest it would be wise to look for some supporting material before acting on the impugned witness's evidence.

The learned judge went on to summarise the relevant principles to be applied in a series of numbered propositions as follows:

(1) Section 32(1) abrogates the requirement to give a corroboration direction in respect of an alleged accomplice or a complainant of a sexual offence simply because a witness falls into one of those categories.

(2) It is a matter for the judge's discretion what, if any, warning he considers appropriate in respect of such a witness, as indeed in respect of any other witness in whatever type of case. Whether he chooses to give a warning and in what terms will depend on the circumstances of the case, the issues raised and the content and quality of the witnesses evidence.

(3) In some cases, it may be appropriate for the judge to warn the jury to exercise caution before acting upon the unsupported evidence of a witness. This will not be so simply because the witness is the complainant of a sexual offence nor will it necessarily be so because a witness is alleged to be an accomplice. There will need to be an evidential basis for suggesting that the evidence of the witness may be unreliable. An evidential basis does not include mere suggestions by cross-examining counsel.

(4) If any question arises as to whether the judge should give a special warning in respect of a witness, it is desirable that the question be resolved by discussion with counsel in the absence of the jury before final speeches.

(5) Where the judge does decide to give some warning in respect of a witness, it will be appropriate to do so as part of the judge's review of the evidence

and his comments as to how the jury should evaluate it rather than as a set piece legal direction.

(6) Where some warning is required, it will be for the judge to decide the strength and terms of the warning. It does not have to be invested with the whole florid regime of the old corroboration rules.

(7) ...Attempts to re-impose the straight-jacket of the old corroboration rules are strongly to be deprecated.

(8) Finally, this court will be disinclined to interfere with a trial judge's exercise of his discretion save in a case where that exercise is unreasonable in the *Wednesbury* sense...

The principles have now been endorsed by the Court of Criminal Appeal in *People (DPP) v. JEM*, Court of Criminal Appeal, February 1, 2000. The applicant in *JEM* sought leave to appeal against his conviction of four counts of sexual assault on a 15 year old girl and one of the main grounds of appeal raised by him was that the trial judge had erred in refusing to give to the jury a corroboration warning in respect of the evidence of the complainant. Denham J., delivering the judgment of the Court, examined the terms of section 7 and emphasised that the warning was no longer mandatory and that the decision whether it should be given is now a matter for the discretion of the trial judge. As to the circumstances where, as a matter of discretion, a judge ought to give a cautionary instruction to the jury and in what terms, she referred with approval to the decision of *Makanjuola*. Although the wording of section 32(1) was not the same as section 7 of the 1990 Act, the learned judge said that the legal principle underpinning both statutes was similar. Thus, she endorsed the principles stated in the numbered propositions set out above with the exception of paragraph 8.

Turning to the facts of the case, Denham J. pointed out that the issue of corroboration had been debated by counsel before the judge. In light of the issues raised, the circumstances and the evidence given, he had exercised his discretion not to give a warning and the learned judge was satisfied that no basis had been advanced upon which the Court could interfere with the trial judge's exercise of his discretion.

The decision in *JEM* is very much to be welcomed in its trenchant reaffirmation that the corroboration warning is no longer mandatory and in its endorsement of the principles laid down in *Makanjuola*. The decision rejects the reasoning underpinning the warning and, by doing so, places Irish law in this area on a path of more rational development which should obviate the necessity for any further legislative intervention (which was being considered as an option: see Department of Justice, Equality and Law Reform, *The Law on Sexual Offences: A Discussion Paper* (1998)).

A couple of comments might be made in passing. The first is that, although the Court did not expressly disavow the dicta in *Molloy* set out above, this decision must now be taken as very much confined to its own facts. Indeed, an examination of the decision discloses the existence of a number of factors which justified the giving of a cautionary instruction of some type. Second, as noted above, the Court refused to endorse proposition 8 of the numbered propositions set out in *Makanjuola*. Although, no reason is giving for not doing so, the use of *Wednesbury* unreasonableness as the standard for review is difficult to comprehend. A better test and one, which it is submitted would find favour with the Irish Courts should the issue arise, is that used by the Australian courts of whether the failure to give a cautionary instruction has given rise to the risk of a miscarriage of justice (see *Bromley v. R* (1986) 161 C.L.R. 315).

IMPROPERLY OBTAINED EVIDENCE

Breach of the Custody Regulations   The Criminal Justice Act 1984 (Treatment of Persons in Custody in Garda Síochána Stations) Regulations 1987 (better known as the "Custody Regulations") lay down minimum substantive and procedural protections for persons in custody designed to ensure their fair treatment. The starting point in considering the effect of a breach of the Custody Regulations is section 7(3) of the Criminal Justice Act 1984 which provides that:

> A failure on the part of any member of the Garda Síochána to observe any provision of the regulations shall not of itself render that person liable to any criminal or civil proceedings or of itself affect the lawfulness of the custody of the detained person or the admissibility in evidence of any statement made by him.

In *DPP v. Spratt* [1995] 1 I.R. 585, [1995] 2 I.L.R.M 117 (Annual Review 1995, 244), O'Hanlon J. interpreted section 7(3) as follows:

> The phrase "of itself" is obviously an important one in the construction of the statutory provisions, and I interpret the sub-section as meaning that non-observance of the Regulations is not to bring about automatically the exclusion from evidence of all that was done and said while the accused person was in custody. It appears to be left to the court of trial to adjudicate in every case as to the impact the non-compliance with the regulations should have on the case for the prosecution.

Subsequently, in *DPP v. Devlin*, High Court, Budd J., September 2, 1998 (Annual Review 1998, 389), it was held by Budd J. that in addition to adjudicating as to whether there has been a breach of the Custody Regulations, the trial judge must go on to adjudicate as to what impact the non-compliance with the regulations has had on the case for the prosecution. In that case, there had been no actual adjudication on the impact of the breach of the regulations on the admissibility of the evidence subsequently obtained and accordingly, the judge had been wrong in dismissing the charge on this basis.

The principles established in *Spratt* and *Devlin* were applied in *DPP v. Cullen*, High Court, Ó Caoimh J., February 7, 2001. The respondent had been charged with drink driving and a case was stated as to whether the District Judge had been correct to dismiss the charge on the basis of a breach of the Custody Regulations had occurred. Having heard all the evidence, the District Judge had made a finding that the respondent had not been handed a notice of his rights while in custody, had not had his rights read out to him, and had not had those rights explained to him. He was, therefore, satisfied that the legal and constitutional rights of the respondent had not been accorded to him on the night in question and in the exercise of his judicial discretion he dismissed the charge.

Ó Caoimh J. concluded that the District Judge had erred in doing so because, having found that a breach of the Custody Regulations had occurred, he had failed to go on to consider the effect of this breach on the prosecution case:

> Before excluding the evidence I am satisfied that a judge of the District Court would have to be satisfied that the impact of the non-compliance with the regulations was one which had a material effect on the case for the prosecution.

He went on to express his doubts whether, given that it was a mandatory requirement for a suspect to give a blood or urine sample, any failure to comply with the Custody Regulations would have any causative link to the evidence obtained thus, justifying its exclusion.

CONFESSIONS

Judges' Rules   As outlined last year in relation to the discussion of the decision in *DPP v. Byrne* [1999] 1 I.L.R.M. 500 (Annual Review 1999, 232) the Judges' Rules were designed to provide clarification of the circumstances in which police officers could question a person and, in particular, as to when a caution was required. To that end, rules 1 and 2 provide as follows:

1. When a police officer is endeavouring to discover the author of a crime there is no objection to his putting questions in respect thereof to any person or persons, whether suspected or not, from whom he thinks that useful information may be obtained.

2. Whenever a police officer has made up his mind to charge a person with a crime, he should first caution such person before asking him any questions, or any further questions as the case may be.

The application of these rules arose for consideration in *Moore v. Martin*, High Court, (Finnegan J.), May 29, 2000. The applicant had been convicted of drink driving arising out of a collision involving the applicant's car and a parked vehicle. A garda, who arrived on the scene was informed by the owner of the parked vehicle that the applicant had left the scene on foot. When the guard caught up with the applicant, he interviewed the applicant who admitted that he had been driving his car at the time of the collision. During the course of this conversation, the garda formed an opinion that the applicant was intoxicated which led to him being arrested.

Finnegan J. rejected the contention put forward by the applicant that the respondent District Judge should have excluded his statement to the garda on the basis that he ought to have been cautioned before being questioned. Finnegan J. referred to rule 1 of the Judges' Rules and stated that he was satisfied that the garda had been doing no more than trying to discover whether or by whom an offence had been committed and that he had been entitled to ask the applicant as to whether or not he had been driving at the relevant time. Therefore, notwithstanding the absence of a caution, the statement made by the applicant in relation to his driving of the car at the relevant time was admissible.

An issue was raised in *People (DPP) v. O'Driscoll*, Court of Criminal Appeal, *ex-tempore*, July 19, 1999 as to the application of rule 7 of the Judges' Rules which provides as follows:

> A prisoner making a voluntary statement must not be cross-examined, and no questions should be put to him about it except for the purpose of removing ambiguity in what he has actually said. For instance, if he has mentioned an hour without saying whether it was morning or evening, or has given a day of the week and day of the month which do not agree, or has not made it clear to what individual or place he intended to refer in some part of his statement, he may be questioned sufficiently to clear up the point.

The appellant challenged the admissibility of a statement made by him, under caution as a result of a question and answer session during which the gardaí had put to him alleged inconsistencies and inaccuracies in his original statement. The appellant argued that this statement had been taken in violation of rule 7 which, it was contended, provides that a suspect making a voluntary statement must not be cross-examined and no questions should be put to him about it except for the purpose of removing ambiguity in what he has actually said. The Court, however, was satisfied that rule 7 refers to the undesirability of cross-examining an accused person while he or she is actually making a statement. In this case, the accused had already made his statement and the gardaí were only putting to him alleged inaccuracies in his original statement.

The Custody Regulations   A number of decisions over the last number of years have clarified the circumstances in which a judge can exercise his or her discretion pursuant to section 7(3) of the Criminal Justice Act 1984 to exclude a statement allegedly taken in breach of the Custody Regulations. The thrust of the case law including *People (DPP) v. Connell* [1995] 1 I.R. 244 and *People (DPP) v. Darcy*, Court of Criminal Appeal, July 29, 1997 (Annual Review 1997, 403) is that a breach of the Custody Regulations is not sufficient, in and of itself, to exclude a statement. To warrant exclusion, there must be some additional factor(s) in the circumstances of the case which indicate that the questioning of the accused was oppressive in some way or that the admission of his or her statement would be unfair. The application of these principles can be seen in two recent decisions of the Court of Criminal Appeal.

In *People (DPP) v. Smith*, Court of Criminal Appeal, November 22, 1999, the applicant submitted that an incriminating statement made by him should not have been admitted because a number of breaches of the Custody Regulations had taken place. The applicant contended, firstly, that he had not been in a fit state to be interviewed. He had vomited in the course of the interview and the doctor who saw him found that he was suffering from gastritis brought on by alcohol he had taken the previous day. However, the doctor had not suggested that this condition required any postponement of the interview and, in the circumstances, the Court was satisfied that there was adequate evidence to support the finding of the trial judge that he had been in a fit state to be questioned. The applicant also complained that the statement did not indicate the time at which the statement had commenced and the time at which it had finished but this was not regarded by the Court as material because these times were established by other evidence.

The third ground advanced by the applicant and one which the Court regarded as more serious was a breach of regulation 12(3) which provides that: "not more than two members shall question the arrested person at any one time and not more than four members shall be present at any one time during the interview". The Court agreed that, since only one person can effectively speak at any give time, this regulation should be construed as providing that, during the course of an interview, only two of the gardaí present may actually question the suspect. However, having regard to the finding by the trial judge that the questioning was not oppressive, the Court did not consider that the statement of the applicant was induced by the fact that three Guards had asked questions. The Court reiterated that the purpose of the regulations is to ensure that a suspect will be treated fairly and that a breach is not, of itself, sufficient to exclude what has been said. Having regard to that and the findings of the trial judge that there was no oppressive conduct, it was satisfied that the statement had been properly admitted.

The appellant in *People (DPP) v. O'Driscoll*, Court of Criminal Appeal, *ex tempore*, July 19, 1999 also sought to rely on various breaches of the Custody Regulations in order to exclude a statement made by him. The trial judge had been satisfied that the questioning had been conducted in a humane and fair manner by the gardaí and he exercised his discretion not to exclude the statement despite the breaches of the Custody Regulations. On appeal, the Court refused to interfere with this exercise of his discretion rejecting the argument made by the appellant that while a trial judge could exercise his discretion so as to waive one breach, he did not have the power to waive a number of breaches. In this case, it was quite clear that the trial judge took the view that the breaches of the Custody Regulations were immaterial and that the questioning had been humane and, in those circumstances, the Court refused to interfere with his decision to admit the statement.

Examination of suspect in custody The applicant in *People (DPP) v. Murray*, Court of Criminal Appeal, April 12, 1999, had been convicted of rape and sexual assault. There was a fundamental conflict between the applicant and the complainant as to what had happened on the night in question and in that context a mark on the applicant's lip assumed some importance. The complainant gave evidence that during the course of the assault she had bitten the applicant on the lip. The explanation which the applicant gave in interviews with the gardaí for the mark on his lip was that it was a cold sore. While the applicant was in custody, he was examined by a doctor for the purpose of obtaining samples for forensic testing in accordance with the provisions of the Criminal Justice (Forensic Evidence) Act 1990. After doing this the doctor spoke to one of the gardaí who asked him if he had noticed a cold sore on the applicant's lip. The doctor informed him that it was not a cold sore and he was asked by the gardaí to examine the applicant again for the purpose of examining his lip. As a result of this second examination the doctor concluded that the mark was most likely made by a bite. At the trial, the applicant objected to the admission of the evidence of this second examination on the ground that it was in breach of the Judges' Rules. The trial judge, while accepting that the examination was in breach of the spirit of the rules, decided to exercise his discretion to admit the evidence.

The Court took the view that there was no question of the second examination constituting an intrusion of the applicant's constitutional right to privacy because the uncontradicted evidence of the doctor was that he had sought and obtained the consent of the applicant to that examination. With regard to the contention made by the applicant that he should have been cautioned by the doctor in accordance with the Judges' Rules, the Court stated that the trial judge had correctly recognised that under the Judges' Rules he had a discretion to admit evidence even where the recommended caution had not been provided. In the circumstances, the Court was satisfied that the trial judge had not erred in the exercise of his discretion.

The Court does not expressly address the issue of whether the trial judge had been correct to take the view that the failure to give the applicant a caution before the second examination constituted a breach of the Judges' Rules but it does not dissent from this view. This is of some considerable interest because the purpose of the caution is to inform an accused of his right to silence/privilege against self-incrimination. Therefore, an extension of the requirement to give a caution to the context of an examination could only be on the basis that a suspect in custody enjoys a privilege against self-incrimination which extends to non-testimonial evidence such as that disclosed by an examination of the accused. This, indeed, was the view taken by Davitt P. in *Sullivan v. Robinson* [1954] I.R. 161, dealing with the results of an examination of a person arrested on suspicion of drunk driving. He said:

> Two legal principles appear to govern this matter. The first is that no one charged with an offence is obliged to incriminate himself or to help the prosecution to convict him. The second is that he is perfectly free to do so if he wishes...Admission or confession may be made by conduct as well as by words. A person charged with driving a car while drunk may in words admit he was drunk at the time. He may also by his conduct, shortly after the time at which it is alleged he was drunk, make such an admission. For instance, he may undertake a test, which a sober man can perform adequately, and by failure to do so confess his incompetence. That seems to me to be as much a confession as if he used words to confess his incompetence.

Therefore, he concluded that similar principles applied to the admission of the results of any tests conducted by a doctor to determine the sobriety of a suspect as applied to the admission of confessions. Thus, the prosecution had to prove that any test, the result of which tended to incriminate him had been voluntarily undergone by the accused. Thus, the accused had to be cautioned (a) that he was not obliged to undergo any test unless he wished to do so; (b) as to the purpose of the test; and (c) that its result might be given in evidence.

The proposition that the privilege against self-incrimination extends to non-testimonial evidence has been rejected by the United States Supreme Court (*Schmerber v. California* (1966) 384 US 757), the Supreme Court of Canada (*R v. Stillman* [1997] 1 S.C.R. 607) and by the European Court of Human Rights (*Saunders v. UK* (1996) 23 E.H.R.R. 313). This body of authority does not bode well for its continued adoption in Irish law should the issue arise for decision again.

RES JUDICATA

Issue estoppel in criminal cases The decision in *People (DPP) v. O'Callaghan*, Court of Criminal Appeal, December 18, 2000, addresses directly for the first time in this jurisdiction the question as to whether issue estoppel is available in a criminal trial for the benefit of an accused. This question, which had been expressly left open by Henchy J. in *Dublin Corporation v. Flynn*

[1980] I.R. 357, has created difficulty in other common law jurisdictions. The House of Lords in *DPP v. Humphrys* decided that it could not be invoked by an accused but the United States Supreme Court in *Ashe v. Swenson* (1970) 397 US 436 and the Supreme Court of Canada in *Gushue v. R* (1979) 106 D.L.R. (3d) 152 reached the opposite conclusion.

The applicant in *O'Callaghan* had been charged with causing damage by fire to a dwelling house without lawful excuse contrary to section 2 of the Criminal Damage Act 1991. His first trial resulted in a hung jury and he was retried a second time and convicted. One of the points raised on his appeal and in respect of which additional submissions were made at the request of the Court of Criminal Appeal was whether the ruling of the trial judge at the first trial that the evidence of a particular witness was irrelevant precluded the judge at the second trial from reconsidering this issue and reaching a different conclusion.

Delivering the judgment of the Court, Hardiman J began by examining the relevant Irish authorities. He discussed at length the decisions in *Kelly v. Ireland* [1986] I.L.R.M. 318 and *Breathnach v. Ireland* [1989] I.R. 489 which involved civil proceedings instituted against the State by two of the persons convicted of the infamous Sallins train robbery. In *Kelly v. Ireland* [1986] I.L.R.M. 318, the plaintiff sought damages for assaults allegedly committed upon him while he was in custody. These allegations had previously been made by him at his trial in a challenge to the voluntariness of his confession but had been rejected by the Special Criminal Court and the defendants pleaded that the matter was, therefore, *res judicata*. O'Hanlon J referred to the decision of the House of Lords in *Humphrys* [1977] A.C. 1, [1976] 2 All E.R. 497 where it was held that estoppel could not be raised by an accused in a criminal trial. One of the main arguments put forward by Lord Salmon against the importation of the concept of issue estoppel into criminal law was the difficulty of identifying the issues in the absence of pleadings defining the issues and judgments explaining how the issues were decided even if identifiable. These difficulties did not, however, arise on the facts before O'Hanlon J as it was possible to identify the issue and there was a judgment of the Special Criminal Court defining the issue and explaining how it had been decided. He therefore held that:

> In the rare case where a clearly identifiable issue has been raised in the course of a criminal trial and has been decided against a party to those proceedings by means of a judgment explaining how the issue has been decided, I would be prepared to hold that such decision may give rise to issue estoppel in later civil proceedings in which that party is also involved. Such estoppel would arise, not only in relation to the specific issue determined (in this case, whether the statement was made freely and voluntarily) but also to findings which were fundamental to the court's decision on such issue.

This passage was subsequently approved and applied by Lardner J. in *Breathnach v. Ireland* [1989] I.R. 489. In that case, the plaintiff brought a civil action claiming damages for, *inter alia*, assault and battery alleged to have occurred while he was in detention. He had challenged the admissibility of his confession on this basis at his trial but the Special Criminal Court held that he had not been assaulted and admitted his confession. His conviction was subsequently quashed by the Court of Criminal Appeal because it was not satisfied beyond a reasonable doubt that the inculpatory statements made by him were voluntary. However, the Court expressly refused to interfere with the findings of fact by the Special Criminal Court on the issue of assault and battery. In the circumstances, Lardner J. was satisfied that the decision of the Special Criminal Court was a subsisting decision on that issue and he, thus, concluded that the plaintiff was estopped from litigating this issue again.

Hardiman J regarded these decisions as authority for the proposition that, in principle, the determination of an issue in criminal proceedings can give rise to an issue estoppel and that a finding on an issue in a criminal trial could constitute an estoppel even though the verdict in that trial was subsequently set aside as a result of a successful appeal, provided that the basis of the appellate judgment did not invalidate the finding alleged to give rise to the estoppel. He pointed out, however, that in each case, the proceedings in which the estoppel was raised were civil proceedings and so the cases were did not decide whether such estoppel could arise in further criminal proceedings. This question had also been left open by the Supreme Court in *Dublin Corporation v. Flynn* [1980] I.R. 357 where it was held that estoppel could not be availed of by the prosecution.

In the absence of a binding Irish authority, the learned judge approached the issue on the basis of principle and took the view that:

> There appears to be no reason in principle suggesting that a discrete, clearly identifiable issue decided in a criminal trial should not give rise to an estoppel in a subsequent criminal trial, if is capable of giving rise to estoppel in a civil action.

He pointed out that this had been the position at common law in England (referring to *Connelly v. DPP* [1964] A.C. 1254) prior to the decision of the House of Lords in *DPP v. Humphrys* [1977] A.C. 1 which had dramatically altered the law in this respect. He also referred to the availability of issue estoppel in criminal cases at common law in the United States (*Ash v. Swenson* (1970) 397 US 436) and Canada (*R v. Grant* (1991) 7 CR (4th) 388). He also adverted to the 'cogent' academic criticisms which made been made of the decision in *Humphrys*. One of the matters which had troubled the Law Lords was that estoppels were mutual in nature and that, therefore, it estoppel was available to the defendant, it would have to be available to the prosecution. However, Choo, *Abuse of Process and Judicial Stays of Criminal Proceedings* (1993) criticised this thesis, arguing that:

It is not at all obvious that, if the doctrine of criminal issue estoppel were part of English law, it must be equally available to both parties. To determine the nature of criminal issue estoppel in the light of its civil counterpart is misguided. Criminal estoppel should be viewed as part and parcel of the double jeopardy principle, and the basis of this principle...does not obtain in civil proceedings.

The judgments of their Lordships also dwelt upon the practical difficulties of applying estoppel in the criminal context, principally the difficulty of identifying the issues which had previous been decided and the precise findings which led to that decision. However, as McDermott (*Res Judicata and Double Jeopardy* (Butterworths, 1999) points out, "even if the application of a particular doctrine may present practical difficulties, it seems strange to use the fact that the doctrine may be able to be invoked successfully in only a few cases to deny its availability in toto." The arguments in favour of the extension of issue estoppel to criminal cases are canvassed at length by McDermott and the one which Hardiman J. regarded as the most relevant was that relating to the role which would be played by issue estoppel in protecting the moral integrity of the criminal process.

   Although the learned judge accepted the practical difficulties of its application and he acknowledged that its application would be rare, he nevertheless concluded that estoppel should be available to an accused:

> Since it seems clearly established at common law, and since its availability in a civil action following a determination of an issue in a criminal case seems established, it appears to this Court that unless and until the Supreme Court is persuaded to give a decision along the lines of *Humphrys*, issue estoppel as between one criminal trial and another should be regarded as available here.

Despite being framed in somewhat timid terms, the decision in *O'Callaghan* constitutes a clear endorsement by the Court of Criminal Appeal of the proposition that issue estoppel may be available to an accused in criminal proceedings. Although Hardiman J. adverts to the possibility of the Supreme Court taking a different view on the matter, this is, perhaps, unlikely give that recent decisions have emphasised the policy basis of *res judicata* and adopted an expansive interpretation (see, for example, *McCauley v. McDermot* [1997] 2 I.L.R.M. 486 (Annual Review 1997, 438).

Cause of action estoppel   Cause of action estoppel is that branch of *res judicata* which, *per* Lord Diplock L.J. in *Thoday v. Thoday* [1964] P. 181, 197, "prevents a party to an action from asserting or denying, as against the other party, the existence of a particular cause of action, the non-existence or existence of which has been determined by a court of competent jurisdiction in previous litigation between the same parties." It, thus, prevents the contradiction of a previous determination as to the existence or non-existence of a cause of action.

Perhaps the best Irish example of its application is to be seen in *White v. Spendlove* [1942] I.R. 224. The defendant in the case had previously brought an action against the plaintiff claiming specific performance of an agreement dated 9th February 1935. In her defence to that action, the plaintiff had pleaded that she had entered into a different contract dated February 12, 1934 for the purchase of the said premises subject to certain conditions precedent. She alleged that these conditions had not been fulfilled and therefore counterclaimed for recission of the alleged agreement and repayment of money which she alleged had been paid on foot of the agreement. The defendant's action was dismissed on the ground that a valid agreement did not exist and the plaintiff not having proceeded with her counterclaim, it was also dismissed by the court. In the instant case, the plaintiff claimed the return of the money allegedly paid on foot of the contract of February 12. Again she alleged that the said agreement was subject to conditions precedent which had not been complied with by the defendant and that, therefore, there had been a failure of consideration. A majority of the Supreme Court held that the plaintiff's claim was based on substantially the same cause of action as her counterclaim in the former action and that she was, therefore, estopped from suing again for recovery of the said sum.

Apart from preventing the contradiction of previous judgments, cause of action estoppel also has the effect of preventing the fragmentation of litigation because of the doctrine of merger or *transit in rem judicatam*. According to this theory, when a judgment as to the existence or non-existence of a cause of action is given, the cause of action is extinguished by that decision and, *per* Dixon J in *Blair v. Curran* (1939) 62 C.L.R. 464, 531-2, "the very right or cause of action claimed…has in the formal proceedings passed into judgment, so that it is merged and has no longer an independent existence". One consequence of this doctrine is that where a suit is brought on a cause of action, the plaintiff must make all claims open to him or her and the defendant must raise all the defences available to him or her because the judgment operates as a comprehensive declaration of all the rights and duties of the parties arising out of the cause of action. Thus, fragmentation of litigation is prevented. Perhaps the best known statement of this principle is that of Wigram VC in *Henderson v. Henderson* (1843) 3 Hare 100, 114:

> … where a given matter becomes the subject of litigation in, and of adjudication by, a court of competent jurisdiction, the court requires the parties to that litigation to bring forward their whole case, and will not (except under special circumstances) permit the same parties to open the same subject of litigation in respect of matter which might have been brought forward as part of the subject in contest, but which was not brought forward, only because they have, from negligence, inadvertence, or even accident, omitted part of their case. The plea of res judicata applies, except in special cases, not only to points upon which the court

was actually required by the parties to form an opinion and pronounce a judgment, but to every point which properly belonged to the subject of litigation, and which the parties exercising reasonable diligence, might have brought forward at the time.

Both the non-contradiction and the non-fragmentation aspects of cause of action estoppel arose in *Ulster Bank Ltd v. Lyons*, High Court, Ó Caoimh J., March 10, 2000. The plaintiff brought summary proceedings against the defendants claiming a liquidated sum consisting of monies allegedly due on foot of two joint accounts. The plaintiff had previously obtained an order for possession against the defendants pursuant to an indenture of mortgage in a mortgage suit commenced by way of special summons but had refrained from enforcing it against the defendants. It argued that the issue of the defendants' indebtedness to the plaintiff had been determined in the earlier proceedings and that the matter was *res judicata*. For their part, the defendants, relying on *White v. Spendlove*, argued that the plaintiff's cause of action was estopped because it was the same cause of action as had been litigated in the earlier proceedings. Alternatively, it was contended that the plaintiff's claim could have been brought in the previous proceedings and was, therefore, estopped by the principle in *Henderson*.

In response, the plaintiff submitted, relying on *McCauley v. McDermott* [1997] 2 I.L.R.M. 486 (Annual Review 1997, 438) that for cause of action estoppel to arise, the issues in the two set of proceedings were required to be precisely the same and, here, they were not even substantially the same. Further, so far as the principle in *Henderson* was concerned, it was argued that the reliefs sought in the instant proceedings could not, by virtue of the Rules of the Superior Courts, have been raised in the earlier special summons proceedings. Conversely, the reliefs sought in the earlier proceedings could not have been sought in the instant proceedings. The plaintiff, therefore, contended that, since it was not possible under the Rules to deal with both matters in the same set of proceedings, the principle in *Henderson* did not apply.

Ó Caoimh J. concluded that, while there were certain similarities between the earlier and the instant proceedings, they were not "substantially the same" and, furthermore, it would not have been appropriate for the relief sought in the instant proceedings to have been included in the earlier proceedings. Accordingly, he was satisfied that the plaintiff was not precluded from maintaining the action. Furthermore, he was of the view that there was no inconsistency between the claim being made in the later proceedings and that made in the earlier proceedings and he distinguished the decisions in *White v. Spendlove* and *Henderson* on that basis.

While, on the facts, the causes of action in the two sets of proceedings would not seem to have been sufficiently similar for cause of action estoppel to arise, it should be noted that the argument made by the plaintiff as to the limitations imposed by the Rules on the joinder of reliefs would not prevent an estoppel from arising in a suitable case. Although it is correct to state that a claim for a liquidated sum can not be made in a mortgage suit instituted by way of special summons, the use of a summary or special summons is not mandatory and a plaintiff can, if he or she wishes, combine the two claims on a plenary summons (*Barden v. Downes* [1940] I.R. 131).

Extradition proceedings   The plea of *res judicata* in *Bolger v. O'Toole*, High Court, O'Neill J., June 8, 2000, failed one of the fundamental tests for issue estoppel, that the issue determined in the previous action and that upon which it was sought to raise an estoppel are identical.

The applicant had been convicted *in absentia* in England of a number of offences and fourteen warrants were issued seeking his extradition. At the hearing before the District Court, the applicant successfully contended that the warrants were defective and that, therefore, his arrest on foot of them was illegal. Subsequently, new warrants were issued which remedied the defects identified and fresh extradition proceedings were brought against him. The applicant then instituted judicial review proceedings seeking to halt the extradition proceedings against him arguing that, once there had been a determination of an extradition application in the District Court, the matter became *res judicata* and a fresh application could not be made.

Although it is not explicit in his judgment, O'Neill J. seems to have rejected the proposition that cause of action estoppel could arise and, instead, concentrated on whether issue estoppel had arisen. The question for the court was, thus, whether the issues for determination in the instant District Court proceedings were the same as those heard and determined in the previous District Court proceedings. A difficulty arose in this regard in that, due to the pre-emptive nature of the judicial review proceedings, it was not yet apparent what issues would arise in the instant District Court proceedings. The learned judge took the view that it would, in the circumstances, be "manifestly premature" to say whether any issue estoppel would arise. However, having regard to the fact that matters raised in the previous proceedings which had led to the accused's discharge had been corrected in the second set of warrants, he ventured the opinion that it was unlikely that these issues would arise for determination again.

Striking out proceedings   In *Ewing v. Kelly*, High Court, O'Sullivan J., May 16, 2000, a number of the defendants brought motions seeking to have the proceedings struck out against them on the ground, *inter alia*, that a number of the issues raised had been decided in previous proceedings and were, therefore, *res judicata*. O'Sullivan J. regarded it was well settled, that where issues raised between parties had been raised and finally dealt with on the merits by a court of competent jurisdiction, such issues should not be tried again and the relevant pleadings should be struck out. On the facts, he was satisfied that this was the case in relation to a number of issues and he made an order striking out the offending pleadings.

MISCELLANEOUS

Res gestae In *People (DPP) v. O'Callaghan*, Court of Criminal Appeal, December 18, 2000, the applicant had been charged with causing damage by fire to a dwelling house without lawful excuse contrary to section 2 of the Criminal Damage Act 1991. He was convicted after being tried twice in relation to the offence. At the first trial, the trial judge had refused to admit the evidence of a particular witness on the ground that it was not relevant. However, the trial judge at the second trial reached a different conclusion, deciding that it was admissible even though it was more prejudicial than probative. The precise basis for this decision was not clear but reference was made to the evidence being relevant as forming part of the *res gestae*.

The Court of Criminal Appeal, in a judgment delivered by Hardiman J., criticised this ruling as unsatisfactory on the basis that the evidence could only be admitted if it was relevant because "relevance is the first and most basic requirement of admissibility". Further, if as appeared to be the opinion of the judge, it had a slight relevance, then the question of whether its prejudicial effect outweighed this probative value had to be addressed. If the probative value of the evidence was outweighed by its prejudicial effect, then this would constitute a strong ground for the exclusion of the evidence. Although no reference was made to any authorities, the conclusion is supported by authority including *People (AG) v. O'Neill* [1964] Ir Jur Rep. 1 where it was held that a trial judge should exercise his or her discretion to exclude relevant evidence where he or she is satisfied that its probative value is outweighed by its prejudicial effect.

Interestingly, the learned judge took the opportunity to criticise the invocation by the trial judge of the concept of *res gestae* as unhelpful in elucidating the reason for the decision. He referred to the description by Stone, "Res Gestae Reagitata" (1939) 55 L.Q.R. 66 of *res gestae* as "the lurking place of a motley crowd of conceptions in mutual conflict and reciprocating chaos" and the infamous statement of Lord Blackburn who advised that: "If you wish to tender inadmissible evidence, say it is part of the res gestae" (quoted in Cross, *Evidence* (5th ed.), p.43, n.13). To these criticisms could be added that of Lord Tomlin in *Holmes v. Newman* [1931] 2 Ch. 112 who described *res gestae* as "a phrase adopted to provide a respectable legal cloak for a variety of cases to which no formula of precision can be applied". Hardiman J. echoed this view, saying that:

> The term is merely an expression of the general proposition that there is no universal formula for all kinds of relevancy. This proposition is not elucidated by the use of this Latin term which, unlike others, have no virtue of precision or historical connotation.

There is a notable paucity of modern Irish authority on *res gestae* and, therefore, the comments of Hardiman J. are interesting insofar as he evinces little enthusiasm for concept and may signal a desire to limit its application to an exception to the hearsay rule.

Function of the trial judge   In *Blanchfield v. Harnett* [2001] 1 I.L.R.M. 193, the applicant brought proceedings by way of judicial review seeking an order of certiorari to quash a number of orders which had been made by the first named respondent District Judge under the Bankers Books Evidence Act 1879. A preliminary objection to the making of such an order was, however, raised by the respondents on the basis that the real purpose behind the application was to render the evidence obtained under the orders inadmissible at the criminal trial. It was argued that this was inconsistent with the regularity of judicial procedures whereby the determination of questions as to the admissibility of evidence, including illegally obtained evidence, was granted exclusively to the trial judge.

It was, therefore, necessary for O'Neill J. to address, at the outset, whether the trial judge in the Circuit Court had jurisdiction to determine the validity of the District Court order or whether the validity of such an order could only be challenged and determined by the High Court on an application for judicial review. Referring to the jurisdiction exercised by a trial judge in criminal proceedings he said:

> In the course of such proceedings issues arise as to the admissibility of evidence and the resolution of such issues rests solely with the trial judge. Where it is alleged that evidence has been obtained illegally the question of whether or not such is the case, i.e. whether an illegality has occurred, is one solely for the trial judge and following upon that whether or not the evidence should be admitted is again one solely for discretion of the trial judge, a discretion to be exercised in accordance with law. In my view the principle of regularity of judicial proceedings requires that all questions relevant to the determination of such issues rests with the trial judge. Otherwise trials would be suspended for lengthy periods while such issues were litigated in other courts...

This was a practice which had been the subject of judicial disapproval in *People (AG) v. McGlynn* [1967] I.R. 232, 239, where Ó Dalaigh C.J. stated that:

> The nature of a criminal trial by jury is that once it starts, it continues right through until discharge or verdict. It has the unity and continuity of a play. It is something unknown to the criminal law for a jury to be recessed in the middle of a trial for months on end, and it would require clear words to authorise such an unusual alteration in the course of a criminal trial by jury.

O'Flaherty J. had referred to this passage in *DPP v. Special Criminal Court*

[1999] 1 I.R. 60 and observed that:

> While this statement applies to criminal trials with a jury, it should be
> regarded as a precept that should, as far as practical, be followed in
> respect of all criminal trials subject to the jurisdiction of courts to grant
> cases stated on occasion.

Applying these authorities, O'Neill J. was satisfied that the exclusive
jurisdiction of trial judges to determine issues as to the admissibility of evidence
was correct in principle as being consistent with the regularity of judicial
proceedings. It necessarily followed that a trial judge asked to adjudicate on
an issue as to the admissibility of evidence had a jurisdiction to hear and
determine all questions of fact and law relevant to the determination of the
issue of admissibility, including questions relating to allegations of breaches
of constitutional rights, allegations of non-compliance with statutory provisions
and all other illegalities. He, therefore, rejected the contention that the trial
judge in a Circuit Court criminal trial could not entertain issues such as those
raised on the case stated because these issues were appropriate to the judicial
review jurisdiction of the High Court:

> Whilst it is the case that there may be a coincidence of issues between
> the jurisdiction exercised by a trial judge in the Circuit Court and a judge
> of the High Court exercising a judicial review jurisdiction, that of course
> does not mean that the trial judge of the Circuit Court is in some way
> usurping a jurisdiction inappropriate to him. The trial judge in a criminal
> trial in the Circuit Court had his own exclusive jurisdiction. It may very
> well be from time to time that he may be asked to try an issue of law for
> the purposes of adjudicating on the admissibility of evidence which in
> other circumstances would be a more usual or appropriate issue for the
> judicial review jurisdiction of the High Court. That fact, however, could
> not prevent a trial judge in the Circuit Court from exercising his own
> exclusive jurisdiction in the course of a criminal trial.

He was, therefore, satisfied that the trial judge in dealing with an issue of
admissibility of evidence obtained on foot of the orders impugned in the instant
case had ample jurisdiction to deal with all questions relating to the legality of
those orders, and there were not any exceptional circumstances which would
justify an application for judicial review.

He bolstered this conclusion by a consideration of the practical effects of
making the orders sought. If, as had been submitted by counsel for the applicant,
a determination by the High Court of the issues raised relating to the legality of
the orders of the District Court would create an estoppel in respect of similar
issues arising on an objection to the admissibility of evidence in the Circuit
Court criminal trial, this would be an impermissible intrusion by the High Court

on the jurisdiction of the trial judge to determine all questions of law and fact related to the admissibility of evidence and would be an unwarranted trammelling of the discretion of the trial judge in relation to the admissibility of evidence. If, on the other hand, the grant of an order of certiorari did not have this effect and if it were open to the Circuit Court trial judge to deal with all issues relevant to the admissibility of evidence obtained on foot of the District Court orders, then it could fairly be said that the granting of an order of certiorari was futile in that it served no useful purpose.

Circumstantial evidence   In cases that go to trial, it is common for the prosecution to have to rely on circumstantial evidence to prove one or all of the facts in issue in the case. In *Thomas v. Jones* [1921] 1 K.B. 22, 48, Atkin L.J. explained the operation of circumstantial evidence as follows:

> Evidence of independent facts, each of them in itself insufficient to prove the main fact, may yet, either by their cumulative weight or still more by their connection of one with the other as links in a chain, prove the principle fact to be established.

In *People (DPP) v. Lafferty*, Court of Criminal Appeal, February 22, 2000, the applicants sought leave to appeal against their convictions for dangerous driving causing death. The prosecution arose out of a head on collision between two cars in which the driver and front seat passenger of one car had been killed. The other car was driven by the first named applicant and the third car involved in the incident was driven by the second named applicant. After the accident the second named applicant had made a cautioned statement to the investigating Garda. He said that he had consumed about seven pints and after an argument with the first named applicant as to the merits of the car he was driving, they had proceeded to race each other. He further stated that in the course of this race he had passed out the first named applicant's car at a speed of approximately 100 miles per hour and that, shortly thereafter, his own car went off the road. Evidence was also adduced by the prosecution that the car in which the deceased had been travelling was being driven at approximately 40 miles an hour.

It was submitted, on behalf of the first named applicant, that the case against him should have been withdrawn from the jury at the conclusion of the prosecution case because there was no evidence from witnesses as to how the accident had occurred and, in particular, there was no evidence as to the speed of the car driven by him or that it was being driven in a dangerous manner. Emphasis was placed on the fact that the statement made by the second named applicant was not evidence against him. For his part, the second named applicant submitted, that while the statement made by him was unquestionably evidence that he had been driving in an extremely dangerous manner on the night of the accident, there was nothing to indicate that this had contributed in any way to the accident.

The judgment of the Court was delivered by Keane C.J. who began by referring to the cardinal principle that the prosecution had to prove each ingredient of the offence against the applicants beyond a reasonable doubt. In the present case, the burden was on the prosecution to establish, in the case of each applicant, that at the time and place specified in the indictment, he had been driving the car in a manner which was dangerous to the public and which had caused the deaths of the deceased. If, at the close of the case for the prosecution, the state of the evidence was such that a jury, properly directed as to the relevant principles of law could not properly convict on it, it was the duty of the trial judge to withdraw the case from the jury.

In the case of the first named applicant, there was no direct evidence as to the manner in which his car was being driven at the time of the accident. In the case of the second named applicant, there was such evidence contained in his statement on which the jury were clearly entitled to rely, but no direct evidence as to the other essential ingredient of the offence, i.e. that the dangerous driving had caused the deaths of the deceased. Accordingly, in both cases, the prosecution relied on circumstantial evidence. He said that such evidence was normally defined as any fact from the existence of which the judge or jury could infer the existence of a fact in issue. No authority had been opened to the court as to the use which could be made of circumstantial evidence in prosecutions for dangerous driving causing death. In England, it had been held that if the speed at which someone was travelling at a particular time was an issue, evidence of the rate at which he was travelling a few moments earlier was admissible as circumstantial evidence (see *Beresford v. St. Alban's Justices* [1905] 22 T.L.R. 1; *Hallet v. Warren* [1929] 93 J.P. 225). However, even in the absence of these authorities, the learned Chief Justice said that the Court would have little difficulty in reaching the conclusion that evidence as to the manner in which a car was being driven at a relatively short time before the accident was admissible as circumstantial evidence in a prosecution for dangerous driving causing death.

Turning to the facts of the instant case, the jury were obliged to consider the possibility that, almost immediately before the collision, the first named applicant had given up any attempt to race with the second named applicant and had been driving in a normal manner at the time the accident occurred and that, coincidentally and with a relatively narrow time spectrum, the car in which the deceased were travelling which had been driven in a normal manner at a moderate speed by a sober driver for a significant part of its journey that evening, was driven in a manner which resulted in a violent collision. If, however, the jury, having given consideration to that possibility, were satisfied beyond reasonable doubt that the accident had not been caused by that conjunction of events, but was a result of the applicant's car being driven at the time of the accident at a wholly excessive speed and at a time when his judgment was impaired by the consumption of alcohol, this was a conclusion which they were entitled to reach. The Court was, accordingly, satisfied that the trial judge had been correct in concluding that these were issues which should properly be determined by the jury and that he was correct in refusing the application for a direction at the close of the prosecution case.

So far as the second named applicant was concerned, the jury were entitled to conclude beyond a reasonable doubt, on the basis of the admission made by him, not merely that he had accepted the challenge by the first named applicant to take part in a race but that he was actively participating in the race at the time when he passed out the first named applicant's car. Since the jury, for the reasons already stated, were also entitled to conclude beyond a reasonable doubt that the first named applicant continued to participate in the race and was so participating when the final collision occurred, it follows that they were also entitled to conclude beyond a reasonable doubt that the second named applicant's admittedly dangerous driving was a causative factor in the collision itself.

Although the conclusion of the court is unexceptionable on the facts of the case, it is somewhat surprising that greater reference was not made to the authorities dealing with circumstantial evidence. In particular, no mention was made of the decision of the Court in *People (AG) v. McMahon* [1946] I.R. 267 that where the case against the accused rests entirely on circumstantial evidence, such evidence in order to ground the conviction must be consistent with the guilt of the accused and must be inconsistent with any rational hypothesis consistent with innocence. In addition, there is no discussion of the nature of the charge to the jury in a case which rests on circumstantial evidence. In *McGreevy v. DPP* [1973] 1 All E.R. 503, the House of Lords held that there is no rule requiring a special or additional direction where the evidence against the defendant is wholly or partially circumstantial and that it suffices to direct the jury that the prosecution has the burden of proving the defendant's guilt beyond reasonable doubt. Some clarification as to whether the same situation obtains in this jurisdiction would have been welcome.

Evidence in mitigation of damages in libel cases   The plaintiff in *Browne v. Tribune Newspapers Plc*, Supreme Court, November 24, 2000, was a detective superintendent in the Garda Síochána. He brought libel proceedings against the defendant on foot of a newspaper article dealing with the circumstances surrounding an incident in County Cavan in which the County Registrar had been shot. The thrust of the article was that the shooting could have been prevented if the gardaí had been more diligent. In their defence, the defendants denied that the plaintiff was identified by the article and pleaded justification and fair comment.

The plea of justification was successful and the plaintiff appealed, seeking an order that the judgment dismissing the plaintiff's claim be set aside. The main ground of appeal advanced was that the trial judge had erred in permitting counsel for the defendant to cross-examine the plaintiff during the trial in order to elicit from him the fact that he had recovered in excess of £80,000 as a result of four previous libel actions and was not, therefore, as he attempted to characterise himself, a reluctant litigant.

The judgment of the Supreme Court was delivered by Keane C.J. who approached this question, firstly, on the basis of principle. He pointed out that cross-examination as to actions for defamation brought by the plaintiff in the past in respect of other unrelated publications was clearly not relevant to the issues of justification, fair comment, the meaning to be attributed to the words complained of, or the identification of the plaintiff. It could, therefore, only be relevant, if at all, to the issue of damages. However, he was of the view that permitting cross-examination of this nature would involve the Court in trying collateral issues. It would, he said, be necessary to permit the plaintiff, in order to correct any damaging impression in the mind of the jury arising from the recovery of damages in earlier proceedings, to permit the plaintiff to give details as to the precise nature of the defamation on the previous occasion, the course that the proceedings had taken, whether any apology had been offered, and the nature of the trial. The defendant would, in turn, be entitled to call rebutting evidence and the Court would find itself in the position of having to conduct a virtual trial within a trial on this issue. The Chief Justice regarded it as "remarkable that the Court would be obliged to try collateral issues of this nature simply in order to determine whether, in the event of the plea of justification failing, the plaintiff's damages should be reduced because of his readiness to bring defamation proceedings in the past". In the absence of any authority on the matter, he would, therefore, have inclined to the view that this cross-examination should not have been permitted.

This conclusion was bolstered by a consideration of the authority on the point. In their *Consultation Paper on the Civil of Defamation* (1991), the Law Reform Commission had identified the evidence which a defendant could lead evidence in mitigation of damages as follows:

(a) Evidence that the plaintiff had a general bad reputation prior to the publication of the defamation;

(b) Under section 26 of the Defamation Act [1961] evidence that the plaintiff has recovered damages, or has bought actions for damages, for libel or slander in respect of the publication of words to the same effect as the words on which the action is founded, or has received or agreed to receive compensation in respect of any such publication;

(c) Under section 17 of the Defamation Act [1961], evidence that the defendant made or offered an apology to the plaintiff before the commencement of the action or as soon afterward as he had an opportunity of doing so, in case the action was commenced before there was an opportunity for making or offering such apology;

(d) Evidence of retractions or corrections by the defendant, or the offer of a right of reply;

(e) Evidence of the conduct of the plaintiff;

(f) Evidence of the circulation of the libel;

(g) Repetition and disclosure of source."

Rejecting any distinction in principle between evidence in mitigation of damages led by the defendant and evidence elicited by him on cross-examination, the Chief Justice took the view that the foregoing passage accurately set forth the law and it was clear that evidence that the plaintiff had instituted proceedings in the past in respect of unrelated publications did not come within any of the categories set out.

Keane C.J. went on to explain that defamation actions are *sui generis* and that the estimation in monetary terms of the damage to a person's reputation was a very different exercise to the assessment carried out by a court in a personal injury action. Given that a jury was being asked to assess damages in respect of damage to the plaintiff's reputation, it was well-established that a plaintiff should not be allowed to recover damages for injury to a reputation that he did not possess. It had, accordingly, been held in the leading English decision of *Scott v. Samson* (1882) 8 Q.B.D. 491, that general evidence of a bad reputation was admissible in mitigation of damages but that evidence of particular facts tending to show the character and disposition of the plaintiff was not. Cave J. summarised the position as follows:

> As to...evidence of facts and circumstances tending to show the disposition of the plaintiff, both principle and authority seem equally against its admission. At the most it tends to prove not that the plaintiff had not, but that he ought not to have, a good reputation and to admit evidence of this kind is in effect, as it was said in *Jones v. Stephen*, 11 Price 235, to throw on the plaintiff the difficulty of showing a uniform propriety of conduct during his whole life. It would give rise to interminable issues which would have but a very remote bearing on the question in dispute, which is to what extent a reputation which he actually possesses has been damaged by the defamatory matter complained of.

The law in Ireland in relation to this issue was less settled. In *Kavanagh v. The Leader*, Supreme Court, March 4, 1955, the position as set forth in *Scott v. Samson* was accepted as settled law. However, in the earlier case of *Bolton v. O'Brien* (1885) 16 LR Ir 97, specific instances of misconduct were admitted with a view to reducing damages. The issue has been addressed by the Law Reform Commission in their report on the *Civil Law of Defamation* (1991) which recommended that the law should be clarified by permitting the defendant to introduce in mitigation of damages any matter, general or particular, relevant at the date of the trial to that aspect of the plaintiff's reputation with which the defamation was concerned.

The Chief Justice conceded that there might be cases where rigid application of the rule in *Scott v. Samson* might lead to the exclusion of a specific act of misconduct which would be plainly relevant in establishing that the plaintiff was claiming damage to a reputation which he did not have. However, the reasons which had led the courts both in Ireland and in England to lean against the introduction of evidence as to specific acts of misconduct in mitigation of damages also pointed to the exclusion of evidence that the plaintiff had instituted proceedings in the past for defamation arising out of other publications relating to wholly different matters. In *Plato Films Limited v. Speidel* [1961] A.C. 1090, Lord Morris had explained that:

> If in a quest to discover or to assess the true character and disposition of a plaintiff a defendant could assert and seek to prove certain deeds which were discreditable to the plaintiff, the latter could hardly be denied the right to counterbalance them by asserting and seeking to prove deeds which redounded to his credit. The limits of roving enquiry would be hard to control. There would be trials within a trial. The last stage of a trial would be far removed from the first.

Keane C.J. opined that this concern must apply with even greater force where the acts of which evidence was sought to be given, i.e. the institution of the proceedings for defamation, were not of themselves discreditable. He rejected, in this regard, the contention made by the defendant that the evidence was being introduced, not in relation to the reputation of the plaintiff, but in relation to the injury and distress which the publication was alleged to have caused him personally. That was one of the matters which the jury was, undoubtedly, entitled to take into account in assessing the damages in an action for defamation. However, he took the view that it would be anomalous if a defendant were to be generally precluded from introducing evidence as to specific acts of misconduct with a view to mitigating the damages in respect of the injury to the plaintiff's reputation, but permitted to introduce evidence of specific acts, whether amounting to misconduct or not, with a view to mitigating the damages payable in respect of the injury to the plaintiff's feelings. Furthermore, this conclusion was strongly reinforced by the provisions of section 26 of the Defamation Act 1961 which provided that in an action for libel or slander the defendant could adduce in evidence in mitigation of damage that the plaintiff had recovered damages or had brought actions for damages for libel or slander in respect of the publication of words to the same effect as the words on which the action was founded, or had received or agreed to receive compensation in respect of such publications. If the contention of the defendant that it was permissible to adduce evidence of the institution by the plaintiff of defamation proceedings in respect of wholly unrelated libels was correct, the provisions of section 26 would be entirely superfluous.

Keane C.J. also rejected the submission, which had found favour with the trial judge, that the cross-examination was permissible as going to credit. He pointed out that the purpose of cross-examination as to credit is to undermine the credibility of a particular witness and, in a case where the plaintiff had not suggested in any way in his direct evidence that this was the first case he had brought for defamation, eliciting from him that he had in fact instituted such proceedings would not in any way affect his credibility. He reiterated again that it would be remarkable if a defendant was to be precluded from cross-examining as to specific acts of misconduct but could be allowed under the guise of a cross-examination as to credit, to introduce evidence of conduct which would not be said to be, of itself, discreditable. He therefore concluded that the trial judge had erred in law in permitting this line of cross-examination and this error had been seriously prejudicial to the plaintiff in enabling counsel for the defendant to portray him to the jury as a person who was in the business of recovering damages for alleged libels however trivial and inconsequential they might be. In the premises, the appeal was allowed and a new trial ordered.

The common law courts have traditionally employed a somewhat accentuated concept of relevance such that evidence which is logically relevant in the sense outlined by Lord Simon in *DPP v. Kilbourne* [1973] A.C. 729, 756, that "it is logically probative or disprobative of some matter which requires proof" may be excluded on policy grounds as being insufficiently relevant. The most common basis on which evidence of marginal relevance may be excluded is where its admission would or might give rise to collateral issues which would distract the court of trial from the main issue and lengthen the proceedings (see, for example, *Agassiz v. London Tramway Co* (1872) 21 W.R. 199). Indeed, some of the exclusionary rules such as the rule against hearsay and the rule against the admission of misconduct evidence can be seen to be based, in part, on the fear of the courts becoming enmeshed in a multiplicity of side issues. Although, as Keane C.J. was at pains to point out, libel actions are *sui generis*, the decision in *Browne* is of interest in that it provides a very good modern example of this fear, on the part of the courts, of collateral issues and the desire to keep trial issues within reasonable bounds.

It might be noted in passing that another ground of appeal which was advanced in *Browne*, was that the trial judge had intervened in the cross-examination by counsel for the plaintiff of one of the witnesses at what was described as "a critical juncture" in such a way as to deprive the cross-examination of its force. While the Chief Justice accepted that there are occasions when interventions by a trial judge in either civil or criminal cases being tried by a jury could be so prolonged and of such a nature as to be unfairly disruptive and even give the jury the impression that he or she was leaning in favour of one side of the case, he was satisfied that this was not so in the instant case.

Family Law

NULLITY OF MARRIAGE

Grounds for a decree   In *G.F. v. J.B. (otherwise known as J.F.)* High Court, March 28, 2000, Murphy J. granted a decree of nullity on the ground of the petitioner's incapacity to enter into or sustain a normal marriage relationship and (on one view of the judgment) his lack of consent where the uncontradicted evidence of the medical inspector appointed by the court and of another psychiatrist was to the effect that the petitioner lacked 'an adequate emotional capacity' to enter into such a relationship.

The petitioner was born in 1964. He formed a relationship with a young woman when he was around twenty-one. She became pregnant and told him that she was having an abortion. This caused him intense anxiety. He had panic attacks and suffered from depersonalisation. He told his parents of the situation; his mother was distressed, his father 'seemed indifferent'. The petitioner consulted a psychiatrist for a time. The judgment does not record any more details about the petitioner's relationship with the young woman. It is clear, however, that the relationship ended around this time.

In 1987 the petitioner formed a new relationship, this time with the respondent. Within a few weeks, she told him that she was pregnant. Murphy J. recorded that the petitioner:

> reacted with great concern. It was a repeat disaster for him. He was concerned for his mother. He was concerned for his new girlfriend. He was determined not to disturb his mother. He would have done anything to avoid that. Yet he had no long term plans.
>
> He decided to tell his parents first that they were getting married and then that she was pregnant so as to bring a solution to the problem. His mother accepted that. He says his father took a sneering attitude and remained distant.

At the time of the wedding, the petitioner 'was still focused on panic attacks and depression. He had no sense of his own worth.' The petitioner was in contact with his psychiatrist six times between the wedding and the birth of his daughter.

The marriage did not work out successfully. The petitioner left the family home six years later. Both he and the respondent established new relationships. The petitioner had a child in his new relationship.

The petitioner's psychiatrist gave evidence of his belief that the petitioner:

> suffered from depersonalisation and was like an antelope incapable of responding to the presence of a lion. In relationships he was possessive, with a high need to be appreciated and with the significant separation anxiety problem he required constant availability.

The petitioner had told the psychiatrist in relation to his marriage that he was being sucked into a situation that he could not handle, that his wife knocked the confidence out of him and that they were fighting all the time. As time went on this was affecting their daughter.

The psychiatrist believed that the basic problem with the petitioner was that he was a very insecure person, who suffered from anxiety and depression, and 'separation anxiety' with an obsessive personality disorder. The petitioner, in his view, was not capable of viewing his life partner as a separate individual:

> There was no mutuality in the relationship. While the petitioner had an intellectual insight into this condition he did not have control over his emotions. He was drawn by an immature set of emotions.

In relation to the petitioner's ability to sustain marriage, the psychiatrist believed that this would be extremely difficult. His personality problems would tend to erode whatever relationship there was. It would 'need a "perfect" partner, a mother figure who was constantly available'.

The medical inspector was willing to go further than this psychiatrist. In his view, the petitioner suffered from gross immaturity. His decision to marry 'depended on his attitude to his parents and not to his own need. His decisions were made on a more proximate need and not on any long-term basis'. Although the petitioner's parents had not forced him into marriage, his inordinate need to please had led him to that decision. He was 'immature and not able to consent'.

The medical inspector believed that the respondent was not supportive. Murphy J. recorded:

> As he perceived it the relationship was doomed. The petitioner would have to find a particular foil: '*a perfect person*'. That person would have to be calm, materialistic. As he perceived it, this was not the relationship that he had formed; it was not conducive to his being able to cope.

No evidence was given by or on behalf of the respondent.

Murphy J. granted the decree of nullity of marriage. He accepted the expert evidence that the petitioner had lacked the emotional capacity to enter into or sustain a normal marriage relationship with the respondent. He went on to note that:

> [i]t would appear also that because of that the petitioner was not fully free in his mind or fully informed to consent to the marriage ceremony with the respondent.

Whether this is a separate ground is not entirely clear since the petitioner's lack of freedom to consent was attributed to a condition which, Murphy J. found, was sufficient in itself to render the marriage voidable. It is hard to see how the petitioner was not fully informed on any relevant fact. There would seem little benefit in letting relational incapacity expand into a second ground for granting a decree of nullity of marriage. Some people may indeed consider that it scarcely warrants recognition as a ground in that, at all events where it is constituted by evidence of emotional immaturity, even to a gross degree. It is interesting to note the difference among the psychiatrists recorded in the judgment as to who would be the 'perfect' wife for this man. In the view of the medical inspector, she would have to be 'calm, materialistic'. According to the other psychiatrist's prescription, she should be 'a mother figure who was constantly available'.

DIVORCE

Grounds for a decree   In *M.McA. v. X. McA.* [2000] 2 I.L.R.M. 48, McCracken J. gave the first authoritative interpretation of the 'living apart' requirement in section 5 (1) of the Family Law (Divorce) Act 1996. Section 5(1) provides as follows:

> Subject to the provisions of this Act, where, on application to it in that behalf by either of the spouses concerned, the court is satisfied that:
>
> (a) at the date of the institution of the proceedings, the spouses have lived apart from one another for a period of, or periods amount to, at least four years during the previous five years;
> (b) there is no reasonable prospect of a reconciliation between the spouses;
> and
> (c) such provisions as the court considers proper having regard to the circumstances exists or will be made for the spouses and any dependent members of the family,
>
> the court may, in the exercise of the jurisdiction conferred by Article 41.3.2° of the Constitution, grant a decree of divorce in respect of the marriage concerned.

The facts of the instant case need to be set out in detail since it was from the totality of these details that McCracken J. determined the question whether the 'living apart' claim should succeed. The parties were married in 1968. There were two grown up children, both of whom worked in the family business. In 1988 the applicant discovered that the respondent was carrying on an affair with another woman. Having been confronted with the applicant's knowledge of the affair, the respondent left the family home. He continued to conduct the affair. In 1989, the applicant consulted a solicitor, who wrote several letters on her behalf to the respondent, threatening family law proceedings. No such proceedings in fact were issued. The respondent provided for his wife who continued to reside in the family home with the children.

In 1991 the respondent ended the affair and returned to live in the family home. The applicant said in evidence that she was glad to have him come back because she had never really accepted that the marriage had ended. The respondent maintained in evidence, however, that his primary motive for returning was that he wanted to develop a better relationship with his son, who was then just 18. Commenting on these differing recollections, McCracken J. observed:

> The applicant certainly hoped that some form of normality could be achieved in the marriage. I think that the respondent did not have any such expectations, even at that stage.

Over the following years, the parties slept in separate bedrooms and never resumed sexual relations. On several occasions they went away on holidays with the children but again slept in separate bedrooms. McCracken J. accepted that, in 1991,

> [w]hen they were in the house together they appear to have had what might be called a civilised relationship, in that they were polite to each other and if both were present at meal times would take their meals together. When he was at home, the respondent would tend to go to bed, or at least to his room early and watch television and he had a separate telephone line installed into his room.

McCracken J. regarded the financial dimension to the parties' lives as having significance to the issue of their living apart. The respondent's business was during this period growing rapidly to the point that he became probably the biggest employer in the town where they lived. Because of his business activities, the respondent became involved in a number of social activities. McCracken J. observed that the parties 'were important people in the town and undoubtedly attended a number of local functions together.' The applicant owned 15% of the shares of the holding company of her husband's business. She also managed a shop in the town which was part of the business. As manager she was paid a wage for her work. In 1991, when the respondent returned to the house, he agreed to pay the applicant £750 per month in cash (which was later increased to £1,000 per month). The applicant's car and motoring expenses were also paid out of the respondent's business.

In 1995, while the parties were still living in the same house, the applicant 'entered into a relationship, including a sexual relationship with another gentleman.' In 1996 the respondent entered into a relationship with another woman. He left the family home the following year to live with her. McCracken J. observed that, '[o]n the evidence it seems that at that time [in 1995 and 1996] neither of th[e parties] was fully aware of the extent of the other's relationships ...'

McCracken J. provided a detailed analysis of the 'living apart' requirement. He noted that the 1996 Act did not attempt a definition of the term but he considered that some assistance could be obtained from English authorities. He acknowledge that these decisions were somewhat complicated by the fact that England's Divorce Reform Act 1969 provides (in section 2(5)) that, for the purposes of that legislation, a husband and wife are to be treated as living apart unless they are living in the same household. (In Ireland, a similar definition is contained in the Judicial Separation and Family Law Reform Act 1989, section 2(3)(a), but significantly neither the Fifteenth Amendment to the Constitution nor the 1996 Act includes a similar definition.)

McCracken J. referred to three English authorities, two relating to the 'living apart' requirement under the 1969 Act and one concerned with the issue of when desertion ends after the resumption of cohabitation of a limited, non-sexual character. He considered that in *Mouncer v. Mouncer* [1972] 1 W.L.R. 321, Wrangham J. had adopted reasoning that applied ' .... a totally physical test' as to whether the parties were living apart but that a different attitude had been favoured by the English Court of Appeal in *Santos v. Santos* [1972] 2 All E.R. 246. There Sachs L.J. had stated (at 255) that the expression 'living apart' contained in grounds (d) and (e) of section 2(1) of the Divorce Reform Act 1969 was:

> a state of affairs to establish which it is in the vast generality of cases arising under those heads necessary to prove something more than that the husband and wife are physically separated. For the purposes of that vast generality, it is sufficient to say that the relevant state of affairs does not exist when both parties recognise the marriage as subsisting. That involves considering attitudes of mind and naturally the difficulty of judicially determining that attitude in particular cases may on occasions be great. But the existence of such a difficulty cannot be in point, for heads (d) and (e) are not the only ones in which the identification of an attitude of mind is required; indeed the whole concept of a breakdown being 'irretrievable' may involve coming to conclusions on attitudes of mind, when an issue is raised under s. 2(3).

In *Bartram v. Bartram* [1949] 2 All E.R. 270, where the issue concerned the termination of desertion, a wife who had deserted her husband was unable to find any other accommodation eighteen months after the desertion had begun. She moved into the house where her husband was living with his mother, but slept in a separate bedroom and as far as possible avoided meeting him except at mealtimes. In holding that the desertion had not been terminated, Bucknill L.J. observed that the desertion could have been brought to an end:

> only if the facts show an intention on the part of the wife to set up a matrimonial home with the husband. If the facts do not establish any intention on the part of the wife to set up a matrimonial home, the mere fact that, as a lodger, she went to live under the same roof as her husband, because she had nowhere else to go, goes not remove the desertion which she had already started and which she continued to run.

McCracken J. gleaned from *Santos* and *Bartram* that, unlike *Mouncer*, they clearly had expressed the view that the intention of the parties was 'a very relevant matter in determining issues such as whether they live apart or whether there has been desertion.'

McCracken J. rejected the argument made on behalf of the applicant that *Bartram* supported the proposition in regard to the instant case that, once the parties had started to live apart, they continued to do so in the legal sense even after the respondent returned to the family home because there was no true reconciliation between the parties. McCracken J. could not accept this as a general proposition for two reasons. First, *Bartram* was concerned with desertion rather than living apart. Secondly, the whole purpose of section 5(1)(a) of the 1996 Act, in prescribing a period of 'living apart' for four of the previous five years, was to allow the parties come together for a short time in an attempt to become reconciled.

McCracken J. did, however, regard *Bartram* as 'a further authority that the court should look to the intention of the parties in considering matters of this nature.'

In a crucial passage, McCracken J. stated:

> "It must be born[e] in mind that the right to a divorce in this country is a constitutional right arising under Article 41.3.2° of the Constitution, and that the 1996 Act sets out the circumstances under which such a constitutional right may be exercised. In construing the Act the court must have regard to the context in which words are used, namely the termination of a matrimonial relationship. Marriage is not primarily concerned with where the spouses live or whether they live under the same roof, and indeed there can be a number of circumstances in which the matrimonial relationship continues even though the parties are not living under the same roof as, for example, where one party is in hospital

or an institution of some kind, or is obliged to spend a great deal of time away from home in the course of his or her employment. Such separations do no necessarily constitute the persons as living apart from one another. Clearly there must be something more than mere physical separation and the mental or intellectual attitude of the parties is also of considerable relevance. I do not think one can look solely either at where the parties physically reside, or at their mental or intellectual attitude to the marriage. Both of these elements must be considered, and in conjunction with each other.

Applying this test, McCracken J. had:

no doubt that, just as parties who are physically separated may in fact maintain their full matrimonial relationship, equally parties who live under the same roof may be living apart from one another. Whether this is so is a matter which can only be determined in the light of the facts of any particular case.

In the instant case, the respondent had categorised his bedroom as his apartment and had given evidence that normally he went away at weekends unless the children were at home; this meant that he would be away for three weekends out of four. He also said that he would see the applicant for only two or three hours in any week and that he felt like a lodger in the house. McCracken J. observed that, on the other hand, it was quite clear that, when the children were in the house, the respondent took a full part in the household arrangements and on a number of occasions had gone on holidays with the applicant and the children.

McCracken J. was satisfied that, from the time he first left in 1998, the respondent had considered the marriage to be at an end and that he did not return with any intention of resuming a normal matrimonial relationship. In contrast, the applicant did not want the marriage to be at an end and hoped that, when he returned in 1991, it would lead to a normal matrimonial relationship. McCracken J. observed:

Marriage involves mutuality, and it is my view on the evidence that when the respondent returned in 1991 he did not intend to return to a marriage, but rather that he wanted to have a better relationship with his children, who were then in third level education. I do not think he ever intended to live together with his wife as husband and wife, and as the phrase 'living apart from one another' is used in the context of a marriage, I think that the respondent never intended to live other than apart from the applicant.

The relevant period, for the purposes of the Act's requirements, was the five-year span between August 1994 and August 1999, from which a four-year period of 'living apart' had to be established. McCracken J. considered that the existence of the applicant's relationship with another man, which began in 1995, was:

> evidence of the mental attitude of the applicant to the marriage in 1995. Whatever she may have hoped for in 1991 when the respondent returned, quite clearly by 1995 she was aware that for all intents and purposes the marriage was at an end, there had been no sexual relations for many years and she, perhaps understandably, was prepared to form a relationship with another person. If I consider the mental and intellectual attitude of the parties, therefore, I am satisfied that the respondent never considered himself to be living together with the applicant in a marriage, and that certainly in the last four years of the marriage the applicant did not consider herself to be living together with the respondent in that same sense. Accordingly I am of the view that the respondent has satisfied the conditions set out in s. 5 of the 1996 Act and I would propose to grant a decree of divorce.

The analysis of the crucial ground for a decree of divorce will be closely studied by persons anxious to divorce who have not been living physically apart from their spouse for the requisite four-year period. It is now open to argue that living apart can occur even where the spouses are residing under the same roof with some degree of communication between them. On the important issue of whether the complete absence of sexual relations is necessary to constitute living apart, the judgment is curiously silent. Although McCracken J. made a finding that the spouses had not had sexual relations during the requisite period, he did not say that this element was a precondition to a finding of living apart. If spouses who maintain a sexual relationship and who live under the same roof can obtain a decree of divorce on the basis of the level of mental withdrawal from the marriage by one or both of them, then the predictions of those who opposed the measure will have proved prophetic. Once one accepts the philosophy that disengagement from the marriage by one spouse should warrant the granting of a decree, albeit after a long period of time, the requirement of proof of actual separation for the duration of the period can begin to look like a futile impediment to the right to turn into actuality the right to move on and seek happiness in another relationship. In the legal process, the deep philosophical structure has a tendency eventually to reveal itself and command obedience. Commentators on the decision have discussed such questions as whether there is a need for one spouse to communicate to the other an intention to terminate *corsortum* or whether both spouses must mentally withdraw from the relationship: see Frank Martin, '"To Live Apart or Not to Live Apart": That is the Divorce Question' [2000] 2 I.J.F.L. 2; Conor Power, 'Case Comment' [2000] 1 I.J.F.L. 22.

Consolidation of proceedings   In *M v. M*, High Court, May 23, 2000, McCracken J. took the view that where a respondent to proceedings for judicial separation subsequently issues divorce proceedings, the two proceedings should then be consolidated. He accordingly made an consolidation order.

ANCILLARY ORDERS

Pension entitlements   In *M v. M*, High Court, May 23, 2000, McCracken J. gave useful guidance as to how a court should exercise its jurisdiction under section 17(2) of the Family Law (Divorce) Act 1996, in relation to pension entitlements. The spouses were very well off. McCracken J., earlier in his judgment had made a property adjustment order transferring the wife's shares in the family company valued at £1,200,000 to her husband and an order for a lump sum payment of the same amount by the husband to the wife. The husband had a private pension trust governed by a deed of trust set up in 1996.

The wife submitted that the percentage of the trust fund to be held for her benefit should be sufficient to produce an amount equivalent to the maintenance payments to her which would cease to be payable on the making of the order. She submitted that the pension should be of an amount, not of the current maintenance, but rather of that sum increased in line with inflation.

McCracken J. observed:

> There are of course a number of imponderables involved. At the moment both parties have substantial assets, but I cannot foresee their circumstances in later years, which means that I do not know whether the maintenance order would be subsequently be varied. I also do not know whether the wife might re-marry, nor do I know whether she may get a substantial benefit from the transfer of life insurance policies. All in all, I do not think it would be correct for me to assume that she is entitled to a permanent income increasing in accordance with the cost of living, or indeed on any other basis such as a fixed percentage increase.

McCracken J. also took into account the fact that he was going to order the transfer of five policies (of £100,000 each) which, if the husband should die before the year 2010, would result in a large lump sum payment to the wife independent of any pension rights. He acknowledged that he should allow for some increase in cost of living. Taking all these facts into account, McCracken J. ordered that 75% of the retirement benefit accrued from the commencement of the private pension trust to the time of the judgment should be paid to the wife.

Business interests   In *M.McA v. X McA.*, [2000] 2 I.L.R.M. 48, McCracken

J. had to make financial orders in relation to a couple where the husband's business, towards which the wife had made an 'initial input', was worth several million pounds. It appeared that, on account of recent competition and the development of other techniques, the business had probably peaked, with little room for further growth in the absence of substantial investment in new technology. Ownership of the holding company was divided between the spouses, with the husband having an 85% interest, the wife 15%.

The spouses agreed that the wife should have the family home as well as an apartment in Tenerife and a house in Dublin and that the husband should have the second home and the apartment where he was living. The wife, moreover, was by agreement given ownership of the shop that she had been managing for many years (and the home adjoining it); the business carried on there was in future to be for her sole benefit.

The spouses also agreed that the husband would acquire the wife's 15% interest in the business at a price to be fixed by the court. McCracken J. accepted that, when valuing the business the essential emphasis should be on estimating the value of the future income rather than of the income in recent years. Accordingly he adopted a multiplier which took account of the increasing competition and changes in technology. This yield a valuation of eight million pounds, which measured the wife's interest at 1.2 million pounds.

McCracken J. noted that this sum was money to which the applicant was entitled as of right, irrespective of her entitlements under the 1996 Act. When addressing the orders that he should make under section 20 of the Act, he bore in mind that, the husband had assets of two million pounds in addition to his interest in the family business. So far as the order for periodic payments was concerned (which it appears the husband was willing to pay, subject to its quantum being fixed by the court), McCracken J. set the figure at £4,500 per month. He took account of the fact that the wife would be separately assessed for tax and that therefore this amount would be taxable in her hands, while noting also that she would undoubtedly have 'a sizeable income' from the lump sum that she would receive from the transfer of her interest in the business to her husband.

Turning to a further lump sum payment, McCracken J. thought it proper to order one having regard to the husband's assets, but he thought that it must be 'fairly limited.' It would not be in the interests of either party to undermine the husband's business potential. Accordingly McCracken J. fixed that order at £300,000.

McCracken J. deferred consideration of matters relating to the pension and life assurance policies pending further submissions.

Variation of separation agreements   The modern legislative code on family law is replete with directions to the court, when making ancillary orders, to 'have regard to' certain specified factors. Section 20(2) of the Family Law (Divorce) Act 1996 sets out twelve factors. Section 20(3) provides that the court, when deciding whether to make an order under any of the provisions referred to in section 20(1), is to have regard to the terms of any separation agreement which has been entered into by the spouses and is still in force.: Precisely what regard that should consist of is not clarified. This is unfortunate as there is a long legislative history, going back to the Family Law (Maintenance of Spouses and Children) Act 1976, of a normative battlefield between the goals of finality and certainty, on the one hand, and that of protecting vulnerable spouses, on the other.

It would be fair to say that the latter concern focused on wives and children as being more likely than husbands to find themselves in a position of financial insecurity. In *MG v. MG*, Circuit Family Court, July 25, 2000, the spouse who was seeking to assert vulnerability in opposition to finality was the husband. He was an accountant who had worked as an administrator. His wife was a senior civil servant. The parties had separated in 1995, entering a separation agreement under which the husband agreed to transfer his interest in the family home (then with a gross value of £200,000) to his wife. That interest was valued at £20,000 representing 20% of the net value of the property. In return for acquiring the husband's interest, the wife undertook to compensate him for that amount by a series of 'complicated arrangements' in the separation agreement, which envisaged payment to the husband on sale of the house, by a process of offsetting it against education fees for the children or by periodical payments over the next decade. The husband also agreed to pay maintenance for the children.

A year later the husband wished to obtain a divorce in the Dominican Republic in order to be able to marry his new partner. He sought his wife's consent to this plan. In consideration of her concurrence the husband offered to waive his entitlement to his share of the family home. A supplemental deed of separation was entered into in March 1996. Under this deed the husband waived his entitlement to be paid the sum of £20,000, which instead was to be held by the wife in trust for the three children. The husband after the divorce, married his new partner.

In 1998 the husband lost his job. He found it difficult to gain employment. He went to live outside Ireland with his new partner becoming employed on short-term contracts. Following the loss of his job the husband had been entitled only to unemployment assistance and was unable to pay the full amount of maintenance under the separation agreement. On his obtaining employment he recommenced payment of maintenance and also paid some of the arrears of maintenance which had built up.

Judge Buckley acknowledged the lack of guidance given the court by section 20(3) as to how to exercise the function of 'hav[ing] regard to' the separation agreement. He went on to observe:

> Where the parties are, as they are in this case, well-educated intelligent persons, who have had the benefit of competent legal advice before

entering into a separation agreement which is of recent date, it seems to me that the court should be slow to make any radical alterations to the terms of such agreement unless there have been sufficient changes in the situations of the parties. It is likely that such agreements will have been in operation for upwards of four years, and that the parties (or at least one of them) and their children will hopefully have adjusted to the new family regime established by that agreement. Making any significant alterations to the arrangements may well cause further distress to the children, who may well see themselves as vulnerable pawns in a renewed conflict between their parents. To the extent that there is a conflict between the statutory, and indeed constitutional, obligations imposed on a court to ensure that proper provision is made for the children of divorcing parents and the statutory obligation to consider every aspect of the parties financial and family situation before granting the decree while 'having regard' for the existing separation agreement I believe that court should be slow to order any changes which would affect the stability of the children's home life which hopefully will have been achieved following the separation agreement...

The first change in circumstances that had taken place after the first separation agreement was the husband's desire to obtain a divorce in order to re-marry his new partner. The second was the loss of his job. The third was that value of the family home had increased substantially between 1996 and 2000, being valued at £800,000 at the time of the judgment.

Judge Buckley commented:

The seeking of a decree of divorce in Ireland by the applicant was certainly foreseeable at the time of the separation and indeed the Divorce Referendum had been passed in Ireland by the time of the supplemental agreement.

The loss by the applicant of his job might have been reasonably foreseeable as he had suffered a similar loss on a previous occasion and indeed had had two significant periods of unemployment during the marriage.

The other major changes in the applicant's situation is that he now lives outside Ireland with his new partner, whom he married in New York having obtained his divorce in the Dominican Republic. Unfortunately she has recently lost her job on health grounds. The respondent has continued to live in the family home, maintaining it as a secure base for the children and has been solely responsible for their welfare. She has found her finances to be 'tight'. The market value of the family home has increased very significantly since 1995 and is now believed to be about £800,000, with a mortgage debt of over £50,000.

Taking all these matters into account, Judge Buckley came to the conclusion that, with one exception, he should not make any alteration to the financial provisions which had been made in the two agreements. The one change he made was in relation to the family home. He did:

> not think it could have been contemplated by the parties at the time of the supplemental agreement that there would be such remarkable increase in residential property values between the date of the supplemental agreement and the date of trial. If it had been contemplated I doubt if the applicant would have so readily surrendered all his interest in the family home.

Accordingly, Judge Buckley directed that on any future sale of the family home the respondent should pay the applicant a sum equal to 10% of the net sale price. This order did not confer any equitable estate in the property on the applicant.

JUDICIAL SEPARATION

Ancillary orders In *C. O'R v. M. O'R*, High Court, September 19, 2000, O'Donovan J. gave guidance on a number of important issues relating to ancillary orders in judicial separation proceedings. The parties had married in 1993, when the applicant wife was aged 22 and the respondent husband was 29. They had three children. They separated in 1997. The respondent started a new relationship. Two children were born to that union. The respondent's father was very rich and the applicant argued that the respondent benefited from this wealth. O'Donovan J. rejected this argument on the evidence. So far as the father's wealth was concerned, he considered that this was not a matter to be taken into account when determining the respondent's support obligation to the applicant and her children. O'Donovan J. observed:

> It may well be that, in the fullness of time, the husband will succeed to a very large proportion of his father's wealth and, if and when that happens, it may well be that the wife and children of the husband will be entitled to a greater contribution from him for their maintenance and support. However, as I interpret the evidence of [the husband's father], while he is not short of affection for his son, he is certainly not disposed to settling large sums of money on him in the short term and neither is he disposed to supplement any shortfall on his son's income so that the husband can make better provision for the support of his wife and children. Accordingly, when determining the reality of the husband's assets and income and the extent to which is will permit him to contribute towards the support of his wife and children, I am excluding

from the equation the fact that the husband's father is a very wealthy man save that I am viewing all commercial transactions between father and son, whether negotiated directly or through the medium of companies controlled by them, with some suspicion, in the sense that I must satisfy myself that they are genuine commercial transactions and that they are not influenced by the relationship.

The respondent, though he was earning a good salary and was involved in a number of business ventures on his own behalf, was falling under some considerable pressure from borrowings. He argued that the family home, should be sold and that a less expensive house be purchased for the applicant and their children. O'Donovan J. concluded on the evidence that this would not be the proper course. He stated that he wished:

> to emphasise that, in coming to this conclusion, I am influenced more by what I perceive to be the better interests of the children of the marriage than I am by the views or wishes of their parents. In this regard, I am aware of my own knowledge how traumatic and disruptive it can be for a child to have to leave surroundings with which he or she has been familiar for most of their lives: surroundings which, in this case, are located in close proximity to their school and surroundings which, in all probability, are located in close proximity to their friends and to go somewhere else, where, in effect, they have to start life all over again. Accordingly, it seems to me that, when there is a breakdown of a marriage and there are children of that marriage, the better interests of those children demand that they should not have to leave the home which they have known all their lives unless the financial position of their parents requires that the family home be sold.

O'Donovan J. did not, however, order that the home be transferred to the applicant. He considered that, given that the marriage had only lasted three and a half years, that both parties had contributed to its breakdown, that they were still relatively young and that the wife had not made any financial contribution, it would be 'a grave injustice' to the respondent to make such an order. Instead O'Donovan J. made an order under section 10 (1)(a)(i) of the Family Law Act 1995 conferring on the applicant the right to occupy the family home to the exclusion of the respondent until the children had completed their full-time education, at which point, in default of mutual agreement, the court would make a further order.

So far as maintenance was concerned, O'Donovan J. questioned the need for the children to attend a crèche between the time that their school day finished and the time that the applicant returned home from work:

> In this regard, while I heard no evidence with regard to the cost of the

crèche which the children are presently attending, again, I have some personal knowledge of the approximate cost of such facilities and I am aware that they are relatively expensive. Accordingly, as the children are no longer infants and, presumably, are as independent as one can expect of a five or a six year old, it occurs to me that it should be possible for [the applicant] to employ someone to collect them from school and look after then for a few hours until she, herself, comes home from work. In that event, I would have thought that the cost involved would be considerably less that the cost of putting the children in a crèche.

In *A.K. v. P.K.* High Court, March 13, 2000, Murphy J. had to deal with a couple, married in 1972, whose children were of full age, though they still 'required and were given support from both [parents]'. The husband was a professional in partnership with another person. A new surgery had recently been built which was attached to the family house. This surgery, owned by the partnership, was valued at £225,000. An old surgery, also jointly owned by the spouses was valued at £75,000.

Murphy J. made a periodical payments order in favour of the wife, under section 8(1)(a) of the Family Law Act 1995, of £375 per week. He also made a property adjustment order under section 9, requiring the husband's interest in the old surgery premises to be transferred to the wife. So far as the new surgery and the family home were concerned, Murphy J. noted that it had not been contested that part of the husband's practice was conducted in the family home. He accordingly granted an order under section 10 conferring on the husband the right to occupy the family home and surgery to the exclusion of the wife for as long as he remained in practice or until he reached 65, whichever was the earlier. At that point, unless the spouses agreed otherwise, the family home would be sold and the net proceeds divided equally between the spouses.

In *P. O'D. v. J. O'D.*, High Court, March 31, 2000, in an elaborate judgment extending to ninety-seven pages, Budd J. held that the wife of a man who had built up an extensive property empire, by her work in collecting rents, cleaning the properties, dealing with workmen and related matters, had contributed sufficiently to what Budd J. characterised as a partnership between the spouses to entitle her to a half share in the property portfolio. He was guided by the approach adopted by McGuinness J. in *J.D. v. D.D.* [1997] 3 I.R. 64. It seems that Budd J. was also affected by the husband's strategy of seeking to disguise the full extent of his beneficial ownership in properties.

CHILDREN

Children born outside marriage   In *EH v. JM*, High Court, April 4, 2000 (Circuit Appeal) an unmarried couple, with two children, separated. The agreement which they drew up amicably was later overtaken by disharmony. Judge Linnane in the Circuit Court, made an order under which the parties were to retain joint custody and guardianship of the children: there is no discussion in Kinlen J's judgment of the father's having previously been made joint guardian under the Status of Children Act 1987. Judge Linnane also made detailed orders regarding the maintenance of the children. By a subsequent order Judge Linnane required that there should be 'no dealings by or on behalf of the [father] in respect of the site' which he had in a rural location until further order. This site had planning permission. The mother was living in rented accommodation.

On appeal to the High Court, Kinlen J. declined to award sole custody of the children to their mother as he was of the opinion that this would not be in their best interest. Kinlen J. reversed the order against dealings in respect of the site on the basis of an undertaking to the court by the father whereby he agreed that he would build a house or bungalow on it within three years.

So far as maintenance was concerned. Kinlen J. made some observations that are worthy of note. The father was a human resource manager; the mother a social worker who had apparently given up work in order to look after the children who, at the time of the High Court judgment were aged nearly sixteen and twelve, respectively. The judgment is not explicit on when she gave up her employment; it notes that, a few months before the speculation in 1996, she 'was a full time social worker'. Kinlen J. observed:

> The [father] maintains that the [mother] could earn much more than she is earning but she insisted that she had to give up work so as to attend to the children. If it ever were valid there is no foundation in the circumstances of today. The children are 16 and 12 respectively. The [father] and the [mother] should meet half the value of the expenses in respect of the children even though her earnings potential is much less than his.

When computing the amount of maintenance that the father should pay, Kinlen J. made no analysis of the amount that the mother might be likely to earn, so this passage should perhaps be understood in general terms rather than as articulating a specific criterion to guide the court. Kinlen J. observed, in the conclusion to this judgment, that:

> [s]ince the Court is concerned only with the well being of the children, the [mother] and the [father] are free agents and owe no duty to each other, other than joint parenting.

The reference to 'free agents' bears an interesting parallel with the concept of *union libre* in French law. Cohabitation is very much at a transitional stage in Irish legal characterisation. The legislature and the courts have been slow to impose mutually binding legal obligations of a proprietary nature but increasingly the legislature is recognising cohabitation in other contexts, such as fatal accident claims and the protection against domestic violence, albeit in a hesitant manner.

Financial support In *M.P. v. A.P.*, Supreme Court, March 3, 2000, parties to litigation under the Guardianship of Infants Act 1964 and the Judicial Separation and Family Law Reform Act 1989 compromised the proceedings on terms set out in a consent which was annexed to an order of High Court. Clause 5 (a) of the consent provided as follows:

> Maintenance of £1,800 nett of income tax per month. £1,400 attributable to Mrs. P. £200 p.m. attributable to each of the children. Same to be increased annually on the basis of the CPI for 1993 and annually thereafter.

Clause 10 provided that:

> Mrs. P will be liable for income tax and any income she may have from whatever source in addition to the maintenance of £1,800 nett of tax per month as adjusted hereafter.

The High Court order provided that:

> the husband do pay to the wife for maintenance the sum of £1,800 per month nett of income tax being the sum of £14,000 in respect of the wife and two equal sums of £200 each in respect of the said infant children respectively, the said sums to be adjusted annually in line with variations if any in the Consumer Price Index using mid-August as a base date.

A dispute later arose between the spouses as to the meaning of these clauses in the consent and the High Court order. Did they mean (as the wife claimed) that the husband was obliged to pay the wife a gross sum which, after deduction of the income tax payable by her, would leave her with the net sum of £1,800 per month? Or did they mean (as the husband asserted) that the tax payable by the wife in respect of the sum of £1,800 was to be deducted by him and transmitted to the Revenue, with the balance being paid to the wife?

In an *ex tempore* judgment, Costello J. rejected the husband's submission and held that the words 'nett of income tax' meant that the wife was entitled to be paid the sum of £1,800 and to be under no liability to income tax in respect of that sum.

On appeal to the Supreme Court, the parties were agreed that provisions in the family law and tax codes requiring maintenance payments to be made without deduction of income tax – the Family Law (Maintenance of Spouses and Children) Act 1976, section 24, Judicial Separation and Family Law Reform Act 1989, section 26, Family Law Act 1995, section 37, Family Law (Divorce) Act 1996, section 31 and the Finance Act 1983, section 3(2)(a) – did not affect the issue requiring determination in the proceedings. Counsel for the husband submitted that the parties had, in effect 'opted out' of the statutory provisions and the wife did not contest this. On the husband's argument, he had agreed to act as agent for the wife, deducting the tax payable by her on the sum of £1,800 and transmitting it to the Revenue on her behalf. Counsel for the husband argued that, if the intention had been as the wife contended, the parties would have adopted the expression widely employed in Irish separation agreements, of 'free of tax' rather than the ambiguous expression that the agreement had used. He contended that the consent should be rectified to embody what the parties had actually intended and that accordingly the case should be remitted to the High Court for oral evidence.

The Supreme Court accepted this argument. Keane CJ (Denham and McGuinness JJ. concurring) observed that, while there was undoubted force in the wife's contention that the words 'nett of income tax' could not be treated as mere surplusage, the expression remained 'unhappily ambiguous'. There was thus a need to have evidence as to the factual matrix in which the consent had been reached.

Health Services

UBALDUS de VRIES, Dublin City University

AMBULANCE SERVICES

Council The National Ambulance Advisory Council (Revocation) Order, 2000 (S.I. 108/2000) dissolves the National Ambulance Advisory Council and revokes the National Ambulance Advisory Council Order, 1998 (S.I. 27/1998) (Annual Review 1998, 446). The Council is replaced by the Pre-Hospital Emergency Care Council, established by the Pre-Hospital Emergency Care Council Order, 2000 (S.I. 109/2000) under the Health (Corporate Bodies) Act 1961 (as amended). The functions of the Council are many-fold. They include recognising institutions for the education and training of emergency medical technicians and conducting examinations leading to the award of N.Q.E.M.T. (National Qualification in Emergency Medical Technology) and awarding persons accordingly.

CORONERS

Anonymous testimony Section 28 of the Coroners Act 1962 provides that a coroner, who does not take depositions at an inquest, must take note of the names and addresses of all persons who give evidence at the inquest. Section 29 provides that the coroner must preserve depositions, notes as well as any other report. It further states that he must provide an applicant with a copy of any such document and may charge a fee for it.

In *Morris and Morris v. Dublin City Coroner* High Court, October 8, 1999 (Kinlen J.) (Annual Review 1999, 310-311), the applicants sought an order for certiorari, quashing the decision of the respondent to allow two witnesses, who were members of the Garda Síochána, to testify anonymously. The applicants also sought an order for certiorari of the decision not to permit the identification of the forensic and ballistic reports, which would identify the weapons used in the killing of the deceased (and thereby the identity of the two Garda officers). Kinlen J. held that, although it was certainly desirable that a coroner would investigate a request for anonymity, he has no such statutory power.

The respondents appealed: *Morris and Morris v. Dublin City Coroner* [2001] 1 I.L.R.M. 125. The Supreme Court allowed the appeal. Keane C.J. (with whom Murphy and Geoghegan JJ. concurred), held that sections 28 and 29 were of no particular relevance in the case. The point at issue was whether the coroner was entitled to make the rulings because of the threats to the personal security of the Gardaí witnesses. The issue was not whether the hearing had to be held in public, as claimed by the appellants. The Chief Justice further held that a coroner could conduct an enquiry in a manner that would serve best the public interest provided he adhered to the legislation and the rules of fair procedures. As the legislation did not provide rules in respect of anonymous testimony, the coroner was entitled to adopt the course he did.

The Chief Justice held, *obiter*, that a coroner's inquest does not fall within the ambit of Article 34.1 of the Constitution. The inquest need not take place in public. The coroner does not exercise any judicial power. However, regardless the silence of the legislation, the common law has established that the public interest is served that an inquest should take place in public (cf. *Garnett v. Ferrand* (1827) 6 B. & C. 611).

DISCIPLINARY PROCEEDINGS – AN BORD ALTRAINAS

The litigation between Anne O Ceallaigh and An Bord Altrainas has come to a close with two Supreme Court judgements. The litigation has been extensively reported upon in the Annual Review 1999, 320-325, which has been reprinted here to the extent of the points of appeal.

Background   The applicant in the many proceedings, Ann O Ceallaigh, has been a registered nurse and domiciliary midwife with An Bord Altrainas. The latter received complaints about her in 1997 and directed the Fitness to Practice Committee to conduct an inquiry under Part V of the Nursing Act 1985. These complaints, four in total, were made by the Master of a maternity hospital and the Matron of a different maternity hospital. Since then, Ms. O Ceallaigh has initiated judicial proceedings on many occasions, challenging the conduct of the disciplinary procedure and the powers of the An Bord Altrainas and its Fitness to Practice Committee.

The issues   The two Supreme Court judgments each dealt with two issues. These were:

— Section 44 – application on suspension. Two questions arose. First, to what extent was the midwife entitled to be informed and heard about the decision to suspend her. Second, what was the proper interpretation of section 44 in respect of the role of the Bord and the High Court.

— Section 38 – referral of complaints. The question here was whether the midwife was entitled to be notified that the complaints would be referred to the Fitness to Practice Committee so that she could be heard.

The two judgments are:

— *O Ceallaigh v. An Bord Altranais*, Supreme Court, 17 May 2000, with
   Hardiman J. giving the leading judgment, with separate opinions of
   Geoghegan and Murphy JJ. This judgment is an appeal from *O Ceallaigh
   v. An Bord Altranais*, High Court, 26 May 1998 (McCracken J.).

— *An Bord Altrainas v. O Ceallaigh*, Supreme Court, 17 May 2000, with
   Barron J. giving the leading judgment, with separate opinions of Denham
   and Murphy JJ. This judgment is an appeal from *An Bord Altrainas v. O
   Ceallaigh*, High Court, 18 May 1999 (Morris P.)).

Section 44 – right to be informed   Section 44 allows the Bord to apply to the
High Court for an order to suspend the nurse from the register if it is satisfied
that it is in the public interest to do so. This hearing must be held in private.

By court order of August 1, 1997, the midwife was suspended as a nurse
and midwife under section 44 pending the conclusion of the Fitness to Practice
Inquiry. This order was varied on a number of occasions. On August 13, 1997
the order was varied to suspend the applicant as a midwife only; her suspension
as a nurse was lifted. The following October (October 2 and 3, 1997), the order
was varied again to allow her to provide midwifery services to certain named
clients. On December 17, 1997, the order was again varied to add certain further
named clients. The order was last varied by order of the President of the High
Court on May 18, 1999, against which the Bord appealed. The midwife also
applied for judicial review in respect of the order.

Both cases – the judicial review before McCracken J., and its appeal, as
well as the appeal to the judgment of Morris P. on May 18, dealt with the proper
interpretation of section 44 of the Act.

Thus, in *O Ceallaigh v. An Bord Altrainas and the Attorney General*, High
Court, May 26, 1998 (McCracken J.), the applicant had challenged the decision
of the Bord to apply for her suspension under section 44. She stated that, under
section 44 the respondent had to be "satisfied" that the suspension would be in
the public interest. She argued that it could not be satisfied without making
reasonable enquiries, particularly from the applicant herself. This meant that
she ought to have been notified of the decision and be entitled to be heard.

The respondent claimed that were the High Court to grant the relief, it would
in effect challenge the previous decisions made by the court to grant the
application for suspension. These decisions could not be but correct. The applicant
had had the opportunity to challenge the decision there. McCracken J. agreed.
Indeed, the applicant had already done so, but unsuccessfully. Thus, as the court
had decided upon the matter, it was not open to the applicant to come back to the
High Court with the same issue by way of judicial review. Morris P. came to a
similar conclusion in his judgment of May 13.

The Supreme Court heard the appeal from the McCracken judgment on May
17, 2000, confirming his decision in respect of section 44. Hardiman J. held

that the midwife had had ample opportunity to air her grievances before the High Court under the various section 44 applications. This meant, according to the judge, that 'it is redundant to entertain further submissions on a matter which has been adjudicated upon by the High Court on two occasions' (page 32 of his judgment).

However, Hardiman J. also stated, perhaps *obiter,* that a section 44 *ex parte* application was an extreme measure and demands prompt action by the Bord, contrary to what had occurred in the present case. He held that an *ex parte* application (page 33 of his judgment):

> should be grounded on a full affidavit which explains in detail the reasons why it is not thus possible, in the Board's view, to the put the practitioner on notice in the ordinary way. It is not however possible to hold that there may not be circumstances, presumably very rare indeed, where the *ex parte* procedure will still be required.

Murphy J. held a more liberal approach towards the Bord's obligation to put a practitioner on notice in respect of a section 44 application. He stated:

> The fact that litigation, whether criminal or civil, may of itself and independent of its outcome cause embarrassment and inconvenience, or even damage, to the intended defendant is not of itself sufficient reason for imposing on the intended plaintiff an obligation to consult with the intended defendant before instituting the proceedings. In many cases it would be appropriate and desirable to warn the intended defendant of the threatened litigation and afford him an opportunity of meeting the claim without the necessity for proceedings. But the failure to adopt that course would not invalidate the proceedings or impinge upon the constitutional rights of the defendant. Inappropriate or precipitated action might be penalised by the order of the Courts in relation to costs or otherwise but would not go to the validity of the action. If the Board is precluded from instituting proceedings under s. 44 without first hearing the intended Respondent that extraordinary restraint must be found in s. 44 itself.

Thus, according to Murphy J., the Bord must concern itself first with the nature of the complaint before making a section 44 application. Does it warrant an application? Does the conduct complained of pose a threat to the public interest? Section 44 does not demand from the Bord to hear the intended defendant. Indeed, once instituted, Murphy J. held that the function of safeguarding the public interest transfers from the Board to the High Court.

This point was reiterated by Geoghegan J. in his judgment. He held that there was no obligation to give prior notification before commencing section 44 proceedings. He held that section 44 was designed to prevent immediate danger to the public. This public interest must be weighed against the right to natural justice of the applicant. The terms of section 44 achieved that balance, according to the judge. However, this raises the issue when the Bord is entitled to make a section 44 application. This was addressed in the appeal from the decision of Morris P. of May 18.

Section 44 – role of Bord and court   The Supreme Court decision in *An Bord Altrainas v. O Ceallaigh*, Supreme Court, May 17, 2000 is an appeal from the decision by Morris P. in *An Bord Altrainas v. O Ceallaigh*, High Court, May 18, 1999.

The High Court decision was the accumulation of many interlocutory procedures in respect of the suspension of the respondent under section 44. At issue was whether the interlocutory orders, suspending the midwife, were to be made permanent. Morris P. held that to decide this, the court had to be satisfied at the present time, and not only at the time the initial section 44 application was made, that suspension would be in the public interest. This also meant, according to the President of the High Court, that the Bord was required to review the position as the case developed to come to a view whether it was in the public interest to apply to the court. He held that, as the Bord had not done so (in fact it was a newly constituted Bord), he had to refuse the application.

The Bord appealed this decision. It submitted that the High Court had erred in law to hold that the Bord had to be satisfied at the trial date that suspension was in the public interest. It also submitted that the court had erred in holding that the Bord ought to have reconsidered the evidence available to it either continually or at the date of the trial.

Denham J. held that the wording of section 44 appears clear. The Bord must be satisfied when it applies to the court. However, by analogy to other injunction proceedings, Denham J. explained that an order might be an interim and subsequent interlocutory order. As matters proceed, fresh evidence may come into the proceedings that may contradict previous evidence. This is, though, a matter for the court to determine. The court keeps its jurisdiction, as the foundation for its jurisdiction is there. To this end, judge Denham allowed the appeal in respect of the first submission. She held that it was not necessary for the Bord 'to reconsider the matter and be satisfied at the time of a hearing [...] that it is in the public interest' to make the application to the court' (page 9 of her judgment). This precondition was met at the time of the first application in 1997. However, this did not absolve the Bord from its obligation to react to new evidence. Denham J. held:

> Where there is a conflict, and where, as here, there is a considerable delay, it would appear appropriate for a professional body to address the changed or changing situation and/or conflicting evidence.

She added that it would be wrong for a court to act on outdated information. On this basis, Denham J. rejected the second submission and upheld Morris P.'s decision that the Bord ought to have reconsidered its position as time proceeded and new evidence came to light. Denham J. also decided not to remit the case to the High Court and regarded the matter closed.

Barron J. carried out a thorough analysis of the aim and function of section 44. He stated that section 44 provides the Bord a right to bring proceedings when it is satisfied that the public interest demands the suspension of a member. Section 44, he held does not constitute an automatic right to obtain an immediate injunction on an *ex parte* application. He held that the Bord cannot sit back and do nothing when an interim or interlocutory order is granted; it must take steps to obtain a final order. To obtain the relief then there must be 'an onus on [the Bord] to satisfy the court that it should be continued and that what it might or might not have been its opinion two years before was immaterial' (at page 42 of his judgment).

An *ex parte* application under section 44, without notifying the person, would depend on the seriousness of the complaint and the urgency to obtain a suspension. However, Barron J. held that the evidence did not suggest that such urgency had arisen. He held (at page 45 and 46 of his judgment):

> Unless the issue as to the need to issue proceedings under s. 44 is adverted to immediately the Board has become aware of the ground which would justify such proceedings, then it is unlikely that such proceedings would be justified. Such ground would generally be apparent from the nature of the complaint itself, but might become clearer in the course of the investigative procedures required. But in all cases, the relevant medical facts must be brought to the attention of those who have the professional competence to understand them.

Matters then to be considered were (i) the nature of the complaint, (ii) the strength of the case and (iii) the appropriate sanction in the event of a finding of professional misconduct (i.e. striking-off the register or suspension). No such evidence had been presented to the court and, thus, Morris P. could not but lift the order, Barron J. held.

Murphy J. dissented, stating that the President of the High Court had erred in law. He held that the Bord was not required to review the original complaints or any additional available information since it had applied for a section 44 procedure. As far as judge Murphy was concerned, the application was properly brought before the court and it was for it to decide whether the injunction should be granted. The High Court was bound to this duty irrespective of the current opinion of the present Bord.

Section 38   Any person, including An Bord Altranais, may apply to the Fitness to Practice Committee for an inquiry into the alleged professional misconduct of a nurse or midwife (section 38(1)). Upon receipt of the application, the

Committee decides whether there is a *prima facie* case to hold an inquiry. The Committee informs the Bord about its findings. The latter then directs the Committee to hold the inquiry or to discharge the nurse (section 38(2) and (3)). The Bord notifies the nurse of the decision and, if an inquiry is to be held, he or she is told about the allegation and the contents of the collected evidence. It also informs the nurse that he or she, and his or her representative, can be present at the inquiry (section 38(4)).

In *O Ceallaigh v. An Bord Altranais*, High Court, May 26, 1998, McCracken J. held that section 38(3) allowed the Committee to decide to hold an inquiry if there was *prima facie* evidence warranting an inquiry. Only when it has decided to do so, an obligation existed to inform the applicant about the complaint. There was no need for the Committee to inform the midwife of its intention to hold an enquiry so that she could be heard. On appeal, the Supreme Court was divided. Hardiman J., with whom Geoghegan J. agreed, held that in the circumstances of the case the Bord should have notified the applicant about the decision to hold an inquiry so that she could be heard. Murphy J. dissented. He held that the Bord was under no such obligation.

Hardiman J. stated that the purpose of the enquiry was a preliminary investigation and designed as a filtering process. It would prevent prohibitive costs, distress and anxiety as well as public knowledge of the complaint. But should the midwife be given an opportunity to be heard at this stage? She had submitted that natural justice and fair procedures required such an approach. She evidenced that this had been done in relation to the first complaint.

Counsel on behalf of the Bord submitted that, according to the academic literature, the courts do not normally accede to a person's request to be heard in respect of an act that commences a sequence of events that might be detrimental to that person's interest. This is not a rigid rule but each separate step, as part of a whole, must be seen to be fair. (Counsel referred to Smith's *Judicial Review of Administrative Action*, 1980, 4th edition (page 199) and Wade's *Administrative Law*, 1988, 6th edition (pages 570-571).) A number of cases were said by counsel to support the general academic proposition. Thus, in *Scariff v. Lieutenant Col. David Taylor and Others* [1996] 1 I.R. 242, *Rees v. Crane* [1994] 2 A.C. 173 and *Murray v Legal Services Commissioners* [1999] 46 N.S.W.L.R. 224, the relevant disciplinary procedures were silent on the issue, as in the present case.

However, Hardiman J. pointed out that in *Rees*, the Privy Council held that the silence might well indicate that the fairness of the matter demanded that the defendant should be informed and heard. The Privy Council also held that in the case the disciplinary body could not rely on the urgency or necessity of the matter not to inform the defendant. Nor could it be said that it had not been possible for it to inform the defendant. The Court of Appeal of New South Wales held essentially the same position in the *Murray* case.

In *State (Shannon Atlantic Fisheries Limited) v McPolin* [1976] I.R. 93, the High Court quashed a report into an accident at sea, as the owner of the vessel had not been heard or given an opportunity to comment. The High Court held that it was irrelevant that someone else (the Minister) would make a decision on the basis of the report for the report not to include the owner's version of events. Hardiman J. held that the case is authority 'for the proposition that, in some circumstances at least, a preliminary inquiry without direct legal effect may give rise to an obligation to apply principles of natural justice' (page 27 of his judgment).

Hardiman J. also rejected the analogy made by counsel for the Bord that its decision was akin to a decision of a policeman or the DPP, relying on the *Rees* decision. He held that the actual complainants against the midwife acted out the role of policeman or DPP. The Bord's decision was more akin to a quasi-judicial decision.

Hardiman J. then reviewed what had happened in respect of the first complaint. There the midwife had been informed about the complaint and asked whether she wanted to comment. Furthermore, a publication by the Irish Nursing Board on the Bord's procedures also included this procedural aspect. A Bord member agreed in evidence that members of the INO would expect this to happen. Hence, this led Hardiman J. to conclude that the applicant would reasonably believe that further complaints would be notified to her.

On the basis of these findings Hardiman J. held that the applicant had not been treated fairly in relation to the section 38 decision to hold an enquiry. He held that the applicant should have been told about the allegations and be given a chance to deal with them. This would not mean that no circumstance exist not to inform a defendant but in the instant case, according to Hardiman J., the Bord could not give any satisfactory explanation why it had not informed the applicant. Nor had it, or would it, suffer any impairment to its ability to discharge its statutory functions.

Geoghegan J. agreed with the Hardiman J. He added that the Bord had not been exercising its statutory power properly. It had failed to make reasonable attempts to notify the applicant and take on board what she might have to say on the issue. Geoghegan J. held (page 2 of his judgment):

> If a professional body is invested with the power of receiving complaints relating to a member of that profession and deciding whether an inquiry should be put in motion the outcome of which might lead to the person complained about being no longer able to practice his or her profession, that body cannot be said to be exercising its power lawfully and fairly without the person complained about being informed of the complaint and the Board having sight of any response to such complaint.

The decision in *Rees*, according to Geoghegan J., allowed for an element of discretion to ensure fairness as regards the application of the general rule that a person need not be heard at the initial stages.

Murphy J. dissented. He considered whether the applicant, in addition to her statutory right to be informed about a pending inquiry, has also an implicit right to be informed and heard in respect of any decision about the complaint, including a decision to hold an inquiry. Murphy J. agreed that the right to be heard is a long-established principle and extends to extra-judicial judgments, decisions and reports. However, he stated that the law is unclear at what moment the right to be heard comes into play. He agreed with the dictum of Lord Slynn of Hadley in *Rees*, who held that ([1994] 2 A.C. 173 at 194 (at page 10 and 11 of Murphy J.'s judgment)):

> silence on procedures [i.e. the right to be heard] in the absence of other factors indicates, or at least leaves open the possibility, that there may well be circumstances in which fairness requires that the party whose case is to be referred should be told and given a chance to comment. It is not *a priori* sufficient to say, as the appellants in effect do, that it is accepted that the rules of natural justice apply to the procedure as a whole but they do not have to be followed in any individual stage. The question remains whether fairness requires that the *audi alteram partem* rule be applied at the commission stage.

However, Murphy J. distinguished the present case from the circumstances in *Rees*. The nurse could not have been suspended by any action of the Bord at this stage, contrary to what had happened in *Rees*, or at any other stage, as the suspension of a nurse is vested in the High Court. The Committee only had to decide whether there was a *prima facie* case to hold an inquiry. On that basis, Murphy J. held that the applicant had no implied right to be informed. He stated that 'there is, or would be, a strange air of unreality if the Committee was required as a matter of statutory interpretation or constitutional necessity to conduct a preliminary inquiry as to whether they should conduct a substantive inquiry' (page 15 of his judgment).

The same issue arose in *An Bord Altrainas v. O Ceallaigh*, Supreme Court, May 17, 2000, which was an appeal from the decision by Morris P. in *An Bord Altrainas v. O Ceallaigh*, High Court, May 18, 1999. Barron J., who gave the leading judgment held, following the case law (as referred to above) that there was no hard and fast rule at what stage a right to be consulted comes into existence. It depended on what was proper and fair. In the present case, Barron J. considered that the Bord should have taken into account to what extent its powers and function impinged on the rights of the respondent. To inquire as to whether there was a *prima facie* case was, according to the judge, a filtering system and a very serious matter for the midwife. He stated that 'it would be unfair for [the Committee] to decide to hold an inquiry without recourse to her having regard to the additional strain such an inquiry would impose' (at page 36 of Barron J.'s judgment). In respect of the first complaint, Barron J. held that fair procedures were followed, as the respondent had been informed about these. In respect of the other complaints he held that no fair procedures were followed.

He held (at page 38 and 39 of his judgment):

> Once the application had been made to the Fitness to Practice Committee, then that body had an obligation to apply fair procedures. That necessitated the making of inquiries. None was made of the respondent. How the inquiry should have developed thereafter and what other procedures should have been adopted would have depended upon the manner in which the respondent treated the complaint, and bearing in mind that the disputed matters of fact did not fall to be decided in the course of such inquiries. Since the respondent was not contacted before the decision was made in each case that there was a *prima facie* case, there was a breach of fair procedures in relation to all three complaints once they had become applications for an inquiry.

Relationship between section 38 and 44   The various judgments of the members of the Supreme Court commented upon the relationship between section 38 and section 44. The question was whether section 38 and section 44 were intertwined. In other words, can the Board seek the suspension of a member under section 44 separate from an enquiry under section 38 or only in pursuance of a section 38 enquiry? It appears that these comments were *obiter dicta*.

The court held that section 44 and section 38 were not inevitably intertwined. Geoghegan J. (in the McCracken appeal) held that situations do exist where an enquiry is unwarranted but suspension is needed. He gave the example of a nurse being temporarily unfit to practice due to illness or injury. Furthermore, the judge distinguished sections 38 and 44. He stated that the former has as its aim the protection of the integrity and competence of the profession, whereas the latter 'is designed to give speedy protection to the public from perceived danger' (page 5 of his judgment). Hardiman J., (in the McCracken appeal) though, was inclined to link section 44 to section 38. He stated that section 44 'seems easier to construe if this is the case, in particular because it envisages the making of an order suspending the affect of registration for a specified period only' (page 5 of his judgment). Barron J. too (in the Morris P. appeal) saw section 44 as providing a 'complementary procedure to that contemplated by section 38' (page 39 of his judgment).

DISCIPLINARY PROCEEDINGS – MEDICAL COUNCIL

Temporary registration   Section 29 of the 1978 Act provides for temporary registration. Temporary registration is designed to allow persons from outside the European Community to engage in medical practice and to obtain clinical experience for a specified period of time. They can be employed in hospitals approved by the Council for this purpose. The person must hold a degree or equivalent qualification, which in the opinion of the Council guarantees a sufficient degree of relevant knowledge and skill. The degree must have been obtained through an examination process. In addition, the person must possess a certificate of experience equivalent to the certificate of experience required for full registration.

A doctor is normally registered for such periods as determined by the Medical Council. Each time, he or she is obliged to apply for re-registration on the temporary register. No appeal lies open to a decision not to allow re-registration, contrary to the position in respect of full registration. The Medical Practitioners (Amendment) Act 2000 amends section 29(2). It provides that temporary registration cannot exceed an aggregate of seven years (it was five years). Nothing in the Act seems to stop the Council from issuing to temporary registered medical practitioners a certificate of full registration. Indeed, full registration can be afforded under section 27 of the 1978 Act.

The procedure of temporary registration raises an issue, which was addressed in a *Anachebe v. The Medical Council*, High Court, July 12, 2000 (Morris P.). In the case, the Medical Council had found the applicant guilty of professional misconduct. It censored the doctor and refused to re-register the doctor for a period of five months upon completion of his current temporary registration period. In effect, the Medical Council suspended the doctor for five months.

Had the doctor been fully registered, the Medical Council could not have suspended him upon a finding of professional misconduct, as only the High Court has this jurisdiction upon an *ex parte* application. This is clearly stated in section 47 of the Medical Practitioners Act 1978. The reason for this is that the sanction of suspension or removal is so grave, and the consequences for a doctor so serious, that they constitute an "administration of justice".

The applicant sought an order of certiorari. A preliminary issue arose whether he could apply to the High Court in the first place. His counsel argued that the Council's decision to refuse re-registration also amounted to an administration of justice, as it had effectively led to his suspension for five months. Section 29 had the same effect as section 47. This meant that the applicant should be entitled to appeal to the High Court, as he had been equally deprived of his constitutional right to earn a livinghood.

The case really turns around the effect and use of section 29 in this case rather than its actual purpose or meaning. As counsel for the Medical Council pointed out, section 29 allows a doctor from outside the EU to come to Ireland for training and falls therefore in a different category of registered medical practitioners, subject to limitations that do not apply to doctors who are fully registered. Section 29 allows for a degree of control and any decision made thereunder cannot be challenged in a court, contrary to a decision to sanction a doctor after he is found guilty of professional misconduct.

The President of the High Court agreed with the respondent. He stated that the power to decline further temporary registration was independent and separate from any powers, which the Medical Council has under the provisions in Part V of the Act, regulating the professional conduct of all registered doctors. The power it had under section 29 derived from its obligation to regulate temporary doctors.

Thus, section 29 lies outside the ambit of the direct jurisdiction of the High Court. But, did the Medical Council not use section 29 as a disciplinary tool to sanction the doctor? Did it use this power for a different reason, other than to regulate training of Third World doctors? If this is accepted the vulnerability of doctors on temporary registration is cruelly exposed. The doctor was subject to a disciplinary enquiry. Specific rules of procedure apply to such an enquiry. If these are not followed, or it appears that these are not followed, a doctor should be entitled to challenge this in court. It appears that the suspension of the temporary registration was too closely linked to the finding of professional misconduct.

MENTAL TREATMENT

Section 260   Section 260 of the Mental Treatment Act 1945 obliges a plaintiff to seek leave from the High Court to sue persons that have been connected with his or her detention under the 1945 Act. Leave will be granted if the plaintiff can show substantial grounds that the defendants or defendants acted unreasonable or in bad faith: indeed, a high burden of proof akin to proving the action itself (cf. *Murphy v. Greene* [1990] 2 I.R. 566). Thus, to establish a mere *prima facie* case is insufficient.

In *Blehein v. St. John of God Hospital (Stillorgan, Co. Dublin)*, High Court, July 6, 2000, O'Sullivan J., held that this interpretation would mean that the court (page 3 of his judgment):

> will be satisfied that there are substantial grounds under the sub-section if credible evidence is presented to it which – if accepted at a full hearing – could reasonably support a case of either bad faith or lack of reasonable care on the part of the proposed Defendant.

In *Blehein*, the applicant had been detained on a number of occasions. The detentions had been arranged for upon the request of his wife. Her life with him had become unbearable because of his (false) belief that she had liaisons with other men. The applicant submitted nine points upon which his detention would be invalid. Three grounds deserve attention.

He claimed breaches of section 185(1) and (4) and section 5(1) of the Mental Treatment Act 1945. Section 185(1) provides that the detention of a private patient is based on the application to the person in charge of the relevant institution. The application must be accompanied by a certificate signed by two medical practitioners who have examined the patient separately within seven days prior to making the application (section 185(4)). Section 5(1) provides that the applicant must take the person to the institution within seven days of the date of the examination. The institution can detain the person for 12 hours or until the application is granted or refused. Section 5(1) further provides that the seven-day period commences from the date of the first examination.

The applicant claimed that no application for detention had been made and, therefore, no detention order could have been made, which meant that his detention had been invalid. He relied on the wording of the relevant application form, which stated that the application refers to the reception of a private patient, not his or her detention. However, counsel for the respondent pointed out that the heading of the form does refer to the reception and detention of private patients. Elsewhere, the form makes reference to reception and detention also. The trial judge thus held that the applicant had no substantial grounds in respect of this claim.

The applicant also submitted that the first detention order had not been made within seven days. He argued that there had been more than two examinations and that the very first examination was much earlier than the seven-day period. However, the trial judge held that this was a wrong interpretation of section 5. He held that section 5 refers to the earlier date of examination of the two examinations by two medical practitioners required for an order of certification and not to the earliest examination by one of them. As an examination must be up-to-date, the latest of a series of (on-going) examinations by one doctor would, accordingly, be the most appropriate.

Third, the applicant claimed that his constitutional rights to fair procedures were breached. He submitted that he had a right to have notice of his detention and its grounds, the right to consult a lawyer and his own medical practitioner, and the right to be heard in advance of his detention. The trial judge held that these procedural rights do not apply to the detention procedure of section 185. O'Sullivan J. held it (at page 12 of his judgment):

> to be quite inconsistent with the operation of these statutory provisions to impose upon them the further mechanism implied by the principle of *audi alteram partem* or other quasi judicial procedures. The legislature had has entrusted the initiation of this mechanism to the professional judgment of two registered medical practitioners and given that the need for some intervention arises, the particular mechanism to be employed is a matter of the legislature.

The Supreme Court decision in *Blehein v. Murphy and others*, Supreme Court, July 13, 2000 is an appeal by the applicant from a previous case (*Blehein v. Murphy and Others*, High Court, July 2, 1999 (Geoghegan J.). (Annual Review 1999, 329-330)). The Supreme Court dismissed the appeal, confirming the decision of the High Court.

Human Rights

ROSEMARY BYRNE, Trinity College Dublin

The emerging position of human rights as a discernible area of domestic law was fortified with a range of important developments in the year 2000. While overlapping with many areas of Irish constitutional, common and statutory law, human rights are specifically the rights and liberties that are anchored in international instruments. The references to international norms, practices and evolving jurisprudence that come from this radical area of international law are progressively achieving prominence in the major debates in Irish law and policy reform.

In 2000 the bedrock was laid for what has the potential to become an alternative institutional mechanism in advanced democracies for fostering the promotion and protection of international human rights. With the passage of the Human Rights Commission Act 2000 (2000 No. 9) the statutory framework was established for an independent national human rights institution in Ireland. Perhaps as a testament to the promise of this body, the early stages of the construction of the Human Rights Commission was surrounded by heated controversy at the end of the year. Nonetheless, the legislation and the fundamental structures and powers it confers has been widely acknowledged as an important model for human rights protection in the State, region and beyond.

HUMAN RIGHTS COMMISSION ACT 2000

Depending upon the capacity of the future Human Rights Commission to realise the expectations of its establishing legislation, the Human Rights Commission Act 2000. may be the most significant act for the promotion and protection of human rights in the State. The unique creation of a national independent human rights institution in Ireland is highlighted by the fact that no other advanced democracy has a similar organisation with the scope of remit as accorded to this future body.(*See* R. Carver, *Performance and Legitimacy: National Human Rights Institutions* (Geneva: International Council on Human Rights) (2000) S. Spencer and I. Bynoe, *A Human Rights Commission: The Options for Britain and Northern Ireland* (London: Institute for Public Policy Research) (1998). The creation of national human rights institutions around the world has become a central policy objective of the U.N. High Commissioner for Human Rights, although their proliferation has been predominantly in developing countries and transitional regimes. By the beginning of 2000, there were 24 national human rights institutions in Africa. (B. Nowrojee, *Protectors or Pretender? Government Human Rights Commissioners in Africa*, (New York: Human Rights Watch) (2001) The most likely reason for their absence in the industrialised states of the North is that it simply has not seemed necessary to create and finance such an institution in countries such as Ireland with highly developed legal traditions advanced by independent judiciaries and strong democratic institutions. Indeed, having designed the forthcoming Commission as a national hallmark institution, it was not long after that the UN High Commissioner for human rights entered the brewing dispute over the need for the government to support the Commission by allocating adequate resources. ("Robinson to Warn on Funds Need," *Irish Times*, October 13, 2000)

Because it is a unique institution in western Europe, when operational the Human Rights Commission may attract the international spotlight. Rather than a reflection of political and legislative innovation, this Human Rights Commission is a by-product of the peace process in the North. The promise to deliver peace for the island of Ireland in the Good Friday Agreement was built upon a foundation of human rights obligations that would provide the framework for achieving reconciliation. (Agreement Reached in the Multi-Party Negotiations, Apr.10, 1998. Also known as the "Belfast Agreement") (*See* R. Byrne, "Changing Modalities: The Implementation of Human Rights Obligations in Ireland after the Good Friday Agreement," *Nordic Journal of International Law* 70, 1 (2001)) Included in the Chapter of the Agreement addressing "Rights, Safeguards and Equality of Opportunity" under paragraph 5 are the provisions that provide for the establishment of a Human Rights Commission in Northern Ireland, which shall:

- keep under review the adequacy and effectiveness of law and practices

- make recommendations to the Government as necessary;

- provide information, and promote awareness of, human rights;

- consider draft legislation referred to them by the new Assembly;

- in appropriate cases, bring court proceedings or provide assistance to individuals doing so.

The parallel obligation to take "Comparable Steps" in the South is set forth in paragraph 9, which requires the Irish government to "establish a Human Rights Commission with a mandate and remit equivalent to that within Northern Ireland".

While the legislation promises that comparable steps will be taken, they have yet to be taken as an establishment day order has not been made. The Irish government is far behind their Northern counterparts. Legislative provision for the Northern Ireland Human Rights Commission was made in the Northern

Ireland Act, 1998. (Section 68 of the Northern Ireland Act 1998; Northern Ireland Act 1998 (Commencement No.1) Order 1999 (S.I. No.340 of 1999) The Northern Ireland Human Rights Commission began its work in March 1999 and it is likely that the Human Rights Commission in the South will not convene until two years after its northern counterpart commenced its work. (*See* "Achievements in Implementation of the Good Friday Agreement- July 16, 2001: A paper by the British and Irish Governments"(http//www.irlgov.ie/iveagh/angloirish/achievements/default.htm).

The Human Rights Commission Act 2000 places the institution at the intersection of national and international rights protection in its clear designation of the interpretation to be accorded to the term "human rights." Human rights are "the rights, liberties and freedoms conferred on, or guaranteed to, persons by the Constitution, and the rights, liberties or freedoms conferred on, or guaranteed to, persons by any agreement, treaty or convention to which the State is a party. (Section 2 of the Human Rights Commission Act 2000).

This dual foundation, combining a national and international rights framework, is paralleled by the two roles it plays in the context of the South, on the one hand, and in the context of all Ireland, on the other. Pursuant to the terms of the Good Friday Agreement a Joint Committee is to be established in conjunction with the Northern Ireland Human Rights Commission. It will serve "as a forum for consideration of human rights issues in the island of Ireland...[and] will consider, among other matters, the possibility of establishing a charter, open to signature by all democratic political parties, reflecting and endorsing agreed measures of the protection of fundamental rights of everyone living in the island of Ireland." ((Agreement Reached in the Multi-Party Negotiations, Apr.10, 1998., para. 10.) As Dillon Malone points out in his annotation of the Act, the prospective all-Ireland charter of Rights should not be confused with the Northern Ireland Bill of Rights. The former would be a declaration of principles, the latter would be a legislative enactment. (P.Dillon Malone, "Human Rights Commission Act 2000", ICLSA R.75: April 2001). Although it will not possess a statutory status, the content of both the forthcoming Charter and the Northern Ireland Bill of Rights will attract notable consideration, as the Good Friday Agreement commits both governments to guarantee a parity of rights across jurisdictions. If honoured by the letter and spirit, it symbolises a striking forfeiture of national sovereignty. This prospect intensifies the focus on the appointment of Human Rights Commissioners and the priorities and agenda of the future Commission.

It is the wide range of functions of the Human Rights Commission that distinguish it from already existing forms of independent human rights institutions in comparable jurisdictions which have either very tightly circumscribed remits, as in the Canada, which deals exclusively with equality issues, or very limited advisory powers, as in France. (See R. Carver, *Performance and Legitimacy: National Human Rights Institutions* (Geneva: International Council on Human Rights) (2000) Under Section 8, the Human

Rights Commission is entrusted with the following functions:

• to keep under review the adequacy and effectiveness of law and practice in the State relating to the protection of human rights;

• if requested by the Minister, examine any legislative proposal and report its views on any implications of such proposal for human rights;

• consult with national or international bodies or agencies having a knowledge or expertise in the field of human rights as it sees fit;

• make recommendations to the Government in relation to the measures which the Commission which the Commission considers should be taken to strengthen, protect and uphold human rights in the State;

• promote understanding and awareness of the importance of human rights in the State and, for those purposes, to undertake, sponsor or commission, or provide financial or other assistance for, research and educational activities;

• prepare and publish reports on research or enquiries it conducts

• conduct enquiries;

• to establish and participate in the joint North/South Committee of representations drawn from the Commissions in both jurisdictions;

• to provide legal and other assistance;

• to institute proceedings for the purpose of obtaining relief of a declaratory or other nature in respect of any matter concerning the human rights of any person or class of persons;

• to appear as an amicus curiae on application to the High Court or the Supreme Court in proceedings that involve human rights "on foot of such liberty being granted";

The restraints on the powers of the Commission through its functions set forth in section 8 reflect the inherent tension of defining a formal space for limited non-governmental intervention in the key processes that fall in the exclusive domain of branches of the executive, legislature and judiciary and the legislature. In some areas, such as the vetting of legislation, the Commission's role was curtailed from having automatic function of vetting all legislation, as this was seen to be an excessive intrusion on the powers of the executive. (P.Dillon Malone, "Human Rights Commission Act 2000" ICLSA R.75: April 2001) Likewise, the innovation of introducing the convention of external parties appearing as a "friend of the Court" is conditioned upon the "absolute discretion" of the Court in each instance. While vesting the Commission with new and unchartered powers for a non-governmental, independent body, the government and legislature has sought to maintain clear boundaries to protect the exclusive powers of each branch.

Absent more expansive powers than those bestowed upon it by its statutorily defined functions, the ultimate effectiveness of the Human Commission will rest upon its influence. The extent of its influence, in turn will rest upon its perceived legitimacy by both governmental and non-governmental spheres. It is from this perspective that the most heated and crippling issue surrounding the creation of the Human Rights Commission in 2000 raises concern. The controversy resulted from the appointment process of the initial Human Rights Commissioners. Under the Act the Commission shall consist of a President and eight other members, four men, and "not less than 4" women. Section 5 states that the Commissioners shall be appointed by the government. Towards this end, the Government appointed a Selection Committee. The terms of the Committee's mandate however, left the final selection of candidates to the unfettered discretion of the government. A list of 16 candidates was presented to the government by the Committee. The first eight names on the list had been unanimously recommended for appointment. After receiving the list, the government exercised its discretion and appointed eight commissioners, yet only one of those appointed as a Commissioner was from the initial list of unanimously endorsed applicants. After the announcement of the appointed Commissioners, the Selection Committee's list of 16 names was leaked to the press and an flurry of fury within the NGO community led the Minister for Justice, Equality and Law Reform to announce that six additional Commissioners would be nominated. Thus the total number of Commissioners climbed to 14, and amending legislation was required. The Minister announced that the necessary legislative amendments to give effect to these developments would be contained in the forthcoming bill for the incorporation of the European Convention on Human Rights, which would be published in 2001.(Press Release, "Minister for Justice, Equality & Law Reform Announces Widening of Representation on the Human Rights Commission, 19 December 2000 http://www.justice.ie/)

It was ironic that the Human Rights Commission, heralded by the government as the "model of its kind, which will set, rather than follow, standards of best practice in this field," barely stumbled its way into being. The lesson is perhaps an enduring one of the importance of transparency and process. Critical attention has focussed on the government's exercise of its statutorily granted discretion in the appointment process. Yet the terms allowing for absolute discretion with respect to the appointments were accepted by legislators in the passage of the Act, as well as by all members of the Selection Committee when they agreed to participate in the creation of the first Commission. The tangible cost was the delayed establishment of the Commission as it requires new amending legislation. The unquantifiable costs may be higher, for the functions of the Commission require a shared perception by all of the legitimacy of the institution in order for it to effectively execute many aspects of its mandate. The intensity of feelings over the appointment process within the human rights community demonstrates the level of commitment to the institutional ideal as well as the height of expectations for the Commission. If it lives up to these, it surely will make its mark on the protection and culture of human rights in Ireland and abroad.

International norms and monitoring bodies have played a role in several evolving areas of national law. While in 1999 the Irish government established an independent Committee to Review the Offences Against the State Act 1939, (hereafter 1939 Act) its final report was not forthcoming in 2000. In the interim, the chorus of those calling for legislative reform was strengthened by two judgements of the European Court of Human Rights and the Concluding Observations of the Human Rights Committee. In *Heaney and McGuinness v. Ireland*, (European Court of Human Rights, Application no. 34720/97, December 21, 2000) and *Quinn v. Ireland*, (European Court of Human Rights, Application no. 36887/97, December 21, 2000) the European Court of Human Rights unanimously held that the applicants conviction and imprisonment under section 52 of the 1939 Act was in violation of the right to a fair trial and presumption of innocence guaranteed under Article 6 of the European Convention on Human Rights and Fundamental Freedoms. The three applicants were arrested on suspicion of terrorist offences and cautioned by the police that they had the right to remain silent. However, pursuant to section 52 of the 1939 Act, they were then asked details about their movements at the times the offences were committed and advised that the failure to answer could itself result in criminal conviction. All three refused to account for their movements and were convicted and sentenced to 6 months imprisonment. In Heaney and McGuinness, the Court found that "the 'degree of compulsion' imposed on the applicants by the application of section 52 of the 1939 Act with a view to compelling them to provide information relating to charges against them under that Act, in effect, destroyed the very essence of their privilege against self-incrimination and their right to remain silent." The Court also rejected the Government's submission that section 52 of the 1939 Act was a proportionate response to the subsisting terrorist and security threat in the State. It held that the security and public order concerns of the Government "cannot justify a provision which extinguishes the very essence of the applicant's rights to silence and against self-incrimination" under Article 6. (*Heaney and McGuinness v. Ireland*, European Court of Human Rights, Application no. 34720/97, December 21, 2000, paras. 55-59.) Under Article 41 (just satisfaction) of the European Convention on Human Rights, the Court awarded the three applicants £4,000 each in respect of non-pecuniary damage, in addition of £9,377.50 for costs and expenses to Heaney and McGuinness and £11, 341.08 to Quinn.

In addition to these judgements from the European Court of Human Rights, further pressure for amendments to, or arguably, the repeal of, the 1939 Act came from the Human Rights Committee in its Concluding Observations on the compliance of the Irish government with its obligations under the International Covenant for Civil and Political Rights.(ICCPR)(Consideration of Reports submitted by States Parties Under Article 40 of the Covenant, Concluding Observations of the Human Rights Committee, Ireland (CCPR/ C0/69/IRL, http://www.irlgov.ie/iveagh/policy/hr/hrcobs.htm) The non-binding observations commented on the 1939 Act under its section identifying "Principal subjects of concerns and recommendations". In paragraph 13 the Committee recommends that the jurisdiction of the Special Criminal Court should be ended, which is in accordance with its Concluding Observations in response to Ireland's First Report under the ICCPR 1993. The Human Rights Committee then stated that under present circumstances at that time, there was no justification for the continued operation of the Special Criminal Court. (Concluding Observations of the Human Rights Committee: Ireland, 03/08/ 93. CCPR/C/79Add.21 (Concluding Observations/Comments)) para. 11). With respect to other provisions, it expresses concern over the operation of the 1939 Act, with specific reference to the following aspects:

• the increased periods of detention without charge that has occurred under the Act's implementation;

• persons may be arrested on suspicion of being about to commit an offence and that the persons arrested are never charged with an offence;

• in circumstances covered by the Act, failure to respond to questions may constitute evidence supporting the offence of belonging to a prohibited organisation.

• legal assistance and advice may not be available until a person has been charged.

The Committee concludes that these provisions are not compatible with Articles 9 (right to liberty and security of person) and 14(3) (g) (right against self-incrimination). It recommends that "Steps should be taken to end the jurisdiction of the Special Criminal Court and to ensure that all criminal procedures are brought into compliance with articles 9 and 14 of the ICCPR.

In the aftermath of the admissibility decision last year in the *Heaney and McGuinness* and *Quinn* cases, the work of the independent Committee established to review the 1939 Act appeared likely to pre-empt any regional or international conclusions about the abridgement of fundamental rights with respect to section 52. However, the delivery of the 3 judgments from Strasbourg and the clear condemnation inherent in Concluding Observations of the Human Rights Committee provides a compelling backdrop which now will undoubtedly constitute a strong shadow over the forthcoming national debate that will ensue with the publication of the review committee's final report.

While compared to larger states within Europe, the number of Irish cases submitted, and ultimately determined in Strasbourg is notably small, 2000 evidenced a striking 57% climb in the number of provisional files opened at the European Court which pertain to Ireland. (Registrar of the European Court of Human Rights, "Statistical Tables by State," Survey of Activities 2000, Table VIII (http://www.echr.coe.int/Eng/EDocs/ 2000%Survey%2000 [Court].pdf). This is in line with the overall increasing trend of individuals throughout the Council of Europe bringing cases to the European Court of Human Rights. The European Court of Human Rights has doubled its productivity in 2000, as compared to 1999, averaging 600 completed cases per month, compared to the earlier average of 300. The workload of the Court increased 40% in 1999, and there was a projected increase of 22% for 2000. (Press Release issued by the Registrar, European Court of Human Rights, September 28, 2000, *http://www.echr.coe.int* /Eng/P.../ Press%20briefing%2028%20Sept%202000%20epress.ht)

Of cases pending, *Croke v. Ireland* was struck out of the list of the European Court following a "friendly settlement" between the Irish government and the applicant. (European Court of Human Rights, Application no. 33267/96, December 21, 2000). At the time that the decision on admissibility was rendered, the applicant was detained in St. Ita's psychiatric hospital. He was admitted to the hospital in 1993 on foot of a reception order under section 184 of the Mental Health Act 1945. In 1995 the applicant commenced Habeas Corpus proceedings pursuant to Article 40 of the Constitution, the basis of which was a challenge to the constitutionality of sections 163, 171, and 172 of the 1945 Act. The grounds for the proceedings were that the making of a Reception Order required judicial intervention and that the indefinite period of detention provided for under section 172 required an automatic and independent review procedure. The High Court held that section 172 fell below the norms required by the constitutional guarantee of personal liberty and consequently its constitutionality was referred by way of a case stated to the Supreme Court pursuant to Article 40.4.3 of the Constitution. The Supreme Court overturned the High Court ruling on the grounds that there were sufficient protections contained in section 172. (*Sean Croke v. Charles Smith, Art O'Connor, Eastern Health Board, Ireland and The Attorney General*, July 31, 1996 by Hamilton C.J.). The applicant argued that the absence of an automatic and independent review of detention either immediately before or after his initial detention, and, the absence of a periodic independent and automatic review of his ongoing detention thereafter, raises issues under Articles 5 (freedom of liberty) and 6 (fair trial). The Irish Government issued a Green Paper in 1992 containing a broad review of mental health legislation in Ireland and a White Paper in 1995, outlining proposed changes to the legislation. The Court unanimously declared the application admissible, as it "raises issues under Article 5 secs.1 and 4 of the Convention, which require determination on the merits.

The European Court reported that the case had been struck out following a friendly settlement in which an agreed (unpublished) compensatory sum is to be paid, to acknowledge the applicant's "legitimate concerns in relation to the absence of an independent formal review of his detention under the Mental

Health Acts". The agreement also specifies that the applicant "has had regard to the expressed intention of the Government of Ireland to secure the enactment into law of the Mental Health Bill, 1999" and that the Irish State "has had particular regard to the very special circumstances of the applicant as the first Irish person to bring this important issue before the Court and the fact that the applicant's claim was initiated prior to the publication of the Mental Health Bill, 1999. (http://www.echr.coe.int/*english*/*2000*/ *dec*/*dec212000* judsepress.htm)

Two additional cases were found to be admissible during the year, illustrating the increasing relevance of the considerable jurisprudence that is coming out of Strasbourg. *D.G. v. Ireland* (European Court of Human Rights, Application No. 0003947/98, Decision as to Admissibility, September 9, 2000) concerns the detention of applicant minor in St. Patrick's Institution, raising issues under Article 3 (inhuman or degrading treatment) Article 5 (lawful arrest or detention, detention of a minor) Article 8 (private and family life) and Article 14 (discrimination). The Grand Chamber ruled as admissible an important case concerning state immunity, *McElhinney v. Ireland* (European Court of Human Rights, Application no. 31253/96, Decision as to Admissibility, February 9, 2000). The applicant claims that he was assaulted by a member of the United Kingdom armed forces on territory in the Republic of Ireland. He argues that by invoking and applying the doctrine of sovereign immunity, the United Kingdom and the Irish courts denied him the right of judicial determination of his compensation claim arising out of the allegations of assault. The applicant complains of a violation of Articles 5 (right to liberty and security), 6 (right to a fair trial) and 13 (right to an effective remedy). He also complains of discrimination, invoking Article 14, because the British courts would not have applied the same doctrine in an action for assault committed by an Irish soldier in the United Kingdom. The Grand Chamber decided that the complaints under Articles 5 and Articles 13 were manifestly ill-founded, yet his complaint under Articles 6 and 14 raises serious questions of fact and law which are of such complexity that there determination should depend on an examination on the merits.

A third case was held to be partially inadmissible, with the examination of remaining issues to be adjourned. The applicants in *Doran v. Ireland* (European Court of Human Rights, Application No. 00050389/00, Decision as to Admissibility, March 30, 2000) complain of violations over the length and fairness of proceedings, as well as the existence of a domestic remedy with respect to legal proceedings brought concerning disputes over a purchase of property. The Court found that it could not decide upon the admissibility of certain complaints raised under Articles 6 (fair trial) and 13 (domestic remedies) with the current file, hence it decided to adjourn their examination. With the forthcoming incorporation of the European Convention on Human Rights, Irish lawyers will soon find a heightened need to keep abreast not only of Irish cases before the European Court, but of the expanding case law that is being generated by the many states in an already expanded Council of Europe. In 1999 the jurisprudence of the European Court of Human Rights exceeded 1000 cases, as compared to the mere 116 judgements that had been delivered in the first three decades of the Court's existence. (*http://www.echr.coe.int/ Eng/EDocs/1999Survey(Court).pdf.,* p. 50)

The Concluding Observations of the Human Rights Committee were issued in July 2000 in response to the Irish Government's submission of a second report under the International Covenant for Civil and Political Rights. In addition to the critique of and consequent recommendations for the 1939 Act discussed above, the Human Rights Committee opined on a wide range of national law and practice, highlighting the tension between national norms and values and international proclamations for monitoring committees. The most striking instance of this appears in paragraphs 16 and 18 of the Concluding Observations which address the rights of women in the Ireland. Paragraph 16 of the Human Rights Committee targets the Article 41 (para.2) of the Constitution of Ireland 1937 (Bunreacht na hÉireann) which "recognises that by her life within the home, woman gives to the State a support without which the common good cannot be achieved. The State shall, therefore, endeavour to ensure that mothers shall not be obliged by economic necessity to engage in labour to the neglect of their duties in the home." The Committee expresses concern that these references "could perpetuate traditional attitudes toward the role of women."(CCPR/C0/69/IRL, *http://www.irlgov.ie/iveagh/policy/hr/ hrcobs.htm at para. 16)*This echoes the conclusions of the Constitution Review Group, which in 1996 recommended that the Article be retained, but revised in a gender neutral form. The Group's recommended wording was as follows: "The State recognises that the home and family life gives to society a support without which the common good cannot be achieved. The State shall endeavour to support persons caring for others within the home." (Constitution Review Group, Report of the Constitution Review Group (Dublin: Government Publications) (1996) pp.333-334) With the impetus of the views of the Human Rights Committee, and the heed that the Human Rights Commission, by virtue of its new mandate, must take of these Concluding Observations, one might anticipate that the Commission would advocate for a modernisation of this constitutional clause to prevent the capacity for it to be used in support of policies that discriminate on grounds of sex.

More controversially, however, is the requirement set forth by the Human Rights Committee that emerges from its expressed concern "that the circumstances in which women may lawfully obtain an abortion are restricted to when the life of the mother is in danger and do not include, for example situations where the pregnancy is the result of rape." (CCPR/C0/69/IRL, http:/ /www.irlgov.ie/iveagh/policy/hr/hrcobs.htm at para. 18). The General Comments of the Human Rights Committee, which provide interpretative statements on the substantive provisions of the ICCPR, interpret the right to life under Article 6 as requiring that States parties "give information on any measures taken by the State to help women prevent unwanted pregnancies, and to ensure that they do not have to undertake life-threatening clandestine abortions."(Human Rights Committee, General Comment 28, Equality of rights between men and women (article 3), U.N. Doc. CCPR/C/21/Rev.1/Add.10 (2000) para. 10) This interpretation of the right to life offers the most striking example of the clash between domestic and international law and policy. Ireland's reservations made to the ICCPR make no reference to the constitutional protection of the unborn child. (Reservations were made with respect to Articles 10(2) (right to liberty and of accused persons to be segregated from the convicted) 14 (fair trial), 19(2) (freedom of expression), 20(1)(prohibition of war propaganda) and 23(4) (dissolution of marriage) In its Second Report submitted to the Human Rights Committee, the Government indicated its intent to remove its reservations with respect to Article 14 and 23(4) in light of the enactment of the Criminal Procedure Act, 1993 and the legalisation of divorce. (Department of Foreign Affairs, International Covenant for Civil and Political Rights, Second Report by Ireland. (Brunswick Press) (1998), para.3.)

It is unlikely that the political process that surrounds the national political dialogue on abortion in Ireland will be circumvented by reliance on the Concluding Observations of the Human Rights Committee. It does however raise interesting questions about the margin of appreciation afforded to governments, the questionable legal status of abortion under international law, as well as the agenda to be adopted by the future Human Rights Commission. While the Concluding Observations of the Human Rights Committee are non-binding, it remains to be seen if they will have greater impact if adopted as guiding declarations by the Human Rights Commission. It highlights the dilemmas caused by clashes between the views of the democratic majority in a State and those of an expert international committee entrusted with monitoring the government's compliance with a specific international treaty. If the greater profile of international human rights instruments and jurisprudence enjoyed in the State translates into greater influence in policy reforms, it beckons greater consideration of the legal reasoning embraced in the findings of these bodies. Unfortunately, because of the limitations of these bodies operating usually by consensus and in committee form, many of the principles developed are presented absent the substantive analysis of the committee's deliberations. Hence, as these Concluding Observations for the Irish report demonstrate, the Human Rights Committee's interpretation of state obligations is without the detailed justification one would expect to find in judicial decisions in common law jurisdictions or in parliamentary debates dealing with issues of comparable import.

Additionally, international treaties and norms appeared in two central legislative developments with the enactment of the Criminal Justice (United Nations Convention Against Torture) Act, 2000 (No.11, 2000) (Hereafter CAT Act) This Act gives effect to the Convention Against Torture and Other Cruel,

Inhuman or Degrading Treatment or Punishment, December 10, 1984. This legislation is part of much wider universal trend to create accountability through domestic courts of the commission atrocities under international law. Many serious violations of international human rights law occur in jurisdictions where the national courts are unable or unwilling prosecute. The trial of General Augusto Pinochet highlighted the emerging trend of attempts to prosecute those accused of having carried out grave human rights violations in national courts of other states. *Regina v. Bow Street Metropolitan Stipendiary Magistrate, Ex Par Pinochet Ugarte* [1998] 4 All E.R. 897 (House of Lords), [1999] 2 All E.R. 97 (House of Lords) This legislation may pave the way the for prosecutions in Ireland of war criminals and perpetrators of human rights abuses in line with the emerging role of national courts in the enforcement of international standards. (For an overview of prosecutions in national courts *see* S. Ratner and J. Abrahms, *Accountability for Human Rights Atrocities in International Law* (Oxford: Oxford University Press) (2001).

Section 2 of the CAT Act defines the offence of torture, which is liable on conviction on indictment to life imprisonment, as an act carried out "within or outside the State". This incorporates the principle of universal jurisdiction for the crime of torture, which under international law is a crime against humanity. The legislation contains an Amendment of Extradition (Amendment) Act 1994 under section 9, which gives effect to one of the central provision in the Convention Against Torture, mandating that if a signatory state fails to prosecute an individual falling under the terms of the Convention, it must extradite the accused to a state willing to do so.

The most rapidly evolving area of human rights law in Ireland continues to be refugee and asylum law. In response to the continuing flow of asylum seekers, the Illegal Immigrants (Trafficking) Act 2000 was passed. This legislation creates an offence of trafficking in illegal immigrants. With the revolution in transportation that has transformed migration in the latter half of the 20th century and the closing of traditional means of legally entering western Europe and North America, human smuggling and trafficking has become a central component of transnational crime. Its persuasiveness is reflected by the fact that it is now addressed on a regional scale by over 30 intergovernmental fora. (J.Morrison, "The Trafficking and Smuggling of Refugees: in end game in European asylum policy", (unpublished) (July 2000).)

Under the Irish Trafficking Act, the offence of trafficking is punishable by a maximum sentence of ten years imprisonment with the further possibility of forfeiture of vehicles used for trafficking. The Act also contains provisions on the deportation process and curtails access to judicial review in immigration and asylum matters. Within 14 days of receiving a deportation order, rejected asylum seekers are required to establish a "substantial" rather than "prima facie" case before leave seeking judicial review is granted. The higher threshold for access to judicial review and the tight time framework within which it must be sought, has caused considerable controversy among non-governmental organisations and lawyers representing asylum seekers and immigrants.(*See* Irish Council for Civil Liberties, Shadow Report Under the International Covenant for Civil and Political Rights, (unpublished) (2000) p. 51) Under Article of the Constitution, the President referred the legislation to the Supreme Court. On August 28, 2000, the Supreme Court opined that the provisions were not repugnant to the Constitution.

The Dublin Convention (Implementation) Order 2000 (S.I. No. 343 of 2000) will also affect the right of asylum seekers to remain in the jurisdiction. However, the Dublin Convention will apply prior to a substantive examination of an asylum seeker's claim. The implementation order gives effect to the 1990 Dublin Convention which provides systematic criteria for determining state responsibility for asylum claims. (Convention Determining the State Responsible for Examining Applications for Asylum Lodged in One of the Member States of the Community , Dublin, June 15, 1990. Entered into force September 1, 1997. OJ 1997 C 254/1. [Hereafter Dublin Convention]. These focus primarily on technical issues of transit and visas. This Implementation Order should be seen against the backdrop of the implementation of the Dublin Convention in other Member States. In the EU, the Dublin Convention framework has failed in its objective to efficiently allow for the transfer of asylum seekers between signatories to the treaty. The Dublin Convention relies extensively upon evidence that asylum seekers have transited through another signatory state. When the realities of modern forced migration encourage asylum seekers to respond by destroying travel documents, this system is unlikely to realise its ambition of redistributing asylum seekers throughout the region. For example, a study by the Danish Refugee Council indicates that in 1999, the number of applicants transferred from and to Austria represented .3% and 4.7% respectively of the total number of asylum seekers that year, compared to 1.3% and 1.3% respectively in Belgium and 1.8% and 3.5% in Germany. The study argues that even these official figures are inflated, as statistics do not consider the number of successfully transferred applicants who do not remain in the responsible country, choosing to move on to another state or returning illegally to the first Member State.(F. Liebaut, ed., *The Dublin Convention: Study of its Implementation in the 15 Member States of the European Union* (Copenhagen: Danish Refugee Council) (1999). (*See also* A. Hurwitz, "the 1990 Dublin Convention: A Comprehensive Assessment," *International Journal of Refugee Law*, 11, 4 (1999) pp. 646-677.

The short comings of the Dublin Convention have been acknowledged by the European Commission and in 2001, a new draft directive will be introduced. Hence it is likely that the life span of the Dublin Convention Implementation Order will be short.

With respect to international treaties, the state both fulfilled outstanding obligations, in ratifying the Convention against the Elimination of Racial Discrimination and the Elimination of Discrimination against Women, as well as created new state obligations with the signing the two new Optional Protocols to the Convention on the Rights of the Child.

Each of the developments in this chapter are defining steps in the transformation of human rights protection in Ireland. Individually, they reflect concrete substantive changes in Irish law, partially shaped by a body of international human rights law with aspirational standards that a decade ago many commentators wrote off as noble but unenforceable. Collectively, these developments are part of a much deeper transition in Irish law and policy. True to the patterns of globalisation, law is less and less insulated from the cross-fertilisation of external principles, practices and the values that inspire them. This does not imply that international and regional norms are superior to, or in most areas, significantly different from, those embraced by Irish law. What it does demonstrate, however, is that the range of participants in debates on societal reforms affecting rights is continually expanding beyond geographical frontiers. The outcome is that fundamental debates in the courts, the Dáil and society at large, will be deepened, and inevitably, enriched.

Information Law and the Ombudsman

ESTELLE FELDMAN, Law School, Trinity College, Dublin

The year 2000 marks the third year of operation of the Freedom of Information Act, 1997: Annual Review 1997, 2 et seq.; Annual Review 1999, 1-3 and 350-357. The decision initially to combine the Office of Information Commissioner with that of the Ombudsman is now clearly recognised as advantageous to the conduct of both offices (see *Annual Report of the Information Commissioner 2000*. Pn 9502 and at http://www.irlgov.ie/oic). Additionally, the Ombudsman has been more regularly exercising certain of his investigative functions resulting in the publication of reports to the Dail and Seanad, Ombudsman Act 1980, section 6(7). Hence, commencing with this Annual Review, the chapter on Information Law will also note relevant activities of the Ombudsman.

INFORMATION COMMISSIONER

High Court Appeals   In July 2000 three separate appeals were heard by the High Court against decisions of the Information Commissioner under the statutory provisions of the Freedom of Information Act, section 42(8): Annual Review 1999, 1–3 and 350–357.

Salve Marine Ltd. v. Information Commissioner, High Court, July 19, 2000, *The Irish Times* July 20, 2000, is an *ex tempore* judgment of Kelly J. In this case, the appellant questioned the Information Commissioner's interpretation of section 6(5)(a) of the Act. Section 6 provides for the right of access to records created subsequent to the commencement of the Act on April 21, 1998 subject to certain exceptions and limitations. Section 6(5)(a) provides a right of access to records created earlier where these are necessary or expedient in order to understand records created after the commencement. Personal information is not subject to this date restriction: Annual Review 1997, 2 *et seq.*; Annual Review 1999, 1–3 and 350 –357.

In denying the appeal, Kelly J. held that the Information Commissioner had correctly interpreted the relevant section in a manner which gave effect to the object of the Act in a purposeful and meaningful way. There were three possible constructions of section 6(5)(a). The word 'understand' could be interpreted in its literal sense – whether the post-commencement document could be literally comprehended. Another construction considered and rejected by the Commissioner was that the fact that an earlier record might throw fresh light on the subject discussed in a later record, or enable the requestor to extend or analyse information in a later record. This did not mean that access to the earlier records was necessary or expedient in order to understand the later records. In the construction employed by the Commissioner, he had determined that the critical question in interpreting the section was whether the pre-commencement documents were necessary to understand the substance or gist of the documents created after the Act commenced. The Commissioner took the view that the fact that a document does not contain all the information which a requestor might wish to have does not mean the substance of the document cannot be understood. This construction was approved by Kelly J.

With regard to the other High Court actions, judgment was delivered in April 2001 in the case of *EH v. Information Commissioner.* Judgment is awaited in relation to the appeal of the Department of Education and Science against the Information Commissioner's decision to release results of Leaving Certificate Examinations for the year. These cases will be analysed in next year's Review.

A lengthy delay in delivering any judgment is particularly unfortunate as the value of information may often diminish over time, a fact recognised by the insertion of a limitation period in the Act regarding reviews. For instance, all requests for access must be acknowledged not later than two weeks after receipt of such request (section 7(2)) and all decisions must be notified not later than four weeks after receipt (section 8(1)). An internal review decision must be notified by the head of the public body concerned not later than three weeks after receipt of the application for review (section 14(4)). Furthermore, generally the Information Commissioner must deliver a decision on an appeal for review 'as soon as may be and, in so far as practicable' within four months during the first three years of the Act's operation, and, subsequently within three months (section 34).

Due to lack of resources the Information Commissioner regularly has not kept within the time limit prescribed. Process may also be responsible for delay in some instances as the Commissioner may require time to exercise his discretion to arrive at a settlement rather than issue a binding decision. In 2000, 235 of 237 decisions were delivered outside the time limit: *Annual Report of the Information Commissioner 2000*, 1.3.

Absence of Appeal to Supreme Court   There is no appeal under the Act to the Supreme Court. By virtue of section 42(8), the decision of the High Court under an appeal or reference under the section is final and conclusive. This is unfortunate for several reasons. In the first instance, the absence of the higher appeal mechanism may contribute negatively to the speed of the delivery of the High Court appeal judgments. It is also the situation that there is a developing use of the Act as a part of legal proceedings in preference, or in addition, to discovery.

More significantly, however, it precludes the possibility of developing a coherent body of law in relation to the Freedom of Information Act. It is too early in the operation of the Act to make a definitive comment on any trend in the substantive issues which might be the subject of High Court appeals. What is obvious, nevertheless, is that if each occasional appeal is heard by a different High Court judge, given the disparate nature of each set of facts, the decisions may go in all directions. While every judge may acknowledge the value of the Freedom of Information Act, if unreported judgments or inordinate delays in delivery of judgments become the order of the day, the onus of interpreting the Act will rest more heavily on the Information Commissioner. For example, in *Salve Marine,* the Commissioner's interpretation and application of section 6(5)(a) is based on his determination of an earlier decision (*No. 98117 Mr. ABE and the Department of Marine and Natural Resources*). In the absence of a reported judgment, it is unclear whether Kelly J. approved of, or, indeed, was indifferent to, the Commissioner's practice of binding himself to his own earlier interpretations. This practice of adopting a system of respect for precedent seems a sensible one in giving a degree of predictability to the Commissioner's adjudicatory functions, which is of benefit to the general public.

Certificates of exemption A Government Minister may exempt a record from the application of the Freedom of Information Act. This occurs where the Minister is satisfied that a requested record is exempt either by virtue of section 23 (relating to law enforcement or public safety) or section 24 (relating to security, defence and international relations) and, is satisfied that the record is of sufficient sensitivity or seriousness to justify issuing a certificate under section 25(1), declaring such a record to be exempt. Any Minister who issues such a certificate must furnish a copy of the certificate and a statement in writing of the reasons why the record to which it relates is an exempt record to the Taoiseach and to such other Ministers as may be prescribed under the Act (25(6)(b)). In addition, the Minister must furnish the Information Commissioner with a yearly report detailing the number of certificates issued by him or her in the year and the provisions of section 23 or 24 of the Freedom of Information Act which applied to the exempt records (section 25(11)). The Commissioner must, in turn, append a copy of these reports to his Annual Report of the year in which the certificates were issued (section 40(1)(b)).

The Information Commissioner has no power of review of a record exempted by a current section 25 certificate(section 25(3)(b) and section 37(8)). However, the requester concerned or any affected person may appeal to the High Court on a point of law against the issue of such a certificate (section 42(2)(a)). Subject to section 25(7), at the expiry of each period of six months or such other prescribed period not exceeding twelve months in length from the commencement of the Act, the Taoiseach with any other Government Ministers standing prescribed must review the operation of the issuing of certificates. No Minister may partake in a review in relation to a certificate issued by him or her, but a Minister may make submissions to the other Ministers participating in the review. If, following a review, the other Ministers are not satisfied that the terms of exemption have been met, they request the Minister concerned to revoke the certificate, and he or she shall do so and inform the requester(section 25(8)). The Taoiseach may, at any time, review the operation of the issuing of certificates in so far as it relates to any other Minister.

In 2000, two certificates were issued, both by the Minister for Justice, Equality and Law Reform. The first, which will expire on February 2, 2002, notes exemption by reason of international relations of the State (section 24(1)(c)) and of matters relating to Northern Ireland (section 24(1)(d)). The second, which will expire on March 29, 2002, notes exemption by reason of the security of the State (section 24(1)(a)): *Annual Report of the Information Commissioner 2000* Appendix II.

OMBUDSMAN

Jurisdiction   Both the Information Commissioner and the Ombudsman deal with matters of administrative accountability. In the *Report of the Constitution Review Group* Pn 2632 May 1996 this is described as:

> the process of ensuring that public service activities and, in particular, the exercise of decision-making powers, whether discretionary or otherwise, are carried out not only in a proper legal manner but fairly and consistently with good administrative practice.

In recognition of the role and performance of the Ombudsman, the Review Group recommended a new Article in the Constitution to confirm the establishment of the Office and ensure the independence of its function and operation. It noted that:

> the Ombudsman must be able to operate without being influenced by Government action. It is not enough for him or her to be independent in fact – he or she must also be seen as such by those who use the office. A constitutional guarantee for this independence would reinforce freedom from conflict of interest, from deference to the executive, from influence by special interest groups, and it would support the freedom to assemble facts and reach independent and impartial conclusions. *Report of the Constitution Review Group*: chapter 17.

The Constitution Review Group recommendations have not been implemented. Nor has the promised Ombudsman (Amendment) Bill yet emerged which would extend the Ombudsman's remit to bodies in the wider public sector such as the public voluntary hospitals, Fás and the Health and Safety Authority. This would be more in line with the function of Information Commissioner. The differences in jurisdiction between the two offices causes some difficulties to people requesting assistance when experiencing difficulties with public administration.

The heads of a Bill approved in 1999 would have extended the Ombudsman's remit to bodies in the wider public sector. The inexplicable failure to implement the relevant legislation is noted by the Ombudsman for the seventh year in succession in his most recent Annual Report: *Annual Report of the Ombudsman 2000*. Pn 9502 and at http://www.irlgov.ie/ombudsman/ :3.6.

Nevertheless, in 2000 the Ombudsman, on foot of positive legal advice, extended his jurisdiction in relation to dealing with the imposition of fines/penalties by bodies within his jurisdiction. Section 4(2) of the Ombudsman Act, 1980 permits the examination of administrative actions of bodies within the remit: *Annual Report of the Ombudsman* 2000: 7 *et seq.*

The Ombudsman's Report records (page 7) that he is examining a complaint in relation to a summary prosecution for failure to have a television licence under section 77(b) of the Postal and Telecommunications Act 1983. A second complaint resulted in the waiver of an 'on the spot' fine imposed by Dublin Corporation for an alleged breach of section 3(1) of the Litter Pollution Act 1997. In relation to the wider issue of 'on the spot' fines imposed by local authorities under the Road Traffic Act 1994 for less serious offences such as parking offences, the Ombudsman is now acting on advice that these actions are administrative in nature. As such these cases do not fall within the terms of the exclusion precluding the Ombudsman from investigating any action where a person has a right of appeal, reference or review before a court (Ombudsman Act 1980, section 5(1)(a)(ii)). The Ombudsman may not examine complaints in relation to fines issued by the Garda Síochána which is listed as one of the bodies outside his remit (Ombudsman Act 1980, Part II, First Schedule).

Local authority planning complaints   In the 2000 Report (page 6) the Ombudsman notes very considerable delays on the part of local authorities in furnishing reports to his Office on planning complaints. He admits that his "overall impression is one of a system which is in a state of collapse." He further notes that the impact of the new Planning and Development Act, 2000 has yet to be observed (see Planning Chapter, 324 *et seq.*).

Section 6(7) investigations   Three recent reports of major national significance have been presented to the Dail and Seanad under the Ombudsman's investigative functions in accordance with section 6(7) of the 1980 Act. These investigations arose from individual complaints, generally of individuals who lack the ability to act on an organised basis to lobby successfully for redress. The first report, *Lost Pension Arrears* was published in June 1999. The Ombudsman highlights that all the complainants were pensioners. The Department of Social, Community and Family Affairs, the Department concerned, was inactive in efforts to resolve the difficulties during the period 1985 to 1996. Rules were applied rigidly and without equity and, where discretion was available the Ombudsman only discovered it by chance.

It is noteworthy in the present context that no High Court action has ever been taken by an aggrieved pensioner who has been refused arrears of contributory pension. Perhaps this inaction is not so much a reflection of weak legal arguments as a reflection of the inability of those concerned to muster the resources to mount a legal challenge: *Lost Pensions Arrears*, 14.

These themes, and the wider issues of abuse of secondary legislation and delegated powers also run through the subsequent reports, *Local Authority Housing Loans*, published in July 2000, and *Nursing Home Subventions*, published in January 2001. In each of these investigations it is clear that the weakest in society have been inadvertently and, most certainly in the case of the Nursing Home Subventions, deliberately, deprived of statutory entitlements involving relatively significant sums of money necessary for their daily living. The issues raised will be dealt with in detail in the 2001 Review.

STATUTORY INSTRUMENTS

Freedom of information Act 1997 *Bodies which came within the scope of the Act during 2000* The Courts Service, the Equality Authority and Eastern Area Health Boards are among the twenty-eight additional government, regulatory, health and voluntary bodies which became subject to the Freedom of Information Act in 2000 by way of three Statutory Instruments.

S.I. No. 67 of 2000 (Prescribed Bodies) Regulations, 2000 prescribe the Courts Service, the Equality Authority, and the Ordnance Survey as separate public bodies for the purposes of the Freedom of Information Act, by their inclusion in paragraph 1(2) of the First Schedule to that Act, and deletion of the reference to the Employment Equality Agency from that Schedule. They also prescribe the Area Health Boards and the Health Boards Executive established under the Health (Eastern Regional Health Authority) Act 1999 as public bodies under the Freedom of Information Act.

The Area Health Boards so prescribed are the Eastern Regional Health Authority Corporate, the East Coast Area Health Board, the Northern Area Health Board and the South Western Area Health Board.

S.I. No. 115 of 2000 (Prescribed Bodies)(No.2) Regulations, 2000 prescribe Radio Telefís Éireann and its subsidiaries RTE Commercial Enterprises Limited, RTE Music Limited and DTT Network Company and Serbhisí Thelefís Na Gaeilge Teoranta (the legal framework for TG4's activities) as separate public bodies for the purposes of the Freedom of Information Act by their inclusion in para 1(2) of the First Schedule to that Act.

In accordance with section 3(5) of that Act, these Regulations apply the Act to non-programme related functions of these bodies only.

S.I. No. 355 of 2000 (Prescribed Bodies)(No.3) Regulations, 2000 prescribe the Combat Poverty Agency, Social Welfare Tribunal, Irish Wheelchair Association, Enable Holistic Services Ireland Limited, the Multiple Sclerosis Society of Ireland, the National Council for the Blind of Ireland, the National

Association for the Deaf, the Chesire Foundation in Ireland, the Independent Radio and Television Commission, An Comhairle Ealaíon, Local Government Computer Services Board, National Safety Council, an Comhairle Leabharlanna, the Irish Water Safety Association, the Fire Services Council and the Office of the Director of Telecommunications Regulation as separate public bodies for the purposes of the Freedom of Information Act, by their inclusion in paragraph 1(5) of the First Schedule to that Act.

Consumer Information Act 1978   S.I. No. 468 of 2000 (Advertisement for Air Fares) Order, 2000 These Regulations provide for transparency in airline advertising, in order to give consumers accurate information about the full price of airline tickets and the availability of the airfares advertised.

Labour Law and Employment Law

DR. UBALDUS de VRIES, Dublin City University

CONTRACT OF EMPLOYMENT

Commencement In *Brennan v. Religious of the Sacred Heart* [2000] E.L.R. 297, the claimant accepted an offer of employment as housekeeper with the respondent. With mutual agreement the initial starting date was postponed by a week; she would start on September 29, 1997. During that week, her father died. She was told that she could start when she felt ready. She started her employment three days later on October 2, 1997. She got paid from October 1, 1997. The contract was terminated on September 30, 1998. The question arose whether the Unfair Dismissals Acts 1977-1993 applied.

In dispute was whether a letter had been written setting out the effective starting date as October 2. The claimant stated she had never received the letter. The Employment Appeals Tribunal held that the contractual employment relationship had come into being on September 29, even though the claimant did not physically work until three days later. The Tribunal determined that a change in the terms of the contract of employment may only be achieved by *consensus ad idem*, which, from the facts, had not been the case (cf. *Mespil Ltd. v. Capaldi* [1986] I.L.R.M. 373).

Frustration of contract In *Zuphen and others v. Kelly Technical Services (Ireland) Ltd. and others* [2000] E.L.R. 277, Murphy J. held that the doctrine of frustration has at its basis ([2000] E.L.R. 277 at 290):

> A supervening event which must be so unexpected and beyond the contemplation of the parties, even as a possibility, that neither party can be said to have accepted the risk of the event taking place when contracting.

In the case, the plaintiffs, South African technicians, had entered into contracts with the defendants, who were recruitment agencies for Eircom plc. The contracts were conditional of the plaintiffs presenting themselves at a certain date with a valid work permit. The contracts were not conditional on the availability of work. Eircom later notified the agencies that the recruits were no longer needed. They informed the plaintiffs of this and told them to return to South Africa. The plaintiffs sued for breach of contract, claiming that the termination of their contracts were null and void. They also claimed that the contracts guaranteed them work for at least one year. The defendants undertook to pay the plaintiffs their contractual salary and sought work for them after these proceedings were initiated.

However, a preliminary issue arose as to whether the contracts had become frustrated with no fault on part of the defendants after they had lost the Eircom contract. Applying the doctrine of frustration, Murphy J. held that the contract was not frustrated. Was there an unexpected event that changed the face of things? Murphy J. held that hardship, inconvenience or material loss do not allow the court to hold a contract frustrated. He held that there 'must have been such a change in the significance of the obligation that the thing undertaken would, if performed, be a different thing from that contracted for' ([2000] E.L.R. 277 at 291). This had not been the case, as the defendants in fact had procured work for the plaintiffs to mitigate their loss. This was an indication, according to the trial judge, that the contract had survived, contrary from what would be demanded by the doctrine of frustration. In addition, the trial judge accepted the plaintiffs' evidence that they would have not come to Ireland had the contract been conditional on work being available.

Furthermore, the trial judge held that in employment contracts (of service) a strict approach of contract law to employment disputes was inappropriate, as it would tend to 'obscure the social implications of certain kinds of conduct or events by reducing them to legalistic principles' ([2000] E.L.R. 277 at 291).

"Of service" or "for services"   The question in *Dower v. Radio Ireland Ltd. (t/a Today FM)* [2001] E.L.R. 1 was whether a change of remuneration and other conditions led to a change of status of the employment contract. The plaintiff had started on a three-month contract as a free lance radio producer and presenter. The contract stipulated that all disputes would be referred to arbitration. He was paid a fixed fee per programme. Later, the pay agreement was converted into an agreement that entitled him to 30.000 pounds per year, paid on weekly invoices. No tax deductions were made. Nor was he part of the pension scheme or entitled to sick pay and holiday pay. He worked for the defendant for more than three years until he received a three-month notice. The plaintiff issued plenary summons. He claimed that his status had changed into an employee after the renewal from time to time of his initially short-term contract. He also claimed that the arbitration clause no longer applied. The defendant sought a stay on the proceedings, claiming that the arbitration clause was still valid.

The point at issue was whether the employment relationship was "of service" or one "for services" so to determine the validity of the arbitration clause. The High Court held that the contract was one "for services" and that the arbitration clause applied. Carroll J. held that the change in his working hours and remuneration did not change his status as an independent contractor. The remuneration could not be deemed a salary but an agreed fee, based on weekly invoices, for a free lance presenter. (cf. *Re Sunday Tribune* [1984] I.R. 505, *Henry Denny and Sons (Ireland) Ltd. v. Minister for Social Welfare* [1998] 1

282 *Annual Review of Irish Law 2000*

I.R. 34 (Annual Review 1997, 483-485 and *Tierney v. An Post* [1999] E.L.R. 293 (Annual Review, 359-360)). The terms of the contract, including the arbitration clause, applied on a rollover basis. Nothing suggested, according to the trial judge, that the parties did not continue to be bound by the same terms.

EMPLOYERS' LIABILITY

Recovery of wages In *Hogan v. Steele and Company Limited, and Electrical Supply Board (notice party)*, Supreme Court, November 1, 2000, the plaintiff, an employee of the notice party, had suffered personal injuries while delivering goods to the defendant. ESB continued paying his wages during the period of his recovery upon an undertaking that they would be refunded if he would recover that sum from the defendant. The plaintiff settled the action with the defendant, which included a sum representing the loss of earnings. The High Court held that the plaintiff was entitled to recover that sum from the defendant but not insofar the sum concerned PAYE, PRSI and pension contributions.

The Supreme Court dismissed the appeal and confirmed the order of the High Court. Keane J. held that only the net wages were recoverable, as anything more would compensate the plaintiff for loss he had never suffered. The Chief Justice quoted with approval the dictum of Kingsmill Moore J. in *Attorney General and others v. Ryan's Care Hire Limited* [1965] I.R. 642., who stated that a tortfeasor:

> is only responsible in damages for the direct injury which he had caused to the person against whom the tort has been committed and not for indirect injuries to a third person who may suffer loss indirectly as a result of the injury to the first person. To this rule there are two exceptions in common law, the actions *per quod servitium amisit* and *per quod consortium amisit*, both anomalous and both apparently based on the conception of a direct injury to quasi-property. They are too long established to be disturbed, but in my opinion should not be enlarged (page 9 of the Chief Justice's judgment).

The substantive issues on employers' liability are dealt with in the Tort Chapter 416 *et seq.*

EMPLOYMENT EQUALITY

Access to employment In *Gleeson v. The Rotunda Hospital and the Mater Misericordiae* [2000] E.L.R. 206 the Labour Court determined that the claimant had made out a *prima facie* case of discrimination. The facts were that Noreen Gleeson had unsuccessfully applied for the post of consultant obstetrician/

gynaecologist. A male candidate had been appointed. At the interview, one of the interviewers noted that the major career developments had taken place in the years when she had her babies. When Dr. Gleeson indicated that she would not be interested to do voluntary work in the Sexual Assault Treatment Unit, one of the interviewers remarked: "that's fine, sink the sisters".

She claimed being discriminated on the grounds of gender. Further to her experience at the interview, she stated that she had higher qualifications than the appointed candidate had, who also had been allowed to amend his curriculum vitae. She also stated that the interview board had not used pre-determined criteria of assessment and consisted of eight males and one female.

The equality officer recommended that the claimant could not establish a *prima facie* case. She appealed and the Labour Court allowed the appeal and determined that the cumulative effect of the facts established a *prima facie* case, such as the claimant's higher qualifications, amendment of the successful male candidate's curriculum vitae, the remarks at the interview and the constitution of the interview board. It further determined that the onus was now on the respondents to justify their decision (cf. *Wallace v. South Eastern Education and Library Board* [1980] N.I. 38). It determined that they had failed to discharge the onus of proof. The claimant was awarded £50,000.00.

The Labour Court further determined that the respondents were jointly liable, as all members of the interview board had signed of, recommending the male applicant for the post. It also warned the respondents that the complete lack of transparency and absence of pre-determined assessment criteria were matters of concern, which demanded correction.

Gender discrimination In *Minister of Justice, Equality and Law Reform v. Jordan* [2001] E.L.R. 24, the question arose whether the claimant had been discriminated against on the basis that he had not been promoted because a higher percentage of female candidates had been placed on a promotion panel. The claimant was a prison officer who was one of 173 candidates for promotion. 31 candidates were put on the promotion panel after a written examination and interviews, 18 of which were women and 13 men. The claimant was not put on the panel. He argued that he had been discriminated against because 54% of the female interviewees had been placed on the panel against 28% of the male interviewees. He also argued that the interview board had been entirely comprised of men.

The equality officer found no discrimination had occurred. The claimant appealed to the Labour Court, which dismissed the appeal. It determined that the case had no substance, as the promotion competition had been conducted fairly based on an objective assessment of all the candidates. It also determined that an all-male interview board, although not desirable, did not automatically suggest a source of discrimination against a male candidate.

Grounds for appeal on a point of law *Davis v. The Minister for Justice,*

Equality and Law Reform, High Court, June 23, 2001 (Quirke J.) is an appeal against the Labour Court, which had held that the applicant had not been discriminated against in respect of its selection of Head of Library Services at D.I.T. (Dublin Institute of Technology). The post had been advertised in 1997. The advertisement sought applicants with relevant experience and qualifications. It also sought applicants with the appropriate "stature, strength of character and communication skills" for what it deemed to be a senior management position. She did not get the position. She claimed gender discrimination. Both the equality officer and the Labour Court dismissed her claim.

This case is an appeal from the Labour Court determination. Section 21(4) of the Employment Equality Act, 1977 allows an appeal to the High Court but only on a point of law. She claimed that, considering the evidence, the Labour Court's determination had been irrational in that no administrative body could reasonably and fairly had come to its decision, and, thus, open to appeal.

The Supreme Court has distinguished between primary and secondary facts (cf. *Henry Denny & Sons (Ireland) Ltd. v. The Minister for Social Welfare* [1998] 1 I.R. 34 (Annual Review 1997, 693) approving *Mara (Inspector of Taxes) v. Hummingbird Ltd.* [1982] I.L.R.M. 421). Normally, the court does not interfere with the former but would approach the latter differently. Thus, the court can reverse the findings of, for example, a rights commissioner for three reasons. First, on the basis of an incorrect interpretation of documents, as the court is similarly equipped to make such interpretations. Second, if these findings were such that no reasonable commissioner would draw. And, third, the commissioner's conclusions show that he or she adopted a wrong view of the law.

The second ground was relied upon in *Faulkner v. The Minister for Industry and Commerce* [1997] E.L.R. 107. However, the Supreme Court held that the Labour Court had material in support of its conclusion that the applicant had not been discriminated against. It further held that (cited by Quirke J. at page 7 of his judgment):

> When reasons are required from administrative tribunals they should be required only to give the broad gist of the basis for their decisions. We do no service to the public in general, or to particular individuals, if we subject every decision of every administrative tribunal to minute analysis

Quirke J. concluded from this that, *prima facie*, a decision of a 'tribunal cannot be challenged on grounds of irrationality if there is relevant evidence before the tribunal which supports its findings' (at page 8 of his judgment). (Cf. *O'Keeffe v. An Bord Pleanála* [1992] I.L.R.M. 237).

Quirke J. held that the appeal must fail. He stated, first, that it was not his function to review the evidence with an aim to adduce the comparative weight. Nor was it appropriate for the High Court to interfere with the findings of the Labour Court on questions of primary facts, as there was substantial evidence before the latter to make these findings. Third, Quirke J. was satisfied that the conclusion that the appellant had not been discriminated against, as a finding on a question of primary fact, had been within the particular expert jurisdiction of the Labour Court based on ample evidence enabling it to reach that conclusion.

Burden of proof In the same case (*Davis v. The Minister for Justice, Equality and Law Reform*, High Court, June 23, 2001 (Quirke J.)) an issue arose as to when the burden of proof would reverse to the respondent. The appellant claimed that the evidence had established a *prima facie* case of discrimination, which would automatically reverse the burden of proof. Quirke J. adopted the test as developed by the House of Lords in *Glasgow City Council v. Zafar* [1998] 2 All E.R. 953. In the case, Browne-Wilkinson L.J. followed the five-step test of Neill L.J. in *King v. Great Britain-China Centre* [1992] I.C.R. 516. These steps are:

1. The applicant must make out his or her case on the balance of probabilities.

2. It is unusual to find direct evidence of discrimination.

3. This means that the outcome of the case depends on what inferences can be properly drawn from the primary facts.

4. This might lead to a possibility of discrimination, which may demand an explanation on the part of the respondent/employer. If such an explanation is not forthcoming or unsatisfactory, the tribunal may legitimately infer discrimination, as a matter of common sense (not law) (cf. *North West Thames regional Health Authority v. Noon* [1988] I.C.R. 813).

5. It would be unhelpful to introduce the concept of a shifting burden of proof. A tribunal should make its findings as to the primary facts, based on the evidence presented to it, and draw such inferences as it sees proper. A tribunal must then reach a conclusion on the balance of probabilities and, while doing so, bear in mind the difficulties an applicant faces with proving discrimination and the fact that it is for the applicant to prove the case.

Quirke J. was satisfied that the Labour Court made its findings as to the primary facts, which were reasonably open to it on the basis of the presented evidence. The inferences it drew from these facts were perfectly reasonable in the circumstances. Quirke J. added that the fact that there was a gender difference between the successful and unsuccessful candidates did not in itself require the court to seek an explanation, as referred to in *Zafar*.

Vocational training Institutions offering vocational training cannot discriminate against prospective candidates in respect of refusing access to the training course, the manner within which the course is provided or the terms upon which training is offered (section 12 of the Employment Equality Act

1998). However, section 12(4) allows certain vocational institutions to discriminate on the religion ground so to ensure the availability of nurses to hospitals and teachers to primary schools under the control of those institutions. Criteria are that these institutions must be established for a religious purpose, and the discrimination must serve the maintenance of the religious ethos of the schools and hospitals. The exception specifically applies to admission to the School of Nursing of the Adelaide Hospital (see: Paragraph 5(*s*) of the Health Act 1970 (Section 76) (Adelaide and Meath Hospital, incorporating the National Children's Hospital) Order 1996). In addition, institutions can apply to the Minister for Health and Children in the case of hospitals and the Minister for Education and Science in the case of primary schools.

The Employment Equality Act 1998 (Section 12) (Church of Ireland College of Education) Order 2000, allows the Church of Ireland College of Education to reserve 32 places in its vocational education courses leading to a degree of Bachelors of Education of the University of Dublin for the purposes of section 12(4).

FAIR PROCEDURES AND NATURAL JUSTICE

Prison services   In *Sheriff v. Corrigan, the Governor of Shelton Abbey, the Minister for Justice and the Attorney General* [20001] 1 I.L.R.M. 67, the Supreme Court held that in disciplinary proceedings concerning prison officers, the Minister's decision is an administrative decision that has a direct bearing on the (rights of the) applicant (the prison officer subject to the disciplinary proceedings). This meant, according to the court, that the rules of natural justice and fair procedure should be adhered to and the extent of these depend on the circumstances of the case; they need not to be similar as those of a court of law.

The court held that the Minister had adhered to the rules of fair procedures. Thus, an oral hearing was not necessary, as the facts were not in dispute. The charge was clear, although not formalised. The applicant had been given the reasons for the charge, the essential facts and a reasonable opportunity to respond to the charge. The Minister could take into account recommendations from a local officer. The preliminary determination by the Minister was confirmed only after representations were heard on the part of the applicant. The penalty subsequently imposed was not disproportionate.

Suspension civil servant   *Deegan, Gavin and Lynch v. The Minister for Finance* [2000] E.L.R. 190 is an appeal from the High Court ([1998] E.L.R. 280 (Annual Review 1998, 276)). In the case, the applicants successfully obtained an order of certiorari quashing the decision to suspend them without pay. The suspension was the result of a fraud investigation. They had claimed that they had not been given notice or informed about the allegations.

O'Higgins J. in the High Court had held that a decision to suspend is a justiciable decision and that fair procedures must be adhered to. The Minister had failed to do so. They had not been properly informed and, therefore, had been unable to state their case. Furthermore, O'Higgins J. had stated that a suspending authority could terminate the suspension of a civil servant under section 13(2) of the Civil Service Regulations Act 1956. Accordingly, O'Higgins J. had held, relying on *Ni Bheolain v. City of Dublin and Others*, High Court, 28 January 1993 ([1998] E.L.R. 280 at 286):

> It should be open, therefore, to a person concerned, to approach the suspending authority and ask him to terminate the suspension under the powers [of section 13(2)]. In order to do so it would be essential that the person would have sufficient detail of the allegations. In the present case I am satisfied that the information given to the three applicants falls far short of being sufficient to enable them to make such representations.

The respondents appealed. The Supreme Court allowed the appeal. Keane C.J. (with whom Murphy and Geoghegan JJ. concurred) distinguished between suspension as a disciplinary sanction and suspension for the purposes of carrying out an inquiry. It held that in respect of the former, a person is entitled the application of fair procedures and natural justice (cf. *John v. Rees* [1969] 2 All E.R. 274). The Chief Justice stated:

> The consequences of such suspension can be extremely serious for the person concerned, involving not merely their right to earn a livinghood but also their right to have their good name protected.

The Chief Justice held that in respect of the latter, the rules of natural justice do not automatically apply (cf. *Lewis v. Heffer* [1979] 3 All E.R. 274). This was the situation in the instant case even though they were not suspended with full pay. They were paid a proportion of their remuneration to which they would normally be entitled on the grounds of hardship. The Chief Justice stated that it was not to say that the rules of fair procedure and natural justice did not apply in the instant case at all. As they were suspended under section 13(2) of the Act, rules of fair procedure did apply, as they were allowed to make representations to have the suspension terminated. Keane C.J. referred to the decision in *Flynn v. An Post* [1987] I.R. 68. Thus, the applicants were entitled to be informed of the reasons of their suspension. This would enable them to make the relevant representations.

The Chief Justice held that on the facts of the case they had been told about the irregularities and knew in sufficient detail the reasons for their suspension and possible disciplinary sanctions so make the relevant representations.

Suspension of salary In *Carr v. The Minister for Education and Science and the City of Limerick Vocational Education Committee*, Supreme Court,

November 23, 2000, the issue arose whether the Minister was entitled under section 7 of the Vocational Education (Amendment) Act, 1944 to suspend the salary of the appellant. Section 7 allows the Minister to suspend and officer, and suspend paying his or her salary, if there is reason to believe that he or she has failed to perform the duties of officer satisfactory or is guilty of misconduct, pending an inquiry.

The Supreme Court held that it was clear that the Minister, or the VEC, has no power to suspend paying an officer's salary on the grounds of unreasonable behaviour or otherwise. There must be a concurrent inquiry that gave rise to the suspension of an officer (and his or her salary). This had not been the case. The suspension of salary could only be done had there been an express statutory provision allowing for this.

The court also held that the Minister could not rely on any common law right to withhold the officer's salary. Counsel for the respondent argued that the orders of *certiorari* or *mandamus* are at the discretion of the court to give. Counsel argued that, considering the wholly unreasonable behaviour of the appellant in respect of the work relationship, the court should set aside the orders. The Supreme Court held that it had such discretion but that in this case, the decision to suspend the appellant's salary had no conceivable statutory basis, which led the High Court with no option but to allow the orders. Such discretion would exist in cases where an applicant has acted unreasonable, but this would also depend on whether the unreasonable behaviour was procedural or substantive. (The court referred to *The State (Abenglen Properties Limited) v. Corporation of Dublin* [1984] I.R. 381 and *Aherne v. The Minister for Industry and Commerce (No. 2)* [1991] 1 I.R. 462.)

The Supreme Court also rejected the argument that the VEC had an implied right under its contract with the appellant to stop paying her salary and that, therefore, it was not obliged to back-pay her after the court imposed the order. Although the court could be tempted to accept the argument (cf. *Miles v. Wakefield Metropolitan District Council* [1987] A.C. 539) it held that of paramount importance in this case was that the Minister had acted *ultra vires* the 1944 Act. It stated that to merely 'quash that decision without making the consequential order for payment of the salary due would not be a proper vindication of the applicant's right' (page 23 and 24 of Geoghegan J.'s judgment).

INDUSTRIAL RELATIONS

Codes of practice   The Industrial Relations Act 1990 (Code of Practice on Voluntary Dispute Resolution) (Declaration) Order, 2000 (S.I. 145/2000) gives legal effect to the code as drafted by the Labour Relations Commission under section 42 of the Industrial Relations Act 1990. The Code will apply to the resolution of labour disputes where there are no negotiating arrangements in place and where collective bargaining does not take place.

The primary objective of the Code is to provide a recognised framework for dispute resolution, which is supported by all parties concerned. The Code prescribes a number of steps that ought to be taken if a dispute arises. First, the matter is referred to the Labour Relations Commissioner. It will appoint an officer to assess the issues in the dispute and will work with the parties with an aim to resolve the dispute. If a resolution cannot be found, the Code prescribes a cooling-off period. During this period, the Labour Relations Commission Advisory Service will continue to work with the parties, attempting to resolve outstanding issues. If no resolution is found during this period, the Labour Relations Commission must submit a written report to the Labour Court. The Labour Court will consider the position of the parties and will issue recommendations on outstanding issues.

The Industrial Relations Act 1990 (Code of Practice on Grievance and Disciplinary Procedures) (Declaration) Order 2000 (S.I. 146/2000) gives legal effect to the code as drafted by the Labour Relations Commission under section 42 of the Industrial Relations Act 1990. The Code provides new grievance and disciplinary procedures, replacing those set out in the Schedule to the Industrial Relations Act 1990 (Code of Practice on Disciplinary Procedures) (Declaration) Order 1996 (S.I. 117/1996) (Annual Review 1997, 498-499).

The primary purpose of the Code is to encourage best practice, providing employers and employees guidelines about the general principles that apply in grievance and disciplinary procedures. The Code is an alternative to local or internal procedures that already exist and adhere to the general principles. It stresses the importance of these principles, in particular those that relate to the principles of fair procedures and natural justice as well as the importance of maintaining good industrial relations between employer and his or her employees. It stresses that grievance and disciplinary procedures should be written in clear and unambiguous language and that copies should be given to employees at the commencement of their employment. The procedures should also be part of any induction programme that might take place in the organisation. All staff, including management, should be aware of the procedures and adhere to them. The general principles include:

— Procedures should be rational and fair.

— The basis for disciplinary action should be clear and sanctions well defined.

— The procedure should allow for an appeal mechanism.

— Procedures should be periodically reviewed and up-dated.

— Procedures should have proper stages, starting with an informal mechanism.

— Procedures should allow for an employee representative.

— Procedures should comply with the rules of fair procedures and natural justice as derived from legislation and the corpus of case law.

— Allegations and complaints should be set out in writing.

— Sanctions should generally be imposed progressively.

— Warning should be removed form the employee's record after a specified period of time.

— Proper records should be kept.

Inquiry into trade dispute   The Industrial Relations Act, 1990 allows the Minister to request the Labour Court or the Labour Relations Commission to conduct an inquiry into a trade dispute if the Minister is of the opinion that the dispute is of special importance (section 38(2)). In *Ryanair v. Flynn and McAuley and Irish Productivity Centre (notice party)* [2000] E.L.R. 161, the court held that the preparation of these reports could not be judicially reviewed.

In the case, the Minister had requested an inquiry into the trade dispute between SIPTU and Ryanair in March 1998 about the terms of the contracts of ground-handling agents. The report concluded that the assertion by Ryanair that its ground-handling staff was better off than their comparators employed elsewhere and who were represented by SIPTU was unfounded. Ryanair sought a declaration that the report was *ultra vires* by virtue of manifest errors and a declaration that the rules of natural justice had not been complied with when preparing the report.

Kearns J. dismissed the application. He held that the court could only intervene by way of judicial review in respect a decision, act or determination that affect a legal right of the applicant. The report did not amount to a decision; there was no "decision" to be quashed. The report was a fact-finding exercise that did not infringe any of the applicant's rights. Kearns J. held that any decision that may be made on the basis of the report was speculative and not a probable consequence interfering with applicant's rights. Kearns J. further held that the respondents were not obliged to act judicially in the preparation of the report. The application, thus, was not justiciable.

Kearns J. made some general comments, *obiter*, on the limits of judicial review.

"Excepted body"   *Iarnród Éireann - Irish Rail v. Holbrooke and others and ILDA* [2000] E.L.R. 109 resulted from industrial action in July 1999. The plaintiff claimed damages for inducement of breach of contract and, alternatively, actionable conspiracy. It also sought a declaration whether the ILDA (Irish Locomotive Drivers' Association) was an "excepted" within the meaning of the Trade Union Act 1941, as amended by the Trade Union Act 1942. Section 2 of the 1942 Act provides that an "excepted" includes a body of all the members employed by the same employer, which carries out negotiations for its members (but no other employee).

O'Neill J. held that the plaintiff had failed to establish any liability on the part of the defendants for the loss suffered by it. The trial judge also held that all members of an "excepted body" must at all times be in employment with the plaintiff. The ILDA extended membership to persons other than the employees of the employer. It could, therefore, not be regarded as an "excepted body". As it did not have a licence to negotiated as required under the Trade Union Act 1941 it was not a representative within the meaning of section 55 of the Railways Act 1924.

O'Neill J. also attempted to clarify the law as to the position of the plaintiff as an employer *vis-à-vis* its employees and employees' representative bodies. He held, *obiter*, that the concept of representation under section 55 of the 1924 Act relates solely to the relationship between the union and its members. It does not permit the consideration of the interests of the employer. Unions, then, who purport to negotiate with the plaintiff must have as their members a substantial majority of the workers in the relevant grades. The plaintiff is entitled to refuse to negotiate if this is not the case. It is not obliged to do so but if it enters into negotiations and an agreement is reached under the aegis of section 55 its terms bind the plaintiff and all the relevant workers.

The ILDA represents 41 per cent of the locomotive drivers who are in employment with the plaintiff.

MINIMUM WAGE ACT 2000

Scope   The National Minimum Wage Act 2000 came into force on April 1, 2000 (National Minimum Wage Act 2000 (Commencement) Order 2000 S.I. 96/2000)). The Act stipulates a minimum hourly rate of remuneration for all employees. It determines the minimum wage and other entitlements, and provides for its review, settlements of disputes, recovery of wages and imposition of penalties. It amends the Terms of Employment (Information) Act 1994, the Organisation of Working Time Act 1997 and the Protection of Employees (Employers' Insolvency) Act 1984.

The Act applies to all contracts of employment of service or apprenticeship and any other contract where one person agrees to carry out work for another (section 2). Thus, the Act applies to contracts of services as well as for services. The Act does not apply to employment of family members or an apprentice within the meaning of the Industrial Training Act 1967 or the Labour Services Act 1987 (section 5).

The Act makes void any term in an existing or future contract of employment that aims at excluding the Act (section 7). Such terms are automatically modified. The Act has retrospective effect in this regard.

Pay reference period   The Act requires employers to use a pay reference period to determine whether an employee is paid no less than the minimum hourly rate of pay. A reference period cannot exceed one calendar month (section 10). An employee's working hours would be the hours of work as determined by what is agreed between the parties. Alternatively it is the total amount of hours the employee works at the place of employment or is required to be available for work and is paid as if he or she is working. The employer must choose whichever of the two is greater (section 8(1)).

Working hours include overtime, time spent travelling on official business and time spent training during normal working hours on a course authorised by the employer. It does not include time spent on call or stand-by at a place other than the place of work. Nor does it include time spent travelling to and from work, time spent on sick leave, annual leave, parental leave, protective leave, adoptive leave, while on strike or lockout, or paid in lieu of notice (section 8(2)).

An employer cannot always control an employee's working hours. If working hours mean the total amount of hours worked, than the employee must keep a written record of the hours worked during each pay reference period and hand this over to his or her employee after the reference period. If he or she fails to do so, the working hours are calculated according to what is normally agreed between the employer and employee (section 9).

National minimum wage   Section 11 allows the Minister for Enterprise, Trade and Employment to declare, by order, a national minimum hourly rate. The Minister takes in account the impact of the proposed rate on employment, economic conditions and national competitiveness. The minimum rate may include allowances for board with lodgings or board or lodgings only. In 2000, the Minister has made two orders (National Minimum Wage Act 2000 (National Minimum Hourly Rate of Pay) Order 2000 (S.I. 95/2000) and National Minimum Wage Act 2000 (National Minimum Hourly Rate of Pay) (No. 2) Order 2000 (S.I. 201/2000)).

Section 12 allows the Minister to review the minimum rate from time to time. The Minister can do so if there is an existing or new national economic agreement that includes recommendations on pay. The Minister must accept or reject such recommendation within three months and account for his or her decision to the Oireachtas. Such an agreement can be express or implied. This follows from section 13. It allows any representative organisation to apply to the Minister with its views as to whether such an agreement exists. It may also apply tot he Labour Court to request it to examine the national minimum wage and make recommendations to the Minister after taking into account all relevant matters such as, for example, movement in earnings, exchange rate movements and the likely impact of any proposed change.

Entitlements   Section 14 stipulates that all employees over 18 are entitled to pay that is on average no less that the hourly minimum wage. Employees under 18 are entitled to 70% of the minimum wage (it could be referred to as minimum youth wage). Section 15 allows an employer to gradually pay the minimum hourly wage over two years when an employee first enters into employment or continues into employment after attaining the age of 18 years. The employer can pay 80% in the first year and 90% in the second year. The employer must take reasonable steps to trace such an employee's employment history to escape liability in any dispute on the rate of pay.

Section 16 provides for trainee rates. An employee who undergoes a course of training or study, which has been authorised by the employer or is prescribed by ministerial regulations, is entitled to a minimum percentage of pay of 75 percent in the first third of the study period, 80 percent in the second and 90 percent the third. Such study periods cannot exceed 12 months. The National Minimum Wage Act 2000 (Prescribed Courses of Study or Training) Regulations 2000 (S.I. 99/2000) prescribe specific criteria in this regard.

Section 17 stipulates that the rate of pay is calculated pro rata in respect of any time that is less than a full hour.

Calculation   The Act does not prevent any lawful deductions from any pay, for example, under section 5 of the Payment of Wages Act 1991. However, these deductions cannot be used to determine the minimum hourly rate. All pay must be included to determine whether an employee is paid the minimum hourly rate except those listed in Part 2 of the Schedule to the Act (for example: overtime premium, service pay, unsocial hours premium) (section 19).

The method of calculating is to divide the gross remuneration in a reference period by the total amount of working hours in that reference period.

Records and statements   Employers must keep records necessary to show that the Act is complied with (section 22). These records must be kept for at least three years. Employers are guilty of an offence if they do not comply with this provision without any reasonable cause. In the absence of records, the onus lies with the employer to prove that the Act is complied with.

Employees are entitled to request in writing a written statement of his or her average hourly rate of pay for any reference period unless the average rate of pay is 150% of the minimum hourly rate or when the request is frivolous or vexatious. The employer must furnish a statement within four weeks. It must include the pay components that are paid or allowed in accordance with Part I of the Schedule to the Act, the working hours, the average hourly rate actually paid and the minimum hourly rate to which the employee is entitled. An employer who fails to comply with the request or provides misleading information is guilty of an offence.

Dispute resolution   Disputes about the minimum hourly rate can be submitted to a rights commissioner without prejudice to any other action (section 24). However, certain criteria must have been fulfilled. Thus, the employee must have received a statement of his average rate of hourly pay or at least requested such a statement. No more than six months must have been elapsed since the statement was obtained. The rights commissioner cannot hear a claim if the employer is under investigation by an inspector under section 33 or 34 or prosecuted for an offence under section 35.

If the rights commissioner can hear the case, the normal fair procedures apply. Thus, he or she will give notice in writing to the employer and will hear the parties to dispute and any evidence offered by them. Any such hearing is held *in camera*. The rights commissioner will male a decision expediently, inform all relevant parties and send a copy of the decision to the Labour Court (section 26). The decision, if in favour of the employee, will require the employer to remedy the employee' position. It can also include a reward (arrears and expenses). The rights commissioner must maintain a register of all decisions, which is available for inspection by any person.

A party may appeal a decision within 6 weeks to the Labour Court (section 27). The Labour Court will send notice to the other party. The appeal takes the form of a rehearing. The Labour Court may take evidence under oath and seek witnesses, who will have the same privileges and immunities as witnesses before the High Court. The Labour Court will determine the appeal and either confirm the appeal or substitute the decision of the rights commissioner as it sees fit. The Labour Court may request the Minister to refer the determination to the High on a point of law only.

(There appears to be a drive to limit the possibility of access to the superior courts by parties to a labour dispute to clarify points of law. It must be questioned whether this is good development, notwithstanding the expertise and status of the Labour Court as a court of law.)

The Act may tempt employers to reduce the employees' hours of work while demanding a similar amount of work or duties from them. If this occurs, the employer must revert the employee's working hours to the position prior to the coming into operation of the Act or declaration of the minimum hourly rate within two weeks. A failure to do so amounts to under-payment and the provisions on dispute resolutions under Part V of the Act apply (section 25).

Enforcement An employee can refer a determination with which an employer does not fully comply to the Labour Court (section 31). The Labour Court may make a determination without hearing the employer or considering any evidence.

Any determination made by the Labour Court may provide that any matter must be remedied within a specific period of time or in a specific manner (section 32). In the absence of a specified period, a situation needs to be remedied within six weeks from the date of notice of the determination. Any failure of the employer to comply and remedy a situation allows the Circuit Court, on application by the employee or his or her trade union, or the Minister, to make an appropriate order without hearing the employer or considering any evidence.

The Minister will appoint inspectors whose task it is to examine or enquire whether employers comply with the provisions of the Act (section 33). In addition, they may be requested by an employee to investigate the employee's allegation that the employer has failed to remunerate him or her in accordance with this Act (section 34). The inspector must advise the employee about the outcome of the investigation. He or she must inform the Minister if the inspector is satisfied that an offence is committed.

The Minister may also request an investigation where the Minister seeks advice under section 39 (This section allows the Minister to initiate civil proceedings on behalf of the employee if it is not reasonable in circumstances to expect the employee to take action).

An inspector cannot investigate a matter that has been referred to a rights commissioner or in matters that arose three years prior to the date of the inspection.

Offences   The employer commits an offence where he or she refuses or fails to remunerate the employee in compliance with the Act. The burden of proof is upon the employer to show that he or she did comply with the Act (section 35). An employer also commits an offence where he or she causes an employee to be victimised (section 36). Further more, a dismissal as a result of a pay dispute will be construed as unfair dismissal under section 6(1) of the Unfair Dismissals Act 1977-1993.

Employer in financial difficulties   An employer may apply to the Labour for an exemption of non-compliance with the Act if the employer experiences financial difficulties. The majority of employees must consent to such an application (section 41).

PARENTAL LEAVE

Entitlement to parental leave   The Parental Leave Act 1998 sets out minimum requirements for parental leave and minimum requirements for time off work on grounds of *force majeure*. It entitles male and female employees to parental leave on the grounds of the birth or adoption of a child for a minimum period of three months. Employees can avail of this right until the child has reached an age up to 8 years (Annual Review 1998, 289-295).

Under the Act, an employee who is the natural or adoptive parent of a child was entitled to a parental leave for a period of 14 working weeks (section 6(1)). The entitlement only applied to children who were born or adopted on or after 3 June 1996 (section 6(2)). This was the date the Directive was issued to the Member States. Thus, children of employees who had reached the age of 2 years and six months on the operational date of the Act (3 December 1998), were deprived of extra parental care under the Act. It was unclear why the Act had chosen 3 June 1996 as the cut-off date. The date, although apparently logical, did not reflect the spirit of the Directive. It also seemed at odds with section

6(3) which provided that an entitlement to parental leave would end on the day the natural child has reached the age of five.

The European Communities (Parental Leave) Regulations 2000 (S.I. 231/ 2000) have rectified this situation and allow parents parental leave who were excluded from this entitlement under section 6(2) of the Act. The Regulations repeal section 6(2) of the Act. The Regulations provide that an employee who is the natural parent of a child born in the specified period is entitled to parental leave (Regulation 3). The specified period is now the period beginning on 3 December, 1993 and ending on 2 June 1996 (Regulation 2(1)).

Adoptive parents are entitled to parental leave in respect of a child born on or after 3 December, 1993 and for whom an adoption order was made during the specified period.

Entitlement to uncontinous leave The Parental Leave Act entitles a parent to parental leave for a period of 14 weeks (section 6(1). Section 7(1) allows parents, in agreement with the employer, to take leave over a number of periods. In *O'Neill v. Dunnes Stores* [2000] E.L.R. 306, the question arose whether the entitlement to uncontinuous leave, as provided in section 7, is an absolute entitlement similar to the absolute entitlement of 14 continuous weeks. In other words, could uncontinuous leave be taken in the absence of an agreement wit the employer? The claimant had asked leave for a period of three weeks. The Employment Appeals Tribunal held that an employee is only entitled to a period of uncontinuous leave pursuant to an agreement with his or her employer.

***Force majeure* leave** The High Court decision in *Carey v. Penn Raquet Sports* Ltd. [2001] E.L.R. 27, overturned the recommendation of the Employment Appeals Tribunal on the proper interpretation of section 23 of the Parental Leave Act 1998. Carroll J. held that entitlement to *force majeure* leave should not be based on an *ex post facto* analysis of the events that gave rise to the leave. Section 23 allows an employee to take *force majeure* leave if, for urgent family reasons, owing to an injury to or the illness of [a family member], the immediate presence of the employee [...] is indispensable'.

In the case, the claimant had taken a day off work to look after her daughter. She had fallen ill and had developed a rash. The plaintiff had decided to bring her to the doctor and than stay at home to observe her. When she subsequently applied for *force majeure* leave, the respondent refused her the leave. She did not produce a medical certificate when asked for. The respondent offered her a half-day's pay. A claim brought by her to the rights commissioner and Employment Appeals Tribunal was dismissed. The Tribunal determined that the event had not been urgent, immediate and her presence at home indispensable to qualify has a *force majeure*. On appeal, Carroll J. looked at the case differently. She held that the fact that the rash turned out not to be serious was no basis to refuse the force majeure leave. Instead, she held that ([2001] E.L.R. 27 at 32):

> the matter should have been looked at from the plaintiff's point of view at the time the decision was made not to go to work. Also the plaintiff could not be assumed to have medical knowledge which she did not possess

The decision really means that, upon interpretation of section 23 of the Act, parents are entitled to *force majeure* leave when their child falls ill, regardless the relative seriousness of the illness, as that can only be determined after medical advice has been sought.

PROTECTION OF EMPLOYMENT

Amendment The European Communities (Protection of Employment) Regulations 2000 (S.I. 488/2000) amend the Protection of Employment Act 1977 (as amended by the Protection of Employment Order 1996 (S.I. 370/1996)). The Regulations give further effect to Council Directive 75/129/EEC on collective redundancies (as amended by Council Directive 92/56/EEC). The Regulations provide for representation of, and consultation with, employees in the absence of a trade union or other employee representative bodies. The Regulations also provide a right of complaint to a rights commissioner where an employer has breached section 9 or 10 of the Protection of Employment Act 1977, failing to properly inform or consult his or her employees. They also increase the levels of fines for offences.

TERMS OF EMPLOYMENT

Employee In *Millen v. Presbyterian Church in Ireland* [2000] E.L.R. 292, the Employment Appeals Tribunal determined that a minister of the Presbyterian Church of Ireland was not an employee within the meaning of the Terms of Employment (Information) Act 1994. The Tribunal stated that the Church does not make appointments but rather the particular congregations of which the Church is made up. That he had been issued with a P60 form did not determine the employment relationship regardless of the descriptions "employer" and "employee" used therein.

TRANSFER OF UNDERTAKINGS

Safeguarding employees' rights The European Communities (Safeguarding of Employees' Rights on Transfer of Undertakings) Regulations 2000 (S.I. 487/2000), gives further effect to Council Directive 77/187/EEC. The Regulations provide for representation of, and consultation with, employees in the absence of a trade union or other employee representative bodies. The Regulations also provide a right of complaint to a rights commissioner where an employer has breached section 9 or 10 of the Protection of Employment Act 1977, failing to properly inform or consult his or her employees. They also increase the levels of fines for offences.

WRONGFUL AND UNFAIR DISMISSAL

Interlocutory injunction In *Howard v. University College Cork* [2000] E.L.R. 8 the court held that the relevant test to allow or disallow an interlocutory injunction was whether there was a fair question to be tried. O'Donovan J. held that the court did not need to review all the circumstances and events that had given rise to proceedings, as these events were irrelevant to any issue, which the judge must decide on the hearing of the application (cf. *Campus Oil Ltd. v. Minister for Industry and Energy (No. 2)* [1983] I.R. 88).

In the case, the plaintiff was professor of German and Head of Department. Her contract stipulated that the function as Head of Department would be for at least five years. Five years later, in 2000, she was informed that the five-year period had expired and that she would not be re-appointed as Head. She argued that the function of Head did not expire by effusion of time. She sought interlocutory relief, restraining the defendants from removing her from the post, appointing someone else to the post and interfering in the performance of her function as Head.

The background to these proceedings were proceedings in respect of alleged bullying and harassment against which the plaintiff claimed relief and which had created a hostile working environment.

Was there a fair question to be tried? O'Donovan J. held that the manner within which the defendants sought to have the plaintiff removed as Head of Department is an issue of law that must be resolved at the trial of the case but not in respect of grating the injunction. O'Donovan J. held that there were fair questions to be tried. These included whether the defendants were obliged to adhere to fair procedures when seeking the plaintiff's removal as Head of Department, whether the plaintiff had legitimate complaints in regard the defendants conducted their investigation in respect of the harassment and bullying allegations.

O'Donovan J. then considered whether the interlocutory injunction could be granted. This depended on whether damages in the trial of the case would be an adequate remedy and where the balance of convenience would lie. The judge held that damages would be inadequate to compensate her for the loss of her reputation. As regards the balance of convenience, O'Donovan held that to appoint a new Head pending the trial of the case would cause more difficulties than solving them and would place a heavy burden on the trial judge. Therefore, he held that the balance of convenience demanded that 'the status quo be maintained'. The defendants would not be irreversibly damaged, nor would the plaintiff be discriminated in her favour.

Notice and type of relief In *Philpott v. O'Gilvy & Mather Limited*, High Court, March 21, 2000 (Murphy J.) the High Court held that the plaintiff had been denied his contractual right to notice upon summary dismissal. It then considered whether injunctive relief as sought by the plaintiff or damages was the adequate remedy. It held that damages would have been the adequate relief. The plaintiff did not, and could not, rely on the protection under the Unfair Dismissal Act 1977. The High Court applied the decision in *Parson v. Iarnrod Éireann* [1997] E.L.R. 203. Murphy J. held (at page 9 and 10 of his judgment):

> If the traditional relief at common law for Unfair Dismissal was a claim for damages then the plaintiff may also have been entitled to declarations and injunctions in aid of his common law remedy. But if such equitable relief has no independent existence apart from the claim for damages for wrongful dismissal then, it seems to me, that there is no other free standing relief which can be claimed at law or equity.

Law Reform

The Law Reform Commission was busy in 2000, producing three Reports and one Consultation paper. In the Torts Chapter of the 2001 Review we shall analyse its *Report on Aggravated, Exemplary and Restitutionary Damages* (LRC 60-2000). In the Chapter on Limitations, below, 319, we discuss its *Consultation Paper on the Law of Limitation of Actions arising from Non-Sexual Abuse of Children* (LRC – CPIG – 2000). Later in this Chapter, below, 303, we examine the Commission's *Report on Statutory Drafting and Interpretation: Plain Language and the Law* (LRC 61-2000).

The Commission also published the *Report on the Rule against Perpetuities and Cognate Rules* (LRC 62-2000) which will be discussed in 2001 Annual Review.

Finally, we may note the publication of the Commission's *Report on the Variation of Trusts* (LRC 63-2000). This Report is designed to be read in conjunction with the Commission's *Report on the Rule against Perpetuities and Cognate Rules*. Its central proposal is that the courts should be given a wide-ranging jurisdiction to approve arrangements varying, resettling or revoking trusts arising under wills, settlements or other dispositions. The Report favours a liberal approach to the subject, preferring criteria uncircumscribed by restrictive qualifications. This approach is probably one that will yield the best results in practice, since the judiciary can be relied on to be sensitive to constitutional considerations. It does, however, raise some interesting issues of constitutional theory, on which our analysis concentrates.

Under existing law, the scope for varying settlements is narrowly defined, arising in only four contexts: the rule in *Saunders v. Vautier* (1841) Cr & Ph 240, 'salvage' jurisdiction, payment of maintenance out of income directed to be accumulated and a compromise jurisdiction arising where there is in existence a genuine dispute as to the interpretation of the terms of a trust. The Commission identifies two areas where difficulties can arise. The first is where it transpires after the trust has come into operation that certain powers, omitted from the trust instrument, are necessary. The Commission identifies as examples of powers that may turn out to be necessary 'the power to sell land or other assets; the power to continue running a business; investment powers wider than those contained in the [Trustee] Act [1893]; and the power to delegate': para. 1.16. The second area relates to changes in family circumstances which were not anticipated by the settlor:

For instance, certain members of the family may become incapacitated or fall on hard times or, alternatively, may inherit money from another quarter. (Para 1.17).

The Commission admits to having 'briefly' considered the possibility that the legislation might give the court power to authorise the redrafting of a trust to help other 'deserving' members of the family who are not beneficiaries and who fall on hard times. It rejected this approach, however, out of concern for the fact that this would diminish

> 'the original beneficiaries' property interests, conferred by the trust instrument ... Any variation, we believe should be conditional on the court taking the view that it is for the benefit of any beneficiary who cannot or will not consent for himself. To go beyond this cardinal principle would be, in effect, to extend indirectly the Succession Act 1965, section 117': para 1.17.

The Commission goes on to address the crucial issue of principle: whether it is proper to give the court jurisdiction to contradict the wishes of the settlor. It takes the view that, '[i]f the objection based on fidelity to the settlor's wishes carries no weight in a *Saunders [v. Vautier]* context then, as a matter of logic and justice, nor should it be treated as insurmountable in a Variation of Trusts context': para 2.07. Perhaps the conclusion does not follow with such inexorable logic. *Saunders v. Vautier* deals with the specific situation where the beneficiaries are of full age and capacity and together entitled to the entire beneficial interest in the trust. If they all agree, they may terminate the trust, without any resort to the court. They may do so because there is a certain futility about forcing them to stay tied to the terms of a trust where their combined interests represent the total beneficial interest. Letting them terminate the trust, provided they all agree, is not based on any social view that it is for their benefit to take this step, other than *a priori* faith that people's view of their self-interest coincides with their objective benefit. It is quite another matter to authorise a court to intervene, on the basis of some value judgment as to the objective benefit, and vary the terms of a trust contrary to the wishes of the settlor and without the consent of some of the beneficiaries. Whatever merit such a power of judicial intervention may have – and certainly the legislatures of an array of common law jurisdictions have perceived such merit to exist – it does not follow logically or as a matter of justice from the rule in *Saunders v. Vautier*.

The Commission addresses the constitutional implications of giving the court a power of variation. It perceives no difficulty so far as the settlor is concerned, since the settlor has no proprietary interest to assert after the trust has come into operation. This is of course true but it is scarcely the whole truth. Constitutional scrutiny should not begin only after the settlor has parted with his or her proprietary interest. It should embrace the entire process in which the settlor seeks to give effect to a particular wish in regard to his or her property. For the court to be authorised to frustrate that wish and to divert the property from the path on which the settlor sent it may be considered to represent a potentially significant interference with the settlor's entitlement, subject to the common good, to do with his or her property what he or she wishes.

The constitutional concerns are enhanced when one takes into account the Commission's proposal, later in the Report (para.6.04) that the court's powers to vary trusts should extend to revocable trusts. Here the settlor clearly can continue to have an interest in the property. It is surely straining matters very far to authorise a court to make an order altering the terms of a trust and contradicting the wishes of a person with a proprietary interest in the trust property.

Perhaps these concerns would be allayed if the court's power of intervention were tightly controlled, being based on circumstances akin to necessity or other pressing justification. In fact the Commission recommends an open-ended criterion for variation of trusts, subject only to a reservation that the court should retain a discretion to refuse approval (paras.4.15-4.16). Moreover the extent of judicial powers of intervention proposed by the Commission is wider than that of the English legislation in embracing re-settlement of a trust rather than drawing the line at variation (para.3.17) and in permitting the court to contradict the substratum of the trust (para.3.19). Both of these extensions are based on the Commission's distaste for involving the courts in 'unnecessary entangle[ment] ... in a difficult area of distinction ...": para.3.17. Yet is it not the fate of courts to entangle themselves in such difficult areas every day?

In addressing what constitutes a benefit, the Commission runs into a troublesome aspect of public policy. Should the courts vary a trust in order to reduce the tax liability of beneficiaries? Is their benefit, at public expense, actively to be fostered by the judiciary? It is one thing for the law to decline to strike down tax avoidance schemes (cf. *McGrath v. McDermott*, [1988] I.R. 258, Annual Review 1988, 356-8); it is another for the courts to endorse the value judgment that the reduction of tax liability is a goal which should be part of the judicial function to seek to achieve.

The present Chief Justice, writing extra-judicially thirteen years ago, evinced caution in this general context: Keane, *Equity and the Law of Trusts in the Republic of Ireland* (1988) 130. South Australia is the only jurisdiction with legislation providing for variation of trusts that deals explicitly with the question: The Trustee Act 1936, section 59E(3)(c) prohibits the court from approving an application for a variation that is 'substantially motivated by a desire to avoid or reduce the incidence of tax.'

The Commission is opposed to such a restriction, on several grounds. It considers that, if tax avoidance is to be tackled, this should be done in a matter that applies equally to other financial arrangements, rather than targeting the variation of trusts specifically. It points to the 'wide-ranging and sophisticated battery of laws which the legislature has enacted over the past decade to deal with tax avoidance, in particular section 811 of the Taxes Consolidation Act 1997, which gives the Revenue Commissioners the power to take necessary steps to ensure that 'the tax advantage resulting from a tax avoidance transaction shall be withdrawn from or denied to any person concerned.' The Commission comments (para.4.19) that:

> [t]he omission of an explicit restriction on tax avoidance from our proposed legislation would not deprive the Revenue of any of its usual powers under this, or any other, section.

Perhaps it could be argued that, in the light of the clear anti-avoidance strategy adopted by the Oireachtas, it would be wrong for the courts to proceed on the basis of a contrary value judgment as to the social responsibilities of citizens. To isolate individualistic norms of benefit and ignore the common good, which is a central constitutional value, might seem mistaken.

The sphere of application of the variation jurisdiction which the Commission contemplates is very broad. It extend to all cases where property is held on trusts arising under any will, settlement or other disposition, including revocable trusts and even trusts that pre-exist the proposed legislation. It summarily disposes (para.6.24) of constitutional anxieties as to the latter category:

> Given that any variation must benefit the person(s) whose consent has not been given to the variation, then it is hard to see that anyone's constitutional property rights or other interest has been violated.

STATUTORY DRAFTING AND INTERPRETATION

In its *Report on Statutory Drafting and Interpretation: Plain Language and the Law* (LRC61-2000), the Law Reform Commission proposes important changes, giving the Oireachtas a far greater role than formerly. Up to now, Interpretation Acts have dealt with relatively narrow rules of interpretation in discrete contexts. The Law Reform Commission, impatient with 'what may be called judicial a-la-cartism' in relation to statutory interpretation, recommends that legislation should prescribe a standard approach for a number of basic points in regard to statutory interpretation, in order to encourage uniformity.

The Commission's preference is for the retention of the literal rule as the primary rule of statutory interpretation. Departure from it would be appropriate, not only in cases of ambiguity or obscurity but also where a literal interpretation would fail to reflect the plain intention of the Oireachtas. Such departure would be permitted only where that plain intention 'can be gathered from the Act as a whole.'

One may, perhaps, wonder about the practical implications of this restriction. Of course, a purposive view of legislation 'as a whole' will enlighten, and possibly transform, the interpretation of its specific provisions. But, if a court encounters a particular provision in a long piece of legislation and that provision is ambiguous or is absurd when given a literal interpretation, the court's resort to a purposive interpretation will in some cases be focused on the particular context of that provision. It may be mistaken to require the court to apply the literal interpretation unless the interpretation based on the plain intention of the Oireachtas can be gathered from the Act as a whole. No doubt, courts are likely to treat this requirement in a formulaic way and will simply adopt a purposive interpretation of the provision even in cases where nothing extra can be derived from a gestaldt approach, but one can question whether it is desirable to force the courts into complying, verbally at least, with this requirement.

One should not discount the benefit of looking at the legislation in its entirety in order to understand the meaning of terms used in particular contexts. The Civil Liability Act 1961 contains provisions in Part II dealing with the survival of actions on death and in Part III dealing with concurrent wrongdoing and contributory negligence. The two parts have only a tenuous connection. Of course, the whole Act can be considered to be dealing with aspects of civil liability but that genus is pretty amorphous. When one digs somewhat deeper, one finds that Part II is modelled on English legislation of 1934 and Part III is based faithfully on model legislation contained Glanville William's *Joint Torts and Contributory Negligence*. Section 7(2), which falls within Part II refers to 'exemplary damages'; in contrast, section 14(4), which falls within Part III, refers to 'punitive damages'. Could it therefore be argued that these two descriptions indicate two separate categories of damages? In *Kennedy v. Ireland* [1988] I.L.R.M. 472, Hamilton P. thought so, since it seemed odd to him that one piece of legislation should contain two separate descriptions unless the Oireachtas intended there to be a categorical distinction between them.

It is only when one identifies the drafting provenance of each of the two Parts that one can reasonably conclude that no such distinction was on the minds of our legislators. Perhaps it could be said that this is a case where the explanation for the dissonance in terminology may be attributed to the *absence* of a coherent 'plain intention' to be gathered from the Act as a whole. On another view the 'plain intention' was to make reforms of the law in separate areas, borrowing from separate foreign statutory models. One would hope that the formula for statutory interpretation proposed by the Commission will ensure that the courts are able to take what might be called a 'sensible' view of legislation, conscious of the realities of the drafting process.

The Commission considers that it is better for it not to make any recommendations 'that would interfere with th[e] area' of penal taxation statutes, where the judicial policy of interpretation has been changing in recent years. It considers that broader principles of natural justice come into play in this area, which it is better to let the judges control.

The Commission goes on to consider in some detail the fascinating question of the interpretation of statutes over time. It is here that the contrast between judicial precedent and statutory interpretation is most stark. No words of a judgment expounding on principles of common law are intended to be frozen in time. They seek to capture the appropriate principles at a crossroads where justice, practicability and common sense coincide. So, for example, the famous rendition in *Donoghue v. Stevenson* [1932] A.C. 562 of the new regime for products liability, in which the privity-of-contract 'fallacy' was abandoned, necessarily expressed the formula for a duty of care in words that inevitably would be revisited and modified: see McMahon & Binchy, *Law of Torts* (3rd ed, 2000), paras 11.11–11.61.

Statutes do not easily permit of such a fluid approach. They are statements of law which, on conventional theory, envisage restatement only through a legislative voice. Judges (again on conventional theory) are not legislators. So, if a judge encounters a statutory provision which obviously calls for restatement, the judge's hands are tied unless (according to the Commission's proposals) the particular provision is ambigous or obscure or a literal interpretation would be absurd or fail to reflect the plain intention of the Oireachtas.

The problem with the passage of time in relation to a statutory provision is that a particular provision, which made perfect sense when it was enacted, can be overtaken by changes in society so that a literal interpretation will yield a highly unsatisfactory outcome. This difficulty is manifestly not the fault of the original legislators, who could not be criticised for having failed to anticipate these changes. Perhaps it might be considered to reflect badly on more recent legislators who neglected to amend the provision in the light of contemporary reality but the truth of the matter is that the corpus of legislation is vast and the process of change can be fitful. One could posit an ideal world where there would be a comprehensive legislative audit of the statute book on an ongoing basis. That idea is not, however, merely impracticable: It runs contrary to the complex phenomenon that a culture represents. Change – of technology, dominant values and more particularly linguistic usage – is an inevitable constituent of a society but that society cannot, and perhaps should not, seek to stand outside itself and attempt to interpret the changes authoritatively as they occur. Only a naive rationalist would propose such a futile exercise.

If the legislature cannot itself provide a comprehensive solution to the problem, can any general rule of interpretation be called in aid? One approach, of course, would be to adopt a purposive interpretation but that strategy, as we have seen, does not commend itself to the Commission. By way of contrast, the literal approach contains strengths but equally weaknesses. Its major strength is that it allows the court to interpret a provision, phrase or word in the light of its contemporary connotation. This can in some cases result in an outcome that is satisfactory even though it is quite inconsistent with what the legislators originally must have intended. Conversely, the literal approach will in many instances yield an unsatisfactory outcome, simply because the words in question, at a surface level, cannot be considered to extend to (for example) a new technological phenomenon, even though it will be clear to the court that the legislators, if living today, would be driven by the logic of the provision and its underlying values and policies to make such an extension.

If we allow, for a moment, the possibility of the courts' intervening to extend, contract or otherwise modify the interpretation of a legislative provision in order to accommodate contemporary reality, the question naturally arises as to the principles on which such an intervention should be permitted and the manner in which the modification should be made. The simplest, and narrowest, approach would be to permit the courts to take into account technological changes subsequent to the enactment of a particular legislative provision when interpreting that provision. Even this seemingly modest proposal is teeming with underlying issues. The relationship between individuals, society and technological change is a complex one. So, for example, changes in the means of communication, such as the development of fax, e-mail, mobile and text message, do not simply supplement the mail, telephone and telegraphs but radically transform social relationships, work patterns and friendship networks in subtle but radical ways. It would be mistaken to have regard merely to the technical character of communication when interpreting legislature provisions which mentioned particular means of communication but which naturally was incapable of anticipating the newer means of communication. Whilst some progress can be made with the criterion of 'functional equivalence' in this context (cf. UNCITRAL's model law on electronic commerce, discussed by the Commission in paras.3.27-328 of its Report) there are dangers when one moves from the narrow and unambiguous context of commerce where shared goals and values may to a large extent be presumed, into the wider world of social relationships.

Another approach would seek to identify the 'essence' of a word and, having done so, apply that essence to new contexts, technological or otherwise, which could not have been identified by the legislators at the time of enactment. This can be a tempting, and plausible, strategy where the word appears to be rooted in a technologically focused context. Even here, however, the task is a philosophical chimera. Words, as such, have no 'essence'. They may have highly, predictable connotations based on sociolinguistic experience to date, but that experience is susceptible to rapid shifts.

What the 'essence' approach seeks to capture is something different, harder to tie down but no less real. This is that legal systems contain, even in their specific provisions, underlying interpretations of the meaning and purpose of human existence and of the values that should govern international relationships. The answer in the *Dredd Scott* case to whether a slave was a 'person' whose rights are protected under the American Constitution was one saturated with philosophical and normative premises. In this context, the Commission refers to a letter by Francis Bennion (1997) 147 New LJ 716), (discussing whether Dolly, the cloned sheep, should be considered to fall within the Animals Act 1971.) One could equally address the crucial questions whether the protection afforded to 'everyone' by Article 2 of the European Convention on Human Rights embraces unborn children, children born with disabilities, the seriously mentally disabled and those who are in a deep coma. The search for a solution through the 'essence' of the word itself seems mistaken. Instead the court should engage in a philosophical enquiry, in which characteristic linguistic usage is an important, but not predominant, source of guidance.

This brings us to the wider question of the interpretation over a period of time of abstract or general concepts of a philosophical or normative kind which appear in statutory provisions. The Commission notes (paras 3.06) that:

> [s]uch words or phrases are 'mobile' in the fullest sense and judges will naturally take a dynamic interpretative approach to these, e.g. 'standards of decency', reasonable behaviour, etc....
>
> Generally ... th[is] typ[e] or wording [does not] cause many difficulties of interpretation. As the intention of the legislature at the time of enactment was clearly that the statute be interpreted in its context at the time of interpretation, there are no competing constructions, i.e. the presumption that 'points towards an updated consruction and the general rule in favour of the purpose of the legislature at the time of enactment, both lead to the same result.

This is no doubt so but one may wonder what implications this has for rules of statutory interpretation. It creates an anomalous distinction, based on the form rather than substance of statutory provisions. If one particular provision manifests a substantive norm using 'mobile' terminology, that norm is allowed to change in application over time but if another particular provision manifests exactly the same substantive norm using 'immobile' terminology, the norm becomes frozen in time, incapable of any change in its application.

The Commission ultimately expresses a preference for the principle of dynamic interpretation of legislation, whereby an updated construction is to be applied to old statutory provisions to make allowances for any changes which have occurred, since the Act's passing, 'in law social conditions, technology, the meaning of words and other matters': para 3.4. The Commission considers that there should be some limit to this dynamic principle. It adopts the proposal of the New Zealand Law Commission, in its Report No 17 1990, *A New Interpretation Act – To Avoid "Prolixity and Tautology"*, that an enactment 'applies to circumstances as they arise so far as its text, purpose and context permit': para. 3.44.

It is hard to predict how courts would discharge their functions under this interpretation model. The reference to changes in 'social conditions' is so general as to give courts a very broad remit, which could in practice swallow up the ostensible general rule of priority for the literal approach. For example, if a statute of sixty years ago gave to members of a tenant's family a right to succeed to the tenant's interest on his or her death, do changes in social conditions over the past six decades mean that the statutory entitlement extends to heterosexual cohabitees or homosexual partners? For a comprehensive analysis, see Fergus Ryan, 'Sexuality, Ideology and the Legal Construction of "Family": *Fitzpatrick v. Sterling Housing Association*' [2000] 3 IJFL 2.

The Commission proceeds to consider the question of internal aids to construction of statutes. Section 11(g) of the Interpretation Act 1937 provides as follows:

> No marginal note placed at the side of any section or provision to indicate the subject, contents, or effect of such section of provision and no heading or cross-line placed at the head or beginning of a Part, section or provision or a group of sections or provisions to indicate the subject, contents or effect of such Part, section, provision or group shall be taken to be part of the Act or instrument or be considered or judicially noticed in relation to the construction or interpretation of the Act or instrument or any portion thereof.

The Commission favours the repeal of section 11(g) and its replacement by a positive statutory authorisation to the court to use intrinsic aids. It sees no merit in the failure to acknowledge the true position in practice, which is that 'it is inconceivable that judges would not notice material which is, after all, on the same printed page as the substantive provision being interpreted. Not to do so would almost require blinkers ...' para 4.23. Moreover, as the Commission observes (para 4.31):

> [i]t is clearly anomalous that the only material which Irish courts are specifically prevented from using in interpretation is published by the Oireachtas itself.

So far as extrinsic aids to construction are concerned, the Commission recommends that the court should have a discretion to make use of certain of such aids, which it specifies in the following closed list:

(a) any document that is declared by the Act to be a relevant document for this purpose;
(b) any relevant report of an Oireachtas committee;
(c) any treaty or other International Agreement referred to in the Act;
(d) any official explanatory memorandum relating to the Bill containing the provision;
(e) the speech made by a Minister on the second reading of a Bill;
(f) any other material from the official record of debates on the Bill in the Dáil or Seanad;
(g) any publication of the Law Reform Commission or other official

body that was published before the time when the provision was enacted;

(h) legislation dealing with the same subject area as the provision being construed;

(i) such other document as the court, for a particular reason, considers essential.

The Commission also recommend that, in determining whether consideration should be given to any extrinsic aid or the weight to be given to it, the court shall have regard, in addition to any other relevant matters, to:

(a) the desirability of persons being able to rely on the ordinary meaning conveyed by the text of the provision taking into account its context in the Act; and

(b) the need to avoid prolonging any legal or other proceedings without compensating advantage.

When one reviews the closed list proposed by the Commission, it is clear that paragraph (i) is intended to give courts some leeway in exceptional cases: cf. para 5.76. Nevertheless, the phrase 'for a particular reason' is scarcely a formidable barrier to an expansive court. There will always be a 'particular reason' for the court's inquisitiveness if that is the key necessary to open the door.

Chapter Six, the final substantive chapter in the Commission's Report, deals with legislative drafting. The Commission recommends a comprehensive programme of plain language reform in Irish statute law and it supports the initiatives of the Parliamentary Counsel to the Government and the Statute Law Revision Unit. It recommends that the following strategies should be adopted where possible and appropriate:

(a) familiar and contemporary vocabulary in legislative drafting;

(b) shorter and less complex sentences;

(c) the active rather than passive voice;

(d) positive rather than negative statements;

(e) the avoidance of multiple cross-references between sections and subsections of the same Act;

(f) the replacement of concepts, such as 'the relevant period', or 'the appropriate date', with more specific information where this would be clearer;

(g) increased use of examples, maps, diagrams and mathematical formulae; and

(h) the highlighting in bold font of terms defined earlier in the enactment.

Whilst these recommendations are largely non-controversial, the Commission is conscious that 'sometimes brevity does not imply clarity; slightly more obscure words may sometimes be appropriate ... Plain language should never be utilised at the expense of legal certainty, particularly where certain words and grammatical constructions, though not in common usage, have acquired a fixed and clear legal meaning': para.6.22.

The Commission goes on to recommend that the Office of the Parliamentary Counsel to the Government should consider including purpose clauses in some Acts of the Oireachtas and to support the view that 'this ought to be done, in particular, where an Act gives effect to European legislation which itself has a purpose clause': para.6.40. Preambles and recitals can achieve the same function but in practice in Ireland has 'tended not to make maximal use' of them: para.6.31.

One should be cautious before offering unquestioning support for this development. The Commission acknowledges that some speakers at the Colloquia which it organised on the subject were – somewhat sceptical about whether the use of purpose clauses would have the desired clarifying effect. The Commission concedes (para. 6.35) that:

> [a]dmittedly, it is difficult to see how a single purpose clause could resolve all, or even most, of the potential ambiguities in a statute. And there may be other problems associated with the use of purpose clauses ... [T]here were some suggestions that a purpose clause could become the focus of debate in the Oireachtas, diverting attention from the substantive provisions of a Bill. There is certainly a perception that such clauses might be open to abuse by members of the Oireachtas, who might propose purpose clauses designed to give legislation the appearance of being something other than it is. Such clauses might not accurately reflect the content of the substantive provisions of a Bill and there may be a danger of conflict between the actual provisions contained in a Bill and its politically motivated purpose clause.

Finally, the Commission turns its attention to explanatory memoranda to Bills. The overall quality of these has undoubtedly deteriorated in the past twenty years. Several fail the test of objectivity, which would allow the most zealous opponent of a Bill to rely on its explanatory memorandum with as much comfort as the Minister who commends the Bill to the House. Particularly impressive examples, still worth close study, are the explanatory memoranda that emerged from the Department of Justice in the Nineteen Sixties, at a time of vibrant law reform against a background of a dearth of Irish academic commentary. The Commission acknowledges this gradual deterioration, stating (para 6.36) that, whilst the use of explanatory memoranda has become more common in recent years,

> some judges have remarked that explanatory memoranda were of more

assistance to interpretation in previous times, when they were published more selectively with some Bill. A factor to be noted is the variation in quality and content of memoranda; this may result from the fact that the memoranda are drafted in the various Departments of State, rather than by the Office of the Parliamentary Counsel to the Government. Very often, these Departments may have little or no in-house legal expertise.

The Commission recommend that, as legislative initiatives proceed through the Houses of the Oireachtas the explanatory memoranda should be updated to take account of the amendments. This is a most welcome recommendation, enhanced by the Commission's proposal that explanatory memoranda should be made available on the internet.

Licensing

INTOXICATING LIQUOR

Millennium arrangements   The Intoxicating Liquor Act 1999 amended the Licensing Acts 1833 to 1997 and the Registration of Clubs Acts 1904 to 1995 to provide for an exemption for owners of on-licences for December 31, 1999, the Millennium New Year's Eve. The 1999 Act came into force on its signature by the President on December 15, 1999. While the 1999 Act facilitated late openings in pubs for the millennium celebrations, the more significant discussion during 1999 in this connection were the overtime rates being sought by employee who were being required to work during the festivities. The effect was that, indeed, many public houses did not take advantage of the 1999 Act.

Intoxicating Liquor Act 2000   The Intoxicating Liquor Act 2000 provided for a number of significant changes in the licensing code, including new opening hours for public houses, provisions on under age drinking and arrangements for seeking new licences. The majority of the Act, other than ss.15, 17 and 27, came into effect on 6 July 2000. Section 27, which relate to special restaurant licences came into effect on 2 October 2000: see the Intoxicating Liquor Act 2000 (Commencement) Order 2000 (SI No.207 of 2000). Sections 15 and 17, which concern under-age drinking, have not been brought into force at the time of writing.

Opening hours   A significant development in the 2000 Act was to introduce permitted opening hours applicable at all time of the year. These are contained in Part 2 of the Act (sections 4 to 12). Prior to the 2000 Act, winter time closing hours were earlier than during summer time, but it was felt that this was outdated and a uniform system was pout in place.

The permitted opening hours applicable after the 2000 Act came into effect are as follows. On Mondays, Tuesdays and Wednesdays: 10.30 am to 11.30 am (and a half hour 'drinking up' time, that is, no alcohol may be sold during this time, but customers may remain on the premises), except on the eve of public holidays, when closing time is 12.30 am (and a half hour drinking up time). On Thursdays, Fridays and Saturdays: 10.30 am to 12.30 am (and half hour drinking up time). On Sundays: 12.30 p.m. to 11.00 p.m. (and a half hour drinking up time). The so-called 'holy hour', from 2.00 p.m. to 4.00 p.m. on Sundays, during which public houses were required to close, was abolished by the 2000 Act. On the eve of a public holiday, Sunday closing is 12.30 am (and a half hour drinking up time).

Under-age drinking   Part 3 of the 2000 Act (sections 13 to 17) provided for more stringent measures aimed at under-age drinking, that is drinking in public houses by persons under the age of 16. The intoxicating liquor code had provided for many years that it is an offence to sell alcohol to persons under the age of 16, but the 2000 Act contains new measures in this area. Thus, section 13 provides that the District Court may order the temporary closure of premises where the licence holder is convicted of selling to under-age customers. The previous defence that the licence holder had a 'reasonable belief' that the customer was not under age was abolished by section 14 of the 2000 Act, leading to an obligation on licensees to be satisfied as to the age of a person before supplying alcohol. Section 15 of the 2000 Act, which relates to the display of notice relating to under-age drinking, is conditional on the making of specific Regulations on this. Section 15 will be brought into operation when such Regulations are made. Section 17 of the 2000 Act, which provides that licence-holders engaged in off-sales of liquor must identify the premises concerned on the containers in which the alcohol is sold, is also intended as a further provision in the law to assist in the curbing of under-age drinking. The Minister for Justice indicated during the Oireachtas debate on the 2000 Act that consultations with representatives of the off-licence trade would take place before this provision was brought into effect.

Altered licensing application provisions   Section 18 of the 2000 Act introduced significant changes in the restrictions on applications for new licences, in particular those dating to the Licensing (Ireland) Act 1902. The 2000 Act abolished the restrictions which create separate licensing arrangements for towns and cities as opposed to rural areas, and the restrictions on new licences were either relaxed or abolished. In general, prior to the 2000 Act, two licences in an area had to be extinguished in order to create a new licence, and the licensing code provided for a number of grounds on which existing licence holders could object on grounds of economic impact on their existing business. This latter provision was considered by the Competition Authority to amount to an impermissible restriction on access to the market under the Competition Acts 1991 and 1996. Under section 18 of the 2000 Act, the entire State is treated as a single licensing unit leading to mobility of licences from rural areas, where there is a recognised over-abundance, to cities and towns which had been severely restricted in the number of new licences which could be created under the '2 for 1' provisions of the previous regime. Section 18 of the 2000 Act introduced a new test of whether the existing public houses in an area are 'adequate' which precludes objections concerning economic impact on existing businesses. The same provisions also apply to applications for off-licences. During the Oireachtas debate on the 2000 Act, the Minister for Justice had referred to the urban areas as being 'under-pubbed.' A further side-effect of the arrangements prior to the 2000 Act was the proliferation of 'super-pubs', that is, extremely large premises which, arguably, were not in keeping with the traditional Irish public house. However, it seems unlikely that the 2000 Act will lead to a return to the smaller public house, especially in urban areas.

Off-licenses   In addition to the provisions on off-licences discussed above, section 32 (which repealed section 47 of the Intoxicating Liquor Act 1988) in effect provides that any premises to which an on-licence or an off-licence is attached engaged in the sale of other products (for example, a supermarket) may sell alcohol from 7.30 am on all weekdays and may open for the sale of other products at any time.

Night clubs   Under the licensing code, night clubs operate by virtue of a 'special exception' order, coupled with a dance hall licence. The 2000 Act abolished the obligation that such premises provide a 'substantial meal' as a condition for a special exemption as well as the requirement that a premises be a hotel or restaurant. The restriction of the granting of a special exemption for any time on a Sunday, that is, after midnight on Saturday night, and after normal closing time on a Sunday evening was also abolished by the 2000 Act. In their place, the 2000 Act provides that special exemption orders will be granted in normal circumstances to 2.30 am unless the District Court considers it expedient, for stated reasons, to grant an exemption for a shorter period. In addition 30 minutes drinking up time will now be permitted after the period of special exemption.

Limitation of Actions

CHILD ABUSE

Over the past few decades there has been a growing international awakening to the reality of child abuse. Medical research four decades ago revealed that children were being subjected to a range of violence and neglect in their domestic environment which had not previously been known, though perhaps was often suspected. Over the past twenty years evidence as to child sexual abuse has become widespread. In the Irish context, there is now greater awareness of the abuse that occurred in some institutions where children were sent with the blessing of the State. A Commission to Enquire into Child Abuse, chaired by Hon Miss Justice Laffoy, has been established: Commission to Enquire into Child Abuse Act 2000.

One of the great difficulties about civil claims for compensation for child abuse is that victims are slow to come forward and initiate litigation. The reasons are complex. Even long into their adulthood the victims may have suppressed their memory of the traumatic events, they may be suffering from post-traumatic stress disorder, the prospect of suing may simply be too daunting or they may not have made the causal connection between their psychological distress and the abuse.

Internationally, courts and legislatures have adopted differing strategies to deal with the phenomenon of child abuse, sexual or non-sexual, in the context of limitation of actions. One approach is to apply the 'discoverability' test. This has resulted in extension of time in Canada, (*M(K) v. M(H)* (1992) 96 D.L.R. (4th) 289 (SCC)) but not in recent decisions of the New Zealand Court Appeal (*T v. H* [1995] 3 N.Z.L.R. 37 (CA). Cf. section *v. G* [1995] 3 N.Z.L.R. 681 and *H v. R* [1996] 1 N.Z.L.R. 299.) These decisions are discussed by the Law Reform Commission in its Consultation Paper, *The Law of Limitation of Actions arising from the Non-Sexual Abuse of Children* (CP 16-2000), paras. 2.099–2.101.

Another approach, now favoured in Ireland in the context of sexual abuse, is the disability model. This concentrates, not on the victim's intellectual *awareness* of the abuse, but on his or her *capacity* to initiate litigation in response to it. If the abuse had weighed so heavily on the victim as to render him or her incapable of doing so for same time, the clock stops during that period and the general limitation rules as to disability apply.

The Statute of Limitations (Amendment) Act 2000, in section 2, inserts a new section 48A into the Statute of Limitations 1957. In simple terms, it

provides that a person bringing an action founded on tort in respect of an act
of sexual abuse committed against him or her during minority is to be treated
as being under a disability while he or she is suffering from any psychological
injury caused by that act or any other act of the transgressor and the
psychological injury is of such significance that his or her will, or his or her
ability to make a reasoned decision, to bring that action is substantially impaired.

The legislation does not define 'psychological injury'. The concept would
appear to embrace a range of conditions broader than mental illness Whether
it goes so far as including any inhibition of freedom of choice or capacity to
act remains to be seen. Yet again we have a case where the law proceeds on
the basis of freedom of the will as the starting premise, which is capable of
being displaced in certain instances. Psychiatric and psychological theories
today generally proceed of a determinist hypothesis. When – as they often do
– experts of a determinist philosophy give evidence, the result can be one of
philosophical, and ultimately legal, incoherence since the law is premised on
a rejection of determinism. Another interpretation of the use of the word 'will'
in the section needs to be considered. The plaintiff must be suffering from a
psychological injury of such significance that 'his or her will ... to bring an
action is substantially impaired.' Could the concept of impairment to a person's
'will to bring an action' be regarded as resting on a different philosophical
premise that that of impairment to a person's will? A contextualised will, with
a specific goal, might be equiparated with 'desire' or 'wish', neither of which
concept is necessarily based on a philosophy of freedom of the will.

An 'act of sexual abuse' is defined as including:

(a) any act of causing, inducing or coercing a person to participate in any
     sexual activity.

(b) any act of causing, inducing or coercing a person to observe any other
     person engaging in any sexual activity, or

(c) any act committed against, or in the presence of, a person that any
     reasonable person would, in all circumstances, regard as misconduct of a
     sexual nature,

provided that the commission of the act concerned is recognised by law as
giving rise to a cause of action. Thus the conduct must constitute a tort or
other violation of a legally protected interest. Since certain kinds of sexual
abuse may not actually involve physical contact, as the definition makes clear,
it may well be that our courts will be called on, and probably prove disposed
to, extend the existing repertoire of torts, such as those of assault and intentional
infliction of emotional suffering, interpret them broadly and, in the odd case
where a lacuna persists, have resort to the strategy of compensating for
infringements of constitutional rights. It seems very likely, in the light of
McDonnell v. Ireland, [1998] 1 I.R. 134 (Supreme Court), that such claims
would be characterised as being 'founded on tort', as the legislation requires.

It should be noted that the legislation applies, not just to claims against the alleged transgressors themselves, but also against those alleged to have been guilty of negligence or breach of duty in respect of the personal injuries caused by the act of sexual abuse. So, for example, if a victim takes a claim against a school or other institution, or indeed the State itself, arguing that the defendant negligently facilitated or failed to prevent the abuse, the Statute of Limitations (Amendment) Act 2000 applies to that claim.

A couple of points of controversy may be noted about the claim against the alleged transgressor. In order to fall within the scope of section 48A the plaintiff must be suffering from any psychological injury that:

> is caused, in whole or in part by th[e] act [of sexual abuse], or by any other act, of the person who committed the first mentioned act ...

It would appear from this language that, to obtain the benefit of the legislation, the plaintiff must actually establish the defendant did what the claim alleges he or she did (unless the plaintiff is relying on a causal connection between the psychological injury and some other act of the defendant, about which we shall have some observations below). How is the court to determine whether the case falls within section 48A without addressing the merits of the claim? Is it to adopt a strategy of hearing the claim in its entirety, without prejudice to dismissing it on the limitations issue at the termination of the proceedings?

Another aspect of the section may be noted. It is drafted in such a way that, in cases where the plaintiff's delay in suing is attributable to psychological injury caused by 'any other act' of the person who committed the act of sexual abuse, that 'other act', in contrast to the act of sexual abuse need not give rise to a cause of action. From the defendant's standpoint this might appear to have a particular difficulty in that what purports to be a threshold test for suspending the operation of the Statute of Limitations would, in practice, fail to prevent any proceedings from being heard. Moreover, it is hard to require a court to dismiss a claim where it is satisfied that the defendant was indeed guilty of the sex abuse complained of but is not so sure that the plaintiff suffered from the requisite psychological injury.

The new disability period prescribed by section 48A applies to actions whether accruing before or after the passage of the legislation. With regard to actions that could not be brought, because the period of disability has ended and the relevant period of limitation thereafter has expired, there is a special, limited, extension. Such actions may be brought not later than one year after the passing of the legislation (June 21, 2000), provided that, after the expiration of the period within which that action could be brought by virtue of the legislation, but prior to March 30, 2000:

(a) the person bringing the action obtained professional legal advice that caused him or her to believe that the action could not, by virtue of the legislation, be brought, or

(b) a complaint to the Garda Siochana was made by or on behalf of the person
in respect of the act to which the action relates.

Section 3 of the Act contains a saver in relation to the court's power to dismiss
an action on the ground of delay where this would be in the interests of justice.
The section gives no guidance to the court as to what weight it should attach to
the fact that legislative policy support the taking of actions, even after a long
time, where disability as defined in the legislation exists.

The Act has generated much analysis. See Cathleen Noctor, 'Statutes of
Limitations (Amendment) Act 2000 – Implications for Parties to Actions
Regarding Child Sexual Abuse' (2001) 19 ILT (ns) 126; Ward, 'Statute of
Limitations (Amendment) Act 2000 and Actions for Child Sexual Abuse' in
Breen, Casey and Kerr (eds.), *Liber Memorialis Professor James C. Brady*
(2001), p. 344.

We must now consider the Law Reform Commission's Consultation Paper,
The Law of Limitation of Actions arising from Non-Sexual Abuse of Children
(CP 16-2000). The policy issues here are considerably more complex as the
parameters of non-sexual abuse, in contrast to sexual abuse, are not so easy to
define. What is sound discipline in the eyes of one person may be a violent
assault on a defenceless child in the eyes of another.

The Commission is not keen on the disability model since it sees difficulties
surrounding resort to psychological evidence. It provisionally recommends a
fixed period of time after a victim of non-sexual abuse reached majority. It is
divided on whether this period should be fifteen years or twelve years with a
supplementary judicial discretion to extend the period for up to three years. In
cases involving claims for both sexual and non-sexual abuse, the limitation
regime more favourable to the plaintiff should apply. In contrast to the
legislation of 2000, the defendant would have to be in a relationship of trust
and dependency with the plaintiff or fall under a supervisory duty or vicarious
liability; claims for non-sexual abuse against strangers would not thus fall
within the extended limitations period provisionally recommended by the
Commission.

DISCOVERABILITY

In *Scanlon v. Ormonde Brick Ltd*, High Court, July 21, 2000, the plaintiff sold
his mine to the defendant in March 1989, reserving to himself any coal deposits
including the pillars exposed in the course of the defendant's abstraction of
shale and fireclay as they became available in the course of the defendant's
operations. In May 1990, the defendant told the plaintiff that it had completed
certain work and that he was free to enter the lands to remove the coal that had
been exposed. After four days of extracting the coal, the plaintiff was informed
by the defendant that no further coal was to be taken from the site. Prolonged

negotiations then took place; it transpired that the source of the difficulty was that there was no statutory mining licence authorising the plaintiff to remove the coal. Subsequent negotiations involving the State Mining Board 'continued for several years.'

In the second week of June, a week after the defendant had been excluded from the lands, local people began to remove coal in an organised commercial way. This involved teams of men working with tractors, trailers and the necessary removal equipment. The plaintiff complained about what was going on to senior officials in the defendant's employment. He forwarded to them the names of those involved but the defendant took no action. The plaintiff also reported the matter to the Garda Síochána but they were also disinclined to take any action in the matter in the light of a longstanding local custom of unofficial removal of coal from mines in the area. Barr J observed that, at Castlecomer, it seemed that 'traditionally the mine owners turned a blind eye to such activities which were never formally sanctioned but were not regarded as pilfering in the strict sense of the term'.

A plenary summons was issued on August 7, 1996. Barr J dealt with the limitation issue by referring to sections 2(a) and 11 (1)(a) of the Statute of Limitations 1957, which, he observed, 'limits loss sustained by the plaintiff to that which occurred during the period ending on the date of issue of the plenary summons…' He noted that the plaintiff had conceded that, soon after he had been prohibited from continuing to remove coal, 'substantial pilfering of coal in commercial proportions commenced and, it seems, continued up to the crucial date from which damages may be claimed, i.e., August 7, 1990.' There was no firm information as to the quantity of coal wrongfully removed during that period of approximately two months but, on the evidence, Barr J. decided that its value should be assessed at £10,000, which was subtracted from the gross amount of damages awarded.

No reference was made to the Statute of Limitations (Amendment) Act 1991 or to the exact moment at which the plaintiff could reasonably have become aware of the pilfering. From Barr J.'s discussion of the plaintiff's response to learning of the pilferings it appears that it must have been close to immediately after it began. Even if it had been a week or two after it started, this would amount to not an insignificant sum of over £1,000 per week.

MORTGAGE AND CHARGE

In *ACC Bank Plc v. Malocco*, High Court, February 7, 2000, some light was thrown on the scope of section 36(1) of the Statute of Limitations 1957, which provides, in paragraph 7, that:

> [n]o action shall be brought to recover any principal sum of money secured by a mortgage or charge on land or personal property (other

than a ship) after the expiration of twelve years form the date when the
right to receive the money occurred.

'Mortgage' is defined in section 2(1) as including an equitable mortgage. In
the instant case, the plaintiffs sought the recovery of moneys due on a loan
agreement under which the defendant agreed to give a first charge on an
identified property. The defendant's solicitors had given an undertaking in
relation to this property to secure the execution of a deed of mortgage upon it
and to register it. The undertaking was expressed to be made in consideration
of the plaintiff's agreeing to draw-down the loan before the completion of the
security formalities.

Section 32(2) of the 1957 Act provides that no action claiming the sale of
land subject to a mortgage or charge may be brought after the expiration of
twelve years from the date on which the right accrued.

Counsel for the defendant argued that, to establish the existence of an
equitable mortgage on foot of the solicitors' undertaking, the plaintiff would
have to surmount two hurdles: that it had a contract for a legal mortgage which
was specifically enforceable and that the circumstances were such that a court
in aid of execution would infer the existence of an equitable mortgage.

Laffoy J. took a different view. She considered that, by the combined
operation of the loan agreement, involving the defendant's agreement to give
a first charge on the property, and the solicitors' undertaking, including the
authority given by the defendant which was embodied in it, an equitable
mortgage over the defendant's interest in the property had been vested. In the
instant case, the right to receive the principal money had accrued on October
14, 1991, the date when the facility was withdrawn and demand was made for
the repayment of the debit balance. The claim for the sale of the land was thus
not statute-barred under section 36. So far as recovery of interest was concerned,
the cut-off date of six years, prescribed by section 37, applied.

FRAUD AND MISTAKE

In *Moffat v. Bank of Ireland*, High Court, November 17, 2000, the plaintiffs
unsuccessfully invoked sections 71 and 72 of the Statute of Limitations 1957
in a claim for conversion of a cheque in 1983. The cheque was from insurers
of a house owned by the plaintiffs and represented the proceeds of a claim
arising from its destruction by fire. The defendant, having received it, lodged
it to the first-named plaintiff's account in reduction of his liabilities without
his having endorsed it. It notified him by letter the day it had so acted. The
first-named plaintiff had expected the cheque to come to him directly and had
hoped to negotiate with the defendant to have some of the proceeds of the
claim going to reduce his liabilities and other portions going towards the

provision of a family home and facilitating his trading. He did not, however, protest at the time.

The proceedings were issued in 1997. The plaintiffs (who represented themselves) argued that section 71, dealing with fraud and fraudulent concealment, and section 72, dealing with relief from the consequences of mistake, applied to their claim.

Finnegan J. had little hesitation in dismissing the first-named plaintiff's claim since he had had full knowledge of all the circumstances attending the defendant's conduct from the time he received its letter to their telling him what it had done with the cheque. The second-named plaintiff's claim was on a different basis. She was the owner of most of the contents of the house which had been destroyed by fire. The settlement cheque, insofar as it related to the contents, was payable to the first-named plaintiff in trust for her, the policy having been effected by the first-named plaintiff in trust for her to that extent.

The trust was, however, one implied by law and not an express trust and accordingly time ran against the second named plaintiff from the date of conversion. She could not rely on sections 71 and 72. Finnegan J went on to observe:

> [T]he bank did not and could not reasonably be expected to advert to the possibility that the second-named plaintiff might have an interest in the proceeds of the contents of the contents insurance. In these circumstances a claim against the bank for knowing assistance of the first-named plaintiff's breach of trust and knowing receipt of the second-name plaintiff's share of the settlement cheque in breach of trust does not lie: see *Lipkin Gorman v. Karpnale Ltd* [1992] 4 All E.R. 512 and *Bank of Credit and Commerce (Overseas) Ltd (In Liquidation) v. Akindele* [2000] 4 All E.R. 321.

ADVERSE POSSESSION

In *Feehan v. Leamy*, High Court, May 29, 2000. Finnegan J. held that the defence of adverse possession had not been sustained in respect of agricultural lands where the second named defendant kept cattle upon them. Finnegan J. considered that he had not the necessary *animus possidendi* to dispossess the plaintiff. For much of the period, the plaintiff had been involved in, ultimately successful, litigation against another party to establish his title to the property. Finnegan J. considered that the second named defendant's state of mind had been that litigation 'was pending and dragging on in relation to the lands which were lying idle and ungrassed'. He must had been to some extent aware of the progress of the litigation. On an occasion when another person's arrival on the lands led to the calling of the Gardaí, the second named defendant had told a member of the Garda Síochána that the lands belonged to a man in America. This answer indicated to Finnegan J 'the absence of the necessary *animus possidendi* – an intention to preclude the true owner and all other persons from enjoyment of the estate or interest which is being acquired'.

ESTOPPEL

In *Ryan v. Connolly*, High Court, February 29, 2000, Kelly J. had to consider whether the defendants were estopped by their conduct from raising a plea based on the Statute of Limitations 1957 where proceedings were initiated four years and three months after a road traffic accident. He observed that the court was being 'asked to exercise the jurisdiction of a court of equity which, over the centuries in appropriate cases, has intervened so as to prevent a defendant from exercising strict legal rights and entitlements in circumstances where it would be inequitable to do so.'

The defendants' insurers had written to the plaintiff's solicitors fifteen months after the accident letting them know that they had concluded the material damage element of the plaintiff's claim directly with the plaintiff's insurers and inviting the plaintiff's solicitors to discuss settlement terms on the personal injury element of the claim. Several other such invitations were made by the defendants' solicitors over the following years, including one made after the limitation period had expired.

Kelly J. was guided by the remarks of Henchy J in the Supreme Court decision of *Doran v. Thompson & Sons Ltd* [1978] I.R. 223 at 225, which represent the *locus classicus* on the issue:

> Where in a claim for damages such as this a defendant has engaged in words or conduct from which it was reasonable to infer, and from which it was in fact inferred, that liability would be admitted, and on foot of that representation the plaintiff has refrained from instituting proceedings within the period prescribed by the Statute, the defendant will be held estopped from escaping liability by pleading the Statute. The reason is that it would be dishonest or unconscionable for the defendant, having misled the plaintiff into a feeling of security on the issue of liability and, thereby, into a justifiable belief that the Statute would not be used to defeat his claim, to escape liability by pleading the Statute. The representation necessary to support this kind of estoppel need not be clear an unambiguous in the sense of being susceptible of only one interpretation. It is sufficient if, despite possible ambiguity or lack of certainty, on its true construction it bears the meaning that was drawn from it. Nor is it necessary to give evidence of an express intention to deceive the plaintiff. An intention to that effect will be read into the representation if the defendant has so conducted himself that, in the

opinion of the court, he ought not to be heard to say that an admission of liability was not intended.

Kelly J. observed that it was clear from that judgment that a twofold test had to be applied:

> Have the plaintiff's legal advisers in fact inferred from the correspondence ... that the Statute would not be pleaded against them and was it reasonable for them to so infer?

The affidavit evidence from one of the plaintiff's solicitors was clearly to the effect that the first requirement of this test had been fulfilled. Kelly J. was satisfied that the second requirement had also been complied with. He stated:

> In all the circumstances it seems to me that the view that was formed by the plaintiff's solicitor was a reasonable one. First of all, he was put on notice that the material damage claim had been concluded directly with the plaintiff's insurer. On a reasonable reading of that correspondence it seems to me that the defendants' insurance company was prepared to settle, and did in fact settle, the part of the claim. That must have been an indication that the invitations to engage in settlement negotiations were being extended in circumstances where the defendants' insurance company had in fact settled the property damage claim.
>
> Taking into account that correspondence and the frequent invitations to engage in settlement negotiations, including one letter which was written after the defence of the Statute was open to the defendants, I have come to the conclusion that it would now be inequitable to allow the defendants' insurance company to plead the Statute of Limitations as against the plaintiff. I am not for a moment saying that the mere fact that an insurance company invites a plaintiff's legal representative to settlement negotiations would be sufficient of itself to bar it from pleading the Statute of Limitations ... I quite accept that it would make life very difficult for insurance companies if they were subsequently precluded from pleading the Statute of Limitations simply by extending an invitation to engage in settlement negotiations.

Accordingly Kelly J. held that the defendants were estopped from raising the defence under the Statute.

DISMISSAL FOR WANT OF PROSECUTION

How pro-active must a plaintiff be? In *Silverdale & Hewett's Travel Agencies Ltd v. Italiatour Ltd t/a Off Shore World Cup '94*, High Court,

November 7, 2000, an issue arose as to how pro-active a litigant should be when his or her solicitor is delaying with the prosecution of a claim. The plaintiff claimed damages for breach of contract. It alleged that it had entered into an agreement with the first named defendant to act as agent for it for the sale in Ireland of travel packages to the 1994 World Cup in the United States of America. It claimed that the agreement had been concluded with the second and third named defendants acting as agents for the first named defendant. The plenary summons had been issued in June 1995, with the statement of claim being delivered against the first named defendant two months later. Thereafter the proceedings became lethargic. Following an order in May 1996 joining the second named and third named defendants as defendants the amended plenary summons was not issued. However, a form of amended plenary summons and statement of claim was served on the second named and third named defendants in October 1996. The failure to issue an amended plenary summons came to light when the solicitors for the second named and third named defendants attempted to enter an appearance in February 1997. While the necessary papers for an application for an extension to the time limited by the Order of May 1996 were drafted the matter was thereafter overlooked and it was only in July 1999 that an Order was made extending the time for the issue of the amended plenary summons and the delivery of the amended statement of claim. The amended plenary summons was thereafter duly served on the second named and third named defendants in August 1999 and the amended statement of claim was delivered on the same date.

In March 2000, the first named defendant issued a motion seeking the dismissal of the proceedings on account of the delay.

Applying the principles set out by Finlay P in *Rainsford v. Limerick Corporation* [1995] 2 I.L.R.M. 561 at 567, Finnegan J. found that the delay of the plaintiff had been both inordinate and inexcusable. The solicitor to the plaintiff had sworn an affidavit in which he frankly accepted responsibility for the delay. There was nothing in any of the affidavits filed on this application to suggest that there existed any personal blameworthiness on the part of the plaintiff beyond that its solicitor, for which it was vicariously liable. This was a factor which Finnegan J. acknowledged had to be taken into account in determining how he should exercise his discretion on the motion.

Finnegan J. stated:

> In considering a party's personal blameworthiness one must look at the circumstances of the party. In the case of an infant plaintiff this circumstance will most likely justify delay during his minority: *O'Donnell v. Merrick* [1984] I.R. 151. In *Guerin v. Guerin* [1992] 2 I.R. 287 Costello P had regard to the circumstances that while the plaintiff was an infant his family lived in one of the poorest sections of the community, permanently unemployed, and were unaware that he the plaintiff had a cause of action. Such considerations have little

application to the plaintiff in the present case which is a considerable commercial enterprise and must be expected to pursue litigation of a commercial nature with reasonable expedition and to that end take steps to ensure that its legal advisors act in an appropriately expeditious manner. Lack of personal blameworthiness in litigation such as this is of less significance than in cases such as *O'Domhnaill v. Merrick* and *Merrick v. Guerin.*

Turning to the question of where the balance of justice lay, Finnegan J. noted that the third defendant had gone into liquidation in 1998. The first named defendant claimed that it had been prejudiced by the delay on the part of the plaintiff in prosecuting the proceedings in that, had the claim been prosecuted diligently, a hearing would have been obtained in advance of the liquidation of the third named defendant. Further, following the liquidation of the third named defendant the second named defendant had taken no interest in the proceedings and the solicitors retained by him and the third named defendant had come off record. The delay, said the first named defendant, had denied the first named defendant the opportunity of obtaining contribution or indemnity from the third named defendant and seriously diminished the possibility of its obtaining contribution or indemnity from the second named defendant.

Finnegan J rejected this argument. Having regard to the third named defendant's trading situation, he was not satisfied as a matter of probability that, had the first named defendant obtained a judgment for contribution or indemnity prior to the liquidation, the third named defendant would have been in a position to satisfy it. In those circumstances, the attitude of the second named defendant to the litigation would not have been different from that which he was actually adopting.

Finally, Finnegan J. noted that the plaintiff instituted the proceedings in June 1995 in respect of an alleged breach of contract in February 1994. The limitation period would not have expired until February 2000. The first named defendant could have issued the motion at a much earlier date – at any time after July 1998 – had it so wished. Rather it chose to delay doing so until the limitation period had expired. Finnegan J. took this fact into account in determining the balance of justice.

In the light of all these factors, Finnegan J. was satisfied that the balance of justice was in favour of allowing the action to proceed. Justice, however, required that he should impose a condition on the plaintiff in prosecuting the action:

> Having elected to join the second named defendant and the third named defendants as defendants rather than to have the first named defendant join them as third parties the action must not be set down against the first named defendant only but must be set down against the first named defendant and the second named defendant so that the first named

defendant's claim for contribution and indemnity can proceed at the same time.

In *Hughes t/a Hughes Engineering International v. Moy Contractors Ltd, De Beer Industrial Diamonds Division (Ireland) Ltd and Garland and Partners*, High Court, January 25, 2000, the first named defendant sought dismissal of a claim for breach of contract, negligence and misrepresentation by reason of the plaintiff's inordinate and inexcusable delay in commencing and prosecuting the proceedings. The plaintiff was a specialist demolition contractor. The first named defendant was the main contractor for works carried out for and on behalf of the second named defendant, a manufacturer with a facility in the Shannon Airport industrial estate. The third named defendants were consulting engineers acting in that capacity in connection with a contract made in 1988 for demolition work at the second defendant's premises. The first named defendant was claiming to be the main contractor for this work.

The plaintiff claimed that it entered the 1988 contract to carry out demolition work of certain concrete pits at the second defendant's premises. The plaintiff claimed that it entered the contract on the basis of representations made by the defendants as to the quality and depth of the pits. It claimed that the concrete turned out to be much thicker than had been represented, with the result that the drill bits ordered for the job were too short and a number of other features were not shown in the drawings. The plaintiff claimed that it advised the third named defendant of the difficulties and that, after further site meetings, it was agreed that additional monies would be paid to carry out the work.

The plenary summons was issued in July 1992 and served over eight months later. The plaintiff's first notice of intention to proceed was served in 1995, the second notice in 1997. The statement of claim was delivered in February 1998. The first named defendant's notice for particulars was served in August of that year; replies were furnished a month later. A motion for judgment in default of defence was entered in February 1999 and re-entered the following May. In July 1999 the second and third named defendants succeeded in their motion to have the action struck out for want of prosecution: see Annual Review 1999, 405-6, 446.

As to the period between 1988 and the issuing and serving of the plenary summons (in 1992 and 1993 respectively), Morris P. was satisfied that the delay could probably be attributed to the reluctance of the plaintiff to serve the proceedings while ongoing negotiations were taking place between the parties. The period of delay from March 1993 to February 1998, when the statement of claim was delivered, counsel for the plaintiff conceded that it was inordinate and inexcusable. The plaintiff's solicitors explained that a number of the staff dealing with the file had been transferred from litigation to conveyancing, with the unfortunate consequence that the file was misplaced for a considerable period of time. Moreover, the claim was a complicated one, which required consultation to prepare the statement of claim. These circumstances had been hampered because the plaintiff was regularly abroad for considerable periods of time. Morris P. had no doubt that, even if the plaintiff's counsel had not made the concession, he could have come to the conclusion that, having regard to the initial lapse of time before the serving of the summons, the additional delay was entirely inordinate and excusable. Morris P. was:

> satisfied that whatever part of this blame may be accepted by the plaintiff's solicitors the plaintiff itself must carry responsibility by reason of the fact that [the plaintiff] was out of the country and apparently took no active steps to advance his claim.

On the questions whether the first named defendant had suffered prejudice as a result of the delay and whether justice required that the action be struck out, the first named defendant argued that two essential witnesses had died and a third witness, aged over seventy, was in poor health and unlikely to be capable of giving satisfactory evidence. Moreover, the fact that the action against the second and third named defendants had been struck out meant that the first named defendant would be left to carry full responsibility to the plaintiff where the primary responsibility to pay the plaintiff would (in the event of a finding of liability) have rested on the second named defendant. The plaintiff responded to the first of these grounds by claiming that other witnesses would be available to support whatever case the first named defendant might make. Morris P. did not agree. He was left in no doubt that the evidence of one of the deceased witnesses and of the elderly witness was central to the entire transaction, since it related to an alleged oral contract in which certain representations were alleged to have been made. Morris P was of the view that to be deprived of essential witnesses in this way grossly prejudiced the first named defendant in the defence of its action and he was satisfied that justice required that the action be dismissed.

Morris P. did not, however, accept the first named defendant's second point, since it was open to the first named defendant to make a claim for contribution or indemnity under the third party procedure if the plaintiff should succeed against it.

Local Government

BUILDING REGULATIONS

Dwellings: disability access   The Building Regulations (Amendment) Regulations 2000 (S.I. No.179 of 2000), made under the Building Control Act 1990 (Annual Review 1990, 404-6) amended Part M of the Building Regulations 1997 (Annual Review 1997, 557-8) by requiring that all new dwellings constructed after January 1, 2001 should be visitable by people with disabilities.

FINANCIAL PROVISIONS

Service charges   The Local Government (Financial Provisions) Act 2000 confirmed the power of local authorities to make charges for services by virtue of the Local Government (Financial Provisions) (No. 2) Act 1983, and validates any such charges made to its enactment. The 2000 Act was enacted against the background of considerable resistance and consequent challenges to the validity of service charges made by local authorities under the 1983 Act, particularly charges for refuse collection services. The 2000 Act came into effect on its signature by the President on 20 April 2000.

LOCAL AUTHORITY OFFICERS

Tenure of office of managers   The Local Government Act 2000 amended the Local Government Act 1991 by the insertion of a new section 47A of the 1991 Act, which provides for an option for the extension of the tenure of office of local authority managers. The 2000 Act came into effect on its signature by the President on July 8, 2000. The Local Government (Tenure of Office of Managers) Regulations 2000 (S.I. No.219 of 2000) sets out the detailed provisions in relation to the extension of tenure of office, and came into effect on July 12, 2000.

Planning Law

GARRETT SIMONS, B.L., Lecturer in Administrative and Planning Law, King's Inns

PLANNING AND DEVELOPMENT ACT 2000

Introduction   The single most significant event of the year 2000 in respect of planning law was the enactment of the Planning and Development Act, 2000. This Act not only represents a consolidation of the Local Government (Planning and Development) Acts 1963 to 1999, it also involves the introduction of a number of radical amendments to the substantive law of planning. To date, only parts of the Act have been commenced and for this reason, and given the scale of the task otherwise involved, it is intended to confine this commentary to those parts of the Act which had been commenced in the year 2000. Before turning to that purpose, it is proposed to consider briefly the decision of the Supreme Court on the Article 26 reference which preceded the President's signing of the Act into law.

Article 26 reference   Article 26 of the constitution provides for the referral of Bills to the Supreme Court for a decision on their constitutionality. By order of June 30, 2000, the President referred Part V of the Planning and Development Bill 1999 to the Supreme Court for a decision on the question as to whether the said part or any provision or provisions thereof was, or were, repugnant to the Constitution. Part V of the Bill established the provision of social and affordable housing as an objective of the planning legislation, and introduced a mechanism whereby the developers of residential development could be required to cede land, at its existing use value, to the planning authority for this objective. Specifically, the Bill provided for the attaching of a condition to a planning permission requiring the applicant, or any other person with an interest in the land, to enter into an '*agreement*' for the transfer of land (up to a maximum of twenty per cent). The requirement was to apply only to lands which were designated for residential use, or for a mixture of residential and other uses, under the statutory development plan. Compensation was to be paid to the landowner for any lands transferred on the following basis. A distinction was to be drawn between lands acquired before the date of the publication of the Bill (August 25, 1999), and lands acquired after that date. In the case of land acquired after that date, the measure of compensation was the value of the land calculated by reference to its existing use on the date of the transfer of ownership of the land to the planning authority on the basis that on that date it would have been, and would thereafter continue to be, unlawful to carry out any development in relation to that land other than exempted development. (In the case of land purchased before the date of the publication of the Bill, the landowner was to be entitled to be paid the sum he had actually paid for the land (together with interest), if higher than the existing use value). The effect of limiting compensation to the existing use value of the lands would be to exclude the '*hope*' value of the land for the purpose of determining compensation. Ordinarily, in determining the quantum of compensation, a property arbitrator would be entitled to have regard to the development potential of the land. For the purpose of compensation under Part V of the Bill, however, no regard was to be had to the fact that the land was zoned for development (whether residential or otherwise), or to the likelihood of planning permission being obtained.

As stated above, the matter was referred to the Supreme Court pursuant to Article 26 of the constitution; *In re Part V of the Planning and Development Bill, 1999* [2000] 2 I.R. 321; [2001] 1 I.L.R.M. 81. A discussion of the constitutional issues argued is well beyond the remit of this annual review of planning law. In very general terms, however, the broad thrust of the arguments might be summarised thus. Counsel assigned by the Supreme Court to argue against the constitutionality of Part V of the Bill submitted that Part V was repugnant to a number of the provisions of the constitution. It was submitted that while it was undoubtedly important, and indeed essential, for the executive and the legislature to do everything within their power to remedy the serious socio-economic problems resulting from the high level of house prices now prevailing, it should not be done by requiring one section of the population – owners legitimately wishing to develop their land, to bear a disproportionate share of alleviating the social ills in question. The Supreme Court rejected these arguments and upheld the Bill as constitutional. The Supreme Court ruled, *inter alia*, that whereas a person who is compulsorily deprived of his or her property in the interest of the common good should normally be compensated at a level equivalent to at least the market value of the acquired property, special considerations were applicable in the case of restrictions to the use of land imposed under the planning legislation, as follows

> Every person who acquires or inherits land takes it subject to any restrictions which the general law of planning imposes on the use of the property in the public interest. Inevitably, the fact that permission for a particular type of development may not be available for the land will, in certain circumstances, depreciate the value in the open market of that land. Conversely, where the person obtains a permission for a particular development the value of the land in the open market may be enhanced. [...]
>
> In the present case, as a condition of obtaining a planning permission for the development of lands for residential purposes, the owner may be

required to cede some part of the enhanced value of the land deriving both from its zoning for residential purposes and from the grant of permission in order to meet what is considered by the Oireachtas to be a desirable social objective, namely the provision of affordable housing and housing for persons in special categories and of integrated housing. […] [The provisions] are rationally connected to an objective of sufficient importance to warrant interference with a constitutionally protected right and, given the serious social problems which they are designed to meet, they undoubtedly relate to concerns which, in a free and democratic society, should be regarded as pressing and substantial.

The Supreme Court decision is open to criticism under two headings. First, the finding that planning permission represents an enhancement of property rights is inconsistent with earlier authorities which had indicated that the very requirement to obtain planning permission actually represented an interference with property rights. Indeed, as recently as the previous year (1999), O'Flaherty J. had stated as follows: '[I]n 1964, the legislature would have been conscious that the enactment of planning control did represent a huge encroachment on the age-old right to hold private property in broadly the same way for the future as they had in the past provided it was not a nuisance, or other in breach of the law'; *Butler v. Dublin Corporation* [1999] 1 I.R 565 at 588; [1999] 1 I.L.R.M. 481 at 490. See also *Waterford County Council v. John A. Wood Ltd.* [1999] 1 I.R. 556; [1999] I.L.R.M. 217.

Secondly, it is the writer's personal view that the Supreme Court decision does not advance any convincing reason for rejecting the argument that the legislation unfairly and invidiously discriminated against landowners who develop their land for *residential* development. It is submitted that a requirement which is confined to residential development only, lacks the generality of regulation which underpins other types of zoning objectives under the statutory development plan. It is invidious to require the developers of residential land to transfer land at a discount in circumstances where the particular social problem to be remedied (i.e. the need for social and affordable housing) is not directly related to the proposed developments, and where the developers of other lands (for example, for commercial or industrial purposes) may take the benefit of planning permission free from this form of planning gain.

At all events, it is idle to speculate on the correctness or otherwise of the Supreme Court decision, for the following reason. Article 34.3.3° of the constitution provides, *inter alia*, that no court shall have jurisdiction to question the validity of any provision of a law, where the corresponding provision in the Bill for such law shall have been referred to the Supreme Court under Article 26. Accordingly, whereas challenges might be made to the implementation of the procedures under Part V of the Planning and Development Act 2000, the constitutionality of same is now unimpeachable.

Commencement orders   Two commencement orders were made under the
Planning and Development Act 2000 in the year 2000, as follows. The Planning
and Development Act 2000 (Commencement) Order, 2000 (S.I. 349 of 2000),
which, in brief, commenced Part V of the Act (social and affordable housing),
and Part IX (strategic development zones) as and from November 1, 2000. It
also commenced the provisions in respect of ministerial guidelines and policy
directives from the same date (November 1, 2000). Other provisions in respect
of development plans and local area plans were commenced from January 1,
2001. The second commencement order (Planning and Development Act 2000
(Commencement) (No. 2) Order 2000 (S.I. No. 449 of 2000) will be considered
in the next Annual Review. Very briefly, it commenced (from January 1, 2001)
provisions in respect of the acquisition of lands; the acquisition of protected
structures; and introduced amendments to the Roads Act, 1993.

The provisions in respect of social and affordable housing; strategic
development zones; and ministerial guidelines and policy directives, are
considered further below under those individual headings.

SOCIAL AND AFFORDABLE HOUSING

Introduction   Part V of the Planning and Development Act 2000, establishes
the provision of social and affordable housing as an objective of the planning
legislation, and introduces a mechanism whereby the developers of residential
development may be required to cede part of their lands, at its existing use
value, to the planning authority for this objective. This is to be achieved in the
context of a statutory housing strategy, and of the statutory development plan.

Land transfer agreement   Section 96 allows for the attaching of a condition
to a planning permission requiring the applicant, or any other person with an
interest in the land, to enter into an *'agreement'* for the transfer of land
(hereinafter referred to as a *'land transfer agreement'* where convenient). Some
flexibility is allowed for, however, in that the developer may *elect* to transfer a
number of built houses, or a number of fully or partially serviced sites, instead.
The provisions of Section 96 are triggered where a development plan objective
requires that a specified percentage of any land zoned solely for residential use
(or for a mixture of residential and other uses) be made available for social and
affordable housing. (The specified percentage cannot be more than twenty per
cent). The mechanics of section 96 are unusual in that matters of basic detail
(including the very identity of the land to be transferred) are not specified by
way of condition attached to the planning permission but rather are left over for
'agreement'. This has the effect that final decisions as to the logistics are
postponed; planning permission is, in effect, granted in principle, in the first
instance, subject to a condition requiring that the developer enter into an
agreement.

In its most basic form, a land transfer agreement will simply identify the land to be transferred. In the event of a dispute in relation to this basic form of agreement, the planning authority; the applicant for planning permission; or any other person with an interest in the land, may refer the matter to An Bord Pleanála for determination. (It appears that this cannot be done until eight weeks have expired from the date of the *grant* of the planning permission).

The position in relation to the transfer of built houses and/or serviced sites is more complicated. It would appear that the developer must *elect* to enter into a land transfer agreement in this form; the default is the transfer of undeveloped land. It is not clear from the legislation as to whether the planning authority is obliged to accept a land transfer in this form in circumstances where the applicant offers it, or whether the planning authority can still insist on the transfer of undeveloped land. (The proposals of the applicant are a mandatory consideration). In the event of a dispute in relation to this type of agreement, the matter is to be referred to a statutory property arbitrator (and not to An Bord Pleanála). (It appears that this cannot be done until eight weeks have expired from the date of the *grant* of the planning permission). In particular, the number and price of houses *or* serviced sites to be transferred are to be fixed by the arbitrator. The fact that the arbitrator is to determine the number of built houses or serviced sites is significant in that it indicates that he has a function in relation to the planning merits of the land transfer agreement, and not just in the determination of the quantum of compensation payable.

Compensation The calculation of compensation differs depending on whether the land was purchased before or after August 25, 1999 (that is, before or after the publication of the Bill). (Further special rules apply in the case of land acquired by gift or inheritance). In brief, in the case of land purchased before August 25, 1999, compensation is payable in the sum of the price paid for the land (together with interest).

In the case of land purchased after August 25, 1999, the compensation payable is the value of the land calculated by reference to its *existing use* on the date of the transfer of ownership, on the basis that on that date it would have been, and would thereafter have continued to be, unlawful to carry out any development in relation to that land other than exempted development.

In circumstances where the land transfer agreement provides for the transfer of built houses or serviced sites, an additional sum must also be paid in respect of the building and/or attributable development costs (to be fixed by the property arbitrator in default of agreement).

STRATEGIC DEVELOPMENT ZONES

Introduction Part IX of the Planning and Development Act, 2000 provides for the designation of strategic development zones. The significance of such a designation is that an expedited procedure for obtaining planning permission applies. Provided that the proposed development would be consistent with the planning scheme in force for the land in question, the planning authority shall grant planning permission. There is no appeal to An Bord Pleanála against a decision on an application for planning permission in respect of development in a strategic development zone.

Procedure The designation is carried out by the government where, in its opinion, specified development is of economic or social importance to the State. The designation order shall, *inter alia*, specify the type or types of development that may be established in the strategic development zone. The relevant development agency then prepares and submits a draft planning scheme to the relevant planning authority. Following a public consultation procedure, the planning authority may make, subject to variations and modifications, the draft planning scheme, or decide not to make the draft planning scheme. The decision of the planning authority may be appealed to An Bord Pleanála. A planning scheme will indicate the manner in which it is intended that the site is to be developed, and, *inter alia*, will indicate the type or types of development which may be permitted; the extent of any such proposed development; and proposals in relation to the overall design of the proposed development, including maximum heights, the external finishes of structures and the general appearance and design.

GUIDELINES AND DIRECTIVES

Guidelines Under Part IV of the Planning and Development Act 2000, the Minister for the Environment and Local Government can issue guidelines to planning authorities regarding any of their functions under the Act, and the planning authorities are required to have regard to those guidelines in the performance of their functions.

Policy Directives Under Part IV of the Planning and Development Act 2000, the Minister for the Environment and Local Government may also issue policy directives to planning authorities regarding any of their functions under the Act, and the planning authorities are required to have regard to any such directives in the performance of their functions.

DEVELOPMENT PLANS

Introduction Although not strictly within the remit of this year's review (2000), it is proposed to consider very briefly some of the changes in respect of the statutory development plan introduced under the Planning and Development Act 2000.

Contents and procedure   The prescribed contents of a development plan are considerably changed under the new Act. The inclusion of zoning objectives is mandatory; the distinction between rural and urban areas is removed. Furthermore, the development plan shall include objectives, *inter alia*, for the provision or facilitation of the provision of infrastructure (including transport, energy and communication facilities, water supplies and waste recovery and disposal facilities); the conservation and protection of the environment; the integration of the planning and sustainable development of the area with the social, community and cultural requirements of the area and its population; and the protection of structures, or parts of structures, which are of special architectural, historical, archaeological, artistic, cultural, scientific, social or technical interest. The breadth of the matters which are to be included in the development plan, and, in particular, the fact that many of same are directed towards prohibiting or limiting development, probably gives *quietus* to the suggestion in the decision in *Glencar Explorations plc v. Mayo County Council* [1993] 2 I.R. 237 that development objectives must be positive in character.

The procedure for making the development plan is also modified. The obligation to make a plan is changed from five to six years. The public consultation process is brought a step back: the planning authority must now invite submissions or observations regarding the review of the existing plan and the preparation of a new plan. In other words, public consultation is now to take place in advance of the draft plan having been finalised. The time limits for the procedure are also tightened. For example, the minimum period for the display of the draft development plan is reduced from three months to ten weeks. There is also no longer any continuous requirement to republish in case of a material alteration cf. *Raggett v. Athy Urban District Council* [2000] 1 I.R. 469; [2000] 1 I.L.R.M. 375 (Annual Review 1999, 425).

Local area plans   The concept of local area plans is put on a statutory footing for the first time under the Planning and Development Act 2000. The legality of non-statutory '*action area plans*' had been open to question under the previous legislation. The Local Government (Planning and Development) Act 1963 imposed a duty on a planning authority to make a development plan, and provided for a comprehensive scheme of public participation: the hiving off of certain matters to action area plans appeared to side step this scheme. (See, also, *Great Portland Estates v. Westminster City Council* [1985] A.C. 661).

A local area plan is required to be consistent with the objectives of the development plan. Although the provisions in respect of compensation under the new Act (Part XII) have not yet been commenced, it is worth noting the significance of the provisions of a local plan in this connection. Compensation is excluded, *inter alia*, where one of the reasons for the refusal of planning permission is that the development would be premature pending the adoption of a local area plan. It is also to be noted that it appears that material contravention of any of the objectives of a local area plan (not just of zoning objectives) is a non-compensatable reason for refusal.

JUDICIAL REVIEW PROCEDURE

Types of decision protected   The special judicial review procedure under section 82(3A) and (3B) of the Local Government (Planning and Development) Act 1963 (as amended by the Local Government (Planning and Development) Act 1992) does not apply to all decisions of a planning authority but only those on an application for planning permission. This principle was re-iterated in the High Court decision in *O'Connor v. Dublin Corporation (No. 1)* [2000] 3 I.R. 420; [2001] 1 I.L.R.M. 58. Kelly J. held that a challenge to a decision of a planning authority in respect of certain matters which had been left over by condition for agreement between the planning authority and the developer, was not subject to the provisions of section 82(3A) & (3B) and was properly brought by way of conventional judicial review. Although not cited, this judgment is consistent with that of the Supreme Court in *State (Fingal Industrial Estates Ltd.) v. Dublin County Council,* Supreme Court, February 17, 1983. The judgment in *O'Connor* highlights an anomaly which can arise on the wording of section 82(3A). Kelly J. stated that it would be strange indeed if the special judicial review procedure were to apply to the decision at first instance made by the planning authority but not to the determination of An Bord Pleanála on appeal. The respective decisions of a planning authority and An Bord Pleanála on the same matter, however, do fall to be treated differently in some circumstances. The special judicial review procedure applies to the decision of a planning authority on an application for planning permission only, but applies to any decision of An Bord Pleanála on any appeal or reference. Thus, for example, in the case of the revocation of planning permission, the decision of the planning authority can be challenged by conventional judicial review, whereas the decision of An Bord Pleanála must be challenged under section 82(3A) & (3B).

Substantial grounds of challenge   The requirement that an applicant for leave to apply for judicial review establish *'substantial grounds'* for contending that the relevant decision is invalid or ought to be quashed has been considered in a number of decisions in 2000. It appears that there are now two lines of authority emerging as to the interpretation of *'substantial grounds'*. The first line (which stems from the decision of the Supreme Court in *Scott v. An Bord Pleanála* [1995] 1 I.L.R.M. 424) seeks to uphold the orthodoxy that there is a qualitative distinction between the function of the court at the application for leave, and its function on the substantive application for judicial review. This is perhaps best illustrated by the oft cited *dicta* of Carroll J. in *McNamara v. An Bord Pleanála* [1995] 2 I.L.R.M. 125 at 130. These *dicta* were expressly approved of by the Supreme Court in *In re Section 5 and Section 10 of the Illegal Immigrants (Trafficking) Bill, 1999* [2000] 2 I.R 360. Reference is also made to the decision in *Ashbourne Holdings Ltd. v. An Bord Pleanála* High Court, March 23, 2000. McCracken J. stated that the applicant does not have to prove his case even on a balance of probability at the preliminary stage, nor should the High Court determine any question of fact, or make any final determination on questions of law. Once substantial grounds of challenge have been established, legal argument becomes a matter for the substantive hearing, and not for the preliminary hearing.

The second line of authority appears to involve an attempt to assimilate the test at the leave stage to that applicable at the substantive hearing. This is illustrated by the decision in *Kenny v. An Bord Pleanála (No. 1)*, High Court, December 15, 2000 (see also *Kenny v. An Bord Pleanála (No. 2)*, High Court, March 2, 2001). McKechnie J. stated that some difference in approach between an application for leave on notice, and one made *ex parte*, may be justified, and that whereas the High Court, on an application for leave, should not attempt to resolve conflicts of fact or express any concluded view on complex questions of law or indeed anticipate the long term result, nonetheless within the existing limitations an evaluation of the factual matrix should be made. McKechnie J. also stated that, at the leave stage, the High Court should, where with certainty it could, form some view of the appropriate statutory provisions and the relevant and material case law. With respect, such an approach while involving a formalistic acknowledgement of the narrow function of the High Court on the leave application brings the High Court at the leave stage tantalisingly close to a final determination. The approach underlying this second line of authority is more evident in the context of the similarly worded provisions of the Illegal Immigrants (Trafficking) Act, 2000. Specifically, Smyth J. in the decision of *P. v. Minister for Justice Equality and Law Reform*, High Court, January 2, 2001; Supreme Court, July 30, 2001 indicated that it is appropriate on the leave stage to consider the prospects of success, and to grant leave only if satisfied that the applicant's case is not merely arguable but is strong; that is to say, is likely to succeed.

It is submitted that whereas the first line of authority is probably more loyal to the literal wording of section 82(3A) and (3B) which does envisage a two stage hearing, the second line of authority represents an attempt to identify the rationale underlying the provisions, and involves a recognition that, under the planning legislation, the application for leave to apply approximates more closely to the full hearing than to the application for leave in conventional judicial review. It is submitted that this narrowing of the gap between the leave stage and the substantive hearing serves to undermine any justification for a separate leave stage. There is little saving in time or cost if the High Court, at the leave stage, is required to consider the application in great depth. Rather than assimilate the leave stage to that of the substantive hearing, it might be better to abolish the requirement for leave entirely. Instead, the time limits prescribed in the Rules of the Superior Courts 1986 as to the exchange of pleadings could be strictly enforced so as to ensure an early and definitive hearing of the matter.

Nature and extent of leave   The provisions of section 82(3A) & (3B) of the

Local Government (Planning and Development) Act 1963 (as amended) are silent as to the effect of the grant of leave. On a strict interpretation, it could be argued that, as in the case of an application for leave to appeal to the Supreme Court (*Scott v. An Bord Pleanála* [1995] 1 I.L.R.M. 424), the grant of leave should be global i.e. it should not necessarily be confined to particular grounds of challenge. If the objective is simply to exclude insubstantial cases then once any ground is shown to be substantial, the statutory threshold has been crossed and leave should be granted on all grounds. In practice, the High Court tends to tailor the grounds of challenge, and to refuse leave in respect of certain grounds. This approach appears to be informed by pragmatism: the excising of grounds on the grant of leave can shorten the substantive hearing, and may provide some justification for there being a separate leave stage. On occasion, the approach can cause difficulty, however. The grounds of challenge may not always be divisible, but may, in fact, interlock, and it may be artificial to seek to separate them out at the leave stage. For example, the concept of administrative unreasonableness is closely allied to the duty to give reasons: see the facts of *Village Residents Association Ltd. v. An Bord Pleanála (No. 3),* High Court, May 5, 2000.

Abuse of process   The High Court has previously identified one of the objectives of the introduction of procedural restrictions on challenges to the validity of decisions in respect of applications for planning permission, as being to ensure that any impugned planning permission becomes absolute at the earliest possible moment. Specifically, McCracken J. in *Irish Cement Ltd. v. An Bord Pleanála,* High Court, February 24, 1998 (Annual Review 1998, 499) stated that the whole system would be open to abuse by allowing lengthy court proceedings to take place while the term of the planning permission was expiring. The more recent decision of *Sean Quinn Ltd. v. An Bord Pleanála* [2001] 2 I.L.R.M. 94 considers the potential for abuse of process in greater detail (albeit in the context of proceedings by way of plenary summons, rather than by way of judicial review). An application was brought to strike out plenary proceedings (seeking declaratory relief) on the grounds that the proceedings comprised an abuse of the process, and were vexatious in nature. Quirke J. held that the jurisdiction to strike out was to be exercised only with great caution, and that the court must be satisfied by way of evidence that the plaintiff in commencing the proceedings (i) had an ulterior motive; (ii) sought a collateral advantage for itself; and (iii) had instituted the proceedings for a purpose which the law does not recognise as a legitimate use of the remedy which had been sought. On the facts, Quirke J. found that the proceedings had been commenced by the plaintiff in a cynical, calculated and unscrupulous fashion for the sole purpose of seeking a commercial advantage over a competitor. The purpose for which the proceedings had been instituted was not to redress a wrong or grievance; to right an injustice; to ensure compliance with the provisions of national or international legislation; to ensure the proper and lawful planning and development of any particular area; or for any other commendable, environmental or civic spirited reason. Accordingly, the plaintiff's claim was dismissed.

Although the decision may well have been justified on its own particular facts, the application of a test requiring the consideration of the motives of an applicant/plaintiff can present conceptual difficulties in the context of environmental litigation. Proceedings challenging a decision to grant planning permission can very often be opportunistic in the following sense: a litigant opposed in principle to the development the subject matter of the proceedings will seize on a procedural defect in an attempt to prise apart the decision, and to prevent the development going ahead. In such cases, although the legal argument will revolve around the procedural point, the litigant may well be more concerned with blocking the proposed development than with the niceties of whether or not, for example, the site notice was defective, or the decision maker had regard to an irrelevant consideration. This is a function of the fact that whereas the court is concerned only with the legality of the decision and not its merits, it is unlikely that proceedings will be brought other than by a person vexed by the merits of the decision. The extent to which it is legitimate for an applicant to rely on substantial grounds of legal challenge for the ulterior purpose of preventing development going ahead, remains to be tested. Relief has, on occasion, been refused as a matter of *discretion* where the applicant had sought to prevent a business competitor opening up near by; *State (Toft) v. Galway Corporation* [1981] I.L.R.M. 439.

The necessity for the bringing on of an interlocutory application to strike out is probably reduced in the case of a challenge to a decision under the planning legislation. The various procedural requirements applicable (in particular, the requirement that an applicant demonstrate substantial grounds of challenge, and a sufficient interest in the matter), together with the fact that judicial review is a discretionary remedy, may well provide sufficient safeguards.

Locus standi   The issue of *locus standi* was considered in the High Court decision in *Seery v. An Bord Pleanála,* June 2, 2000. Order 84, rule 20(4) of the Rules of the Superior Courts 1986 provides that an applicant should have a sufficient interest in the matter to which the judicial review application relates. The High Court in *Seery v. An Bord Pleanála* adopted a traditional approach to the question of standing. The applicants were the owners of lands adjacent to the proposed development. It was sought to challenge the decision to grant planning permission on the ground, *inter alia*, that a site layout plan misstated the separation distance between the applicants' lands and those houses on the proposed development closest to those lands. The notice party developers sought to challenge the applicants' interest in the proceedings on the basis that the applicants had not claimed to have been personally misled by any error in the site layout plan. Finnegan J. held that the applicants were affected by the planning permission granted: their dwelling immediately adjoined the proposed development, and at all times the applicants had expressed a concern about the proximity of the houses on the proposed development to their own dwelling house. Finnegan J. accordingly found the applicants to have standing.

The decision in *Seery v. An Bord Pleanála* appears to treat the right to bring an application (*locus standi*) as being distinct from the arguments which might be made on the application (*jus tertii*). It seems to be implicit in the decision that it was not necessary for the applicants to demonstrate that the alleged non-compliance affected them directly, it was sufficient that the applicants were damnified by the fact of planning permission having been granted. It is submitted that such a generous approach to *locus standi* results in the discretionary nature of the judicial review remedies, and the statutory criterion of '*substantial grounds*', assuming greater significance. Even if not relevant to the issue of *locus standi*, the fact that an applicant was not personally prejudiced by the alleged defect may nevertheless be relevant to the exercise of the High Court's discretion to withhold relief (*Cunningham v. An Bord Pleanála*, High Court, May 3, 1990), or to the statutory requirement of '*substantial grounds*' (*Blessington & District Community Council Ltd. v. Wicklow County Council* [1997] 1 I.R. 273).

Service: mandatory parties   Section 82 (3B) of the Local Government (Planning and Development) Act 1963 (as amended by the Local Government (Planning and Development) Act 1992) provides that an application for leave to apply for judicial review is to be on notice to certain prescribed parties. In the case of a challenge to a decision of the planning authority on an application for planning permission, the planning authority and the applicant for planning permission should be on notice. In the case of a challenge to a decision of An Bord Pleanála on any appeal or reference, An Bord Pleanála, the planning authority, and the other parties to the appeal or reference should be on notice. The extent, if any, to which the High Court can dispense with the requirement for service of all the prescribed parties was considered in the decision of *Murray v. An Bord Pleanála* [2000] 1 I.R 58. In that case, judicial review proceedings challenging a decision of An Bord Pleanála had not been served on the planning authority. Quirke J. ruled that the High Court had no discretion to waive or relax in any respect the statutory requirement of service which he found to be mandatory. This appears to be the case even where the party not served is prepared to waive its entitlement to service. The decision in *Murray v. An Bord Pleanála* must be contrasted with that in *McCarthy v. An Bord Pleanála* [2000] 1 I.R. 42 (Annual Review 1998, 502). In that latter case, Geoghegan J. appears to have accepted a submission by counsel that in enacting the Local Government (Planning and Development) Act 1992, the legislature did not introduce some new kind of judicial review application different from conventional judicial review but was merely altering the procedure and requirements for obtaining leave, and that the question as to who were necessary notice parties fell to be determined on an *ad hoc* basis, as in the case of conventional judicial review. It may be that the two decisions can be reconciled on the basis that the facts of *McCarthy* are distinguishable from those in *Murray* in that in the former case, unusually, there were a number of co-appellants before An Bord Pleanála and reasons of pragmatism would suggest that a multiplicity of parties might delay judicial review proceedings and defeat the purposes of the Local Government (Planning and Development) Act 1992.

Notice party: costs   The fact that section 82(3A) & (3B) of the Local Government (Planning and Development) Act 1963 (as amended by the Local Government (Planning and Development) Act 1992) requires that an application for judicial review is to be on notice to certain prescribed parties, may present difficulties in terms of any award of costs. Although the general principle is that costs follow the event, a judge may be reluctant to award two sets of costs (those of the respondent planning body, and of the notice party developer) against an unsuccessful applicant. Indeed, the House of Lords has indicated that the developer will not normally be entitled to his costs unless he can show that there was likely to be a separate issue in respect of which he was entitled to be heard, or unless he has an interest which requires separate representation: the mere fact that he is the developer will not of itself justify a second set of costs in every case; *Bolton Metropolitan District Council v. Secretary of State for the Environment* [1995] 3 P.L.R. 37.

The fact that the developer is a mandatory party under section 82(3A) & (3B) might suggest that a different approach should apply in this jurisdiction. Certainly, the Supreme Court have indicated, in the context of conventional judicial review, that a notice party is entitled to security for costs. (See also *Village Residents Association Ltd. (No. 2) v. An Bord Pleanála* [2000] 4 I.R. 321; [2001] 2 I.L.R.M. 22). In an *ex tempore* judgment in *Spin Communications v. Independent Radio and Television Commission,* Supreme Court, April 14, 2000, Keane C.J. held that a notice party with a vital interest in the outcome of proceedings was entitled to security for costs. The judgment is interesting in that the entitlement to security for costs (and possibly to an award of costs) appears to derive from the mere fact that the notice party has an interest in the proceedings, and is not expressly predicated on the notice party being in a position to advance arguments on points which might not otherwise be addressed.

Even if it were the case that only one set of costs should be awarded, it does not necessarily follow that it would be the respondent decision maker i.e. either the planning authority or An Bord Pleanála, who should receive costs. If the test is which person is the proper party to advance the argument, it might well be that in respect of certain arguments, the notice party developer is the *legitimus contradictor*. For example, a number of cases have been disposed of on the basis of procedural points in relation to time limits, and the service of documents. As the Supreme Court have indicated in *K.S.K. Enterprises Ltd. v. An Bord Pleanála* [1994] 2 I.R. 128 that time limits are for the benefit of the developer, perhaps such points are more properly made by the notice party developer.

Pre-emptive costs order   The High Court confirmed that it has jurisdiction, in appropriate cases, to deal with costs at an interlocutory stage in a manner which ensures that a particular party will not be faced with an order for costs against him at the conclusion of the proceedings. Specifically, in *Village Residents Association Ltd. v. An Bord Pleanála (No. 2)* [2000] 4 I.R. 321; [2001] 2 I.L.R.M. 22, Laffoy J. interpreted Order 99, rule 5 of the Rules of the Superior Courts 1986 (which provides that costs may be dealt with by the court at any stage of the proceedings or after the conclusion of the proceedings and that an order for the payment of costs may require the costs to be paid forthwith, notwithstanding that the proceedings have not been concluded), as allowing, in principle, for the making of a pre-emptive or protective costs order. On the particular facts of the case, however, Laffoy J. refused to make such an order, for the following reasons. First, the challenge was not brought by a public interest litigant in the strict sense, in that the members of the applicant company had a private interest in the outcome of the proceedings. Secondly, any issue of public importance was not sufficiently immediate to justify a pre-emptive costs order. Thirdly, the court did not have sufficient appreciation of the merits of the application at the interlocutory stage to conclude that it would be in the public interest to make a pre-emptive costs order. The fact that the applicant had satisfied the statutory criterion of '*substantial grounds*' at the leave stage was not, on its own, a circumstance from which one could conclude that it was in the public interest to insulate the applicant company from a future award of costs without awaiting the outcome of the challenge. Fourthly, the applicant had sought a pre-emptive costs order against a non-public body (the notice party developer).

Security for costs   The principles governing an application for security for costs against a limited liability company in judicial review proceedings under the planning legislation were considered in *Village Residents Association Ltd. v. An Bord Pleanála (No. 2)* [2000] 4 I.R. 321; [2001] 2 I.L.R.M. 22. The decision is authority for a number of points of general application, as follows. First, the fact that an applicant company has established '*substantial grounds*' for challenge on the application for leave to apply for judicial review does not constitute a special circumstance which could justify not making an order to provide security. Every applicant is required to overcome the statutory threshold, and, in any event, it was well settled that the strength or otherwise of a party's case is generally not an appropriate consideration on an application for security for costs, unless the case of the plaintiff or applicant is unanswerable in which circumstances security should be refused. Secondly, in terms of the timing of an application for security for costs, there does not appear to be any requirement that an application for security be made in advance of the application for leave to apply for judicial review. Delay is only relevant to an application for security for costs where the applicant has altered its position to its detriment by reason of the application for security not having been made earlier. Thirdly, an allegation that the true purpose of the moving party in seeking security was to stifle the applicant company's legitimate claim, would not generally, on its own, justify refusing security. (It is, of course, the case that any stifling effect does not follow from the making of the order for security for costs *per se*, but from the failure of the members of the applicant company to demonstrate their commitment by providing the necessary funds to support the company's application).

The decision also confirms (following the decision in *Lancefort Ltd. v. An Bord Pleanála* [1998] 2 I.R. 511) the principle that, as in the case of an appeal to the Supreme Court, it is appropriate on an application for security for costs in the context of judicial review proceedings to consider whether the grounds on which the applicant company has been granted leave give rise to a question of law of public importance.

A further aspect of this decision *viz.* the question whether the provision of security for costs might be a *quid pro quo* for allowing *locus standi* to limited liability companies, had been considered previously (Annual Review 1999, 418).

Undertaking as to damages   Order 84, rule 20(6) of the Rules of the Superior Courts 1986 provides that if the High Court grants leave to apply for judicial review, it may impose such terms as to costs as it thinks fit, and may require an undertaking as to damages. These provisions were considered in detail, in the context of conventional judicial review proceedings, in *Broadnet Ireland Ltd. v. Office of the Director of Telecommunications Regulation* [2000] 3 I.R. 281; [2000] 2 I.L.R.M. 241. Laffoy J. ruled that in considering whether or not to exercise its discretion to require an undertaking as to damages as a condition to the grant, or the continuance, of leave to apply for judicial review, the essential test was whether such requirement was necessary to mitigate injustice to parties directly affected by the existence of the pending judicial review application. Laffoy J. went on to state that, in her view, if, in substance, the existence of the application for judicial review has an effect similar to that of an interlocutory injunction in private litigation – that activity which would otherwise be engaged in is put 'on hold' pending final determination of the controversy, with resulting loss and damage – it would be appropriate for the High Court to require an applicant to give an undertaking to make good that loss and damage if it were ultimately to be found that the applicant's case was unsustainable, provided that there was no countervailing factor arising from the public nature of the jurisdiction which the High Court exercises under Order 84.

Of particular significance to challenges under the planning legislation, is the fact that Laffoy J. indicated that it was not necessary that interlocutory injunctive relief be sought (whether in the form of a stay under Order 84, rule 20(7)(a) or otherwise) in order for the provisions of Order 84, rule 20(6) to be triggered: the chilling effect of the existence of the judicial review proceedings *per se* might be sufficient.

These principles have been applied in the context of judicial review proceedings under the planning legislation in *Seery v. An Bord Pleanála (No. 2)* [2001] 2 I.L.R.M. 151. Finnegan J. held that the grant of leave to challenge the validity of a grant of planning permission had like effect upon the notice party developers as the grant of an interlocutory injunction: it would have been commercial folly to embark upon the development envisaged by the planning permission sought to be impugned while the judicial review proceedings were pending. Turning then to a consideration of whether there were any countervailing factors arising from the public nature of the jurisdiction which the High Court exercises under Order 84, Finnegan J. held that the whole tenor of the applicants' objection to the proposed development related to a small portion of the proposed development which would overlook the applicants' own dwelling house. In the circumstances, it did not seem that the application had the necessary public nature to constitute a countervailing factor.

In so ruling, Finnegan J. held that there was no distinction in principle between conventional judicial review, and the special procedure applicable under section 82(3A) & (3B) of the Local Government (Planning and Development) Act, 1963 (as amended). It is respectfully submitted that this finding is correct. The special procedure under section 82(3A) & (3B) is not a stand alone procedure, but was expressly grafted onto the conventional judicial review procedure under Order 84. It is also the case that the intention of the legislature has been identified by the Supreme Court as entailing, *inter alia*, an objective to confine the opportunity of persons to impugn by way of judicial review decisions made by planning authorities (*K.S.K. Enterprises Ltd. v. An Bord Pleanála* [1994] 2 I.R. 128). It would be contrary to this policy to attempt to compensate for the introduction of a more restricted procedure under section 82(3A) & (3B), by removing elements of the existing procedure under Order 84.

Stay on proceedings   Under Order 84, rule 20(7)(a) of the Rules of the Superior Courts 1986, the High Court may direct that the grant of leave to apply for judicial review shall operate as a stay on the proceedings in respect of which the judicial review application relates. The application of Order 84, rule 20(7)(a) to judicial review proceedings challenging a grant of planning permission may present difficulties. The term '*proceedings*' would not appear to be apt to embrace circumstances where a planning authority or An Bord Pleanála has determined a planning application or appeal; once its decision is made, the planning authority or An Bord Pleanála is arguably *functus officio*, and there are no '*proceedings*' extant before it. The reality is, of course, that it is the developer whom it is sought to restrain by securing a stay.

The application of Order 84, rule 20(7)(a) was considered tangentially in two decisions in the year 2000. In the first, *Village Residents Association Ltd.*

v. An Bord Pleanála (No. 2) [2000] 4 I.R. 321; [2001] 2 I.L.R.M. 22, Laffoy J. indicated that it might be open to an applicant in judicial review proceedings to seek a stay on the decision, but that it would first be necessary to join the developer in the proceedings. (The facts of the case were unusual in that the mandatory notice party, the applicant for planning permission, was only the lessee of the premises, and at least some of the development was to be carried on by the freeholder who was not yet a party to the proceedings). In the second decision, *Broadnet Ireland Ltd. v. Office of the Director of Telecommunications Regulation* [2000] 3 I.R. 281; [2000] 2 I.L.R.M. 241, Laffoy J., in an *obiter dicta*, appeared to approve the decision of the Court of Appeal in *R. v. Pollution Inspectorate ex parte Greenpeace Ltd.* [1994] 1 W.L.R. 570. The Court of Appeal decision suggested, *inter alia*, that the courts should look to the substance rather than to the form, and if the real purpose of an application for a stay on a decision was to prevent a third party from carrying out an activity, then the court should apply the same principles to the application as would have been applicable had the application been for an interlocutory injunction.

The upshot of the two decisions would appear to be that, in circumstances where a third party is affected, there is little difference in approach as between the principles to be applied to an application for a stay under Order 84, rule 20(7)(a), and those governing an application for an interlocutory injunction. It would also seem to follow, by analogy, from the substance of the ruling in *Broadnet Ireland Ltd. v. Office of the Director of Telecommunications Regulation* [2000] 3 I.R. 281; [2000] 2 I.L.R.M. 241 in relation to Order 84, rule 20(6) that an undertaking as to damages will be required in order to secure a stay or interlocutory injunction. If this is correct, then it may be necessary to distinguish the earlier *ex tempore* judgment in *Lancefort Ltd. v. An Bord Pleanála* February 13, 1998 (Annual Review 1998, 505), and to confine it to its own special facts. In particular, the irreversible nature of the development works concerned, involving as they did the possible destruction of a listed building, and the fact that the developer had not indicated an intention to commence development to the trial judge, might well be pointed to as distinctions.

Exhaustion of rights   The existence of a statutory right of appeal to An Bord Pleanála presents a person seeking to challenge a decision of a planning authority with a choice of remedies: to appeal to An Bord Pleanála, or to seek judicial review in the High Court. The High Court has a discretion, however, to refuse relief in circumstances where an appeal to An Bord Pleanála would have been the more appropriate remedy. Generally, An Bord Pleanála does not have jurisdiction to determine other than simple questions of law, nor to provide redress for breaches of natural and constitutional justice (*State (Abenglen Properties Ltd.) v. Dublin Corporation* [1984] I.R. 381). The decision in *Electricity Supply Board v. Cork County Council,* High Court June 28, 2000 provides the most recent example of the application of the exhaustion of rights principle. The case concerned a challenge to a decision to revoke a planning permission. A statutory right of appeal lies against the decision of the planning authority to An Bord Pleanála. The applicant elected to challenge the decision of the planning authority by way of judicial review, and a point was raised as to whether relief should be refused as a matter of discretion. Finnegan J. held that as the impugned decision had been made in breach of the rules of natural and constitutional justice, judicial review was appropriate. This aspect of the decision is unexceptionable, and is consistent with other recent authorities such as, for example, *Eircell Ltd. v. Leitrim County Council* [2000] 1 I.R. 479; [2000] 2 I.L.R.M. 81 (Annual Review 1999, 421). There is, however, another aspect of the judgment which merits further consideration. Finnegan J. had found that as works pursuant to the planning permission had previously commenced, the power to revoke the planning permission could not have been properly exercised. The interpretation of the provision of the legislation which restricts the circumstances in which planning permission can be revoked is properly a matter of law for the High Court, and, accordingly, would justify an application for judicial review. Somewhat surprisingly, then, Finnegan J. appeared to suggest that this error would not of itself have entitled the applicant to judicial review of the respondent planning authority's decision.

JUDICIAL REVIEW: SUBSTANTIVE LAW

Standard of review The distinction between questions of law, and questions of fact and degree, is of particular importance in the context of judicial review of planning decisions. If a challenge to a planning decision is based on an allegation that the decision is unreasonable or irrational, the applicant must overcome the very stiff threshold prescribed under *O'Keeffe v. An Bord Pleanála* [1993] 1 I.R. 39. (See, for example, *de Faoite v. An Bord Pleanála,* High Court, May 2, 2000). If, however, a challenge is based on an allegation that the planning authority or An Bord Pleanála have exceeded some other limitation on jurisdiction, one expressly imposed by statute, then the matter is a question of law for the courts. The principles in *O'Keeffe* are only applicable to a challenge to the exercise of a discretion conferred by statute (such as the decision to grant or refuse planning permission). If, conversely, the legislation imposes a requirement or restriction on a planning authority or An Bord Pleanála, then the question of whether or not there has been compliance with that requirement, or if that restriction has been breached, is a matter for the courts. The fact that the planning authority or An Bord Pleanála may be of the view that there has been such compliance or that there was no breach is irrelevant. In such circumstances, the courts are neither bound by the decision of the planning body nor inhibited by the *O'Keeffe* principles. (See generally Simons *'The unreasonable planning authority: A review of the application of O'Keeffe v. An Bord Pleanála'* Parts I and II (2000) 7 I.P.E.L.J. 164; (2001) 8 I.P.E.L.J. 26).

The principles above are well explained in the decision in *O'Connor v. Dublin Corporation (No. 2),* High Court, October 3, 2000. In that case, the applicant sought to challenge a 'decision' of the planning authority in respect of certain matters which had been left over, by condition attached to planning permission, for agreement between the developer and the planning authority. The applicant argued that what was agreed by the planning authority materially altered the development in respect of which An Bord Pleanála had granted planning permission, and was not a faithful implementation of the conditions attached to that planning permission. The respondent planning authority argued that any decision it had taken to agree the matters under the conditions was one within jurisdiction, and hence was only open to review on the basis of irrationality. O'Neill J. rejected this submission. In his view, the function of the planning authority in agreeing the matters left over for agreement under the planning permission was wholly and radically different from the jurisdiction exercised by a planning authority in making its decision to refuse or grant planning permission. The latter exercise was clearly of a judicial nature and involves an extensive discretion. Conversely, the former function was a limited one and of a ministerial nature. The planning authority was confined in this exercise solely to the ascertainment of the true and correct meaning of the conditions and, consequent on that, confined in its agreement to proposals which faithfully adhered to and implemented those conditions. Such an approach, O'Neill J. held, excluded the reasonableness test laid down in *O'Keeffe v. An Bord Pleanála* [1993] 1 I.R. 39.

It is respectfully submitted that the course adopted by O'Neill J. was correct, and that the decision of the planning authority was properly subject to full blooded judicial review, not the attenuated form of review applicable under the *O'Keeffe* principles. There is a temptation on the part of planning authorities to invoke the protection of the *O'Keeffe* principles in respect of all their acts. The careful analysis in *O'Connor v. Dublin Corporation (No. 2)* indicates, however, that this is not appropriate in all cases, and it is hoped that this distinction between those decisions which attract the lower standard of review (questions of fact and degree) and those which do not (questions of law), will provide guidance in future cases.

An example of a decision falling on the other side is that of the High Court in *de Freitas Waddington v. An Bord Pleanála,* High Court December 21, 2000. In that case, Butler J. held that the *O'Keeffe* principles governed a challenge based on an allegation that there had not been compliance with procedural requirements under the EC (Natural Habitats) Regulations 1997.

A less extreme example is to be found in the decision in *Kenny v. An Bord Pleanála (No. 1),* High Court, December 15, 2000. McKechnie J. held that once the statutory requirements had been satisfied, the High Court should not concern itself with the qualitative nature of an environmental impact statement, nor the debate on it before the oral hearing. Further, the fact that the planning authority and An Bord Pleanála were satisfied with the environmental impact statement, with the inspector and An Bord Pleanála also being happy with the evidence, both documentary and oral, produced at the oral hearing, in his view concluded the matter. With respect, although this decision may well be correct on its facts, it is submitted that the principle may overstate the matter somewhat. An Bord Pleanála has a statutory obligation to consider the adequacy of the environmental impact statement: the regulations do not, however, appear to confer a statutory *discretion* on An Bord Pleanála in this regard. Accordingly, it is open to argument that the adequacy of an environmental impact statement is open to review by the courts. The intention of the legislature must be the overriding consideration, and the fact that review of a particular type of decision might necessitate the High Court examining broad factual issues cannot *per se* indicate that the matter is only open to the attenuated form of review provided for under *O'Keeffe v. An Bord Pleanála* [1993] 1 I.R. 39.

An interesting variation on the question of the standard of review is to be found in the decision in *Costigan v. Laois County Council*, Supreme Court, April 7, 2000. The planning authority were considering exercising a discretionary power *viz.* the amendment of the statutory development plan, in a particular way. Legal advice was then taken on the point; this advice was to the effect that the proposed re-zoning would be unlawful. The planning authority decided not to proceed with the re-zoning, and that decision was subsequently challenged in judicial review proceedings. The applicant argued, *inter alia*, that the applicant, as a person interested, should have been consulted on the selection of the barrister to give the legal advice. It had also been contended in the notice of appeal that the planning authority had unlawfully delegated its decision making power to its legal advisers. Both these submissions were ultimately rejected by the Supreme Court. The facts of the case present a conundrum. The decision to amend the development plan, as the exercise of a statutory discretion, is subject only to limited review under the principles set out in *O'Keeffe v. An Bord Pleanála* [1993] 1 I.R. 39. But if the exercise of this discretion is tainted by an incorrect interpretation of the law, albeit one based on [erroneous] legal advice, should some remedy not be available? The Supreme Court held that the planning authority was entitled to seek legal advice but that that advice was in no sense binding: the planning authority was entitled to reject or accept the legal advice. With respect, this might be taken as suggesting that the interpretation of a matter of law could itself be cloaked within the statutory discretion, and that the planning authority was free to plumb for either interpretation provided it acted reasonably. It is submitted, however, that a planning authority can have no discretion as to questions of law, and if it were the case that the exercise of a discretionary power was influenced by a misunderstanding of the law, then that error of law would vitiate the decision. If necessary, this could be characterised as the taking into account of an irrelevant consideration. For example, to modify radically the facts of the instant case, if it were to be established that a planning authority held off making an otherwise desirable amendment to its development plan on the basis of an erroneous view of the law (whether based on legal advice or not), then it would seem that that decision should be open to challenge.

Presumption of validity   McKechnie J. stated in *Kenny v. An Bord Pleanála (No. 1)*, High Court, December 15, 2000 that it would be incorrect for the High Court to assume that a planning authority, which as a matter of law ought to be aware of its functions and responsibilities, including its limitations, when dealing with conditions leaving matters over for agreement, would exceed its role in the implementation of the conditions attached to a planning permission.

Duty to give reasons   There is a statutory duty (section 26(8) of the Local Government (Planning and Development) Act 1963) to give reasons in respect of a decision on an application for planning permission. The duty which applies to An Bord Pleanála is broader than that imposed on a planning authority: the latter is required to state reasons only in respect of a refusal or the imposition of conditions. An Bord Pleanála must specify the reasons for its decision, irrespective of whether the decision is to grant or to refuse planning permission. In practice, the statement of reasons for decisions tends to be formulaic. Notwithstanding the fact that the duty to give reasons is an express statutory requirement, the courts appear to have condoned a perfunctory approach to the giving of reasons. The test to be applied is what an intelligent person who had taken part in the appeal, or had been appraised of the broad issues which had arisen, would understand from the decision, the conditions and the reasons (*O'Keeffe v. An Bord Pleanála* [1993] 1 I.R. 39). It would also seem that the duty to state reasons may be discharged by incorporating, by reference, the inspector's report (*Ní Éili v. Environmental Protection Agency,* Supreme Court, July 30, 1999).

The duty to give reasons fell for consideration in two reserved decisions in 2000. The first, *Village Residents Association Ltd. v. An Bord Pleanála (No. 3),* High Court, May 5, 2000 involved an application of the traditional principles set out above. The applicant company, in brief, had complained that An Bord Pleanála had failed to address in its statement of reasons, the issue of whether or not the proposed development would represent a material contravention of the development plan. Laffoy J. held that while An Bord Pleanála did not *explicitly* state that the proposed development would not conflict with the zoning policy, it was to be *inferred* from the decision taken as a whole (and, in particular, a condition requiring omission of part of the development) that An Bord Pleanála was of the view that provided the drive-thru element of the proposed restaurant was omitted, the development would not be in conflict with the zoning objective.

The second decision, *Stack v. An Bord Pleanála,* High Court, July 11, 2000 is potentially more radical. (The decision arose on an application for leave to apply for judicial review, and accordingly it was not necessary for the court to determine the issue definitively). The applicant had sought leave to argue that a decision of An Bord Pleanála was *ultra vires* on the ground that the stated reasons were inadequate in that no guidance was provided as to future applications. Specifically, the decision was ambiguous in that it could be interpreted as meaning simply that the instant development proposal was defective, or, alternatively, that no development would be permitted on the site. Counsel for An Bord Pleanála responded by submitting that it was neither necessary or indeed desirable that An Bord Pleanála should by its decision set down markers for future applications because it might then be held to be estopped from refusing a future application. O'Neill J. granted leave to apply for judicial review on this ground, ruling that it was arguable that the legal authorities to date had dealt more with the form of the decision (prescribing merely that the decision, taken in its entirety, must be capable of demonstrating to an intelligent person who was aware of the issues raised, what the reasons for the decision were), rather than the essential content of the reasons for a decision. O'Neill J. went on to speculate that the principles laid down in *Save Britain's Heritage v. Number 1 Poultry Ltd.* [1991] 1 W.L.R. 153 might represent a development of the law in the area, which had not yet happened in this jurisdiction.

Finally, two procedural issues arose on the decision in *Village Residents Association Ltd. v. An Bord Pleanála (No. 3),* High Court May 5, 2000, as follows. First, Laffoy J. indicated that, in circumstances where the statutory obligation was to give reasons contemporaneous with the decision, she found it difficult to determine what weight should be given to reasons advanced by An Bord Pleanála at a time subsequent to the decision. (The decision of the Supreme Court in *O'Keeffe v. An Bord Pleanála* [1993] 1 I.R. 39 had suggested that there might be a requirement on an applicant to seek an elaboration or explanation of the reasons, in advance of taking judicial review proceedings). Secondly, Laffoy J. indicated that even were she wrong in concluding that the reasons stated were sufficient, relief would in any event be refused as a matter of discretion, as follows. The underlying rationale of the statutory duty to give reasons was to facilitate the invocation of the High Court's supervisory jurisdiction. As the applicant had been refused leave to challenge An Bord Pleanála's decision on the grounds of irrationality or procedural grounds, and as An Bord Pleanála had, in effect, 'passed muster' on the substantial and fundamental issues arising on the appeal, it would not be just or fair to quash its decision on the adequacy of reasons ground at the suit of a person who had not participated in the appeal process.

Legislative amendments: transitional provisions   Generally when legislation is either amended, or repealed, transitional provisions govern the interregnum before the coming into full effect of the new legislation. Two decisions in the year 2000 illustrate the difficulties that can arise in this regard. In the first decision, *O'Flynn Construction Company Ltd. v. An Bord Pleanála* [2000] 1 I.R. 497, the curious wording of the secondary legislation in question had the result that insofar as certain pending appeals were concerned neither the old nor the new statutory instrument applied. More specifically, the Local Government (Planning and Development) General Policy Directive (Shopping) 1998 provided that it was to come into force on a particular date (June 10, 1998), and, further, that this directive was to replace the previous 1982 directive. An Bord Pleanála apparently made a concession that the new directive would not apply to applications/appeals which where pending prior to its coming into operation. An Bord Pleanála instead sought to rely on the old directive. The High Court held that the replacement of the old directive involved its revocation, and that none of the transitional provisions of the Interpretation Act 1937 applied. (In particular, Geoghegan J. held that an application for planning permission was not to be regarded as a legal proceeding). Accordingly, the decision of An Bord Pleanála had to be quashed. The judgment was ameliorated somewhat by the fact that Geoghegan J. remitted the matter to An Bord Pleanála for re-determination, and indicated that An Bord Pleanála would be entitled to note both the existence and the terms of each of the statutory instruments and to take the view that the directive was only revoked in the context of a substituted directive with more extensive provisions and that those provisions which were common to both directives represented ministerial, and therefore, in a sense, public policy.

The second decision involved a more rigid approach. In *Kenny v. An Bord Pleanála (No. 1)*, High Court, December 15, 2000, an issue arose as to whether legislative provisions *viz.* the Local Government (Planning and Development) Act 1999, which had been commenced after the initial application for planning permission but before the subsequent appeal to An Bord Pleanála was determined, applied to the appeal. McKechnie J. held that to interpret the legislation so as to apply to a pending application would be to give it retrospective effect. McKechnie J. also held that when proceedings under a statutory regime had been commenced, those involved in or affected thereby, have a right to see that process through to a conclusion, under the law as it was at the date of its commencement. With respect, it may be that the breadth of this statement fails to acknowledge the fluid nature of the decision making process under the planning legislation, or the fact that an appeal to An Bord Pleanála is heard *de novo*. Given the delays involved in the planning process, it often happens, for example, that a development plan will have been amended or varied before a decision is given on an appeal. The better view must be that An Bord Pleanála may give effect to the current provisions of the development plan, rather than to be locked into those of the previous development plan. Reference is also made to the transitional provisions under the Planning and Development Act 2000: Section 265(4) appears to treat the date of an appeal as being as significant in terms of determining the applicable law, as the date of the initial application.

ENFORCEMENT

Section 27 injunction: procedural limitations   A number of decisions in 2000 have emphasised the procedural limitations on relief available under section 27 of the Local Government (Planning and Development) Act 1976 (as amended). In particular, the sentiments of the Supreme Court (expressed in *Mahon v. Butler*

[1997] 3 I.R. 369; [1998] 1 I.L.R.M. 284; and *Waterford County Council v. John A. Wood Ltd.* [1999] 1 I.R. 556; [1999] 1 I.L.R.M. 217 (Annual Review 1999, 519)) to the effect that summary proceedings under section 27 are not appropriate where novel questions of law and complex questions of fact are involved, have been applied. For example, in *Dublin Corporation v. Lowe*, High Court, February 4, 2000, Morris P. indicated, *obiter*, that proceedings under section 27 would have been inappropriate where there was an issue to be tried as to a pre-1964 use of lands: this issue could only be tried on full plenary hearing. (A curious aspect of the decision in *Dublin Corporation v. Lowe* is that Morris P. also appears to suggest, citing *Dublin County Council v. Kirby* [1985] I.L.R.M. 325, that it would be inappropriate to grant mandatory relief under Section 27(1). With respect, any such finding would run counter to the express wording of the section, and would seem to ignore the amendments introduced by the Local Government (Planning and Development) Act 1992). Reference is also made to the decision in *Fingal County Council v. R.F.S. Ltd.* High Court February 6, 2000. Morris P. found that there were a variety of issues of a factual nature which remained to be resolved as to a pre-1964 use, and that given that the onus of proof rested with the applicant to establish facts from which the High Court could raise a probable inference that the premises had been used at and immediately prior to the October 1, 1964 otherwise than in the manner in which they were now used, the applicant had failed to discharge the onus.

Section 27 injunction: discretion   The discretionary nature of the relief under section 27 of the Local Government (Planning and Development) Act 1976 (as amended) is illustrated by the decision in *Eircell Ltd. v. Bernstoff*, High Court, February 18, 2000. Proceedings had been brought under section 27 of the Local Government (Planning and Development) Act 1976 (as amended) alleging a technical breach of planning permission. Specifically, it was alleged that certain conditions which required various matters to be attended to *'prior to the commencement of development'*, had not been complied with in time. The applicants argued that the requirements in question were conditions precedent to the commencement of development, that they should be strictly interpreted, and that subsequent compliance did not render legal what was already an unlawful development. Barr J. refused the relief sought, stating that no court should make an order which is potentially futile, and if the development were to be declared unlawful, there was no doubt that application would be made to the planning authority for a retention planning permission and in the circumstances would be granted for the asking. (It might also be observed that the wording of section 27(2) suggests that the relief under that part of section 27 is intended to be prospective only: the court can make such order as necessary to ensure that the development is carried on in conformity with the planning permission).

The question of whether or not delay could constitute a discretionary factor was considered in *Dublin Corporation v. Lowe*, High Court, February 4, 2000.

Morris P. appeared to accept, in principle, a submission that notwithstanding a statutory outer time limit of five years, unreasonable delay on the part of the applicant planning authority could be interpreted as acquiescence. On the facts, however, Morris P. found that the applicant planning authority had acted entirely reasonably in holding off the institution of proceedings pending the determination of an application for planning permission.

In *Westport U.D.C. v. Golden,* High Court, December 18, 2000, Morris P. held that in the exercise of its discretion under section 27 of the Local Government (Planning and Development) Act 1976 (as amended), the High Court is entitled to take into account the extent to which the respondent itself contributed towards the situation upon which the court is asked to exercise its discretion. If through no fault of its own, a respondent stumbles upon a situation where the Fire Safety Regulations require that certain works be maintained notwithstanding the fact that such works are not authorised by planning permission, then in those circumstances the discretion might be exercised in favour of refusing the relief sought in the interests of doing justice between the parties. Where, however, as in the instant case, the respondent deliberately set out to disregard the planning procedures and sought to avoid the service of a warning notice, the court should not exercise its discretion in favour of the respondent when to do so would lend support to uncooperative conduct.

The *ex tempore* judgment of the High Court in *Grimes v. Punchestown Developments Company Ltd.,* High Court, June 21, 2000 (Record No. 2000/60 M.C.A.) examined in some detail the various factors which may operate on the High Court's discretion on an application under section 27. The decision arose in the context of an application under section 27 to restrain the holding of a pop concert. The proceedings had not been initiated until very shortly before the event was scheduled to take place. In brief, Herbert J. indicated that the High Court was entitled to take the following considerations, *inter alia,* into account: (i) the fact that the applicant was not resident in the area and would not in any way suffer any injury from the events complained of, and that there was no evidence of any concern by persons closely connected with the area; (ii) the attitude of the planning authority; (iii) the *bona fide* belief of the respondents that planning permission was not required: while not in any way conclusive, it could be taken into account on the basis that it would be unjust and disproportionate to insist on the letter of the law being observed where there was no evidence of any significant damage to, or interference with, the proper planning and development of the area; and (iv) evidence to the effect that the event sought be to enjoined had been widely publicised for a very considerable period, and the applicant did not take any steps until shortly before the event was to take place.

Section 27 injunction: costs The costs of bringing the proceedings, up to and including the first day, were awarded against a respondent who subsequently made a concession in respect of part of the development in respect of which relief had been claimed; *Fingal County Council v. R.F.S. Ltd.,* High Court, February 6, 2000.

Section 27 injunction: undertaking as to damages   Some confusion has arisen as to whether or not an undertaking as to damages is required under section 27. The confusion arises from the fact that the application proceeds by way of originating notice of motion, grounded on affidavit. Accordingly, a Section 27 application partakes of some of the characteristics of an application for an interlocutory injunction in plenary proceedings. This might suggest that, as in the case of an interlocutory application, an undertaking as to damages should be a *quid pro quo* for the granting of an injunction. This would, of course, be to miss the vital distinction between section 27 and plenary proceedings. In the case of section 27, final orders are made on the basis of the originating notice of motion and the affidavit evidence; generally, there will be no plenary hearing (*Mahon v. Butler* [1997] 3 I.R. 369; [1998] 1 I.L.R.M. 284). Thus the High Court will have determined the issues between the parties definitively. This is to be contrasted with the grant of an interlocutory injunction where the High Court will only have made a preliminary finding that there is a *prima facie* case: the final resolution of the issues must await the full hearing. The purpose of the undertaking as to damages is to allow the court to make interlocutory orders safely, by ensuring that the other side will be compensated if it subsequently transpires that an order was made which the moving party was not entitled to. In the case of section 27, conversely, the court generally will have determined the legal issues before making any order, and the question of an undertaking as to damages will not normally arise. There is, however, the possibility of interlocutory relief under section 27(3) i.e. a holding order can be made even before the Section 27 proceedings are determined, and relief of this type would, it is submitted, require the giving of an undertaking as to damages. The *ex tempore* judgment of the High Court in *Grimes v. Punchestown Developments Company Ltd.,* High Court, June 21, 2000 (Record No. 2000/60 M.C.A.) suggests that, in an appropriate case, the court can require an undertaking as to damages.

DEVELOPMENT – EXEMPTED DEVELOPMENT

Advertising hoarding   The decision in *Dublin Corporation v. Lowe,* High Court, February 4, 2000 is of practical significance to those using their premises for the exhibition of commercial advertisements. Morris P. held that the removal and replacement of an advertising hoarding (so as to facilitate a changeover between third party advertisers) represented a break in continuity so as to destroy any established use rights. Morris P. held that there must, in planning terms, be a significant difference between a temporary removal for repair and maintenance, with the intention of the original or repaired structure being reinstated after such repair, and the removal of such a structure with no intention of its reinstatement by its owner but the replacement of a different (albeit similar) structure by a third party. Such an abandonment occurred even where the period of time during which there was no structure amounted to no more that some days.

The decision is noteworthy in that the advertisement was treated as development by *works*. Section 3 of the Local Government (Planning and Development) Act 1963 provides, *inter alia*, that the use of any structure for the exhibition of advertisements constitutes a *material change in use*. If the facts were approached on the basis of development by material change in use, a different result may have followed. Whereas it may have been the case that there was no intention to reinstate the *original* advertising hoarding works, there does appear to have been a clear intention to continue the use for advertising display, and this should have been sufficient to rebut any finding of abandonment. Insofar as any works were concerned, same may well have constituted exempted development (whether under section 4(1)(g) of the Local Government (Planning and Development) Act 1963, or otherwise). Although the distinction in the context of enforcement proceedings between development by works, and development by material change in use, was to an extent collapsed by the Supreme Court decision in *Kildare County Council v. Goode* [1999] 2 I.R. 495; [2000] 1 I.L.R.M. 346 (Annual Review 1999, 427), it is submitted that the present decision goes too far.

Land reclamation   The spreading of spoil, clay and earth so as to lay a rough path or road does not constitute land reclamation within Part III, Class 9 of the Second Schedule of the Local Government (Planning and Development) Regulations 1994. The exemptions in respect of '*field drainage*', and '*removal of fences*', respectively, do not extend to interfering with the drainage of an adjoining landowner, or to the removal of boundary fences to the detriment of adjoining landowners. Nor does the fact that the work in question may eventually benefit and enhance lands and make them more suitable and more convenient for use for agricultural purposes bring the works within the exemption for the use of land for the purposes of agriculture under section 4 of the Local Government (Planning and Development) Act 1963; *Dolan v. Cooke,* High Court, February 20, 2000.

Extension of dwelling house   The exemption provided for in respect of the extension of a dwelling house was increased to forty square metres; Local Government (Planning and Development) Regulations 2000 (S.I. No. 181 of 2000). Certain conditions and limitations apply, however.

Pop concerts   The staging of a one day pop concert was found not to require planning permission in the *ex tempore* judgment of the High Court in *Grimes v.*

Punchestown Developments Company Ltd., High Court, June 21, 2000 (Record No. 2000/60 M.C.A.). Herbert J. applied the provisions of section 40 of the Local Government (Planning and Development) Act 1963, holding that there was evidence before him that Punchestown racecourse had been put to various uses prior to October 1, 1964, in addition to its principal use which related to horse racing, and equestrian events. In the alternative, Herbert J. held that if there was a change of use involved, it was not a *material* change in use as the use was a transient use of a type which fell full square within the decision in *Butler v. Dublin Corporation* [1999] 1 I.R 565; [1999] 1 I.L.R.M. 481.

REVOCATION OF PLANNING PERMISSION

Works Under section 30 of the Local Government (Planning and Development) Act 1963, a planning authority may revoke or modify a planning permission if there has been a change in circumstances relating to the proper planning and development of the area since the date of the decision to grant planning permission. There are a number of restrictions on the exercise of this power, including the following: where the planning permission relates to works, the power to revoke may only be exercised before those works have commenced. (Special provision is made in the case of works which, consequent to the making of a variation of the development plan, would contravene such plan: the power to revoke can be exercised at any time before those works have been completed). The nature of the works required was considered by the High Court in *Electricity Supply Board v. Cork County Council,* June 28, 2000. Finnegan J. held that the manufacture of site specific steel constituted 'works' for the purpose of section 30.

Procedural fairness The decision in *Electricity Supply Board v. Cork County Council,* June 28, 2000 is also authority for the proposition that the beneficiary of the planning permission was entitled either to have sight of the materials circulated in connection with an application to revoke the planning permission, or, at the very least, to have a sufficiently detailed statement of the contents thereof to enable it to make submissions in relation thereto.

DEFAULT PLANNING PERMISSION

Validity of application Under section 26(4) of the Local Government (Planning and Development) Act 1963, planning permission is deemed to have issued, by default, in circumstances where the planning authority has failed to notify a decision within two months of the date of a valid planning application. In order to avail of such a default planning permission, it is necessary that the application for planning permission have been in full compliance with the regulations. On a number of occasions, the courts have declined to allow a default planning permission on the basis of relatively minor defects: see, for example, *Creedon v. Dublin Corporation* [1983] I.L.R.M. 1. The strictness with which the regulations will be applied is evidenced by the decision in *Walsh v. Kildare County Council,* High Court, July 29, 2000. Article 18 of the Local Government (Planning and Development) Regulations 1994 provides, *inter alia,* that an application for planning permission shall state the name and address of the applicant, and indicate the address to which any correspondence relating to the application should be sent. The applicant had indicated an address in a rural area which although apparently sufficient to allow the postal service to deliver registered letters, proved not to be detailed enough to allow personal service. Specifically, the address given was, in fact, that of the applicant's married sister, and thus when an official from the planning authority was unable to find the address, inquiries under the applicant's own name proved unsuccessful in eliciting more specific directions. As a result, a request for further information (which would have stopped the two month time period running) was not served until after the two month time period had already elapsed. Finnegan J. held that although the applicant had acted in good faith, had he adopted the simple device of giving his address care of his sister or brother-in-law, the official would have located the address given without undue difficulty. Finnegan J. also held that the provisions of section 7 of the Local Government (Planning and Development) Act 1963 (which prescribe a number of modes of service for notices etc.) were intended to give the planning authority a *choice* as to the manner in which it could give notice: if the address given by an applicant for planning permission was inadequate to afford the planning authority a choice of the full range of options for giving notice then notwithstanding that the applicant may have acted in good faith, the application is bad. Accordingly, no default planning permission arose.

Material contravention of development plan   Another of the restrictions which the courts have placed on the operation of these provisions is to hold that a default planning permission is not available in respect of development which would represent a material contravention of the development plan; *State (Pine Valley Developments Ltd.) v. Dublin County Council* [1984] I.R. 407. This was relied upon as an alternative ground for refusing the default planning permission sought in *Walsh v. Kildare County Council,* High Court, July 29, 2000.

COMPENSATION

Notice excluding compensation   The refusal of planning permission attracts a *prima facie* entitlement to the payment of compensation. Compensation is excluded, however, where the development for which planning permission is refused is of a specified class or description, or where the reason or one of the reasons for refusal is a prescribed reason. Moreover, the planning authority may, not later than three months after the claim is received, serve a notice stating that notwithstanding the refusal of permission to develop land, the land in question is in their opinion capable of other [beneficial] development; section 13 of the Local Government (Planning and Development) Act, 1990. For this purpose, other development means development of a residential, commercial or industrial character, consisting wholly or mainly of the construction of houses, flats, shops or office premises, hotels, garages and petrol filling stations, theatres or structures for the purpose of entertainment, or industrial buildings (including warehouses), or any combination thereof. Compensation is not then payable on a claim where such a notice is in force in relation to the claim. A Section 13 notice continues in force for a period of five years unless, *inter alia*, before the expiration of that period, an application for permission to develop the land to which the notice relates in a manner consistent with the development specified in the notice is refused. Finally, the provisions of section 13 assume a particular significance in that, once the matter proceeds to arbitration, there is a statutory presumption that planning permission would not be granted for [beneficial] development of the kind prescribed under section 13.

The issue arose in *Arthur v. Kerry County Council* [2000] 3 I.R. 407; [2000] 2 I.L.R.M. 414 as to whether or not, in circumstances where an application for permission to develop the land in a manner consistent with the development specified in the notice is refused, the planning authority was entitled to serve a further section 13 notice. McGuinness J. summarised the opposing arguments as follows. If section 13 were to be interpreted literally, it would, on a practical level, be impossible for a planning authority to issue a second notice, even where appropriate, for the reason that the three month time limit would have long since expired. The alternative construction, however, had the danger that a developer might unjustly be denied compensation by the issue of repeated notices. Ultimately, McGuinness J. favoured a strict interpretation of the provision, and held that the refusal of planning permission annulled the section 13 notice, and the claim for compensation revived and fell to be considered.

The decision illustrates the practical difficulties with the section 13 procedure. As in the case of its statutory predecessor, the undertaking to grant planning permission, a section 13 notice suffers from the artificiality of being based on a notional planning permission being available for the land in respect of which the decision to refuse planning permission relates. The judgment in *Arthur v. Kerry County Council* confirms that the planning authority only has one shot at employing a section 13 notice. Special care will have to be taken, in drafting such notices, to state the beneficial development with precision: the broader the terms of the notice, the greater the permutations of application which will be consistent with the other development specified in the notice, and thus the greater the risk that planning permission will be refused and the notice annulled. To put the matter another way, it should be easier for the planning authority to anticipate the outcome of an application (and appeal to An Bord Pleanála) in respect of a specific development, than to say, for example, that residential or industrial development *simpliciter* would be granted planning permission.

Another issue which arose on the facts of *Arthur v. Kerry County Council*, but which did not need to be decided, was whether the notice must be confined to the land to which the decision to refuse related or could include other lands. The better view would appear to be that the notice must relate to the same lands: not an area greater or smaller.

APPLICATION FOR PLANNING PERMISSION

Name and address of applicant   The requirement under Article 18 of the Local Government (Planning and Development) Regulations 1994 to state, *inter alia*, the name and address of the applicant, and to indicate the address to which any correspondence relating to the application should be sent, obliges an applicant to state the address with sufficient particularity so as afford the planning authority a choice of the full range of options for giving notice. The applicant had indicated an address in a rural area which although apparently sufficient to allow the postal service to deliver registered letters proved not to be detailed enough to allow personal service; *Walsh v. Kildare County Council,* High Court, July 29, 2000.

Site or layout plans   There were 'substantial grounds' for arguing that a layout plan which significantly misrepresented the size and location of a neighbouring dwelling house, and the distance between same and those houses on the proposed development closest to it, rendered the application for planning permission invalid; *Seery v. An Bord Pleanála,* High Court, June 2, 2000.

Modified plans   Article 17 of the Local Government (Planning and Development) Regulations 1994 provides, *inter alia*, that a planning authority has a discretion to require further public notice of an application for planning permission. A question arose in *Irish Hardware Association v. South Dublin County Council,* High Court, July 19, 2000 as to whether a planning authority was required to exercise this power in circumstances where the applicant for planning permission submits modified plans for the proposed development. Butler J. ruled that a planning authority can grant planning permission for something which was substantially different from that which was originally applied for. Butler J. further held that he did not accept that the modification in issue amounted to a materially different development, and that, as to re-advertising, he was satisfied that anyone interested in retail warehousing in the area in question was properly put on notice in the first instance and that all information concerning any modifications of the original plan was available on the public file.

ENVIRONMENTAL IMPACT ASSESSMENT

Adequacy of environmental impact statement The decision in *Kenny v. An Bord Pleanála (No. 1),* High Court, December 15, 2000 suggests that the adequacy of an environmental impact statement (as opposed to the separate issue as to whether or not an environmental impact statement is required) is a question of fact and degree for the planning authorities and An Bord Pleanála.

Local authority development The EC (Environmental Impact Assessment) (Amendment) Regulations 2000 facilitate the transfer of the function of certifying environmental impact assessment of local authority own development from the Minister for the Environment and Local Government to An Bord Pleanála.

Practice and Procedure

HILARY DELANY and RAYMOND BYRNE

ABUSE OF PROCESS/NO REASONABLE CAUSE OF ACTION

In *Moran v. Oakley Park Developments Ltd* High Court, March 31, 2000 O'Donovan J. applied well established principles in refusing to dismiss the plaintiff's claim pursuant to the inherent jurisdiction of the court on the basis that it did not disclose a reasonable cause of action or that it was frivolous or vexatious. He stated that for the purpose of adjudicating on the relief sought, he must assume that the facts pleaded in the statement of claim and asserted in the grounding affidavit were true. Having referred to a number of authorities, O'Donovan J. stated that while the jurisdiction to dismiss should be sparingly exercised and only in clear cases, if having considered all the relevant documentation, the court is satisfied that a plaintiff's claim must fail, then it is a proper exercise of its discretion for the court to strike out proceedings on the grounds that their continued existence cannot be justified and manifestly causes irrevocable damage to the defendant. O'Donovan J. adopted the summary of the law set out by Macken J. in *Supermac's Ireland v. Katesan (Naas) Ltd*, High Court, March 15, 1999 (see now the Supreme Court decision [2001] 1 I.L.R.M. 401, below) and then considered the plaintiff's case as set out in the statement of claim. He concluded that while, in the light of the authorities he had considered, he had to admit to having certain reservations about the matter, on balance he was satisfied that the plaintiff had an arguable case which was neither frivolous nor vexatious.

In *Ewing v. Kelly,* High Court, May 16, 2000 O'Sullivan J. considered motions brought by a number of defendants in an action seeking an order dismissing the plaintiff's claims against them. He summarised the relevant legal principles as being that in so far as the application is based on allegations that the pleadings disclosed no reasonable cause of action he must assume that all of the relevant matters pleaded by the plaintiff will be established by him and said that he must take account of any amendment of the actual pleadings which could 'save' the case being made by the plaintiff. In addition, if as in the case before him, the defendants had made it clear that they intended to plead the Statute of Limitations and such a defence is one which in the circumstances must inevitably succeed, O'Sullivan J. said that he should take this into account. Further, if issues raised between the same parties had already been finally dealt with on the merits by a court of competent jurisdiction, such issues should not be tried again and the relevant pleadings should accordingly be struck out. He added that in so far as the applications before him were grounded on the inherent jurisdiction of the court, if he came to the conclusion that it was inevitable that the claim must fail, then he should strike it out, but bearing in mind that the court should be very slow to exercise such a jurisdiction. Finally, O'Sullivan J. said that where applications are grounded on the allegation that the pleadings are unnecessary or scandalous or tend to embarrass, prejudice or delay a fair trial, he must have regard to the relevance of the material on the issues raised. Applying those principles to the facts of the case before him, O'Sullivan J. concluded that the claims against the first, second, third, fourth, fifth and sixth named defendants must be struck out. He further ordered that the seventh, eighth and ninth named defendants, who were facing motions for judgment in default of defence, should have two weeks in which to file their defences.

In *Supermac's Ireland Ltd v. Katesan (Naas) Ltd* [2001] 1 I.L.R.M. 401 (SC), the Supreme Court declined to strike out a claim for specific performance, even though the defendant raised some questions over whether there was a sufficient note or memorandum in place for the purposes of the Statute of Frauds. The Supreme Court (affirming Macken J. in the High Court) held that the defendant had failed to convince the court that the plaintiff would be unable to overcome the difficulties raised by the defendant and that, in any event, the matters raised appeared to more appropriately resolved by allowing the claim to proceed to hearing.

COSTS

High Court costs where Circuit Court had no jurisdiction   In *Rodgers v. Mangan*, July 15, 1996 (the judgment having been generally circulated in 2000), Geoghegan J. held that, where relief initially being sought could only have been obtained in the High Court, it was correct to allow High Court costs, even where damages were subsequently awarded and were substantially below the High Court monetary jurisdiction floor. The plaintiff had sought injunctive relief to prohibit the defendant from operating a bus service along a specified route, but did not initially seek damages and an interlocutory injunction was granted in the case in 1994. At the full hearing an injunction was no longer necessary and the plaintiff was awarded £3,000 damages and the costs of the action. The defendant then claimed that Circuit Court costs should be awarded in relation to the injunction and District Court costs in relation to the plenary hearing on the basis of section 17 of the Courts Act 1981, as amended by section 14 of the Courts Act 1991. Geoghegan J. disagreed and awarded costs of the action to be taxed as High Court costs.

He held that there was no justification for subdividing the costs, since the costs were the costs of the action as a whole and as the District Court has no jurisdiction to grant injunctions the costs at the very least must be Circuit

Court costs. Moreover, the injunction to which the plaintiff would have been entitled was not an injunction to restrain interference with property or the enjoyment of property but with the wrongful causing of financial loss by a wrongful activity. Since this was not included in the category of actions referred to in the Third Schedule of the Courts (Supplemental Provisions) Act 1961, the Circuit Court would not have had jurisdiction by virtue of section 22 of the 1961 Act. Indeed, Geoghegan J. noted that, prior to the Courts of Justice Act 1924, the Circuit Court did not have jurisdiction to grant a primary injunction unrelated to property, likewise there is no jurisdiction under section 22(5) of the 1961 Act by reference to the earlier Courts of Justice Acts.

Pre-emptive costs order   In *Village Residents Association Ltd v. An Bord Pleanála (No.2)* [2001] 2 I.L.R.M. 22 (HC) Laffoy J. considered the circumstances in which the Court may make a pre-emptive costs order. The background was that the second respondent (McDonald's Restaurants of Ireland Ltd) had been granted permission by An Bord Pleanála for the development of a restaurant in Kilkenny city. The applicant had been incorporated with the object of, *inter alia*, the preservation and protection of the amenities and environment in the locality and was granted leave to apply by way of way of judicial review proceedings seeking to quash the decision of An Bord Pleanála: see *Village Residents Association Ltd v. An Bord Pleanála* [2000] 2 I.L.R.M. 59 (HC). The respondents then applied for an order that the applicant provide security for their costs pursuant to section 390 of the Companies Act 1963. This was granted by Laffoy J. who also considered at length, but rejected, the arguments made by the applicant for a pre-emptive costs order.

Laffoy J. noted that it had not been argued that the Court lacked jurisdiction to make a pre-emptive costs order. She referred to section 14 of the Courts (Supplemental Provisions) Act 1961, which provided that the jurisdiction vested in and exercisable by the High Court was to be exercised so far as regards pleading, practice and procedure generally, including liability to costs, in the manner provided by the rules of court in force when the Act of 1961 came into operation. She also noted that Order 99 of the Rules of the Superior Courts 1986 empowers the Court to make an order for costs at any time. However, she considered that the Court's discretion as to costs should normally be exercised on the basis that costs follow the event.

She accepted that it was difficult in the abstract to identify the type or types of case in which the interests of justice would require the court to deal with the costs issue by making a pre-emptive order and that it would be unwise to attempt to do so. Nonetheless, she also approved the views expressed by Dyson J. in *R v. Lord Chancellor, ex p. Child Poverty Action Group* [1998] 2 All E.R. 755 (citing in turn the views of Hoffman LJ in *McDonald v. Horn* [1995] 1 All E.R. 961) that it would not generally be appropriate to make such an order in litigation *inter partes* and that they should be confined to 'public interest challenges' in which the party seeking such an order had no private interest. Laffoy J. held that the criteria applied by Dyson J. must at least be met, namely that the issues raised in such a case are truly of general public importance and that the court must have a sufficient appreciation of the merits of the case to conclude that it is in the public interest to make the pre-emptive costs order. In the instant case, none of these criteria had been met, since the members of the applicant company had a private interest in the outcome of the case nor were the issues raised truly of public importance. Laffoy J. also stated that, since the second respondent was a private company, not a public body, she did not see why it should be penalised in costs in the context of a challenge by the applicant to the planning decision of the first respondent.

Security for costs: amount of security The question of the amount of security for costs which should be furnished by a plaintiff where a defendant seeks security pursuant to section 390 of the Companies Act 1963 has been considered recently in a number of decisions. In *Gibson v. Coleman* [1950] I.R. 50 Dixon J. had said that he did not believe that the use of the word 'sufficient' imported a different norm in relation to the amount of security to that implicit in the simple criterion of 'security for costs' and he expressed the view that the fact that an application might be brought pursuant to the Companies Act should not affect the amount of security fixed. In *Thalle v. Soares* [1957] I.R. 182 Kingsmill Moore J. made reference to the fact that Dixon J. had rejected the idea that there was any difference between the measure of security to be given under the Companies Act and where a plaintiff is resident out of the jurisdiction and said that he was unable to take that view. He stated that '[t]he statute lays down reasonably precise instructions as to the measure of security while the rule makers and the judges seem studiously to have avoided any approach to definiteness, leaving each case to be decided by an uncontrolled discretion'.(at 192)

This issue was considered by McCracken J. in *Lismore Homes Ltd v. Bank of Ireland Finance Ltd,* High Court, March 24, 2000 in a decision recently upheld by the Supreme Court (October 5, 2001). McCracken J. referred to the *dicta* of Kingsmill Moore J. and also to the decision of the English Court of Appeal in *Innovare Displays plc v. Corporate Broking Services Ltd* [1991] B.C.C. 174, 179 where Legatt LJ had expressed the view that the equivalent section 'does not mean... complete security. It can only mean security of a sufficiency in all the circumstances of the case to be just'. However, McCracken J. pointed out that the English authorities did not seem to be compatible with the decision in *Thalle*. He said that while it is arguable that the use of the word 'may' in section 390 gives a general discretion to the court, on the whole he thought it more likely that the word referred to the making of the order for security rather than the amount thereof. McCracken J. expressed the view that if the discretion was intended to be in relation to the amount, the word 'sufficient' would not have been used. However, it was used in the section and he stated that its only logical construction was that it meant sufficient for the costs of the defendant if he were successful in his defence. While it was customary to require security of approximately one third of the probable costs where the plaintiff was out of the jurisdiction, McCracken J. stated that he did not see how under any circumstances this could be called 'sufficient security' and he concluded that 'the section can only mean that the security required must approximate to the probable costs of the defendant should be succeed'. These principles were subsequently applied by McCracken J. in *Windmaster Developments Ltd v. Airogen Ltd.* High Court, July 10, 2000 in which the defendants sought an order pursuant to section 390 of the Companies Act 1963 that the plaintiff should provide security for the defendants' costs. McCracken J. referred to his judgment in *Lismore* and to the fact that he had held that the words 'sufficient security' in section 390 meant that the security required was to approximate to the probable costs of the defendant should it succeed and assessed the security on that basis.

A similar conclusion was reached by the Supreme Court in *Hot Radio Co. Ltd v. Independent Radio and Television Commission,* Supreme Court, April 14, 2000 although it should be pointed out that Keane CJ merely concluded that it was just in the case before him to order the full measure of security because there was no suggestion that the action would be stifled by such an award. Keane C.J. referred to the *dicta* of Kingsmill Moore J. in *Thalle v. Soares* but pointed out that it might be regarded as *obiter* since the learned judge was dealing with a case brought pursuant to the Rules of Court and not the Companies legislation. The Chief Justice then referred to the decision of the English Court of Appeal in *Innovare Displays* and said that it was clear that in that case a matter which weighed significantly with the court was the fact that there was a danger the claim would be stifled if security for costs at the full measure was ordered; the opinion of the court was that sufficient security meant security sufficient in all the circumstances to be just. Keane CJ then stated that even applying those criteria and assuming that this view of the law was to be preferred to the view expressed by McCracken J., it was just in the case before him to order the full measure of security because there was no suggestion that the action would be stifled by the award of this amount. Therefore it is not possible to draw any firm conclusions from the decision of Keane C.J. in *Hot Radio* as to whether the approach of McCracken J. or the English courts might be followed in the future. On the facts of the case before him both tests led to the same conclusion but on balance it would appear that Keane C.J., although he avoided expressing a preference for either option, favoured the "sufficient in all the circumstances to be just" approach. This view has been borne out by the recent decision of the Supreme Court in *Lismore Homes Ltd v. Bank of Ireland Finance Ltd*, Supreme Court, October 5, 2001.

Security for costs and corporate plaintiffs Established principles about where the onus of proof should lie where an application for security for costs is brought against a company were applied by Barr J. in *Wexford Rope and*

Twine Co. Ltd v. Gaynor, High Court, March 6. 2000. Inability to discharge its liabilities to the defendants should he fail was conceded by the plaintiff. The onus then passed to the plaintiff to establish special circumstances why it should not have to provide security which it could not do. It failed to establish a *prima facie* case that inability to give security derived from the wrongdoing of the defendants or that there had been an unreasonable delay on their part. Barr J. concluded that in the case before him it was reasonable for the defendants to await the statement of claim in order to ascertain precisely what was being alleged against them before bringing an application for security. Barr J. concluded that in all the circumstances, the defendants were entitled to the orders for security for costs which they sought.

In *Broadnet Ireland Ltd v. Office of the Director of Telecommunications Regulation* [2000] 2 I.L.R.M. 241, Laffoy J. held that a statutory body, such as the respondent, was entitled to the benefit of the provisions on security for costs in section 390 of the Companies Act 1963. In that case, she ordered the applicant to provide security for costs in a judicial review of the respondent's decision refusing it a broadband telecommunications licence. She also ordered it to provide an undertaking as to damages, secured by its parent company, since the judicial review proceedings involved applications for interlocutory relief, in effect, seeking to overturn the granting of licences to other companies.

Taxation: bias   In *deRossa v. Independent Newspapers plc (No.2)*, High Court, March 7, 2000, Geoghegan J. reversed a ruling of a Taxing Master for apparent bias. The case arose from the libel proceedings brought by the plaintiff, which resulted in an award of £300,000 in his favour. In the taxation, the Taxing Master had made a nil assessment in respect of the non-party discovery costs made by the Workers Party, of which the plaintiff had been a member. Geoghegan J. held that many of the colourful remarks contained in the Taxing Master's first costs ruling would not give any confidence to the Workers Party that there would be an unbiased assessment. Concluding that there was enough evidence to have enabled the taxing master to have awarded considerably more than nil and it was thus erroneous and unjust, he directed that in the exceptional circumstances of this case it should be dealt with by the other taxing master.

Taxation: judicial review or motion to review   In *Bula Ltd v. Taxing Master* [2000] I.R., McGuinness J. held that, in general, matters such as individual items and quantum arising out of a taxation of costs were best dealt with by the motion to review under Order 99, rule 38(3) of the Rules of the Superior Courts 1986 and that it was inappropriate to deal with those matters by judicial review. But where the manner of the taxation was being challenged, this was a suitable matter for judicial review proceedings. In this case, she held that judicial review lay where the Taxing Master had purported to apportion costs between parties where such apportionment formed no part of the order of the court. She held that, as had been held in *McGauran v. Dargan* [1983] I.L.R.M. 7, it was appropriate to order that the liability for costs was joint and several. Nonetheless, she held that many other matters raised by the applicants, such as whether the Taxing Master had erred in his decision to allow the costs of three senior counsel for the third respondent (the State), were suitable for review under Order 99 of the 1986 Rules. On this point, she held that the Taxing Master had not erred on this; not was his decision to award a higher brief fee to one of the senior counsel unjust within the meaning of section 27 of the Courts and Court Officers Act 1995.

Taxation: significance of case not fully taken into account   In *Bloomer v. Law Society of Ireland (No.2)* [2000] I.R., Geoghegan J. dealt with an appeal against the taxation of costs in a case in which the plaintiffs had successfully challenged the former exemption from the FE-1 'Entrance' examination of the defendant: see *Bloomer v. Law Society of Ireland* [1995] 3 I.R. 14 (HC); [1997] I.R. (SC) (Annual Review 1996, 567-8). In his judgment, Geoghegan J. held that the Taxing Master had acted correctly in many aspects of the taxation of the costs in this case, but that he had fallen into some error on a number of points, in particular by failing to take into account the significance of the case and its complexity. Nonetheless, taking account of the increased discretion of the Taxing Master under section 27 of the Court and Court Officers Act 1995, the decisions he had made were left largely undisturbed.

In global terms, the Taxing Master had substantially reduced the fees being claimed by the plaintiffs' solicitor and counsel for the hearings in the High Court and the Supreme Court. Taking account of the views expressed in *Smyth v. Tunney* [1999] 1 I.L.R.M. 211, *Tobin & Twomey Services Ltd v. Kerry Foods Ltd* [1999] 1 I.L.R.M. 428 and *Minister for Finance v. Goodman*, High Court, October 8, 1999, Geoghegan J. held that in considering whether the Taxing Master had erred in the exercise of his powers under section 27 of the 1995 Act, it had to be seen whether, in arriving at his decision, he had regard or excessive regard to some factor which he either should not have had regard to or which he should have had much less regard. It had then to be considered whether there had been some significant factor to which the Taxing Master ought to have had regard to and which he either had no regard at all or insufficient regard. It also had to be considered whether the Taxing Master had fallen into error in either law or jurisdiction. Moreover it had to be decided whether the taxation was unjust. In relation to any given item in the taxation which was in controversy, Geoghegan J. held that the justice or injustice of the decision would be determined by the amount involved.

As to the solicitor's instruction fee, he accepted that while it was difficult to attempt to review it, this had to be done if the evidence warranted it. In this context, it was necessary to examine how the Taxing Master approached his assessment of the instructions fee and, above all, how he approached his own review of taxation. There were three criteria upon which the fee had to be determined, namely, any special expertise of a solicitor, the amount of work done and the degree of responsibility borne. In the instant case, even if the Taxing Master had fallen into limited error in underplaying the importance of the case, the importance he attached to it could not be described as unjust; and the Taxing Master had correctly attached weight to the fact that the case had been barrister-led.

As to counsel's fees, Geoghegan J. held that it was entirely right that senior counsel's brief fee on the appeal to the Supreme Court should bear no relationship to the brief fee on the hearing of the action and that the Taxing Master had been correct to reduce it as he had done. As to the relationship between the brief fee and refresher fees, he held that, in a complex High Court action the complexity should normally be reflected in the main in the brief fee, rather than in the refresher. This is because the brief fee covers preparation for the case. In this particular case there were a number of matters which had to be freshly attended as the case progressed. The day-to-day running of the case was extremely difficult and in all the circumstances, the Taxing Master had been correct in increasing the refresher fee on his review, but, there was no justification for him (Geoghegan J.) making it any higher.

A specific issue arose in the case as to whether senior counsel in the case had done work normally done by a solicitor, in this case taking statements in Belfast from the plaintiffs. It happened that senior counsel for the plaintiffs spent part of his professional time in the Republic and part in Belfast, and was thus available to deal with the plaintiffs. The Taxing Master had appeared to query whether this aspect of counsel's part in the case had amounted to breach of the Code of Conduct of the Bar. Geoghegan J. did not accept this view of the matter. He accepted that a barrister could never be allowed on taxation a fee or any element of a fee which covered work which he was prohibited from doing by the rules of his profession; and he also noted that work involving direct contact with clients could only devalue the solicitor's instruction fee. But he also accepted that, within certain parameters and provided it did not breach the Code of Conduct, a barrister's brief fee could be increased because of unusual work which he did in connection with the case. In this respect, the Taxing Master had fallen into error with regard to senior counsel's brief fee in that neither his rulings in the original taxation nor on the review of taxation indicated that he adequately appreciated the importance of the case. On balance, therefore, the brief fee that had been allowed to senior counsel was either unjust or was not within such a reasonable range that it ought not be interfered with under the 1995 Act.

The restrictions placed by section 27 of the 1995 on the ability to challenge a taxation of costs were also apparent in *Superquinn Ltd v. Bray UDC*, High Court, May 5, 2000. Kearns J. noted that, since the review had to be carried out subject to the additional powers of the taxing master in the 1995 Act, and since the taxing master had a duty to examine the nature and extent of work in any particular case and make his own reasonable assessment on the merits accordingly, this meant that former 'no go' areas no longer existed. Following the approach in *Smyth v. Tunney* [1999] 1 I.L.R.M. 211, he held that the 1995 Act imposed a heavier burden on a party seeking to challenge the taxing master's ruling than had been the case previously. Under section 27 of the 1995 Act, the Court could only intervene if satisfied the taxing master erred to the extent that his decision was unjust. Although he accepted that the court's jurisdiction was limited, Kearns J. adjusted upwards some of the figures claimed by the solicitors for the first and fifth named defendants for their solicitor's instruction fee and counsel's brief fees; but he reduced the refresher fees.

DELAY (DISMISSAL FOR WANT OF PROSECUTION)

The principles set out in *Rainsford v. Limerick Corporation* [1995] 2 I.L.R.M. 561 relating to the circumstances in which a claim may be dismissed for want of prosecution were applied again in *Silverdale and Hewetts Travel Agencies Ltd v. Italiatour Ltd* [2001] 1 I.L.R.M. 464 (HC), in which Finnegan J. refused to dismiss the proceedings. A point initially highlighted by Finlay P in *Rainsford v. Limerick Corporation* [1995] 2 I.L.R.M. 561 which resurfaced in *Silverdale* is that the extent of a litigant's personal blameworthiness for delay may be material to the exercise of the court's discretion. In *Silverdale* Finnegan J. stressed that in considering a party's personal blameworthiness the court must look at the circumstances of the party. He stated that in the case of an infant plaintiff, this circumstance will most likely justify delay during minority, as in *Ó Domhnaill v. Merrick* [1984] I.R. 151. In addition, in *Guerin v. Guerin* [1992] 2 I.R. 287 (Annual Review 1992, 436) Costello J. had had regard to the fact that while the plaintiff was an infant his family lived in one of the poorest sections of the community and was unaware that he had a cause of action. However, as Finnegan J. stated such considerations had little application to the plaintiff in the case before him, which was a commercial enterprise of considerable size, and which must be expected to pursue litigation with reasonable expedition and to that end to take steps to ensure that its legal advisors act in an appropriately expeditious manner.

In *Glynn v. Rotunda Hospital* High Court, April 6, 2000 O'Sullivan J. applied the now well established principles set out in *Primor plc v. Stokes Kennedy Crowley* [1996] 2 I.R. 459, 475-476 (Annual Review 1995, 401) in relation to the circumstances in which a claim should be dismissed for want of prosecution in a medical negligence claim brought by plenary summons in January 2000 in relation to the circumstances surrounding the plaintiff's birth in 1981. He also referred to the fact that the Supreme Court had addressed the issue of whether the court has jurisdiction to dismiss an action brought within the statutory limitation period in *Ó Domhnaill v. Merrick* [1984] I.R. 151 and *Toal v. Duignan (No. 2)* [1991] I.L.R.M. 140 (Annual Review 1990, 394-8) and that it had concluded that there is such jurisdiction if there has been inordinate and inexcusable delay and if a failure to do so would result in an unjust trial and an unjust result. O'Sullivan J. stated that the fact that the plaintiff was in her minority during all the relevant period of what he concluded had been inordinate and inexcusable delay and the fact that some of the material of relevance had not been available to the plaintiff's advisors during the period of delay, were features of the case which must be weighed in the balance in deciding whether the interests of justice required that the plaintiff be permitted to continue with her claim. He also noted that whilst it was not a 'documents only' case, full contemporaneous records were available and that some but not all of the relevant medical personnel were available to give evidence. O'Sullivan J. concluded that bearing in mind the value to be attached to the survival of full notes together with an 'authoritative contemporaneous medical professional witness', he had not been persuaded that the probability was that if the plaintiff's case proceeded, the delay would lead to an 'unjust trial and an unjust result' (*per* Finlay C.J. in *Toal v. Duignan (No. 2)*). Accordingly he refused to dismiss the plaintiff's action for want of prosecution.

DISCOVERY

Interpretation of new discovery rule Increasing dissatisfaction with the manner in which Order 31, rule 12 of the Rules of the Superior Courts 1986 was being utilised culminated in the substitution - by the Rules of the Superior Courts (No.2) (Discovery) 1999 - of a new Order 31, rule 12 with effect from August 3, 1999, which substantially altered the discovery process in a number of material ways. First, the written application seeking voluntary discovery is now required to specify the precise categories of documents in respect of which discovery is sought and must also set out reasons why each category of documents is required. It should be noted that a proviso to rule 12(4) sets out that where, by reason of the urgency of the matter, the consent of the parties, the nature of the cases or any other circumstances which seem appropriate to the court, it may make an order as appears proper, without the necessity for prior application in writing. Secondly, the notice of motion is required to specify the precise categories of documents in respect of which discovery is sought. Thirdly, motions for discovery must now be grounded on an affidavit which shall verify that the discovery sought is necessary for disposing fairly of the matter or for saving costs and shall furnish the reasons why each category of documents is required to be discovered. These new requirements have resulted in a number of important changes both in relation to the type of order of discovery being sought and to the manner in which the court's discretion will be exercised. It will no longer suffice to seek a general order for discovery seeking all relevant documents in the other party's possession or power and precise categories of documents will have to be specified. In addition, while under the original rule 12(1) the onus of establishing that an order for discovery was not necessary appeared to lie on the party against whom discovery is sought, the substituted rule clearly requires the party seeking the order to verify that the discovery is necessary and to furnish reasons why each category of documents is required to be discovered.

A number of useful indications in relation to the manner in which these new provisions are likely to be interpreted can be found in the judgment of Morris P. in *Swords v. Western Proteins Ltd* [2001] 1 I.L.R.M. 481 (HC), which concerned an appeal from an order of the Master that the defendants should make discovery. At the hearing of the motion, the Master had adjourned the case to enable the plaintiff's solicitors to file a supplemental affidavit and he subsequently ordered the defendants to make discovery of, *inter alia*, an accident report form and all documents relating to the reporting and investigation of an accident in which the plaintiff was involved up to the date when the defendant was made aware of the plaintiff's intention to bring legal proceedings in relation to the accident. Counsel for the defendant submitted that the Master had misdirected himself in allowing discovery of these documents. Counsel referred to the new rule introduced in 1999 and in particular Order 31, rule 12(4) which precludes the court from making an order for discovery unless the applicant shall have previously applied by letter requesting that discovery be made voluntarily, specifying the precise category of documents in respect of which discovery is sought and furnishing the reasons why each category of documents is required to be discovered. In addition, the rule requires that a reasonable period of time for discovery must be allowed and the party requested must have failed or refused to make discovery. Counsel submitted that the letters written by the plaintiff's solicitor made no attempt to specify the precise category of documents in respect of which discovery was sought, that no reason had been furnished setting out why each category of documents was required to be discovered and that no reasonable period of time for discovery had been allowed. In addition, counsel contended that when the matter first came before the Master, the grounding affidavit failed to verify that discovery of the documents sought was necessary and that it did not give reasons indicating why each category was required to be discovered. He submitted that while a supplemental affidavit filed by the plaintiff may have done this, the Master had been wrong in law in adjourning the matter to enable such an affidavit to be filed.

Morris P. stated that he was satisfied that the amendment to Order 31, rule 12 had been made for the purpose of addressing a problem which had given rise to delay and potential injustice over a number of years. He continued as follows (at p.487):

> Accordingly I believe that [the new O.31, r.12] imposed a clearly defined obligation upon a party seeking discovery to pinpoint the documents or category of documents required and required that party to give the reasons why they were required. Blanket discovery became a thing of

the past. The new rule was brought into being to ensure in the first instance that the party against whom discovery was being sought would, upon receipt of the preliminary letter, be in a position to know the document or category of documents referred to and be able to exercise a judgment on whether the reasons given for requiring those documents to be discovered was valid. He would then be in a position to know if he was required to comply with the request. If he disputed his obligation to make discovery the court would know by reference to this letter precisely why the moving party sought the documents in question and the grounds upon which the moving party believed that the documents sought to be discovered might help to dispose fairly of the cause or save costs.

Morris P. expressed the view that if the letter of application did not comply with the rules then the Master had no power to make a determination even where an elaborate affidavit is filed in support of the application. In his opinion the Master derived his jurisdiction to determine the questions which arose between the parties from the identification of the issues in the applicant's originating letter or letters. This is an important point and illustrates that considerable thought must be put into the contents of the letter seeking voluntary discovery and that the specific requirements of the rules must be complied with at this stage and not just when the grounding affidavit is being drawn up.

Applying these principles to the case before him, Morris P stated that in as much as the plaintiff's solicitor's letter had identified the documents as "accident report book/record details", no effort had been made to specify the precise categories of documents sought or to furnish adequate reasons why discovery was being applied for. In the view of Morris P the Master's order which translated this into "accident report form and all documents relating to the reporting and investigating of the accident in which the plaintiff was involved up to October 1, 1997" was an elaboration which was not justified. In addition, Morris P. was satisfied that there had been a failure on the part of the plaintiff's solicitors to furnish reasons why each of the categories of documents was required to be discovered. Even a second letter sent after the shortcomings in the original had been pointed out by the defendant's solicitor failed to remedy the omission.

Turning to the submissions made in relation to the requirements of rule 12 as to the contents of the affidavit, Morris P pointed out that when the matter came before the Master the only affidavit was that of the plaintiff's solicitors which neither verified that discovery was necessary for the purpose of disposing fairly of the cause or matter or to save costs nor did it furnish reasons why each category of documents was required. However, the solicitor had obtained leave from the Master to file a supplemental affidavit which in the view of Morris P. complied with the requirements of the rule. He added that he had no doubt that it was within the Master's jurisdiction to give the plaintiff an opportunity to file a supplemental affidavit to enable him to comply with the Rules of Court. In response to a further argument put by counsel for the defendant that the limits of the Master's jurisdiction in this regard are as set out in Order 31, rule 12(2), Morris P. stressed that in his view the Master had an overall jurisdiction to adjourn a case if the interests of justice required it and that his authority was not derived solely from the provisions of rule 12(2).

Morris P. concluded by saying that the jurisdiction to make an order for discovery is confined to circumstances in which the Master is of the opinion that there has been compliance by the applicant with Order 31, rule 12(4)(1) and that on an appeal to the High Court its jurisdiction was also so limited. In view of the fact that he had held that there had been a failure on the part of the applicant to comply with the Rules, Morris P. stated that accordingly he had no jurisdiction to make the order for discovery sought by the plaintiff.

A number of important points emerge from this judgment which should be borne in mind by any party seeking to obtain discovery. First, Morris P. obviously placed considerable importance on the requirements relating to the content of the application in writing seeking voluntary discovery. He stated quite clearly that in his view the Master derived his jurisdiction to determine the issues which arose from the identification of the issues in the originating letter and that even an elaborate affidavit filed subsequently could not make up for earlier deficiencies.

Secondly, it is clear from his judgment that Morris P. was adopting a strict approach to the requirement that the letter seeking voluntary discovery should specify the precise categories of documents in respect of which discovery was sought and furnish reasons why each category of documents was required to be discovered. While the Master's order clearly specified the categories of documents sought with more particularity than the plaintiff's solicitor's letter, the view of Morris P. that such elaboration should not be permitted is clear evidence of strict standards being applied by the courts in relation to the contents of such letters. However, a more flexible approach can be discerned in the attitude adopted by Morris P. towards the issue of filing a supplemental affidavit to deal with any shortcomings in the original one filed. His conclusion that it was within the Master's jurisdiction to give the plaintiff an opportunity to take this step was a pragmatic one and in his view was in the interests of saving time and costs.

Relevance of documents In *Aquatechnologie Ltd v. National Standards Authority of Ireland* Supreme Court, July 10, 2000 the appellant sought discovery of certain documents against the first named respondent and appealed against an order of the High Court refusing to order discovery of the documents sought. In upholding the decision on the High Court on this point, Murray J. considered the question of what documents might be relevant within the meaning of Order 31, rule 12(1) which requires a party to make discovery of documents which are or have been in his possession or power 'relating to any matter in question therein'. Murray J. quoted the *dicta* of Brett LJ in *Compagnie Financiere et Commerciale du Pacifique Peruvian Guano Company* (1882) 11 Q.B.D. 55, 63 to the effect that 'every document relates to the matters in question in the action, which not only would be evidence upon any issue, but also which, it is reasonable to suppose, contains information which *may* - not which *must* - either directly or indirectly enable the party requiring the affidavit either to advance his own case or to damage the case of his adversary.' Murray J. expressed the opinion that there was nothing in that statement which was intended to qualify the principle that documents sought on discovery must be relevant, directly or indirectly to the matters in issue between the parties in the proceedings. He added that an applicant for discovery must show that it is reasonable for the court to suppose that the documents contain information which may enable the applicant to advance his own case or to damage that of his adversary. As Murray J. stated: 'an applicant is not entitled to discovery based on mere speculation or on the basis of what has been traditionally characterised as a fishing expedition'. Applying these principles to the facts of the case before him, Murray J. concluded that the documents sought were not relevant to the issue in dispute and he stated that the order of the High Court should be upheld in this respect.

Further and better discovery The circumstances in which a court may reach the conclusion that there are further documents in existence which are relevant to the action and in the possession of the deponent were also set out by Brett L.J. in *Compagnie Financiere et Commerciale du Pacifique v. Peruvian Guano Co.* (1882) 11 Q.B.D. 55 in the following terms. He stated that the question must be whether from the description either in the first affidavit itself or in the list of documents referred to in that affidavit or in the pleadings, there are still documents in the possession of the party making the original affidavit which contain information which may, either directly or indirectly enable the party requiring the further affidavit either to advance his own case or to damages the case of his adversary. These principles were approved by Herbert J. in *Spring Grove Services (Ireland) Ltd v. O'Callaghan* High Court, July 31, 2000 which concerned an application for further and better discovery. Herbert J. also rejected an argument that the trial would be unnecessarily and unreasonably delayed by the motion before the court or that it had been so delayed by previous applications for discovery. He distinguished the facts of the case before him from those in *Brooks Thomas Ltd v. Impac Ltd* [1999] 1 I.L.R.M. 171 (Annual Review 1998, 543) and said that there was no evidence to suggest that the plaintiffs had not been 'getting on with the case and achieving finality' in the words of Lynch J. in *Brooks Thomas*. Herbert J. then proceeded to order that the plaintiff was entitled to discovery of most, but not all of the documents and records specified.

Reference should also be made to the views expressed by Finlay C.J. in *Bula Ltd v. Crowley* [1991] 1 I.R. 220, 223 (Annual Review 1990, 432) where he stated that 'a court should be satisfied, as a matter of probability, that an error has occurred in an omission from an affidavit of discovery of documents on the basis of irrelevancy before making any order for further discovery'. These principles were applied by the Supreme Court in *Phelan v. Goodman* [2000] 2 I.L.R.M. 378 where the Court concluded that the evidence was insufficient to satisfy it that relevant documents were or had been in the possession of the defendant which should have been but had not been discovered by him.

JUDICIAL PENSIONS

The Courts (Supplemental Provisions) (Amendment) Act 2000 provided for the grant of full pension rights to a judge of the High Court who on his retirement on July 9, 2000 would not have accumulated the necessary 15 years' service as a judge which would entitle him to a full pension. For this purpose, the 2000 Act amended Part I of the Second Schedule to the Courts (Supplemental Provisions) Act 1961. While couched in general terms, the 2000 Act was enacted to provide a full pension for Flood J, who had been appointed a High Court judge in October 1991 and thus fell short of the 15 year period of service on his retirement July 9, 2000. Flood J. was continuing to chair a Tribunal of Inquiry at the time of his retirement, and it was envisaged he would continue to do so until well into 2002.

REMITTAL

In *MW v. DW* [2000] 1 I.L.R.M. 416, the Supreme Court exercised its discretion not to remit a family law case to the Circuit Court. Under Order 70A of the Rules of the Superior Courts 1986, as inserted by the Rules of the Superior Courts (No.3) 1997, the High Court (and, on appeal, the Supreme Court) may remit such proceedings to the Circuit or District Court where it considers such an order to be 'in the interests of justice.' The petitioner had initiated judicial separation proceedings in 1998 in the High Court. The respondent sought an order remitting the action to Cork Circuit Court on the grounds, *inter alia*, that he was suffering from ill health and would find it difficult to travel, the parties, the witnesses and the solicitors resided in Cork, the rateable valuation of the family home was less than £200 and that the costs incurred in the High Court would eat up the family assets. The petitioner resisted the application on the grounds of delay, that seventeen orders had already been made in the High Court, that the respondent was covert in relation to his affairs, that he travelled widely on business, that there would be considerable delay in hearings in Cork and that the High Court was the appropriate venue for the case having regard to the respondent's wealth (his assets exceeding £1.8 m). The High Court had refused to remit the action, and the Supreme Court upheld this decision on appeal.

While the Court held that the delay in seeking the order to remit was not such as to weigh against the respondent, the issue of delay in general in the case was an important factor in considering the interests of justice. The Court held that time was an important aspect of this case; also important was access to court for interim and interlocutory applications to process the case, the probability being that proceedings in Cork would take longer. The court had a discretion and that discretion should be exercised to remit if that be in the interests of justice, but in the circumstances the refusal to remit was just. Delivering a concurring judgment, Barron J. commented on a specific aspect of the case, namely that the petitioner had repeatedly sought discovery in the case. His view (supported by Barrington J.) was that, instead of bringing a motion for discovery when such a motion would otherwise be appropriate, the party should instead press on with the hearing and at the same time warn the other party of the failure to make full disclosure at the time.

RULES OF COURT

The following rules of court were made in 2000.

District Court   The following Rules were made in 2000 concerning the District Court.

Attachment and committal The District Court (Attachment and Committal) Rules 2000 (S.I. No.196 of 2000) amended Order 46B of the District Court Rules 1997, as inserted by the District Court (Attachment and Committal) Rules 1999, by the addition of a form of endorsement to orders of the District Court indicating the consequences of non-compliance with the order. They came into effect on July 27, 2000.

Offences against the State The District Court (Offences Against the State (Amendment) Act 1998) Rules 2000 (S.I. No.166 of 2000) amended Order 17 of the District Court Rules 1997 by the addition of an application and warrant to further detain a person arrested under section 30 of the Offences Against the State Act 1939, as amended by section 10 of the Offences Against the State (Amendment) Act 1998. They came into effect on June 12, 2000.

Revenue: venue The District Court (Taxes Consolidation Act, 1997) Rules 2000 (S.I. No.238 of 2000) substituted a new Order 38, rule 2(7) in the District Court Rules 1997 on the venue for an application to the District Court by an authorised officer of the Revenue Commissioners under section 908A of the Taxes Consolidation Act 1997, as inserted by section 207 of the Finance Act 1999, and amended by section 68 of the Finance Act 2000.) The came into effect on August 25, 2000.

Circuit Court   The following Rules were made in 2000 concerning the Circuit Court.

Domestic violence The Circuit Court Rules (No.1) (Domestic Violence Act 1996) 2000 (S.I. No.104 of 2000) provide for the making of applications under the Domestic Violence Act 1996. They came into effect on April 28, 2000.

Parental leave The Circuit Court Rules (No.2) (Parental Leave Act 1998) 2000 (S.I. No.208 of 2000) added a new Order 63C to the Circuit Court Rules 1950, and they prescribe procedures in respect of applications under section 22 of the Parental Leave Act 1998 for the enforcement of decisions of a Rights Commissioner or determinations of the Employment Appeals Tribunal pursuant to the 1998 Act. They came into effect on 28 July 2000.

High Court   The following Rules were made in 2000 concerning the High Court.

Family proceedings The Rules of the Superior Courts (No.4) (Amendment of Order 70A) 2000 (S.I. No.327 of 2000) substituted a new Order 70A, rule 28 into the Rules of the Superior Courts 1986 to the effect that the provisions of Order 119, rules 2 and 3 (insofar as they relate to the wearing of a wig and gown), shall not apply to any family law cause, action or proceeding under Order 70 or 70A of the 1986 Rules. They came into effect on November 19, 2000.

Powers of attorney The Rules of the Superior Courts (No.1) (Powers of Attorney Act 1996) 2000 (S.I. No.66 of 2000) inserted a new Order 129 into the Rules of the Superior Courts 1986 and prescribe procedures in relation to enduring powers of attorney under the 1996 Act. They came into effect on March 8, 2000.

Taxation review The Rules of the Superior Courts (No.3) (Documentation for Review of Taxation) 2000 (S.I. No.329 of 2000) amended Order 99, rule 28(5) of the Rules of the Superior Courts 1986 and removed the requirement on the Taxing Master, on an application for an Order to review taxation of costs, to transmit to the High Court with his report the original Bill of Costs, notice of objections and any other material documentation. Instead, the party seeking a review of taxation must produce to the Court duly certified copies of such documentation. They came into effect on November 19, 2000.

Tender offer in lieu of lodgment The Rules of the Superior Courts (No.5) (Offer of Payment in Lieu of Lodgment) 2000 (S.I. No.328 of 2000) inserted a new Order 22, rule 14 into the Rules of the Superior Courts 1986. The new Rule provides for the making by qualified parties of an offer of tender of payment in lieu of lodging money in Court. The new provision came into effect on November 19, 2000. This is probably the most significant rule change for personal injuries actions in terms of its potential scope since the introduction of disclosure rules in 1997 (see Annual Review 1997, 593-8, and Annual Review 1998, 549-51). They can also be seen as part of the overall aim of providing for more effective access to civil justice. Although not as revolutionary in scope as the UK Woolf Reforms, they indicate some steps are being taken in this area.

Courts-Martial Appeal Court The Rules of the Superior Courts (No.2) (Courts-Martial Appeal Court Rules (Amendment)) 2000 (S.I. No.105 of 2000) amended rules 4(1) and rule 8 of the Courts-Martial Appeal Court Rules 1993, which, as amended, have now been inserted into the Rules of the Superior Courts 1986 as Order 86A. They came into effect on April 28, 2000.

SERVICE OUT

Sovereign immunity In *Adams v. Director of Public Prosecutions*, High Court, April 12 2000; Supreme Court, March 6, 2001, the High Court and, on appeal, the Supreme Court held that the British Home Secretary was entitled to claim sovereign immunity in a case that had an extradition background. The applicant had been extradited from Northern Ireland to face larceny charges, on which he was convicted and sentenced. On his release, he was charged on a number of counts of rape and sexual assault. It was accepted that, under the rule of speciality which applies under the Extradition Act 1965, such charges could not have been brought without the issuing of a waiver by the British Home Secretary. The necessary waiver had been issued. The applicant applied for judicial review, seeking an order of prohibition. In the course of the application, he sought to serve the proceedings on the Home Secretary. On an *ex parte* application to the High Court, leave to serve under Order 11 of the Rules of the Superior Courts 1986 was granted. The Home Secretary then applied to set aside the order and to dismiss the proceedings against him. The High Court and, on appeal, the Supreme Court acceded to the application.

In the High Court, Kelly J. noted that (as set out in *Brennan v. Lockyer* [1932] I.R. 100) the only circumstances in which the court could exercise the 'exorbitant jurisdiction' permitting service of its process outside the State were those contemplated by O.11 of the 1986 Rules. In the instant case, he considered that there was no ground for arguing that, by issuing the waiver, the Home Secretary had impliedly waived his entitlement to sovereign immunity. Citing the decision of McCracken J. in *Voluntary Purchasing Groups Inc v. Insurco*

Ltd. [1995] 2 I.L.R.M. 145 (Annual Review 1995, 389), he held that it would be unjust to deny a party, against whom an *ex parte* order had been made, the opportunity of applying to the court to set it aside. He added that it was wrong that, in the *ex parte* application, the court's attention had not been drawn to the relevant legislation and case law which would have indicated that service out was precluded. Kelly J. set aside the order granting leave to bring proceedings against the Home Secretary as well as the direction authorising service on the British ambassador in Dublin. In addition, any purported service in London was null and void. On appeal, the Supreme Court in 2001 dismissed the appeal, holding that the Irish courts had no jurisdiction to review the powers exercised by the Home Secretary, since he was exercising powers conferred on him by United Kingdom legislation. The Court held that it was unsustainable to suggest that Irish legislation, namely the Extradition Act 1965, had created this power. Having dismissed the appeal, the Court noted that that the applicant was free to pursue his claim in this jurisdiction against the remaining respondents and, if necessary, to pursue any challenge in the United Kingdom against the Home Secretary.

SUPREME COURT

Constitutional issues not raised in High Court   In two cases, the Supreme Court emphasised that while in exceptional circumstances it would consider constitutional issues which had not been argued in the High Court, this jurisdiction would be exercised sparingly. In *Blehein v. Murphy* [2000] 1 I.L.R.M. 481, the plaintiff had been refused leave by the High Court pursuant to section 260 of the Mental Treatment Act 1945 to issue proceedings against the respondents, two doctors, his wife and three members of the Garda Síochána in respect of his admission to hospital in 1987. On appeal, he sought to amend his notice of appeal to the Supreme Court in order to include a claim that section 260 was invalid having regard to the provisions of the Constitution. He further sought to adjourn the hearing of the appeal in order that he could serve notice on the Attorney General under Order 60, rule 1 of the Rules of the Superior Courts 1986. The defendants contended that the issue of the constitutionality of section 260 had not been raised by the plaintiff in the High Court, and that he was attempting to begin a constitutional action on appeal. The Supreme Court refused the applicant leave to amend his grounds of appeal.

The Court stated that the parties, including the Attorney General, had the right to have issues argued fully in the High Court. The Court accepted that, in exceptional circumstances, such as those in *Attorney General (SPUC Ltd) v. Open Door Counselling Ltd(No.2)* [1994] 2 I.R. 333 (Annual Review 1993, 160, 440, 446), it would consider issues of constitutional law which had not been argued in the High Court. But it held that there were no exceptional circumstances in the present case to invoke the exception to the rule and it noted that Article 34.3.2 of the Constitution did not envisage that cases would routinely raise the issue of the validity of a law for the first time in the Supreme Court. Finally, the Court noted that the Mental Treatment Act 1945 enjoyed a presumption of constitutionality as it was passed after the enactment of the Constitution of Ireland 1937.

In *Dunnes Stores (Ireland) Co v. Ryan*, Supreme Court, February 8, 2000, the Court took a similar line, albeit against a slightly different background. The applicant had instituted judicial review proceedings seeking, *inter alia*, an order of *certiorari* quashing the decision of the second respondent (the Minister for Enterprise, Trade and Employment) to appoint the first respondent as an authorised officer under the Companies Act 1990 to examine the books and records of the applicant. The applicant also sought a declaration that section 19 of the 1990 Act, under which the appointment was made, was invalid having regard to the provisions of the Constitution. The High Court found that the first respondent had been validly appointed but that he had then acted unreasonably in the manner in which he went about examining the records. On appeal and cross-appeal, the Supreme Court set aside the High Court order in its entirety and remitted the proceedings to the High Court for a determination of the issues in respect of which leave to apply for judicial review had been granted, including, if necessary, the constitutional issues.

The Court accepted the correctness of the principle in *Murphy v. Roche* [1987] I.R. 106 (Annual Review 1987, 83-5) and *Brady v. Donegal County Council* [1989] I.L.R.M. 282 (Annual Review 1988, 125) that where the issues between parties could be determined and disposed of by the resolution of an issue of law other than constitutional law, the court should proceed to determine the other issue first. If that determination disposes of the case, then the Court should refrain from expressing any view on any constitutional issue that might have been raised. In the instant case, however, the Court noted that this was not the situation here. Once the High Court had concluded that the appointment of the first respondent was *intra vires* the 1990 Act, the Supreme Court held that the applicant was entitled to have the issue as to the constitutionality of section 19 of the 1990 Act determined. Since that did not happen in the High Court, it was not now open to the Supreme Court to determine an issue of constitutional law which had not been the subject of adjudication in the High Court. On that basis, the High Court order was set aside and the case remitted for a full re-hearing, as indicated above.

Prison Law

A most welcome publication in 2000 was Paul Anthony McDermott's *Prison Law* (Round Hall Ltd, 2000), a comprehensive discussion of prison law as it affects prisoners.

PRISON OFFICERS

Disciplinary procedures In *Sheriff v. Corrigan* [2001] 1 I.L.R.M. 67 (SC), the Supreme Court dismissed an application to review disciplinary action against the applicant, a prison officer. The applicant, then assistant chief officer in a prison, had become involved in a dispute in 1994 about a claim for expenses in the sum of £5.96 made by another officer which had, ultimately, been paid by the relevant clerical officer in the prison. The clerical officer had then queried the payment and the applicant had written a letter in response to this query, referring to the clerical officer as a 'scab', on the basis that he had passed an official picket during an industrial dispute by prison officers in 1988. The Minister for Justice instituted disciplinary action against the applicant, in which the applicant was charged with conduct to the prejudice of good order, contrary to rule 99 of the Rules for the Government of Prisons 1947. Although the applicant made an apology in writing, the Minister decided to downgrade the applicant to prison officer as a disciplinary penalty under rule 99. The High Court dismissed the applicant's judicial review claim, which was based on failure to comply with the rules of natural justice. The Supreme Court affirmed.

The Court accepted that, while the Minister's decision was administrative, the applicant's interests had been directly affected by the decision. Thus, the requirements of natural justice had to be met, in line with the particular circumstances of the case. In the instant case, the Court noted that while it was not best practice for the Minister to have before him papers of which the applicant was unaware (in this case the views of the prison governor), the requirements of natural justice were met in that the applicant was given due notice, informed of the relevant charge, the reasons and essential facts, and he was given a reasonable opportunity to present his response. There was no need in the circumstances of this case to have an oral hearing, and the penalty was not disproportionate.

TEMPORARY RELEASE

In *Corish v. Minister for Justice, Equality and Law Reform*, High Court, January 13, 2000 O'Neill J. held that the refusal of temporary release to a prisoner based on the category of prisoner was *ultra vires* the Criminal Justice Act 1960. The applicant had been refused temporary release from prison under the Temporary Release of Prisoners (Castlerea) Rules 1998 (made under the 1960 Act) on the grounds that it was the policy not to grant this 'to offenders serving sentences for the supply of drugs.' The applicant claimed that to refuse on the grounds of a category of persons who were ineligible was contrary to the 1998 Regulations, and, alternatively that the 1998 Regulations themselves were *ultra vires* section 2(1) of the 1960 Act. O'Neill J rejected the first argument but held with the applicant on the second.

He held that Article 4 of the 1998 Regulations empowered the Minister to deal with prisoners on a category basis and to apply a policy which affected a whole class of prisoners. But he also held that there was nothing in section 2 of the 1960 Act which allowed the Minister to deal with prisoners on a category basis. Rather, it was intended by the 1960 Act that prisoners be dealt with on an individual basis rather than by category. Thus, Article 4 of the 1998 Regulations was *ultra vires* the power conferred on the Minister in section 2(1) of the 1960 Act. It may be noted that the Criminal Justice (Temporary Release of Offenders) Bill 2001 seeks to provide further grounds on which the power in the 1960 Act may be exercised. We will return to this in a future Review when and if the 2001 Bill is enacted.

Restitution

EOIN O'DELL, Trinity College, Dublin.

THE PRINCIPLE AGAINST UNJUST ENRICHMENT

In the *Bricklayers' Hall* Case (*Dublin Corporation v. Building and Allied Trades Union* [1996] 1 I.R 468; [1996] 2 I.L.R.M. 547 (SC); on which see O'Dell [1996] *Restitution Law Review* §134; "Restitution and *Res Judicata* in the Irish Supreme Court" (1997) 113 *LQR* 245; "Bricks and Stones and the Structure of the Law of Restitution" (1998) 20 *D.U.L.J.* (*n.s.*) 101) Keane J. identified four "essential preconditions" for personal liability in restitution: whether there has been

> [(i)] an enrichment of the defendant [(ii)] at the expense of the plaintiff ... [(iii) in circumstances in which the enrichment can] be regarded as 'unjust' and [(iv)] whether there are any reasons why ... restitution should nevertheless be denied to the plaintiff. ([1996] 1 I.R. 468, 483-484; [1996] 2 ILRM 547, 557-558; see the 1996 Review, 502).

This principle against unjust enrichment (see O'Dell (1993) 15 *D.U.L.J.* (*n.s.*) 27) is at the heart of the modern law of restitution and will be used to organise the discussion of this year's cases.

AT THE PLAINTIFF'S EXPENSE

Restitution for wrongs Law Reform Commission *Report on Aggravated, Exemplary and Restitutionary Damages* (LRC 60-2000; LRC, Dublin, 2000) concluded "in favour of the availability of restitutionary damages in Irish law for all torts and breach of contract, in cases where the defendant has derived a profit from the commission of the tortious or contractual wrong against the plaintiff. The Commission does not recommend the enactment of legislation regarding restitutionary damages at this point, but considers that the development of the law in this area should be left to the common law ..." (para.6.48; pp.103). For the reasons given in the analysis of the Commission's prior *Paper* on the issue, this is entirely to be welcomed (see the discussion of the Law Reform Commission *Consultation Paper on Aggravated, Exemplary and Restitutionary Damages* (Law Reform Commission, Dublin, 1998) in the Annual Review 1998, 557-566). In principle, no one should be allowed to profit from wrongdoing, and damages in the restitution measure for tort or breach of contract (on which, see, *e.g.*, *AG v. Blake* [2001] 1 A.C. 268 (HL)) have the effect of stripping the wrongdoer of the profits of his wrongdoing.

UNJUST

Compulsory discharge An enrichment will *prima facie* be unjust where the plaintiff did not consent to the defendant's receipt thereof (see, *e.g.*, O'Dell (1998) 20 *D.U.L.J.* (*n.s.*) 101, 107-110, see Annual Review 1996, 518-519 and Annual Review 1999, 461-471). A plaintiff will not consent where he has been coerced; where he has been compelled to discharge the debt of another, the compulsion is the unjust factor, and the discharge of the defendant's debt constitutes the enrichment. Restitution for the compulsory discharge of the debt of another features in the background to *Hogan v. Steele and the ESB (notice party),* Supreme Court, November 1, 2000.

An employee was injured in the course of his employment with the notice party, who continued to pay him while he was out of work recovering. He had no automatic contractual entitlement to the payments in question, but there was a contractual obligation on the plaintiff to repay such amounts out of any damages for loss of earnings recovered from the defendant. In the High Court ([2000] 1 I.L.R.M. 330 (HC) (see Annual Review 1999, 465-471)) Macken J. had no difficulty in holding that "the plaintiff suffered a loss of earnings, that the defendant is obliged to pay the sums so lost to the plaintiff, and that plaintiff is, in turn, obliged to repay the same to the notice party" ([2000] 1 I.L.R.M. 330, 343). On appeal, the Supreme Court affirmed.

In both courts, the question was faintly raised whether, if the employee had no contractual duty to repay his employer, the employer might nevertheless have an alternative claim. In the Supreme Court, Keane C.J. (Hardiman and Geoghegan JJ. concurring) approved the views of Kingsmill-Moore J. in *Attorney General v. Ryan's Car Hire Limited* [1965] I.R. 642 (SC) that "a tortfeasor ordinarily is only responsible in damages for the direct injury which he has caused to the person against whom the tort has been committed and not for indirect injuries to a third person who may suffer loss indirectly as a result of the injury to the first person. To this rule there are two exceptions in common law ... [which] in my opinion should not be enlarged" to include the kind of claim which the employer sought to make in *Ryan*; the employer in *Hogan* sought to make a similar claim which similarly failed. It last year's Review it was argued that the law of restitution provided no route by which the employer could recover from the tortfeasor: if the employer is not compelled to pay the employee's wages, but does (as in *Hogan v. Steele* itself) then there is no unjust factor of compulsion; whilst, if the employer is compelled to pay the employee (as often happens), then the employee suffers no loss for which the defendant tortfeasor can be liable, the employer's payment of the wages does not discharge any debt owed by the defendant, and there is thus no enrichment. The absence of enrichment in such a case was confirmed by the Supreme Court in *Attorney General v. Ryan's Car Hire Limited* (on which see the discussion in (1998) 20 *D.U.L.J.* (*n.s.*) 101, 111-113). Hence, there is no cause of action in restitution to set up a possible third exception to the general rule stated in *Ryan* and approved in *Hogan*. (Finally, for the sake of completeness, it should be noted that it was also concluded in last year's review that there is no cause of action in restitution by the employer against the employee based on the unjust factor of failure of consideration).

PROPRIETARY CLAIMS

Unjust enrichment of the defendant, at the expense of the plaintiff, simply gives rise to a personal obligation on the part of the defendant to make restitution to the plaintiff of the value of the enrichment received. It is, therefore, *prima facie* a legal personal claim. It does not give rise to a proprietary obligation to hold the very thing received for the plaintiff. For such a proprietary claim, there must be something more than merely an unjust enrichment of the plaintiff at the expense of the plaintiff, or there must be something else which would give rise to a separate but parallel proprietary claim (see (1998) 20 *D.U.L.J.* (*n.s.*) 101, 160-180).

The trust is often pressed into service to justify proprietary restitution. The controversial speech of Lord Browne-Wilkinson in *Westdeutsche Landesbank Girozentrale v. Islington LBC* [1996] A.C. 669, 705 identifies the defendant's knowledge of the plaintiff's claim as a sufficient reason to elevate the plaintiff's personal claim to a proprietary one by means of a constructive trust. Again, if subrogation or resulting trusts are restitutionary (see, respectively, Mitchell, *The Law of Subrogation,* (Oxford, 1994); Chambers, *Resulting Trusts,* (Oxford, 1997)) then satisfaction of their terms provides the additional element to elevate the plaintiff's claim. If, however, they are not restitutionary, then they provide alternative separate but parallel proprietary claims, potentially restitutionary in pattern, but not responding to unjust enrichment.

In *Barclays Bank v. Quistclose Investments*, Lord Wilberforce held that arrangements "for the payment of a person's creditors by a third person [can] give rise to a relationship of a fiduciary character or trust, in favour, as a primary trust, of the creditors, and secondarily, if the primary trust fails, of the third person" ([1970] A.C. 567, 581). This is a formulation which has been followed in courts in Canada (see Klinck "The *Quistclose* Trust in Canada" (1994) 23 *Can. Bus. L.J.* 45), New Zealand (the leading case is *General Communications v. Development Finance Corporation of New Zealand* [1990] 3 N.Z.L.R. 406 (NZ HC and CA); on the High Court judgment, see Maxton "The *Quistclose* Trust in New Zealand" (1989) 13 *N.Z.U.L.R.* 303; see also *Re Securitibank Ltd* [1978] 1 N.Z.L.R. 97 (NZ HA: Barker J); *Foreman v. Hazard* [1984] 1

386 *Annual Review of Irish Law 2000*

N.Z.L.R. 586 (NZ CA); *Dines Construction Ltd v. Perry Dines Corporation* (1989) 4 N.Z.C.L.C. 65,298 (NZ HC; Ellis J)) and Australia, where it has been approved in the High Court (*Daly v. Sydney Stock Exchange* (1985-1986) 160 C.L.R. 371 (HCA) 379-380 *per* Gibbs C.J.; *Australasian Conference Association Ltd v. Mainline Constructions Pty Ltd* (1976-1978) 141 C.L.R. 335 (HCA) 353 *per* Gibbs A.C.J. (Jacobs and Murphy JJ. concurring)) and applied in many important lower court decisions (see, especially, in *In re Associated Securities Ltd* [1981] 1 N.S.W.L.R. 743; *Ausintel Investments Australia Pty Ltd v. Lam* (1990) 19 N.S.W.L.R. 637 (NSW CA); *Re Australian Elizabethan Theatre Trust* (1991) 102 A.L.R. 681; see generally Rickett "Different Views on the Scope of the *Quistclose* Analysis: English and Antipodean Insights" (1991) 107 *L.Q.R.* 608; on the last case, see also Burns "The *Quistclose* Trust: Intention and the Express Private Trust" (1992) 18 *Monash U.L.R.* 147).

Quistclose was early approved and applied in Northern Ireland (see *In re McKeown* [1974] N.I. 226 (Q.B.D.; Lord MacDermott)) but its progress in Ireland has been fitful. *In re Kayford Ltd (In Liquidation)* [1975] 1 W.L.R. 279 – a case which is not strictly speaking an application of *Quistclose* (see, *e.g.*, Rickett (1991) 107 *L.Q.R.* 608, 609) though it is a close cousin which is often treated with it (see, *e.g.*, *In re Goldcorp Exchange* [1995] 1 A.C. 74 (PC) 100 *per* Lord Mustill) – was applied by Kenny J. in *Murphy Bros v. Morris* (1963-1993) Ir.Co.L.Rep. 99 (October 6, 1975), whilst this case and *Carreras Rothmans Ltd v. Freeman Mathews Treasure Ltd* [1985] 1 Ch. 207 (Ch. D. ; Peter Gibson J.) – an important application of *Quistclose* – were applied by Costello J. in *Glow Heating v. Eastern Health Board* (1988) 6 *I.L.T.* 237 (March 4, 1988). Furthermore, in *Jackson v. Lombard and Ulster Bank* [1992] 1 I.R. 94, a bank lent money to a broker to allow the company for which it was acting to pay insurance premiums. The brokers paid the premia, but the company encountered financial difficulties, and the broker negotiated the cancellation of the policies and obtained a partial refund of the premia. The plaintiff had been appointed receiver of the firm, pursuant to a 1985 debenture, and sought the repaid premiums in priority to the defendant bank. In the course of holding that they were caught by the debenture on foot of which the receiver had been appointed containing a valid fixed charge over "book debts and other debts", Costello J. rejected an argument for the bank that the broker held the money on trust for the bank ([1992] 1 I.R. 94, 101-102). The trust pleaded by the bank was plainly a *Quistclose* trust, and it failed not in principle but on the facts (a claim of similar structure was unsuccessful in *Re Miles* (1988) 85 A.L.R. 218, but successful in *Re McKeown* (above) and *Re EVTR* [1987] B.C.L.C. 646 (CA); noted Maxton "A Further Endorsement of the *Quistclose* Trust: *Re EVTR*" [1988] *N.Z.L.J.* 31). *Quistclose* itself was mentioned in argument before the Supreme Court in the *Bricklayers' Hall* case, though not in the decision of Keane J. But, taken together, these cases constituted powerful evidence that the wind was blowing strongly in favour of an Irish judicial approval of *Quistclose* at an appropriate opportunity.

That opportunity arose in *In re Money Markets International Stockbrokers Ltd.*, High Court, October 20, 2000, Carroll J. Money Markets International, a stockbroker, negotiated a call option on shares from K and H Options Ltd in favour of some of its clients. MMI debited the relevant clients' accounts, but made no corresponding payment to K and H. In the winding up of MMI, K and H argued that MMI held the relevant payments on trust for them. Carroll J. rejected this argument.

Section 52 of the Stock Exchange Act, 1995 requires brokers to lodge client funds to client accounts, and section 52(5)(a) (as amended by section 78 of the Investor Compensation Act 1998) provides that "[n]o liquidator … or creditor … shall have or obtain any recourse or right against a client's money … until all proper claims of the client … against the client's money … have been satisfied in full". In an earlier decision in the Money Markets winding up, Laffoy J. held that "… the effect of section 52(5)(a) is to ring-fence the funds in the client money bank account and preserve them for the client creditors who provided them. … The entire fund [in the client account] is impressed with a trust in favour of the client creditors of MMI and the plaintiff has and will have no recourse or right against any part of that fund, save in the unlikely eventuality that there is a surplus after satisfaction in full of all proper claims of the client creditors" (*In re Money Markets International Stockbrokers Ltd* [2000] 3 I.R. 437, 447-448; see also 454). The clear and unambiguous meaning of the section was "that the beneficial claims of client creditors have to be satisfied in full before anybody else, even a contributor to the ultimate balance, has a call on the funds" ([2000] 3 I.R. 437, 449-450).

Section 52(7)(a) (as amended by section 64 of the Investor Compensation Act 1998) similarly provides that "[n]o liquidator … or creditor … of an investment business firm shall have or obtain any recourse or right against clients money … until all proper claims of clients … against client money … have been satisfied in full". Carroll J. interpreted section 57(2)(a) consistently with Laffoy J.'s interpretation of section 57(5)(a) and therefore excluded the claim of the creditors before her. Given that the subsections apply equally to exclude the claims of a "liquidator … or creditor" then this must be right. In the claim before Laffoy J., the liquidator had sought to argue that some of the money in the client account was in fact owned by MMI, but Laffoy J. rejected this claim on the basis of the wording of the statute. Similarly, in the claim before Carroll J., the outside creditor, K and H, had sought to argue that some of the money in the client account was in fact held in trust from them, but following Laffoy J.'s lead, Carroll J. rejected this claim on the basis of the wording of the statute (though it has to be said that Carroll J. did admit, *obiter*, to a slightly less absolutist view of the relevant subsection, it was in a respect which does not touch upon the issues which arose in the case itself).

However, even on the text of section 52(5)(a) and section 52(7)(a), there may in fact be a relevant difference between the two cases. What is ring-fenced, according to the subsections is "client's money" (section 52(5)(a)) or "client money" (section 52(7)(a)) (the slight difference in wording arises for grammatical reasons having to do with the construction of the subsections; there is no substantive difference between them). When MMI allowed to remain in the account money which they were otherwise entitled to withdraw, on the application of the principle that a fiduciary must be taken to have acted consistently with fiduciary duties, MMI must be taken to have intended to make up the shortfall in the account, and therefore the money left by MMI in the account became client money. For example, in *In re Hallett's Estate* (1880) 13 Ch. D. 696 (CA) an insolvent solicitor had misappropriated funds from his marriage settlement and a client, and the Court of Appeal held that they were able to trace the funds into the bank account into which they had been lodged. Jessel MR held that "[w]henever an act can be done rightfully the man who has done it is not allowed to say, as against the persons entitled to the property or the right, that he has done it wrongfully. That is the universal law. ... where a man does an act which may be rightfully performed, he cannot say that the act was intentionally and in fact done wrongly" ((1880) 13 Ch. D. 696, 727). Hence, when Hallett withdrew from the mixed fund in the bank account, it was "perfectly plain that he cannot be heard to say that he took away the trust money when he had a right to take away his own money" (*ibid.*, see also *Shanahan's Stamp Auctions v. Farrelly* [1962] I.R. 386 (HC) 425-429, 443 *per* Budd J.; *In re Irish Shipping* [1986] I.L.R.M. 518 (HC) 521, 523 *per* Carroll J.). Conversely, where a solicitor, having dissipated trust funds, then makes further lodgements to the account, "the only possible inference is that [the solicitor] intended the [lodgment] to be a replacement of moneys which he had wrongfully withdrawn from the client account" (*Re Hughes* [1970] I.R. 237, 242 *per* Kenny J.). In both cases, the fiduciary solicitor is taken to have acted consistently with his fiduciary duties, in not withdrawing trust funds (*Hallett*) or in reconstituting the trust (*Hughes*). Similarly, in the application in *Money Markets International* before Laffoy J., the stockbroker must be taken to have acted consistently with its fiduciary duties in making up the shortfall at which it allowed the client account to operate (on MMI's operation of the account, see [2000] 3 I.R. 437, 447-448). In which case, the money that it left in the client account becomes "client's money" against which, by virtue of section 52(5)(a), it has no claim.

However, if the argument on behalf of K and H in the application before Carroll J. were correct that MMI held money on trust for them, it is difficult to see how it could properly have constituted "client money" for the purposes of section 52(7)(a). Indeed, the attraction of the trust for claimants against an insolvency is that the property is owned in equity by the beneficiary of the trust and thus brings such a claim outside the ambit of the liquidation (see, e.g., *Shanahan's Stamp Auctions v. Farrelly* [1962] I.R. 386, 444-445, 448 *per* Budd J; Oakley, "Proprietary Claims and Their Priority in Insolvency" [1995] *C.L.J.* 377). Hence, the money claimed by MMI in the application before Laffoy

J. could never have been anything except client's money, whereas the argument on behalf of M and H before Carroll J. raises this question squarely. Of course, it may be that the effect of the statutory regime embodied in section 52 (as amended) is to preclude even trust claims against the client account, but because of the point of distinction between the issues before Laffoy J. and Carroll J., more was required in the latter application than simply applying the decision in the former. However, since Carroll J. also held that no trust in fact arose this distinction falls away on the facts, but its impact could be crucial in a future case in which a creditor could otherwise assert a trust claim against the client account.

K and H had argued that, when MMI debited approximately £321,620 from the individual clients' accounts in respect of the options purchased from K and H, this had the effect of crystallising K and H's interest in the money which was therefore held by MMI on resulting or constructive trust for them. Carroll J. held that the debit entry in an individual client account could not be construed as a declaration of trust. MMI had no authority to create a trust, and none of the clients themselves created any trust in favour of K and H. Since the money was never paid out in accordance with the terms of section 52 of the 1995 Act (as amended) it never ceased to be client funds. In particular, she held that no *Quistclose* trust arose because no special fund for the money had been created (in this respect, distinguishing *Quistclose*, *Carreras Rothmans*, and *General Communications*). The importance of this holding is that *Quistclose* and its progeny were accepted and applied, although no such trust arose on the facts. This stage of the *Money Markets International* liquidation then is the express Irish adoption of the *Quistclose* principle.

Although a segregated fund is often useful in determining whether a trust exists (see, *e.g.*, *Walker v. Corboy* (1990) 19 N.S.W.L.R. 382 (NSW CA)), and this applies in particular in the context of a *Quistclose* trust (see, *e.g.*, *Re Nanwa Gold Mines Ltd* [1955] 3 All E.R. 219 (Ch. D., Harman J.); *Re Australian Elizabethan Theatre Trust* (1991) 102 A.L.R. 681, 689 *per* Gummow J.), this is not necessary in either context (see, *e.g.*, *Commissioner of Inland Revenue v. Smith* [2000] 2 N.Z.L.R. 147 (NA CA) (statutory express trust, account not necessary); *Stephens Travel Service International Pty Ltd v. Qantas Airways* (1988) 13 N.S.W.L.R. 331 (NSW CA) (*Quistclose* trust, no segregated account). The key to this issue resides in the intentions of the parties, and segregation into a separate bank account is merely one fact – albeit an important one – from which an inference that the parties intended a trust can be drawn: as Megarry J. put it in In Re *Kayford* "[p]ayment into a separate bank account is a useful (*though by no means conclusive*) indication of an intention to create a trust ..." ([1975] 1 W.L.R. 279, 282, emphasis added; see also *Thiess Watkins White Ltd v. Equiticorp Australia Ltd* [1991] 1 Qd. R. 82, 84 *per* de Jersey J.). The absence of a separate fund then at best raises an inference that the parties did not intend a trust, and in *Money Markets*, this inference would have been reinforced by all of the other considerations referred to by Carroll J: in particular, as she interpreted the effect of section 52, the money coming from the client account had to be paid to K and H or it remained client money; no "halfway house arrangement" by which a trust arose over money in the account was possible under the legislation.

However, though now established as an element of Irish law, there are still many unanswered questions regarding the operation of the *Quistclose* trust. For example, when can the lender enforce the primary trust against the borrower and when can the intended beneficiary of the loan do so. Millett's prescription (Millett "The *Quistclose* Trust: Who Can Enforce It?" (1985) 101 *L.Q.R.* 269) was adopted by the New Zealand Court of Appeal in *General Communications*, which was referred to but not analysed by Carroll J., though it seems not to have attracted itself to the Court of Appeal in *Twinsectra Ltd v. Yardley* [1999] Lloyds Rep. Bank. 438 (CA).

Again, Birks has argued that the secondary trust in the *Quistclose* relationship is restitutionary (see Birks, *An Introduction to the Law of Restitution,*(Oxford, 1989) 225-226, 387, 461-462) and he has been followed in this by Chambers (*Resulting Trusts*, chapter 3). If so, then *Quistclose* provides one example of the additional elements necessary to elevate a plaintiff's otherwise personal claim to a proprietary one. Indeed, some aspect of this debate might have been before Carroll J., as immediately after rejecting the plaintiff's claim based upon *Quistclose*, she commented that "it is not possible to impose a constructive trust on the grounds of unjust enrichment or any other equitable ground". No equitable doctrine other than *Quistclose* is considered in her judgment, so it may be that she considered this sentence as a further reason why the *Quistclose* claim failed. If so, then this sentence constitutes tentative Irish judicial support for the Birks/Chambers view of the *Quistclose* trust. On the other hand, Worthington (*Proprietary Interests in Commercial Transactions* (Oxford, 1996) chapter 3) sees both limbs as based on the parties' mutual intentions and hence not restitutionary, whilst the essentials of the analysis from which Birks struck out to *Quistclose* have been challenged by Mee, *The Property Rights of Cohabitees,* (Hart, 1999) 256-260, though without reference to Birks' extension of the analysis to *Quistclose*. There is merit in these criticisms; after all, the key fact for Lord Wilberforce in enforcing a secondary trust in *Quistclose* itself was the mutual intentions of the parties ([1970] A.C. 567, 580-582). If they are correct, then the secondary *Quistclose* trust is not restitutionary; it would not then respond to unjust enrichment, but it would provide an alternative separate but parallel proprietary claim. The resolution of these – and other related – issues now awaits the Irish courts in the wake of the adoption of the *Quistclose* analysis by Carroll J. in *Money Markets International*.

Safety and Health

CHEMICALS

General chemical safety The European Communities (Classification, Packaging, Labelling and Notification of Dangerous Substances) Regulations 2000 (S.I. No. 393 of 2000) gave effect in consolidated form to Directive 67/548/EEC on the classification, packaging and labelling of dangerous substances, that is, single chemicals, as most recently amended in 2000 by Directive 00/32/EC. They revoked and replaced the European Communities (Classification, Packaging, Labelling and Notification of Dangerous Substances) Regulations 1994 to 1998 (see Annual Review 1998, 570) and came into effect on November 29, 2000. The Classification, Packaging and Labelling Regulations (CPL Regulations) require manufacturers of chemicals to notify the Health and Safety Authority where new chemicals are placed on the market and to submit detailed technical dossiers on the chemicals (this requirement has been in place in preceding Regulations since 1981). They also require manufacturers of all chemicals to classify chemicals according to the criteria (explosive, flammable etc) in the 1967 Directive, as amended, to package and label them in accordance with the requirements of the 1967 Directive and to ensure that appropriate Material Safety Data Sheets (MSDSs) are provided to users.

The European Communities (Dangerous Substances and Preparations (Marketing and Use) Regulations 2000 (S.I. No.107 of 2000) gave effect in consolidated form to Council Directive 76/769/EEC on the marketing and use of chemicals and preparations, that is single chemicals and chemical compounds, as most recently amended by Directives 99/43/EC, 99/51/EC and 99/77/EC. They revoked and replaced the European Communities (Dangerous Substances and Preparations (Marketing and Use) Regulations 1998 and came into effect on April 5, 2000. By contrast with the CPL Regulations, above, the Marketing and Use Regulations are primarily confined to imposing complete bans on certain chemicals, such as PCBs and PCTs, or imposing severe restrictions on their use, such as excluding the use of certain chemicals in toys.

Cosmetics The European Communities (Cosmetic Products) (Amendment) Regulations 2000, the European Communities (Cosmetic Products) (Amendment) (No.2) Regulations 2000 (S.I. No. 150 of 2000) and the European Communities (Cosmetic Products) (Amendment) (No.3) Regulations 2000 (S.I.

No. 203 of 2000) amended the European Communities (Cosmetic Products) (Amendment) Regulations 1997 (Annual Review1997, 666-7) to implement further Directives updating the principal EC Directive on the manufacture, marketing and sale of cosmetic products, 76/768/EEC. The (No.3) Regulations gave effect to Directive 2000/41/EC, which postponed the date on which the ban on the testing of animals in respect of any ingredient or combination of ingredients used in cosmetic products comes into force. The Regulations are overseen by the Irish Medicines Board.

Petrol stores The Dangerous Substances (Retail and Private Petroleum Stores) (Amendment) Regulations 1999 (S.I. No.424 of 1999), made under the Dangerous Substances Act 1972, amended the Dangerous Substances (Retail and Private Petroleum Stores) Regulations 1979 in order to provide enhanced safety requirements in certain circumstances for petrol filling stations constructed before the 1979 Regulations came into effect. They also enable such older outlets to be licensed on a transitional basis until December 31, 2001, while ensuring the maintenance of safety management controls. The Regulations came into effect on January 1, 2000.

FOOD SAFETY

(See also Agriculture and Food Chapter, *supra*, 8).

Beef: standards and traceability The National Beef Assurance Scheme Act 2000 provided for the establishment of the National Beef Assurance Scheme. The scheme was enacted against the background of the BSE crisis in the agri-food sector and the need to reinforce consumer confidence in this area. The 2000 Act provides for the development of common standards for the production, processing and trade in Irish cattle and beef for human consumption and for the manufacture and trade of feedingstuffs. This is being done through a process of registration, inspection and approval under the auspices of An Bord Bia, the Food Board, and also through improved animal identification and traceability for Irish cattle. The National Beef Assurance Scheme Act 2000 (Commencement) Order 2000 (S.I. No.130 of 2000) brought Part V of the Act into effect on May 29, 2000. The National Beef Assurance Scheme Act 2000 (Commencement) (No.2) Order 2000 (S.I. No.414 of 2000) brought sections 20 to 22 of the Act into effect on December 22, 2000.

Extraction solvents in foodstuffs The European Communities (Extraction Solvents in Foodstuffs and Food Ingredients) Regulations 2000 (S.I. No.141 of 2000) gave effect to the 'Framework' Directive, 88/344/EEC, as amended by Directives 92/115/EEC, 94/115/EC and 97/60/EC. They specify by name the substances which may be used as extraction solvents and their condition of use. The 2000 Regulations revoked the Health (Extraction Solvent in Foodstuffs) Regulation 1995 (Annual Review 1995, 441) and came into effect on May 25, 2000.

Infant foods   The European Communities (Processed Cereal-Based Foods and Baby Foods for Infants and Young Children) Regulations 2000 (S.I. No.142 of 2000) gave effect to Directive 96/5/EC, as amended by Directive 98/36/EC and Directive 99/39/EC. They revoked the European Communities (Processed Cereal-Based Foods and Baby Foods for Infants and Young Children) Regulations 1998 (Annual Review 1998, 572) and came into effect on May 25, 2000.

Labelling and packaging   The European Communities (Labelling, Presentation and Advertising of Foodstuffs) Regulations 2000 (S.I. No.92 of 2000) consolidated with amendments the implementation of Directive 79/112/EEC, as amended, the 'Framework' Directive in this area. The 1979 Directive, as amended, requires food labelling to conform with certain requirements to provide consumers with information on the nature and characteristics of certain foodstuffs, such as lists of ingredients, storage conditions, the 'best before' or 'use by' date, depending on the nature of the food and lot or batch numbering. They revoked and replaced the European Communities (Labelling, Presentation and Advertising of Foodstuffs) Regulations 1982 to 1997 and came into effect on March 29, 2000. They precede the ongoing debate at EU level on the labelling of GM foods, on which legislative proposals are being prepared by the European Commission.

Food premises: hygiene standards   The European Communities (Hygiene of Foodstuffs) Regulations 2000 (S.I. No. 165 of 2000) gave effect to Directive 93/43/EEC, as amended by Directives 96/3/EC and 98/28/EC on the hygiene of foodstuffs and lay down comprehensive food hygiene obligations on proprietors of any food business, whether public or private. They came into effect on June 7, 2000 and revoked and replaced the European Communities (Hygiene of Foodstuffs) Regulations 1998 (Annual Review 1998, 571). The definition of food business includes the preparation, processing, manufacturing, packaging, storing, transportation, distribution, handling or offering for sale or supply of foodstuffs. The 2000 Regulations, like their 1998 predecessors, are more comprehensive in scope than the Food Hygiene Regulations 1950, as amended, though no reference whatsoever is contained in the 2000 Regulations to the 1950 Regulations. Be that as it may, the 2000 Regulations may be seen as a radical transformation on this area. They impose a general duty on the proprietor of a food business to carry out the business in a hygienic way. The Regulations also set out detailed requirements concerning the premises in general, rooms where food is prepared, foodstuffs, transportation, equipment, food waste, water supply, personal hygiene and training of staff. Proprietors must ensure that a system of Hazard Analysis and Critical Control Points (HACCP) is developed and maintained. The Food Safety Authority of Ireland is also empowered to issue Guides to Good Hygiene Practice under the 2000 Regulations (under the 1998 Regulations, this was the function of the Minister for Health). The 2000 Regulations, in giving effect to Directive 96/3/EC, lay down requirements to ensure the protection of the public health and safety of food in the case of the bulk carriage of cooking oils or fats by sea. Unlike with the Food Hygiene Regulations 1950, responsibility for enforcement of the 2000 Regulations is in the hands of the Food Safety Authority of Ireland, unlike the position under the 1998 Regulations which imposed this duty on health boards, and in particular environmental health officers.

LABORATORIES

General The European Communities (Good Laboratory Practice) (Amendment) Regulations 1999 (S.I. No.294 of 1999) amended the European Communities (Good Laboratory Practice) Regulations 1991 (Annual Review 1991, 367) to give legal effect to Directives 1999/11/EC and 1999/12/EC. They also take into account the change of name of the Irish Laboratory Accreditation Board (ILAB) to the National Accreditation Board (NAB), the body responsible for accrediting laboratories for the purposes of the 1991 Regulations. The 1999 Regulations came into effect on September 17, 1999.

MANUFACTURING STANDARDS

Explosive atmospheres The European Communities (Equipment and Protective Systems Intended for Use in Potentially Explosive Atmospheres) Regulations 1999 (S.I. No.83 of 1999) implemented the 1994 Directive on Equipment and Protective Systems Intended for Use in Potentially Explosive Atmospheres, 94/7/EC, setting down the technical standards for such equipment.

Pressure equipment The European Communities (Pressure Equipment) Regulations 1999 (S.I. No.400 of 1999) implemented the 1997 Directive on Pressure Equipment, 97/23/EC, setting down the technical standards for such equipment. They came into effect on December 16, 1999.

MARINE SAFETY

Irish Water Safety Association The Irish Water Safety Association (Establishment) Order 1999 (S.I. No.361 of 1999), made under the Local

Government Services (Corporate Bodies) Act 1971, established the Irish Water Safety Association as a corporate body with effect from November 26, 1999. It enables the Association to provide services to the Minister for the Environment and Local Government, and local authorities, in relation to the promotion of public awareness of water safety, the advancement of education in relation to the prevention of accidents in water and other services relating to water safety.

OCCUPATIONAL SAFETY

Asbestos The European Communities (Protection of Workers) (Exposure to Asbestos) (Amendment) Regulations 2000 (S.I. No.74 of 2000) amended the European Communities (Protection of Workers) (Exposure to Asbestos) Regulations 1989 and 1993 (Annual Review 1989, 378, and Annual Review 1993, 505) in order to further implement Article 7 of Directive 87/217/EEC on the prevention and reduction of environmental pollution by asbestos. They also amend the requirements of the plan provided for in the 1989 Regulations which must be prepared prior to any demolition work involving asbestos. They also extend the length of time that medical records and the occupational health register must be maintained from 30 years to 40 years. The 2000 Regulations came into effect on March 23, 2000.

Fishing The Safety, Health and Welfare at Work (Fishing Vessels) Regulations 1999 (S.I. No. 325 of 1999), made under the Safety, Health and Welfare at Work Act 1989 (Annual Review 1989, 379-93), belatedly implemented Directive 93/103/EEC on the minimum health and safety requirements applicable to work on board fishing vessels. In view of the unusual employment relationships in fishing, especially share fishing, the 1999 Regulations are not confined to imposing duties on employers and employees, but also focus on the duties of self-employed persons. They came into effect on October 19, 1999.

Major accident hazards The European Communities (Control of Major Accident Hazards Involving Dangerous Substances) Regulations 2000 (S.I. No.476 of 2000) implemented, belatedly, Directive 96/82/EC on the control of major accident hazards involving dangerous substances (the 'Seveso II' Directive), with effect from December 2000. The failure to implement the 1986 Directive, due to have been implemented in December 1998, had led to enforcement proceedings being initiated by the European Commission. The 2000 Regulations impose very specific obligations concerning on-site and off-site emergency plans in places of work where large concentrations of chemicals are either stored in a depot or used in a manufacturing process. The various threshold amounts of chemicals which trigger the 2000 Regulations are set out in Schedules to the Regulations. Enforcement of the 2000 Regulations is shared across a range of bodies, such as the Health and Safety Authority, local authorities and the Environmental Protection Agency. Although categorised here as occupational safety Regulation, they could also be categorised as environmental as well as planning Regulations. The 2000 Regulations revoke and replace the European Communities (Major Accident Hazards of Certain Industrial Activities) Regulations 1986 to 1992 (see Annual Review 1992, 527), which had implemented Directive (82/501/EEC), as amended (the original 'Seveso' Directive).

Night work and shift work The main elements of the 1993 EC Working Time Directive, 93/104/EC, were implemented by the Organisation of Working Time Act 1997 (Annual Review 1997, 502-8). Articles 9 to 13 of the 1993 Directive were implemented by the Safety, Health and Welfare at Work (Night Work and Shift Work) Regulations 2000 (S.I. No.11 of 2000), which replaced with minor changes the Safety, Health and Welfare at Work (Night Work and Shift Work) Regulations 1998 (Annual Review 1998, 575). The 1998 Regulations had come into force on February 1, 1999 and the 2000 Regulations came into force on January 25, 2000. The 2000 Regulations are largely identical to the 1998 Regulations and were made primarily to clarify that the medical checks for night workers applied at the pre-employment stage. Regulation 5 requires employers to take such steps as, having regard to the nature of the work, are appropriate for the protection of the safety and health of an employee who is a night worker and or a shift worker. As indicated by section 16 of the 1997 Act, Regulation 6 of the 2000 Regulations states that an employer must carry out a risk assessment to determine if any night workers are exposed to special hazards or a heavy physical or mental strain. This risk assessment must take account of the specific effects and hazards of night work and have regard to the risk assessment requirements in section 12 of the Safety, Health and Welfare at Work Act 1989 (Annual Review 1989, 379-93) (which deals with risk assessments for the safety statement).

Regulation 7 of the 2000 Regulations requires employers before an employee is employed to do night work and at regular intervals while the employee is employed in night work to make available to the employee, free of charge, an assessment of the effects, if any, on the employee's health. The health assessment must be carried out by a registered medical practitioner or a person acting under his or her supervision. If the employee is entitled to such an assessment from the State, the employer must facilitate this. The person carrying out the assessment must endeavour to detect if the employee's health is being or will be adversely affected by night work. The employer and employee is to be informed by the person carrying out the assessment of their opinion whether the employer is fit or unfit to do night work. If of the opinion that the employee is unfit for night work by reason only of the particular conditions under which it is performed, the employer and employee must be informed of the person's opinion of what changes could be made which would result in their being able to consider the employee fit to perform that work. The health assessment must comply with requirements of medical confidentiality. Regulation 7 also states that if an employee employed on night work becomes ill or otherwise exhibits symptoms of ill-health which are recognised as being connected with the fact that they perform night work, the employer must whenever possible assign the employee duties that do not involve night work and to which they are suited. As indicated, Regulation 7 also clarifies that any reference to an employee in Regulation 7 itself also refers to a person who the employer proposes to employ as a night worker.

The Regulations do not actually state that the employer should transfer the employee to day work, although the heading for Regulation 7 is 'Health assessment and transfer to day work' and the Explanatory Note to the Regulations refers to the requirement to 're-assign such workers to day work suited to them whenever possible.' In any event, the 1993 Directive specified that the employer must, in the situation described, whenever possible transfer the employee to day work.

Pregnant employees The Safety, Health and Welfare At Work (Pregnant Employees Etc.) Regulations 2000 (S.I. No.218 of 2000), made under the Safety, Health and Welfare at Work Act 1989 (Annual Review 1989, 379-93) revoked and replaced the Safety, Health and Welfare At Work (Pregnant Employees Etc.) Regulations 1994 (Annual 1994, 406). The 2000 Regulations in large measure replicate the provisions of the 1994 Regulations, in order to implement the occupational safety and health provisions of Directive 92/85EEC, the maternity protection Directive (largely implemented by the Maternity Protection Act 1994). The single difference between the 1994 and 2000 Regulations is that the list of chemical, physical and biological agents and work processes listed in the Regulations as requiring risk assessments to determine whether pregnant employees and breastfeeding mothers may engage in such work is stated to be 'non exhaustive', in accordance with the terms of the 1992 Directive. This had been omitted from the 1994 Regulations. The 2000 Regulations came into effect on June 30, 2000.

Radiation: ionising The Radiological Protection Act 1991 (Ionising Radiation) Order 2000 (S.I. No.125 of 2000) is discussed separately, below.

RADIOLOGICAL (NUCLEAR) SAFETY

The Radiological Protection Act 1991 (Ionising Radiation) Order 2000 (S.I. No.125 of 2000), which came into effect on May 13, 2000, sets out the licensing system which the Radiological Protection Institute of Ireland (RPII) administers for exposure to ionising radiation sources and also specifies the relevant protective and preventive measures for persons, whether employees or members of the public, exposed to radioactive sources and other forms of radiation. In summary, the Order specifies the detailed arrangements required of employers to prevent radioactive contamination of workers and the public. The 2000 Order implemented the 1996 Directive on the protection of employees from ionising radiation, 96/29/Euratom, and the 1990 Directive on the protection of outside workers from ionising radiation, 90/641/Euratom. The 2000 Order replaced a number of Orders and Regulations which had implemented previous Directives on radiological safety, namely the European Communities (Ionising Radiation) Regulations 1991 (Annual Review 1991, 375-6), the Radiological Protection Act 1991 (General Control of Radioactive Substances, Nuclear Devices and Irradiating Apparatus) Order 1993 (Annual Review 1993, 482-3) and the European Communities (Protection of Outside Workers from Ionising Radiation) Regulations 1994 (Annual Review 1994, 406-7). These were formally revoked by the European Communities (Revocation of Regulations Relating to Ionising Radiation and Protection of Outside Workers from such Radiation) Regulations 2000 (SI. No.131 of 2000), with effect from May 16, 2000.

Scope of 2000 Order   Article 3 of the 2000 Order provides that it applies to any work activity that involves a risk from ionising radiation, whether from an artificial or natural source, where natural radionuclides are being processed. This includes:

• custody, production, processing, handling, holding, storage, use, manufacture, importing into or exporting from the European Union, distribution, transportation, recycling, re-use or other disposal of radioactive substances and nuclear devices

• custody, distribution or use of irradiating apparatus, including x-ray sets for industrial radiography or for medical diagnosis or treatment and electron microscopes

• work involving exposure to radon gas concentrations in excess of 400 Bq m^{-3} over a three month period or other natural sources of radiation resulting in an effective dose in excess of 1mSv in a 12 month period

• any other practice specified by the RPII.

Some provisions of the Order apply to protecting air crew on an aircraft where their exposure to cosmic radiation involves an effective dose in excess of 1mSv in a 12 month period. This definition is sufficiently wide to include hospitals, laboratories, universities and industrial and other employers who use various sources of ionising radiation and who expose their employees to certain naturally occurring forms of radiation, such as radon and cosmic radiation. The Order also applies to the operation of a nuclear reprocessing plant or uranium mining, but such activities are not currently undertaken in the State.

Licensing system   In general, the 2000 Order requires that the activities to which it applies cannot be carried out unless a licence has been obtained from the RPII. The application must be made at least one month before the activity commences. The format for the licence application is set out in Schedule 1 of the Order.

Measurement of exposure and categorisation of persons exposed   Exposure to radiation sources is measured using a number of complex formulae, specified in the 2000 Order. The becquerel (Bk) is the standard unit of measurement of radioactivity and corresponds to one disintegration per second. The other significant measurement of exposure is the sievert (Sv). This is the unit measuring the impact on the human body of the energy absorbed from ionising radiation and which could thus have a damaging effect on a person's health. The milliSievert (mSv) is the unit used in the 2000 Order for determining dose limits for those exposed to ionising radiation.

Those exposed to radiation are categorised into four groups for the purpose of the 2000 Order: exposed workers, outside workers, apprentices and students and members of the public.

Justification principle, risk assessment and dose constraints   Article 8 of the 2000 Order provides that a licence will be granted only if the RPII considers that it complies with the justification principle, that is, where the RPII approves it as being justified by its economic, social or other benefits in relation to the health detriment it may cause. In this context, Article 9 of the 2000 Order requires an undertaking to ensure that all exposures to ionising radiation sources are kept 'as low as reasonably achievable', taking into account economic and social factors. This legal test is similar to the 'reasonably practicable' test set out in the Safety, Health and Welfare at Work Act 1989. Article 9 of the 2000 Order also requires undertakings to conduct a risk assessment, acceptable to the RPII, of the exposure it proposes to undertake, in order to identify the protective measures needed to restrict exposures to ionising radiation. This is similar to the risk assessments required under the Safety, Health and Welfare a Work Act 1989.

Dose limits   Article 10 of the 2000 Order requires that the undertaking must ensure that persons are not exposed to radiation levels in excess of the dose limits specified in Schedule 2 of the Order (subject to special exemptions that may be obtained under Article 12). Schedule 2 sets out the relevant dose limits. These limits are in some respects similar to those contained in the European Communities (Ionising Radiation) Regulations 1991, which the 2000 Order replaces, but some of the limits have been considerably reduced. The general dose limit of 20 mSv for an exposed worker in the 2000 Order is the same as that contained in the 1991 Regulations; but the limit for pregnant employees of 1 mSv for the remainder of the pregnancy in the 2000 Order contrasts with a limit of 5 mSv in the 1991 Regulations.

Organisational arrangements   The 2000 Order requires undertakings to ensure that appropriate organisational arrangements are in place to protect persons against radioactive contamination. These include:

- classifying areas as 'controlled areas' (where specified systems of work are required for those entering) or 'supervised areas' (where the activities should be kept under review with the possibility of reclassifying as a controlled area)

- preparation of radiation safety procedures, a written statement of procedures

- classification of exposed workers into Category A and Category B workers (Category A workers being those likely to be exposed to more than 6mSv in a period of 12 months; or to more than one third of the other dose limits specified for exposed workers in Schedule 2; Category B workers being all other exposed workers)

- appointment in writing of one or more radiation protection advisers, whose name must be forwarded to the RPII for inclusion in the RPII's register of radiation protection advisers

- provide information and instruction to workers on the precautions taken by the undertaking to comply with the 2000 Order and of the risks associated with exposure to ionising radiation

- monitoring of the working environment to ensure compliance with the 2000 Order, including the dose limits

- individual dose monitoring of exposed workers, students and apprentices, including individual records of such monitoring and retention of such records until the persons are 75 years of age or for 50 years after the worker has ceased work involving exposure, whichever is the later

- the provision of medical surveillance for Category A workers, including retention of records until the workers are 75 years of age or for 50 years after the worker has ceased work involving exposure, whichever is the later

- ensuring that outside workers are covered by the preventative measures, including the provision of an individual radiation passbook to such outside workers

- maintaining an inventory of radioactive substances, nuclear devices and irradiating apparatus

- identifying whether natural radiation sources, in particular radon, are present in a place of work and to take appropriate remedial measures

- where the employer is an air operator, conduct an evaluation of the extent of exposure of air crew from cosmic radiation and to take appropriate measures to reduce exposure likely to cause harm to such crew

- ensuring that the best possible protection of the general population is in place, in particular by ensuring that the dose limits set out in Schedule 2 for the general population are met

- preparing plans to deal with a radiological emergency, that is, a situation that requires urgent action to be taken to protect workers or the public at large.

TOBACCO

Control of advertising The Tobacco Products (Control of Advertising, Sponsorship and Sales Promotion) (Amendment) (No.2) Regulations 2000 (S.I. No.215 of 2000), made under the Tobacco Products (Control of Advertising, Sponsorship and Sales Promotion) Act 1978, further prohibit the publication or distribution in the State of newspapers, periodicals or magazines where such newspapers, periodicals or magazines contain any advertisements for tobacco products. They came into effect on July 11, 2000.

Social Welfare Law

GERRY WHYTE, Law School, Trinity College, Dublin

SOCIAL WELFARE ACT 2000

In addition to providing for the annual increases in welfare payments and for changes in social insurance contributions, the Social Welfare Act 2000 provided for, *inter alia*, improvements in the Family Income Supplement scheme, changes in the method of assessing capital for the purpose of social welfare means-tests and the introduction of new schemes of Carer's Benefit, Widowed Parent Grant and special contributory pensions for people with pre-1953 insurance.

Part I contains the usual provisions for short title, construction and continuance of instruments while Part II provides for the annual changes in welfare rates and in the calculation of social insurance contributions. Sections 8(1)(d) and 8(1)(f), providing for a reduction in the employer social insurance contribution, were brought into effect on December 21, 2000 by the Social Welfare Act 2000 (sections 8(1)(d) and 8(1)(f)) (Commencement) Order 2000 (S.I. No. 471 of 2000).

Part III (sections 10-12) provides for the new Carer's Benefit scheme which is designed to assist people (other than the self-employed or persons earning less than £30 per week) who wish to leave the workforce temporarily in order to look after older people or people with disabilities in need of full-time care and attention. To qualify, a person must, *inter alia*, have been in employment for at least three months, working at least 38 hours per fortnight, prior to commencing full-time care duties and must have at least 156 paid contributions since entry into insurance. In addition, the claimant must also have at least 39 paid contributions during the last complete contribution year before the beginning of the benefit year which includes the first day for which benefit is claimed or at least 39 paid contributions during the calendar year immediately prior to the first day for which benefit is claimed or at least 26 paid contributions in each of the last two complete contribution years before the beginning of the benefit year which includes the first day for which benefit is claimed. The benefit will be payable for a period of up to fifteen months in respect of the same care recipient, during which time the claimant's employment rights will be protected. Provision is also made for the payment of a respite care grant. (Arising out of the introduction of this scheme, a number of consequential amendments to the Social Welfare (Consolidation) Act 1993 are effected by section 11) This Part was brought into effect on October 26, 2000 by the Social Welfare Act 2000 (Part III and Section 28) (Commencement) Order 2000 (S.I. No. 339 of 2000).

Part IV (sections 13-15) provides for a new Widowed Parent Grant, payable to a newly widowed parent on the death of his/her spouse where the death occurs on or after December 1, 1999. To qualify, a claimant must have at least one qualified child residing with him/her and also be entitled to either bereavement grant, widow's (contributory) pension, widower's (contributory) pension, one-parent family payment, or widow's or widower's (contributory) pension payable by virtue of Council Regulation 1408/71 or by virtue of a reciprocal agreement with another State. For the purposes of this payment, the divorced spouse of the deceased is treated as his/her widow/widower. (Arising out of the introduction of this scheme, section 13 effects a number of consequential amendments to the Social Welfare (Consolidation) Act 1993.)

Part V provides for various improvements to a number of social welfare schemes. Section 16 provides for the payment of special rate Old Age (Contributory) Pension to certain insured persons with pre-1953 insurance who failed to qualify for a contributory old age pension or who qualified for a minimum rate pension only. Claimants with at least five years' paid contributions shall now be entitled to have every two contributions paid prior to 1953 counted as three contributions for the purposes of each of the contribution conditions for old age (contributory) pension. The pension payable amounts to 50% of the ordinary old age (contributory) pension. By virtue of Social Welfare (Consolidated Payments Provisions) (Amendment) (No.7) (Increase for Qualified Adult) Regulations 2000 (S.I. No.124 of 2000), claimants of such pensions with adult dependants will also be entitled to the payment of reduced Qualified Adult Allowance increases. Section 17 amends the rules for the assessment of capital for all of the social assistance schemes in the social welfare code other than Supplementary Welfare Allowance. Now the first £10,000 of a capital sum is disregarded, the weekly value of any sum between £10,000 and £20,000 is assessed at £1 per each £1,000, the weekly value of any sum between £20,000 and £30,000 is assessed at £2 per each £1,000 and the weekly value of any sum in excess of £30,000 is assessed at £4 per each £1,000. This change will benefit claimants with capital who claim any of the relevant social assistance payments as it reduces the amount of means attributed to capital. This section was brought into effect on various dates in October 2000 by the Social Welfare Act 2000 (Section 17) (Commencement) Order 2000 (S.I. No. 311 of 2000). (Similar changes were introduced by Social Welfare (Consolidated Payments Provisions) (Amendment) (No.12) (Capital Assessment) Regulations 2000 (S.I. No.313 of 2000), Social Welfare (Liable Relative) Regulations 2000 (S.I. No.314 of 2000) and Social Welfare (Rent Allowance) (Amendment) (No.1) Regulations 2000 (S.I. No.315 of 2000) for the purposes of determining whether qualified adult allowance is payable, of calculating the contribution due to the Department by a liable relative and of determining eligibility for rent allowance, respectively.) Section 18 provides for a number of changes in the means test for the Farm Assist scheme, including a reduction in the assessment of a farmer's net income from self-employment from 80% to 70% and an increase of £100 in the amount of income disregards for child dependants. Section 19 makes similar changes in the assessment of income of certain low-income fishermen for the purposes of Unemployment Assistance. Both of these sections were brought into effect on 27 September 2000 by the Social Welfare Act 2000 (Sections 18 and 19) (Commencement) Order 2000 (S.I. No. 312 of 2000). Section 20 enables the Minister to provide by regulation for the retention of the full rate of child dependant allowances where a claimant's income is less than £135 per week. Heretofore a claimant whose weekly income was between £60 and £105 only qualified for 50% of such allowances. Section 21 provides for the payment of full-rate Disability Allowance to certain people in residential care. Heretofore, such claimants only qualified for half-rate Disability Allowance. The section also provides for an extension of the disregard of rehabilitative earnings to those in self-employment. This last aspect of section 21 was brought into effect on April 3, 2000 by the Social Welfare Act 2000 (Sections 21(3) and 27) (Commencement) Order 2000 (S.I. No. 101 of 2000) and the Social Welfare (Consolidated Payments Provisions) (Amendment) (No.4) (Rehabilitative Employment) Regulations 2000 (S.I. No. 103 of 2000) – see below, p.000. Section 22 provides for an increase in the annual Respite Care Grant from £200 to £300. Section 23 enables the Minister to make regulations providing for the return of social insurance contributions paid by a spouse making enforceable maintenance payments. Section 24 provides that a former claimant of Deserted Wife's Allowance who was transferred to the then new Lone Parent's Allowance in 1990 and ultimately to the One-Parent Family Payment Scheme in 1997 shall resume her entitlement to Deserted Wife's Allowance when she ceases to have a qualified child residing with her, providing that she continues to satisfy the remaining conditions of that scheme. Section 25 effects a number of changes in the payment after death arrangements by providing that where a claimant is in receipt of either Old Age (Contributory) Pension or Retirement Pension and his/her spouse/partner is in receipt of either Old Age (Contributory) Pension, Retirement Pension, Old Age (Non-Contributory) Pension or Blind Pension, the claimant will continue to receive his/her spouse/partner's full pension for a period of six weeks following the death of such spouse/partner. In addition, a claimant of One-Parent Family Payment will continue to receive such payment for a period of six weeks following the death of the claimant's last remaining qualified child. Heretofore only the increase in respect of such child was payable. Section 26 provides for a weekly disregard of £25, for the purpose of the means test for Rent and Mortgage Interest Supplement payable under the Supplementary Welfare Allowance scheme, from any net gain in income experienced by a person receiving unemployment payment who takes up casual or part-time work. The section also provides for disregards in the case of claimants of Carer's Allowance who qualify for such supplements and also empowers the Minister to provide for the disregard of a certain amount of any allowances payable for attending approved training courses. Finally section 27 repeals the provision whereby a person entitled to Unemployment Benefit is generally disqualified for receipt of

Unemployment Assistance. This change was introduced to permit Community Employment workers who revert to the Live Register after completing a period on a CE scheme to re-qualify for long-term Unemployment Assistance which includes secondary benefits not payable with Unemployment Benefit. The Social Welfare Act 2000 (Sections 21(3) and 27) (Commencement) Order 2000 (S.I. No. 101 of 2000) brought section 27 into effect on April 3, 2000.

Part VI of the Act contains a number of miscellaneous changes to the social welfare code. Section 28 amends the definition of a care recipient for the purposes of Carer's Allowance and provides that Carer's Allowance and Carer's Benefit shall not be payable simultaneously in respect of the same care recipient. This section was brought into effect on October 26, 2000 by the Social Welfare Act 2000 (Part III and Section 28) (Commencement) Order 2000 (S.I. No. 339 of 2000). Section 29 provides for the charging to the Social Insurance Fund of expenditure incurred in relation to the Free Electricity Allowance, Free Television Licence, Free Telephone Rental Allowance, Free Fuel Allowance, Free Natural Gas Allowance and Free Bottled Gas Allowance, thus transferring the cost of these schemes from the Exchequer. The section makes similar provision for expenditure under the Medical Card system on dental treatment for insured persons who otherwise qualify for Dental Benefit and also provides for the reimbursement from the Fund to the Department of the cost of benefit involved where persons opt for a higher rate of Unemployment Assistance or Old Age (Non-Contributory) Pension than the corresponding social insurance payment. Section 30 provides for the application of different rates of qualified adult allowance under Blind Pension payable in respect of spouses aged under and over sixty six years of age. Section 31 enables the Minister to provide by regulation that certain categories of claim for Supplementary Welfare Allowance shall be determined by the Department of Social, Community and Family Affairs rather than by the Health Board. Section 32 adds the National Breast Screening Board to the list of specified bodies entitled to use the Personal Public Service Number and also provides for the sharing of information by educational bodies with the Minister for Education and Science where such information is required by the Minister in order to enable him/her to provide education in accordance with section 6(b) of the Education Act 1998. The section also elaborates on different situations in which authorised bodies may share personal data pursuant to sections 223 to 233I of the Act. This section was brought into effect on July 31, 2000 by the Social Welfare Act 2000 (Section 32) (Commencement) Order 2000 (S.I. No.264 of 2000). Section 33 repeals section 218(2) of the Social Welfare (Consolidation) Act 1993 providing for penalties for continuing offences.

Part VII (section 34) provides for an increase in the weekly exemption threshold for the payment of the Health Contribution pursuant to the Health Contributions Act 1979.

In Part VIII, section 35 amends the Pensions Act 1990 to address concerns regarding the practice of integrating social welfare pensions with occupational retirement pensions on an ongoing basis, post retirement, under a total income approach, while section 36 repeals section 3A of the 1990 Act providing penalties for continuing offences.

REGULATIONS

Thirty regulations relating to income maintenance schemes were promulgated during 2000. They are as follows:

Social Welfare Act 1999 (Sections 29 and 30) (Commencement) Order 2000 (S.I. No. 47 of 2000) – This Order brought sections 29 and 30 of the Social Welfare Act 1999, dealing with time limits for appeals in relation to social welfare entitlements to the Circuit Court and with the investigation of claims for Supplementary Welfare Allowance by officers of the Criminal Assets Bureau, into effect on February 14, 2000.

Social Welfare (Consolidated Payments Provisions) (Amendment) (Increase for Qualified Adult) Regulations 2000 (S.I. No.81 of 2000) – These regulations provide for an increase in the income range up to which tapered increases in respect of qualified adults are payable. They also provide for extending these tapered increases to the Old Age (Contributory) Pension, Retirement Pension and Invalidity Pension.

Social Welfare (Consolidated Payments Provisions) (Amendment) (No.2) (Homemakers) Regulations 2000 (S.I. No.82 of 2000) – These regulations extend the time limit within which an application to become a Homemaker for the purposes of Old Age (Contributory) Pension may be made.

Social Welfare (Consolidated Payments Provisions) (Amendment) (No.3) (Disregard From Spouse's Earnings) Regulations 2000 (S.I. No.83 of 2000) – These regulations provide for an increase in the disregard applicable to the earnings from insurable employment of the spouse of a claimant or beneficiary of Disability Allowance, Unemployment Assistance, Pre-Retirement Allowance and Farm Assist.

Social Welfare Act 2000 (Sections 21(3) and 27) (Commencement) Order 2000 (S.I. No. 101 of 2000) – This Order brings sections 21(3) and 27 of the 2000 Act into effect on April 3, 2000.

Social Welfare (Consolidated Supplementary Welfare Allowance) (Amendment) Regulations 2000 (S.I. No.102 of 2000) – These regulations provide for an increase in the amount of weekly earnings disregarded from employment of a rehabilitative nature in the assessment of means for the purposes of Supplementary Welfare Allowance.

Social Welfare (Consolidated Payments Provisions) (Amendment) (No.4) (Rehabilitative Employment) Regulations 2000 (S.I. No. 103 of 2000) – These regulations provide for amendment of the means test for Disability Allowance and Blind Pension by increasing the disregard of earnings from rehabilitative employment to £75 per week and by extending this disregard to income from self-employment of a rehabilitative nature in the case of Disability Allowance.

Social Welfare (Consolidated Payments Provisions) (Amendment) (No.3) (Carers) Regulations 2000 (S.I. No.106 of 2000) – These regulations exempt claimants of Carer's Allowance and people providing full-time care and attention in respect of which Constant Attendance Allowance or Prescribed Relative's Allowance was payable from certain contribution conditions governing entitlement to Disability Benefit.

Infectious Diseases (Maintenance Allowances) Regulations 1999 (S.I. No.157 of 1999) – These regulations provide for increases in the maximum rates of maintenance allowances payable to persons being treated for certain infectious diseases.

Social Welfare (Occupational Injuries) (Amendment) Regulations 2000 (S.I. No.120 of 2000) – These regulations provide for the annual increases in the reduced rates of certain occupational injuries benefits.

Social Welfare (Rent Allowance) (Amendment) Regulations 2000 (S.I. No.121 of 2000) – These regulations provide for increases in the amount of means disregarded for the purposes of the Rent Allowance scheme payable pursuant to the Housing (Private Rented Dwellings) Act 1982. The changes come into effect on May 4, 2000.

Social Welfare (Consolidated Payments Provisions) (Amendment) (No.5) (Increase in Rates) Regulations 2000 (S.I. No.122 of 2000) – These regulations provide for the annual increase in the reduced rates of certain social insurance payments, in the rates of tapered increases in respect of qualified adults and in the minimum weekly rate of Maternity Benefit and Adoptive Benefit. They also amend the yearly average bands for receipt of reduced rate Old Age (Contributory) Pension and Retirement Pension.

Social Welfare (Consolidated Payments Provisions) (Amendment) (No.6) (Family Income Supplement) Regulations 2000 (S.I. No.123 of 2000) – These regulations provide for an increase in the minimum weekly payment of Family Income Supplement from £5 to £10.

Social Welfare (Consolidated Payments Provisions) (Amendment) (No.7) (Increase for Qualified Adult) Regulations 2000 (S.I. No.124 of 2000) – These regulations provide for the payment of reduced Qualified Adult Allowance increases in respect of the new half-rate Old Age (Contributory) Pension for claimants with pre-1953 insurance – see section 16 above.

Social Welfare (Consolidated Payments Provisions) (Amendment) (No.8) (Late Claims) Regulations 2000 (S.I. No.159 of 2000) – These regulations provide for the extension of the period within which a claim for benefit may be made where the delay in making the claim is due to incorrect information given by the Department, the person being so incapacitated that s/he was unable to pursue the claim or a force majeure. The regulations also provide for an extension where the person is currently in financial difficulties and for the defeat of any right to benefit where it is not claimed within six months of the due date of the order or cheque, unless there is good reason for the delay.

Social Welfare (Consolidated Payments Provisions) (Amendment) (No.9) (Loss of Purchasing Power) Regulations 2000 (S.I. No.160 of 2000) – These regulations provide for payments to be made to claimants in respect of loss of purchasing power where payment of benefit has been delayed for a period in excess of twelve months due solely or mainly to circumstances within the control of the Department. The regulations also provide for compensation for incidental expenses, up to a limit of £50, where the expenses are incurred as a result of such delay.

Social Welfare (Consolidated Payments Provisions) (Amendment) (No.10) (Sale of Residence) Regulations 2000 (S.I. No.232 of 2000) – These regulations increase the disregard, in certain circumstances, of the amount of money derived from the sale of a principal residence for the purposes of the means-test for the Old Age (Non-Contributory) Pension, Widow's or Widower's (Non-Contributory) Pension or One-Parent Family Payment.

Social Welfare (Consolidated Contributions and Insurability) (Amendment) (Credited Contributions) Regulations 2000 (S.I. No.263 of 2000) – These regulations provide for the award of credited contributions for periods in respect of which a member of a local authority gives up insurable employment to serve temporarily as Cathaoirleach of a local authority or as Chairman of a Health Board or Vocational Education Committee.

Social Welfare Act, 2000 (Section 32) (Commencement) Order 2000 (S.I. No.264 of 2000) – This order provides that section 32 of the 2000 Act will come into effect on 31 July 2000.

Social Welfare (Consolidated Payments Provisions) (Amendment) (No.11) (Child Benefit) Regulations 2000 (S.I. No.265 of 2000) – These regulations provide that, in cases of shared custody of a qualified child who resides on a part-time basis with each of his/her parents, payment of Child Benefit will be made to the parent with whom the child resides for the greater part. The regulations also provide for the extension of the period for back-dating Child Benefit claims to six months.

Social Welfare Act 2000 (Section 17) (Commencement) Order 2000 (S.I. No. 311 of 2000) – This Order brought section 17 of the Social Welfare Act 2000 into effect on various dates in October 2000.

Social Welfare Act 2000 (Sections 18 and 19) (Commencement) Order 2000 (S.I. No. 312 of 2000) – This Order brought sections 18 and 19 of the Social Welfare Act 2000 into effect on September 27, 2000.

Social Welfare (Consolidated Payments Provisions) (Amendment) (No.12) (Capital Assessment) Regulations 2000 (S.I. No.313 of 2000) – These regulations amend the existing method of assessing capital for the purpose of calculating a spouse's weekly income in order to determine whether a qualified adult allowance is payable. The new formula is the same as that provided for in section 17 of the 2000 Act.

Social Welfare (Liable Relative) Regulations 2000 (S.I. No.314 of 2000) – These regulations make a similar change in the assessment of capital for the purposes of calculating the contribution payable to the Department by a liable relative.

Social Welfare (Rent Allowance) (Amendment) (No.1) Regulations 2000 (S.I. No.315 of 2000) – These regulations make a similar change in the assessment of capital for the purposes of the Rent Allowance scheme.

Social Welfare (Consolidated Contributions and Insurability) (Amendment) (No.1) (Carer's Benefit) Regulations 2000 (S.I. No.338 of 2000) – These regulations provide for the award of credited contributions to claimants of the new Carer's Benefit. It also provides that modified contributions paid by public servants and members of the Defence Forces shall be reckoned for the purposes of Carer's Benefit.

Social Welfare Act 2000 (Part III and Section 28) (Commencement) Order 2000 (S.I. No. 339 of 2000) – This Order brought Part III and section 28 of the Social Welfare Act 2000 into effect on October 26, 2000.

Social Welfare (Consolidated Payments Provisions) (Amendment) (No.13) (Carers) Regulations 2000 (S.I. No.340 of 2000) – These regulations provide for the extension of existing claims and payments provisions to the Carer's Benefit scheme, prescribe the circumstances in which a carer is to be regarded as providing full-time care and attention, detail the conditions to be satisfied by a non-resident carer and provide for medical examination of the care recipient and for disqualification for Carer's Benefit and Carer's Allowance for failure to co-operate with this requirement. The regulations also amend the residency conditions which apply to a non-resident carer in the case of Carer's Allowance by deleting the "close proximity" requirement.

Social Welfare (Temporary Provisions) Regulations 2000 (S.I. No.374 of 2000) – These regulations provide for the payment of a Christmas bonus to long-term social welfare claimants.

Social Welfare Act 2000 (Sections 8(1)(d) and 8(1)(f)) (Commencement) Order 2000 (S.I. No. 471 of 2000) – This Order brought sections 8(1)(d) and 8(1)(f) of the Social Welfare Act 2000 into effect on December 21, 2000.

The Irish superior courts do not appear to have decided any cases concerning the operation of the social welfare code during 2000. During that year, the Department of Social, Community and Family Affairs produced a report entitled, *Review of the Qualifying Contributions for the Old Age (Contributory) and Retirement Pensions* (Pn.8888). This report identified four major issues relating to eligibility for these pensions – (a) the operation, in relation to contribution conditions, of the yearly average test to determine eligibility; (b) the pension entitlements of homemakers; (c) the use of pre-1953 contributions and (d) information issues. The Social Welfare Act 2000 has already addressed some of the Report's proposals in relation to these issues, namely, the recognition of contributions made prior to 1953 and the rationalisation of the rates bands for both pensions. The Report also recommended, *inter alia*, switching from the yearly average test (whereby the claimant must have a certain minimum yearly average of contributions paid or credited since entering insurance) to a Total Contributions Approach which relates entitlement to pension to the total number of contributions over a lifetime and improving entitlement for homemakers by providing them with credited contributions for the purposes of the old age (contributory) pension and by retrospectively extending existing provisions allowing for the disregard of periods spent working in the home for the purposes of applying the yearly average test. These issues will be addressed further by the Department in the second phase of its review process.

Tort

DUTY OF CARE

Control test   *Shinkwin v. Quin-Con Ltd and Quinlan*, [2001] 2 I.L.R.M. 154 represents the first decision of the Supreme Court in a number of years to address the conceptual dimensions of the duty of care. The facts were simple. The plaintiff, an employee of the first named defendant company, suffered severe injuries to his hand in an accident at the factory premises where he worked. The first named defendant was uninsured and had no assets. The second named defendant was 'the effective sole shareholder and effective day-to-day manager' of the company. The plaintiff sued both defendants and was awarded over £30,000 against them. The crucial question on appeal related to the second defendant's liability.

The background to the accident should be mentioned. The plaintiff was aged twenty. Having come originally to the factory on a FÁS training programme, he was put to work on wood-working machines about eight months before the accident. He used an electric circular saw with a jig. The saw was not adequately guarded. On the fateful day, as he was moving the jig while the saw was in motion, the jig shifted suddenly. His right hand came in contact with the saw, resulting in the loss of three fingers and part of his thumb.

The plaintiff had received no training in the use of the machine and no warnings as to the dangers inherent in the work. In particular he had not been warned to stop the circular saw before adjusting the jig.

The trial judge imposed liability on both defendants. He considered that the second defendant had owed the plaintiff a duty of care 'as manager of the factory premises'.

On appeal by the second defendant, his counsel argued that the fact that he was virtually the sole owner of the business did not impose a duty of care on him. The duty to provide a safe system and a safe place of work was an obligation imposed directly in law on the first defendant as employer of the plaintiff. The decision of the High Court, if allowed to stand, would open the door too wide and establish a new basis of liability for factory managers. Whilst a fellow employee was admittedly liable personally for any direct negligent act causing injury in the work place, the second defendant should be regarded 'merely in the guise of manager'. The faults attributed to him were mere acts of omission; persons in such positions did not attract personal liability. Counsel relied on the judgment of Barron J. in the High Court in *Sweeney v. Duggan* [1991] 2 I.R. and of the Supreme Court on appeal [1997] 2 I.R. 531. See

McMahon and Binchy, Law of Torts (3rd ed., 2000), paras. 10.30–10.39.

Counsel for the plaintiff relied on the neighbour principle established in *Donoghue v. Stevenson* [1932] A.C. 562. The first defendant was not merely the sole effective shareholder of the plaintiff's employer; he was also the effective and only manager. Counsel for the plaintiff laid special emphasis on the complete control exercised by the second defendant over the plaintiff and the plaintiff's workplace. He drew attention to *Tulsk Co-operative Livestock Mart Limited v. Ulster Bank Ltd*, High Court, May 13, 1983, where Gannon J. had observed:

> In every case in which a claim for damages is founded in negligence it is essential to examine the circumstances which bring the parties into relation with each other and in which the risks of reasonably foreseeable harm can be identified, and the extent to which each or either has control of the circumstances, with a view to determining what duty of care, if any, may exist, the nature and extent of the duty, and whether and to what extent there may have been a breach of duty of care ....

Fennelly J. (Keane C.J. and Geoghegan J. concurring) approached the issue by taking two points at opposite ends of a spectrum. On the one hand, a person might be the sole effective and controlling sharehholder in a business run by a company but have no involvement in its day-to-day operations. Clearly he would not, without more, be responsible to employees injured by the negligent acts of the company. To do so would disregard the principle of limited liability. On the other hand, employees owed their fellow employees a duty to exercise at least such care in the performance of their work as not to cause direct injury to the fellow workers.

It seemed to Fennelly J. that the second defendant fell between these two stools:

> He is the effective sole shareholder and effective day to day manager. I would reduce the issue to this: did he involve himself so closely in the operation of the factory and, in particular, in the supervision of the plaintiff as to make himself personally liable for any of the acts of negligence which injured the plaintiff?

The evidence disclosed that the plaintiff had dealt personally with the second named defendant from the beginning. Whilst it was true that the second named defendant's two sons were more physically active on the factory floor and he was often absent from the premises, nevertheless, it was he who, about eight months before the accident, had approached the plaintiff about using all the machines.

He was always in and out of the machine area if the shop was busy, saw the plaintiff using the machine and the difficulties he had in moving the jig. He worked with the plaintiff on the machine on at least one occasion. He repeatedly warned the employees, on his own evidence, that there was no insurance and as aware of a history of accidents that made it impossible to get insurance. He gave instructions about not playing football for the same reason. All of these factors, even though partially disputed by the plaintiff, demonstrate the intimate involvement of the second defendant in the management of the factory and the supervision of the plaintiff, in particular, and his consciousness of the danger of accidents. It is in this context that his concession, in cross-examination, that he was in undisputed control of the factory becomes significant.

Fennelly J. noted that in *Ward v. McMaster* [1988] I.R. 337 at 349, McCarthy J. had declared his unwillingness to 'dilute the words of Lord Wilberforce ...'. Fennelly J. observed:

> We are here concerned only with the first stage of the two stages adopted by Lord Wilberforce in the passage from *Anns v. Merton London Borough* [1978] 728 at 752...

It will be recalled that Lord Wilberforce expressed the first stage as follows:

> First, one has to ask whether, as between the alleged wrongdoer and the person who as suffered the damage there is a sufficient relationship of proximity or neighbourhood such that, in the reasonable contemplation of the former, carelessness on his part may be likely to cause damage to the latter ...

One must quote the crucial element of Fennelly J's judgment *in extenso*:

> The criterion of 'control' which is proposed in this case is not an addition to the test for the existence of proximity. The open textured language of Lord Wilberforce leaves wide scope for argument as to the character of 'proximity or neighbourhood'. Clearly it involves more than a mere test of foreseeability of damage. The assessment of the relevance of control as well as its nature and degree will depend on the circumstances. Ó Dálaigh CJ in *Purtill v. Athlone UDC* [1968] I.R. 205 at 213 noted that 'the defendants employees were in charge and control of the detonators..' which caused injury to the plaintiff in that case. In my opinion some assessment of the element of control, in the sense of 'control of the circumstances', mentioned by Gannon J. in the *Tulsk* case, is a useful guide to the decision as to the existence of a duty of care. A person cannot be held liable for matters which are outside his

control. He will not be, as the defendant in *Ward v. McMaster* was not, in control of the plaintiff's independent actions and should be responsible in law only for matters which are within his own control.

In my view, the second defendant, on the particular facts of this case, placed himself in a relationship of proximity to the plaintiff. He had personally taken on a young and untrained person to work in a factory managed by him and personally put him to work upon a potentially dangerous machine over which he exercised control to the extent of giving some though completely inadequate instructions to the workers. He was bound to take appropriate steps to warn the plaintiff of such obvious dangers as failing to stop the circular saw from revolving while adjusting the jig or to ensure that it was guarded. In his supervision and instruction of the plaintiff, he failed to do these things and was consequently negligent.

Fennelly J. distinguished *Sweeney v. Duggan*, where the plaintiff failed in his claim that the principal shareholder and quarry manager of a company which employed the plaintiff owed him a duty of care in negligence to inform him that the company was not adequately insured from industrial accidents. Fennelly J. commented:

It emerges clearly from the judgment of Murphy J. on the appeal that the claim failed because the defendant, Duggan, could not be under a greater obligation to the plaintiff in respect of insurance than was the company, which was the employer. The plaintiff failed to establish that such a term should be implied into his contract of employment. Hence, this claim also failed against Duggan.

Here the plaintiff makes his claim directly in negligence against the second defendant, not as employer or as shareholder but as a person who had placed himself by his own actions in such a relationship to the plaintiff as to call upon himself the obligation to exercise care.

Fennelly J. did not think it necessary, on the facts of the case, to express an opinion on the issue as to the potential exposure generally of factory managers to personal liability. Counsel for the second named defendant had pointed to the serious implications of such liability for insurance and industrial relations. Fennelly J. considered it nonetheless relevant to observe that there had never been any doubt as to the right of the employer to be indemnified by an employee who, in the course of his or her employment, negligently causes injury to another. In this context he referred to what McCarthy J. had said in *Sinnott v. Quinnsworth* [1984] I.L.R.M. 523 at 537.

In the light of the holding that the second named defendant was liable under the *Donoghue v. Stevenson* neighbour principle, Fennelly J. considered it unnecessary also to decide whether, as the plaintiff had argued, the second named defendant was his employer.

Shinkwin is subjected to strong critical analysis by Austin Buckley, 'Employer's Liability and the Personal Liability of the Manager Beyond the Corporate Veil' (2001) *Commercial Law Practitioner* 13.

Public policy   In *Gayson v. Allied Irish Banks Ltd*, High Court, January 28, 2000, the plaintiff, a substantial farmer, sued the defendant bank for damages for alleged negligent advice given to him by the bank not to avail himself of the tax amnesty of 1988. In its ongoing relationship with the plaintiff, Geoghegan J. found that the bank was clearly implicated in the tax evasion regarding the plaintiff's moneys 'as a consequence of its own activities, encouragement and advice' but Geoghegan J. was equally certain that at all material times the plaintiff himself was well aware that the moneys were being hidden for tax purposes and that the moneys would in ordinary way be subject to tax.

In 1986 the DIRT was introduced for the first time. A senior officer of the bank (who was not the manager) had a discussion with the plaintiff. She explained to the plaintiff about the DIRT and suggested that the provision by him to the bank of a genuine overseas address such as the English address of his sister 'would get us over the technicalities of the last budget'. He then provided the bank with his sister's English address. The bank at all material times knew well that the plaintiff was living in Ireland rather than with his sister in England. As Geoghegan J. observed: 'All the bank was doing was substituting a pseudo genuine English address for a totally bogus one.'

In August 1988 a national tax amnesty was announced. The plaintiff gave evidence to the effect that he had asked the senior officer of the bank whether there was 'anything in the amnesty for us' but had been advised to leave his money where it was as the amnesty would cost him a good deal of money.

The core of the plaintiff's claim was reliance and negligent misrepresentation under the principle articulated in *Hedley Byrne & Co Ltd v. Heller and Partners Ltd* [1964] AC 465: see McMahon & Binchy, *op cit.*, paras.10.50–10.141. Geoghegan J. quoted from *Charlesworth on Negligence*, 9th ed., p. 93 to the effect that:

> as a result of the decision in *Hedley Byrne & Co Ltd v. Heller and Partners Ltd*, it must not be assumed that, upon every occasion, when economic loss is a foreseeable consequence of a careless statement, an action will lie, even in the absence of a duty recognised at law. On the contrary, the overriding principle is that the existence of such a duty, independent on any question of carelessness and foreseeability, must still be established; indeed it will be an essential fact to be proved in any given case that the defendant had assumed responsibility for giving his opinion, advice or, even information.

Geoghegan J. was satisfied that any such conversation which the plaintiff had with the senior officer of the bank was on an 'off the cuff' nature and that it would never have reasonably occurred to either of them than any answer given by her could have given rise to an action against the bank. Accordingly no liability could be imposed in negligence Geoghegan J. considered that, even if the bank official had not been speaking in a casual conversation, the bank should still not be held responsible by reason of the principle of vicarious liability. While there was abundant evidence of the bank being actively involved in the plaintiff's tax evasion and therefore in illegality, the kind of illegal advice given by the bank in connection with setting up particular types of deposit accounts was intimately connected with the banking business and was of a totally different order from direct advice given to the plaintiff as to whether he should avail himself of the amnesty or not:

> The bank is in no sense in the business of advising customers as to whether they should avail of a tax amnesty or not. If, therefore, [the senior officer] gave such advice in circumstances that went beyond a mere casual conversation as I have indicated, she was, to use the traditional terminology, 'on a frolic of her own'. The bank could not be vicariously liable for the advice.

A further reason for not imposing liability on the bank was that there was no clear evidence that the plaintiff was necessarily and exclusively relying on the advice of the bank's senior officer:

> He was probably in two minds himself as to whether he would avail of the amnesty or not and he decided not to but I think that that was his own independent decision.

Fourthly, and Geoghegan J. observed, 'perhaps most importantly', Geoghegan J. considered that as a matter of public policy the courts would not hold that there was an actionable duty of care owed by the senior officer, even if she was acting as agent of the bank, in these circumstances.

> Once she was being asked to advise on two possible options and one of those options was clearly illegal, I would take the view that an actionable duty of care does not arise. It might be a different matter if the plaintiff was entirely innocent and never in any sense understood that he was evading tax or perhaps even what an amnesty was but none of that applies here.

No duty to company   In *Murphy v. Proctor*, High Court, October 11, 2000, Kelly J. held that a solicitor advising two personal clients who were purchasing a shop owed no duty of care to a company that they formed several months later with a view to developing the property. We analyse this decision below 441-443.

EMPLOYERS' LIABILITY

'Non-delegable' duty of care   In *Armstrong v. William J. Dwan & Sons Ltd*, High Court, February 8, 1999, Morris P. evinced no enthusiasm for the idea that an employer should be held under a 'non-delegable duty of care' such as to render him liable, in essence vicariously, for the negligence of the repairer of a vehicle used by his employee. This approach is consistent with that adopted by the House of Lords in *Davie v. New Morton Board Mills Ltd* [1959] A.C. 604, by Walsh J. in the Supreme Court decision of *Keenan v. Bergin* [1971] I.R. 192, at 199, and (implicitly) by Murphy J. in an *ex tempore* judgment in *McCarthy v. Garda Commissioner*, Supreme Court, February 27, 1998. See the 1998 Review, 622-3. It is not so easy, however, to reconcile this approach with the expansive definition of the employer's duty by O'Flaherty J. in *Connolly v. Dundalk Urban District Council,* November 18, 1992:

> The common law duties to take reasonable steps to provide safe plant and a safe place of work – I speak of the place of work as being part of the employer's property, which is the instant case – are such that they cannot be delegated to independent contractors so as to avoid the primary liability that devolves on employers to make sure that these duties are carried out. These are responsibilities which cannot be put to one side; they must remain with the employer. They are owed to each individual employee. That is not to say, of course, but that the employer on occasion is entitled to and very often should get the best expert help that he can from an independent contractor to perform these duties. If he does so and the contractor is negligent, causing injury to an employee, the employer retains a primary liability for the damage suffered though if he is not himself negligent he may obtain from the contractor a contribution to the damages and costs which he has to pay which will amount to an indemnity.

In *Everitt v. Thorsman Ireland Ltd* [2000] 1 I.R. 256, Kearns J. addressed the issue. The plaintiff, a general assistant employed by the first defendant, was trying to open the lid of a bin with a lever provided for that purpose when the lever snapped and broke, causing him to fall backwards. Both bin and lever had been supplied to the first defendant by the second defendant. The lever broke because its material was too weak and because the diameter of its tube was too small. The likelihood of such a fracture could not, however, be apparent to a lay person. An expert witness went so far as to say that even an engineer looking at the implement would not have spotted the relevant defect.

Kearns J. referred to *Davie* and quoted from O'Flaherty J.'s judgment in *Connolly*. He noted that this passage was *obiter*. Careful reading of it conveyed to Kearns J. that O'Flaherty J. had 'recognised that the actual common law duty is 'to take reasonable steps to provide safe plant and a safe place of work', and in the particular case (which concerned premises and not a tool) the employers were in any event found to be in default in two respects.' Kearns J. went on to observe:

> What further steps could the employer have taken in the instant case? Short of having the lever assessed by an expert in metallurgy or breaking the lever with a view to determining its maximum stress resistance it is difficult to see what could have been done. It was a newly purchased tool which appeared strong enough for the job and had been purchased from a reputable supplier and there is no suggestion to the contrary.

Accordingly the plaintiff's claim at common law (though not from breach of statutory duty failed against the first defendant.

It now appears that the weight of judicial authority is firmly against applying the principle of a non-delegable duty of care to cases where goods are supplied, or repaired, by an outside contractor, even where there is an ongoing commercial relationship between the parties. Where, however, the outside contractor actually comes onto the employer's premises to effect the supply or repair, it is possible that the principle may still have some vitality. *Connolly* gives it support. It is also worth noting that the principle received Judge Spain's approval in the context of occupiers' liability in *Crowe v. Merrion Shopping Centre Ltd*, (1995) 15 I.L.T. (ns) 302 (Circuit Court), analysed in Annual Review 1995, 518-9.

Duty of persons other than employer Earlier in the chapter, above 411, we examine the important decision of the Supreme Court in *Shinkwin-Quin-Con Ltd and Quinlan* [2001] 2 I.L.R.M. 154 imposing liability in negligence on a person who was 'the effective sole shareholder and effective day to day manager' of a company in respect of injuries sustained by the company's employee. The Court emphasised this position of control as generating sufficient proximity of relationship to warrant placing him under a duty of care.

Unsafe system of work In *McSweeney v. J.S. McCarthy Ltd*, Supreme Court, January 28, 2000, the perennial issue in employer's liability litigation of the extent to which paternalistic values should take priority over mollycoddling employees fell for consideration. The plaintiff was thirty four years old. He was a fully classified painter and decorator, having passed an apprenticeship of five years with the defendant company. He was injured when the ladder on which he was working slipped from under him on a tiled factory floor. The ladder was not secured at either the top or the bottom and no one was holding it at its base.

The essence of the plaintiff's case in negligence was that the defendant had failed to provide him with a safe system of work. The defendant's reply, successful at trial in the High Court, was that the plaintiff had been engaged in what was 'essentially a one man job', that he had sufficient experience to carry it out, that he was well aware of the danger of climbing an unsecured ladder and that he knew that the foreman (who was on the premises, but some distance away) would hold the ladder if asked.

The Supreme Court upheld the plaintiff's appeal. Murray J. (Hamilton C.J. and Barron J. concurring) observed that it was:

> well established that an employer is under a common law duty to provide his employees with a reasonably safe system of work. I know of no principle which exempts an employer from this duty only because their employee(s) are experienced, or know or ought to have known, of the dangers inherent in the work. Certainly, there are many factors which come into play in assessing where, in the circumstances of the particular case, the system of work was reasonably safe or not. Among these are the experience of the workman concerned, the level of danger involved, its complexity and so on.

As regards a safe system of work, Murray J. elaborated on the theme as follows:

> [T]he expression 'a safe system of work' is not susceptible to a single all embracing definition. One may look at what it encompasses.
>
> The word 'system' may in this context be said to comprehend a set of procedures according to which something is done; an organised scheme or method. (See *New Oxford English Dictionary*, Oxford University Press, 1998).
>
> The organisation of procedures or methods according to which the work of an employee(s) should be carried out necessarily involves foresight and forethought on the part of the employer.
>
> It is the employer who assigns the work; he sets the scene, so to speak. He is in control at this point. If follows that an employer must have addressed, in advance, the foreseeable risks inherent in the work which the employee is being required to carry out, so as to ensure that the method or procedures to be followed in carrying out the work are sufficient so as to reasonably protect him from those risks. The extent of the duty will evidently vary considerably according to the circumstances of the case. In cases where the work is complex and/or highly dangerous the duty may involve the establishment of an elaborate system which is strictly supervised and enforced. In other circumstances a mere warning or specific instruction may suffice.

In the instant case it was foreseeable that the plaintiff at some point in the course of his duties that day would require the assistance of someone else to secure the ladder at its foot when he had to mount it since climbing an unsecured ladder was inherently dangerous. It is agreed between the parties that, in the circumstances of the case, it would be placing too onerous a duty on the employer to contend that he should have provided the plaintiff during his entire period of work with an assistant ready to hold the ladder, as the isolated need arose.

Murray J. observed:

> The reality of cases like the present is that both employer and employee had an opportunity to consider how the work should be carried out, whether it involved any dangers, and, if so, how they should be avoided. [D]enying liability because only the employee was present is in effect to seek to plead some sort of last opportunity rule. This, however, is not the basis of liability. Admittedly, the employee is more proximate to the events leading up to the circumstances in which the injury occurred. But this is not the test of liability. The test is dependent upon control of the work.
>
> In the ordinary case, it is the employer who controls the work and liability on the part of the employer derives from his control. That does not mean that the employee cannot also be liable to the extent that he or she is in control or should be regarded as being in control.
>
> If both have an opportunity to consider how the work should be done, what dangers might arise and how to avoid them, as between them, it is the employer who will normally exercise, or be required to exercise, primary control. That was the case here where the defendant's foreman had the task of determining and assigning the work to be done.

In the instant case when the plaintiff arrived at a point where he needed the assistance of a fellow worker to secure the ladder, the only person who could be considered reasonably to be available for this task was his foreman.

> The carrying out of the plaintiff's work safely, therefore, required some co-ordination between him and the foreman who had assigned the work to him.
>
> … This was not the case of an employee failing to observe a safe system of work. As the evidence clearly shows, there was no system of work. On the evidence of the foreman … the plaintiff was left entirely to his own devices and had to devise his own method of work.

While the experience and competence of the employee was a relevant factor in considering whether, in the circumstances, a system of work had been made reasonably safe, his experience could not be a reason for ignoring completely the duty to ensure that there was a safe system of work in place and leaving it up to the employee rather than the employer to devise such a system or whether there should be such a system:

> It is clear from the caselaw on employers' liability that workmen will be tempted to take risks on the spur of the moment in order to get on with the job, particularly when that risk is a momentary or transient one, such as was the case here. It is to protect him from such foreseeable risks from an inherent danger that a safe system of work is required.

It was at all times foreseeable that the plaintiff, working without assistance, was likely to need such assistance to secure the ladder for access to one or more points at which he had to work and during one or more stages of his working day. The foreman had not inspected the site to identify when or where this was likely to arise or how the plaintiff should deal with this situation or how he might or should be contacted by the plaintiff when assistance was needed. A straightforward but specific instruction to postpone the work until the plaintiff sought out and located the foreman, whatever delay was involved, would have been one means of addressing it. There might have been alternative procedures, but the defendants, in any case had done nothing.

Each case depended upon its own facts. This was a case where both parties had been in a position to consider whether any problems might arise and to determine how the work should be carried out in safety. There could be other cases where an employee might be solely liable for what occurred.

Murray J. considered that the instant case could be distinguished from *Fennell v. E. Stone & Sons Ltd.* [1967] I.R. 204. There, the plaintiff was a general labourer engaged in carrying out renovation work to premises, dismantling and moving scaffolding from one room to another. While doing so, he caused an electric lamp to fall on his head. There was nothing intrinsically dangerous about the layout of the rooms. What occurred was something which could have been avoided with a little care. It was held that the employers were not insurers and were not negligent because they had not in effect warned their employee to be careful in the course of what he was doing.

Murray J. observed that *Fennell* was:

> a further illustration of the principle of control. It was the plaintiff himself who was actually in control of what he was doing. Neither was there an inherent danger in the work. His employer could not be responsible for every trivial aspect of his work which might cause him difficulty and which he was perfectly capable of avoiding.

> In this case the circumstances are otherwise. Assigning a man on his own to use a ladder to work at a height poses immediately the question as to how he or she is to mount an unsecured ladder, whether it is for the purpose of tying it at the top or getting to his place of work. That was an inherent danger which was primarily, though not

exclusively, under the control of the defendants as the employers...

Since there was a foreseeable danger to a workman left on his own and to his own devices when using a ladder to climb such heights, the defendants were under a duty to provide a reasonably safe system to work. They didn't do so and their failure to do so was a causative factor in the accident which gave rise to the plaintiff's injuries.

Accordingly the Supreme Court, reversing the High Court, found the defendant company liable in negligence at common law. It also found the defendant in breach of its statutory duty to the plaintiff. It reduced the award by 40% to take account of the plaintiff's contributory negligence.

It must be said that this decision sets a very high standard for employers. if control is to be the test, surely the experienced and skilled employee was the person who was in truth the one exercising control over the operation? Any reminder by his employer of his entitlement to call for assistance before mounting his ladder would in practice surely be redundant.

NERVOUS SHOCK

The issue of liability for negligently caused psychiatric damage 'nervous shock' continues to fascinate the courts throughout the common law world: see McMahon & Binchy, *op. cit.,* Chapter 17.

A distinction between 'primary' and 'secondary' victims has gained currency in the British courts in recent years. Those who are primary victims benefit from the characterisation in two ways: they may obtain compensation for unforeseeable psychiatric injury and they are not subject to the policy limitations prescribed by the House of Lords in *Alcock v. Chief Constable of South Yorkshire Police* [1992] 1 A.C. 310. It is thus a matter of some practical significance whether a plaintiff is characterised as a primary or secondary victim. The essence of the distinction appears to be based on whether or not one was a foreseeable participant in the accident which generated the psychiatric injury: if one was, and sustained physical injury or psychiatric injury, compensation for the injury will be forthcoming.

Several criticisms have been made of this distinction. Two may be mentioned. It extends the scope of liability too far in one respect, by requiring a defendant to compensate a plaintiff for entirely unforeseeable psychiatric injury merely because the defendant risked causing, but did not in fact cause, physical injury to the plaintiff. If a distinction is to be made between physical and psychiatric injuries for the purposes of remoteness of damage, this outcome cannot easily be supported unless one has to resort to the 'egg shell skull' rule. Secondly, and of greater relevance in the present context, the judicial acceptance of a distinction between primary and secondary victims is likely to have the effect of writing in stone the policy limitations prescribed in *Alcock*, removing the possibility, in the short term at least, of the courts' moving to embrace a more flexible proximity criterion or, more radically, the reasonable foreseeability test favoured by Lord Bridge in *McLoughlin v. O'Brian* [1983] 1 A.C. 410. Moreover, as the British, case-law shows, judicial consideration of the scope of duty owed to such claimants as police and fire fighters who suffer 'nervous shock' I the course of their employment can get side-lined into a semantic debate about whether they can aspire to the rosette of a 'primary victim' characterisation.

In *Curran v. Cadbury Ireland Ltd* [2000] 2 I.L.R.M. 343 (Circuit Court), Judge McMahon noted the criticisms that the English Law Commission had made of the distinction between primary and secondary victims. He observed:

> For my own part, I am not convinced that the separation of victims into these two categories does anything to assist the development of legal principles that should guide the courts in this complex area of the law. Hamilton CJ (with whom Egan J. agreed) did not refer to the distinction in *Kelly v. Hennessy* [1996] 1 I.L.R.M. 321, the leading Irish case on the matter, and while Denham J. in the same case used the term 'secondary victim' to describe the aftermath relatives who were plaintiffs in that case; her primary focus was naturally on the plaintiffs before her rather than on persons who are more directly involved in the accident.

In the instant case, Judge McMahon awarded compensation to the plaintiff, who sustained psychiatric injury when, on turning on a machine where she worked, she believed with good reason that she had killed or seriously injured a fellow employee who was working inside the machine without her knowledge. It was clear that, on Denham J's definition of a primary victim, the plaintiff came within its scope. The plaintiff had unwittingly become an essential link in the causative chain that resulted in injury to her colleague. Her injury was foreseeable in the circumstances.

Judge McMahon's subtle analysis of the subject, ranging widely over the common law world and academic texts, has provoked detailed discussion: see, e.g., Dunne, 'Secondary Victims and Nervous Shock', (2000) 5 Bar Rev 383.

BREACH OF STATUTORY DUTY

Employers' duty in respect of work equipment In the section on Employer's Liability earlier, we discussed *Everitt v. Thorsman Ireland Ltd.* [2000] 1 I.R. 256, where Kearns J. rejected the motion of a 'non-delegable duty of care' resting on an employer in respect of equipment supplied by a third party. The manner in which he disposed of the employee's claim for breach of statutory duty makes it plain that employers' immunity from common liability will be of no practical advantage to them since they will be impaled on statutory liability.

The plaintiff employee had been knocked over when a lever he was using to open the lid of a bin snapped and broke. The lever, supplied to the plaintiff's employer by another person, had a latent defect which the employer could not reasonably be expected to have discovered.

The plaintiff's claim for breach of statutory duty rested on two regulations in the Safety, Health and Welfare Act At Work (General Application) Regulations 1993 (S.I. No. 44). Regulation 19, in Kearns J.'s view 'imposes virtually an absolute duty on employers in respect of the safety of equipment provided for the use of their employees.' It provides in part as follows:

It shall be the duty of every employer to ensure that—

> (a) the necessary measures are taken so that the work equipment is suitable for the work to be carried out or is properly adapted for that purpose and may be used by employees without risk to their safety and health. . . .

Regulation 20 obliges employers to comply with the requirements of the Fifth Schedule which includes, as requirement 7, the following:

> Where there is a risk of rupture or disintegration of parts of work equipment, likely to pose significant danger to the safety and health of employees, appropriate protection measures shall be taken.

Kearns J. concluded:

> Accordingly, while there is no blameworthiness in any meaningful sense of the word on the part of the employer in this case, these Regulations do exist for sound policy reasons at least, namely, to ensure that an employee who suffers an injury at work through no fault of his own by using defective equipment should not be left without remedy. As O'Flaherty J. pointed out [in *Connolly v. Dundalk Urban District Council* Supreme Court, November 18, 1992] an employer in such a situation may usually, though not always, be in a position to seek indemnity from the third party who supplied the work equipment.

Accordingly Kearns J. imposed liability on the employer for breach of statutory duty.

In *Rogers v. Bus Atha Cliath*, Circuit Court, January 2000, the questions of an employer's duty to provide safe equipment and a safe system arose in the context of a bus driver being assaulted on two separate occasions in February and November 1995. There had been a dramatic increase in the number of serious assaults on bus drivers in the Dublin area in the period 1991-5. As far back as 1985, the vulnerability of bus drivers had been recognised by the employers who met with the drivers, the unions and Gardaí to discuss the problem. Various solutions were proposed as to how the driver in one-person buses might be protected. Some of these were installed but were vetoed by the drivers who, in one case, said the modified structure was too claustrophobic and, in another, that the perspex surround caused a glare. A horizontally sliding screen was then adopted, but after trials in November 1993 it was found to have two faults: first, the driver did not use it frequently, and second, it was not totally secure in so far as a determined assailant could get around it. Eventually by the middle of 1995 an agreed structure was adopted and all new buses were fitted with this structure, and all existing stock was scheduled for modification. The plaintiff's bus had not been fitted with the structure when he was attacked in February and again in November 1995. Judge McMahon held that the employers had acted reasonably in all the circumstances: they recognised the problem, they addressed it seriously, they spent considerable amounts of money in trying to design an acceptable frame, they continuously discussed the proposed solutions with the workers and the unions and, when finally an acceptable solution was devised, they began to implement the solution in a reasonable fashion.

The plaintiff further argued that, given the bad record of assaults on the plaintiff's particular route, the employers should have prioritised the conversion of his bus. Judge McMahon did not accept this argument, and in any event, he held that, even had the conversion been done, this would not have deterred the assailant since, the new agreed screens were not assault-proof and the assailant in the November assault, wearing a balaclava and armed with a butcher's knife, would have as easily rounded the proposed screen as he did the existing one.

Employer's duty to make work conditions safe   In *McSweeney v. J.S. McCarthy Ltd.*, Supreme Court, January 2000, an employer was held liable for breach of statutory duty (as well as common law negligence: see above 000-000) where an employee, an experienced painter and decorator, fell from a ladder which ought to have been held secure at its base by another person. The employee had not sought the assistance of his foreman, who was in the general area but not immediately accessible. The foreman had not specifically told the employee to call him.

Section 37(1) of the Factories Act 1955, as amended by section 12 of the Safety in Industry Act 1980 and section 73(3) of the Construction (Safety, Health and Welfare) Regulations 1975, provides as follows:

> Every place at which any person has at any time to work shall be made safe and kept in a safe condition and in addition to the foregoing there shall, so far as is reasonably practicable, be provided and maintained safe means of access to and egress from every such place.

426   *Annual Review of Irish Law 2000*

Section 73(3) of the Construction Regulations 1975 provides in part as follows:

> [W]here it is impracticable as regards a ladder standing on a base to comply [with other requirements of the section] ... a person shall be stationed at the foot of the ladder when in use to prevent it slipping.

It was not disputed that these provisions applied to the place and work which the plaintiff was carrying out at the time of the accident. Nor was it disputed that the unsecured ladder, at the time when it was used by the plaintiff, constituted an unsafe means of access to the place at which he had to work within the meaning of section 37.

The defendant argued that the work which the plaintiff had been asked to carry was essentially a one person job, that he was aware of the danger of climbing an unsecured ladder and knew that the foreman would come and hold it for him if requested to do so. Accordingly, the defendant contended, he had the means at his disposal to ensure that the ladder was made safe for use by getting the foreman to hold it for him and therefore there was no breach of statutory duty.

In the view of Murray J. (with whom Hamilton C.J. and Barron J. concurred), this argument sounded in contributory negligence rather than constituting grounds for relieving the defendant of the statutory duties specifically imposed on the employer. Murray J. observed:

> It is for the protection of persons in the workplace that statutory duties such as those contained in the aforementioned provisions are expressly imposed on employers in specific situations envisaged in those provisions and they cannot be abandoned and delegated to an employee by leaving him to his own devices such as happened here. It seems to me that it would be a negation of such statutory protection if an employer were allowed to leave it to the employee to ensure that the statutory provisions in question were observed because he should be considered capable of doing so. This would be to treat the statutory provisions and regulations as imposing a duty on the employee rather than the employer.

Contributory negligence In *McSweeney v. J.S. McCarthy Ltd.*, Supreme Court, January 28, 2000, a skilled worker and experienced painter and decorator who fell from a ladder because no one was holding it at its base was found to have been guilty of contributory negligence both in respect of his action for negligence at common law and his claim for breach of statutory duty. So far as the latter claim was concerned, section 125(7) of the Factories Act 1995, as amended by section 8 of the Safety in Industry Act 1980, was held applicable. This requires employees to whom these Acts apply to take reasonable care for their own safety. Murray J. (Hamilton and Barron JJ. concurring) stated:

> In apportioning degrees of fault, the courts have traditionally adopted a more lenient view of the contributory negligence of a workman when there is a breach of statutory duty on the part of the employer.
>
> In this case, however, the conduct of the plaintiff amounted to more than mere 'inadvertence' referred to in the authorities. It consisted of a deliberate act in his part when he knew of the risk involved.
>
> Having regard to the particular circumstances of this case I am satisfied that the negligence and breach of statutory duty of the plaintiff contributed substantially to the injury which he sustained.
>
> I would apportion degrees of fault under both headings as 40% to the plaintiff and 60% to the defendants …

In the instant case, it is clear that the same test – at least in its verbal expression – applied to the plaintiff both in respect of his common law claim and his action for breach of statutory duty: he was to take 'reasonable care' for his own safety. Yet, as Murray J. acknowledged, the test for employees' contributory negligence in actions for breach of statutory duty is 'more lenient' than that applicable to common law negligence claims. The reason for this, historically, is that paternalistic legislation in respect of employees' safety has been respected by the courts on the basis that its underlying policy would be frustrated by too zealous an application of the doctrine of contributory negligence. Yet this can create a certain dissonance. If an employee succeeds in both his claim for negligence and his action for breach of statutory duty, could the court find him 60% responsible in his common law claim and only 40% responsible in his action for breach of statutory duty? If so, is it right that he should be awarded 60% of his damages?

The statutory provisions requiring employees to take reasonable care for their own safety could have been interpreted as having abolished the difference in judicial policy as between negligence claims and actions for breach of statutory duty. A close reading of Murray J's analysis suggests that this is not his interpretation of their effect.

Delegation of duty Section 57(2) of the Civil Liability Act 1961 provides that '[i]t shall not be a defence in an action for breach of statutory duty merely to show that the defendant delegated the performance of the duty to the plaintiff.' In *Connell v. McGing*, High Court, December 8, 2000, Lavan J. invoked this section when holding that a discussion that had taken place between the defendant and his crew members on a fishing vessel as to certain safety alterations that ought to be taken in relation to the vessel could not exempt the defendant from liability for breach of statutory duty (the judgment not referring to the particular statutory provision imposing the duty in question). Lavan J. stated:

> The defendant cannot escape liability for breach of his statutory duty

by arguing that he diluted his obligation to provide a safe workplace by discussing the matter with his employees.

However, while delegation of a statutory duty is not a special defence this does not mean that the defendant will always be fully liable in every case where there is apparent delegation. The principles of contributory negligence still apply.

Lavan J. referred to *Ginty v. Belmont Supplies Ltd.* [1959] 1 All E.R. 414, where Pearson J. observed (at 423-4):

> In my view, the important and fundamental question in a case like this is not whether there was delegation, but simply the usual question: Whose fault was it?

In the instant case, the plaintiff claimed that, while in the course of his employment with the defendant on board the defendant's fishing boat, situated off the County Donegal coast, he was hauling in a fishing net on board the vessel, the negligence of the defendant, his servants or agents as employer led to the plaintiff's being dragged along the deck of the vessel, resulting in injury.

Lavan J.'s view of the evidence was that what was in operation on the day of the accident was a dangerous operation to the knowledge of the defendant. Lavan J. went on to reject the defence of contributory negligence, on the basis that the plaintiff had 'acted in a moment of crisis'.

STANDARD OF CARE

Protection of another's property from theft In *Scanlon v. Ormonde Brick Ltd.*, High Court, July 21, 2000, an interesting issue arose as to the extent to which one person is obliged to exert himself or herself to protect another's property from theft. Matters were complicated by the existence of a contractual relationship between the parties, coupled with a social tradition, undisturbed by the Garda Síochána, of turning a blind eye to the unauthorised removal of coal from mines.

The plaintiff had sold his mine to the defendant, reserving to himself any coal deposits, including the pillars exposed in the course of the defendant's removal of shale and fireclay. Shortly after the coal had been exposed by the defendant's operatives and the plaintiff was given the opportunity to remove it, he was prevented from continuing to do so because, it transpired, there was no statutory mining licence authorising him to do so. Subsequent negotiations involving the State Mining Board continued for seven years until 1997. In the meantime teams of men working with tractors and trailers and the necessary equipment removed the plaintiff's coal 'in an organised commercial way'. The plaintiff complained about this to the defendant, forwarding the names of those who had engaged in the removal but no action was taken to prevent the trespass. He also exposed the matter to the Garda Síochána but they were disinclined to take any action in the matter in the light of a longstanding local custom of unofficial removal of coal from mines in the area. Barr J. described this custom as follows:

> A pertinent historical note relating to coal-mining at Castlecomer is that over the years a custom developed whereby miners and their families regarded themselves as being entitled to enter the mining areas and remove the coal for their own use. The unauthorised removal of anthracite by miners was in some cases more extensive and they engaged in the sale of coal thus obtained. It seems that traditionally the mine owners turned a blind eye to such activities which were never formally sanctioned but were not regarded as pilfering in the strict sense of the term.

The plaintiff suffered losses approaching £100,000 as a result of this unauthorised removal.

Barr J. did not regard the defendant's failure to protect the plaintiff's coal from being pilfered as a breach of an implied term in the contract for the sale of the lands. He preferred to invoke the analogy of bailment, 'which may exist independent of contract.' He addressed the issue, under that characterisation, as follows:

> What duty did the defendant as bailee owe to the plaintiff as bailor of the coal? It was held by Barron J. in *Sheehy v. Faughnan* [1991] I.L.R.M. 719 that a bailee owes a duty to a bailor to take reasonable steps to prevent loss to the bailor, and where loss has occurred, the onus of proof is on the bailee to show that it did not occur through lack of reasonable care on his part...

Applying the judgment of Barron J. in *Sheehy v. Faughnan* Barr J. was satisfied that in the instant case the defendant had a duty to take reasonable steps to prevent loss to the plaintiff through pilfering of his coal from the defendant's lands:

> The fact that large scale pilfering over a protracted period of time without significant let or hindrance by the defendant was happening, even though from the beginning it was made aware of what was going on, itself indicates that reasonable efforts were not made by or on its behalf to protect the plaintiff's coal. The line taken on behalf of the defendant …. was that they denied having any liability to protect coal from being unlawfully taken by third parties from the lands. However, they did not regard themselves as having any obligation to stop the pilferers. It was

contended (as was the fact) that the defendant had complied with the fencing requirements set out in clause 7 of the special conditions of the contract and that that was all they were required to do ... I am satisfied that special condition 7 did not limit their liability in the matter of protecting the coal .... It is obvious that such fencing did not and would not protect the lands from coal pilfering and that substantially more was required to provide reasonable protection of the plaintiff's interest. That obligation was all the more obvious and important bearing in mind that, as the defendant was aware, the value of the coal in question was in effect part of the agreed purchase price....

Although securing the ... gates by ensuring that they could not be lifted off their hinges was probably a relatively simple matter, it was not until the mid 1990's that any steps were taken in that regard. It also emerged in evidence that no action was taken to increase the height of the main gate .... until after the coal had been removed from that area. [It was] conceded in evidence that the digging of a trench at the boundary of the ... lands would have prevented unauthorised tractors and trailers being brought onto [them] which was fundamental to the illegal removal of coal on a commercial scale. The defendant had appropriate machinery on the site to carry out such works but failed to do so ... Another alternative which was open to the defendant was to negotiate with the plaintiff the purchase of his interest in the coal in question thus avoiding the risk of deterioration in their relations with the local wrongdoers....

The onus is on the defendant to show that it took reasonable care to secure coal on its land ... for the benefit of the plaintiff in accordance with the contract . . ., 1989. The evidence establishes that in breach of contract and in breach of duty as bailee it failed to do so in consequence of which the plaintiff suffered substantial loss. This finding is borne out by the fact that, although the identify of the primary culprits was known to the defendant from the beginning, nothing of any significance was done to restrain the wrongdoers or to protect the plaintiff's interest for several years when it was too late.

Barr J.'s judgment gives rise to a few observations. First, there would have seemed to have been a straightforward claim for breach of contract on the facts of the case. It is not clear from the judgment whether the action included such a claim. The standard criteria for determining whether to imply a term of due care in protecting the plaintiff's coal from depradation would appear comfortably to yield such a conclusion.

Secondly, one may doubt whether the relationship between the parties was truly one of bailment since the coal was not personal property when still attached to the ground (unless one were, unconvincingly, to identify the short period of time *after* the coal had been severed from the realty by the pilferers while it still remained on the defendant's lands). Barr J. acknowledged that the bailment characterisation was by way of analogy. It nonetheless was treated as involving a shift of onus on to the defendant to show that it had used reasonable care. That is a somewhat potent effect for an analogy.

Thirdly, the defendant's obligation in relation to protecting the coal could be regarded as involving an issue of either the *standard*, or the *duty*, of care. The former identifies four factors and makes a value judgment, after due consideration of these factors as to whether the defendant fell below the appropriate standard of care. The latter approach uses more metaphysical (or, at all events, metaphorical) language: it seeks to establish whether there was a relationship of sufficient 'proximity' or 'neighbourhood' between the parties to impose a duty of care in the circumstances. Barr J. appears to have favoured the former approach. The four factors relevant to an assessment of the standard of care are: the *probability* of a detrimental occurrence taking place, the *gravity* of the threatened damage, the *social utility* (or lack of utility) of the defendant's activity and the *cost* of preventing damage. See McMahon & Binchy, *op. cit.*, paras. 7.25–7.54.

In the instant case, there clearly was a high probability of the pilfering of the plaintiff's coal in the absence of proper preventative strategies. There was a social custom of pilferage, in relation to which apparently not only mine owners but also the Garda Síochána turned a blind eye. From the month of June 1990 this probability had translated into certainty since the plaintiff had actually gone so far as to give to the defendant the names of the culprits. The gravity of the threatened damage was high: just short of £100,000 worth of coal. The social utility of the defendant's activity was neutral so far as the issues of the case were concerned. The defendant did not, it seems, argue that it should have deferred to the local custom of pilferage. Finally, Barr J. gave a comprehensive analysis of the cost of preventing the loss. It is clear from this that the defendant had failed to take simple and, it seems, not cost-prohibitive steps to avoid the risk of continuing pilferage.

So far as the duty of care was concerned, there surely was sufficient proximity of relationship between the parties to withstand any contention that the defendant was relieved of an obligation to take reasonable steps to protect the plaintiff's property from theft. It is true that the duty of care is circumscribed in three respects that might appear to be relevant to the case: these relate to *omissions* to act, the *activities of third parties* and *economic loss*. Traditionally, the law of negligence has been slow to impose affirmative obligations to assist the interests of others, particularly so where these interests are of an economic character. Moreover, there has been a strong judicial reluctance to hold one person legally responsible for the conduct of third parties who are acting outside the reach of the net of vicarious liability. Thus, in *Doherty Timber Ltd v. Drogheda Harbour Commissioners* [1993] 1 I.R. 315; [1993] I.L.R.M. 401, the defendants were absolved of liability where a consignment of timber, which had been left with their permission on the quayside, was set on fire by children who had access to the area, which was not protected by any system of security.

Flood J. held that no duty of care arose under the criterion set out in the Supreme Court decision of *Ward v. McMaster* [1988] I.R. 337. Whilst it was undoubtedly foreseeable that the goods might be damaged by either the deliberate or accidental conduct of third parties,

> the reality was a bare permission which caused no further obligations on the part of the harbour commissioners for the very simple reason that it would be virtually impossible to effectively implement ... Further, the consignee being the person primarily involved, it was for him to evaluate and assess the risk of damage to his goods.

Interestingly Flood J. also rejected the plaintiff's claim based on bailment on the basis that the bare permission by the defendant to have the goods deposited on its premises did not involve the degree of control necessary to create a bailment.

Clearly the facts in *Scanlan v. Ormonde Bricks Ltd* pointed in the other direction so far as the duty of care was concerned. The defendant was in a contractual relationship with the plaintiff which carried with it, if not an implied term to take reasonable care to protect his coal from being pilfered, certainly a sufficient degree of proximity of relationship to generate a duty of care in negligence.

Occupiers' liability In *Guckian v. Genport t/a Sachs Hotel*, High Court, November 2, 2000, a case involving an accident in May 1995 – two months before the Occupiers' Liability Act 1995 came into force on July 17, 1995 – the plaintiff, a patron at the defendants' night-club, tripped on a defect in the tiling at the top of the steps at the entrance. O'Donovan J. imposed liability observing that this was

> a defect of which the defendants were aware, or ought to have been aware, and, accordingly, should have recognised that it was a potential source of danger to persons frequenting their night-club; a danger which it seems to me that they took no steps to avoid.

Whilst O'Donovan J. did not in express terms characterise the defect in the tiling as an 'unusual danger', his remarks are otherwise close to the language of Willes J. in *Indermaur v. Dames* (1866) L.R. 1 C.P. 274, in respect of the duty owed by an invitor to an invitee. It seems clear enough that the outcome of the case would have been the same had the plaintiff been characterised as a 'visitor' under the 1995 Act, to whom a 'common duty of care' would be owed.

PROFESSIONAL NEGLIGENCE

Dentists In *Hamilton v. Cahill*, High Court, February 15, 2000, (Circuit Appeal) O'Higgins J. dismissed a claim of negligence by a patient against a dentist who had extracted one of her teeth. The essence of the claim was that the defendant had been negligent in failing to advert the fact that he had left a portion of the root of the extracted tooth in the jaw and in failing to take proper steps to remedy the situation. O'Higgins J. held that the defendant had not fallen below the requisite standard of care in his interpretation of the x-rays taken before and after the operation. In O'Higgins J's view, this was:

> fatal to the plaintiff's case. Absent any warnings of difficulty provided by the x-ray, the fact that the tooth was fractured 9even where coupled with the plaintiff's symptoms) was not in itself sufficient to alert the defendant to a potential problem. Indeed, such case has not been made.

Doctors and Hospitals In *Geoghegan v. Harris*, High Court, September 14, 2000, where a patient sued his dentist alleging negligence in the performance of implants and bone graft procedures, Kearns J, in an elaborate judgment, came to the conclusion of fact relating to the procedure adopted, that the defendant had transgressed a five millimetre barrier zone between the tips or apices of the plaintiff's lower frontal incisor teeth and the upper margin of the bone graft. He left over for further submission consideration of a number of other factual issues as well as questions of where the onus of proof lay in their regard and whether any issue as to legal causation arose. Kearns J. had already resolved an issue of informed consent to treatment in favour of the defendant on causal grounds.

In *O'Mahony v. Tyndale*, High Court, April 7, 2000, Quirke J. held that the defendant hospitals system for recording the condition and treatment of neonates immediately after birth 'was wholly inadequate and did not accord with proper and appropriate medical practice in that respect.' He dismissed the plaintiff's case, however, on the ground of lack of proof of causal connection between the hospital's negligence and the plaintiff's disability.

In *Wolfe v. St. James's Hospital,* High Court, November 22, 2000 Barr J. imposed liability in negligence on the defendant for the failure to diagnose a phaeochromocytoma, which resulted in the death of a patient. The patient had suffered from 'panic attacks' from time to time over a period of years. Having attended another hospital, he later became a patient at the defendant hospital in 1989, where he was successfully treated. He returned in 1991, when an ulcer was cured. No attempt was made at that time to investigate fully the possible source of his 'panic attacks'. Some time later he died.

Even though the condition was rare and hard to detect, Barr J. found that the doctor treating the patient had failed in his duty of care.

The symptoms which were known to [the doctor] are serious and, as previously stated, included nausea, vomiting, abdominal pain, headaches, shaking and loss of normal pallor. If they had been investigated it would have been discovered (a) that the attacks also included severe sweating; (b) that they had been happening in severe form since later 1988 and, crucially, (c) that they had become acute three years after Mr. Wolfe lost his permanent job in 1985. There is no evidence or expert testimony to connect the time lag between the onset and continuance of severe symptoms in 1988 and the loss of employment in 1985. In my view no clinician of comparable status and sill if acting with ordinary care would have failed to investigate 'panic attacks' having such severe associated symptoms. Having done so, he/she would have contemplated at least a possibility that the attacks from late 1988 were unrelated to the plaintiff's loss of employment in 1985 and that in fact they may have been caused by an as yet unidentified abdominal ailment. Once that possibility presented itself prudence would indicate that appropriate abdominal tests should be carried out. If that had been done in the instant case Mr. Wolfe's phaeo tumour would have been discovered and surgically treated with probable success.

In 1989 [the doctor's] tentative diagnosis of a viral infection did not explain the known symptoms of the attack which the patient had suffered – far less the full nature of such attacks if investigated. In my view he or his team should have investigated the attacks and, if so, would have discovered that they were unlikely to have any connection with the patient's loss of employment in 1985 and may have had a purely physical cause associated with the abdomen. It was negligent as defined in *Dunne's* case not to carry out that investigation, or to have it carried out by some other appropriate expert. Likewise, when Mr. Wolfe returned to [the doctor's] care in 1991 the 'panic attacks' from which he was suffering ought to have been investigated – all the more so that they were similar to those with which he had presented in 1989.

It has to be said that this holding appears to involve the application of a standard of care more stringent than used to be adopted in medical negligence litigation in Ireland. With the recent decision of the Supreme Court in *Collins v. Mid Western Health Board* [2000] 2 I.R. 154, it suggests that the bar for defining negligence in this context may be been lowered.

Informed consent   The extent to which a medical practitioner is obliged to inform his or her patient of the nature of proposed treatment – of its risks and the chances of success – is a question that has given rise to much analysis in the past couple of decades. Important philosophical and social questions are involved: at the base is a clash between the values of autonomy and paternalism.

What is the proper test for deciding whether the doctor has given sufficient information to the patient? Three principal solutions have been proposed. The first resolves the question by reference to the generally accepted practice in the medical profession. This approach stresses the fact that the decision of what to tell the patient has traditionally been regarded as primarily a matter of medical judgment and discretion. The second solution, at the other end of the spectrum, concentrates on the patient's right of self determination in regard to what is to be done to his or her body. It requires full disclosure of all material risks incident to the proposed treatment, so that the patient, rather than the doctor, makes the real choice as to whether treatment is to be carried out. As was stated in *Miller v. Kennedy* (1975) 85 Walsh 2d 151, 530 P 2d 334:

> 'The patient has the right to chart his own destiny, and the doctor must supply the patient with the material facts the patient will need in order to intelligently chart that destiny with dignity'

The third approach lies in between these two extremes. While tilting somewhat towards the first, it defers to customary medical practices of disclosure save where disclosure of a particular risk 'was so obviously necessary to an informed choice on the part of the patient that no reasonably prudent medical man would fail to make it': *Sidaway v. Governors of the Bethlem Royal Hospital* [1985] A.C. 871 at 900 (per Lord Bridge).

Courts in other jurisdictions have shown no unanimity on this matter. In England, in *Sidaway*, different members of the House of Lords favoured each of these positions: Lord Diplock the first, Lord Scarman the second, and Lords Bridge and Keith the third. The initial response in the courts in England below the level of the House of Lords to the competing views expressed in *Sidaway* was to favour Lord Diplock's approach. The general principle of reliance on customary medical practice when determining a medical negligence claim, on which Lord Diplock's approach was based, has since been rejected by the house of Lords in *Bolitho v. City and Hackney Health Authority* [1998] A.C. 232, in which their Lordships were careful to avoid becoming embroiled in a debate on informed consent. It might have been expected that the Bridge-Keith approach would move into the ascendancy since it is most easy to harmonise with the *Bolitho* philosophy on medical treatment. There are indications, however, that Lord Scarman's test, based on disclosure of material risks, may ultimately triumph in England. Cf. *Pearce v. United Bristol Healthcare NHS Trust* [1999] PIQR 53 (CA), analysed by Grubb (1999) 7 Med. LR 61. See also Kennedy & Grubb (eds.) *Principles of Medical Law* (1998), paras 3.136-3.138.

This liberal approach has been favoured by the Supreme Court of Canada in *Hopp v. Lepp* (1980) 112 D.L.R. (3d) 67 and *Reibl v. Hughes* (1980) 114 D.L.R. (3d) 1 and the High Court of Australia in *Rogers v. Whitaker* (1992) 175 Comm LR 479. In Ireland the subject was first addressed substantively by the Supreme Court in 1992, in *Walsh v. Family Planning Services* [1992] I.R.

796. For analysis of the decision, see the 1992 Review, 558-68. It cannot be said that *Walsh* left the law in a clear or satisfactory state.

Summarising the decision as a whole it may be observed that the Diplock approach in *Sidaway* found no support in *Walsh*. The Bridge/Keith approach was endorsed by Finlay C.J. and (less certainly) by McCarthy J. The Scarman approach was endorsed by O'Flaherty J., with whom Hederman J. concurred. So far as elective treatment is concerned, Finlay C.J., while formally remaining within parameters of the Bridge/Keith approach, postulated a degree of judicial policing of the disclosure requirement that brings it, in substance, far closer to the materiality test favoured by Lord Scarman in *Sidaway* and O'Flaherty and Hederman JJ. in *Walsh*. Similarly McCarthy J. tilted towards a materiality test in relation to elective treatment.

It is not perhaps surprising that in later decisions the High Court judges found difficulty in locating a clear *ratio* in *Walsh*.

The O'Flaherty/Hederman flag was raised in the most recent High Court analysis of the duty of disclosure in *Geoghegan v. Harris* [2000] 3 I.R. 536. This decision represents the most sophisticated and closely-reasoned discussion of the subject of an Irish court. For a comrehensive analysis of the judgment see Ciaran Cravey, 'Consent to Treatment by Patients – Disclosure Revisited' (2000) 6 Bar Review 56, 111.

The plaintiff complained that a dental implant procedure, involving a bone graft taken from his chin, had been carried out negligently by the defendant, leaving him with chronic neurapathic pain in his chin. He also claimed that the defendant had failed to disclose to him the risk that pain of this character might result from this procedure. Kearns J, with the consent of the parties, delivered a judgment on the latter issue first, leaving to a later date the issue of negligence.

Kearns J. subjected *Walsh v. Family Planning Services Ltd* to a serious critical scrutiny. He expressed his opposition to the approach favoured by Finlay C.J. since he did not consider that the *Dunne* test for medical treatment in general, which in essence the Chief Justice applied in *Walsh*, could convincingly be so extended. Kearns J. observed:

> Where the medical professional standard is adopted, subject to a caveat or saver, then, to me at least, it makes no great sense to oust from any meaningful role the views of the self-same medical practitioners as to the materiality of a risk or the need for a warning. Their views are received and relied upon in ordinary medical negligence cases. Who else can supply evidence of inherent defects? To substitute its own view, effectively in opposition to the experts on whose views, at least in the first instance, it purports to rely, the Court sets at nought the professional standard test and the result in the instant case is that the defendant must be found to be in breach of duty when not a single expert from either side believes a warning to be necessary.

Kearns J. quoted passages from the Supreme Court judgments in *Roche v. Peilow*, [1985] I.R. 232, which dealt with the court's power to override an established professional customary practice. That case had involved a claim for negligence against a solicitor. Henchy J. had expressed the view that a person could not be considered to be acting reasonably if he mindlessly followed the practice of others when, if he had given the matter thought, he would have realised that the practice in question was 'fraught with peril' for his client and was readily avoidable or remediable. McCarthy J. had considered it was the solicitor's duty to warn against 'a clear and present danger' of financial loss for the client. Kearns J. placed emphasis on the quoted phrases. In a crucial passage, he stated:

> *Roche v. Peilow* strongly suggests that the exception should only operate where a high onus is met and the defect, ignored or tolerated by the approved practice of a profession, relates to an obvious risk or danger, which is in very marked contrast to the instant case. The exception is there to address an obvious lacuna in professional practice usually arising from a residual adherence to out-of-date ideas. It seems an inappropriate mechanism to find fault with medical practitioners for failing to warn of very remote risks which for that very quality cannot be regarded an obvious or 'clear and present danger' even on due consideration. It is yet another reason to think that the third principle in *Dunne,* though suitable for medical treatment, is perhaps inappropriate in the distinctly different context of disclosure. One must surely conclude that the more remote the risk, the harder it is to judge any practice of not disclosing it to be 'blind, lax or inherently negligent'. The converse approach adopted in *Walsh* was justified by reference to the elective nature of the surgery, but that consideration ... is more appropriate to the issue of causation than any duty of disclosure, where the seriousness of the consequences and the frequency of the risk are the real concern.

Perhaps this analysis can be debated. There is nothing illogical or implausible in a court's conclusion that, in particular circumstances, it is obviously necessary for a doctor to disclose to a patient a very small risk relating to the proposed treatment. It is not the risk that must be obvious; what is essential is that the situation be one in which disclosure is obviously necessary. Whether disclosure of a small risk is obviously necessary involves a value-judgment on the part of the court. If a small risk of very serious injury is an element of a particular treatment, where the patient has other options, one could envisage a court's concluding that disclosure was 'obviously necessary' thus keeping requirements as to disclosure in broad harmony with the approach favoured in *Dunne.*

What is interesting about the passage just quoted from Kearns J.'s judgment is that Kearns J. did not regard the elective nature of the proposed treatment as a distinctive reason for expanding the range of disclosure of risks. He proceeded on the basis that in relation to both elective and non-elective treatments, there is an obligation restiring on the doctor to give a warning to the patient of any material risk that is a 'known complication' of an operative procedure carefully carried out, even if the risk of its occurrence is very small. The only proviso or clarification that Kearns J. considered necessary was that:

> clearly the duty must be confined to such consequences or consequence which may be described as foreseeable or predictable consequences arising from such complications. Mere coincidental and unrelated risks, for example, could not properly fall within the compass of any duty, any more than consequences which might flow from the practitioner's negligence.

In the instant case, Kearns J. held that nerve damage had to be characterised as a 'known complication' of the procedure, 'be it implants *per se,* or bone grafts, in the chin area'. The particular symptom of neuropathic pain was 'a subdivision, not in a different species of risk or unrelated risk'. It was 'foreseeable as a consequence of damaging nerves and certainly those nerves' with which this case is concerned'. Once that was established, the fact that the particular manifestation of the nerve damage was very remote and unusual - 'one in multiple thousands' - was legally immaterial, since it was within the range of what was known or should be known by the medical practitioner.

What is not entirely clear from Kearns J.'s judgment is whether the materiality test should require disclosure of 'known complications' in every case. In favour of the view that it does, it can be argued that, if a risk of 'one in multiple thousands' had to be disclosed in the instant case by reason of its being a known complication (in the sense of being a complication capable of being identified in advance), there would seem no obvious reason in principle for setting the bar higher in another case. As against this, Kearns J. did make it clear that the disclosure standard he prescribed was to apply in the instant case, and his judgment contained an important passage in which he appeared to accept that what must be disclosed is less than every possible known risk and will depend on the particular circumstances of each case:

> The application of the reasonable patient test seems more logical (than that of *Dunne)* in respect of disclosure. This would establish the proposition that, as a general principle, the patient has the right to know and the practitioner a duty to advise of all material risks associated with a proposed form of treatment. The court must ultimately decide what is material. 'Materiality' includes consideration of both (a) the severity of the consequences and (b) statistical frequency of the risk. That both are critical is obvious because a risk may have serious consequences and yet historically or predictably be so rare as not to be regarded as significant by many people. For example, a tourist might

be deterred from visiting a country where there had been an earthquake causing loss of life, but if told the event happened fifty years ago without repetition since, he might well wonder why his travel agent caused him unnecessary worry by mentioning it at all.

The reasonable man, entitled as he may be to full information of material risks, does not have impossible expectations nor does he seek to impose impossible standards. He does not invoke only the wisdom of hindsight if things go wrong. He must be taken as needing medical practitioners to deliver on their medical expertise without executive restraint or gross limitation on their ability to do so.

The decision in *Walsh* effectively confines the test of materiality to severity of consequences only ...

However, [there is a] possibility that at times a risk may become so remote, in relation at any rate to the less than most serious consequences, that a reasonable man may not regard it as material or significant. While such cases may be few in number, they do suggest that an absolute requirement of disclosure in every case is unduly onerous, and perhaps in the end counter productive if it needlessly deters patients from undergoing operations which are in their best interests to have.

As pointed out by Mr. Healy *Medical Negligence: Common Law Perspectives* (1999), p 99: 'materiality is not a static concept'. If the assessment of materiality is to abide a rule of reason, any absolute requirement which ignores frequency seems much at variance with any such rule.

Every case it seems to me should be considered in the light of its own particular facts, evidence and circumstances to see if the reasonable patient in the plaintiff's position would have required a warning of the particular risk.

Looking at Kearns J.'s analysis of the issue of duty of disclosure in its entirety, it seems clear that he favours the 'material disclosure' test and that he envisages that this involves a very wide range of disclosure of risk, at all events where what is at stake is the risk of serious injury or death. Precisely how this translates into practice in specific cases other than the instant case awaits further judicial analysis.

The final, and crucial, issue in the case was that of causation. If a patient would still have embarked on the treatment had the dentist (or doctor) made the proper disclosure then he or she will have no right of action since the failure to disclose did not result in any injury that would not otherwise have occurred. In determining whether the patient would have undergone the treatment, is it good enough to rely on what the patient says or should a more objective test be adopted to avoid the risk of self-deception on the part of injured patients? Kearns J. discussed decisions from the United States and Canada which favoured the objective 'prudent patient' test, as well as decisions from Australia favouring the subjective plaintiff-centred test. Noting that English decisions also favoured the subjective test, he eventually adopted a hybrid test.

In the first instance, the court should consider the problem from an objective point of view by asking itself what a reasonable person, in the plaintiff's position would have done if properly informed. Taking account of the plaintiff's position would involve having regard to the plaintiff's age, pre-existing health, and family and financial circumstances assessed, though personal to the plaintiff'. The objective test would sometimes have to yield to a subjective test, 'but only when credible evidence, and not necessarily that of the plaintiff, in the particular case so demands.'

Kearns J., having considered that, wherever possible, the court should look beyond the testimony of the parties for credible confirmation, went on to observe:

> If this dual and combined approach smacks of pragmatism, so be it. It is in my view well justified if it achieves a better result in terms of deciding what probably would have occurred. At the end of the day it seems to me that the different approaches are more about methodology than any legal principle. It is an exercise in 'fact construction'. In any such hypothetical though necessary exercise, there are dangers in dogmatically adopting one approach to the exclusion of the other, and certain aids to analysis would be forsaken by doing so.

This passage makes it plain that Kearns J. was applying causal criteria that are faithful to the general approach in negligence litigation which is to enquire into what would have been the position if the negligent act had not taken place. In the context of the issue of informed consent, that question can be answered by reference to the particular plaintiff: what would this plaintiff have done had he or she been told of the risks involved in the proposed treatment? Kearns J. was surely correct to place emphasis on the objective facts external to the parties' testimony, in determining the answer to the question but, in doing so, he was conscious that this was not transforming the test into that of a hypothetical 'prudent patient'. At the end of the day, the judicial definition is about how the plaintiff in the proceedings would have acted if properly informed.

Kearns J, expressing his agreement with Dr. White's analysis, in *Medical Negligence Actions*, (1996), p. 190, of the issue of the relevance of the elective character of the treatment to the duty of disclosure and causation, respectively, went on to re-emphasise that he considered that the significance of the elective dimension lay in causation rather than the duty to inform. It was obvious common sense to hold that a person might forego surgery when he had a real choice in the matter but, even in making a decision as to whether or not to undergo elective surgery, the reasonable man would be very greatly influenced by the statistical likelihood of the particular adverse consequence ever taking place:

> If the risk is virtually off the spectrum, then I believe a reasonable man might accept or disregard such a risk where it is not in the more serious category and when he has regard to the perceived benefits attaching to the proposed procedure.

In the instant case, Kearns J., placing more emphasis on the objective than the subjective factors, in view of their greater reliability, concluded that, had there been proper disclosure, the plaintiff would still have undergone the treatment. He had been keen to have it and his conduct clearly suggested that he was not going to be put off by some very remote risk when balanced with the perceived benefits of the procedure. Accordingly Kearns J. held against the plaintiff on the causation issue, with the result that no liability attached to the defendant in respect of the claim based on lack of disclosure of risk.

It is fair to say that no other Irish judge has examined the issue of informed consent to treatment in as thorough and philosophical manner as Kearns J. did in *Geoghegan v. Harris.*

Lawyers   In *Murphy v. Proctor*, High Court, October 11, 2000, Kelly J. dismissed proceedings in negligence taken by purchasers of a shop against their solicitor. The purchasers, who were the first and second plaintiffs, claimed that the defendant had failed to make it clear to them that the property they were buying did not include a right to immediate possession of its forecourt. After a detailed review of the evidence, in which he made it clear that he preferred the defendant's evidence, Kelly J. rejected the claim. He accepted that the defendant had advised the purchasers that the forecourt as identified on the map which he had produced to them:

> was not part of the premises that they were buying as such. This explanation was given in non-legal language. It did not involve the defendant telling them that the interest in the forecourt was with Dublin Corporation and that they had a reversion which would fall in some hundred years hence. I quite accept the common sense approach of the defendant when he indicated that he put the advice to them in non-technical language and made it clear that they were not getting the forecourt as part of the premises.

There had undoubtedly been a discussion relating to the use of the forecourt by the vendor. Kelly J. accepted that the defendant had told the purchasers that there would probably be no problems with continuing that use but that it could not be guaranteed.

Two other issues of potentially general legal interest arose but neither generated liability in the circumstances. The first concerned the time of the planning searches in respect of the premises. The search was carried out *after* the signing of the contract and before the closing of the sale. It demonstrated that a year previously an enforcement order had been made by the planning authority requiring the removal of a sign and the steel cage on the forecourt and the discontinuance of the forecourt for use as a fuel storage area within two months. When this appeared on the search a discussion took place about it. The defendant had no great concern in respect of the enforcement notice, regarding it as being really directed to the way in which canisters had been stored in steel cages at times when the shop was closed. His understanding was that the vendor had changed the method of storage so as to keep the canisters within the confines of the shop at night and that that satisfied the planning authority.

The essence of the purchasers' claim in this context was that, if the defendant had carried out the planning search before the signing of the contract, as they argued he should have done, this would have demonstrated the existence of the enforcement order. Kelly J. rejected this claim on causal grounds. He said:

> Whatever may have been the conveyancing practice in 1989 in this regard (and I do not propose to make any finding on this topic) I cannot see how the [purchasers] can demonstrate any loss would flow to them even if it had been appropriate to carry out such a planning search. What it would have demonstrated was the existence of an enforcement notice in respect of part of the premises that was not in practical terms in sale. The fact is that on the [date the contract was signed] the defendant was fully aware of what was being sold. He had read the title that day. He had prepared the deed in draft form. It was subsequently engrossed without amendment. He had told the [purchasers] that the forecourt was not in sale. If the defendant had not been aware on [that date] of what was being purchased then maybe the enforcement notice might have set him off on a train of enquiry or jogged his memory in some way. But that is not the case here. I find the [purchasers] have not made out a case in this regard.

The issue therefore still remains open for future judicial consideration. Earlier decisions have addressed the question of when particular searches should be made in conveyancing practice: see, e.g. *Roche v. Peilow* [1985] I.R. 232. In the instant case Kelly J. made no reference to what evidence (if any) had been addressed as to professional practice on the matter.

The second issue that arose in the instant case concerned the defendant's possible liability in negligence to the third plaintiff, a company formed by the first and second plaintiffs several months after the purchase, with a view to redeveloping the premises. Kelly J. held that the defendant owed no duty of care to the company. He did:

not accept that at ... any of the [meetings before the purchase] was the defendant alerted to any intentions with the [first and second] plaintiffs might have had with a view to redeveloping the premises in the future ...

I am also satisfied that there was not at th[ese meetings] any mention of an intention on the part of the [first and second] plaintiffs to form the third named plaintiff company. In fact that company was not formed until many months afterwards and the defendant had no part in its formation. I am therefore satisfied that at no time did the defendant owe any duty of care to the third named plaintiff.

The reason for exempting the defendant from such a duty of care appears to have been its lack of foreseeability or proximate nexus to the defendant. The mere fact that a company (or, indeed, a human being) comes into existence after one has acted is not in itself a reason preventing a possible duty of care from falling upon one. Provided the requirements of proximity and foreseeability are met, such a duty of care may arise.

NEGLIGENT MISREPRESENTATION

Ingredients of the tort In Annual Review 1998,173-4, Eoin O'Dell analysed the decision of Morris P in *Wildgust v. Bank of Ireland and Norwich Union Life Assurance Society*, High Court, July 28, 1998. See also the 1998 Review 633-4. There the essence of the plaintiff's case against the second named defendant was that one of its representatives had represented to certain bankers from whom the first named plaintiff had obtained a loan secured by a life insurance policy that the policy had been reinstated because payment had been made in respect of it when this was not in fact the case. Morris P declined to grant a non-suit as he considered that this amounted to a claim for negligent misrepresentation but, as the claim, in his view, had not been made out with sufficient clarity on the pleadings, he made an order granting the plaintiffs liberty to amend their statement of claim, penalising them in costs and putting the case back for new hearing.

The plaintiffs appealed to the Supreme Court, arguing that the statement of claim had in fact made out a claim for negligent misrepresentation and that the case should have been allowed to proceed as the defendants were aware of the substance of the claim: [2001] 1 I.L.R.M. 24.

McGuinness J. ((Denham and Murphy JJ concurring), rejected the former, but accepted the latter argument. She addressed the former argument as follows:

I cannot accept that this in any way sets out a claim of negligent misstatement under *Hedley Byrne* principles. It does not state the duty of care owed by the second named defendant to the plaintiffs. It does not state that the communication in question was made to the plaintiffs, or at least to agents of the plaintiffs. It does not state that the plaintiffs, or indeed Hill Samuel Bank Ltd, relied on the communication or that Norwich Union knew that they would rely on it: nor does it clearly set out that the plaintiffs acted to their detriment in reliance on the communication. It does not even set out that the communication was untrue. All of these things would be normal elements in the pleading of a claim of negligent misstatement and are material facts rather than matters of law. Even given the subsequent details provided in the replies to particulars it could not be clear to the defendants on the basis of the pleadings that they had to meet a claim of negligent misstatement. [Counsel for the second defendant] is, I consider, justified in arguing that paragraph 13 and the following paragraphs appeared to him to be part of the plaintiffs' allegation of *mala fides* on the part of the second named defendant.

Accordingly in my view the learned President of the High Court was correct in holding that on the pleadings he was 'unable to find any case based upon negligent misstatement or broadly based on the *Hedley Byrne v. Heller* principle'.

The import of this analysis is that the Supreme Court is not disposed at present to subsume negligent misrepresentation under a more general rubric of negligence based on the proximity principle. The tendency in that direction, evident in *Forshall v. Walsh,* Supreme Court, 31 July 31, 1998 (noted in Annual Review 1998, 633) appears to have been halted.

Scope of advice and reliance   Earlier in the Chapter, in the section on Duty of Care, above, 415, we analyse the important decision of *Gayson v. Allied Irish Banks Ltd*, High Court, January 28, 2000, in which Geoghegan J. addressed a number of issues relating to the tort of negligent misrepresentation. One of these was the scope of the bank's advisory functions. Geoghegan J. held that this did not extend to advising customers on whether or not they should avail themselves of a tax amnesty. On the evidence in the case, Geoghegan J. held that the plaintiff had not relied on any such advice. Moreover, as a matter of public policy the courts should not recognise that an actionable duty of care arose as to advice where one of two possible options was clearly illegal.

ROAD TRAFFIC ACCIDENTS

Changing lanes   In *Sherry v. Smith*, High Court, December 20, 2000, an accident took place on the Naas dual carriageway when the plaintiff's vehicle, travelling at around 90 miles per hour, collided with the defendant's vehicle, travelling at a much slower speed. The defendant was in the process of changing lanes. He had used his indicator but had not seen the plaintiff's vehicle. The plaintiff had a measurement of 125 ml of alcohol per ml of blood when breathalysed after the accident.

Johnson J. imposed liability on the defendant. He observed:

> The evidence is that at no time was the defendant aware that the plaintiff was on the roadway at all. There is a duty on persons moving from one laneway to another to ensure [when] they are so doing that they do so without causing embarrassment or danger to any other road user. In order to carry out their obligations on foot of this requirement it is necessary that they should check carefully the mirrors to ensure that it is safe to so do and I find the defendant did not so do.

Johnson J. reduced the damages by 75%, however, to take account the plaintiff's contributory negligence in driving at excessive speed having consumed alcohol, both factors in combination making him unable to respond effectively to the emergency created by the defendant.

Roundabouts In *Pierce v. Mitchell Ltd*, High Court, October 11, 2000, a collision occurred at a roundabout which was not marked in traffic lanes. The plaintiff and the defendant driving separate vehicles – a car and a goods vehicle – entered the roundabout travelling more or less in parallel in the same direction. When on the roundabout, closer to its fulcrum than the defendant, the plaintiff indicated her intention to leave the roundabout onto a road directly opposite to the point that she and the defendant had entered the roundabout. The defendant's goods vehicle bumped into her car as she sought to execute this manoeuvre. The defendant had intended to come off the roundabout at the next exit, which was in the direction of Tallaght. Imposing liability, Herbert J. observed:

> If the …. defendant saw the plaintiff's indicating left, as he ought to have done had he been keeping a proper lookout, and also observed the position of her car, he must have realised that if he drove across the first exit a collision with the plaintiff's car was almost inevitable. I accept the evidence of the plaintiff and [her passenger] that the …. defendant did not indicate right, sound the horn of his vehicle or even flash the headlights of the vehicle or give any indication whatsoever of his intention to continue across the first exit. In my judgment 'conditions dictated', the phrase used in the Rules of the Road, that the plaintiff was entitled to be in the position she was on the roundabout and to follow the course which she intended and signalled.
>
> I agree with counsel for the defendan[t] that in the circumstances and having regard to the Rules of the Road the goods vehicle was not occupying an incorrect position on the roundabout in continuing to

travel in the outside or left notional lane. However, in my judgment this did not give the goods vehicle right of way over the plaintiff's vehicle. The collision, on the evidence, occurred entirely in the mouth of the inside or right lane of the exit dual carriageway. The plaintiff's vehicle had almost completed its turn into this lane prior to the collision. At any point after the two vehicles had entered the roundabout travelling more or less in parallel, the goods vehicle would have had to turn across the path of the car if it intended to travel in the direction of Tallaght so long as the car was continuing straight ahead. In all the circumstances the .... defendant was obliged to be very aware of the presence and position of the plaintiff's car and to have slowed down or even stopped in response to the plaintiff's signal and permitted her to pass safely in front of his vehicle and continue into the exit from the roundabout. In my judgment, having regard to the evidence, and on the balance of probability the sole cause of this collision was a lack of due care and attention on the part of the ... defendant.

Pedestrians   In *Kelly v. Bus Átha Cliath – Dublin Bus*, Supreme Court, March 16, 2000, the plaintiff pedestrian was injured when struck by a bus as it was making a turn around a corner where there was a pedestrian crossing controlled by traffic lights. The bus went over his foot, resulting in the need to have it amputated. The plaintiff claimed that the accident occurred when he was standing on the pavement. He said that he did not see the bus approach as he was looking at a fire engine some distance away. The bus driver's evidence was that the plaintiff had walked onto the side of the bus well out on the roadway as the bus was negotiating the turn. This evidence was supported by another bus driver who was immediately behind the bus involved in the accident.

Johnson J. found wholly for the plaintiff. He did so on the basis that if the accident had happened as the defendant claimed:

> ... there would have been a major, as far as I am concerned, space between the side of the bus and the pavement and there is no reason why one and if not both drivers should not have seen the plaintiff walking off the pavement in what appears to be an empty space.

Johnson J.'s central finding of fact in the case was expressed as follows:

> Now, under those circumstances, I feel on the balance of probabilities, with a certain amount of doubt, I am satisfied that the bus mounted the pavement and collided with the plaintiff's leg in the manner in which the plaintiff described.

The defendant appealed, on the basis that there had been clear evidence, from both bus drivers, that they had indeed seen the plaintiff before the impact and that this evidence was clearly inconsistent with the inference drawn from the proposition that neither driver had seen the plaintiff 'in what appears to be an empty space'.

The Supreme Court, by a majority, upheld the appeal and ordered a retrial. Hardiman J. (Keane C.J. concurring) considered that, consistently with the approach adopted in *Hay v. O'Grady* [1992] 1 I.R. 210, at 217-8, it was not possible to imply from the trial judge's findings that he had rejected the evidence of the second driver.

> It was open to the learned trial judge to accept or reject this evidence. Either course would constitute a finding of primary fact, and its rejection was crucial to the inference that the impact occurred on the pavement. Only this finding would lead directly to a result wholly in favour of the plaintiff.

Murphy J., dissenting, interpreted Johnson J.'s remarks on the crucial issue of what the drivers had said differently. He did not consider that Johnson J. had been intending to assert that neither driver had claimed to have seen the plaintiff before the accident occurred:

> It is frequently difficult to reconstruct satisfactorily the atmosphere of a High Court trial or the emphasis placed by counsel or witnesses on different matters in the course of the trial. I suspect that the concern which the learned trial Judge sought to convey in the [crucial] passage ... have quoted from his judgment was the failure of either driver to see the plaintiff 'walking off the pavement'. The judge had said there was or would have been 'a major ... space between the side of the bus and the pavement' and it seems to me that he believed in those circumstances at least one of the drivers should have seen [the plaintiff] 'walking off the pavement'.

> That interpretation is consistent with the actual words used in the judgment and avoids the improbable inference that the learned trial judge had over looked the evidence given by a crucial and emphatic witness.

Extrinsic evidence In *Furey v. Suckau* High Court, July 14, 2000, in fatal accident proceedings, the plaintiff's claim depended on 'extrinsic evidence and the theories of various engineers and members of ... An Garda Siochana.'. An accident took place on the main Roscommon to Athlone Road as the defendant was seeking to make a right turn with his camper van. Ó Caoimh J, after a detailed analysis of the evidence, concluded that the deceased driver in relation to whose death the claim was made had been travelling at excessive speed. The defendant was not, however, free from blame as he had failed to position his vehicle in the correct position on the road as he was executing the turn. Ó Caoimh J. held that a deduction of 80% should be made from the damages awarded to take account of the deceased driver's contributory negligence.

Contributory negligence   In *Callaghan v. Bus Átha Cliath/Dublin Bus*, High Court, December 1, 2000, a massive reduction of 90% was made for the plaintiff driver's contributory negligence when he collided with a bus on a dual carriageway. The bus driver was attempting a right U-turn on a dual carriageway with a left junction. There were traffic lights at the junction. The road markings indicated straight ahead and to the left. Thus, the bus driver was attempting to proceed inconsistently with these markings. He gave no hand signals and did not use the hazard lights. The plaintiff was coming behind the bus, travelling well in excess of the 40 mph limitation,. His own estimate was between 55 and 60 mph; that of another car driver whom he passed was 70 mph. He said he panicked when he saw the bus going broadside, slammed on his brakes and geared down. He turned to veer through the inside lane but traffic would not yield. He did not remember seeing an indicator on the bus which the other car driver saw. The bus driver gave evidence that, while he had intended to execute a U-turn he realised that there would not be enough room to do so and decided to continue straight.

Murphy J. noted that it was clear from the detailed evidence in the case that the bus 'was not presenting broadside to the plaintiff in any degree.' He observed:

> While one cannot condone any road user seeking to execute a U-turn where the road markings clearly indicated straight on nor approve indecisiveness, yet this was to the cause of the accident. If the bus had to stop because of traffic lights or because somebody or animal was attempting to cross the road then the same objective circumstances would have prevented themselves to the plaintiff.

Murphy J. found relevance in the decision of *Sinnott v. Quinnsworth Ltd*, [1984] I.L.R.M. 523 where a car ran into a bus coming the opposite way which was not as close as possible to the left hand side of the road. The Supreme Court had overturned a 20% finding of blame on the part of the bus driver, preferring to ascribe total blame to the car driver. O'Higgins CJ observed that

> [t]o suggest to a jury ... that a driver to a vehicle on the roadway has at all times [a] general duty to drive as close as practicable or possible to his leftside is to mislead.

In the instant case, Murphy J. noted that:

> the bus driver was attempting to execute a right hand turn which was counter indicated by the traffic arrows. There is, accordingly, evidence to support some minor degree of blame on the part of the defendant.

The 90% reduction is greater than the norm in cases of this type. The bus driver was engaging in a significantly careless activity, albeit at a slow speed and (though Murphy J. made no express finding to this effect) having used the indicator. *Sinnott* is not very close on its facts (ignoring the irrelevant fact that a bus was involved in both cases) since in *Sinnott* a finding of fault on the part of the bus driver had been premised on a clearly untenable assumption that his duty had been to drive as close to the left side as possible. No similar consideration arose in the instant case. The bus driver was on the right hand side of the road, in the course of, or immediately having abandoned, an attempt to engage in an illegal and dangerous manoeuvre.

Emergency vehicles In the Annual Review 1993, 537-8, we analysed O'Hanlon J.'s judgment in *Strick v. Treacy,* High Court, June 10, 1993, imposing liability in negligence on the driver of a fire tender and a Garda car driver for an accident at a road junction. It is clear that drivers of emergency vehicles have no immunity from being sued, though of course the high social utility of their work will be taken into account in determining whether they fell under the appropriate standard of care: see McMahon & Binchy, *op. cit.,* paras 7.38-7.43.

In *O'Keeffe v. Ladola and Dublin Corporation*, Circuit Court, 12 January 2000, the plaintiff was a passenger in a bus which collided with an ambulance flashing its emergency light. The bus driver was approaching a main road intersection intending to turn right. He slowed down looking first to his right and then to his left. A motorist coming from the bus could emerge across the motorist's path. The bus driver did not look to his right again, but moved into the junction. An ambulance driving fast in an emergency struck the bus from the right. The bus driver, if he looked to his right, had a clear view for 300 yards on the main road. The ambulance driver was travelling at forty miles per hour in a thirty mile an hour speed zone, and had his strobe lights and siren operating. The ambulance had come through a red light some distance back from the scene of the crash and from some seventy yards back had a full view of the bus emerging. Girls travelling in the bus saw the ambulance approaching as the bus drove into the junction. Judge McMahon held the bus driver liable for eighty per cent and the ambulance driver twenty per cent.

TRESPASS TO LAND

It is well established that trespass to land is a tort infringing possession. What constitutes possession depends naturally on the evidence in each case.

In *Feehan v. Leamy*, High Court, May 29, 2000, the plaintiff was held to have been in possession of agricultural lands where the evidence was that, although he had no cattle on the lands and only visited the property on several occasions every year, he would park his car and stand on the road or in the gateway looking over the hedge or gate onto his fields. He was never prevented from doing this by the second named defendant. Finnegan J. applied the presumption that the plaintiff's title extended from the centre of the road; accordingly, 'when standing at the gate looking into the lands the plaintiff was in fact standing on his own lands.' For much to the time, the plaintiff was involved in litigation against another party seeking to establish – as in fact he ultimately did – his title to the property. In looking over the fence or gate, Finnegan J. considered that 'the plaintiff was exercising all the rights of ownership which he wished to exercise in respect of the lands pending the determination of the litigation'. It has to be said that this is an unusually broad interpretation of what constitutes possession.

TRESPASS TO GOODS

The issue of the defence of lawful authority in relation to the defence of trespass to goods was canvassed in *Mongan v. South Dublin County Council*, High Court, October 13, 2000, where the applicant, in judicial review proceedings, contested the legality of the seizure of the applicant's horses by the employees of the respondent council and their detention outside its functional area. Ó Caoimh J. held that the seizure and detention were lawful under section 37(3) of the Control of Horses Act 1996. The applicant was a member of the Traveller Community. Traveller traditions and culture include a strong emphasis on owning horses. The applicant argued that this love of horses should be respected by the law. Ó Caoimh J. acknowledged this cultural dimension but considered it:

> important for the applicant and any other member of the Travelling Community to realise that changes have been affected in the law by the Control of Horses Act 1996 and notwithstanding his wishes to maintain traditions and culture that these traditions and culture can only be maintained within the terms of the law.

Nevertheless Ó Caoimh J. expressed the hope that the respondent council might be in a position to assist the applicant and other members of the Travelling Community to maintain their traditions and culture 'within reasonable limits.'

PASSING OFF

In *Sweeney v. National University of Ireland Cork t/a Cork University Press* [2001] 1 I.L.R.M. 310, Smyth J. granted an interlocutory injunction against the infringement in the plaintiff's copyright in the works of James Joyce and against passing off a work that was not by James Joyce as such a work. Smyth J.'s analysis concentrated on the former claim. The parties did not dispute that there existed a fair question to be tried. Both of them relied on Laffoy J.'s judgment in *Symonds Cider and English Wine Co Ltd v. Showerings (Ireland) ltd* [1997] 1 I.L.R.M. 481. In the instant case, the defendant had entered into unsuccessful negotiations with the plaintiff for permission to publish a number of pieces from James Joyce's works in anthology. The plaintiff had indicated that the licence fee would be £7,000 sterling.

Smyth J. considered that, in copyright cases such as this, the balance of convenience lay in favour of granting an interlocutory injunction:

> The nature of copyright is such that while the owner may voluntarily permit licence or consent to the use in whole or part of a protected work (for a fee or otherwise) it is a right that cannot be wrested from the owner by a person even tendering the fee in full. The terms and conditions, if not agreed upon, cannot be imposed by the applicant proceeding in the face of objection and seeking to publish in whole or part a protected work in the hope or knowledge that it can pay a sum of money. The courts cannot by failing to recognise and uphold the right condemn – most particularly at interlocutory stage when so many facts are in dispute, and points of law require determination – the owner of the right to be content until the hearing of the action to permit the breach of a right in respect of which there is a statutory presumption.

Smyth J. said nothing specific on the issue of passing off but the injunction awarded appears to have embraced this claim as well as that in relation to copyright.

In *Local Ireland Ltd. v. Local Ireland-Online Ltd.* [2000] 4 I.R. 567, the plaintiffs took passing off proceedings for an interlocutory injunction against the defendant, who had had registered a domain name similar to that of the plaintiffs. The first named plaintiff had built up an Internet information service, covering the whole island of Ireland, featuring some 1700 towns and villages and with 3000 subject classifications. This website was the second most busy website in the state, with approximately 205,000 separate site visits per month.

The first named plaintiff has spent over half a million pounds on advertising its business name and services in Ireland and abroad. The first named plaintiff had also invested over £3 million in employing persons to devise software, to gather and present information and to negotiate and conclude agreements with local partners or franchises.

The plaintiffs' claim was summarised by Herbert J. as follows:

> The similarity of the business names and associated domain names, the similarity of the logo of the first named defendant and the first named plaintiff, and the similarity of the services offered, that is, 'a subscription listing of commercial undertakings accessible through the central website of the provider', would, as a reasonable probability, result in customers and prospective customers of the first named plaintiff being misled into thinking that the services offered by the defendant or one of them was as a branch or licensee of the first named plaintiff or was otherwise linked with or connected to the first named plaintiff.

Counsel for the defendants argued that the plaintiffs, having adopted a business name containing words in common use, were not entitled to an unfair monopoly in those words and that accordingly the court should accept the differences in the business names, getup and logos, even if the court should consider them to be small, as none the less sufficient to distinguish the business of the defendants from that of the plaintiffs.

The parties did not consent too treat the hearing as the trial of the action. In such circumstances, having regard to the decision of the Supreme Court in the *Campus Oil Limited v. The Minister for Industry and Energy (No.2)*, [1983] I.R. 88, Herbert J. considered that he should not inquire into the merits of the case:

> Provided that the plaintiffs, upon whom the onus of proof lies, have shown to the satisfaction of this Court, that there is a fair *bona fide* question to be tried as between them and the defendants and that if they are correct in this contention . . . the continuance of the defendants' activities until the trial and determination of the action is likely to cause substantial damage to them for which an award of damages at the trial would not be adequate compensation, I am obliged, as the law now stands, to determine this application solely on the balance of convenience, that is on the relevant extent of the damage to one or other party if the injunction is or is not granted.

Herbert J. considered it:

> somewhat regrettable that in the present case where most if not all of the relevant facts appears to be before the court on affidavit, . . . the parties by agreeing to treat the hearing of this motion as the trial of this action, 'did not use the interlocutory injunction as a simple quick and relatively and cheap way of asking the Court who is right'. (See Kerly's, Law of Trade Marks and Trade Names (12th ed., 1986), p. 322, n.84).

Herbert J. was satisfied that the plaintiffs had raised a strong *prima facie* case in that as regards the business name, '*Local Ireland*', and its associated domain names there already existed in Ireland as well as abroad 'a large body of the public which in the words Barron J. in the case of *Muckross Park Hotel Ltd. v. Randles and Others*, High Court, November 10, 1992 'know it and what it stands for', namely the Internet information services of the plaintiffs'. Herbert J. was also satisfied that the plaintiffs' had made out a strong *prima facie* case that they had a very valuable reputation in the business name, '*Localireland*' or '*Local Ireland*', and its associated domain names.

Herbert J. was also satisfied that the plaintiffs had made out a fair *bona fide* case to be tried that the use by the defendants of the business name, '*Locally Irish*', and its associated domain name '*locallyirish.com*', was so close to the business name and domain name of the first named plaintiff that no sufficient distinction could reasonably be said to exist between them, particularly having regard to the similarity of the relevant service – 'the subscription listing of commercial undertakings accessible through the central web of the provider'. – carried on by the first named plaintiff and the first named defendant and that as a matter of reasonable probability the public was likely to be similarly misled.

Having regard in particular to *Polycell Products Ltd. v. O'Carroll* [1959] Ir. Jur. Rep. 34 and *Mitchelstown Co-operative Agricultural Society Ltd. v. Golden Vale Food Products Ltd.*, High Court, December 12, 1985, Herbert J. was satisfied that the plaintiffs had made out a strong *prima facie* case that on the balance of probability, if customers and potential customers were misled as alleged, the plaintiffs as a reasonably foreseeable consequence of the misrepresentation on the part of either of the defendants would suffer in the interval pending the hearing and determination of the action 'serious permanent injury to or a complete swamping and loss of their reputation for which an award of damages at the trial of the action would be an altogether inadequate compensation to the plaintiffs.'

Although he was satisfied that the defendants intended in good faith to defend the claim and that their defence was neither frivolous nor vexatious, Herbert J. considered that the balance of convenience lay in favour of granting an interlocutory injunction:

> The defendants would not be excluded from the market in the relevant services. They would be perfectly at liberty to continue to offer the relevant services under a new business name and domain name.

For a thorough analysis of the decision, see Stephen Dodd, 'Passing Off, Domain Names and Injunctive Relief' (2001) 8 Commercial Law Practitioner 79.

DEFAMATION

Justification   In *Murphy v. Times Newspapers Ltd.* [2000] 1 I.R. 522, three
important issues fell for consideration. The first might well be characterised
as the corollary of *Hulton & Co v. Jones* [1910] A.C. 20. It will be recalled
that in *Hulton* the House of Lords made it clear that, if the defendant intended
to refer to a particular person and another person shows that he or she was
understood to be the object of the defendant's assertations, it would afford no
defence to show that the defendant had not intended to refer to that other
person. In *Murphy*, the defendants had alleged in their newspaper, The Sunday
Times, that '[t]he IRA's Army Council last February appointed a farmer in the
Republic called 'Slab' Murphy (which is not his real name), to be its operation
commander for the whole of Northern Ireland.' The plaintiff in the instant
proceedings, Patrick Murphy, as well as his brother Thomas, sued the
defendants. Separate trials were ordered. In Thomas Murphy's action, the
defendants conceded that the words complained of had been understood by
people to refer to him. Their plea of justification, however, proved successful
and Thomas Murphy's claim was accordingly dismissed.

   In the instant case the plea of justification in the defence delivered in the
present proceedings was as follows:

> If the description Slab Murphy is applied to the Plaintiff, which is denied,
> the words complained of are true in substance and in fact, insofar as
> they assert that the plaintiff was a prominent member of the provisional
> I.R.A.

A motion was brought on behalf of the plaintiff seeking an order that the plea
of partial justification contained in the defence be struck out. O'Higgins J.
dismissed the application and the plaintiff appealed to the Supreme Court.

   It was argued on behalf of the plaintiff that, since the jury in the first action
had found that, so far as the imputation that the plaintiff in that action was a
prominent member of the provisional I.R.A. was concerned, it was true in
substance and in fact, the defendants should not be allowed to maintain in the
instant proceedings that it was also true in substance and in fact concerning
the plaintiff in these proceedings. The article, the plaintiff's counsel argued,
was plainly written about one person only and it would be an abuse of process
for the defendants in the instant proceedings to say that it was true in substance
and in fact concerning this plaintiff.

   Keane J. (Murphy and Barron JJ. concurring) stated:

> That proposition is, in my view, wholly unsustainable. If the defendants
> are in the position that two plaintiffs in successive actions can satisfy
> the jury that an article, although clearly written about one person, was
> capable of being understood, and was, understood, to refer to each of

the plaintiffs, the defendant is entitled to rely on whatever defences are open to him at law, including a defence in these proceedings that, although he never intended the words to refer to the plaintiff in these proceedings, they are nonetheless true concerning him, so far as the allegation of being a prominent member of the I.R.A. is concerned. That conclusion flows inevitably from the fact that the intention of the writer is immaterial when one is determining whether the words complained of are not only defamatory but were understood to refer to the particular plaintiff concerned. If the proposition contended for represented the law, the plaintiff in these proceedings, assuming that he satisfied the jury that the words were understood by one or more persons to refer to him and were defamatory, could recover damages, although the defendants were in a position to adduce evidence before the jury that the allegation in question was true. The object of the law of defamation is to compensate plaintiffs about whom defamatory statements that have been published which are untrue: not to compensate them for defamatory statements which are true.

It is conceded on behalf of the plaintiff that no question of issue estoppel or *res judicata* arises. Nor is it a case in which the defendants in any sense can be said to be abusing the process of the court by invoking the defence of justification, as they did in the earlier case. It is the plaintiffs in the two sets of proceedings who elected to sue, claiming, in each instance, as was their right, that the words complained of were published of and concerning and, in each case, claiming that they were capable of meaning and did mean, *inter alia*, that the plaintiff concerned was a prominent member of the provisional I.R.A. The defendants in pleading partial justification in the second proceedings brought by a different plaintiff are in no sense seeking to circumvent a decision in an earlier case, as happened in *McCauley v. McDermott* [1997] 2 I.L.R.M. 486 ....

The second issue related to the defendants' entitlement to plead partial justification in a case where, as it was said, there was simply one broad charge – the plaintiff was the operations commander for the whole of Northern Ireland and had planned a bombing campaign in Britain. Keane J. considered that the plaintiff's argument that the defendants should *not* be entitled to make such a plea was also clearly unsustainable:

The statement of claim pleaded that the words complained of had four distinct defamatory meanings and were understood to have those meanings. At common law, where the words complained of contained more than one charge or were otherwise severable, the defendant could justify part only of the defamatory words but remained liable to pay damages in respect of the part not justified: see *Clarke v. Taylor* (1836)

2 Bing. N.S. 654. Since the enactment of s. 22 of the Act of 1961, again modelled on a corresponding provision in the English Defamation Act, 1952, partial justification may now provide a complete defence in the following circumstances set out in the section:

> 'In an action for libel or slander in respect of words containing two or more distinct charges against the plaintiff, a defence of justification shall not fail by reason only that the truth of every charge is not proved, if the words not proved to be true do not materially injure the plaintiff's reputation having regard to the truth of the remaining charges.'

In the present case, the defendants seek to prove the truth of one only of the charges. If they fail to establish the truth of that charge, the jury will go on to consider the question of damages. If they succeed, it will then be a matter for the jury to decide whether the charges they have not proved do not materially injure the plaintiff's reputation, having regard to the truth of the charge which they have established.

The final issue concerned the defendants' entitlement to rely on section 22 of the Act of 1961 where it had not been expressly pleaded in the defence. Under Order 19, rule 3 of the Rules of the Superior Courts 1986:-

> Every pleading shall contain, and contain only, a statement in a summary form of the material facts an which the party pleading relies for his claim or defence, as the case may be, but not the evidence by which they are to be proved...

Keane J. observed:

> That has been done in the present case and extensive particulars furnished in addition. The defendants are not required to plead matters of law which are well within the knowledge of the plaintiff's legal advisers.

Damages

Jury instructions   In the 1999 Review 516-23, we analysed the Supreme Court decision of *de Rossa v. Independent Newspapers Ltd* [1999] 4 I.R. 432. There the court sought to characterise the constitutional protection of free speech as co-extensive with the guarantee afforded by Article 10 of the European Convention on Human Rights. It saw no need to prescribe that the trial judge in defamation cases should give more specific directions to juries as to how to calibrate the quantum of damages than had been given traditionally. *de Rossa* is now before the European Court, which may well take a somewhat different approach. See further Patrick Leonard, 'Irish Libel Law and the European Convention on Human Rights' (2000) 5 Bar Rev. 410; Michael Kealey, 'Hold the Front Page!' (2001) 95 L. Soc. Gazette No. 2, p.8.

The Supreme Court returned to the issue in *O'Brien v. Mirror Group Newspaper*, on October 25, 2000. In this case, the defendants published in one of their newspapers allegations that the plaintiff, 'a well known and successful business man', had paid a Minister of the Government a bribe of £30,000 to secure the awarding of a radio licence and that the plaintiff had secured the awarding of a mobile telephone licence in circumstances that gave rise to a suspicion of bribery or corrupt practices. The jury held that these allegations amounted to actionable defamation and awarded damages of £250,000.

The defendants appealed to the Supreme Court, contending that the damages awarded were excessive. They argued that the appropriate test for determining whether to set aside an assessment of damages was whether the assessment was one which a reasonable jury would have thought necessary to compensate the plaintiff and establish his reputation. Specifically, they claimed that the trial judge had misdirected the jury in failing to have referred (or allowed counsel to refer) to three matters derived from the English decisions of *Ranzen v. Mirror Group Newspapers Ltd* [1994] Q.B. 670 and *John v. MGN* Ltd [1996] 2 All E.R. 35 and which had already been canvassed thoroughly in *de Rossa*. These were the purchasing power of the award that the jury might be minded to make and the income it would produce; by way of comparison, the compensation scales in personal injury cases and previous libel awards made or approved by the Supreme Court; and the level of awards counsel and the trial judge respectively considered to be appropriate. Counsel for the appellants argued that the rules of law or practice restraining counsel and the trial judge in defamation trials from offering guidance of this nature were inconsistent with the provisions of the Constitution. Finally they asserted that the size of the award was an infringement with the defendants' right to freedom of expression, in breach of Article 40 of the Constitution and Article 10 of the European Convention on Human Rights.

Having regard to the *stare decisis* principle, the defendants had a formidable task in trying to persuade the Supreme Court to depart from *de Rossa,* only fifteen months previously. This clearly proved too serious an obstacle for the majority. Keane C.J., Murphy and O'Higgins JJ. concurring, acknowledged that 'a different view could legitimately be taken' from that expressed by Hamilton C.J., in *de Rossa* but he had 'no doubt that that fact of itself could not justify this court in overruling the decision'.

In the light of this, the appeal could not succeed on the ground that the trial judge had not followed the guidelines laid down by the Court of Appeal in *John* and had directed the jury as to the law in accordance with *De Rossa.*

The Chief Justice went on to consider whether the award should nonetheless be set aside as disproportionately high, having regard to the law laid down in *Barrett v. Independent Newspapers Ltd* [1986] I.R. 45 and *de Rossa.* He thought it proper for the Court, '[no] doubt [exercising] a degree of caution', to make comparisons with earlier defamation awards that had reached the Court on appeal. The allegations in the instant case were undoubtedly seriously defamatory and justified the award of substantial damages:

> However, the case must be approached, in my view, on the basis that the damages awarded are in the highest bracket of damages appropriate in any libel case. They are comparable to the general damages awarded in the most serious cases of paraplegic or quadriplegic injuries and, relatively speaking, are in the same bracket as the damages awarded in *De Rossa.* The libel, however, although undoubtedly serious and justifying the award of substantial damages, cannot be regarded as coming within the category of the greatest and most serious libels which have come before the courts.

The instant case could be distinguished from *de Rossa* in several respects. The libel in *de Rossa* could not have been of a more serious character, alleging that the plaintiff had 'supported some of the vilest activities of totalitarian regimes in the twentieth century and was personally involved in or condoned serious crime'. On any view this was a significantly more damaging and serious libel than the admittedly serious allegation against the plaintiff in the instant case. The circulation of the newspaper in *de Rossa's* case was well over seven times as large as in *O'Brien.* Mr. De Rossa was more widely known to the public than the plaintiff in the instant case. Finally, there was a difference in the manner in which the two proceedings had been conducted: in *de Rossa,* the plaintiff had been subjected to prolonged and hostile cross-examination while in *O'Brien* the plea of justification had not apparently been seriously pressed and the cross-examination of the plaintiff had been gentle.

On these grounds, Keane C.J. concluded that the award was disproportionately high and should be set aside. Denham, Murphy and O'Higgins JJ .concurred, on the issue of setting aside the award. There was thus a majority in favour of this course.

Denham J. arrived at her conclusion by a route different from that of the Chief Justice. She considered it proper to revisit *De Rossa* on the basis of the importance of the questions whether Irish law was in breach of Article 10 of the European Convention on Human Rights and whether further information and guidance should be given to juries than had been countenanced in *de Rossa.* She reiterated the views that she had expressed on these issues in *de Rossa.* On the issue of the amount of the award she was in agreement with Keane C.J. that it was excessive.

Geoghegan J. differed from his colleagues on that issue though he agreed with the Chief Justice that the Court should not entertain arguments to the effect that *de Rossa* had been wrongly decided. Geoghegan J. identified important differences between appeals in defamation cases and appeals from an award in personal injury litigation:

> In the case of personal injuries an appeal court can determine with some confidence what would be the range of awards which a reasonable jury (or, nowadays, a reasonable judge) might make. This the appeal court can do because although every personal injury case is different from every other personal injury case there are also great similarities. A broken hip case relates to some extent at least to every other broken hip case. A loss of an eye case relates to some extent at least to every other case of loss of an eye etc. Members of the court from their experience at the Bar and/or experience as trial judges and indeed experience of previous similar appeals may with some confidence form a view as to what the legitimate spectrum of awards could be. In the case of a libel appeal, however, the appeal court although it has to engage in the same exercise, . . . can only do so with diffidence rather than confidence.

It is not easy to predict the future for defamation law in Ireland. It may be that the European Court of Human Rights will find that Irish law in relation to the process of arriving at an award of damages in defamation proceedings violates Article 10 of the Convention. In any event, the statutory incorporation of the Convention into Irish domestic law, subject to the provisions of the Constitution, may also act as a source of encouragement to the judiciary to be more sensitive to the requirements of Article 10.

The movement towards greater emphasis on the Convention's norms is not necessarily all in one direction, however. There is good reason to expect that Irish courts will place greater emphasis on the value of privacy over the coming years. In that regard, we may yet find an interesting debate leading to an ultimate synthesis of the norms protected by Articles 8 and 10 of the Convention. Cf. English, *'Confidentiality and Defamation'*, Chapter 11 of R. English & P. Havers (eds.), *An Introduction to Human Rights and the Common Law* (2000).

Evidence of mitigation of damages In the Evidence Chapter, above, 237, Declan McGrath analyses in detail the important case of *Browne v. Tribune Newspapers Plc*, Supreme Court, November 24, 2000.

Discovery In *McDonnell v. Sunday Business Post Ltd.,* High Court, February 2, 2000, the position of a defendant in defamation proceedings who seeks discovery of documents was analysed. The case was based on the old procedure, prior to the changes effected on August 3, 1999: see the 1999 Review, 452-3. In *McDonnell*, the defendant published in its newspaper on March 29, 1998 'a hard hitting broad ranging attack on the plaintiff in regard to his appointment to the position as Group Chief Executive of the Córas Iompair Éireann ... group of companies and his handling of that position to date.' Within days the plaintiff sued for libel, detailing twenty four defamatory assertations which the article allegedly contained. The defendant sought wide-ranging discovery. O'Sullivan J. stated:

> No authority has been opened to me which establishes that in seeking discovery in the context of, *inter alia*, a plea of fair comment, a defendant must support its application with an affidavit setting out the evidence upon which it intends to rely in establishing the facts referred to in such a plea.
>
> Subject, of course, to such a plea not amounting to a 'fishing expedition' or otherwise offending the principles applicable to discovery. I cannot agree that the absence of such an affidavit disentitles the defendant to an order for discovery.

The fact that a discovery might be comprehensive and wide-ranging did not, in O'Sullivan J.'s view, mean that *ipso facto* it was an exploratory or fishing operation. Such a characterisation would apply where there was 'no stated objective or delimitation by reference to the pleadings.' In the instant case, in general the list of categories of documents sought were capable of being, and in all but one case had been, specifically related to paragraphs in the plaintiff's pleadings. The defendant was not, therefore, engaging in an exploratory or fishing expedition. On the contrary, in the vast majority of instances, specific documents were identified with a reasonable degree of precision.

Nor was O'Sullivan J. persuaded that compliance by the plaintiff with any order made along these lines would be so onerous as to unfair on him. It was the plaintiff who had cast the proceedings broadly and declined to accept the Master's invitation to narrow them so as to limit the scope of discovery.

The defamation proceedings related to an article that was published in the defendants newspaper on March 29, 1998. O'Sullivan J. thought it proper to restrict discovery to a six month period before the plaintiff's appointment and cease on 29 March 1998, with the modification that if a document had been in draft form before the date of the publication it would also be discoverable:

> Thus the annual accounts of the group or any of the companies in the group would be discoverable if, on or before the 29th March 1998, there was in existence an earlier draft or working papers in relation thereto.

Inspection of documents We shall in the next Review analyse Kelly J.'s decision in *Cooper Flynn v. Radio Telifis Éireann* [2001] 1 I.L.R.M. 208, on inspection of confidential bank records where the defendant in defamation proceedings had pleaded justification.

INFRINGEMENT OF CONSTITUTIONAL RIGHTS

In *Sinnott v. Minister for Education*, High Court, October 4, 2000, Barr J. awarded damages to a young adult with severe autism for the State's breach of its duty to honour its constitutional obligation to provide him with education and training appropriate to his particular situation. He also awarded his mother compensation. The precise basis on which the mother's award was made is not entirely clear. It appears to derive from the State's obligation to protect the Family, under Article 41 of the Constitution (p. 56 of Barr J.'s judgment) and from the view that Article 40.1 had been violated because the mother, her family and in particular her plaintiff son were 'entitled to equality of treatment by the State and ought not to be deprived without just cause of basic advantages which the State provides for others': p. 57. The separate idea that the mother, as a foreseeable victim of the State's breach of its constitutional obligation to her son, also appears to have grounded her entitlement to compensation, in Barr J.'s analysis: pp 63-64.

The Supreme Court on July 12, 2001, reversed Barr J.'s judgment, both in respect to the son and his mother's claims. We shall analyse this decision in detail in the 2001 Review. It represents a most important holding on the remit of the State's obligation in respect of primary education, as well as the doctrine of the separation of powers. So far as concerns this mother's claim, this was perceived as a derivative one, parasitic on that of her son's, and accordingly not sustainable. It must be said that such a formalistic approach can be seen as unduly individualistic and atomistic. Tort law has always been conscious of the fact that wrongful injury to one person may cause foreseeable consequential injury to another who is closely related to him or her. That is the basis of the old actions for loss of *consortium* and *per quod servitium amisit*, for example. The whole development of the negligence action for 'nervous shock' is premised on the foreseeability that one person will suffer injury consequential on the injury to another and on the justice of compensating him or her for that humane response. Moreover, the idea of compensating a rescuer for injury sustained in going to the assistance of another negligently put in peril is based on a similar value judgment that foreseeable victims of a wrong may be sufficiently close to warrant compensation. The Supreme Court itself required this in *Philips v. Durgan* [1991] 1 I.R. 89, analysed in the 1990 Review, 493-500.

This is not to suggest that every constitutionally protected right of one person should give rise to a host of consequential rights to compensation in others, but rather to go no further than denying the absoluteness of a principle of rejecting such a claim. If it is to be rejected in any particular case, the rejection must be based on due consideration of the values underlying it and their degree of rootedness in the constitutional value system rather than on formalistic grounds.

DAMAGES

Loss of earnings   In *Hennessey v. Fitzgerald*, High Court, December 13, 2000, a somewhat complicated issue arose, involving a collision between economic rationality, psychological needs and legal principles relating to computation of loss of earnings, the duty to mitigate and the financial version of the 'egg shell skull' principle.

The plaintiff was a qualified fitter, who had returned to England in 1992 to take over his father's workshop. He started his own business, involving the purchase, dismantling and resale of constituent parts of lorries. While 'undoubtedly a skilled and hardworking fitter', he had little managerial skills and the business was generating only a modest profit – less than what he would have earned as a fitter.

In 1997 the plaintiff was involved in a traffic accident caused by the negligence of the defendants. This involved a serious injury to his right arm, as well as hand, face and head injuries. These injuries rendered him incapable of carrying out many of the functions required of a qualified fitter, though he was still capable of light work.

The plaintiff suffered from depression as a result of his injuries. This led to what McCracken J. described as 'almost [a] fixation with wanting to continue the business against all the odds', in an attempt to keep the depression at bay. The business lost money at a considerable rate and there was no real prospect of its being turned around.

Complicating the assessment of his loss, the evidence indicated that, even if the accident had not occurred, the business would not have prospered. McCracken J. had 'no doubt that the plaintiff could have made considerably more money by working for somebody else.' The business had lost £35,000 since the accident. The plaintiff sought compensation for this loss. McCracken J. dealt with this issue by segmenting this claim, which related to loss of income to date, from the claim for future losses. He stated:

> The plaintiff chose to try to continue the business after the accident. That was his choice, and clearly it was the wrong choice. However, I do not think that the consequences of that wrong choice can be visited on the defendant. It is clear from the evidence that the plaintiff has for some considerable time been told that this business could not succeed, and has ignored all advice given to him, and apparently still intends to continue to ignore it. He is, of course, entitled to do so, but he is not entitled to a free run at the expense of the defendant. Accordingly, in relation to past loss of earnings, and on the basis that he ought to have shut down the business, I am prepared to award him the difference between earnings which he would have made as a fitter and earnings which he was capable of making had he sought employment when he was fit to return to work. Indeed, I think this is being generous to the

plaintiff, because it is arguable that he should bear the entire loss which arose from him having decided to carry on the business.

In relation to future loss of earnings, McCracken J. concluded that the plaintiff 'clearly would have continued his business, probably for some years'. His income during this period would not have been as great as if he had been in employment. The amount awarded under this heading was calculated on the basis that the plaintiff's income would have been at this lower amount.

McCracken J. thus did not penalise the plaintiff for his persistence in continuing to run a loss-making business before judgment, invoking the same disposition to persist in a loss-making business as a reason for reducing his compensation for future loss. It is difficult to identify a clear basis in principle for this approach. If the plaintiff's actual stubbornness in acting in an economically irrational manner between the accident and judgment could be ignored, the finding that he would have been equally stubborn in future years if the accident had not occurred seems out of harmony with that approach.

It should be noted that, while McCracken J. referred to the fact that the plaintiff's depression almost certainly explained this persistence in continuing a business against all the odds, he did not base his approach towards calculating damages for loss of earnings on this fact. Accordingly, he did not address the question of the extent to which a psychological or psychiatric disturbance which affects the quality of economic prudence in judgment of a plaintiff should protect the plaintiff from a reduction in damages for negligent failure to mitigate damages (cf. McMahon & Binchy, *op. cit.,* paras 20.24–20.33). On principle if a psychiatric condition caused by the defendant's negligence renders the plaintiff less capable of exercising such prudence, the plaintiff's compensation, whether for losses up to judgment or for future losses, should not be reduced.

We must address a further consideration in this context, which weighs against that approach. McCracken J. in calculating future losses, concluded that the plaintiff, *had there been no accident*, would still have persisted with a loss-making business for some years into the twenty-first century. If this is so, it is hard to see how that irrationality, which was not attributable to the plaintiff's depression, should not have the effect of reducing the compensation for loss of earnings up to judgment as well as afterwards.

In *Fields v. Woodland Products Ltd.*, Supreme Court, July 16, 1999, where the plaintiff's action for negligence and breach of statutory duty included a claim for loss of earnings, the Supreme Court held that the defendant was entitled to discovery of documents, records and memoranda in respect of the plaintiff's income tax returns for the relevant years. Delivering an *ex tempore* judgment with which Murphy and Barron JJ. concurred, Keane J. stated:

> I understand and I am sure everyone perfectly understands that income tax matters are undoubtedly confidential to the tax payer and the Revenue. But when parties come to litigate, the situation changes to

that extent. The other party, if the tax returns relate to an issue in the proceedings and are in that sense relevant to the proceedings, is clearly entitled to inspect them and make what use is appropriate from his point of view in his defence of the proceedings but for no other purpose. It has been said on more than one occasion in the High Court and in this court that parties may not make use of the discovery process for any purpose other than the litigation and that should and one hopes does go without saying. That appears to me to represent the law.

Collateral benefits   Collateral benefits raise important issues of policy. The mathematical starting point is clear: a plaintiff should be compensated only for losses which he or she has sustained. If compensation is to extend further, there must be good social reasons why this simple principle of compensation should be modified. The concept of collateral benefits seeks to identify the cases in which such a good reason exists. It acknowledges that the plaintiff is not in fact out of pocket in relation to the loss for which he or she claims compensation for nonetheless countenances the payment by the defendant to the plaintiff for that 'loss', allegedly but not actually incurred.

Why should the courts contemplate compensating the plaintiff for such a loss? Severral answers are forthcoming. It would inhibit the policy of encouraging people to seek insurance cover against loss if they were to find that their prudence operated against the quantum of damages they would otherwise obtain. Private charitable efforts would be thwarted and the social policies of the State would also suffer. For all of these reasons, the courts have declined to make deductions for certain types of benefits accruing to a plaintiff.

Employers were of course aware of judicial thinking in this area. When addressing the question of providing a humane response to an accident which their employee sustained they were anxious to prevent defendants from taking advantage of their humanity.

What employers sought to create was an obligation on their part to pay wages to an injured employee which, if the employee successfully sued a wrongdoer in tort, would not be deducted from the amount that the wrongdoer would have to pay the employee. They had to tread a narrow line, avoiding a characterisation by the court that the plaintiff employee had not in fact suffered any loss of earnings because the contract of employment between the employee and the employer provided for the payment by the employer to the employee of full (or reduced) wages during the period when the employee was unable to work on account of an injury that might have been caused tortiously by another.

In *Hogan v. Steele & Co Ltd.; Electricity Supply Board Notice Party* [2000] 4 I.R. 587, the plaintiff was tortiously injured when on the defendant's premises. His employer, the notice party, paid him wages while he was out of work; he undertook to refund them in the event of his recovering compensation for them. The defendant contended that this mode of payment resulted in no loss for which the defendant had an obligation to compensate.

Macken J. held that the plaintiff was entitled to recover the sums in respect of the loss of wages from the defendant. His employer had subtracted from the amount it paid him during the time he was out of work the normal deductions for PAYE, PRSI and contributions in respect of his pension. Macken J. held that these deductions were not recoverable from the defendant. The employer appealed to the Supreme Court, arguing that the amount awarded to the plaintiff should not have been subject to these deductions.

Counsel for the employer argued that the decision in *British Transport Commission v. Gourley* [1955] 3 All E.R. 796 which had been followed in this country in *Glover v. BLN Limited (No. 2)* [1973] I.R. 432 was undoubtedly authority for the proposition that, in some cases at least, damages in respect of loss of earnings should be calculated on the basis of the net loss after deducting tax. He submitted, however, that it was unduly simplistic to treat this as a universal rule. Both of those cases were dealing solely with the question of the loss sustained by the plaintiff. Different considerations arose where a third party made the payments as part of the process of paying the plaintiff the full amount of his wages during the period of his absence from work as a result of the injury and thus avoiding undue hardship to him. (It is not clear whether reference was also made to the Supreme Court decision of *Cooke v. Walsh* [1984] I.L.R.M. which endorsed *Glover's* approach. See also McMahon & Binchy, *op cit.*, paras. 44.101–44.106).

Counsel for the defendant submitted that the defendant's liability in damages was confined to the actual loss sustained by the plaintiff. The defendant owed no duty, either tortious or contractual, to the ESB. To allow a third party to recover damages from an admitted wrongdoer to which he was only entitled, if at all, as a result of an agreement between himself and the injured party was inconsistent with the statement of the law by Kingsmill Moore J., speaking for the Supreme Court in *Attorney General v. Ryan's Care Hire Limited* [1965] I.R. 642. It should be noted, however, that the claim for compensation in the instant case was by the plaintiff not his employer. His employer's interest in the outcome of the case sprang from the fact that, if the plaintiff was entitled to be compensated by the defendant for the amounts deducted he would be obliged by virtue of his undertaking to refund them to the employer.

The Supreme Court affirmed Macken J. Keane C.J. (Hardiman and Geoghegan JJ. concurring) stated:

> It is beyond argument, in my view, that the plaintiff will be fully compensated in this case by the payment to him of the wages that he would have earned after deducting PAYE, PRSI and pension contributions. His obligation under the undertaking was to refund to the ESB '*the total amount so advanced [to me during my absences from duty arising out of my accident]*' out of any monies which he might recover from the defendant. To require the defendant to pay more than that sum would be to compensate the plaintiff for a loss which he

had never suffered. It would, of course, have been open to the ESB to require the plaintiff to include in his claim the gross wages to which he would have been entitled during his absence from work because of the injury without any deduction for PAYE, PRSI or pension contributions. Whatever might have been the position if such an agreement had been entered into, there is no legal basis, in its absence, on which either the plaintiff or the ESB could recover those sums from the defendant. Unlike the net wages, these were payments which had been applied for particular purposes by the ESB on behalf of the plaintiff and, in the absence of any agreement, were irrecoverable.

The Chief Justice found support for this approach from the decision of the English Court of Appeal in *Franklin v. the British Railways board* [1994] P.I.Q.R. 1, where Nolan J. had stated:

> It seems to me quite inappropriate to describe the sums handed over by the respondents to the Inland Revenue and the Department of Social Security in discharge of an accepted statutory duty as constituting in any sense of the word a 'loan' which is 'repayable' by the appellant to the respondents. So far as both the respondents and the appellant are concerned the amounts paid over in tax and national insurance contributions have gone forever as a matter of law, if their accepted treatment was correct. The only sum which can in any way in a sense be described as 'repayable' as between the respondents and the appellant is the sum of £5,550.92 which the appellant in fact received and which he has duly repaid. No doubt it would be possible for A and B to make an agreement under which A will pay B's tax on his behalf, in return for B's promise of reimbursement, and such an agreement might broadly be described as involving a loan by A to B, but it seems to me that ... the payments of tax and national insurance contributions by the respondents in the present case stand on a different footing.

Counsel for the ESB had argued that the pension contributions were in a different category. Keane C.J. could not see any difference in principle:

> as was the case with the PAYE and PRSI payments, they were deducted by the ESB for specific purposes, admittedly more directly to the benefit of the plaintiff, and were not in any sense a 'loan' to him which he was obliged to repay to them.

As to the broader grounds on which the ESB sought to base their claim in the present case, Keane C.J. was satisfied that they could not be reconciled with the statement of the law by Kingsmill Moore J. in *Attorney General & Other v. Ryan's Car Hire Limited* [1965] I.R. 642, to the effect that:

> ... a tortfeasor ordinarily is only responsible in damages for the direct injury which he has caused to the person against whom the tort has been committed and not for indirect injuries to a third person who may suffer loss indirectly as a result of the injury to the first person. To this rule there are two exceptions in common law, the actions *per quod servitium amisit* and *per quod consortium amisit*, both anomalous and both apparently based on the conception of a direct injury to quasi-property. They are too long established to be disturbed, but in my opinion should not be enlarged.

Hogan gives rise to several observations. First, it was surely beyond argument on existing judicial authority, that the defendant should not have been called on to compensate the plaintiff in the full amount of his loss of earnings. The Supreme Court in *Cooke v. Walsh* had resolved that issue sixteen years previously when it held (*per* Griffin J.) that 'it is 'take home pay' and not gross pay that should have been used as the multiplicand. Had the plaintiff been uninjured, he would have to pay income tax on the wages he would earn, and PRSI and other deductions would be made from his wages and therefore the sum that would be considerably less than [the gross amount of his wages].' It would of course have been open to the plaintiff (or the notice party) to challenge this approach on its merits, since it results in what is arguably an unjust windfall for defendants. It is worth noting that the courts in Canada and several states of the United States of America do not deduct the value of income tax from the gross sum awarded to plaintiffs for loss of earnings: see, e.g., *Cunningham v. Wheeler*, [1994] 1 S.C.R. 359.

What was not open to the plaintiff or the employer to argue was that a private contractual agreement between the employer and the plaintiff as regards what sum the plaintiff would pay to the employer in the event that he successfully sued the defendant should be capable of *increasing* the extent of the defendant's liability to compensate the plaintiff.

It should be noted that *Franklin v. British Railways Board* involved a claim by the British Railways Board, the employer of Mr. Franklin, to recoup from him deductions for tax and national insurance which it had made in the context of a sick pay arrangement somewhat similar to that in *Hogan*. A major difference was that the British Railways Board was itself liable in tort to Mr. Franklin for having caused the injury in relation to which the sick pay was required. The idea that Mr. Franklin should have to subsidise his tortious employer would seem to many a travesty of justice. Of course *Franklin* involved an interpretation of the terms of the agreement between Mr. Franklin and his employer to find out whether as a matter of contract law, he had undertaken such an obligation. The English Court of Appeal found that he had not. *Franklin* has little to do with *Hogan*, where the issue was one of tort law, not of contract. Even if Mr. Hogan's contract with the ESB could be interpreted as involving such an undertaking on his part to make such a recoupment, this would be *res inter alios acta* so far as the defendant was concerned.

Finally, one should perhaps hesitate before concluding that *Hogan* represents the last word on the issue of liability for negligently caused pure economic loss where that loss is sustained by an employer of a direct victim of the negligent party who suffers physical injury as a result of that negligence. There are good reasons for judicial caution about casting the net of liability for pure economic loss too widely but there are equally compelling reasons why the courts should disdain from *a priori* exclusions of meritorious claims. To engage in this latter course would seem inconsistent with the flexibility of approach envisaged in *McShane Wholesale Fruit and Vegetables Ltd. v. Johnston Haulage Co Ltd.* [1997] 1 I.L.R.M. 86 as well as possibly running into difficulties under Article 6 of the European Convention of Human Rights, as interpreted in *Osman v. United Kingdom* (1988) 29 E.H.R.R. 245.

Special damages In *Tobin v. St James's Hospital* High Court, January 29, 2000 the plaintiff had a birthmark on her cheek and temple, which consisted of a port wine stain on the skin. She underwent laser treatment which, the defendant conceded, was negligently given, resulting in burns on her face. Kelly J. awarded her £20,000 for pain and suffering and a further £60,000 for future pain and suffering. He noted that the plaintiff who was aged sixteen, would have to undergo further treatment under general anaesthesia. The effect of the burns was to remove the prospect that the birthmark could be lightened to the point of being practically incapable of being noticed with effective use of make-up.

***Reddy v. Bates* reduction** In *Hennessy v. Fitzgerald*, High Court, December 13, 2000, discussed above, 461, McCracken J. invoked *Reddy v. Bates* to make a reduction of 10% to the award of damages for future loss of earnings. The plaintiff was a qualified fitter with several years' experience. McCracken J. considered that this quantum of reduction was 'very generous to the plaintiff'. No similar reduction was expressly made in calculating the quantum of loss of earnings up to judgment.

General damages In *Crawford v. Kane*, High Court, April 7, 2000, the plaintiff suffered a significant soft tissue whiplash injury in a traffic accident in 1996. This caused him substantial discomfort and pain as he travelled about 40,000 miles a year in his practice as a solicitor. The medical evidence was to the effect that a complete recovery could take up to five years from the time of trial. Barr J. concluded that the plaintiff would suffer 'a significant degree of ongoing pain and discomfort' which might continue for about another year. He awarded general damages for 'pain, suffering and disablement', in the sum of £30,000.

In *Brennan v. Lissadell Towels Ltd*, Supreme Court, November 15, 2000, an award by McGuinness J. of £70,000 for pain and suffering to the time of judgment and a further £60,000 for future pain and suffering was unhesitatingly upheld. The plaintiff, aged forty at the time of the accident, with three young children, had fractured her elbow in a fall in her employer's car park. She developed paraesthesiae of her hands, with associated clumsiness and loss of grip. She also developed persistent pain over her neck, which was aggravated by any movement. These injuries ruined her artistic ability. She became depressed 'to a quite disabling degree'. She suffered from a pre-existing degenerative condition; the symptoms provoked by the accident, in the view of a medical expert 'could represent a premature onset by approximately five to ten years.'

Hardiman J. (Denham J. and Fennelly JJ. concurring) considered that the award for general damages was:

> by no means excessive. The plaintiff has a condition of constant pain, a significant loss of function and insomnia, all of which contribute to depression and have made it impossible for her to work. This in turn feeds back into the depression. She has in effect suffered the loss of her previous lifestyle, of her independence and her physical integrity. These are serious matters and must have been acutely felt in the earlier stages. With the aid of counselling and medication she has come to terms with them to some degree. She is suffering considerable pain some thirteen years earlier than, on the evidence, it might have been expected to become symptomatic, and it might have become symptomatic only much later or never. The loss of her work plainly means much more to her than the loss of the associated income and this is a real substantial and continuing loss.
>
> Considering the sum awarded for general damages as a whole, it seems impossible to criticise it in light of all the evidence. The consequences of this relatively simple accident on the particular plaintiff were indeed severe. Whether one regards the peak of severity as having already occurred, during the plaintiff's period of adjustment to her dramatically altered lifestyle, or as occurring in the future due to the continuation of certain of her symptoms is to some extent a question of impression. Since the overall figure seems proportionate to the complaints, I would not disturb the findings of the learned trial judge, who saw the plaintiff and her advisers, on the basis that consideration of the case on paper might suggest a greater incidence of pain and suffering into the future.
>
> It should be emphasised that, in this case, the substantial sum awarded to the plaintiff was justified by the exceptional and, on the whole, uncontested evidence of comprehensive destruction of the plaintiff's quality of life, which was quite out of proportion to the original comparatively minor injury to her right radial bone. As a consequence of the combination of depression and post traumatic stress disorder

and associated pain, she suffered the loss of her satisfying and personally rewarding employment and disruption of her family and marital life. Even if the onset of her physical symptoms is to be regarded as an acceleration of the effects of an underlying condition, her depression was considered by her medical advisers to be likely to be permanent.

In *Hennessey v. Fitzgerald*, High Court, December 13, 2000, (discussed above 461-463), McCracken J. awarded £40,000 general damages to the time of judgment and a further £6500 for future general damages where the plaintiff had suffered a permanent serious injury to his arm involving the dislocation of his right radius at the elbow and a comminuted fracture of the ulna, as well as injuries to his hand, back and head. The plaintiff also suffered serious depression, which could well worsen if his business should fail (as seemed probable).

In *Whelan v. Mowlds*, High Court, October 12, 2000, Lavan J. awarded general damages of £10,000 where the plaintiff suffered a low to medium grade pain and discomfort in the right sacro-ipiac and coccygeal bones of her body when accidentally kicked while participating in a swimming lesion. The accident occurred in October 1996. The plaintiff's medical treatment was completed in the months and her physiotherapy treatment was completed in 1998. Lavan J. considered that 'a very large subjective element' must have been involved in the plaintiff's complaints since the latter date, though he did not believe that she was exaggerating her symptoms.

Exemplary damages In *Crawford v. Kane* High Court, April 7, 2000, Barr J. awarded £7,000 exemplary damages (in addition to £34,750 compensatory damages) to a driver into whose vehicle the defendant had collided from the rear. The defendant was found to have been untruthful in his asserting that the plaintiff had reversed his car into the defendant's vehicle and that the plaintiff (who was in fact a teetotaller) had smelt of alcohol.

Barr J. considered that:

> [t]his sinister conduct raises an issue as to whether in all the circumstances the plaintiff is entitled to exemplary damages arising out of the reprehensible behaviour of the defendant. I am satisfied that he is entitled to be compensated on that basis. In coming to that conclusion I have also taken into account the persistence of the defendant in falsely swearing that after the accident the plaintiff smelt of alcohol.

Barr J. observed that the law as to exemplary damages in this jurisdiction had been defined in the judgments of the Supreme Court in *Conway v. Irish National Teachers Organisation* [1991] 2 I.R. 305. There Finlay CJ had specified the three headings of damages in Irish law which were 'potentially relevant to any particular case'. The Chief Justice had described the third of these as follows:

Punitive or exemplary damages arising from the nature of the wrong which has been committed and/or the manner of its commission which are intended to mark the court's particular disapproval of the defendant's conduct in all the circumstances of the case and its decision that it should publicly be seen to have punished the defendant for such conduct by awarding such damages, quite apart from its obligation, where it may exist in the same case, to compensate the plaintiff for the damage which he or she has suffered.

Barr J. also referred to his own earlier judgments in *Lyons v. Elm River Limited and Another*, February 16, 1996 and *F.W. v. British Broadcasting Corporation*, March 25, 1999. He had:

no doubt that the facts which I found bring the instant case within the ambit of the foregoing precept enunciated by Finlay C.J. in *Conway v. INTO* and amply justify an award of punitive damages.

In *Guckian v. Genport t/a Sachs Hotel*, High Court, November 2, 2000, O'Donovan J. gave no indication that he regarded the award of exemplary damages as being subject to the *Rookes v. Barnard* limitations when he reluctantly declined to make an award of this character. The plaintiff, a patron of the defendant's night-club, had been injured when she tripped on a depression in the tiling as she was entering the premises. An engineer acting on her behalf photographed the entrance area on May 10, 1995, twelve days after the accident. On May 10, 1996, he again photographed the area; they showed that the defect in the meantime had been repaired. In subsequent letters from the defendant's solicitors at the time, it was asserted that no repairs had been carried out on the location in the aftermath of the accident. This was untrue, as the defendant's proprietor at the material time conceded; he became aware of the fact that the assertions in the letters were untrue but he did not appraise the plaintiff's advisers of that fact until he came to give evidence at the hearing. O'Donovan J. regarded this as intolerable. He observed:

[T]o be frank, I have grave reservations that [the then proprietor] was not aware of those misstatements long before he conceded that he was aware of them ... I find it difficult to accept that [the] existence [of the defect] would not have been brought to the attention of senior members of the staff ... or [the General Manager of the hotel at the material time] before instructions were given to write the letters of the 22nd of January 1999 and the 13 April 2000 to the plaintiff's solicitors ... I am afraid that I question the *bona fides* of the instructions which led to those two letters being written.

O'Donovan J. awarded the plaintiff £51,500 compensatory damages. He went on to observe:

> In the light of the manner in which the defendant met this claim and,
> particularly, the fact that they appear to have attempted to hide the fact
> that there was a defect in the tiling at the entrance to their night-club at
> the material time, I was sorely tempted to accede to an application on
> behalf of the plaintiff's advisors to award punitive or exemplary damages
> in this case. However, somewhat reluctantly I am not persuaded that,
> reprehensible though it was, the defendants' conduct was sufficiently
> inappropriate to justify such an award.

The logical implication of this passage appears to be that, if the defendants'
conduct had indeed been 'sufficiently inappropriate' to justify an award of
exemplary damages, it would not have been necessary for the claim to have
run the gauntlet of the *Rookes v. Barnard* limitations which, it seems, would
have inevitably thwarted it. Manifestly there was no question of unconstitutional
or arbitrary action by servants of the State; nor had the defendants sought to
invest in the commission of the tort; not did any statutory provision confer a
right to exemplary damages.

Public policy   In the 1998 Review, 659-664, we analysed *Fitzpatrick v. Furey
and Motor Insurances Bureau of Ireland* High Court, June 12, 1998, when
Laffoy J, in fatal accident proceedings, held that public policy considerations
precluded her from quantifying the dependency claim on the basis of the total
income of the deceased, which included some income that had not been
mentioned in declarations to the Revenue Commission by the deceased and,
subsequent to his death, by his widow, the plaintiff in the proceedings. The
effect of the decision was that no compensation was made for the amount of
undeclared income to which the dependants would have been entitled after tax
had been duly deducted. We suggested that this degree of penalty was excessive
in the light of public policy issues involved. See also Binchy, 'Comment: Tort
– Public Policy – Awards in Tort Litigation' (1998) 20 D.U.L.J. 240.

   The issue was revisited in a number of decisions in 2000. In *Downing v.
O'Flynn* [2000] 4 I.R. 383, fatal accident proceedings were taken in relation
to a young man who operated a fruit and vegetable retail business prior to his
death. He had been previously living with a young woman whose household
consisted of three children, in relation to one of whom the decease was *in loco
parentis*. The evidence in the case was that he used to contributed £150 a
week to his girlfriend's household as well as giving his mother around £1,000
per annum. Returns had never been made to the Revenue Commissioners but
on foot of the accounts prepared after his death the Revenue Commissioners
applied a nil liability. If the accounts accurately reflected the income of the
deceased he could not have able to make the payments that he had in fact
made.

McGuinness J. awarded compensation on the basis that the child in regard to whom the deceased had been *in loco parentis* lost a benefit of £37.50 per week, which represented a quarter of the deceased's contribution to the household, and that the deceased's mother's loss was £1,000 per annum. The defendant appealed on the basis that these payments must necessarily have been made out of undeclared income. Reliance was placed on a passage from McGuinness J.'s judgment in which she had noted that the accountant who had prepared the accounts after the death of the deceased had acknowledged that the accounts

> were not complete and this would be a fairly common experience, I would think, in a small retail business like this that the accounts are not all that terribly reliable. Indeed, it is not unknown, I am sure, to counsel on all sides, for money in this type of small business to be extracted from the till in cash which does not always go accurately through the accounts....

The Supreme Court unanimously dismissed the appeal. The judges first addressed Laffoy J.'s approach in *Furey v. Fitzpatrick and Motor Insurers Bureau of Ireland*. Each of them expressed their disagreement with it. Referring to what Laffoy J. had stated on the issue, Denham J. was:

> satisfied that this may not be the correct approach in assessing loss for dependants on declared and undeclared income. Of course the circumstances of each case should be considered. However, in general it would appear appropriate to calculate the loss to the dependants (which has been sustained because of the action of the defendant) on the actual income. If the income, or part of it, has not been declared or taxed then the sum should be analysed to achieve a net figure, net of tax. This net figure would then be the basis on which the loss to the dependants may be calculated.

Murray J. stated his opposition to the approach adopted by Laffoy J. in the following terms:

> It seems to me that public policy intends that persons who have suffered financial loss as a result of the wrongful act of another be compensated for their actual loss and no more. In my view, therefore the application of the fundamental principle of *restitutio in integrum* is a sufficient basis to exclude, in assessing claims for loss of future income, including those which incorporate an element of undeclared earnings, any element based on gross rather than net income after all lawful deductions.
>
> In short, damages in personal injury or fatal accident cases are, in principle, simply compensation for actual loss and this is particularly

evident in the case of special damage. In this context, once liability and actual financial loss have been established the duty in law of the wrongdoer to compensate the injured party by way of damages cannot be abated by the fact that the claim is based, in whole or in part, on undeclared income, once the actual future loss is calculated by reference to the net income after tax. Moreover, it could be said that answerability of the taxpayer to the Revenue authorities for the sole fact of a failure to make a return of income (as opposed to taking account of the tax liability) is truly *res inter alios acta.*

Geoghegan J. also considered that, in assessing loss of future contributions to dependants in fatal accident litigation, the Court should assume that, 'had the deceased lived he would have probably paid his taxes as and from his death, whatever might have been his conduct before his death.' He thought that, in *Fitzpatrick,*

> both sides wrongly argued it on foot of 'public policy consideration' whereas the true analysis should have been as to whether the trial judge had before her sufficient evidence in relation to undeclared income that she could quantify what would have been the net amount of that income if tax were paid. I think that the learned trial judge should have assumed that the deceased would have paid tax had he survived. Public policy considerations did not dictate that the entire of the £6,000, if properly proved, should be disregarded. It is not necessary for the courts to take such a severe view as apart from anything else it could work great hardship and injustice to other hypothetical cases. The true principle is that a defendant should never have to compensate for alleged loss of monies which ought to have gone to the Revenue Commissioners and should not have been retained by the deceased. But the principle does not beyond that.

Applying these principles to this instant case, all members of the Court were satisfied that McGuinness J.'s award should be sustained. They did so on several grounds. The amount awarded in favour of the child was modest. As Denham J. observed, whatever might be said of the figure of £150, it was 'difficult to imagine a sum for the child being less than £37.50. On any view [it] would have been available to the child'. McGuinness J.'s remarks should, Geoghegan J. thought, be interpreted as indicating a view that there was 'plenty of surplus money in reality and that contributions of the amount alleged could have been afforded by the deceased...' rather than involving a finding that they could only have been made out of untaxed income. Denham J. was, moreover, of opinion that the evidence supported a finding that the deceased's business, which was 'successful and . . . growing', would have continued to develop had he survived.

The Supreme court's approach in *Downing v. O'Flynn* provokes a couple of observations. First, there is no indication of a general rejection by the court of the *ex turpi causa* defence in tort litigation. It clearly continues to have a role in relation to illegally obtained income. Thus Denham J. distinguished the instant case on this ground from *Burns v. Edman* [1970] 2 Q.B. 541, where the deceased's income consisted of the proceeds of crime.

Secondly, the decision does not appear to account in express terms to a judicial amnesty to tax evaders. In *Downing* the deceased had not made any false returns. His only default was not to have kept incomplete accounts. But what would be the situation where the deceased had consciously evaded his or her full tax liability over a period of years in circumstances that indicated clear *mala fides* on his or her part? Denham J.'s judgment retains sufficient flexibility to treat that case different from the instant appeal since she cautioned that 'the circumstances of each case should be considered.' Murray and Geoghegan JJ.'s remarks seemed to take a more absolute position in unqualified terms which did not appear to discriminate on the basis of the issue of the deceased's *bona fides*.

Successive actions   In *Hayes v. Callanan*, High Court, March 25, 1999, Smith J. applied the principle recognised in *Brunsden v. Humphrey* (1884) 14 Q.B. 151, that, where a single wrong involves infringements of different interests, the injured party may take separate proceedings in respect of these infringements. In the instant case the plaintiff, who had been involved in a traffic accident, successfully sued the defendants in District Court proceedings for damage to her vehicle. She later took High Court proceedings in respect of personal injuries allegedly suffered in the accident. The defendants' insurers sought to resist this other claim on the basis that the plaintiff had already had her day in court and that, if they had been aware of her intention to launch this claim, they would have appealed the District Court judgement which, as well as imposing liability on the defendants had found the plaintiff free of any contributory negligence.

Smith J. had to consider whether the later proceedings were contrary to public policy and an abuse of the process of the courts. He held that they were not, observing that it seemed to him:

> desirable, if possible, that the legal liability of parties to an accident should be litigated upon as soon as possible after the occurrence of the accident. The advantages of an early trial in relation to liability is that the recollection of events relating to the accident is fresh in people's minds and witnesses are more likely to be available to give evidence in Court. As time lapses so does one's recollection of events. One frequently hears in Court witnesses say that their recollection in relation to certain matters is far from clear because of the passage of time.
>
> By the same token it seems to me that it is also desirable that plaintiffs

who suffer material damage, in addition to personal injuries, should not have to wait many years before they are compensated for such losses. Frequently such plaintiffs have to take out loans to cover the losses arising out of a traffic accident until such time as the matter is litigated in Court....

From the memorandum as prepared by [the] solicitor for the defendant after the District Court case it seems to me that it is unlikely that there would have been any such finding of contributory negligence against the plaintiff but that again is only my view of the matter.

Personal injury claims for damages cannot be rushed. They must be allowed to mature so that a proper and accurate prognosis can be made by professional witnesses in the case.

If I were to rule that the plaintiff is estopped from bringing these proceedings I consider that a great injustice could be done to the plaintiff and in doing so I am bearing in mind that of necessity there must be some injustice done to the defendant's insurers.

Smith J. held that the plaintiff's claim was not barred by cause-of-action estoppel and that the defendant was not entitled to plead accord and satisfaction. The plaintiff's claim for 'personal injuries, loss and damage' in the High Court was accordingly permitted to proceed in the High Court in spite of her successful District Court claim for material damage to her car.

Future decisions will have to address more subtle questions of characterisation than arose in the instant case. Is an interest in physical security separable from that in physiatric integrity? Does the interest in one's life differ from that in one's bodily integrity? And how does the lexicon of infringement of constitutional rights harmonise with the segmentation of 'interests' in tort law?

Transport

AIR TRANSPORT

Airport bye-laws: disability   The Airport (Amendment) Bye-Laws 1999 (S.I. No.469 of 1999), made under the Air Navigation and Transport Act 1988, inserted a new Buy-Law into the Airport Bye-Laws 1994, requiring service providers and others conducting business at Cork Airport, Dublin Airport and Shannon Airport to do all that is reasonable necessary to accommodate the needs of persons with a disability by providing certain treatment or facilities. They came into effect on November 5, 1999.

Airport terminal charges   The Irish Aviation Authority (Terminal Charges) Regulations 2000 (S.I. No.202 of 2000), made under the Irish Aviation Authority Act 1993, re-enacted, in consolidated form and with amendments, the Irish Aviation Authority (Terminal Changes) Regulations 1999. The 2000 Regulations came into effect on July 1, 2000.

Balloons, airships etc.   The Irish Aviation Authority (Tethered Balloons, Airships, Free Balloons and Kites) Order 1999 (S.I. No.422 of 1999), made under the Irish Aviation Authority Act 1993, specified in detail the regimes for the operation of tethered balloons, airships, small balloons and kites, with effect from January 7, 2000.

En route obstacles   The Irish Aviation Authority (En Route Obstacles to Air Navigation) Order 1999 (S.I. No. 423 of 1999), made under the Irish Aviation Authority Act 1993 (Annual Review 1993, 584-5), defined the obstacles to en route air navigation in the State with effect from January 7, 2000.

Noise certification   The Irish Aviation Authority (Noise Certification And Limitation) (Amendment) Order 1999 (S.I. No.421 of 1999), made under the Irish Aviation Authority Act 1993, amended and updated the Air Navigation (Noise Certification and Limitation) Order 1984 by incorporating revised standards and recommended practices into the 1984 Order on the certification of noise levels from aircraft, with effect from January 7, 2000.

MERCHANT SHIPPING

Life-saving equipment   The Merchant Shipping (Life-Saving Appliances) (Amendment) Rules 1999 (S.I. No.368 of 1999), made under section 427 of the Merchant Shipping Act 1894, as amended, prescribe that every ship to which the Rules apply, that is, those less than 40 feet in length, shall carry no less than two lifebuoys and a lifejacket of specified dimensions for each person onboard. The Rules came into effect on April 1, 2000.

ROAD TRANSPORT

Manufacturing standards   The European Communities (Motor Vehicles UN-ECE Type Approval) Regulations 2000 (S.I. No.147 of 2000) gave effect to Decision 97/836/EC which provided for accession by the EC to the revised UN/ECE Agreement on motor type approval. They make provision for administrative arrangements for the granting of type approval for a motor vehicle, component or part based on the UN/ECE regulations and came into effect on May 26, 2000. Further Directives in this area were implemented by the European Communities (Motor Vehicle Type Approval) (No.2) Regulations 2000 (S.I. No.180 of 2000), with effect from July 3, 2000. The European Communities (Agricultural or Forestry Type Approval) Regulations 2000 (SI No.188 of 2000) implemented the most recent Directives concerning the manufacturing standards for forestry tractors and their components, with effect from June 23, 2000.

Registration plates   The Vehicle Registration and Taxation (Amendment) Regulations 1999 (S.I. No.432 of 1999) prescribed an amended format, dimensions and technical specifications of registration plates to be displayed on vehicles, with effect from December 22, 2000.

Taxi licences   In *Humphrey v. Minister for the Environment* [2001] 1 I.L.R.M. 241 (HC), Murphy J. found to be invalid the Road Traffic (Public Service Vehicles) (Amendment) Regulations 2000 (S.I. No.3 of 2000). The 2000 Regulations had purported to introduce a 'liberalised' taxi regime by which local authorities could issue a greater number of taxi plates. While the 2000 Regulations were struck down, we will postpone discussion of this area until the 2001 Review, in view of the finding that further Regulations on the same issue, the Road Traffic (Public Service Vehicles) (Amendment) (No.3) Regulations 2000 (S.I. No.367 of 2000), were upheld in 2001.

Subject Index